# The Income Tax and Business Decisions

FOURTH EDITION

# The Income Tax and Business Decisions

## AN INTRODUCTORY TAX TEXT

William L. Raby, Ph.D., C.P.A.

*Director–National Tax Services,*
*Touche Ross & Co.*

PRENTICE-HALL, INC., Englewood Cliffs, N.J. 07632

*Library of Congress Cataloging in Publication Data*

Raby, William L (date)
The income tax and business decisions.

Includes index.
1. Income tax—United States. 2. Business tax—
United States. 3. Taxation—United States. I. Title.
HJ2381.R313 1978 336.2'4'0973 77-25840
ISBN 0-13-454363-7



Printed in the United States of America

10 9 8 7 6 5 4 3 2 1

Prentice-Hall International, Inc., *London*
Prentice-Hall of Australia Pty. Limited, *Sydney*
Prentice-Hall of Canada, Ltd., *Toronto*
Prentice-Hall of India Private Limited, *New Delhi*
Prentice-Hall of Japan, Inc., *Tokyo*
Prentice-Hall of Southeast Asia Pte. Ltd., *Singapore*
Whitehall Books Limited, *Wellington, New Zealand*

# Contents

Preface ix

Prologue: The Chronicles of Sexat 1

## 1

## THE BROAD PATTERN

1 The Tax Battlefield 11

*The Arithmetic of Tax Controversy. Who Are the Tax Experts? Taxpayer versus Government. Automatic Data Processing (ADP). Congress and the Tax Law. The Treasury Department. The Taxpayer's Burden of Proof. Penalty Provisions in the Tax Law. The Statute of Limitations. Tax Practice as a Profession. C.P.A.'s in Tax Practice. Case Excerpts. Questions and Problems.*

2 Concepts of Income 32

*The Net-Worth Approach to Income. Consumption as Income. The Accountant's Concept. Income Concepts and Business Decisions. Tax Concepts versus Accounting Concepts. Case Excerpts. Questions and Problems.*

# 2

# THE SCAFFOLDING OF THE INCOME TAX

3 The Corporation Income Tax 55

*The Corporation Tax of 1909. The 1913 Act. Two Views of the Corporation. A Simple Computation of Corporate Income Tax. The Balance Sheet. Some Exceptions to the Simple Situation. The Simple Return Complicated. Unreasonable Accumulation of Earnings. The Role of the Corporation in the U.S. Income Tax. Double Taxation of Corporate Income and Internal Investment. Pricing Policy. Comment. Questions and Problems.*

4 The Small Business Corporation 78

*A Small Business Corporation Return. Why Elect Small Business Corporation Treatment? Why Avoid Small Business Corporation Treatment? Case Excerpts. Questions and Problems.*

5 Partnerships 99

*A Rose by Any Other Name... What Is a Partnership? The Aggregate Concept of the Partnership. The Conduit Nature of the Partnership Return. The Reconciliation Schedule (Schedule M, Figure 5-2). Partners' Salaries and Interest Payments. Self-employment Income. The Entity Concept of the Partnership. Relative Importance of Partnerships. Case Excerpts. Questions and Problems.*

6 The Individual Income Tax 118

*The Business Income of an Individual. Social Security Tax on the Self-employed. The Individual Return.*

*A Joint Return Versus Separate Returns. Deductions: Itemized Versus Standard. Filing Requirements. Tax-law Concepts for the Individual Income Tax. How to Fill in Declaration of Estimated Tax. The Individual Income Tax Evaluated. Questions and Problems.*

7 Fiduciary Income Tax 146

*Operation of the Trust. Income Tax Savings. Tax Problems of a Decedent. Summary. Case Excerpts. Questions and Problems.*

# 3
# A CLOSER LOOK AT THE DETAILS

8 Capital Gains 163

*Capital Gains in the U.S. Tax Law. Capital Losses. Depreciable Property. "Special" Capital Gains Provisions. The Corporate Tax Shelter. Minimum Tax on Tax Preferences. Capital Gains and Decisions. Summary. Case Excerpt. Questions and Problems.*

9 The Timing of Income 182

*Installment Sales. Cost Recovery. Contractors. Restricted Property. Income Averaging. Operating Losses. Multiple Entities. Cash Basis. Case Excerpts. Questions and Problems.*

10 Depreciation 202

*Depreciation in Tax Accounting. Some Implications of Cost Depreciation. Patterns of Depreciation. Depreciation Recapture. Useful Life. Tax*

*Depreciation and Capital Budgeting. Investment Credit. Depreciation and Selling Prices. Sale and Leaseback. Accounting Problems and Depreciation. Case Excerpts. Questions and Problems.*

11 Investment Credit 221

*Introduction. Credit versus Deduction. Effectiveness of Investment Credit. Investment Credit Description. Accounting for the Investment Credit. Details of the Investment Credit. Complexities of the Investment Credit. Some Sample Effects on Decisions. New Jobs Credit. Conclusion. Questions and Problems.*

12 Depletion and the Costs of Exploration and Development 237

*Depreciation versus Depletion. Exploration and Development. Oil and Gas, and the Investors. Case Excerpts. Questions and Problems.*

13 Minimum and Maximum Tax 249

*Minimum Tax. Minimum Tax and Recapture. Summary. Maximum Tax on Personal Service Income. Impact of Minimum and Maximum Tax. Summary. Questions and Problems.*

14 How the Tax Law Affects the Investor 261

*Real Estate. Securities. SBIC's and SBC's. Natural Resources. Holding Companies. At Risk. Cattle Investments. Case Excerpts. Questions and Problems.*

15 Taxation of Employee Benefits and Retirement Income 296

*Trusteed Benefit Plans. Employee Stock Ownership Plans (ESOPs). Annuities. Tax Treatment of Employee Distributions. Pension Plans for the Self-employed and the Professional. Annuities for Employees of Tax-exempt Organizations. Commercial Annuities. Credit for the Elderly. Benefit Plans and the Small Business. Case Excerpts. Questions and Problems.*

16 Inventory—Especially LIFO 314

*How Inventory Affects Income. How Macy Tried to Use LIFO. Tax LIFO and Accounting LIFO. Why Isn't Everyone on LIFO? Miscellaneous LIFO Effects. Case Excerpts. Questions and Problems.*

17 Corporate Organizations, Reorganizations, Distributions, and Liquidations 336

*Birth of a Corporation. Acquisition of a Subsidiary. The Consolidated-Return Question. A Stock Redemption. A Property Dividend. Public Underwriting. Losses and New Management. Losses and Merger. Summary. Does the Tax Law Induce Mergers? Accounting for Business Combinations. Conclusion. Case Excerpts. Questions and Problems.*

18 Foreign Tax Matters 360

*U.S. Citizens Abroad. The 1976 Tax Reform Act. Who Pays the Bill? Foreign-Tax Credit. The Nonresident Alien and U.S. Taxes. Foreign Operations of U.S. Corporations and Subsidiaries. Foreign-Tax Credits of Corporations. Tax Treaties. International Tax Planning. Case Excerpts. Questions and Problems.*

19 Estate Taxes, Gift Taxes, Trusts, and Insurance 388

*Transfer Tax. Bypassing An Estate. The Transfer Tax Credit. Extension of Time for Payment of Estate Tax. Redemption of Stock to Pay Estate Taxes. State-Law Caution. Charitable Contributions. Short-Term Trusts. Insurance. Case Excerpts. Questions and Problems.*

# 4

# A LOOK AT TAX PRACTICE AND POLICY

20 Handling the Tax Audit 415

*The Field Audit. The District Conference. The Appellate-Division Conference. The Court Battle. Case Excerpts. Questions and Problems.*

21 Tax Fraud 430

*How Fraud Cases Come About. The Crucial Moment. Constitutional Problems. Privileged Communication. The Burden of Proof. Defending the Fraud Case. Conviction and Punishment. Case Excerpts. Questions and Problems.*

22 Tax Research and Planning 458

*The Basic Tax Service. Beyond the Basic Service. Education for Research. Some General Thoughts on Research. Three Approaches to Research. How to Evaluate Cases. How to Get and Use Private Rulings. Research Methodology. How to Analyze Tax-Planning Problems. Case Excerpt. Questions and Problems.*

23 Tax Reform 483

*U.S. Taxation of Foreign Income. Credits Instead of Deductions. Capital Recovery Allowances. Negative Income Tax. Capital Gain Provision. Adapting to Inflation. Reliance on Other Taxes. Conclusion.*

Appendix: Quantitative Aspects of Decision Making 500

*Identification of the Problem. The Search for Alternative Approaches. Information and Quantification. Qualitative Review of Alternatives. Follow-Through. Illustrative Situations. Reflecting the Tax Factor. Conclusion.*

Index 515

# Preface

This book focuses on tax provisions affecting business and investment decisions. Its primary emphasis is the income tax, but it also explores transfer taxes inasmuch as they impact the estate planning process.

The effect of a tax law provision is a mixture of the statute, its interpretation by the government and by taxpayers, the manner of its administration, and the way in which it interacts with other aspects of the real world, including other tax provisions. Thus, even though this is an introductory text, it pays substantial attention to tax practice considerations.

There are limitations, however, as to what can be done in an introductory book. The approach here is to present tax facts in the context of meaningful relationships in order to form a general pattern which is easily retained and provides a foundation for later learning through study and experience. Thus, much detail has been sacrificed in the interests of keeping the subject comprehensible.

The book assumes that the reader has a minimum knowledge of accounting. Accountants who plan to specialize in tax work will find in this book the conceptual fundamentals of tax practice that will allow them to obtain the greatest benefit from more advanced course work. For accountants not intending to specialize in tax work, and for the business executive or entrepreneur, this book surveys the broad rules of income taxation, including the interaction between the government and the taxpayer, and it provides some understanding of the complexities and uncertainties inherent in the U.S. approach to taxation. In a tax world where specific facts are often outdated even before they are learned, it is most important that both the executive and the accountant develop a sense of the pattern of income taxation, of the evolution of the various components of the pattern, of how tax provisions affect decisions, and of where and how to find the resources needed to handle a tax problem.

The "game" of taxation is played with wealth. To understand taxation from a micro viewpoint, one must see how much wealth is to be taken, and from whom, and why what is done is done as it is. Because most taxpayers would prefer paying reduced taxes, taxation inevitably produces a conflict situation overtly or covertly, between the individual (or the business) and the government. From this conflict flows the interest and excitement which those with some modicum of tax sophistication find ever-present as they observe the tax scene, and which people engaged in tax practice find a major reward of their daily work.

By now, it has become impossible to keep track of all the contributions that constitute this book. I do, however, want to give particular recognition to Professor Warren Higgins, of the University of Connecticut, for his constant and invaluable feedback over many years, and to my colleagues in Touche Ross & Co. (especially Jim Crumlish, Eli Gerver, Israel Press, Gerald Padwe, Bill Rosenberg, and Allan Weiss) who played a role in helping me get it all together for this fourth edition. Persons using or considering this book as a teaching text should obtain from the publisher the related Teacher's Manual, which includes many teaching aids and suggestions as well as solutions to problems and answers to questions. (Questions and problems marked * require the student to do some research outside of this book—see the Teacher's Manual.)

*William L. Raby*

# The Income Tax and Business Decisions

# Prologue: The Chronicles of Sexat

Excerpt from *The Chronicles of Sexat,* an undiscovered manuscript relating the history of a nonexistent race of men.

In the days long gone of the Oldest Ones, the Chief was a man like other Men. If he lived better than most, the strength of his arm and the sureness of his aim were the cause. So it was in the beginning.

Nothing, though, endures unchanged. The Men, who had lived each to himself, sharing only a common area, found that hunting animals for food was a wasteful way of life. Chief Abab it was, wiser than those who came before, who found that a constant supply of food and hides could be had by refraining from slaughter and instead tending and breeding flocks.

Before this, there had been little that one man could take from another, for little had anyone to take. But now the herds became the wealth of Men. The Chief became a judge, who must decide the causes of his people, one against another. He became a warrior, the leader of his people in defending the flocks from Barbarians. He became wealthy, for each of the Men must pay to him a tribute of one ewe and one ram each year. This tribute was the first tax.

For forty years, and forty times forty, this was the pattern of the life of Men. But, in time, there came change. No longer did each man have his own flock to tend. With the passing of the generations, some men obtained more than their brethren. And, for some, their children added yet more, and their children's children. Alas, in time some there were with no flocks to tend, while others had more than they could care for. Then they who had none became the servants of they who had much, that they might indeed remain alive, and their families with them.

Still the tribute of the chief remained the same—one ram and one ewe per man per year. There were those who muttered that the tax had created the servant class—taking, as they would explain, all of the property of him who had but two animals, and an unnoticed portion from him who had thousands.

Then came the elders to the Chief Morat, and spoke long to him of the evil that took from one man his entire sustenance, while taking from another that which he would not miss at all. So had they spoken to other chiefs before, without success. But Morat could see that those who had much were acquiring even more until even now some there were whose wealth rivalled that of the Chief himself.

"Taxation must be borne equally," decreed Morat, "but one way of taxing each man the same may be less equal than another." So saying, he decreed that the annual levy should be one ram and one ewe per hundred head, the figure which the elders had opined would raise the same amount of tribute as one ewe and one ram per year per man.

It was shortly thereafter that the great Feasts of Sexat were first begun, to be held each year in the days just prior to the annual count of the flocks for the purposes of the levy. The new way of raising the tax was a popular one among the mass of Men, who had few in their flocks or none. They could gorge themselves at the annual feasts, as the owners of large flocks tried to eliminate all but the best, not wishing to be taxed on the rest. Those who grumbled were few, being mainly those whose flocks were large. But in time it came to be seen that the wisdom of the now-legendary Morat was indeed that of a Chief of Chiefs, for the flocks grew larger, were healthier, yielded more—and the elders laid credit to the fact that only the best were allowed to live and to breed.

Racing with the passing years over the prairies of time came new changes in the ways of Men. No longer did they range the pastures beyond the horizon, grazing until a range was depleted and then moving on. No longer lived they in the portable huts of latticework covered by skins. The land was seized upon, and divided among the Men. They raised foodstuffs from the soil, and grew new feeds for the herds. They lived in buildings built solid, of sweat and stone and timber. Some of these were as small as the huts of yore, while others were like to a small mountain in size.

Many of those who had no land, or who lost their land, lived perforce in the area surrounding the Chief, and lived there by their ingenuity in doing to or for others. Some made cloth and some made clothes. Those there were who had a way with wood, and became carpenters, while others became metal-smiths, and still others baked bread, made wine, dug wells, told stories, and did a hundred and one things for which a man might find others willing to pay—in grain, in cattle, or in kind. Some there even were whose ways of eking a living could not be seen, and yet who lived. So came the City into being, without plan and with little at first to promise. But it was always there for those who had nowhere else to turn, and later for those who turned to it as a place of opportunity.

At first, all trade in the city was a matter of individually struck bargains. One artisan would exchange a pair of sandals for a six-month-old kid, while for half a bushel of grain a dwelling place might be obtained for a fortnight. But this grew unwieldy. How does one conduct an inn when forty separate arrangements have to be haggled in the course of a day?

Seeing this, the Chief decreed that one male goat, full-grown, should be deemed a measure of value, to be called a "buck." All things were to be measured in terms of bucks. Soon, men of wealth issued slips of paper containing the promise to redeem the signed slip for so many "bucks." These soon circulated freely from hand to hand, thus eliminating the need for actual goats with which to conduct trade, and making possible prices, such as one-half buck, which would have been impossible (or at least messy) where live animals were involved.

Thus, money came into being as the city grew. Some there were who complained that there were more promises to deliver bucks floating around than there were bucks available for delivery, but the system of money worked and their complaints were soon ignored—especially as the complainers were no less assiduous in collecting the paper bucks than were the general run of Men. All things now were measured in terms of money.

The Chief, since the people were his people and were there about him, was protector, ruler, and judge of the City. Yet he pondered long about this problem: The tax he levied, which by now was in money terms, was based upon the flocks, while the thrust of his efforts was against the tangles and miseries of the city.

So, too, complained the herders. And they had another cause of complaint. Some there were, wiser or more aggressive than the rest, who had over the years traded flocks for land. These rented to tenants the right to graze. Now most of the land was held in this wise. Between the tax and the rent, complained the herders, it was increasingly difficult to survive. True it was that, while the number of Men had grown, those who herded had not grown in number at the same pace, nor had their herds. Yet, though the herds grew slowly, the tax need soared, from the money equivalent of one ram and one ewe per hundred, to two per hundred and then three and then five per hundred.

The Chief in those days was Taro, of the line of Morat. He saw that what the herders said was true, saw also that his own power as chief could disappear as the tax derived declined.

"Even now," he said to his elders, "there are those who live in the City, owning shops and much land, who would be as a Chief."

Much they thought, and long they pondered. The seasons passed while they wrestled with their plans.

"These are new days," proclaimed Taro at last. "A new day poses new problems, and new problems require new solutions. He who will not go forward with us must slide backward alone."

The tax of the future, decreed Taro, was to be based upon each man's ability to pay.

"Only so," said he, "can we ensure that the needs of all will be met, while the burdens of taxation fall only on those able to bear them."

The new tax was to be based on income. "We shall tax the fruit," explained Taro, "leaving the tree untouched that it might produce more fruit again, rather than being consumed by the tax." Thus would the destructive effects of previous taxes be avoided.

The higher the income, the higher the rate of tax. "To a man who has no food," Taro pointed out, "an amount sufficient to sustain life has an incalculable value. But as the man eats, the value of each successive bite becomes less and less. Soon the man can eat no more, and there is to him no value to more food at that moment. For Men as a whole, it would be better if the last food of that man who has a surfeit were taken from him to become the first food of one who had little or none—there would thus be more happiness, more satisfaction, more fulfillment among the people.

"And while it may, at first approach, appear that the tax is unfair, since one pays at a rate higher than another, this is not, in fact, the case. As my revered ancestor, the Great Chief Morat, well said, one type of equality may be less equal than another. The quantity of what we take may be unequal relative to the total quantity of income, but the value to the person from whom it is taken is a constant proportion of the quantity involved. The value of added income gets less and less to him who already has a sufficiency, thus requiring that, if he is to bear a fair share of the tax burden, the percentage of the added income that is taken in tax must constantly be increased. Thus the rate of tax, in terms of the values taken from our people, is quite equal."

Thus spake Taro. With ninety and nine of each hundred, the idea of such a tax was felt to be right and fair. Only the hundredth complained, for he was the man of great income. And Taro was content, for now no man would be allowed to rival the Chief. Henceforth, greater and greater amounts of income would not mean greater and greater power, but only larger and larger amounts of tax to pay. Thus, in simplicity of concept, was born the income tax. It has been borne ever since.

All of Taro's counselors had agreed to the tax on income. It came, therefore, as somewhat of a shock to Taro when, once the nature of the new tax had been proclaimed, his counselors were unable to agree on how the exaction was to be taken.

The first matter on which they divided was the question of "When?"

"Ignoring for the moment the question of *what* is income," said Rum, the elder, "it should certainly be plain that it is the nature of Man to spend his income as fast as he gets it. In fact," he said, thinking perhaps of his mate, "a substantial portion of the populace undoubtedly would spend it even before they got it, if only they could figure out some way to do *that*." He paused and then concluded, "Any tax which is imposed must therefore be taken from what they get before they even get it. If too much is taken, let them then file a claim with the Chief and obtain a refund. Each man's interest in his own wherewithal will ensure that only the correct amount is retained."

"Are we to insult our people by this assumption that they are unable to manage their own funds?" objected another elder. "Let each compute, at the end of each year, the amount that he owes. Let him then pay it to the Chief."

To these words, Taro paid great heed. Both elders were a little right and a little wrong, he concluded. But this he did not say directly to them, for Taro was wise. "Look you," he said to them, "that you each draft up the ordinances setting forth the manner in which this income tax shall be determined and collected. For whatever the strength of our argument for what we do, it still remains that we must be able to so set it down that each Man will know. There must be no question as to what he is to pay, when he is to pay it, or what the penalty will be if he pays it not. Further, I would not have it that half of the people must be set to checking on whether the other half have paid their just tax. The rules must be simple to enforce. Nor would I have it that the tax should cause Men to buy and sell solely because of advantages they reap under the tax, when without the tax it would not advantage them to either buy or sell."

The elders separated, each to his own home, to ruminate and to meditate. At the call of Rum, they met in solemn conclave a fortnight later. The discussion waxed and waned for hour upon hour, until Rum, tired but still conscious of his duty as chairman, put his finger on the basic point of difference.

"Our first problem," he said, "is that we cannot agree on what it is we are talking about. We have no difficulty with the idea of a tax, for this is an exaction by the Chief to meet his needs. But the idea of income we seem to variously approach.

"Some of you would say that a man's income is the wealth that flows to him. You would put a value on that which he owned at the beginning of the year and the end. The increase would be added to what he had spent during the year, and thus his income computed.

"Others of you would say almost the same, but would somehow exclude from the tax the unusual things that increase wealth. Thus, if the value of land owned by a man increased, you would not tax that increase, being content instead to tax the rent alone derived from the land. The fruit of the tree you would tax, but if the tree itself were to be sold, its proceeds would not be taxed.

"Then there are the philosophers among you, led so worthily by the elder Fisher. You would turn the matter somewhat about, for, as you state and we all would agree, income is in the last analysis consumption. Money gives us the right to command things to be used for our satisfactions. It is the use of that right, not its obtaining or retention, which is the essence of consumption and, hence, of income. Therefore, not the inflow but the outflow of wealth constitutes the real measure of income and should be the basis for tax. The tax should be on spending. And not on all spending, but only on consumption spending. Money spent on food would be consumption, while money loaned to another at interest would not be subject to tax.

"Now hear me," continued Rum, "for I care not which of these thoughts we might embrace. I wish only that we follow the dictates of our beloved Chief, that what we decide upon be certain, yet simple; productive, yet neutral in effect.

"The first school of thought I shall call the Net Worth school. We can accept the essence of your concept. Yet it is far from simple to apply. I at one time had a fire in my house, which some of you may recall. When I went to the Chief to claim recompense for my loss, I was hard put to prove the value of much of what I had. Yet this would needs be done by every man every year. To check his calculation of the tax, his net worth calculation would needs be checked as well. For the general run of Men, this would be too much.

"But the net worth concept is worthy. As an audit tool it will reveal to us who has lied about his income under whatever concept of income we finally adopt. Thus we shall prove his falsehood, by showing that his income reported was less than the increase in net worth plus his consumption.

"Those of you who emphasize the regularity approach to income are forgetful of the Chief's admonition that the tax should not change the behavior of our people. If the gains from speculation in land are not subject to tax, while the rentals from land are taxed, there will be many who will cease to use the land and instead bend their energies to speculative orgies, especially as the rate of tax goes up and up. If half of a Man's income should be taken in tax . . ." at which statement a loud chorus of derision arose at the very thought of such an event, "one dollar of speculative income would equal two dollars of earned income.

"And as to you, elder Fisher," concluded Rum, "I bow to the wisdom you have attained from staring across the waves in the long years at sea, and I admit the justice and rightness of your remarks. But, paradoxical though it may seem, to tax spending would be to encourage saving. This the artisans in the shops would never accept. For it is spending, and the rapid flow of funds from one person to the next, which makes feasible the existence of the City."

Then spoke the Secretary, not properly an elder at all, a mild-mannered man whose task it was to record the words spoken at meetings of this type.

"Among the merchants," said he, "it is the custom to keep a record of the transactions that occur. When an item of merchandise is sold, then is the selling price considered income, but only to the extent that it exceeds the cost of the thing which has been sold. The ups and downs of value concern them not, for their attention is focused only on what is given and what is taken at the time a thing changes hands. They are practical men. To them, value is a speculation about the future until it is embodied in a sale. Their records are practical records. Since there are two parties to every transaction, even a man who wished to conceal his income would be hard pressed to be sure that he could succeed. The price between buyer and seller is a definite amount, and therefore, unlike value, not subject to argument."

"You speak of things I know not," said Rum, "although I am minded that in those shops where my wife doth buy, I have indeed seen scribblers pushing quills across dry and dusty books. But how, pray tell, would you then solve our problem and define income?"

"We will look to the transactions that occur," explained the Secretary. "For a business, they can only be of two types, it would seem. First would be those wherein the business hath purchased goods or services from others. Merchandise for resale, rent of the store premises, the compensation of the clerks—these would all be of the first category. The second category would be those transactions wherein the business hath sold goods or services to others. Money, or something that can be expressed in terms of money, is involved in all of those transactions.

"The excess of the money received over the money paid out would be our measurement of income!"

"Indeed, it sounds simple," said Fisher. "I presume the income of an individual would then simply be the money received from either goods or services?"

"I would so presume," said Rum. "But I can see great problems in applying this approach. What of the cost of the merchant's merchandise which had not yet been sold? What of the cost of a thing when it is sold in a year later than that in which it is bought? What of the cost of something which is used up over a long period rather than sold at all?"

Then up spake the oldest of the elders, hitherto silent. "It is late, and the meeting has been long. We are seeking to raise a tax, not to perceive a divine revelation. And I am tired. Let us accept the Secretary's idea, which is the only one of those you have discussed that I can understand. Then let the administrators work out the details."

And so it was decided.

After reading the minutes of the meeting, the Chief appointed the Secretary to the new post of Collector of the Income Tax.

Mindful of the complexity of the real world compared to the world of words on paper, the Collector proceeded to meet with the merchants, the grazers, and the landowners to determine the manner of defining income. As problems were discussed, he wrote down rules, until soon the rules composed a book. This book, the Tax Code, as changed from time to time, has been handed down from generation to generation of Collectors and taxpayers.

But the new income tax was not many years old before the Chief was besieged with petitioners. Some of these were businessmen. These claimed that their businesses were so vital to the chiefdom that they needed special tax treatment. Most of these the Chief denied. Individuals clamored for the right to deduct expenses as offsets to their income, arguing that if a business were entitled to deduct the cost of the merchandise it sold in computing its income, a person should be entitled to deduct the cost of his food. These, too, the Chief denied. But when the medicine men joined with the elders in petitioning for the right to deduct amounts paid for the care of the sick, the Chief finally capitulated. Soon the money lenders had rallied public support and the Chief allowed interest to be deducted before computing the tax.

In fact, with the passing years, as more and more little exceptions crept into the Tax Code, it grew to be a book of massive size. The Collector spent more and more of his time wrangling with taxpayers as to whether they could take advantage of one or more of the exceptions. He, too, became a frequent petitioner of the Chief, pleading for limitations on the exceptions. But his success in obtaining limitations only made the Tax Code larger, more complex, more productive of confusion.

# 1

# THE BROAD PATTERN

*Tax rules become arbitrary gibberish unless they can be seen as part of a meaningful pattern. In Chapters 1 and 2, we shall completely ignore the specific rules of the tax law. Instead, we shall investigate the nature of income and of income taxes, and we shall examine the way in which tax laws develop and are administered.*

# 1

# The Tax Battlefield

## THE ARITHMETIC OF TAX CONTROVERSY

The Internal Revenue Code specifically allows taxpayers to deduct expenses in connection with the determination, collection, or refund of any tax. The effect of a provision of this sort is to encourage tax controversy—with the encouragement increasing as the tax bracket rises.

Assume a taxpayer is in a 60 percent tax bracket. He is contemplating carrying through a transaction that has about a 50 percent chance of being upheld for tax purposes. The cost he will incur if he goes ahead will be $10,000. But his after-tax cost will be only $4,000 because 60 percent of the $10,000 will be recovered as a tax deduction. How much potential saving is needed before the transaction appears justified?

The "value" of the tax plan will be one-half the total possible saving, since this is the probability of actually attaining the saving. Thus we get an equation: $0.5X = \$4{,}000$; and the potential tax saving must, in this case, be $8,000. But notice that the $8,000 minimum potential tax benefit is actually less than the $10,000 of cost that must be incurred to achieve the saving! How can spending $10,000 to save $8,000 be explained as a benefit? The costs of achieving the saving are deductible, while the tax saving itself is tax-free income.

Now change the bracket of our taxpayer. If the taxpayer is in a 20 percent tax bracket, the after-tax cost of $1,000 spent seeking tax savings would be $800. Assuming the same 0.5 probability of actually getting the saving sought, we would discover that our taxpayer would have to be able to save $1,600 to have a chance to break even. If his tax-saving potential were that large, however, he would probably not be in a 20 percent bracket.

We can deduce some general rules, to which there will be exceptions. In general, the higher the taxpayer's tax bracket, the greater the likelihood that tax plans involving a high risk of tax controversy will appear justified; the lower the taxpayer's tax bracket, the less likelihood that tax plans involving a risk of controversy will appear warranted.

These generalizations are supported by an analysis of the income sources and deductions of taxpayers in various tax brackets. The higher the tax bracket, the greater the proportion of income from sources that possess some tax-saving potential. The higher the tax bracket, the greater the probability that deductions will be itemized. At the other extreme, the opportunities for tax saving are pretty slim for a taxpayer whose sole source of income is wages subject to withholding and who takes the standard deduction.

## WHO ARE THE TAX EXPERTS?

The federal income tax is imposed by the national government. It's administration started relatively small, and then it grew explosively during World War I. Its administrators worked closely with the certified public accountants who helped taxpayers determine income and comply with the horrendous complexities of the rapidly changing tax law. The accountants responded to the challenge of this task and generally became recognized as the professionals skilled at dealing with tax problems. They became the fastest-growing twentieth-century profession. They practiced on an even footing with lawyers in the Bureau of Internal Revenue and before the Board of Tax Appeals (now called the Tax Court). Most of the business gravitated to the C.P.A.'s.

With World War II, the number of taxpayers swelled enormously. For the first time, the individual income tax yielded more than the corporate. High rates of both profits and taxes led to fantastic amounts being involved in individual tax controversies. Lawyers began to play a more and more active role in these controversies. In 1942 the lawyers were successful in prohibiting future admission to practice before the Tax Court to C.P.A.'s not already admitted, except after passage of a stiff examination. (Since 1943, only about 100 C.P.A.'s have passed this Tax Court exam; few even bother to take it.)

Law and public accounting are not regulated by the national government. Each state determines its own requirements for admission to the practice of law. Each state determines its own definition of what constitutes the practice of law. The states are quite jealous of their prerogatives.

Each state determines its own requirements for use of the title of "Certified Public Accountant." The fact that the work of the C.P.A. is not so much affected by state as by national considerations is reflected, however, in the fact that all the states use the same examination (prepared and graded by the American Institute of Certified Public Accountants) to determine competency. It is interesting to note that no state effectively regulates the practice of public accounting in the same manner as it regulates the practice of law. The C.P.A. certificate is more a right to use a title than a license to do things prohibited to persons who are not C.P.A.'s.

Similarly, no state has been able to limit to C.P.A.'s and attorneys the right to prepare federal tax returns or to represent taxpayers in matters involving such returns. Some states have tried, but such legislation has generally been held unconstitutional. However, the states can register or license the non-lawyer, non-C.P.A. tax-return preparers (e.g., as is being done in California and Oregon).

There are some 150,000 C.P.A.'s and 300,000 attorneys in the United States. In addition, about 18,000 people are enrolled to practice before the Internal Revenue Service (the tax-collecting arm of the Treasury Department) either as the result of passing an annual examination or because of their past I.R.S. employment experience. Since only a small percentage of the attorneys or C.P.A.'s prepare tax returns, the bulk of the tax work for individual taxpayers and small businesses may well be done by these 18,000 and by an estimated 300,000 unenrolled tax-return preparers, most of whom do tax work on a seasonal or part-time basis.

The federal government has the right to determine who may prepare returns, but legislation directing the Treasury Department to promulgate rules regulating return preparation has not passed Congress. The problem of regulating 300,000 unenrolled tax-return preparers would be immense. However, all preparers must now identify themselves (by their social security numbers) on the returns they prepare, and they are subject to sanctions for negligence, fraud, and unauthorized disclosure of information. But this is still a far cry from federal licensing or regulation.

The Treasury Department does have rules relating to which unenrolled tax-return preparers are allowed to represent the taxpayer at the lowest levels within the department—that is, in dealing with the revenue agent who is making a field audit or an office audit. The rules require that such preparers must observe the ethical standards of enrolled practitioners, or they will not be allowed to represent their clients at this lowest level.

Because a primary pressure on the revenue agents in the field is to get a settlement from the taxpayer, it does not appear that these rules relating to preparers have had much effect on standards of practice. From the viewpoint of the agent intent on disposing of a case amicably, dealing with a person who is not enrolled—however that person obtains his clients or conducts his practice—may be preferable to dealing with the taxpayer directly or with an enrolled practitioner not familiar with the tax return under audit. Thus, agents often deal with whoever prepared the return, justifying that person's presence on the basis of his or her explaining how the return was prepared, without being overly technical as to the difference between witnessing and advocating or supporting a position taken.

Who are the tax experts? At the level of return preparation, there really is no way to tell—except by the recommendation of other professionals and by local reputation. For tax planning or the handling of tax controversies, a C.P.A. or an attorney who specializes in tax work usually is the best qualified professional.

## TAXPAYER VERSUS GOVERNMENT

Does it make any difference whether the taxpayer has competent tax help? Many believe that it is only the willingness of taxpayers to fight unwarranted assessments and to protest occasional high-handed behavior by revenue agents that prevents the administration of our tax system from becoming a bureaucratic throttler of economic freedom.

For the taxpayer, arguing can pay off! A taxpayer who is not satisfied with the deficiency proposed by a revenue agent can have an informal conference (at which, however, he cannot be represented by an unenrolled person) with an experienced I.R.S. agent whose job it is to settle controversies and who has more discretion than the field agent—especially in cases where not over $2,500 is involved for the year. These conferences are held in most large and medium-size cities. If not satisfield he can then take his protest to the Appellate Division of the Internal Revenue Service of the United States Treasury Department. Beyond that, he can take the matter to court.

The results are interesting. Looking only at cases handled by the Appellate Division for a recent year, we find that the taxpayer fared reasonably well. Of a net (deficiency plus penalty, less overassessment) of $920,882,000 in proposed deficiencies involved in cases that had not yet been docketed before the Tax Court, taxpayers were able to get a reduction to $219,995,000. Cases that were docketed before the Tax Court but that were settled before being tried involved a net of $307,631,000 in proposed deficiencies. The taxpayers wound up having to pay only $82,852,000—or about 28 percent of the amounts proposed. (Too much should not be made of these numbers. Many controversies involve *when* not *whether* something should be taxed or deducted.)

In district court suits, for the same year, the taxpayer won part or all of what he was contending for in 215 out of 516 cases, a 0.417 batting average. In the Court of Claims, the taxpayer got part or all of what he was arguing for in 22 out of 70 cases. The Tax Court cases that actually went all the way through trial to a decision resulted in the taxpayer having to pay 34 percent of the taxes originally proposed, although the taxpayer won part or all of what he was seeking in only 204 out of 417 cases (for a 0.489 batting average).

The organization of the appeals procedure looks like this:

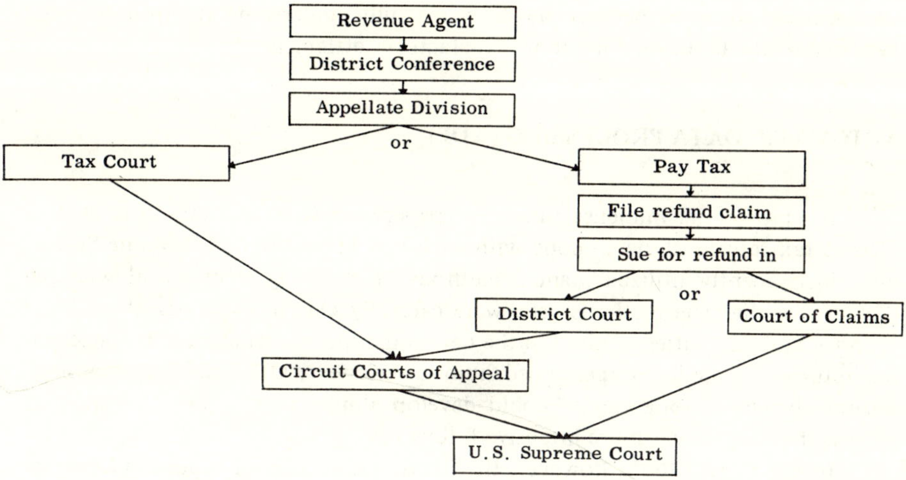


FIGURE 1-1
Organization of Appeals Procedure

More cases go the Tax Court route than the refund-claim route. Decisions of the Tax Court or of the district court can be appealed to the appropriate circuit court of appeals. Out of 243 such appeals decided in a recent year, the government won 170. Decisions of the courts of appeal and of the Court of Claims can be appealed to the United States Supreme Court. The Supreme Court declines to hear many tax cases. In a typical year, it may hand down decisions in five tax cases, of which the government may win three.

The pattern of tax controversy is thus one of substantial compromises achieved at the administrative level; Treasury Department dominance over the taxpayer by a slight margin at the trial-court level; and government dominance over the taxpayer when appeals are taken from lower-court decisions.

One problem of the taxpayer who utilizes incompetent tax help may be that he is, in effect, waiving his chance of winning a tax concession that a better-qualified practitioner might be able to obtain for him. First, the unqualified person is frequently unable to analyze the client's tax affairs, especially as to proposed transactions, so as to push for the best tax results within the framework of the law. Wishing to avoid controversy, many times he decides doubtful items against his client while preparing returns. There are no deficiencies when the returns he prepares are audited. Why should there be? A person will never receive any speeding tickets if you fix his engine so that it cannot go faster than 15 miles an hour. He's not likely to get very far either.

Second, when the returns of the unqualified preparer are audited, he tends to advise settlement with the revenue agent even under circumstances in which the taxpayer could beneficially protest the agent's proposed deficiency. The agent may do this because he cannot handle the controversy beyond the agent-level himself, or even because he does not fully understand the opportunities available to the taxpayer for a more satisfactory settlement.

## AUTOMATIC DATA PROCESSING (ADP)

In spite of its immense inflow of paperwork (over 80 million individual income tax returns alone to cope with each year), the Internal Revenue Service until just recently utilized manual methods of checking returns and selecting them for audit. The methods used were carefully chosen. Analysis of statistics on prior audit activities resulted in the determination of test standards for selecting returns for audit. Experienced human reviewers, after looking at enough returns through a long career, could develop almost a sixth sense for spotting returns that could bear more intensive follow-up.

In the early 1960's, however, the I.R.S. was successful in getting Congress both to pass enabling legislation and to appropriate the money to take a giant step in United States tax administration.

Henceforth, each taxpayer had to have a number. For individuals and employers with Social Security numbers, the tax numbers were to be the Social Security numbers. Those without numbers would have to get them. Critics facetiously linked the requirement of numbers for tax purposes with telephone all-number dialing, and foresaw a day when names would disappear. "Can you imagine saying, '87451789, I love you?'" Mythology would have to be translated into modern guise. Helen of Troy would become 360-14-3404 of area code 518. Tarzan would grunt, "Me 472-05-9876; you 865-04-3201."

The numbers are necessary so that the computers could function. Each person's tax history is recorded on tape, with the information coded by account number and cross-checked by also using the first four digits of the person's name to catch situations where a number might be incorrectly reported. Persons paying wages, interest, dividends, and so forth, file reports showing the name and account number to which payment was made. The computer cross-checks the income being paid against the income being reported. Discrepancies ultimately lead to investigation.

Much of the information was already required but simply could not be processed in the precomputer era. Even with computers, progress has been slow.

In the past, refund checks had sometimes gone out based on false withholding statements or had gone to persons owing the government taxes for other years. The computer cross-checks and prevents such errors. Returns for audit are already selected by programming predetermined standards, many of them arrived at by analyzing computer-compiled statistics previously either unobtainable or obtainable only after long work. Gross profit ratios on business returns, net profit ratios, ratios of various types of expenses to one another and to various types of income, of bad debts to sales, of inventory to sales, and so forth, are all brought into play in selecting which business returns get a human going-over.

At the same time, revenue agents, already highly trained in taxes, are becoming specialists in various industries and trades. When they come in to audit the returns the computer has selected, they are familiar with the taxpayer's operation. This should make life easier for taxpayers and tax practitioners, in that explanations of peculiar trade customs would be held to a minimum. But more knowledgeable agents also tend to raise more sophisticated tax issues.

Even a small data-processing system requires time to iron out the "bugs." The I.R.S.'s giant-size ADP started in one region and was gradually extended to cover the whole country and all taxpayers. As a by-product of ADP, there has been more insistence on filling out tax forms uniformly, on following standard operating procedures, on adapting the individual to the system. The predictable result was a certain amount of confusion. Tax practitioners, tax administrators, and taxpayers all suffered from frustrations that for some seemed almost unbearable. But the system does work, in spite of errors made from time to time by the human beings who manipulate it, create the input, and work with the output. The operation of a U.S. tax system that each year involves more pieces of paper, more dollars, and more complex concepts would probably be impossible without ADP.

## CONGRESS AND THE TAX LAW

The basic tax law is the Internal Revenue Code, which is a small part of the United States Code. The last stem-to-stern overhaul of the Internal Revenue Code took place in 1954, and the present code is thus referred to as the Internal Revenue Code of 1954. Congressional action since 1954 has consisted of making amendments–some of them quite sweeping and substantial–to this Internal Revenue Code of 1954.

Back in the first year, 1913, of our modern income tax (the Civil War income tax having been a predecessor), a Republican senator, Elihu Root, commented, "No one understands the income tax law except persons who have not sufficient intelligence to understand the questions that arise under it." True of the simple tax law of 1913, that statement is even truer today. If to simplify something is to falsify it, practically none of our elected representatives can escape having a false understanding of the income tax since it is almost literally impossible to even think about the income tax without simplifying generalizations. (See Chapter 23 on Tax Reform.)

As a result, congressmen rely heavily on the know-how of the staff of the Joint Committee on Internal Revenue Taxation. These staff people are the tax-research and legislation drafting force for the Congress. In addition, the Treasury Department, which is probably the most active of the tax lobbies, has its staff of experts who present their analyses, recommendations, and comments to both the House Ways and Means Committee, where tax legislation is initiated, and the Senate Finance Committee, where it frequently receives substantial surgery. (It is not uncommon to find that the patient fails to survive the operation.)

Thus, although any member of the House may introduce tax legislation, the bills that receive action in the House Ways and Means Committee are normally bills introduced by members of the committee. If the president desires that a particular tax measure be enacted, it will be presented to the committee. Where a tax bill seems of substantial public interest, the committee will hold public hearings. Any person can present his views at these hearings, although normally the people who put in an appearance or submit statements are representatives of trade or professional organizations, college professors, taxpayers or organizations that would be directly affected, and government officials.

After all this, the committee votes on the bill. It may vote to report it out to the House. It may vote to table the bill, a procedure that usually kills it. Or it may vote against the bill, which also kills it, but with a greater degree of finality. The bill may be amended in the committee, of course. If the bill passes the House, it then goes over to the Senate, where a somewhat similar but less lengthy procedure takes place with the Senate Finance Committee and the Senate itself.

Assuming that a bill finally passes the Senate, it is likely to differ in some respects from the bill that passed the House. The House may accept the changes made by the Senate—which is unlikely—or a Conference Committee of senators and representatives may meet to work out a compromise between the two versions. The Conference Committee version of the bill is normally accorded quick passage by both houses. Once the president signs the bill, it becomes a public law, and the various sections of the Internal Revenue Code are effectively amended as of whatever date or dates may be specified in the bill.

The House Ways and Means Committee, the Senate Finance Committee, and the Conference Committee will each have prepared committee reports explaining what they think the provisions of the bill mean and what each provision accomplishes. When an amendment is made to a bill, the congressman who made it may have made some remarks explaining the intent of his amendment. These will appear in the *Congressional Record,* which is a daily newspaper chronicling the doings in Congress.

The law itself is the best explanation of what Congress has put into the law. But if one wants clarification of the law, the committee reports are initially the only explanations available.

## THE TREASURY DEPARTMENT

Because it is charged with administering the law, the Treasury Department faces the problem of interpreting what the law means. It does this in a variety of ways of varying significance. The Treasury Regulations, which are part of a larger group of administrative regulations called the Code of Federal Regulations, are the most formal and official interpretations. Unless they are clearly contrary to the underlying law itself, these regulations have the force and effect of law. The complexity of some of the provisions of the tax law can be inferred from the length of time it takes the Treasury Department to issue regulations. Some parts of the 1954 act, for instance, have not yet had final regulations issued interpreting them.

The Treasury Department, through a sub-unit, the Internal Revenue Service, also interprets the law in preparing the tax-return forms to be filled in by various classes of taxpayers and in preparing the instructions that accompany or supplement these forms. Upon request, the Internal Revenue Service will consider issuing an interpretation on a prospective transaction, setting forth what its tax effects may be. These are called *private rulings*, and about 40,000 of them are issued annually. Where substantial amounts of money are involved and the tax results are uncertain, many tax practitioners consider obtaining a private ruling to be inexpensive insurance. Although it is not legally binding upon the Internal Revenue Service, by long-established policy such a ruling will be adhered to in regard to the taxpayer to whom the ruling is furnished. Unfortunately, many taxpayers have found to their sorrow that such rulings are not necessarily effective when applied to taxpayers other than those to whom issued.

The ruling process is not without its critics. The Internal Revenue Service, with minor exceptions (for instance, with respect to tax-free transfers of property to or from foreign corporations), is not directly by law to furnish any rulings at all. Thus, the I.R.S. views the issuance of a ruling as a favor to a taxpayer, and not as a right of the taxpayer. The result is that there are many types of transactions on which the I.R.S. will be unwilling, at any given moment, to issue rulings. Critics contend that any taxpayer should be able to obtain a binding advance ruling on any proposed transaction that involves a substantial (to the taxpayer) amount of money. They feel that rulings should be issued by a separate body.

Through the process of auditing returns, the Internal Revenue Service is also forced to make many interpretations. With or without justification, decisions have to be made. Some people express surprise at the large number of tax cases that go to court each year. The truly surprising thing is that so few cases result from the over 100 million returns of various types that are processed annually. However, the litigation policy adopted by the Internal Revenue Service is also a type of interpretation of the law. Because of the diversity of the tribunals to which a taxpayer may carry a case, and because there are so many appellate jurisdictions to which appeal may be made, the Internal Revenue Service will frequently take a position of disagreeing with, and refusing to follow, court decisions. In so doing, the I.R.S. seeks to actively shape the judicial interpretation of the tax law by encouraging litigation on a particular point in a number of jurisdictions, hoping that its position will be upheld by some court. If the I.R.S. can create a conflict of decisions among the circuit courts of appeal, or between the Court of Claims and a circuit court of appeal, it may be able to obtain a Supreme Court review of the particular issue. By and large, as noted previously, the Supreme Court, and the appellate courts to a lesser extent, tend to favor the government in tax cases, as contrasted with the lower courts, which are more inclined to favor the taxpayer—so that this policy of the government has, on balance, been successful.

In tax litigation, the I.R.S. is represented by its own attorneys (regional counsel) in matters before the Tax Court, whereas the government is represented by attorneys from the Tax Division of the Justice Department in cases before the district courts and the Court of Claims, as well as before the appeals courts.

## THE TAXPAYER'S BURDEN OF PROOF

In contesting a tax deficiency, the taxpayer has one great advantage and one great disadvantage. The existence of the first is the rationale for the second.

The great advantage of the taxpayer over the government is that he controls most of the evidence and can thus preserve and produce the evidence most favorable to his version of what happened. To offset this rather substantial advantage, the tax law attaches a presumption of correctness to the determinations made by the Internal Revenue Service, whether or not supported by any evidence.

Thus, if a revenue agent proposes a deficiency in taxes on the basis that the taxpayer claimed charitable contributions of $1,000 that the revenue agent is disallowing as deductions, the government is not put in the untenable position of proving that the taxpayer did *not* make these contributions, or that the organizations to which the contributions were made were *not* tax-exempt. The taxpayer has the burden of affirmatively proving both that he made the contributions and that the organizations were of the type described in Section 170 of the Internal Revenue Code.

This burden of proof on the taxpayer is not a constant burden. Within the administrative process it will vary, depending on the person with whom the taxpayer is dealing. Some revenue agents seem to want proof beyond the shadow of any doubt. Others are satisfied with almost anything tending to support the deduction claimed.

The Tax Court tends to take the position that the burden of proof is more a burden of going forward with the evidence; therefore, a taxpayer's unsubstantiated but credible (and unrefuted) testimony may be all he needs on certain types of issues.

In a suit for refund in a district court, on the other hand, the exact burden of proof that is imposed may vary pretty much with the judge, if the trial is without a jury. It is only by suing for a refund in district court, incidentally, that a taxpayer is able to obtain a jury trial in a tax case.

## PENALTY PROVISIONS IN THE TAX LAW

Arguing with the government may pay off, but the taxpayer may well wonder what risks he takes. As long as neither fraud nor negligence is involved, the taxpayer will be charged interest on any deficiencies in tax. The interest runs from the date the tax payment was due. Because the interest is deductible, the cost of this type of "borrowing" from the government is less than that of "borrowing" from many alternative sources. Because the interest is deductible, the actual cost after tax gets less and less as the taxpayer's tax bracket gets higher and higher. Amounts paid for tax advice or in connection with tax controversies are also deductible, of course.

A charge is also made for substantial underpayment of estimated tax. This charge is *not* interest and is not deductible.

These two charges (on deficiencies and underpayments of estimates) are subject to adjustment every two years to keep them in line with prevailing interest rates. The rate charged was 7 percent in 1977.

Filing a return late will result in a penalty of 5 percent a month, up to a maximum of 25 percent of the tax, unless reasonable cause can be shown for failing to file the return on time. Advice of a competent tax adviser that no return was necessary is sometimes reasonable cause. Where a return cannot be filed on time because of illness, inability to obtain necessary information in time to prepare the return, and so forth, an extension of time for filing the return can be obtained *if* requested before the date the return is due.

Where a deficiency in tax is deemed to be caused by negligence or results from intentional disregard of the tax rules, an additional penalty of 5 percent can be imposed. Penalties, of course, unlike interest, are not deductible.

Finally, there is a civil fraud penalty that applies if any part of a deficiency is due to fraud. This penalty is 50 percent of the deficiency, even though part of the deficiency is not fraudulent.

Although normally no deficiency can be assessed on a return after three years have passed from the date the return was due, there is *no* time limit on assessment of a deficiency where any part of it is due to fraud. Of course, the burden of showing, by a preponderance of the evidence, that there has been fraud rests upon the government. (See Chapter 21.)

Criminal fraud is different from civil fraud. Penalties for criminal fraud are not based on the amount of tax involved; they consist of fines and/or imprisonment. The government must prove its case in a criminal tax matter beyond a reasonable doubt, as in any other criminal proceeding.

## THE STATUTE OF LIMITATIONS

In general, the Internal Revenue Service has three years from the date a tax return is due (or the date filed, if filed after the due date) within which to audit the return and assess any deficiencies. The taxpayer has the same period within which to file a claim for refund if he feels he has overpaid his tax.

To the general three-year rule, there are exceptions of which the government can take advantage. A six-year statute of limitations applies if the taxpayer omits 25 percent or more of his gross income. It matters not that the omission is completely innocent. If the taxpayer's return is fraudulent, then there is no statute of limitations at all. In 1949, the government collected a deficiency (plus interest, plus a 50 percent civil fraud penalty) on a 1924 return when it was able to show that some part of the deficiency was due to fraud.

A taxpayer may have to pay additional tax after filing his return—usually as the result of an I.R.S. audit. At this time, little of the three-year period may remain, since that is measured from the date the return is filed. To give the taxpayer a break in such a situation, he can file a claim for refund at any time within two years of paying a tax, regardless of the three-year statute of limitations. Where either the taxpayer or the government adopts an inconsistent position, resulting in an item being twice taxed, twice deducted, or something similar, a special exception to the statute of limitations may be invoked.

Criminal penalties may be imposed for willful violations of the tax laws. The statute of limitations on these is normally six years from the date of commission of the criminal act. In a tax offense, this would commonly mean six years from the date of the filing of the return.

## TAX PRACTICE AS A PROFESSION

The largest single employer of tax people is, quite naturally, the Internal Revenue Service, with over 70,000 employees scattered over the United States (and a few in other parts of the world). Although its headquarters are in Washington, less than 10 percent of these employees are actually stationed in the District of Columbia. The principal professional jobs within the Internal Revenue Service are those of the revenue agent, revenue officer, special agent, estate tax attorney and tax auditors. Compensation in these jobs is on a par with similar nongovernment jobs, ultimately ranging to over $35,000 per year, and there ar certain intangible advantages to government employment. Each job has an intensive training and internship program.

The job of the *internal revenue agent* is essentially an auditing one. An agent works with corporate executives, accountants, attorneys, businessmen, and taxpayers themselves, examining their records and investigating other sources of information in attempting to determine their correct federal tax liability. Four years of college, including a major in accounting, is required, but this need not include any specific training in taxes.

The position of *revenue officer* likewise requires four years of college, but the major field of study may be in any business-related subjects, including accounting, business administration, business economics, finance, and law. The work consists essentially of collection activities, including the working out of arrangements for payment by financially harassed taxpayers, as contrasted with the revenue agent's auditing activities.

The *special agents* are the Dick Tracys of the Internal Revenue Service. They investigate possible tax frauds and other criminal violations of the tax laws. Their training program covers the skills needed to document, evaluate, and organize evidence; to prepare reports of findings; to conduct surveillance of suspects, interrogate witnesses, make arrests, and conduct raids.

To qualify for a job as special agent, you must have either a law degree or four years of college study, the latter including twelve semester hours of accounting. Because of the sensitive nature of the special agent's job, a personal interview and a written test measuring investigative aptitudes are also required.

The job of the *estate tax attorney* involves determining the value, ownership of interests, and taxability of estates left by decedents and of gifts made by people during their lifetimes. The work involves reviewing financial data, wills, trust indentures, and other legal documents, and contact with trust officers, bank officials, attorneys, executors, and officials of federal, state, and probate courts. Because of the nature of the work, a law degree is required of estate tax attorneys—and this is the only Internal Revenue position of those under discussion for which the normal business curriculum, with some concentration in accounting, does not furnish adequate education.

The *tax auditor's* work is similar to that of the revenue agent but concentrates more on individual-taxpayer returns. Usually, the taxpayer comes to the office to talk with the tax auditor, rather than having the tax auditor come to his office or home for an audit, as in cases handled by the revenue agent. Four years of college study are required, with a major in accounting, economics, finance, business administration, or law preferred.

Most of the tax positions outside the Internal Revenue Service are with accounting firms. These firms range from large, international organizations with thousands of employees to individual practitioners with no employees. With the smaller firms, a new employee is expected to be almost immediately productive, and a fairly extensive college background in accounting and taxes is therefore desirable. The larger firms have training programs, plus a system by which the new employee works under fairly close supervision for the first year or two. Some of these larger firms have been known to hire outstanding students who have no background at all in accounting.

With a large C.P.A. firm, a person interested in tax work can look forward to being assigned to the firm's tax department after a year or two of experience in auditing work. As a tax specialist, his income within the firm can rise to the range of $20,000 to $35,000 per year within seven or eight years. If he becomes a partner, he can expect his income to range from $40,000 on up. Many partners in the larger firms earn more than $100,000 per year.

Working for a small accounting firm generally involves more varied tax work in the earlier stages of a career. But many small firms also do a substantial amount of what is known as "write-up" work which is looked down upon by many accountants as not much more than "mere" bookkeeping. They tend to do only a limited amount of the type of auditing done by the larger firms. Within two or three years, the ambitious and able accountant with the small firm may be thinking of achieving partnership status or of going into practice on his own account. As a partner in a small C.P.A. firm, or as an individual practitioner, he can expect to earn anywhere in the range of $25,000 to over $100,000 per year. Without the C.P.A. certificate, it is still possible to become an individual practitioner, but the financial potential is usually limited, since certain types of services will not normally be handled by the noncertified accountant. To the tax man desiring to specialize in tax work and not interested in auditing, passing the Internal Revenue Service enrollment examination will qualify him to operate on the same level as the C.P.A. in dealing with the I.R.S. but will not give him the public prestige that the C.P.A. enjoys.

Many attorneys specialize in tax practice. Because there are probably not over 5,000 or 6,000 who really could be described as full-time tax attorneys, it is difficult to generalize as to their incomes. Most of them have spent several years working for the Justice Department tax division (which handles tax cases in the district courts and the Court of Claims) or the Regional Counsel's office of the Internal Revenue Service (which handles Tax Court cases), but many are also former regular or special agents. Some have been with the Tax Court, and still others served an internship with a prominent tax lawyer.

In addition, an increasing number of industrial and financial concerns have set up their own tax departments to handle their own tax problems. This represents recognition of the fact that tax considerations permeate almost any business decision and need to be reflected in the thinking that precedes a decision. Compensation of professional tax employees of these companies is comparable to that paid by the large C.P.A. firms to tax department personnel—and, in fact, many of these people are former tax department personnel of C.P.A. firms.

The various state governments, and their subdivisions with taxing powers, also frequently employ tax people, although many of these jobs are not of professional caliber and do not offer professional-level compensation.

The percentage growth in numbers of persons engaged in tax work has been extremely high throughout this past half-century. Although the growth may level off somewhat, it is likely that the number of jobs requiring some technical tax knowledge will continue to increase for many years into the future.

**C.P.A.'S IN TAX PRACTICE**

From time to time, the right of C.P.A.'s to engage in federal tax practice has been challenged. State courts have in the past tended to take the position that a C.P.A. furnishing tax advice except as incidental to preparation of a tax return, or rendering of other accounting services, or representing a taxpayer in proceedings before the Internal Revenue Service, might be engaged in the unauthorized practice of law. Federal courts, in the few cases that had come before them, were inclined to take the position that practicing before the Internal Revenue Service in accordance with Treasury Department rules was not within the jurisdiction of state laws.

In 1963, a Supreme Court decision in a case involving a patent agent appeared to lay to rest any danger that nonlawyers would be charged with practicing law in representing clients before the Internal Revenue Service or the Tax Court. In that case (*Sperry* v. *State of Florida,* 83 S. Ct. 1322), the Court unanimously declared that "a State may not enforce licensing requirements which, though valid in the absence of federal regulation, give the State's licensing board a virtual power of review over the federal determination that a person or agency is qualified and entitled to perform certain functions, or which impose upon the performance of activity sanctioned by federal license additional conditions not contemplated by Congress. . . ."

## CASE EXCERPTS

*U.S.* v. *McCormick* (CA2 1933) 13 AFTR 410 (67 F. 2d 867)
*Commissioner* v. *Newman* (CA2 1947) 35 AFTR 857 (159 F. 2d 848)
*Kurio v. U.S.*, 27 AFTR 2d 71-301 (D.C-Tex. 1971)
27AFTR 2d 71-301 (281 F. Supp. 252)
*McGowan* v. *Commissioner,* 67 T.C.–No. 43 (1976)

*U.S.* v. *McCormick*
(CA2 1933) 13 AFTR 410 (67 F.2d 867)

. . . . The defendant contends that he should have been acquitted because he voluntarily filed delinquent returns. . . . The most that can be said for defendant on account of his disclosure and payment of taxes is that such acts tended to show innocence. The argument is stronger that they only showed a desire to place himself in a safer position when it had become certain that his illegal acts were about to be discovered. . . .

*Commissioner* v. *Newman*
(CA2 1947) 35 AFTR 857 (159 F. 2d 848)

L. Hand, CIRCUIT JUDGE (dissenting). . .

Over and over again courts have said that there is nothing sinister in so arranging one's affairs as to keep taxes as low as possible. Everybody does so, rich or poor; and all do right, for nobody owes any public duty to pay more than the law demands; taxes are enforced extractions, not voluntary contributions. To demand more in the name of morals is mere cant. . . .

*Kurio* v. *U.S.*
27 AFTR 2d 71-301 (D.C.-Tex. 1971) (281 F. Supp. 252)

The purpose of the computer processing system is not only to process perfect returns with dispatch, it is also to process and correct imperfect returns with dispatch. The Court recognizes that an imperfect or an eccentric return will require more time for processing, and does not criticize the IRS computer system, or the officials in charge of such system, for attempting to correct mistakes and examine unusual features. On the other hand, in its original opinion the Court did criticize the IRS system and its supervisors for the absence of procedures permitting errors and eccentricities to be detected and corrected promptly. Such remains the opinion of this Court. That a return is imperfect is no justification for any appreciable delay in processing it. Until the officials in charge of the IRS processing system accept this truth, other taxpayers will be oppressed by that system just as the record reveals plaintiff was oppressed. . . .

Under IRS procedures, the purpose of diverting "unsuitable" returns to the Error Resolution Branch is to correct errors made during processing and to request the taxpayer to correct errors, omissions, and discrepancies detected during processing. Notations made on the Sheetrock return by a specialist before it reached the Error Resolution Branch reflected that payment of the indicated balance due had accompanied the return, but that the depositary receipts and tabulations substantiating the claimed adjustments were missing. Thus the IRS procedures then in effect required personnel in the Error Resolution Branch, upon receipt of the "rejected" Sheetrock return, to search for the missing depositary receipts (the existence and transmittal of which were clearly shown in the space provided on the return) and adjustment substantiation, and *if unable to locate them, to notify the taxpayer of their absence and request an explanation.*

Testimony at trial indicated that IRS procedure requires Error Resolution Branch personnel to mail a notice to the taxpayer requesting any missing substantiation. If there is no reply, the request is furnished to personnel in the Tax Assister section in the Houston IRS office, who make two attempts to contact the taxpayer. If the local personnel are unsuccessful, they notify the

Service Center, which resolves the ambiguity against the taxpayer and adjusts his tax liability accordingly.

At trial the IRS official who described such procedure referred during his testimony to an internal IRS memorandum apparently reflecting that attempts to contact plaintiff had been unsuccessful. The memorandum was not offered in evidence. *The record does not reflect that the taxpayer plaintiff was ever contacted.* It reflects only that the return was not perfected, and that it was again marked with a "Reject" stamp by some clerk somewhere within the Service Center .... *Although the back of the return identified the missing depositary receipts by serial number, date, and amount, there is no evidence that anyone ever attempted to obtain substantiation of the deposit credits claimed by plaintiff, either from the Federal Reserve System or from plaintiff himself. Nor is there any evidence that anyone ever attempted to obtain substantiation of the claimed adjustments from plaintiff.*

Proof that something never happened is difficult to make. However, I am convinced from my examination of the rejected Sheetrock return, the other internal IRS documents introduced in evidence at trial, and the internal procedure of the IRS to record each such action, that any effort to substantiate the claimed deposits or adjustments would have been reflected by an appropriate notation on the return. On the whole record, plaintiff's prompt response whenever requests for information were addressed to him, White's long acquaintance with many of the Houston IRS personnel and their knowledge that he represented plaintiff, and the absence of any affirmative indication on the Sheetrock return or elsewhere in the record that any notification was ever sent, *I find that the IRS never sought plaintiff's help in its effort to process his Sheetrock return.* This failure of the IRS to contact plaintiff and promptly resolve the error referred to the Error Resolution Branch had a disastrous effect on plaintiff's posture before the IRS. It was the immediate cause of the incomplete recordation in the computer both in the Austin Service Center and the National Computer Center of what had transpired, the transfer of the credits out of the 1965 account, significant subsequent transactions, and other consequences adverse to plaintiff which were not of his making.

As a result of intentional conduct, known mistakes in the statement of plaintiff's tax liabilities for 1963, 1964 and 1965 remained uncorrected and consequently, the liens filed against plaintiff to secure such liabilities also remained uncorrected. The existence of these liens subjected plaintiff to severe economic compulsion.

*McGowan* v. *Commissioner*
67 T.C.–No. 43 (1976)

I.R.S. disallowed deduction by an employee of the $72 withheld from his wages and paid to the Rhode Island temporary disability insurance fund. The employee appealed the I.R.S. decision to the Tax Court. In order to avoid an unfavorable Tax Court decision, the I.R.S. conceded the question just prior to trial. Because so many taxpayers in Rhode Island and in other states (e.g. California) with similar plans would be affected, the taxpayer asked the Tax Court to hand down a decision in spite of the I.R.S. concession.

Several factors conjoin here to dictate our rejection of respondent's offer of concession in the best interests of justice. As discussed later in this opinion, respondent first issued an administrative ruling on this question in 1943. I.T. 3607, 1943 C.B. 110. That ruling was modified in 1944 by another published ruling, I.T. 3663, 1944 C.B. 110, and remained in force for more than 30 years thereafter without further modification. Respondent abruptly reversed his position in 1975 through the issuance of Rev. Rul. 75-148, 1975-1 C.B. 64, despite the absence of any significant change in the underlying statutory provisions upon which his earlier rulings rested. This abrupt shift in position, standing alone, would not necessarily run counter to the interests of justice if it were grounded on sound legal principles and fully explained to the inquiring public. In this instance, however, we recognize that respondent's abrupt reversal concerning the Rhode Island contributions was effected without commensurate reversals in rationale being applied with respect to a series of comparable rulings pertaining to foreign tax credits which are mentioned later . . . .

Another factor causing us to reject respondent's offer of concession is the very language of Rev. Rul. 75-148. Not only does that ruling fail to address the primary issue presented for decision by petitioner's motion in a comprehensive manner, but its statement of position also appears invalid. Despite respondent's admission in his notice of concession that this ruling currently is being reconsidered, we are not inclined to believe that such review is being undertaken with the expedience dictated by the circumstances surrounding this case. Many taxpayers in Rhode Island will be affected by the outcome herein and the time for filing another year's return is rapidly approaching for most of them. We continuously have emphasized our desire to reach a speedy determination from the moment petitioner's motion for summary judgment was filed on October 15, 1976. Although respondent (1) reconsidered his original position in 1975 when the most recent ruling was published, (2) has been involved in a lengthy administrative dispute on this point with petitioners during 1976, and (3) has been litigating this case before us since July 26, 1976, he continues to claim as late as December 6, 1976, that more time is needed to resolve the issue administratively. Moreover, his repeated attempts to obtain continuances have run counter to our expressed desire to quickly resolve the issue. We think the interests of justice now demand a more expeditious resolution of the issue than respondent has been willing to provide. Therefore, we conclude that our rejection of respondent's Notice of Concession represents a valid exercise of judicial discretion . . . .

Respondent has deliberately avoided any attempt to support the correctness of Rev. Rul. 75-148. This is not too surprising because it is our firm conviction that the revenue ruling is defective for various reasons. It erroneously holds that employees' contributions to the Rhode Island temporary disability insurance fund are not "taxes." Yet with intrinsic inconsistency it concludes that employers' (secondary or derivative) contributions to the same fund are "taxes." It fails to consider whether the employees' contributions qualify as State "income taxes" under section 164(a)(3). It is plainly inconsistent with respondent's rulings on foreign tax credits. In concluding that such contributions are nondeductible personal expenses under section 262, it fails to give any attention to the clear holding of this Court – and respondent's own position – that an employee is engaged in a trade or business. David J. Primuth, supra; and Rev. Rul. 72-463, 1972-2 C.B. 93. In addition, Rev. Rul. 75-148 is fundamentally wrong in its conclusion that employees' payments under the Rhode Island law are "similar" to employees' payments under the New York law. The two laws are entirely different. And, finally, a long-standing administrative interpretation (here two rulings in existence for over 30 years), applying to a substantially re-enacted statute, is deemed to have received congressional approval and has the effect of law. * * *

All in all, we perceive no sound or rational legal basis for sustaining the validity of Rev. Rul. 75-148. In our judgment the ruling is invalid and, in fairness to thousands of Rhode Island employees, it should be revoked immediately. To let linger the uncertainty created by respondent's inaction would show a careless and callous disregard of the rights of these individuals. They seek a definitive answer. They are entitled to have it.

Accordingly, we will grant petitioners' motion for summary judgment.

## QUESTIONS AND PROBLEMS

1. Your father opened his own business last year and is now looking for someone to assist him in preparing his federal income tax return. He also thinks he may need some advice on how to save taxes. He has several people in mind, from among whom he is going to make a choice:

   *A* advertises "Tax returns prepared. Results guaranteed" in the classified section of the newspaper.

   *B* has a sign on his office door: "Public Accountant. Enrolled to practice before the Internal Revenue Service."

   *C* is a lawyer engaged in general practice.

   *D* is a certified public accountant engaged in general practice.

   *E* is a real estate office with a sign, "Tax Returns Prepared," in the window.

   Explain briefly the tax qualifications each of these persons has demonstrated he possesses.

2. What are the only two federal bodies that give examinations testing an applicant's ability in federal tax law and accounting?

3. Does the federal government regulate the practice of law? Of public accounting?
4. A person not a lawyer is normally prohibited by state law from doing the things that a lawyer is peculiarly qualified to do. Do the states generally prohibit persons not C.P.A.'s from doing the things that C.P.A.'s are peculiarly qualified to do?
5. "Tax planning and tax controversy cost both the taxpayer and the government money. It would be better in the long run if taxpayers were not given the right to appeal the decisions of revenue agents. After all, the revenue agents are not paid on a commission basis, they have no axe to grind, and so their decisions should be fair!" Discuss the pros and cons of this argument.
6. Costs of tax planning and tax controversy are deductible—including fees paid. Jerry Keaton is in a 60 percent tax bracket. His tax adviser has come up with a tax plan that has only a 1 out of 4 (0.25) chance of success. If it fails, Jerry will have to pay the $20,000 of tax he will save if the plan succeeds, plus 7 percent interest for two years (deductible, of course). Fees and costs of $8,000 will be necessary to resolve the tax controversy that is sure to develop. Will Jerry be better off adopting the plan or not adopting it? Would your answer be the same if Jerry were in a 20 percent tax bracket?
7. A taxpayer wishes to contest a proposed tax deficiency without first paying the tax. Describe the steps he would take after being unable to reach an agreement with the revenue agent. Who can represent him?
8. A taxpayer feels that he would find a more sympathetic attitude toward his position from a jury. However, a jury trial is available only in a U. S. district court in a tax case, and then only if requested by the taxpayer. Describe the steps the taxpayer would have to take after being unable to reach agreement with the revenue agent. Who can represent the taxpayer in a district court suit?
9. What is the function of taxpayer individual-account numbers in the ADP system? If a person received dividend income but failed to report it on his individual return, would the computer spot this? If a physician received a substantial portion of his fees from patients in cash, how would the computer spot this?
10. Trace briefly the journey of a tax bill through Congress—from the committee to which it will first be referred to final signature by the president.
11. What is the function of the Joint Committee on Internal Revenue Taxation?
12. Describe the role of the Treasury Department as:
    (a) Lobbyist for tax legislation
    (b) Interpreter of the tax laws
    (c) Collector of the revenue
    (d) A party to federal tax litigation

13. The Tax Court was created in 1924 to provide an independent administrative body to which appeals of Treasury Department tax decisions could be taken without the necessity of suing for a refund. More recently, it has been proposed that the function of issuing regulations interpreting the tax law should be entrusted to an independent commission rather than to the Treasury. What might be some of the arguments, pro and con, on such a proposal?
14. Dave Keefe filed his 1974 income tax return on April 15, 1975. It is now 1979, and he is thinking about destroying his canceled checks, receipts, etc., supporting the items on the 1974 return. Is he justified in doing this?
15. Distinguish the job of the revenue agent from that of the special agent. Is a C.P.A. certificate or a law degree required for either of these jobs?
16. In addition to I.R.S., what other possible employment opportunities are there for a person interested in a tax career? Does it appear that most tax jobs demand a high degree of specialization in tax work while the person is still in school, or does it appear that most of the specialized training is acquired after leaving school?
17. In addition to attorneys and C.P.A.'s, other persons enrolled to practice before the I.R.S. are allowed to represent taxpayers at all levels within the Internal Revenue Service.

    (a) Does this mean that tax-return preparation is restricted to such persons?

    (b) Does this mean that only such persons can represent a taxpayer when his return is being examined by a revenue agent or tax examiner?

    (c) Since practice before the I.R.S. involves representing taxpayers, and since the Internal Revenue Code is a law, should not such representation be limited to lawyers as being the practice of law?
18. "Once a case reaches the point of litigation, it is not uncommon for the attorneys for a government agency to approach their task with the attitude that their objective is to win their case and bring the recalcitrant to heel. Like career soldiers, they are professionals doing a job and there is no personal enmity involved in the actions they take." Contrast this statement with the comment that "the function of any government official must first be scrupulous fairness, with doubts being resolved in favor of the taxpayer. For the government to wrongfully deprive a taxpayer of his property, or the right to use it, is as reprehensible as for the government to deprive him of his civil liberties. Personal freedom without protection of property rights is meaningless in a complex industrialized urban society." How do the *Kurio* and *McGowan* cases relate to these two statements?

# 2

# Concepts of Income

Back in the year 1930, a former mop boy with a scar on his face dominated the booze and gambling underworld in Chicago. Al Capone, then only 35, was treated like bad weather: People said, "How terrible!" but nobody did anything. No one ever did convict Al Capone (alias Al Brown) of murder. They never convicted him of violating the Prohibition Act. They never convicted him of violating any law against gambling.

A concept, and a lot of hard work by Treasury Department agents, sent Al Capone to jail. But hard work alone had failed to win conviction (or even indictment) for most of his crimes. A charge of income tax evasion succeeded. The public was satisfied; Capone had been "gotten." A new wrinkle had been added to the old saw that "the power to tax is the power to destroy."

## THE NET-WORTH APPROACH TO INCOME

Our concern is with the concept we referred to, for its application is not limited to criminals. Income, according to this concept, is the amount that could be consumed by an individual or distributed by a business to its owners, and still leave the person or the business as well off at the end of the year as at the beginning. Its application in tax matters to people like Al Capone, Jake Guzik, Al Nitti, Johnny Torrio, Willie Bioff, and Mickey Cohen is based on the fundamental assumption that all inflows of wealth are taxable income unless specifically excluded from that category by the tax law—and the related proposition that the burden of proving that any such exclusions apply rests on the taxpayer. This concept is called the *net-worth method* in taxes.

In a criminal net-worth case, the special agent (an I.R.S. agent who specializes in violations of the tax laws) decides that the taxpayer's returns and records do not fairly reflect his income. He tries, therefore, to set up a meaningful balance sheet, showing the taxpayer's assets and liabilities, as of a basic date—say, January 1, 1979. He may get help in doing this from financial statements that the taxpayer has furnished to banks or other credit grantors. But racketeers, as opposed to the many more legitimate businessmen who are charged with tax evasion, seldom furnish balance sheets to anyone.

The suspect, of course, is in a dilemma when it comes to helping the agent gather data. If he cooperates, the information he gives may prove to be what convicts him. If he had large amounts of assets on January 1, 1979, the next question would be, "Where did they come from?" If he gives false information, this can result in conviction on a criminal charge. The usual result is that he gives no information.

The special agent attempts to build a balance sheet as of the end of each year from the base date to the present—say, as of December 31, 1981, December 31, 1982, December 31, 1983, and December 31, 1984. The more recent the date, the easier it is for him to get accurate information. Let's say that the base-date balance sheet showed total assets of $1,500,000 and liabilities of $500,000, or a net worth of $1,000,000. The balance sheet at December 31, 1984, showed a net worth of $1,600,000. Thus, net worth increased by $600,000.

The agent also works on the amounts spent during the four years. Perhaps the taxpayer has a nonworking ranch in Arizona, a penthouse apartment on Chicago's Gold Coast, and a mansion in Ft. Lauderdale. It is hard to hide a lavish standard of living. Perhaps the agent can show that the taxpayer spends at least $100,000 a year in ways that are nondeductible. For four years that amounts to $400,000.

The net-worth increase of $600,000 plus the consumption expenditures of $400,000 indicate income of $1,000,000 for the four years. The tax returns show $200,000. The books and records maintained are obviously incomplete and demonstrably inaccurate. The likelihood of the government's obtaining a conviction on a tax-evasion charge is good.

### *Defects in the Net-Worth Concept*

As a basic technique for computing taxable income, the net-worth concept is used only as a last resort. Some taxpayers keep no records; others falsify or destroy their records. Without some such administrative tool as the net-worth approach, a taxpayer might be rewarded for successfully concealing his records.

The net-worth approach is time-consuming, expensive, and lacking in precision when used as a substitute for adequate books and records. But it is a useful audit tool when books and records are maintained and is routinely utilized as an automatic control technique on partnership and corporation returns, as we shall see in later chapters.

While the net-worth approach employed in taxes is related to what we might describe as the net-worth approach to defining income in economics, the two are not identical. In taxes, net-worth calculations are used to approximate taxable income. In spite of the differences, our understanding of the meaning of income would be incomplete if we did not explore the economist's net-worth approach to income determination.

To arrive at net worth, we deduct the taxpayer's liabilities from the value of his assets. But what is "value"? Well, there are different types of value. One type is "fair market value." This is the amount that a willing buyer would be willing to pay, with full knowledge of all relevant facts and under no compulsion to buy, and that a willing seller would be willing to accept, again with full knowledge of all the facts and under no compulsion to sell.

This concept of value is not practical because it can easily be figured only if an active, publicized market exists for the thing to be valued, or if the person doing the figuring is omniscient. It also begs the question. As a buyer, why would I be willing to buy a particular thing? If I am dealing with personal things, consumption things, it is because I expect that the satisfaction I will get from that thing will exceed the satisfaction that I could get from any other thing or combination of things that I could buy for the same amount of money. This is hardly an easily determined amount for something I already possess, such as my old pipe, for which nobody else would have the slightest use. For business things, perhaps, the reason for my willingness to buy may be clearer. I will put up a dollar now if I will get back from that investment more dollars than I can get back from any other comparable investment open to me at the moment. Thus, the value of a thing in this context will be the present worth of all the future cash flows that the thing will produce.

Value, in other words, is essentially a speculation about the future. Only in this way can we explain why, within a period of one year, common stock of IBM can sell for as much as \$400 a share and as little as \$200. Appraisal of the future by the investing public shifts, and as it shifts, from moment to moment, values climb and dive.

To be a practical concept for income taxation, a concept of income must be certain enough in its application to most situations to keep controversy to a minimum. If we cannot calculate what George should pay, how can we make George pay it? If it costs \$5 to convince George by this concept that he should pay \$3 in income taxes, the concept is hardly a practical one. The net-worth approach is neither simple nor objective enough for widespread use.

## CONSUMPTION AS INCOME

At the opposite pole in economic theory from the net-worth approach to income is an approach emphasizing "satisfaction." Money is viewed as merely a convenient mechanism, a device for allocation of real wealth. But, in this "satisfaction" or "consumption" approach, money is also used to measure satisfaction in quite a direct and objective manner. The amount spent on consumer goods and services is the amount of a person's income. To this must be added the use value of the durable goods that he owns. Thus, not the purchase but the use of a house or a car would be income. The source of what is spent is immaterial. Because a business can't consume anything (for all its size, General Motors can't even eat a toasted cheese sandwich), only people would have income, of course.

There are strong differences of opinion as to how certain and simple a tax on expenditures would be. A flat-rate tax, as contrasted with a "progressive" tax in which the tax rate would rise as the amount of expenditures rose, would probably be quite simple. It would merely be an excise, or sales, tax on all consumption transactions. We already have federal excise taxes on many types of transactions. And most of the states impose sales and/or use taxes on the bulk of consumption transactions.

Many contend that such a tax, even with a progressive feature, would be unfair to those who must (or think they must) consume all they earn merely to live, as compared with those with larger incomes (or smaller appetites), who could invest and reinvest a part of their incomes tax free. Certainly an expenditure approach to defining income for tax purposes would encourage saving and discourage consumption. Thus, the expenditure approach runs counter to the political philosophy that a high level of consumer consumption is to be desired and consumer saving is not.

Offsetting this is the advantage of consumption taxes over income taxes when it comes to foreign trade. In such countries as France and West Germany, for instance, the general excise taxes are not imposed on exports. Companies in such countries are therefore able to sell to foreigners at prices below those that (including the tax) they charge their fellow countrymen. A United States company, however, presumably must reflect the income tax load it pays in its price structure. This increases its prices relative to its French or German competitor. To add insult to injury, the U.S. company selling into France or Germany must pay an additional import tax. Imposing a tax on consumption would eliminate the U.S. company's reflecting income tax considerations in its pricing policies. The company could thus sell abroad on a more competitive footing. Furthermore, because foreign imports would encounter the same consumption tax as U.S. products, the company's domestic sales position would not be weakened as substantially as many feel it is now (but see Chapter 18 on foreign tax matters and Chapter 23 on tax reform).

## THE ACCOUNTANT'S CONCEPT

The problem of determining income was not spawned by the advent of the United States income tax. England had an income tax as early as 1799, France had an income tax throughout the eighteenth century, and Florence, Italy, had an income tax in the fifteenth century—but the problem of determining income existed entirely independent of tax considerations.

The problem seems inevitable whenever two or more people join together to conduct any enterprise for profit. In a simple, one-shot venture, the problem is not acute. If X and Y pool their resources, rent an empty lot in early December, buy some Christmas trees, and burn whatever trees remain on January 2, they can figure their profit quite easily on January 2. Theirs is a self-liquidating venture. They start with cash and end with cash. But few modern businesses are one-shot endeavors.

The British Companies Acts of the 1840's and 1850's brought the problem of income to a head and gave birth to the public accounting profession as we know it today. Under those acts, distributions to corporate shareholders that were not from profits (net income) were forbidden. To insure that net income was properly determined, provision was made for an annual audit. Thus, the public accounting profession was early charged with the mission of determining what was income legally available for dividends to shareholders.

The problem of determining income also existed in the area of trust accounting. Where property was held by a fiduciary with the income therefrom to go to one person and the corpus (principal or capital), upon death of the life tenant, to go to another person (the remainderman), it obviously made a difference whether a given inflow was properly called income or considered capital in nature, and whether a given outflow was an expense chargeable against the life tenant or a capital item to be borne by the remainder interest. One of the early Supreme Court decisions on the modern United States income tax (*Towne* v. *Eisner;* see excerpt at the end of this chapter) brought a fiduciary accounting concept to bear on an income tax problem in dealing with a stock dividend.

A one sentence definition of *income,* as the financial accountant might see it, would probably be something like this: Income for a period is the excess of the consideration received, in completed transactions involving the furnishing of goods or services, over the sum of (1) the costs of the assets used up in providing those goods or rendering those services, and (2) any losses sustained during that period. Losses, in this context, would be the using up of assets without the receipt of a full consideration, as, for instance, through a fire that was only partially compensated for by insurance.

The financial accountant's concept of income differs substantially from the economist's, because the purpose of his work differs. The economist deals with value, which is essentially a speculation about the future. He is concerned with the ways in which scarce resources are allocated. He uses money as a measure of value. The accountant deals with transactions and events, which is to say that he deals with the past. He uses money as a symbol. Money provides a common denominator for the diverse things that get involved in transactions.

The financial accountant is concerned with measuring the flow of transactions through the individual enterprise. His objective is that contractual rights of the various claimants to corporate income and assets be fairly reflected, and that those who are responsible for the enterprise assets be able to show a proper performance of their stewardship. This is not all of modern accounting, but this aspect of accounting, as ancient in its origin as the separation of ownership and control, still underlies the concepts employed by practicing accountants.

Let us contrast the net-worth approach of the economist and the transactional approach of the accountant. A factory building is purchased at a cost of $110,000, including $100,000 for the building itself and $10,000 for the land on which it stands. In the accountant's symbolism, one building equals $100,000; land equals $10,000. When half the utility of the building (based on estimates of useful life) has been used up, the accountant's symbolism might show: One-half building equals $50,000; land equals $10,000.

By this time, the fair market value of the building may be $70,000, and that of the land $40,000.

If the property is now sold for $100,000, the economists might say that at the start of the year involved, what we owned had a value of $110,000, whereas at the end of the year we had only $100,000, and therefore a loss of $10,000 was sustained. The accountant, however, deals with the symbols derived from the original transaction—not with the constantly changing values. He would show $50,000 (one-half building) plus $10,000 (land) being exchanged for $100,000, resulting in a gain of $40,000.

Because he deals with transactions, not with values, the accountant would have recorded the transaction in which the property was purchased. A derivative of the original transaction was the necessity of recording the periodic expiration of part of the cost of the building, since the original transaction included an expenditure of $100,000 for the use of a building for *x* years. His record was unaffected by happenings that were not transactions, that did not involve exchanges between the particular accounting entity and the outside world. Thus, he would not have recorded the changing property values, because there were no exchanges to which this particular accounting entity was a party. Finally, when a sale transaction occurs, its effect is measured relative to the previous transactions. Thus, the flow of transactions, rather than value changes is measured. At any time, the financial records also fulfill their stewardship function. The responsibility that was assumed as the result of the basic transaction was to account for one building plus some land. From this point of view, the fluctuating values of land and building were irrelevant. However, once the land and building were disposed of, a new accountability—for purchasing power—was created.

It should be noted that in this "historical cost" use of money as a symbol, the fact that a dollar at one point in time does not equal a dollar at another point in time disturbs many accountants. Although they would retain the use of the dollar as a symbol, they would like to adjust the dollar to represent a more constant common denominator.

The Trueblood report, an in-depth look at accounting objectives published by the American Institute of C.P.A.'s in 1974, called for accounting records that would "serve primarily those users who have limited authority, ability, or resources to obtain information and who rely on financial statements as their principal source of information about an enterprise's economic activities." This report strongly emphasized information that would help the reader assess the prospects of receiving cash—for a stockholder, cash from dividends; for a creditor, cash from interest and the sale or maturity of the debt obligation.

In late 1976, the Financial Accounting Standards Board (FASB) was still wrestling with the question, "What are the objectives of financial accounting?" In addition to the "historical cost" approach to measuring assets and liabilities, and their changes, the FASB saw four other approaches:

1. Current cost—what it might cost today to replace an asset or to replace its productive capacity;
2. Current exit value—the amount that could be raised currently by sale of the asset or the amount needed to remove the liability;
3. Expected exit value—the cash the company expects to receive from holding an asset; and
4. Present value of expected cash flows—the technique already in use in handling capitalization of leases.

## INCOME CONCEPTS AND BUSINESS DECISIONS

How do you measure the success of a business? Depending upon your view of the function of business in a free society, your answer might range from "service to society" to "profit distributed to the shareholders." The first is difficult to measure—except as you may argue that society rewards most richly those businesses that best serve its wants, in which case profit would be the measure—whereas the dividends paid can provide only a long-run test of success. In the long run, presumably, the profit or net income of the business will approximate the amount available for distribution to shareholders In the short run, however, dividends may be low because the business is reinvesting earnings internally, or because the business has earned a lower than normal profit; dividends may be high because earnings are high, but they may also be high because the business is making no provision for the future or is actually distributing capital to its shareholders.

The business normally reports its earnings to outsiders in accordance with generally accepted accounting procedures. When you read in *The Wall Street Journal* or *Barron's* or your morning newspaper that the X Company has earned

$2.70 per share for the year just ended, you are reading a report based on accounting concepts of income. The financial statements that a borrower furnishes to a bank are accounting-based statements. To the extent, therefore, that a management is consciously aiming at results that will meet the actual or implied standards of performance set for the business by stockholders, credit grantors, regulatory bodies, and other interested parties (not excluding employees, who may, for instance, be covered by a profit-sharing plan), the management must take into account in its decisions the effect on the profit that will be reported in the financial statements.

If the firm's planning and control procedures, particularly the planning budget, are integrated by preparing projected financial statements to see what the results of the planned operation would look like when set into the framework of the accounting concept of profit, and are then revised to lead to more acceptable results, the impact of accounting concepts may seep down to the decisions made at the lowest supervisory levels within the organization.

At the level of national policy, perception of profitability by Congress, regulatory bodies, the anti-trust division of the U.S. Department of Justice, and various other publics, not excluding labor unions, in itself has effects on business profits. Thus, if high reported profits in an industry result in attempts to eliminate the excess profits–through taxes, divestations, price controls, increased labor costs, or government contract renegotiation–then the accounting concept will prove to be a self-defeating measurement. Then, also, managers may be stimulated to find ways of reporting lesser earnings.

Accounting concepts of income, therefore, however limited or inadequate they may be, do have indirect effects on business decisions. These same concepts of income have been instrumental in shaping the rules for determining taxable income. By so doing, they have affected business decisions in a direct way–for the income tax is a drain on cash as well as an operating expense, and its control is one of management's responsibilities.

## TAX CONCEPTS VERSUS ACCOUNTING CONCEPTS

The political concept of income is a product of the pressure of administrators toward specific, workable rules and of taxpayer groups toward special treatment for themselves and their problems. In the United States, difficulty was encountered in formulating a political concept of income in the years prior to 1918. The tax act of 1918, and the regulations amplifying and interpreting it, adopted the accountant's transactional approach for the determination of taxable income. The basic approach is still the matrix of the Internal Revenue Code. It is retained because it is workable. It means that revenue and expenses are to be determined on the basis of completed transactions between a taxpayer and an outside party. Increments in value not realized through transactions are not income. Declines in value, not actually sustained as losses through transactions, are not deductible.

But even though the tax law's approach is essentially the transactional approach of the accountant, there are numerous differences between accounting concepts of income and tax concepts of income. In fact, much of this book—indeed, much of the study of taxation—is devoted to the study of the areas where commercial accounting and tax accounting fail to coincide. However, it is easy to be overimpressed with the differences and to lose sight of the fact that probably over 95 percent of the dollar amounts of business gross income and business deductions reported on tax returns *are* determined in accordance with generally accepted accounting procedures.

A major cause of divergence between accounting and taxes can be traced to one little word. That word is *accrue.* To an accountant, items accrue with the passage of time and the receipt or rendering of services. The purpose of accrual accounting is to match with earned income the costs used up in producing that income. Being conservative, the accountant generally follows the maxim, "Never anticipate income; always provide for expenses."

To a tax man, however, something accrues when the amount involved becomes fixed and definite. Thus (see the *Schlude* case at the end of this chapter), the amounts received by a dance studio for lessons to be rendered at some future time would accrue as accounting income only as the lessons were furnished, whereas from a tax viewpoint income would accrue when either cash or a negotiable note was received.

On the other hand, consider the case of a warranty on a consumer product. From past experience, the manufacturer can estimate the probable warranty expenses he will incur relative to a given year's sales. An accountant would set up a liability for these warranties, based upon the best estimates possible, and would reduce profit in the year of sale by the warranty expense to be incurred in future years relative to such sales. For tax purposes, however, the liability does not exist until actual claims have been filed under the warranty contract, and therefore no deduction can be taken in the year of sale.

Other differences between accounting and taxes result from specific legislative enactment. Most of these, like the differences in interpreting the word *accrue,* result in shifting the timing of items, although not the amount. But some, such as the provisions relating to tax-free exchanges and percentage depletion, produce differences that are differences in amount, even viewed over a number of years, and not just differences in timing.

Because it is expensive to keep two sets of books, and because there is more likelihood of a tax treatment being challenged if it differs from the accounting treatment, one subtle effect of differences between accounting and tax concepts of income is to move accounting concepts of business income closer to tax concepts, especially in the accounting for smaller business units. We shall note this effect at several specific points later in the book.

Concepts of equity, objectives of national policy, and pressures from special-interest groups (including the administrators of the law itself), together with hundreds of thousands (perhaps millions) of administrative decisions, plus thousands of court decisions, have all been instrumental in twisting and shaping the income tax law into the highly complex labyrinth of rules, exceptions to the rules, exceptions to exceptions, modifications of the exceptions to the exceptions, and so forth, *ad fatiguum,* that we know today.

Added to the transactional approach to taxes in the United States is a basic point of view. This is that all inflows of assets, except to the extent of recoveries of amounts invested, constitute income unless specifically provided otherwise in the law. Contrariwise, no outflows or using-ups of assets result in deductions unless specifically so authorized in the law. Because of this point of view, the burden of proof falls on the taxpayer to show that he is entitled to exclude from income something he has received. It also devolves upon him to prove that he is entitled to those deductions that he claims.

The excess of includable income over allowable deductions, then, constitutes taxable income. Or, to put it bluntly, taxable income is whatever the Congress says it is; or whatever the administrators say that Congress said or intended to say; or whatever the courts say the Constitution, rules of judicial construction of statutes, and requirements for protection of the revenue may finally determine it to be.

Thus, the political concept of income for tax purposes can be adequately grasped only by a review of the entire structure of the tax law, its administration, and its judicial interpretation. And that is really the major purpose of this entire book.

## CASE EXCERPTS

Stock dividends as income—*Towne* v. *Eisner,* 3 AFTR 2959 (1918)
Embezzlement proceeds as income—*James* v. *U.S.,* 7 AFTR 2d 1361 (1961)
Gift or compensation?—*Madonna and James E. Colwell, v. Comm.* 64 TC 584 (1975)
Gift or contribution to corporate capital— *Federated Department Stores, Inc.,* v. Commissioner (CA6 1970) 25 AFTR 2d 70-1269.
Accrual accounting in taxes—*Schlude* v. *Commissioner,* 11 AFTR 2d 751 (1963)

### *Towne* v. *Eisner*
38 S. Ct. 158, 3 AFTR 2959 (1918)

Mr. Towne received a dividend of common stock on common stock of the same corporation. The tax law did not specifically cover such an item. The government contended that the stock dividend was income in the amount of its fair market value, like any other dividend. The taxpayer (the plaintiff) argued that he had received nothing that could be described as income.

We cannot doubt that the dividend was capital as well for the purposes of the Income Tax Law as for distribution between tenant for life and remainderman. What was said by this Court upon the latter question is equally true for the former. "A stock dividend really takes nothing from the property of the corporation, and adds nothing to the interests of the shareholders. Its property is not diminished, and their interests are not increased. . . . The proportional interest of each shareholder remains the same. The only change is in the evidence which represents that interest, the new shares and the original shares together representing the same proportional interest that the original shares represented before the issue of new ones." *Gibbons* v. *Mahon,* 136 U.S. 549, 559, 560, 10 Sup. Ct. 1057, 14 L. Ed. 525. In short, the corporation is no poorer and the stockholder is no richer than they were before. *Logan County* v. *United States,* 169 U.S. 255, 261, 18 Sup. Ct. 361, 42 L. Ed. 737. If the plaintiff gained any small advantage by the change, it certainly was not an advantage of $417,450, the sum upon which he was taxed. It is alleged and admitted that he receives no more in the way of dividends and that his old and new certificates together are worth only what the old ones were worth before. If the sum had been carried from surplus to capital account without a corresponding issue of stock certificates, which there was nothing in the nature of things to prevent, we do not suppose that anyone would contend that the plaintiff had received an accession to his income. Presumably his certificate would have the same value as before. Again, if certificates for $1,000 par were split up into ten certificates each, for $100, we presume that no one would call the new certificates income. What has happened is that the plaintiff's old certificates have been split up in effect and have diminished in value to the extent of the value of the new.

*James* v. *U.S.*
81 S. Ct. 1052, 7 AFTR 2d 1361 (1961)

Prior to 1961, a clear distinction existed between the tax treatment given embezzled funds and that given other sums illegally obtained. The embezzler was viewed as owing the money to his victim, and the act of embezzlement was equated to the borrowing of money—albeit without the knowledge or consent of the owner. The *James* decision abolished this legalistic distinction. Yet the effect of this quite logical abolition of an untenable distinction was to further punish the victim of the embezzlement and to render it almost impossible for him to recover any of the money he had lost.

When a law-abiding taxpayer mistakenly receives income in one year, which receipt is assailed and found to be invalid in a subsequent year, the taxpayer must nonetheless report the amount as "gross income" in the year received. *United States* v. *Lewis, supra; Healy* v. *Commissioner, supra.* We do not believe that Congress intended to treat a law-breaking taxpayer differently. Just as the honest taxpayer may deduct any amount repaid in the year in which the repayment is made, the Government points out that, "if, when, and to the extent that the victim recovers back the misappropriated funds, there is of course a reduction in the embezzler's income." . . .

We should not continue to confound confusion, particularly when the result would be to perpetuate the injustice of relieving embezzlers of the duty of paying income taxes on the money they enrich themselves with through theft while the honest people pay their taxes on every conceivable type of income. . . .

**DISSENTING OPINION**

MR. JUSTICE BLACK, whom MR. JUSTICE DOUGLAS joins, concurring in part and dissenting in part. . . .

. . . the *Wilcox* holding in no way violates the sound principle of treating "gains" of honest and dishonest taxpayers alike. The whole basis of the *Wilcox* opinion was that an embezzlement is not in itself "gain' or "income" to the embezzler within the tax sense, for the obvious reason that the embezzled property still belongs, and is known to belong, to the rightful owner. It is thus a mistake to argue that petitioner's contention is "that all unlawful gains are taxable except those resulting from embezzlement."

The rightful owner who has entrusted his funds to an employee or agent has troubles enough when those funds are embezzled without having the Federal Government step in with its powerful claim that the embezzlement is a taxable event automatically subjecting part of those funds (still belonging to the owner) to the waiting hands of the Government's tax gatherer. We say part of the *owner's* funds because it is on the supposed "gain" from them that the embezzler is now held to be duty-bound to pay the tax and history probably records few instances of independently wealthy embezzlers who have had non-stolen assets available for payment of taxes.

There has been nothing shown to us on any of the occasions when we have considered this problem to indicate that Congress ever intended its income tax laws to be construed as imposing what is in effect a property or excise tax on the rightful owner's embezzled funds, for which the owner has already once paid income tax when he rightfully acquired them. . . . If Congress ever did manifest an intention to select the mere fact of embezzlement as the basis for imposing a double tax on the owner, we think a serious question of confiscation in violation of the Fifth Amendment would be raised. All of us know that with the strong lien provisions of the Federal income tax law an owner of stolen funds would have a very rocky road to travel before he got back, without paying a good slice to the Federal Government, such funds as an embezzler who had not paid the tax might, perchance, not have dissipated. An illustration of what this could mean to a defrauded employer is shown in this very case by the employer's loss of some $700,000, upon which the Government claims a tax of $559,000.

It seems to be implied that one reason for overruling *Wilcox* is that a failure to hold embezzled funds taxable would somehow work havoc with the public revenue or discriminate against "honest" taxpayers and force them to pay more taxes. We believe it would be impossible to substantiate either claim. . . . And, as already indicated, to the extent that the Government could be successful in collecting some taxes from embezzlers, it would most likely do so at the expense of the owner whose money had been stolen.

It follows that, except for the possible adverse effect on rightful owners, the only substantial result that one can foresee from today's holding is that the Federal Government will, under the guise of a tax evasion charge, prosecute people for a simple embezzlement. . . . Here the embezzler has already pleaded guilty to the crime of embezzlement in a state court, although the record does not show the punishment he has received. Were it not for the novel formula of applying the Court's new law prospectively, petitioner would have to serve three years in federal prison in addition to his state sentence. This graphically illustrates one of the great dangers of opening up the federal tax statutes, or any others, for use by federal prosecutors against defendants who not only can be but are tried for their crimes in local state courts and punished there. If the people of this country are to be subjected to such double jeopardy and double punishment, despite the constitutional command against double jeopardy, it seems to us it would be far wiser for this Court to wait and let Congress attempt to do it. . . .

*Madonna J. and James E. Colwell v. Commissioner*
64 TC 584 (1975)

> A newspaper stereotyper who was not a member of the striking union nevertheless observed its picket line. That union made payments to the stereotyper and to other employees of the struck newspaper who signed cards stating they were out of work and without income because of the strike. Should the stereotyper consider these payments a nontaxable gift or taxable income?

To determine what motivated the ITU to provide the benefits, we rely heavily on the lack of awareness of, or even any inquiry into, the petitioner's financial status on the part of the ITU.

Respondent concedes that a gift excludable under section 102 (a) can be made to persons without the slightest financial need. However, he argues and we agree, in the case involving union strike benefits paid to a striking worker who is not a member of the striking union, in order for the payments to be excludable under section 102 (a), it must be shown at the outset that the union first inquired into the recipient's financial status and found him in need. This is necessary because strike benefits inherently are designed to meet economic need arising only because of the strike. They are paid precisely to help those unemployed by a strike, not from a charitable impulse, but from the self-interested desire to ensure the economic feasibility of the strike. Thus, unless the union inquires into the personal needs of the recipient and makes its payments according to that need, it is impossible to distinguish any benefits as being paid primarily out of a detached and disinterested generosity or other charitable impulse rather than from the desire to ensure the effectiveness of the strike.

In the record before us, we must find that the ITU made the payments to promote the success of the strike. We cannot say that the benefits proceeded from charity or other generous impulse. Consequently, they are not excludable from petitioner's 1970 income under section 102 (a).

*Federated Department Stores, Inc.* v. *Commissioner*
(CA6, 1970) 25 AFTR 2d 70-1269.

Sharpstown owned a 2500-acre tract of unimproved land in Houston, Texas, on 115 acres of which it contemplated constructing a shopping center with the remainder to be devoted to residential and commercial purposes. Sharpstown was of the view that its venture would be more successful if taxpayer would construct and operate a department store in the shopping center. As inducement, Sharpstown offered to convey ten acres in its shopping center area to taxpayer and also to pay taxpayer $200,000 per year for ten years. The agreement was executed and taxpayer constructed a department store in the shopping center at a cost of $1,956,339. Neither taxpayer nor its shareholders owned an interest in Sharpstown; neither Sharpstown nor its shareholders owned an interest in taxpayer.

In the fiscal years 1963 and 1964, taxpayer received payments from Sharpstown of $200,000 and $400,000, respectively. The Commissioner included these amounts in taxpayer's income for the years in question. The Tax Court, however, held these payments excludable from taxpayer's income under Section 118 of the Internal Revenue Code, 26 U.S.C. § 118(a). That section provides: "In the case of a corporation, gross income does not include any contribution to the capital of the taxpayer." This resulted in a reduction in the deficiencies originally assessed by the Commissioner, and it is from this holding by the Tax Court that the Commissioner appeals.

The narrow question presented is whether the payments received by taxpayer from Sharpstown were contributions to taxpayer's capital within the purview of Section 118. We agree with the Tax Court that they were.

The Commissioner argues that Section 118 cannot be used to exclude from taxpayer's income the payments in question because (1) the payments were motivated by Sharpstown's own financial interests rather than by concern for the general welfare of the community; and (2) Sharpstown is not a governmental unit or civic group which allegedly is a prerequisite to the applicability of Section 118.

The Senate Finance Committee Report (83rd Cong., 2d Sess., S. Rept. No. 1622 (1954)), contains the following comment on the purpose of Section 118:

> "[ Section 118] deals with cases where a contribution is made to a corporation by a governmental unit, chamber of commerce, or other association of individuals having no proprietary interest in the corporation. In many such cases because the contributor expects to derive indirect benefits, the contribution cannot be called a gift; yet the anticipated future benefits may also be so intangible as to not warrant treating the contribution as a payment for future services."

Treasury Regulation Section 1.118-1 also provides that Section 118 does not apply to any money or property transferred to a corporation in consideration for goods or services to be rendered.

The payments by Sharpstown to taxpayer were admittedly made with the expectation that the existence of taxpayer's department store would promote Sharpstown's financial interests. However, this expectation was clearly of such a speculative nature that any benefit necessarily must be regarded as indirect. In all the cases relied on by the government, the contributions had a reasonable nexus with the services which it was the business of the recipient corporation to provide. Such is not this case. Under these circumstances, we agree with the Tax Court that any benefit expected to be derived by Sharpstown was so intangible as not to warrant treating its contribution as a payment to taxpayer for future services.

In a somewhat different factual setting, the Supreme Court has held that contributions received to induce a taxpayer to locate factories in a certain area are contributions to capital. *Brown Shoe Co. v. Commissioner* [50-1 USTC [5958], 339 U.S. 583 (1950). Although *Brown Shoe Co.* was decided before the enactment of Section 118, the legislative history of Section 118 makes it clear that it restates existing law as developed through administrative and court decisions. 3 U.S. Code Cong. & Ad. News 4825 (1954).

We do not agree with the Commissioner's assertion that Section 118 has no application unless the contribution is made by a governmental unit or civic group. The Senate Report referred to herein expressly states that Section 118 is also to apply to contributions made to a corporation by an association of individuals having no proprietary interest in the corporation. Our conclusion is not inconsistent with Treasury Regulation Section 1.118-1 as is contended by the Commissioner. In pertinent part, that regulation provides:

> "Section 118 also applies to contributions to capital made by persons other than shareholders. For example, the exclusion applies to the value of land or other property contributed to a corporation by a governmental unit or civic group for the purpose of inducing the corporation to locate its business in a particular community . . ."

The reference in the regulation to a government unit or civic group obviously is only one example of the applicability of Section 118 to a contribution made by a nonshareholder, and by express language is not intended to be exclusive of other posible applications.

The judgment of the Tax Court is affirmed.

*Schlude* v. *Commissioner*
83 S. Ct. 601, 11 AFTR 2d 751 (1963)

The controversy turns upon the accounting method employed by a partnership in which the taxpayers were equal partners. Since a partnership is not a taxable entity, the partners being liable in their individual capacities for their distributive share of partnership income . . . , the proper statement of the partnership's income affects only the tax liabilities of the partners individually. However, as there is no other dispute in the case, for convenience the discussion will center upon the partnership's accounting method without further mention of its effect upon the respective tax liabilities of the partners.

Taxpayers, husband and wife, formed a partnership to operate ballroom dancing studios (collectively referred to as "studio") pursuant to Arthur Murray, Inc., franchise agreements. Dancing lessons were offered under either of two basic contracts. The cash plan contract required the student to pay the entire down payment in cash at the time the contract was executed with the balance due in installments thereafter. The deferred payment contract required only a portion of the down payment to be paid in cash. The remainder of the down payment was due in stated installments and the balance of the contract price was to be paid as designated in a negotiable note signed at the time the contract was executed.

Both types of contracts provided that (1) the student should pay tuition for lessons in a certain amount, (2) the student should not be relieved of his obligation to pay the tuition, (3) no refunds would be made and (4) the contract was noncancelable. The contracts prescribed a specific number of lesson hours ranging from five to twelve hundred hours and some contracts provided lifetime courses entitling the student additionally to two hours of lessons per month plus two parties a year for life. Although the contracts designated the period during which the lessons had to be taken, there was no schedule of specific dates, which were arranged from time to time as lessons were given.

Cash payments received directly from students and amounts received when the negotiable notes were discounted at the bank or fully paid were deposited in the studio's general bank account without segregation from its other funds. The franchise agreements required the studio to pay to Arthur Murray, Inc., on a weekly basis, 10 percent of these cash receipts as royalty and 5 percent of the receipts in escrow, the latter to continue until a $20,000 indemnity fund was accumulated. Similarly, sales commissions for lessons sold were paid at the time the sales receipts were deposited in the studio's general bank account.

The studio, since its inception in 1946, has kept its books and reported income for tax purposes on an accrual system of accounting. In addition to the books, individual student record cards were maintained showing the number of hours taught and the number still remaining under the contract. The system, in substance, operated as follows. When a contract was entered into, a "deferred income" account was credited for the total contract price. At the close of each fiscal period, the student record cards were analyzed and the total number of taught hours was multiplied by the designated rate per hour of each contract. The resulting sum was deducted from the deferred income account and reported as earned income on the financial statements and the income tax return. In addition, if there had been no activity in a contract for over a year, or if a course were reduced in amount, an entry would be made canceling the untaught portion of the contract, removing that amount from the deferred income account, and recognizing gain to the extent that the deferred income exceeded the balance due on the contract, i.e., the amounts received in advance. The amounts representing lessons taught and the gains from cancellations constituted the chief sources of the partnership's gross income. The balance of the deferred income account would be carried forward into the next fiscal year to be increased or decreased in accordance with the number of new contracts, lessons taught and cancellations recognized.

Deductions were also reported on the accrual basis except that the royalty payments and the sales commissions were deducted when paid irrespective of the period in which the related receipts were taken into income. Three certified public accountants testified that in their opinion the accounting system employed truly reflected net income in accordance with commercial accrual accounting standards. . . .

The studio sought to defer its cash receipts on the basis of contracts which did not provide for lessons on fixed dates after the taxable year, but left such dates to be arranged from time to time by the instructor and his student. Under the contracts, the student could arrange for some or all of the additional lessons or could simply allow their rights under the contracts to lapse. But even though the student did not demand the remaining lessons, the contracts permitted the studio to insist upon payment in accordance with the obligations undertaken and to retain whatever prepayments were made without restriction as to use and without obligation of refund. At the end of each period, while the number of lessons taught had been meticulously reflected, the studio was uncertain whether none, some or all of the remaining lessons would be rendered. Clearly, services were rendered solely on demand in the fashion of the American Automobile Association and Automobile Club of Michigan cases.

Moreover, percentage royalties and sales commissions for lessons sold, which were paid as cash was received from students or from its note transactions with the bank, were deducted in the year paid even though the related items of income had been deferred, at least in part, to later periods. In view of all these circumstances, we hold the studio's accrual system vulnerable under Section 41 and Section 446(b) with respect to its deferral of prepaid income. Consequently, the Commissioner was fully justified in including payments in cash or by negotiable note in gross income for the year in which such payments were received. If these payments are includible in the year of receipt because their allocation to a later year does not clearly reflect income, the contract installments are likewise includible in gross income, as the United States now claims, in the year they become due and payable. For an accrual basis taxpayer "it is the right to receive not the actual receipt that determines the inclusion of the amount in gross income," *Spring City Co.* v. *Commissioner,* 292 U.S. 182, 184-185; *Commissioner* v. *Hansen,* 360 U.S. 446, and here the right to receive these installments had become fixed at least at the time they were due and payable.

## DISSENTING OPINION

MR. JUSTICE STEWART, with whom MR. JUSTICE DOUGLAS, MR. JUSTICE HARLAN, and MR. JUSTICE GOLDBERG join, dissenting.

As the Court notes, this case is but the most recent episode in a protracted dispute concerning the proper income tax treatment of amounts received as advances for services to be performed in a subsequent year by a taxpayer who is on an accrual rather than a cash basis. The Government has consistently argued that such amounts are taxable in the year of receipt, relying upon two alternative arguments: It has claimed that deferral of such payments would violate the "annual accounting" principle which requires that income not be postponed from one year to the next to reflect the long-term economic result of a transaction. Alternatively, the Government has argued that advance payments must be reported as income in the year of receipt under the "claim-of-right doctrine," which requires otherwise reportable income, held under a claim of right without restriction as to use, to be reported when received despite the fact that the taxpayer's claim to the funds may be disputed.

As I have elsewhere pointed out, neither of these doctrines has any relevance to the question whether any reportable income at all has been derived when payments are received in advance of performance by an accrual-basis taxpayer. The most elementary principles of accrual accounting require that advances be considered reportable income only in the year they are earned by the taxpayer's rendition of the services for which the payments were made. The Government's theories would force upon an accrual-basis taxpayer a cash basis for advance payments in disregard of the Federal statute which explicitly authorizes income tax returns to be based upon sound accrual accounting methods. . . .

It seems to me that this decision, the third of a trilogy of cases purportedly decided on their own peculiar facts, in truth completes the mutilation of a basic element of the accrual method of reporting income—a method which has been explicitly approved by Congress for almost half a century.

## QUESTIONS AND PROBLEMS

1. Explain why each of the following would or would not constitute an item includible in income within the accounting concept of income:
   (a) James borrows from the Athens National Bank $1,000, secured by his car. The car is worth only $700 because, unknown to the bank, it was in an accident.
   (b) Peterson owns a thriving college book store. His investment in the store, after adjustment for reinvested profits and withdrawals, is $15,000. He receives and rejects a firm offer to buy the store for $25,000.
   (c) Assume that instead of rejecting the offer in (b) above, Peterson accepts it. What would be the amount of his income?
   (d) Ajax Corporation sells common stock to a group of investors. They pay $200,000 for stock with a par value of $50,000.
   (e) Swenson lives in a house that he owns free and clear. The value of the house is $30,000. If Swenson had to pay rent for such a house, a fair rental value would be $300 per month.
   (f) Zippo Corporation receives an order from a customer, accompanied by a check for $10,000. The items ordered are all custom made and it will be about two months until the order can be filled.
   (g) On January 2, 1964, Hill bought 200 shares of Anvil Corporation stock for $5,000. At December 31, 1978, Anvil stock is worth $200 per share. Hill continues to hold his stock, anticipating a further rise in price.
   (h) The Baxter Corporation bills a customer for $300 for merchandise that has been shipped to the customer. The merchandise cost $200.
   (i) Baxter Corporation collects the $300 in (h) above.
2. Review the *Colwell* case excerpt at the end of this chapter. Then restate and change the facts so that they might support the conclusion that Mr. Colwell received a gift from the ITU rather than taxable income.
3. Smith owned 100 shares of Hyphen Corporation stock on July 1, 1978, when Hypen declared and paid a stock dividend of one share of additional stock for each ten shares held. Under the rationale of *Towne* v. *Eisner,* will Smith be deemed to have realized income for tax purposes? For any other purposes (accounting, economics)?

4. An electric company requires that its customers reimburse it for one-half the cost of extending its lines to serve them. Under the federal income tax concept of income, are the amounts received by the electric company income? Should the electric company be allowed to take depreciation on the full cost of extending the lines, or only on the cost of extension reduced by the amount received from the customer? How about the customer? Does he inclur an expense for such a payment, does he acquire a depreciable asset, or what?
5. The dissenting opinion in *James* v. *U.S.* argues that the ultimate financial sufferer from taxing embezzlement proceeds as income to the embezzler will be the *victim* of the embezzlement! Explain the reasoning underlying this conclusion. What if the victim gets a tax deduction for the loss?
6. Contrast the concept of "accrue" underlying the majority opinion in the *Schlude* case with the concept of "accrue" employed in commercial accounting that underlies the dissenting opinion.
7. Many theorists have advocated an approach to computing income based upon the net-worth concept of the economists. Discuss some of the practical problems that might be encountered in implementing such an approach if it were applied to all taxpayers. Would a net-worth approach eliminate the need for accounting for individual transactions?
8. Poodle spends $10,000 per year on consumption items. His assets and liabilities at the beginning and end of the year are:

| | *Jan. 1* | *Dec. 31* |
|---|---|---|
| Cash | $ 5,000 | $ 7,000 |
| Investments | 30,000 | 33,000 |
| Total assets | 35,000 | 40,000 |
| Due to brokers | 10,000 | 12,000 |
| Misc. payables | 3,000 | 3,000 |
| Total liabilities | 13,000 | 15,000 |

The investments are shown at their cost, which is also their fair market value. What was Poodle's income for the year?

9. Barnes lives in a furnished apartment and has no personal possessions except his clothing and toilet articles. For our purposes, we will assume that these have a constant value of $1,000. During the year, Barnes had the following inflows:

| | |
|---|---|
| Salary from his employment | $6,000 |
| Inheritance from his uncle | 2,000 |
| Gain on sale of stock (the gain being excess of selling price over original cost) | 1,000 |
| Dividends and interest | 500 |

During the year, he also had the following outflows:

| | |
|---|---|
| Living expenses | $4,000 |
| Invested in securities | 3,500 |
| Purchased automobile | 2,000 plus old car |

He had no debts at either beginning or end of the year, but owned:

| | *Cost* | *Value* |
|---|---|---|
| January 1– | | |
| Securities | $10,000 | $10,000 |
| Automobile | 3,000 | 500 |
| Cash | 0 | 0 |
| December 31– | | |
| Securities | $12,000 | $19,000 |
| Automobile | 2,000 | 1,500 |
| Cash | 1,500 | 1,500 |

(a) Compute Barnes' income on a net-worth approach as in economics and on a transactional approach.

(b) What was the cost of the stock Barnes sold during the year?

10. In the ordinary tax matter, the taxpayer has the burden of proving the correctness of the return he filed. An alternative approach would be to require the government to prove the return was incorrect. Why isn't the taxpayer assumed to be innocent (and his return presumed to be correct) until he is proven guilty (and his return shown to be incorrect)?

11. Some people see barter (also called *reciprocal trade*) as the wave of the future. At a simple level, a carpenter builds a bookcase for a dentist in exchange for dental work for his children, or a restaurant swaps free meals for advertising in a newspaper or on a radio or TV station. More complex deals require the service of brokers, who might handle the swap of TV time for TV sets, trade the TV sets for hotel and restaurant service credits, swap these for toothpaste to a company that could use the credits to pay for facilities for sales meetings, and ultimately sell the toothpaste to a discount chain. In such a sequence, who realizes income—and when? How about the carpenter/dentist swap?

12. Discuss the problems you might see if the four additional measurement concepts (additional, that is, to the present historical cost) were to be considered for income-tax purposes. In doing so, contrast each concept with historical cost as to the manner of measuring income, objectivity of measurement, and any inequities that might be created among different categories of taxpayers (e.g., would it reduce reported corporate income without affecting the income of wage earners or retired persons?).

# 2

# THE SCAFFOLDING OF THE INCOME TAX

*Chapters 3 through 7 are designed to introduce you to the basic framework of the federal income tax. You will see how the income tax applies to the income of corporations, partnerships, fiduciaries, and individuals. In the process, you will learn to prepare simple tax returns for these types of taxpayers.*

*The objective of getting you involved with the tax-return forms is not, however, to teach you the details of tax return preparation. Rather, it is to help you grasp the tax patterns of the different taxable entities. Then, you will be ready to go on to Part Three, where we shall discuss the specific peculiarities of various types of transactions important in business and investment decisions.*

# 3

# The Corporation Income Tax

The dominant view of the corporation in the United States tax structure was formed in the first decade of this century and embodied in the corporation excise tax of 1909. This view was shaped by what the public thought of corporations. Corporations were poisoners of food, deluders of the ill, exploiters, and corrupters.

Why did Americans view corporations in this harsh way? This had been the era of "trust-busting" and of the "muckrakers"—writers bringing out into public view the skeletons in the corporate closets, of which there were many. A House of Representatives investigation of the United States Steel Corporation produced a majority report charging that financial manipulations disregarded stockholder rights, flaunted the public interest, and produced exorbitant securities profits for the manipulators at the expense of the average investor.

Upton Sinclair's *The Jungle*, had helped produce the Meat Inspection Act. Samuel Hopkins Adams laid bare the patent medicine business and helped obtain passage of the Pure Food and Drug Act of 1906. An investigation of the insurance industry, led by Charles Evans Hughes, resulted in sensational exposures that led to state reform laws.

## CORPORATION TAX OF 1909

An income tax had been held unconstitutional by the Supreme Court in 1895. But the temper of the country strongly favored an income tax—not only to raise revenue, but on equitable grounds as a way of "getting at" the "malefactors of great wealth." William Howard Taft was president in 1909. He had been selected as the successor to Theodore Roosevelt on the ground that he was a moderate. He opposed the income tax, as did most conservative Republicans.

But Taft was an astute politician; he saw that the clamor for an income tax was so deafening that if one were not passed, something else would have to be offered to appease the public.

The corporation excise tax of 1909 (an excise tax on income) was the result. It originated in the Senate as an amendment to a tariff bill, thus shocking traditionalists who took seriously the constitutional mandate that revenue bills originate in the House. Liberals disliked it because they felt that it hurt the chances of getting an all-inclusive income tax passed. Conservatives disliked it because they felt that it was simply an income tax in the form of an excise tax, and hence would provide an entering wedge for an all-embracing income tax. But middle-of-the-roaders accepted it as a temporary compromise and businessmen reluctantly endorsed it for a two-year term as being the lesser of two evils. The *Congressional Record* (44:3344) recorded one of President Taft's additional justifications for the corporation excise tax:

> If now, by a perfectly legitimate and effective system of taxation, we are incidentally able to possess the government and the stockholders and the public of the knowledge of the real business transactions and the gains and the profits of every corporation in the country, we have made a long step toward that supervisory control of corporations which may prevent a further abuse of power.

In this day of mandatory annual reports to shareholders, detailed filings of information available for public inspection with the Securities and Exchange Commission, and a multitude of financial reporting services, it is difficult to appreciate the cloak of secrecy then shrouding the operations of corporations.

As is the case so often, the unknown is both hated and feared. Corporations were repositories of great wealth, and the extent of their wealth and power was magnified in the public mind out of all proportion because of the secrecy with which they operated. To many, they represented power without responsibility, and any measure that might contribute to their control was deemed to be good in and of itself without regard to any other merit it might possess. Initially, therefore, the 1909 excise tax required that corporate tax returns be made available for public inspection. In 1910, this was changed to authorize the inspection of returns only upon the order of the president.

## THE 1913 ACT

By the time the Sixteenth Amendment to the Constitution was finally ratified in 1913, permitting the imposition of an income tax, the taxation of the income of corporations was firmly entrenched. The Revenue Act of 1913 simply carried over the essential features of the excise tax on corporate income and merged it with the income tax. Thus, as happens so often in politics and in taxes, a temporary compromise became a permanent feature, enshrined side by side with what the compromisers sought to avoid.

## TWO VIEWS OF THE CORPORATION

We have two extreme points of view that tangle in any discussion of corporate income taxation. First, we have those persons who feel that the corporation is not itself a proper subject for income taxation, because it functions only as an economic middleman and cannot really have income, since it cannot consume. Many of these persons tend to take the position that the corporate income tax is borne by the shareholders of the corporation. Their argument would be that prices are determined by the variable (or marginal) costs of doing business. Because an income tax does not affect these variable costs, it cannot affect prices, and hence cannot be shifted to customers in the same manner as can other types of taxes.

Perhaps an oversimplified example may illustrate the point. Copper Corporation owns fixed assets and produces copper. The market price at any given time is beyond its control. All Copper can do is produce or not produce.

It has fixed costs of $100,000 per year, and it costs an additional $28 to produce a pound of copper. If the market price of copper is $27 a pound, there will be no production. If the market price is $29 there will be production to the extent of the capacity of Copper to produce. An income tax—whether of 5 percent or of 55 percent—will not affect that decision. If Copper can produce 1,000,000 pounds per year, it will produce that 1,000,000 pounds at any price greater than its $28-per-pound incremental cost, regardless of the tax rate:

| *Price* | *Revenue* | *Before-tax Profit* | *Tax* | *After-tax Profit* |
|---|---|---|---|---|
| $28.10 | $28,100,000 | None | None | None |
| 29.00 | 29,000,000 | $900,000 | $495,000 | $405,000 |

*Conclusion:* In perfect competition, where the sellers cannot affect price, an income tax cannot be passed on to the consumer and hence must be absorbed by the stockholders.

In the middle of this argument as to who bears the tax, we have those who view the corporation as an economic middleman, but who also face the implications of an economy in which perfect competition is not dominant. They argue that the income tax is passed on to the consumer. Corporations set prices to achieve desired after-tax rates of return, so the price includes the tax, and the tax is really a capricious sort of excise tax on consumers.

At the extreme we have those persons who point to the tremendous concentrations of wealth, economic power, and income (in the accounting sense) in corporations and conclude that the taxation of corporate income is preferable to the taxation of individual income. The large modern corporation is an autonomous institution, they would argue, run by professional managers who view stockholders as just another claimant for a share in the flow of wealth that the corporation controls. Growth, share of market, total assets, return on investment, and the personal satisfaction and prestige that these bring to the professional managers are the operational goals of the corporations, and stockholder benefits or social benefits are simply incidental results. We are living in an age in which legal title to property is relatively unimportant, they would argue, and economic control of the flow of wealth is all-important. Control, not consumption, is the key. Because the corporation controls, the corporation must be taxed.

There is some merit to each of these points of view. It depends upon which corporations you look at. Focus your attention on small corporations and you see a picture different from what you will see when you look at the very largest. Automobile manufacturing differs from home building. Retailers have a different kind of business from that of oil wildcatters. It is hard to make meaningful generalizations in the midst of the rich diversity of our American economy.

There is also, of course, what might be described as the political view of the corporation income tax. From this point of view, the very uncertainty as to who really pays it—the consumer or the stockholder or whoever—is perhaps its greatest merit. There are strong political advantages to being able to impose a tax that is not clearly perceived as being paid by the people who pay it.

In any event, we do have a corporation income tax, and so our job must be to understand its workings in addition to its effects.

## A SIMPLE COMPUTATION OF CORPORATE INCOME TAX

Let us look at the income statement of The Simple Corporation (page 64) and then see how the same figures would appear on a corporation income tax return, Figure 3-1 (page 59).

The corporation is a legal entity; it is also a taxpaying entity. Since the essential concepts of income determination for tax purposes are accounting concepts, it should not surprise us that the Simple Corporation income tax return is built around an income statement similar to those encountered in any introductory accounting text. Some of the items have been rearranged, that is all.

Approximately 1,400,000 corporation income tax returns are filed annually. But only 42,000 or so of these returns show taxable net income of over $100,000. It is probable that nine out of ten of the corporations with net

Form **1120**

Department of the Treasury
Internal Revenue Service

**U.S. Corporation Income Tax Return**

For calendar year or other taxable year beginning ............................, 19 , ending ............................, 19 ........

(PLEASE TYPE OR PRINT)

| Check if a— | Name | D Employer Identification No. |
|---|---|---|
| A Consolidated return ☐ | THE SIMPLE CORPORATION | 36-3601434 |
| | Number and street | E County in which located |
| B Personal Holding Co. ☐ | 77 SUNSET BOULEVARD | MOON |
| C Business Code No. (See page 7 of instructions.) | City or town, State, and ZIP code | F Enter total assets from line 14, column (D), Schedule L (See instruction R) |
| | VALHALLA, ARIZONA | $ 511,000 |

IMPORTANT—Fill in all applicable lines and schedules. If the lines on the schedules are not sufficient, see instruction N.

| | | |
|---|---|---|
| GROSS INCOME | 1 Gross receipts or gross sales 575,000 Less: Returns and allowances 8,000 | 567,000 |
| | 2 Less: Cost of goods sold (Schedule A) and/or operations (attach schedule) | 359,000 |
| | 3 Gross profit | 208,000 |
| | 4 Dividends (Schedule C) | |
| | 5 Interest on obligations of the United States and U.S. instrumentalities | |
| | 6 Other interest | |
| | 7 Gross rents | |
| | 8 Gross royalties | |
| | 9 Net gains (losses)—(separate Schedule D) | |
| | 10 Other income (attach schedule) | |
| | 11 TOTAL income—Add lines 3 through 10 | 208,000 |
| DEDUCTIONS | 12 Compensation of officers (Schedule E) | 20,000 |
| | 13 Salaries and wages (not deducted elsewhere) | 42,000 |
| | 14 Repairs (do not include capital expenditures) | 1,000 |
| | 15 Bad debts (Schedule F if reserve method is used) | 3,000 |
| | 16 Rents | 8,000 |
| | 17 Taxes (attach schedule) | 3,000 |
| | 18 Interest | |
| | 19 Contributions (not over 5% of line 28 adjusted per instructions—attach schedule) | 2,000 |
| | 20 Amortization (attach schedule) | |
| | 21 Depreciation (Schedule G) | 5,000 |
| | 22 Depletion | |
| | 23 Advertising | 20,000 |
| | 24 Profit sharing, stock bonus, pension and annuity plans (see instructions) | |
| | 25 Other employee benefit plans (see instructions) | |
| | 26 Other deductions (attach schedule) | 7,000 |
| | 27 TOTAL deductions on lines 12 through 26 | 111,000 |
| | 28 Taxable income before net operating loss deduction and special deductions (line 11 less line 27) | 97,000 |
| | 29 Less: (a) Net operating loss deduction (see instructions—attach schedule) | |
| | (b) Special deductions (Schedule I) | |
| | 30 Taxable income (line 28 less line 29) | 97,000 |

**Schedule J** **Tax Computation**

| | |
|---|---|
| 1 Taxable income (line 30, page 1) | 97,000 |
| 2 Enter line 1 or $25,000, whichever is lesser. (Members of a controlled group, see instructions) | 25,000 |
| 3 Line 1 less line 2 | 72,000 |
| 4 Enter line 3 or $25,000, whichever is lesser. (Members of a controlled group, see instructions) | 25,000 |
| 5 Line 3 less line 4 | 47,000 |
| 6 20% of line 2 | 5,000 |
| 7 22% of line 4 | 5,500 |
| 8 48% of line 5 | 22,560 |
| 9 Income tax (Sum of lines 6, 7 and 8 or alternative tax from separate Schedule D, whichever is lesser) | 33,060 |

FIGURE 3-1
A Simple Corporation Income Tax Return

income under $100,000 keep their accounting records on the same basis as they file their tax returns. For this majority (in number) of corporate taxpayers, the computation of the corporate income tax is little more involved than the Simple Corporation calculation on page 59.

THE SIMPLE CORPORATION
Summary of Income and Expenses
Year Ended December 31, 19X1

| | | |
|---|---|---|
| Gross Sales | | $575,000 |
| Less: | | |
| Sales returns and allowances | $ 8,000 | |
| Provision for collection losses | 3,000 | 11,000 |
| Net Sales | | $564,000 |
| Cost of Goods Sold: | | |
| Inventory, January 1, 19x1 | $ 24,000 | |
| Purchases | 366,000 | |
| Cost of Goods Available | $390,000 | |
| Inventory, December 31, 19x1 | 31,000 | 359,000 |
| Gross Margin | | $205,000 |
| Operating Expenses: | | |
| Sales salaries | $ 52,000 | |
| Office salaries | 10,000 | |
| Rent | 8,000 | |
| Repairs and maintenance | 1,000 | |
| Taxes (except federal income) | 3,000 | |
| Advertising | 20,000 | |
| Depreciation | 5,000 | |
| Contributions and donations | 2,000 | |
| Insurance | 1,000 | |
| Delivery expense | 2,500 | |
| Store supplies | 500 | |
| Miscellaneous | 3,000 | 108,000 |
| Net Profit Before Federal Income Tax | | $ 97,000 |

## THE BALANCE SHEET

Of course, the tax calculation is not all there is to a corporation tax return—even a simple one. Supporting schedules have to be filled in or attached to the return, explaining or providing details on certain items of income or deduction. Furthermore, a balance sheet and a reconciliation of retained earnings must be filled out. (See Figure 3-2.)

### *Everything Comes from Somewhere*

The tax-return balance sheet is an accounting balance sheet, with some slight rearrangement to emphasize data important for tax administration. The

Form 1120 — Page 4

**Schedule L — Balance Sheets**

| ASSETS | Beginning of taxable year (A) Amount | Beginning of taxable year (B) Total | End of taxable year (C) Amount | End of taxable year (D) Total |
|---|---|---|---|---|
| 1 Cash | | 51,800 | | 60,000 |
| 2 Trade notes and accounts receivable | 43,000 | | 52,000 | |
| (a) Less allowance for bad debts | 7,500 | 35,500 | 9,000 | 43,000 |
| 3 Inventories | | 24,000 | | 31,000 |
| 4 Gov't obligations: (a) U.S. and instrumentalities | | | | |
| (b) State, subdivisions thereof, etc. | | | | |
| 5 Other current assets (attach schedule) | | | | |
| 6 Loans to stockholders | | | | |
| 7 Mortgage and real estate loans | | | | |
| 8 Other investments (attach schedule) | | 270,000 | | 350,000 |
| 9 Buildings and other fixed depreciable assets | 63,000 | | 63,000 | |
| (a) Less accumulated depreciation | 31,000 | 32,000 | 36,000 | 27,000 |
| 10 Depletable assets | | | | |
| (a) Less accumulated depletion | | | | |
| 11 Land (net of any amortization) | | | | |
| 12 Intangible assets (amortizable only) | | | | |
| (a) Less accumulated amortization | | | | |
| 13 Other assets (attach schedule) | | | | |
| 14 Total assets | | 413,300 | | 511,000 |
| **LIABILITIES AND STOCKHOLDERS' EQUITY** | | | | |
| 15 Accounts payable | | 22,000 | | 34,000 |
| 16 Mtges., notes, bonds payable in less than 1 yr. | | | | |
| 17 Other current liabilities (attach schedule) | | 4,000 | | 5,000 |
| 18 Loans from stockholders | | | | |
| 19 Mtges., notes, bonds payable in 1 yr. or more | | | | |
| 20 Other liabilities (attach schedule) | | 12,300 | | 33,060 |
| 21 Capital stock: (a) Preferred stock | | | | |
| (b) Common stock | 20,000 | 20,000 | 20,000 | 20,000 |
| 22 Paid-in or capital surplus | | | | |
| 23 Retained earnings—Appropriated (attach sch.) | | | | |
| 24 Retained earnings—Unappropriated | | 355,000 | | 418,940 |
| 25 Less cost of treasury stock | | ( ) | | ( ) |
| 26 Total liabilities and stockholders' equity | | 413,300 | | 511,000 |

**Schedule M-1 — Reconciliation of Income Per Books With Income Per Return**

| | | | |
|---|---|---|---|
| 1 Net income per books (97,000-33,060 | 63,940 | 7 Income recorded on books this year not included in this return (itemize) | |
| 2 Federal income tax | 33,060 | (a) Tax-exempt interest $ | |
| 3 Excess of capital losses over capital gains | | | |
| 4 Income subject to tax not recorded on books this year (itemize) | | 8 Deductions in this tax return not charged against book income this year (itemize) | |
| 5 Expenses recorded on books this year not deducted in this return (itemize) | | (a) Depreciation . . $ | |
| (a) Depreciation . . . . $ | | (b) Depletion . . $ | |
| (b) Depletion . . . . $ | | 9 Total of lines 7 and 8 | |
| 6 Total of lines 1 through 5 | 97,000 | 10 Income (line 28, page 1)—line 6 less 9 | 97,000 |

**Schedule M-2 — Analysis of Unappropriated Retained Earnings Per Books (line 24 above)**

| | | | |
|---|---|---|---|
| 1 Balance at beginning of year | 355,000 | 5 Distributions: (a) Cash | |
| 2 Net income per books | 63,940 | (b) Stock | |
| 3 Other increases (itemize) | | (c) Property | |
| | | 6 Other decreases (itemize) | |
| | | 7 Total of lines 5 and 6 | |
| 4 Total of lines 1, 2, and 3 | 418,940 | 8 Balance at end of year (line 4 less 7) | 418,940 |

FIGURE 3-2

Balance Sheet and Reconciliation of Retained Earnings

balance sheet, therefore, shows the assets of the corporation, valued basically at their unexpired cost and the sources of those assets.

The liabilities are sources of assets in the sense that the corporation has been able to retain assets owing to the willingness of creditors (including the tax collector) to defer receipt of payment. The $511,000 total assets of the Simple Corporation came from:

| | |
|---|---|
| Trade creditors | $ 34,000 |
| Expense accruals | 5,000 |
| Federal income tax | 33,060 |
| Original investment | 20,000 |
| Retained earnings | 418,940 |

The changes in retained earnings are traced through a separate schedule. If the only changes, as in the Simple Corporation, are the taxable income reported on the return and the tax liability also reported on the return, the return hangs neatly together. Unless some of the figures are falsified, it appears that everything has been accounted for. The balance sheet and surplus reconciliation provide a type of net-work cross-check.

## SOME EXCEPTIONS TO THE SIMPLE SITUATION

In our simple situation we dealt only with revenue and expense in the accounting meaning of those terms. But tax accounting has its own special exceptions; some of these have been inserted to achieve equity among different types of taxpayers, some to further social policies believed desirable, some to stimulate certain types of economic behavior, and some because they are simply politically expedient. We shall look at three of these exceptions now.

1. To reduce the double taxation of corporate earnings somewhat, a special deduction is allowed corporations of 85 percent of dividends received by them from corporations paying United States income tax on their earnings.

The rationale is simple. The corporation pays an income tax. If it pays a dividend, that dividend will be taxed to the recipient. But the second corporation is no more a consumer than is the first. Its earnings, in turn, will presumably be ultimately distributed—and the dividends it pays will be subject to tax.

Visualize two corporations, A and B. B owns some stock in A, amounting to a 1 percent interest. Assume that all earnings are paid as dividends:

| | *No Special Deduction* | *After 85% Deduction* |
|---|---|---|
| 1% of A's net taxable income | $10,000 | $10,000 |
| 1% of A's income tax | 4,800 | 4,800 |
| Available for B | $ 5,200 | $ 5,200 |
| B's tax (at 48%) | 2,496 | 374* |
| Available for B's shareholders | $ 2,704 | $ 4,826 |

* 48% X 15% = 7.2%

If the amount available for B's shareholders is actually distributed to them, this will constitute taxable income to them, of course. Without the 85 percent special deduction, the shrinkage of the original $10,000 income before it could be spent by a stockholder to whom it would be taxed at 30 percent would be over 81 percent. Even with the 85 percent credit, the shrinkage still would amount to over 66 percent.

2. Limits may be put on certain types of deductions. Thus, the deduction for charitable contributions of a corporation is allowed only to the extent that contributions do not exceed 5 percent of net income before deducting contributions (and before taking the 85 percent dividends-received deduction).

3. Because of the separation of powers between the federal and state governments, it was long believed that the federal government did not have the power to tax interest from the bonds or notes of states or their subdivisions. This opinion was prevalent at the time the income tax amendment to the Constitution was ratified in 1913, and it still has staunch supporters. As a result, the law has always contained an express exemption of such interest from federal income tax. Even though it is probably constitutional to tax such interest today, it might be politically inexpedient to change a tax rule of such long standing.

## THE SIMPLE RETURN COMPLICATED

Let's complicate the Simple Corporation's tax return a bit and see what difference it makes. We still have $97,000 of profit before income taxes, but now our income statement looks like this:

THE SIMPLE CORPORATION
Summary of Income and Expenses
Year Ended December 31, 19X1

| | | |
|---|---|---|
| Gross Sales | | $534,000 |
| Less: | | |
| Sales returns and allowances | $ 8,000 | |
| Provision for collection losses | 3,000 | 11,000 |
| Net Sales | | $523,000 |
| Cost of Goods Sold: | | |
| Inventory, January 1, 19X1 | $ 24,000 | |
| Purchases | 366,000 | |
| Cost of Goods Available | $390,000 | |
| Inventory, December 31, 19X1 | 31,000 | 359,000 |
| Gross Margin | | $164,000 |
| Operating Expenses: | | |
| Sales salaries | $ 52,000 | |

| | | |
|---|---|---|
| Office salaries | 10,000 | |
| Rent | 8,000 | |
| Repairs and maintenance | 1,000 | |
| Taxes (except federal income) | 3,000 | |
| Advertising | 16,000 | |
| Depreciation | 5,000 | |
| Contributions and donations | 6,000 | |
| Insurance | 1,000 | |
| Delivery expense | 2,500 | |
| Store supplies | 500 | |
| Miscellaneous | 3,000 | 108,000 |
| Pretax Operating Profit | | $56,000 |
| Other Income: | | |
| Dividend income | $20,000 | |
| Interest income | 21,000 | 41,000 |
| Net Profit Before Income Tax | | $ 97,000 |

What we have done with the Simple Corporation is to shift some of its income from operating income to investment income, and to shift $4,000 of what had been advertising expense to the category of charitable contributions. In order to prepare the corporate tax return for Simple now, we shall need to know more about the dividend income and the interest income.

Generally, interest is as fully taxable as any other income. However, interest paid by the states or their subdivisions, as we have seen, is fully exempt from federal income tax. Let us assume that the interest income of Simple is received from revenue bonds issued by a toll road that is a subdivision of a state. (We could have assumed that the bonds were issued by a city, a county, a school district, a sewer district, and so forth, or any other nonfederal political body, with the same tax effect.)

Figure 3-3 shows what the tax return would now look like.

Instead of a tax of $33,060, we have only $15,732 to pay. Our dollars of accounting income were identical, but their tax treatment differed in the two situations. Let's account for the difference between these two tax liabilities:

| | | |
|---|---|---|
| Tax liability, situation 1 | $33,060 | |
| Tax liability, situation 2 | 15,732 | $17,328 |
| 48% of: | | |
| Dividends-received deduction of $17,000 | $ 8,160 | |
| Interest exempt from tax of $21,000 | 10,080 | |
| Subtotal | $18,240 | |
| Less: 48% of 1,900 (6,000–4,100) of excessive contributions | 912 | $17,328 |

Form **1120**
Department of the Treasury
Internal Revenue Service

**U.S. Corporation Income Tax Return**
For calendar year 19 or other taxable year beginning ........................., 19 ending ........................., 19.......
(PLEASE TYPE OR PRINT)

Check if a—
A Consolidated return ☐
B Personal Holding Co. ☐
C Business Code No. (See page 7 of instructions)

Name: THE SIMPLE CORPORATION
Number and street: 77 SUNSET BOULEVARD
City or town, State, and ZIP code: VALHALLA, ARIZONA

D Employer identification number: 36-3601434
E Date incorporated: 1/1/70
F Enter total assets from line 14, column (D), Schedule L (See instruction R) $

IMPORTANT—Fill in all applicable lines and schedules. If the lines on the schedules are not sufficient, see instruction N.

| | | | |
|---|---|---|---|
| GROSS INCOME | 1 Gross receipts or gross sales 534,000 Less: Returns and allowances 8,000 | 1 | 526,000 |
| | 2 Less: Cost of goods sold (Schedule A) and/or operations (attach schedule) | 2 | 359,000 |
| | 3 Gross profit | 3 | 167,000 |
| | 4 Dividends (Schedule C) | 4 | 20,000 |
| | 5 Interest on obligations of the United States and U.S. instrumentalities | 5 | |
| | 6 Other interest | 6 | |
| | 7 Gross rents | 7 | |
| | 8 Gross royalties | 8 | |
| | 9 (a) Net capital gains (attach separate Schedule D) | 9(a) | |
| | (b) Ordinary gain or (loss) from Part II, Form 4797 (attach Form 4797) | 9(b) | |
| | 10 Other income (see instructions—attach schedule) | 10 | |
| | 11 TOTAL income—Add lines 3 through 10 | 11 | 187,000 |
| DEDUCTIONS | 12 Compensation of officers (Schedule E) | 12 | 20,000 |
| | 13 Salaries and wages (not deducted elsewhere) | 13 | 42,000 |
| | 14 Repairs (see instructions) | 14 | 1,000 |
| | 15 Bad debts (Schedule F if reserve method is used) | 15 | 3,000 |
| | 16 Rents | 16 | 8,000 |
| | 17 Taxes (attach schedule) | 17 | 3,000 |
| | 18 Interest | 18 | |
| | 19 Contributions (not over 5% of line 30 adjusted per instructions—attach schedule) | 19 | 4,100 |
| | 20 Amortization (attach schedule) | 20 | |
| | 21 Depreciation (Schedule G) | 21 | 5,000 |
| | 22 Depletion | 22 | |
| | 23 Advertising | 23 | 16,000 |
| | 24 Pension, profit-sharing, etc. plans (see instructions) (enter number of plans ► ..........) | 24 | |
| | 25 Employee benefit programs (see instructions) | 25 | |
| | 26 Other deductions (attach schedule) | 26 | 7,000 |
| | 27 TOTAL deductions—Add lines 12 through 26 | 27 | 109,100 |
| | 28 Taxable income before net operating loss deduction and special deductions (line 11 less line 27) | 28 | 77,900 |
| | 29 Less: (a) Net operating loss deduction (see instructions—attach schedule) — 29(a) | | |
| | (b) Special deductions (Schedule I) 85% x 20,000 — 29(b) 17,000 | | 17,000 |
| | 30 Taxable income (line 28 less line 29) | 30 | 60,900 |

**Schedule J** **Tax Computation**

| | |
|---|---|
| 1 Taxable income (line 30, page 1) | 60,900 |
| 2 Enter line 1 or $25,000, whichever is lesser. (Members of a controlled group, see instructions) | 25,000 |
| 3 Line 1 less line 2 | 35,900 |
| 4 Enter line 3 or $25,000, whichever is lesser. (Members of a controlled group, see instructions) | 25,000 |
| 5 Line 3 less line 4 | 10,900 |
| 6 20% of line 2 | 5,000 |
| 7 22% of line 4 | 5,500 |
| 8 48% of line 5 | 5,232 |
| 9 Income tax (Sum of lines 6, 7 and 8 or alternative tax from separate Schedule D, whichever is lesser) | 15,732 |

Corporation Tax Return Complicated

The excessive contributions are computed by taking as allowable contributions 5 percent of the excess of total income over deductions other than the contributions and the special deduction for dividends received.

| | | |
|---|---|---|
| Total income | | $187,000 |
| Total deductions | $109,100 | |
| Deduct contributions | 4,100 | 105,000 |
| Basis for limitation | | 82,000 |
| Limitation (5%) | | $ 4,100 |

By looking at the balance sheet and retained earnings reconciliation that will result, we can see how the corporate tax return provides a measure of internal control over its own accuracy. See Figure 3-4.

Note that, on the earnings reconciliation, the tax-free interest (which was not reported anywhere in the tax computation) shows up as a separate item. Similarly, the contributions in excess of 5 percent must be separately stated. In fact, we can generalize and say that any transaction or entry that affects a balance-sheet account without having its effect fully offset against some other balance-sheet account (other than retained earnings) will have to appear either on Schedule M or in the computation of taxable income.

If we borrow cash from a bank, the increase in the asset account "Cash" is fully offset by the increase in the liability account "Notes Payable." Schedule M does not get involved, therefore. If we owe $200,000 of "Bonds Payable" and we are able to retire them for $160,000, the $40,000 gain on retirement will either show up in the gross income (where it belongs) or it will have to be shown on Schedule M, if the balance-sheet part of the return is to be balanced out.

Of course, the $40,000 could merely be carried as a balance in the "Bonds Payable" account and everything would still balance out. But in the auditing of the corporate return, such an error (or attempt at tax evasion, if it was intentional) would be easily spotted. With the exception of the figure for "Inventory," most of the balance-sheet-account balances can be readily checked when an audit is made. Thus, individual transactions do not have to be painstakingly investigated. Instead, the balance-sheet accounts can be reviewed against supporting data, the Schedule M items can be looked into, and those specific areas of income and deductions where experience indicates tax problems tend to lie can bear the brunt of the examination.

## UNREASONABLE ACCUMULATION OF EARNINGS

One question that a review of the Simple Corporation return would immediately raise would result from the lack of dividends coupled with the size of the retained earnings and the investments in securities. Because a corporation might refrain from paying dividends simply because it would want to keep its stockholders' taxes down, the law imposes a penalty tax of 27½ to 38½ percent

Form 1120 — Page 4

**Schedule L — Balance Sheets**

| ASSETS | Beginning of taxable year (A) Amount | Beginning of taxable year (B) Total | End of taxable year (C) Amount | End of taxable year (D) Total |
|---|---|---|---|---|
| 1 Cash | | 51,800 | | 60,000 |
| 2 Trade notes and accounts receivable | 43,000 | | 52,000 | |
| (a) Less allowance for bad debts | 7,500 | 35,500 | 9,000 | 43,000 |
| 3 Inventories | | 24,000 | | 31,000 |
| 4 Gov't obligations: (a) U.S. and instrumentalities | | | | |
| (b) State, subdivisions thereof, etc. | | | | |
| 5 Other current assets (attach schedule) | | | | |
| 6 Loans to stockholders | | | | |
| 7 Mortgage and real estate loans | | | | |
| 8 Other investments (attach schedule) | | 270,000 | | 350,000 |
| 9 Buildings and other fixed depreciable assets | 63,000 | | 63,000 | |
| (a) Less accumulated depreciation | 31,000 | 32,000 | 36,000 | 27,000 |
| 10 Depletable assets | | | | |
| (a) Less accumulated depletion | | | | |
| 11 Land (net of any amortization) | | | | |
| 12 Intangible assets (amortizable only) | | | | |
| (a) Less accumulated amortization | | | | |
| 13 Other assets (attach schedule) | | | | |
| 14 Total assets | | 413,300 | | 511,000 |
| **LIABILITIES AND STOCKHOLDERS' EQUITY** | | | | |
| 15 Accounts payable | | 22,000 | | 34,000 |
| 16 Mtges., notes, bonds payable in less than 1 yr. | | | | |
| 17 Other current liabilities (attach schedule) | | 4,000 | | 5,000 |
| 18 Loans from stockholders | | | | |
| 19 Mtges., notes, bonds payable in 1 yr. or more | | | | |
| 20 Other liabilities (attach schedule) | | 12,300 | | 15,732 |
| 21 Capital stock: (a) Preferred stock | | | | |
| (b) Common stock | 20,000 | 20,000 | 20,000 | 20,000 |
| 22 Paid-in or capital surplus | | | | |
| 23 Retained earnings—Appropriated (attach sch.) | | | | |
| 24 Retained earnings—Unappropriated | | 355,000 | | 436,268 |
| 25 Less cost of treasury stock | | ( ) | | ( ) |
| 26 Total liabilities and stockholders' equity | | 413,300 | | 511,000 |

**Schedule M-1 — Reconciliation of Income Per Books With Income Per Return**

| | | | |
|---|---|---|---|
| 1 Net income per books (97,000-15,732) | 81,268 | 7 Income recorded on books this year not included in this return (itemize) | |
| 2 Federal income tax | 15,732 | (a) Tax-exempt interest $ 21,000 | |
| 3 Excess of capital losses over capital gains | | | 21,000 |
| 4 Income subject to tax not recorded on books this year (itemize) | | 8 Deductions in this tax return not charged against book income this year (itemize) | |
| 5 Expenses recorded on books this year not deducted in this return (itemize) | | (a) Depreciation . . $ | |
| (a) Depreciation . . . . $ | | (b) Depletion . . $ | |
| (b) Depletion . . . . . $ | | | |
| Contributions exceeding 5% | 1,900 | 9 Total of lines 7 and 8 | 21,000 |
| 6 Total of lines 1 through 5 | 98,900 | 10 Income (line 28, page 1)—line 6 less 9 | 77,900 |

**Schedule M-2 — Analysis of Unappropriated Retained Earnings Per Books (line 24 above)**

| | | | |
|---|---|---|---|
| 1 Balance at beginning of year | 355,000 | 5 Distributions: (a) Cash | |
| 2 Net income per books | 81,268 | (b) Stock | |
| 3 Other increases (itemize) | | (c) Property | |
| | | 6 Other decreases (itemize) | |
| | | 7 Total of lines 5 and 6 | |
| 4 Total of lines 1, 2, and 3 | 436,268 | 8 Balance at end of year (line 4 less 7) | 436,268 |

FIGURE 3-4

Balance Sheet and Surplus Reconciliation Complicated

on what are described as unreasonable accumulations of earnings. The tax is imposed only on the after-tax earnings for the current year, to the extent deemed excessive, and not on the balance of the retained earnings account.

Although the law is not limited by its terms to corporations with a few shareholders, the practical application of it is such that it will normally apply only in a situation where there are a few large shareholders in a position to control corporate dividend policy (even though there may also be a large number of small shareholders).

A corporation is allowed to accumulate up to $150,000 of retained earnings without any need to show a business purpose. But when its retained earnings pass the $150,000 mark, it may have to establish the fact that failure to pay substantial current dividends is for good business reasons, if it hopes to avoid the penalty tax.

## THE ROLE OF THE CORPORATION IN THE U.S. INCOME TAX

We have already referred to the 1909 excise tax act. This imposed a tax of 1 percent on net income in excess of $5,000. It raised $35 million in 1912, its best and last year. The corporate excise tax was merged with the income tax in 1913. By 1918, rates were up to 12 percent. From 1943 to 1945, with a special tax imposed on "excess" profits, top corporate rates reached 80 percent. In 1974, the first $25,000 of corporate income was being taxed at 22 percent, and a 48 percent rate applied to earnings in excess of $25,000. Beginning in 1975 and through 1978 corporate tax rates are 20 percent on the first $25,000 of taxable income, 22 percent on the second $25,000 of income and 48 percent on earnings in excess of $50,000.

In 1951, corporate income taxes raised over $20 billion in one year for the first time in our history, and since then they have raised amounts of from $17 to $40 billion. Any discussion of the corporate income tax has to face the fact that this is a substantial sum—exceeded only by the income taxes collected from individuals. Until World War II, the corporate income tax raised more dollars annually than did the individual income tax.

At the same time, the position of the corporation in our economy must be of concern. In the private sector of the economy, the corporation is the prime vehicle for capital investment. Presumably, anything that artificially hampers capital investment tends to slow our rate of economic growth, and the rate of growth has come to seem quite important. We shall return to this topic in Part Three of this book.

There is also the question of which corporations we are talking about when we discuss the role of the corporation in the United States income tax. Out of $77 billion of corporate taxable net income in one recent year, less than 5,400 corporations accounted for over $57 billion. These 5,400 corporations paid some $25 billion of the $32 billion that was raised that year. The

66 corporations with taxable net incomes of over $100 million each had $23 billion of aggregate taxable net income and paid $10 billion in income tax. At the other end of the scale, some 1,013,000 corporations, which had taxable net incomes of less than $25,000 each (including loss corporations), paid less than $1.5 billion in aggregate income taxes.

Thus, the corporate income tax raises most of its "take" from large corporations, using income as a test of size. If we use total assets as a test of size, we get the same result. Almost 90 percent of the corporate tax comes from the 6 percent of corporations with assets of over $1 million each. As we shall see in Chapter 6, this is the reverse of the situation we encounter in the individual income tax.

The level of corporate taxable income tends to rise and fall with the business cycle. In periods of prosperity, the amount collected from the corporate income tax (assuming that rates remained constant) would rise, whereas in recessions the amount collected would fall. Since countercyclical fiscal policy is widely advocated, the corporate income tax, which drains purchasing power from the economy during prosperity to a much greater degree than during a recession, seems to many an admirable automatic fiscal tool.

## DOUBLE TAXATION OF CORPORATE INCOME AND INTERNAL INVESTMENT

Corporations, as mentioned earlier, cannot consume. They are merely economic middlemen. But they are peculiar middlemen—especially the bigger and older corporations. They come to have a life of their own, in the sense that any big organization tends to develop a life of its own.

Managers do what they think is best for the organization (with appropriate attention to their own careers, of course). To top managers of large corporations, stockholders are just another claimant for corporate assets. Dividends decrease the wealth controlled by the corporation. So dividend policies are calculated in terms of their effect on market values of the stock, on stockholder and financial press criticism of the corporation, and on the possibilities of obtaining new financing on favorable terms, if future financing is contemplated. Although corporate earnings may "belong" to the shareholders in a legalistic sense, it is a rare publicly owned corporation that can justify paying out all those earnings in dividends. It is better for the organization to plow earnings in excess of a reasonable dividend rate back into the business. And what is good for the organization is also defensible as being for the good of the shareholders in the long run.

Assume that we are the managers of a corporation. We could pay out our earnings in dividends. We have analyzed our shareholders, and we find that our average shareholder pays an effective tax of 30 percent on each dollar of dividend income that he receives from us. We can invest that dollar internally. If we do so, the market value of our stock will increase by approximately one dollar (not immediately, but in the long run).

Our internal investment can be made at a return of 5 percent after taxes. Our average stockholder would take his dividend and invest it at 5 percent after taxes. But we have a dollar to invest, whereas he will have only 70 cents.

If the corporation, year after year, keeps and reinvests the dollar, the difference between what it will accumulate and what the stockholder could accumulate may be quite impressive:

| | *Corporation, $1 per year* | *Stockholder, $.70 per year* |
|---|---|---|
| After 5 years | $ 5.526 | $ 3.868 |
| After 10 years | 12.570 | 8.799 |
| After 20 years | 33.066 | 23.146 |

This assumes that the corporation and the stockholder have available to them investments offering the same 5 percent after-tax return. If, more realistically, we assume that the corporation can earn the greater return, then the gap becomes greater. If we assume that the corporation earns 10 percent after taxes and the stockholder 5 percent, then these are the dramatic results:

| | *Corporation, $1 per year* | *Stockholder, $.70 per year* |
|---|---|---|
| After 5 years | $ 6.105 | $ 3.868 |
| After 10 years | 15.937 | 8.799 |
| After 20 years | 57.275 | 23.146 |

We conclude that we can do more for our average stockholder by retaining his dollar and investing it for him than by turning it over to him for investment. Thus, this double-taxation aspect of our tax structure tends to encourage the expansion of existing successful corporations and intensify their search for profitable investment opportunities.

## PRICING POLICY

If our corporate managers take pride in their work, they are shooting at some sort of standard. Most commonly in big corporations today, that standard tends to be the after-tax return on investment. Where pricing is at all discretionary, "target" prices are set by reference to the desired rate of return on investment. Given a "target" rate of return, the effect of a given tax structure will be to force prices above what they would otherwise be. If, in the absence of taxes, a selling price of $2,000 would produce a net profit of $100, which would provide a satisfactory return on investment, then a 50 percent corporate income tax would force the price to $2,100 in order to achieve a before-tax profit of $200 and an after-tax profit of $100.

Varied approaches are employed in corporate measurement of return on investment. Whereas measuring return on investment in individual projects involves essentially the type of cash-flow procedure in which the time value of money is reflected, corporate return on investment is likely to lean heavily on accounting and budget figures as its data.

Where accounting concepts are being used in this type of evaluation, differences in the time value of money cease to be reflected. Thus, if depreciation is taken more rapidly for tax than for accounting purposes, accepted accounting practice requires showing the total tax ultimately payable as an expense and the tax deferred as a liability. The fact that the deferred tax is a non-interest-bearing liability of indefinite duration makes no difference to its valuation. In a decision-making focus, where data from the accounting statements prepared for outsiders are used to compute return on investment in arriving at prices, the tax expense deducted on the income statement in arriving at projected income is unaffected by the difference between a tax payable in three months and a tax that may not be payable for ten years, if ever.

The result is that pricing decisions may be less affected by tax considerations than investment decisions. A present tax deduction at the expense of a future tax deduction foregone may have little impact on a pricing decision, although it would raise the profitability perceived in an investment situation in which the time value of money was reflected.

Assume that a corporation must pay a total of $500,000 in income taxes over the next five years. From a strictly accounting viewpoint, it makes no difference whether it pays the $500,000 at the rate of $100,000 per year or makes the entire payment in one amount at the end of the fifth year. But from a management point of view, it does make a difference. If the corporation would have to borrow the tax money at 7 percent, then there is a measurable advantage to postponing the payment. It will save interest on the first year's tax for four years, the second year's for three years, etc., by not having to pay (and borrow) the $100,000 per year. The five-year payment postponement is $70,000 better, computed as follows:

| | |
|---|---|
| 7% of $100,000 for four years | $28,000 |
| 7% of $100,000 for three years | 21,000 |
| 7% of $100,000 for two years | 14,000 |
| 7% of $100,000 for one year | 7,000 |
| Total interest saved | $70,000 |

But what if the business would not have to borrow to pay the tax? The same approach still applies. The $100,000 would be invested in something if not used to pay the tax, and the amount it would earn is still the cost of having to pay the $100,000 now rather than later.

For an extended discussion of this business of the time-adjusted value of money, see the Appendix.

## COMMENT

The relationship between tax treatment and financial accounting is often complex. Take, for instance, research and development expenses.

Prior to 1954, the accounting treatment utilized by a company pretty much determined the tax treatment that would be allowed. It became common practice for research and development costs to be charged to expense in the year incurred. In 1954, specific statutory authorization for deducting such costs as current expenses was inserted in the tax law, so that it was no longer necessary to expense them for accounting purposes to be able to take a tax deduction.

The reasoning was that if research were set up as an asset and its costs amortized over some reasonable (even though arbitrary) period, management would be getting a more meaningful message and would face one less temptation to indulge in window dressing.

Most companies continued to charge research and development costs to expense in the year incurred. But there were enough companies, able to expense research for tax purposes regardless of the financial statement treatment, which capitalized substantial amounts of these expenses to induce the Financial Accounting Standards Board twenty years later to decide that research and development was hence to be charged to expense as incurred. The rationale was that only in this way could abuses be avoided. Thus, the financial statement treatment which the tax provision implicitly encouraged resulted in excesses which, in turn, resulted in changing the financial statement treatment.

We shall mention other examples of the interaction between financial and tax accounting, for example, in the discussion of LIFO inventory in Part Three. At this point, however, what we are trying to say is that taxes may even influence management decisions in institutionalized organizations through the influence of tax procedures on accounting concepts and procedures.

## QUESTIONS AND PROBLEMS

1. In *Pollack* v. *The Farmers' Loan & Trust Company* (15 S. Ct. 912, 3 AFTR 2602), the Supreme Court held the 1894 income tax act unconstitutional

on the ground that it violated Article 1, Section 9(4). That provision in the Constitution provides that "no capitation or other direct tax shall be laid, unless in proportion to the census. . . ." That being the case, how was it that an income tax could be constitutionally imposed on the corporations in 1909?

2. "Imposition of an income tax on corporations has no detrimental effect on the economy, because corporations do not consume and all that is taxed is their profits–that is, the surplus over and above the amounts necessary to induce them to produce goods or render services." What assumptions underlie a statement like this, and what would be some of the arguments of the contrary point of view?

3. A balance sheet is not necessary in order to compute a corporation's income tax. Why, then, is a corporation required to provide a balance sheet with its tax return?

4. Items that are treated differently in computing taxable income, on the one hand, and financial income, on the other, will be reflected in Schedule M of the corporate return. Name three such items. (*Note:* The special deduction for dividends received is *not* reflected in Schedule M, because Schedule M shows taxable income before special deductions, and therefore this should not be counted as one of the three items.)

5. If corporations were allowed to deduct dividends paid shareholders in computing taxable income (as compared with the present situation where such a deduction is not allowed the ordinary corporation), which of the following effects would seem likely?

   (a) Increased pressure on the corporation to invest internally

   (b) Increased pressure on the corporation to pay out all surplus funds as dividends, obtaining funds for subsequent growth or expansion from new financing

   (c) An increase in dividends until the amount of working capital retained in the corporation approximated the amount that would have been retained in the absence of the change in tax treatment

   (d) Enhancement of the desirability of investment in corporate stocks by:

      (1) Organizations not subject to tax, such as pension funds, charitable foundations, etc.

      (2) High-bracket individual taxpayers

      (3) Corporate investors

      (4) Individual investors primarily concerned with income

   (e) Other?

6. The statements for the Sadler corporation (a retail store) at December 31, 19X1 are as follows:

## SADLER CORPORATION
### Balance Sheet
### December 31, 19X1

*Assets*

| | | |
|---|---|---|
| Cash | | $ 10,000 |
| Accounts receivable | $ 75,000 | |
| Less allowance for doubtful accounts | 5,000 | 70,000 |
| Inventory, 12/31/X1 | | 95,000 |
| Land | | 3,500 |
| Building | 97,000 | |
| Less accumulated depreciation | 20,500 | 76,500 |
| Machinery & equipment | 83,000 | |
| Less accumulated depreciation | 42,000 | 41,000 |
| Other Assets | | 4,000 |
| Total Assets | | $300,000 |

*Liabilities*

| | | |
|---|---|---|
| Accounts payable | $ 37,000 | |
| Notes payable—due 12/31/X3 | 50,000 | $ 87,000 |

*Stockholders' Equity*

| | | |
|---|---|---|
| Common stock ($100 par) | $ 10,000 | |
| Retained earnings | 203,000 | 213,000 |
| Total Stockholders' Equity & Liabilities | | $300,000 |

## SADLER CORPORATION
### Income Statement
### For Year Ended December 31, 19X1

| | | |
|---|---|---|
| Income: | | |
| Sales | $950,000 | |
| Dividends | 4,000 | $954,000 |
| Expenses: | | |
| Cost of goods sold | 585,800 | |
| Salaries (Employees) | 90,000 | |
| Salaries (Officers) | 55,000 | |
| Advertising | 34,000 | |
| Miscellaneous deductions | 28,000 | |
| Contributions | 23,000 | |
| Depreciation | 9,700 | |
| Local taxes | 8,000 | |
| Repairs | 6,000 | |
| Bad debts | 4,000 | |
| Interest | 2,500 | 846,000 |
| Net Income before Taxes | | $108,000 |

You are given the following added information:

Inventory of 12/31/X0 was $87,000; Purchases were $593,800.

The retained earnings figure shown reflects a $20,000 cash dividend paid in July, 19X1 and charged to retained earnings.

The dividend income was received on stock purchased during the year as a temporary investment and sold for the exact amount for which purchased. You are to prepare the corporate return on Form 1120, making such assumptions as you wish about address and other incidental information requested. Fill in Schedules A (Cost of Goods Sold), L, and M, but no other supporting schedules need to be filled in. You will thus prepare the income statement portion of the return, the computation of tax, the ending balance sheet (note the necessity of setting up the ending tax-liability figures on the balance sheet), and the surplus reconciliation. You need insert no figures for the beginning balance sheet, but you will need to compute the beginning figure of retained earnings.

7. What effect would varying the ending inventory have on the after-tax profit of the Sadler Corporation?

8. The Bravado Development Corporation operates an amusement center named Bravado Park. Its primary source of income is rent from concessionaires. All its stock is owned by a Mr. Drago. The corporate financial statement at 12/31/X1 showed.

BRAVADO DEVELOPMENT CORPORATION
Balance Sheet
December 31, 19X1

| | | |
|---|---|---|
| *Assets* | | |
| Cash | | $ 4,200 |
| Rent Receivable | | 19,600 |
| Investments | | 256,000 |
| Land | | 528,000 |
| Building & Equipment | $975,000 | |
| Less accumulated depreciation | 370,000 | 605,000 |
| Prepaid Expenses | | 4,700 |
| Total Assets | | $1,417,500 |
| *Liabilities* | | |
| Accounts Payable | $ 1,200 | |
| Notes Payable—Current | 249,000 | |
| Mortgage Payable—Noncurrent | 613,000 | $ 863,200 |
| *Stockholders' Equity* | | |
| Common Stock | $400,000 | |
| Retained Earnings | 154,300 | 554,300 |
| Total Liabilities & Stockholders' Equity | | $1,417,500 |

BRAVADO DEVELOPMENT CORPORATION
Income Statement
For Year Ended December 31, 19X1

| | | |
|---|---|---|
| Income: | | |
| Rental income | $523,000 | |
| Municipal bond interest | 8,000 | |
| Other interest income | 1,100 | $532,100 |
| Expenses: | | |
| Depreciation | 170,000 | |
| Advertising | 167,300 | |
| Officers' salaries | 63,000 | |
| Property taxes | 47,500 | |
| Repairs | 45,000 | |
| Interest | 33,000 | |
| Miscellaneous | 29,000 | |
| Other salaries | 24,000 | |
| Pension & profit sharing | 16,000 | 594,800 |
| Net Loss | | $ (62,700) |

If an amount is paid as interest in connection with a loan made to acquire or carry securities the income from which is not subject to tax, the interest paid on such a loan is not deductible. The municipal bonds were originally purchased as a temporary investment of funds, but the bonds were not sold when cash was needed, because of the availability of a relatively low-interest loan for the amount needed. The interest paid to continue carrying the municipal bonds amounted to $3,000 of the total interest paid.

You are to prepare the corporate return on Form 1120, making such assumptions as you wish about address and other incidental information requested. Supporting schedules (except for L and M) are not to be filled in.

9. Based on the following information, prepare on Form 1120 a tax computation using rates on the form and a Schedule M for the ABC Corporation:

ABC CORPORATION
Income Statement
For Year Ended December 31, 19X1*

| | | | |
|---|---|---|---|
| Income: | | | |
| Sales | $1,940,000 | | |
| Less sales returns & allowances | 40,000 | $1,900,000 | |
| Miscellaneous income | | 26,000 | $1,926,000 |
| Expenses: | | | |
| Cost of goods sold | | 1,550,000 | |
| Depreciation | | 53,100 | |
| Officers' salaries | | 35,000 | |
| Other salaries | | 32,000 | |
| Local taxes | | 9,000 | |
| Contributions | | 5,500 | |

| | | |
|---|---:|---:|
| Insurance premiums | 3,000 | |
| Repairs | 1,000 | |
| Interest expense | 400 | 1,689,000 |
| Net Income before Taxes | | $ 237,000 |

*The Miscellaneous Income Account is made up of interest ($10,000) received from local banks and the tax refund, interest ($1,000) from the State of Ohio Bonds, and the proceeds ($15,000) from a life insurance policy received on the death of a corporate officer. The proceeds of such insurance policies will not be taxable because the premiums paid on life insurance policies of which the corporation is a beneficiary are not deductible. The Charitable Contributions Account includes a $500 state political contribution which is nondeductible for tax purposes. The interest expense was the cost of borrowing the money necessary to purchase the Ohio State Bonds. The insurance premium account reflects the cost of life insurance policies on corporate officers with the corporation as beneficiary. The firm estimated its federal income tax expense for the year at $85,000 and paid that amount during the year.

# 4

# The Small Business Corporation

One view of the corporation is that it is merely an economic middleman. From this point of view, as we have said, it is logical to conclude that the income of the corporation is really the income of its shareholders. It should not be too surprising, therefore, to discover that some corporations can elect to have their income treated in exactly that fashion.

These corporations are variously labeled "Subchapter S" or "Sub S" corporations (after the Internal Revenue Code subchapter that gave them birth), "tax-option" corporations (inasmuch as they have exercised their option to be treated in this fashion), or by the ambiguous title used on the tax return form, "Small Business Corporations." We shall find later that "Small Business Corporation" has still another meaning for another tax purpose.

There are over 200,000 such firms, or roughly one out of nine of the corporations presently filing income tax returns. And although the law restricts this optional treatment on the basis of sources of income and number of shareholders, not on total income or total assets, these are, in fact, relatively small businesses, compared to regular corporations. In one recent year, only ten Small Business Corporations had assets of $10 million or more, whereas 14,341 regular corporations had assets of $10 million or more.

To elect the optional tax treatment, the corporation must have no more than ten shareholders (fifteen shareholders after the corporation has been a Sub S for five taxable years or during the first five years of the election if shareholders in excess of ten up to fifteen acquire their stock through inheritance), who must be either individuals, estates, grantor or voting trusts or any trust for 60 days after receiving stock under a will; and all the shareholders must consent to the optional tax treatment. If another corporation were a stockholder, or more then one class of stock is issued, the optional tax treatment could not be elected. A Sub S election will be terminated if a new shareholder affirmatively refuses to consent to the election within 60 days.

Not more than 20 percent of the corporation's gross receipts can originate from such investment sources as dividends, rents, royalties, interest, annuities, and gains on stocks or other securities; and more than 20 percent of gross receipts must be derived from within the United States.

After we have illustrated the tax treatment accorded these corporations, we shall discuss some of the reasons, pro and con, for their use or their avoidance.

## A SMALL BUSINESS CORPORATION RETURN

Remember the Simple Corporation in the preceding chapter? Figure 3-3 (page 69) shows the income statement part of the return we prepared when that firm had dividend income.

Now, let us put the same data on a Form 1120-S, which is the return form for the Small Business Corporation (Figure 4-1). There are minor rearrangements of the data, but the two returns are essentially identical through line 28.

The regular corporation return shows space for special deductions, for the income tax itself, and for credits against the tax. The Small Business Corporation has no need for such data, for it normally pays no income tax and gets no special deductions for dividends received. Instead, it has what might be described as a "distribution schedule," showing how its income is allocated among its shareholders (see Figure 4-2). There are situations, however, when the Small Business Corporation will have to pay tax on its capital gains income. These situations are discussed in Chapter 8.

The individual stockholders report the corporation's income on their personal income tax returns. John Doe would report $77,900 of ordinary income on his individual income tax return, thereby picking up, as his own income, the entire net taxable income of the corporation. He must, of course, also report the $20,000 he received as wages.

The balance sheets on the two types of corporate returns are just about identical. (See Figures 4-3 and 4-4.) Notice that there is only one line for capital stock on the Small Business Corporation return (Figure 4-4) because a Small Business Corporation may not have more than one class of stock outstanding. Notice, too, that no income tax liability appears on the balance sheet of the Small Business Corporation. This is the normal situation, although the beginning balance sheet in the first year as a Small Business Corporation will often show a tax liability carried over from the prior year, when the corporation was taxed as a regular corporation. Comparison of the two corporation balance sheets shows that we had a liability at the beginning of the taxable year for income taxes of $12,300 on the regular corporation balance sheet (Figure 4-3). The $15,732 year-end income tax liability disappears when we assume that we have switched to being a Small Business Corporation, and our earnings on

Form **1120S**

Department of the Treasury
Internal Revenue Service

**U.S. Small Business Corporation Income Tax Return** for calendar year 19 or

other taxable year beginning ................, 19 ending ................, 19......
(PLEASE TYPE OR PRINT)

| | | |
|---|---|---|
| A Date of election as small business corporation: July 1, 19X0 | Name: THE SIMPLE CORPORATION | C Employer identification no.: 36-3601434 |
| B Business Code No. (see page 7 of instructions): 608 | Number and street: 77 Sunset Boulevard | D Date incorporated: 1/1/70 |
| | City or town, State, and ZIP code: Valhalla, Arizona | E Enter total assets from line 14, column D, Schedule L: $ 511,000 |

**IMPORTANT**—All applicable lines and schedules must be filled in. If the lines on the schedules are not sufficient, see instruction N.
**Note:** *If section 465 (deductions limited to amount at-risk) applies, see instruction for line 28.*

| | | | |
|---|---|---|---|
| GROSS INCOME | 1 | Gross receipts or gross sales 534,000 **Less:** Returns and allowances 8,000 | 526,000 |
| | 2 | **Less:** Cost of goods sold (Schedule A) and/or operations (attach schedule) | 359,000 |
| | 3 | Gross profit | 167,000 |
| | 4(a) | (a) Domestic dividends | 20,000 |
| | 4(b) | (b) Foreign dividends | |
| | 5 | Interest on obligations of the U.S. and U.S. instrumentalities | |
| | 6 | Other interest | |
| | 7 | Gross rents | |
| | 8 | Gross royalties | |
| | | 9 Gains and losses (attach separate Schedule D (Form 1120S) and/or Form 4797): | |
| | 9(a) | (a) Net short-term capital gain reduced by any net long-term capital loss | |
| | 9(b) | (b) Net long-term capital gain reduced by any net short-term capital loss (if more than $25,000, see instructions) | |
| | 9(c) | (c) Ordinary gain or (loss) from Part II, Form 4797 | |
| | 10 | Other income (see instructions—attach schedule) | |
| | 11 | TOTAL income—Add lines 3 through 10 | 187,000 |
| DEDUCTIONS | 12 | Compensation of officers (Schedule E) | 20,000 |
| | 13 | Salaries and wages (not deducted elsewhere) | 42,000 |
| | 14 | Repairs (see instructions) | 1,000 |
| | 15 | Bad debts (Schedule F if reserve method is used) | 3,000 |
| | 16 | Rents | 8,000 |
| | 17 | Taxes (attach schedule) | 3,000 |
| | 18 | Interest | |
| | 19 | Contributions **(not over 5% of line 28 adjusted per instructions—attach schedule)** | 4,100 |
| | 20 | Amortization (attach schedule) | |
| | 21 | Depreciation (Schedule G) | 5,000 |
| | 22 | Depletion (attach schedule) | |
| | 23 | Advertising | 16,000 |
| | 24 | Pension, profit-sharing, etc. plans (see instructions) (enter number of plans ▶ ........) | |
| | 25 | Employee benefit programs (see instructions) | |
| | 26 | Other deductions (attach schedule) | 7,000 |
| | 27 | TOTAL deductions—Add lines 12 through 26 | 109,100 |
| | 28 | Taxable income (line 11 less line 27) (see instructions) | 77,900 |
| TAX | 29 | Income tax on capital gains (Schedule J) | |
| | 30 | Minimum tax (see instructions—attach Form 4626) | |
| | 31 | Total tax (add lines 29 and 30) | |
| | 32(a) | 32 **Credits:** (a) Tax deposited with Form 7004 (attach copy) | |
| | 32(b) | (b) Tax deposited with Form 7005 (attach copy) | |
| | 32(c) | (c) Credit for U.S. tax on special fuels, nonhighway gas, and lubricating oil (attach Form 4136) | |
| | 33 | TAX DUE (line 31 less line 32). See instruction G for depositary method of payment ⟶ | |
| | 34 | OVERPAYMENT (line 32 less line 31) ⟶ | |

Under penalties of perjury, I declare that I have examined this return, including accompanying schedules and statements, and to the best of my knowledge and belief it is true, correct, and complete. Declaration of preparer (other than taxpayer) is based on all information of which the preparer has any knowledge.

Date ........ Signature of officer ........ Preparer's signature (and employer's name, if any) ........ Date

Title ........ Identifying number (see instructions) ........ Address and ZIP Code

FIGURE 4-1
Form 1120-S (Return for the Small Business Corporation)

Schedule M-1 are merely $15,732 greater. But we will have to make some assumption about that $12,300. If we assume that the corporation has been a Small Business Corporation all along and therefore owes no income tax, we

Form 1120S (1976) Page **3**

**Schedule K** **Computation of Undistributed Taxable Income and Summary of Distributions and Other Items**

**Computation of Corporation's Undistributed Taxable Income**

| | | |
|---|---|---|
| 1 Taxable income (line 28, page 1) | | 77,900 |
| 2 **Less: (a)** Money distributed as dividends out of earnings and profits of the taxable year | 12,300 | |
| (b) Tax imposed on certain capital gains (line 31, page 1) | | 12,300 |
| 3 Corporation's undistributed taxable income | | 65,600 |

**Summary of Distributions and Other Items (attach additional sheets if necessary)**

| 1. Name and address of each shareholder | 2. Social security number | 3. Stock ownership: Number of shares | Period held: From | Period held: To | 4. Compensation | 5. Percentage of time devoted to business |
|---|---|---|---|---|---|---|
| A John Doe | 360-14-3404 | 200 | 1/1/X1 | 12/31/X1 | 20,000 | 100 |
| B | | | | | | |

| | |
|---|---|
| 4 Actual dividend distributions taxable as ordinary income (Do not include amounts shown on line 6) | 12,300 |
| 5 Actual dividend distributions taxable as long-term capital gains (after tax) | |
| 6 Actual dividend distributions taxable as ordinary income and qualifying for dividend exclusion | |
| 7 Nondividend distributions | |
| 8 Undistributed taxable income—taxable as ordinary income or (loss) | 65,600 |
| 9 Undistributed taxable income—taxable as long-term capital gain (after tax) | |
| **10 Investment credit property** | Cost or basis |

| Property Qualified for Investment Credit | | | |
|---|---|---|---|
| Basis of new investment property | (a) 3 or more but less than 5 years | | |
| | (b) 5 or more but less than 7 years | | |
| | (c) 7 or more years | | |
| Qualified progress expenditures | 1974 and 1975 | (d) 7 or more years | |
| | 1976 | (e) 7 or more years | |
| Cost of used investment property | (f) 3 or more but less than 5 years | | |
| | (g) 5 or more but less than 7 years | | |
| | (h) 7 or more years | | |

**11 Interest on investment indebtedness:**

FIGURE 4-2

Form 1120-S (Distribution Schedule)

might assume that the stockholders who did have to pay income tax personally on the corporate earnings withdrew the $12,300, to make tax payments. The $12,300 would thus have been a cash dividend paid during the year—and we will so treat it.

Another difference between the two balance sheet forms relates to retained earnings. The balance sheet for the Small Business Corporation contains an additional classification of retained earnings, "shareholders' undistributed taxable income." Unfortunately for the people who design tax return forms, the Small Business Corporation has two types of retained earnings. Two retained-earnings reconciliations would prove cumbersome, so instead, the Small Business Corporation reconciles only its regular retained-earnings account (see Figure 4-4).

The differences between the two types of retained earnings are of substantial significance. Retained earnings (line 24, Figure 4-4) represents amounts on which the shareholders have never paid income tax. For example, the end-of-the-year amount of $219,100 consists of retained earnings accumulated prior to electing to be treated as a Small Business Corporation, plus tax-free income and less nondeductible expenses of the corporation since election (such as the $21,000 of tax-free interest received, less the $1,900 nondeductible part of the charitable contributions). Any dividends paid out of this retained earnings will

Form 1120 — Page 4

**Schedule L — Balance Sheets**

| ASSETS | Beginning of taxable year (A) Amount | Beginning of taxable year (B) Total | End of taxable year (C) Amount | End of taxable year (D) Total |
|---|---|---|---|---|
| 1 Cash | | 51,800 | | 60,000 |
| 2 Trade notes and accounts receivable | 43,000 | | 52,000 | |
| (a) Less allowance for bad debts | 7,500 | 35,500 | 9,000 | 43,000 |
| 3 Inventories | | 24,000 | | 31,000 |
| 4 Gov't obligations: (a) U.S. and instrumentalities | | | | |
| (b) State, subdivisions thereof, etc. | | | | |
| 5 Other current assets (attach schedule) | | | | |
| 6 Loans to stockholders | | | | |
| 7 Mortgage and real estate loans | | | | |
| 8 Other investments (attach schedule) | | 270,000 | | 350,000 |
| 9 Buildings and other fixed depreciable assets | 63,000 | | 63,000 | |
| (a) Less accumulated depreciation | 31,000 | 32,000 | 36,000 | 27,000 |
| 10 Depletable assets | | | | |
| (a) Less accumulated depletion | | | | |
| 11 Land (net of any amortization) | | | | |
| 12 Intangible assets (amortizable only) | | | | |
| (a) Less accumulated amortization | | | | |
| 13 Other assets (attach schedule) | | | | |
| 14 Total assets | | 413,300 | | 511,000 |
| **LIABILITIES AND STOCKHOLDERS' EQUITY** | | | | |
| 15 Accounts payable | | 22,000 | | 34,000 |
| 16 Mtges., notes, bonds payable in less than 1 yr. | | 4,000 | | 5,000 |
| 17 Other current liabilities (attach schedule) | | | | |
| 18 Loans from stockholders | | | | |
| 19 Mtges., notes, bonds payable in 1 yr. or more | | | | |
| 20 Other liabilities (attach schedule) | | 12,300 | | 15,732 |
| 21 Capital stock: (a) Preferred stock | | | | |
| (b) Common stock | 20,000 | 20,000 | 20,000 | 20,000 |
| 22 Paid-in or capital surplus | | | | |
| 23 Retained earnings—Appropriated (attach sch.) | | | | |
| 24 Retained earnings—Unappropriated | | 355,000 | | 436,268 |
| 25 Less cost of treasury stock | | ( ) | | ( ) |
| 26 Total liabilities and stockholders' equity | | 413,300 | | 511,000 |

**Schedule M-1 — Reconciliation of Income Per Books With Income Per Return**

| | | | |
|---|---|---|---|
| 1 Net income per books (97,000–15,732) | 81,268 | 7 Income recorded on books this year not included in this return (itemize) | |
| 2 Federal income tax | 15,732 | (a) Tax-exempt interest $ 21,000 | |
| 3 Excess of capital losses over capital gains | | | 21,000 |
| 4 Income subject to tax not recorded on books this year (itemize) | | 8 Deductions in this tax return not charged against book income this year (itemize) | |
| 5 Expenses recorded on books this year not deducted in this return (itemize) | | (a) Depreciation . . $ | |
| (a) Depreciation . . . . $ | | (b) Depletion . . $ | |
| (b) Depletion . . . . . $ | | | |
| Contributions exceeding 5% | 1,900 | 9 Total of lines 7 and 8 | 21,000 |
| 6 Total of lines 1 through 5 | 98,900 | 10 Income (line 28, page 1)—line 6 less 9 | 77,900 |

**Schedule M-2 — Analysis of Unappropriated Retained Earnings Per Books (line 24 above)**

| | | | |
|---|---|---|---|
| 1 Balance at beginning of year | 355,000 | 5 Distributions: (a) Cash | |
| 2 Net income per books | 81,268 | (b) Stock | |
| 3 Other increases (itemize) | | (c) Property | |
| | | 6 Other decreases (itemize) | |
| | | 7 Total of lines 5 and 6 | |
| 4 Total of lines 1, 2, and 3 | 436,268 | 8 Balance at end of year (line 4 less 7) | 436,268 |

FIGURE 4-3
Balance Sheet and Surplus Reconciliation from Chapter 3

be taxable to the shareholders receiving them. Thus, the $21,000 that was tax-free interest income when received by the corporation will at some future date be taxable income if distributed to the shareholders. This loss of the

Form 1120S **Page 4**

**Schedule K-1** **Shareholder's Share of Undistributed Taxable Income, etc.** (Complete a separate Schedule K-1 (Form 1120S) for each shareholder. See page 5 of instructions, and also back of Copy C, Schedule K-1 (Form 1120S).)

**Schedule L** **Balance Sheets**

| ASSETS | Beginning of Taxable year (A) Amount | (B) Total | End of Taxable year (C) Amount | (D) Total |
|---|---|---|---|---|
| 1 Cash | | 51,800 | | 60,000 |
| 2 Trade notes and accounts receivable | 43,000 | | 52,000 | |
| (a) Less allowances for bad debts | 7,500 | 35,500 | 9,000 | 43,000 |
| 3 Inventories | | 24,000 | | 31,000 |
| 4 Gov't obligations: (a) U.S. and instrumentalities | | | | |
| (b) State, subdivisions thereof, etc. | | | | |
| 5 Other current assets (attach schedule) | | | | |
| 6 Loans to shareholders | | | | |
| 7 Mortgage and real estate loans | | | | |
| 8 Other investments (attach schedule) | | 270,000 | | 350,000 |
| 9 Buildings and other fixed depreciable assets | 63,000 | | 63,000 | |
| (a) Less accumulated depreciation | 31,000 | 32,000 | 36,000 | 27,000 |
| 10 Depletable assets | | | | |
| (a) Less accumulated depletion | | | | |
| 11 Land (net of any amortization) | | | | |
| 12 Intangible assets (amortizable only) | | | | |
| (a) Less accumulated amortization | | | | |
| 13 Other assets (attach schedule) | | | | |
| 14 Total assets | | 413,300 | | 511,000 |
| **LIABILITIES AND SHAREHOLDERS' EQUITY** | | | | |
| 15 Accounts payable | | 22,000 | | 34,000 |
| 16 Mtges, notes, bonds payable in less than 1 year | | | | |
| 17 Other current liabilities (attach schedule) | | 4,000 | | 5,000 |
| 18 Loans from shareholders | | | | |
| 19 Mtges, notes, bonds payable in 1 year or more | | | | |
| 20 Other liabilities (attach schedule) | | | | |
| 21 Capital stock | | 20,000 | | 20,000 |
| 22 Paid-in or capital surplus | | | | |
| 23 Retained earnings—appropriated (attach schedule) | | | | |
| 24 Retained earnings—unappropriated | | 200,000 | | 219,100 |
| 25 Shareholders' undistributed taxable income previously taxed | | 167,300 | | 232,900 |
| 26 Less cost of treasury stock | | ( ) | | ( ) |
| 27 Total liabilities and shareholders' equity | | 413,300 | | 511,000 |

**Schedule M-1** **Reconciliation of Income Per Books With Income Per Return**

| | | | |
|---|---|---|---|
| 1 Net income per books | 97,000 | 7 Income recorded on books this year not included in this return (itemize) (a) Tax-exempt interest $ 21,000 | 21,000 |
| 2 Federal income tax | | 8 Deductions in this tax return not charged against book income this year (itemize) | |
| 3 Excess of capital losses over capital gains | | | |
| 4 Income subject to tax not recorded on books this year (itemize) | | | |
| 5 Expenses recorded on books this year not deducted in this return (itemize) Contributions Exceeding 5% | 1,900 | 9 Total of lines 7 and 8 | 21,000 |
| 6 Total of lines 1 through 5 | 98,900 | 10 Income (line 28, page 1)—line 6 less line 9 | 77,900 |

**Schedule M-2** **Analysis of Unappropriated Retained Earnings Per Books (line 24 above)**

| | | | |
|---|---|---|---|
| 1 Balance at beginning of year | 200,000 | 5 Distributions out of current or accumulated earnings and profits: (a) Cash | 12,300 |
| 2 Net income per books | 97,000 | (b) Stock | |
| 3 Other increases (itemize) | | (c) Property | |
| | | 6 Current year's undistributed taxable income or net operating loss (total of lines 8 and 9, Schedule K) | 65,600 |
| | | 7 Other decreases (itemize) | |
| | | 8 Total of lines 5, 6, and 7 | 77,900 |
| 4 Total of lines 1, 2, and 3 | 297,000 | 9 Balance at end of year (line 4 less line 8) | 219,100 |

FIGURE 4-4
Balance Sheet and Reconciliation, Small Business Corporation Return

tax-free nature of income as it passes through the corporation to the shareholder is characteristic of the regular corporation as well as of the Small Business Corporation.

The retained earnings on line 25, labeled "Shareholders' undistributed taxable income previously taxed," is the corporate retained earnings on which the stockholders have paid income tax. The amounts shown on the distribution schedule are, you recall, picked up as income on the individual returns of the stockholders. Since these amounts have been already taxed once to the shareholders in the year earned by the corporation, they may now be distributed to shareholders by the Small Business Corporation without the shareholder incurring additional income tax.

A reconciliation of the retained earnings on line 25 at the beginning and the end of the year would show:

| | |
|---|---|
| Line 25, beginning of year | $167,300 |
| *Add:* Taxable income for year | 77,900 |
| | $245,200 |
| *Deduct:* Cash dividend paid | 12,300 |
| Line 25, end of year | $232,900 |

## WHY ELECT SMALL BUSINESS CORPORATION TREATMENT?

The imagination and ingenuity of taxpayers and their advisers is almost infinite. By allowing corporations to avoid paying tax if their shareholders will elect to report the corporate income as their own, Congress intended merely to remove tax considerations as a factor in the choice of the legal form that a particular enterprise might adopt. But even a simple provision added to the law fits into a framework that is already complex, and hence even such a provision can have unexpected consequences. The Small Business Corporation provisions, not being entirely simple in themselves, have thus spawned a certain degree of complexity.

It is true, however, that a major reason for choosing Small Business Corporation treatment fits naturally into the congressional intention. For business reasons—limited liability, employee incentive through stock ownership, relatively greater ease of handling corporate stock rather than diverse business assets in estate planning, and raising capital through stock sale to friends and relatives who might not wish the risks of a partnership—it may be desirable to conduct a business in corporate form. Yet the owners of the business may need or want to withdraw substantially all of its earnings. As a regular corporation, they would find the corporate earnings subject to at least a 20 percent tax and the dividends paid subject to at least a 14 percent tax, a combined total tax of 31 percent. (How can 20 plus 14 total 31? The corporation can distribute only its after-tax income. Therefore, the 14 percent applies to 80 percent [100 – 20] of the corporate income and is 11.2 percent of that income.) As a Small Business Corporation, the same earnings might be subject to a tax of only 14 percent.

So, to, the corporation may become faced with a possible penalty surtax for unreasonable accumulation of earnings. In that case, the lowest bracket tax would be 20 percent on the corporate income, and a possible additional 27½ percent on the corporate income after taxes–a combined tax load of 42 percent. If the stockholders are in a lower tax bracket than this–and most stockholders are–then the Small Business Corporation election may appear prudent.

This election would also appear prudent when the corporation is formed for a project that will last only a relatively short time. Thus, if the corporation were formed to subdivide a tract of land and it was estimated that the entire operation would be liquidated within five years of its beginning, the double corporate taxation might appear too burdensome. Again, the minimum regular corporate tax would be at least 20 percent, with an additional tax on the shareholders upon liquidation of from 7 to 35 percent of the after-tax profits that had accumulated–a total effective tax rate of from 25.6 to 48 percent.

Then, of course, there are the business operations that will probably produce a loss in their early years. With a regular corporation, such a loss is of no immediate benefit to a new organization. But the stockholders of the Small Business Corporation get to deduct such losses on their personal tax returns. Thus, to the extent of their personal tax rate, they can put the government in the position of sharing in their losses and, through tax reduction, of helping to finance them. The cumulative total of such losses claimed by a stockholder cannot exceed his original investment in the stock of the corporation, plus the amounts he has loaned to the corporation, plus his share of any corporate earnings less any amounts withdrawn as dividends or loan repayments.

An unincorporated business may desire employee fringe benefits for its owner-operators–for example, pension and profit-sharing plans in which the employer gets a current tax deduction for his contributions to the plan, and the employee pays no taxes until he starts drawing benefits from the plan (see Chapter 15). For a Small Business Corporation, these are obtainable subject to special limitations without the necessity of incurring the corporate double tax.

There are other uses of the Small Business Corporation that may not fit the congressional intention quite so neatly. These three examples are indicative of the factors involved:

1. The Small Business Corporation's stock can be given to other members of the stockholder's family. The advantage here is that the income will be taxed to these other members at a lower tax rate since taxation is based on stock ownership. Thus, a father may give 10 percent of the family corporation's stock to each of his three school-age children, pulling income from his own 36 percent tax bracket down into their zero to 20 percent tax brackets. Recognizing this possibility, the law provides that where this is done, the family member active in the business must be paid reasonable compensation for his services. To the extent that he is not, the income for tax purposes may be reallocated to him. Thus, if corporate earnings were $50,000 before taxes, and the father paid no

salary to himself, he could not shift $5,000 (10 percent) of the $50,000 to each of the three children. Assuming that a reasonable salary for his services was $20,000, then the most income that he could shift to the children would be $3,000 (10 percent of [$50,000–$20,000]) to each.

2. A taxpayer who conducts an unincorporated business as a proprietorship may have trouble drawing full Social Security benefits as long as he has substantial self-employment income—that is, profit from his business. If he incorporates the business, however, he is no longer self-employed. If he renders few services and the corporation pays him no salary, he has no earned income. The net income of the corporation, on which he will have to pay income tax, is deemed to be dividend income. But investment income (including dividend income) has no reduction effect on Social Security benefits. Thus, an older person may find that the Small Business Corporation reduces the chance that the Social Security Administration will challenge his right to draw Social Security benefits while still enjoying complete use of the profits of his business.

3. Another use of the Small Business Corporation is to spread income out over a period of years. The classic example is the construction contractor who can obtain two contracts. The potential profit, $120,000 on each, will be realized like this:

| | *No. 1* | *No. 2* |
|---|---|---|
| 1979 | $60,000 | |
| 1980 | 60,000 | $120,000 |
| 1981 | 0 | 0 |

Because of the graduation in individual tax rates, which we shall discuss in a later chapter, he will pay more tax by receiving the profit this way than if he could somehow contrive to have the profit spread out so that some part of it would fall into 1981. The profit on job No. 2, for tax purposes, will be recognized when the job is finished, which will be in March 1980. How to defer it?

In this situation, a Small Business Corporation for contract No. 2, which will liquidate on completion of the contract, can effectively shift any desired portion of that profit to 1981. Any new corporation has the right to elect what its accounting year shall be. We have assumed that our contractor's tax year was the regular calendar year. The Small Business Corporation, however, will elect a fiscal year ending, say, January 31.

The undistributed profit of a Small Business Corporation is deemed to be a dividend distributed to its shareholders as of the last day of the corporation's tax year. The $120,000 is taxable income in the corporation's return for the fiscal year within which March 1980 falls. This would be the fiscal year running from February 1, 1980, through January 31, 1981.

Thus, if no dividends are paid to our contractor during 1980, he will wind up picking up the $120,000 as 1981 income. He would thus have:

| | *No. 1* | *No. 2 (Corporation)* |
|---|---|---|
| 1979 | $60,000 | |
| 1980 | 60,000 | |
| 1981 | | $120,000 |

Or, by paying a cash dividend prior to December 31, 1980, he can throw as much of the $120,000 into 1980 as he wants to. His optimum distribution over the three years may be $60,000, $90,000, $90,000. To achieve this merely requires a $30,000 cash dividend sometime between March 1980 and December 1980.

A somewhat similar strategem was once possible with partnerships, but it has been forestalled by a requirement that a new partnership must adopt the same fiscal year as all its principal partners. Similar "loophole-closing" legislation may ultimately be expected if this aspect of the Small Business Corporation gets too much use.

## WHY AVOID SMALL BUSINESS CORPORATION TREATMENT?

The double taxation of corporate earnings arouses many persons to a level of passionate excitement. It is sometimes disconcerting to a theoretician, sincerely upset by the inequity of double taxation, to be told that most corporations that could eliminate it have not chosen to do so. It is estimated that perhaps 800,000 corporations are eligible to elect Small Business Corporation treatment; and, with minor changes in capital structure, elimination of stock held by trusts, and slight alterations in the sources of receipts, several hundred thousand more could make themselves eligible. Yet only 25 percent of these have done so. Why?

Certainly, the complexity of the Small Business Corporation provisions is a partial answer. Small corporations, all other things being equal, tend to have limited access to tax advice, and many of them simply shy away from anything they do not fully understand. But there are other and better reasons, too.

Some small corporations hope to become big corporations. They can justify accumulating their earnings and so have no worry about paying a penalty surtax for unreasonable accumulations. They do not plan on liquidating in any foreseeable future. If the corporate income before salaries is large enough so that substantial salaries can be paid the stockholders for their services as officers, the first $50,000 of the balance will be taxed to a regular corporation at a 21 percent rate. If Small Business Corporation treatment were elected, the effective tax rate on the same income might be 35 or 40 percent, or even higher, rather than 21 percent.

Other corporations have types of income that make it impossible for them to be Small Business Corporations. Many have substantial rental receipts. These may be offset by heavy amounts of depreciation and interest on mortgages, leaving them with little net rental income. But if the gross receipts are more than 20 percent from rentals, and/or other passive sources, the election cannot be made, or if previously made, cannot stay in effect.

In some corporations, there are stockholder conflicts that make the unanimous consent of the stockholders difficult to obtain, or that make it possible for one stockholder to hold a club over the head of the others if the election is made. By simply transferring some of his stock to a trust (other than a grantor or voting trust or any trust for a period of 60 days in which it receives stock under a will) any stockholder can invalidate the Small Business Corporation election as to the year in which such a transfer takes place and the five subsequent years. Thus, when there is stockholder conflict, the Small Business Corporation election may prove so potentially unstable that it is not worth making.

The conflict between state and federal tax concepts may be a minor cause of some corporations avoiding Small Business Corporation treatment. Most state income tax laws do not recognize the Small Business Corporation on its income. As a regular corporation, the corporation may have obtained a deduction for state income tax purposes for the federal income tax it paid. Now it pays none and gets no deduction. On the other hand, the increased federal income tax being paid by the stockholders may or may not be of state income tax benefit to them.

## CASE EXCERPTS

*James L. Stinnett, Jr., et al.,* 54 TC 20 (1970)
*Joe E. Borg,* 50 TC 257 (1968)
*Edwin D. Davis,* 64 TC 1034 (1975)

### *James L. Stinnett, Jr., et al*
### 54 TC 20 (1970)

> A Small Business Corporation can have only one class of stock outstanding. The Internal Revenue Service took the position that where the stockholders loaned money to the corporation, this would constitute a type of preferred stock if the corporation would not otherwise have been adequately capitalized.

The statute contemplates that the stockholders of a subchapter S corporation would make advances or lend money to the corporation, and for the purpose of reflecting losses deducted by the stockholders in their returns, any resulting debt is treated as a part of the stockholder's "investment." The losses which are charged to that investment can only be attributable to the interest of the stockholder represented by the common stock.

If we look to the effect of section 1376(b)(2), it thus becomes apparent that for purposes of subchapter S, the statute treats debt owing to a stockholder, whether or not regarded as equity for other purposes, as a part of that stockholder's equity interest in the corporation. Debt owing to a non-stockholder is treated differently.

That is not to say that an instrument called a "note" may not by its very terms be something else. However, where the instrument is a simple installment note, without any incidents commonly attributed to stock, it does not give rise to more than one class of stock within the meaning of section 1371 merely because the debt creates disproportionate rights among the stockholders to the assets of the corporation.

We do not have to decide whether the notes involved in this case might nevertheless be treated as "equity" for other purposes. We are not here concerned with the treatment of interest paid on those notes. In fact, no interest was paid. Nor are we concerned with characterizing the transaction to determine whether petitioners might have a bad debt loss in the event of worthlessness. We are not even concerned with the question whether such debt may not be treated differently under other provisions of the tax laws, even in the case of a corporation which has elected to be taxed under subchapter S. For example, there might be situations in which earnings accumulated prior to qualification under subchapter S are sought to be distributed to a stockholder-creditor of the corporation in the "guise" of repayment of debt.

All we are called upon to decide is whether the corporation (International Meadows) had outstanding more than "one class" of stock within the meaning of section 1371 of the Code. In the corporate or formal sense clearly the corporation did not. There can be no question that under the laws of the State of California the corporation had outstanding 100 shares of common stock and nothing more. The only real question is whether in the "tax sense"—in order to carry out the legislative intent—we are required to disregard the form of the incorporation in order to reach a different conclusion.

The statute does not prescribe any rules which we may look to for guidance. The underlying rationale of the "thin capitalization" doctrine seems to be, however, going back to *Gregory* v. *Helvering,* 293 U.S. 465 [14 AFTR 1191], that the court will disregard the form of the transaction where it is to some degree lacking in substance *and* a failure to do so would serve to frustrate the purpose of the taxing statute. As we have pointed out, this is not that type of case. In fact, the only result of a contrary holding on this case would be to defeat an election which the Congress clearly intended to be of benefit to the small and frequently "thinly capitalized" business.

*Joe E. Borg*
50 TC 257 (1968)

Losses of a Small Business Corporation can only be used by shareholders to the extent they have invested in the corporation—either in its common stock or through loans to the corporation. The Tax Court had previously held that a mere guarantee of a corporate debt was not a loan to the corporation for this purpose. Mr. and Mrs. Borg, the chief stockholders of Borg Steel, a Small Business Corporation, are the petitioners in this case.

In 1958, Borg Steel needed additional funds and as a separate entity it sought a loan from the bank. The loan was refused. As a condition to making the loan, the bank insisted that petitioners pledge and mortgage all of their oil and gas interests and other personal assets, assign individual life insurance policies and execute a personal endorsement on the note which in fact, petitioners contend, constituted petitioners comakers of the note and imposed upon them primary liability for payment thereof. Petitioners argue that as "a matter of law and by its express terms this obligation is more than the ordinary 'endorsement'; it is more than a guarantee; it is more than an unconditional and absolute guarantee of payment; it is in fact an agreement 'to be bound by all the provisions hereof and to assume and perform all the obligations therein contained *in like manner as the makers thereof.*' " On this ground petitioners would have us distinguish *William H. Perry, supra.*

Petitioners misconstrue our decision in *Perry*. The basis for our decision was not that the taxpayers' liability was secondary. Rather, it was that, under Missouri law, a guarantor does not have a debt due from the debtor until the guarantor performs on his contract of guaranty. "The statutory language plainly refers to a debt of the corporation which runs to the shareholder. There is nothing in the statutory wording, nor the regulations, nor the committee reports which warrants an inference that a shareholder's contract of guaranty with corporate creditors is tantamount to an 'indebtedness of the corporation to [him],' " *William H. Perry, supra* at 163.

Under the statutes and case law of Oklahoma it is apparent that petitioners were sureties rather than guarantors of the corporate note. The Oklahoma statutes define a surety as one who "at the request of another, and for the purpose of securing to him a benefit, becomes responsible for the performance by the latter of some act in favor of a third person, or hypothecates property as security therefor." Okla. Stat. Ann., tit. 15, sec. 371 (1966). An early Oklahoma case held that where the undertaking endorsed on a note was "For value received, I hereby guaranty the payment of the within note," waiving demand and protest, the endorsement was that of a surety rather than a guarantor. *Walter A. Wood Mow. & Reap. Co.* v. *Farnham*, 1 Okla. 375, 33 Pac. 867 (1893). The distinction between a surety and a guarantor does not aid petitioners, however, for, under Oklahoma law, no cause of action arises until the surety makes at least part payment on his undertaking. See Okla. Stat. Ann., tit. 15, secs. 381-382 (1966); *Miller* v. *National Surety Co.*. 159 Okla. 76, 14 P. 228 (1932); *Jones* v. *Nelson*, 156 Okla. 236, 10 P. 2d 408 (1932).

Borg Steel owed nothing to petitioners by reason of their endorsement, and it would continue to owe nothing to them until and unless they paid part or all of the obligation. "While the sum of money may be payable upon a contingency, yet in such case it becomes a debt only when the contingency has happened, the term 'debt' being opposed to 'liability' when used in the sense of an inchoate or contingent debt." *Gilman* v. *Commissioner*, 53 F. 2d 47, 50 (C.A. 8, 1931). Accord, *United States* v. *Virgin*, 230 F. 2d 880 (C.A. 5, 1956); *Brown-Rogers-Dixson Co.* v. *Commissioner, 122 F. 2d 347 (C.A. 4, 1941). It* follows that the sums borrowed by the corporation from the bank did not give rise to "indebtedness of the corporation to the shareholder" and cannot be used in computing petitioners' allowable portion of the corporate net operating loss.

*Edwin D. Davis*
64 T.C. (No. 100) (1975)

> Taxpayer, an orthopedic surgeon, formed two corporations, each 90 percent owned by his children, to perform X-ray and physical therapy services. The corporations elected to be taxed as small business corporations; the I.R.S. attempted to tax Dr. Davis on all of the income.

Dr. Davis testified that his reasons for forming the corporations were:

(1) To provide security for his children in view of his marital difficulties and his personal health problems;

(2) To insulate him personally from damage suits arising from negligent use of the potentially dangerous X-ray and physical therapy equipment; and

(3) To separate the personnel problems into the X-ray and physical therapy functions and away from the personnel problems of his medical practice. Respondent counters with alternative remedies to the concerns of Dr. Davis. He could have made cash gifts to his children; he could have purchased liability insurance to insulate him from liability arising from the negligent use of the X-ray and physical therapy equipment; and he could have issued mandates to resolve the personnel problems.

We do not agree with respondent that Dr. Davis' purposes were tenuous. The transfer of valuable property rights with a known potential to produce income seems a logical reason to establish the corporations and give the stock to his children instead of giving cash which would have to be invested. Using the corporate form to insulate the taxpayer from liability has long been recognized as a valid reason for incorporating. *Sam Siegel*, 45 T.C. 566 (1966). It is especially applicable here because Dr. Davis had recently experienced the possibility of liability caused by serious burns received by a patient who was receiving heat therapy. We find Dr. Davis explanation of resolving personnel differences by separation of the operations a plausible and satisfactory reason.

Respondent's reliance upon *Kimbrell* v. *Commissioner, supra,* is unavailing. In that case the corporations merely executed contracts, hired employees, negotiated loans, and collected interest thereon, and filed income tax returns. In the instant case the corporations X-rayed patients and administered physical therapy to patients.

Moreover, a taxpayer is not required to continue one form of business organization which results in the maximum tax on business income. *Polak's Frutal Works, Inc.*, 21 T.C. 953, 974-975 (1954).

Respondent contends that the earnings of the corporations should be taxed to Dr. Davis because he had control over the earning of the profits by performing the services. The facts are otherwise. Dr. Davis prescribed the type of X-ray or X-rays to be made for each patient and he prescribed the physical therapy to be administered. The X-ray prescriptions to the corporation were no different than were those to a radiologist he referred patients to before he owned X-ray equipment or those given to the hospital when he would prescribe X-rays for a patient who was admitted to the emergency room. We see little difference in prescribing X-rays or physical therapy and prescribing drugs to be compounded by a pharmacist. Dr. Davis' division of his endeavors is not particularly unusual. It is common knowledge that an orthopedic surgeon does not himself normally take X-rays nor does he administer physical therapy. If, on the other hand, Dr. Davis attempted to separate his diagnostic work from his surgery, this would be unusual because a doctor personally performs both of these services for a patient. The income of the corporations was generated by the services of persons employed by the corporations not by the services performed by Dr. Davis. Dr. Davis' direct services to the corporations were minimal. Under section 61, we conclude that the corporations controlled the capacity to produce the income through their employees and they, not Dr. Davis, are taxable on that income. *Ronan State Bank,* 62 T.C. 27 (1974).

. . .In his notices of deficiency the Commissioner allocated the net taxable income of the corporations to Dr. Davis. In his brief the Commissioner contends that the corporate employees were adequately compensated for the services they performed and that he advocated allocation only of the net taxable income of the corporations to Dr. Davis because the corporations' contributions of earning that portion of the income were minimal. This line of reasoning is fallacious. The corporations were paid fees comparable to those charged by other X-ray laboratories and physical therapists in the community and those fees were received by the corporations for the services performed by their employees, not Dr. Davis. Again, the analogy to the pharmacist is appropriate. The X-ray technician, the physical therapist, and the pharmacist all carry out prescriptions made by the doctor. Respondent's blanket characterization of the tasks of the employees of the corporations which include the X-ray technician and the physical therapist as "routine" is not warranted. Both are specialists trained to carry out a doctor's order just as a pharmacist fills a prescription. As pointed out above in our discussion of section 61, the division of Dr. Davis' practice into medical practice, X-ray, and physical therapy is not unusual in that the different endeavors are frequently engaged in by separate persons or entities. It is also not unusual in the respect that X-ray laboratories and physical therapists rely on referrals for their business. Again, we see a close analogy to the better-known relationship of doctor and pharmacist. The entire arrangement was comparable to others in the community except that Dr. Davis was in the position to forward business to the corporations. For example, before he owned X-ray equipment, he referred his patients to a radiologist which did not give him a referral fee in return. The radiologist performed no service for the patient different from what the X-Ray corporation now performs; i.e., in both instances the X-rays were interpreted and acted upon by Dr. Davis. Based on all the evidence we conclude that petitioners have made an adequate showing that the Commissioner abused the discretion granted to him by section 482 in allocating the net taxable income of the corporations to Dr. Davis . . .

As a final "string to his bow" the Commissioner relies upon section 1375(c) which permits him to allocate from one shareholder in a "Small Business Corporation" (subchapter S corporation) amounts treated as dividends which should be allocated to other shareholders who are members of the shareholders' family to reflect the value of services rendered to the corporation by such shareholders. The purpose of section 1375(c) is to tax each shareholder of a subchapter S corporation on the full value of the income he earns. No deflection of that income is to be permitted through artificial salary or dividend payments. S. Rept. No. 1983, 85th Cong., 2d Sess. (1958), 1958-3 C.B. 1143-1144; *Charles Rocco*, 57 T.C. 826, 831 (1972).

> In determining the value of services rendered by a shareholder, consideration shall be given to all the facts and circumstances of the business, including the managerial responsibilities of the shareholder, and the amount that would ordinarily be paid in order to obtain comparable services from a person not having an interest in the corporation. * * * [Sec. 1.1375-3(a), Income Tax Regs.]

The determination is factual and tests applied to ascertain the value of the shareholder's services include "the nature of the services performed, the responsibilities involved, the time spent, the size and complexity of the business, prevailing economic conditions, compensation paid by comparable firms for comparable services, and salary paid to company officers in prior years." *Walter J. Roob,* 50 T.C. 891, 898,899 (1968).

As in *Charles Rocco, supra* at 832, we need not decide whether section 1375(c) requires petitioner to merely overcome the presumptive correctness of the Commissioner's determination or requires him to prove that the Commissioner abused his discretion (if section 1375(c) provides the Commissioner with the same authority he possesses under section 482) because here we find that petitioners have satisfied both tests.

The Commissioner allocated 100 percent of the net taxable income of the subchapter S corporations to Dr. Davis. The undisputed testimony is that he did not actually spend more than 20 hours per year in direct duties to the corporations, which is minimal.

Respondent would have us consider the referral activities of Dr. Davis as being personal services rendered by him to the corporations. This we will not do.

. . . Accordingly, we find that none of the net taxable income of X-Ray and Therapy was taxable to petitioners Edwin D. Davis and Sandra W. Davis for the taxable years 1966 and 1967.

## QUESTIONS AND PROBLEMS

1. The Plaza Corporation operates an apartment building. Its preferred stock is owned by seven persons, and six other persons own its common stock. Name three reasons why the Plaza Corporation could not elect to be taxed as a Small Business Corporation. Can these problems be overcome?
2. The Gaylord Rubber Corporation has total assets of $50 million and annual sales of $94 million. All its outstanding stock is held by Mr. Sylvester Gaylord and his two sons. Sylvester draws a salary of $100,000 a year from the corporation, and each of his two sons draws $75,000. All three men are married.
   (a) Is there anything in the information given that would preclude the corporation electing to be treated as a Small Business Corporation?
   (b) Is there anything in the information given that would indicate it would be disadvantageous for the shareholders to make such an election?
3. The undistributed income of a Small Business Corporation (showing taxable income) is allocated among shareholders in proportion to ownership of stock as of the last day of the year. Losses, on the other hand, are allocated on the basis of days of stock ownership; for example, if you owned all the corporate stock, but owned it only 1/10 of the year, only 1/10 of the loss for the year would be allocated to you, whereas 9/10 would go to the owner or owners of the stock during the balance of the year. What could be the purpose of introducing such a complication into the law?
4. Describe the two types of retained earnings of a Small Business Corporation in terms of their source and of their effect when distributed to shareholders.
5. When a shareholder in a Small Business Corporation disposes of his stock, the line-25 retained earnings attributable to him is not transferred to the purchaser. What would be the rationale of a provision such as this?

6. Prepare a Form 1120S for the Sadler Corporation. The stock of the corporation is entirely owned by George Sadler. The beginning-of-the-year retained earnings consisted of $30,000 of line-24 retained earnings and $85,000 of line-25 retained earnings. The firm's financial statements are below:

SADLER CORPORATION
Balance Sheet
December 31, 19X1

| | | |
|---|---|---|
| *Assets* | | |
| Cash | | $ 10,000 |
| Accounts receivable | $ 75,000 | |
| Less allowance for doubtful accounts | 5,000 | 70,000 |
| Inventory, 12/31/X1 | | 95,000 |
| Land | | 3,500 |
| Building | 97,000 | |
| Less accumulated depreciation | 20,500 | 76,500 |
| Machinery & equipment | 83,000 | |
| Less accumulated depreciation | 42,000 | 41,000 |
| Other assets | | 4,000 |
| Total Assets | | $300,000 |
| *Liabilities* | | |
| Accounts payable | $ 37,000 | |
| Notes payable–due 12/31/X3 | 50,000 | $ 87,000 |
| *Stockholders' Equity* | | |
| Common stock ($100 par) | 10,000 | |
| Retained earnings | 203,000 | 213,000 |
| Total Liabilities and Stockholders' Equity | | $300,000 |

SADLER CORPORATION
Income Statement
For Year Ended December 31, 19X1

| | | |
|---|---|---|
| Income: | | |
| Sales | $950,000 | |
| Dividends | 4,000 | $954,000 |
| Expenses: | | |
| Cost of goods sold | $585,800 | |
| Salaries (employees) | 90,000 | |
| Salaries (officers) | 55,000 | |
| Advertising | 34,000 | |
| Other deductions | 28,000 | |

| | | |
|---|---|---|
| Contributions | 23,000 | |
| Depreciation | 9,700 | |
| Local taxes | 8,000 | |
| Repairs | 6,000 | |
| Bad debts | 4,000 | |
| Interest | 2,500 | $846,000 |
| Net Income Before Taxes | | $108,000 |

You are given the following additional information: Inventory of 12/31/X0 was $87,000. The retained-earnings figure shown reflects a $20,000 cash dividend paid in July, 19X1 and charged to retained-earnings. The dividend income was received on stock purchased during the year as a temporary investment and sold for the exact amount for which it was purchased. (Compare your answer to this question with the answer you gave for Question 6 in the preceding chapter.)

7. Using the information shown, prepare a Schedule M of Form 1120S for the Coleman Company. This is the first year that the Coleman Company has elected to be a Small Business Corporation.

Analysis of Retained Earnings

| | *Dr.* | *Cr.* |
|---|---|---|
| Balance 1/1/X1 | | $325,000 |
| Net earnings for 19X1 before taxes | | 110,000 |
| Reserve for contingencies restored to retained earnings | | 50,000 |
| Dividends paid | $40,000 | |

A review of the corporate transactions for the year disclosed:

(a) The corporation received interest of $1,000 on City of Portland bonds.

(b) Contributions of $30,000 were deducted.

(c) The corporation paid interest of $800 on funds borrowed to purchase the City of Portland bonds.

(d) An amount of $1,200 was paid on insurance policies covering officers of the corporation. The corporation owns the policies and is the beneficiary. An asset account, "Cash surrender value of corporate life insurance," was debited for $300, representing the 19X1 increase in cash surrender value of the policies, while the remaining $900 was charged to expense. Because the proceeds of such insurance are not normally taxable, no deduction is allowed for premium payments on life insurance where the corporation is a beneficiary.

(e) During the year the corporation wrote off as an expense $5,000, representing a decline in value of certain land it held as an investment. At the beginning of the year, the land was worth $25,000; at the end of the year, only $20,000.

8. Based on the Coleman Corporation Schedule M in Problem 7, calculate the amount of line-24 and line-25 retained earnings at 12/31/X1.
9. Using the information shown below, prepare a Schedule M-1 of Form 1120S for the ABC Corporation and show the amounts of 12/32/X1 retained earnings on lines 24 and 25 of the ending balance sheet. This is the first year of the Small Business Corporation election.

Retained Earnings Account

| | *Dr.* | *Cr.* |
|---|---|---|
| Balance 1/1/X1 | | $300,000 |
| Net profit, per books | | 152,000 |
| Cash dividends paid | ? | |
| Refund of 19X0 income tax | | 13,000 |
| Balance 12/31/X1 | $390,000 | |
| | $465,000 | $465,000 |

ABC Corporation
Income Statement
For Year Ended December 31, 19X1

| | | | |
|---|---|---|---|
| Income: | | | |
| Sales | $1,940,000 | | |
| Less sales returns and allowances | 40,000 | $1,900,000 | |
| Miscellaneous income | | 26,000 | $1,926,000 |
| Expenses: | | | |
| Cost of goods sold | | 1,550,000 | |
| Depreciation | | 53,100 | |
| Officers' salaries | | 35,000 | |
| Other salaries | | 32,000 | |
| Local taxes | | 9,000 | |
| Contributions | | 5,500 | |
| Insurance premiums | | 3,000 | |
| Repairs | | 1,000 | |
| Interest expense | | 400 | 1,689,000 |
| Net Income Before Taxes | | | $ 237,000 |

The Miscellaneous Income Account is made up of interest ($10,000) received from local banks and the tax refund, interest ($1,000) from the State of Ohio bonds, and the proceeds ($15,000) from a life insurance policy received on the death of a corporate officer. The Charitable Contributions Account includes a $500 state political contribution which is nondeductible for tax purposes. The interest expense was the cost of borrowing the money necessary to purchase the Ohio State bonds. The Insurance Premium Account reflects the cost of insurance policies on corporate officers with the corporation as beneficiary. The shareholders estimated their federal income tax for the year at $85,000 and used corporate checks to send their payments in quarterly. The accountant deducted their total payments from the $237,000 net income before taxes of the firm and transferred the $152,000 balance to the Retained Earnings Account.

10. The *Stinnett* case (see excerpt) discusses the "thin capitalization" doctrine. Explain why a regular corporation may want to treat as debt rather than stock an amount of investment in it. Does this explanation apply to a Small Business Corporation? Explain.
11. What might the stockholder have done differently in the *Borg* case in order to obtain a deduction for the corporate losses? Describe your suggestion step by step, and explain how the economic effect of your proposed restructuring of the transaction would be the same, or substantially the same, as the actual transaction. Also explain why the tax result would be different.
12. "I understand federal tax law," says one tax person, "so that it really does not matter whether I know anything about state law." But his colleague at the next desk disagrees. "Federal tax questions involve state law," he says, "and if you don't know state law, you should confer on many points with a lawyer who does." Using the *Borg* case as a point of reference, explain which statement you think should prevail.
13. Using the *Davis* case (see excerpt) as a point of reference, discuss the importance of business purpose, economic substance, and ability to produce credible evidence in successfully taking advantage of tax law provisions. If Dr. Davis was in a 50 percent tax bracket, while the children were in 20 percent tax brackets, how much tax per year could he save by his tax plan if the two corporations together earned $80,000?

# 5

# Partnerships

## A ROSE BY ANY OTHER NAME . . .

A real estate broker, trying to sell a large office building, had a brilliant idea. Instead of trying to find a purchaser able and willing to swing a $2 million proposition, he would divide the building up into units and try to sell 2,000 thousand-dollar units! The building had an appraised value of $6 million, and there was a $3 million mortgage against it. The deal looked quite attractive.

How to set up the deal? A corporation was considered, since individual investors would be reluctant to personally assume liability on the $3 million mortgage. But a regular corporation might run into a snag. Investors in a building would want to receive a cash return on their investment. This would necessitate dividends, and thus the double taxation of corporations would cut the effective cash return to the investors.

A Small Business Corporation was out of the question. All the receipts of the building were rentals; and as we have seen, if more than 20 percent of the receipts are from such passive sources as rents and dividends, then the Small Business Corporation election can't be made.

How about a partnership? No tax is imposed on the partnership, but instead each partner picks up his share of the partnership income on his individual tax return. One of the disadvantages of the partnership, however, is the unlimited liability of the partners for partnership debts. This liability feature, the realtor's lawyer informed the broker, could be avoided by forming a limited partnership. The limited partners would not be active in the partnership business and could lose no more than the amount of their investment in the partnership. Of course, added the lawyer, there would have to be a general partner who would be liable for the debts of the partnership. But the general partner could be a corporation.

So the broker duly formed a dummy corporation (one with no assets) to become a general partner and proceeded to sell limited partnership interests in the office building. We shall pass over the problems he encountered with the state securities commission. Ultimately, the whole deal was consummated, the broker had his commission, and everyone was happy.

The limited partnership made regular cash distributions to the limited partners, and a partnership tax return was duly filed. All ran smoothly until the day the Internal Revenue Service stepped into the picture. This limited partnership, they said, was not a partnership at all for federal income tax purposes.

Vainly the broker pointed to the state law defining what a partnership was and to the fact that the limited partnership had complied with all its provisions. Federal taxation deals with substance and not with form, he was told. Any organization that has more corporate than noncorporate characteristics is a corporation, no matter what state law calls it. A corporation typically differs from a partnership in having these characteristics:

1. *Continuity of life.* The death of a stockholder has no effect on the legal existence of the corporation, nor, under state law, would the death of a limited partner affect the legal existence of the limited partnership. Because the general partner was a corporation, it could not die.
2. *Centralization of management.* The general partner, the corporation, actually managed the partnership business. In fact, to retain their limited-partnership status under the state law, the limited partners had to refrain from participating in the day-to-day operations of the building. The partnership agreement stripped them of all management rights.
3. *Liability for debts limited to the property in the business.* The limited partners, under state law, were not personally liable for partnership debts. Although the corporate general partner was liable, its liability was meaningless since it had no substantial assets.
4. *Free transferability of ownership interests.* The limited-partnership interests, under state law, were freely transferable. The general partner's interest was not literally transferable without terminating the partnership; but because it was a corporation, its stock was freely transferable. Thus, in essence, all the ownership interest in the partnership was freely transferable.

The distributions to the partners were deemed to be nondeductible dividends to shareholders, and a tax deficiency was collected from the partnership. The tax was computed on the basis that the partnership was a regular corporation. If losses had been sustained rather than gains earned, adverse tax consequences would also have followed from a determination that the organization was a corporation. As a partnership, the losses would have been deducted on the returns of the individual partners. When the partnership status was thrown out, deficiencies in tax would result against the individual partners through disallowing these loss deductions.

If the corporate general partner had had substantial assets in addition to its partnership interest, then the status of the limited partnership for tax purposes would likely have been that of a partnership.

## WHAT IS A PARTNERSHIP?

The name given an organization obviously does not entirely control its treatment for federal income tax purposes. Thus, the I.R.S. will treat as a corporation both a corporation created as such under state laws and also any other organization more similar to a corporation than to a partnership or trust. (In Chapter 7 we shall talk about trusts.)

Partnerships, in turn, are broadly defined to include syndicates, groups, pools, joint ventures, and other organizations not classifiable as corporations, in addition to organizations that would be labeled partnerships under state law.

Characteristics of the typical general partnership under state law would include the ability of each partner to act as an agent of the partnership (for example, to enter into contracts); the unlimited personal liability of each partner for partnership debts; the fact that the death, insanity, bankruptcy, or withdrawal of any partner acts to terminate the partnership; and the fact that the partners share profits (and/or losses) equally or in some agreed-upon manner. These are characteristics that are already relatively familiar to you. Less familiar may be such terms as *syndicates, pools,* and *joint ventures.*

*Syndicate* usually refers to an undertaking for a specific purpose that requires a relatively large aggregate of capital. Thus, to distribute corporate securities, an underwriting syndicate is often formed. Such a syndicate is a group of security houses, each of which agrees to take a stipulated portion of the security issue involved. Management of the syndicate is usually lodged in the hands of one or a few members of the group. Once the underwriting terminates, that particular syndicate is concluded. Syndicates are also found in the real estate business and in oil, gas, and other mineral undertakings requiring large amounts of capital.

*Pools,* on the other hand, tend to be associated with specific trading activities. Thus, several persons or organizations might "pool" their funds to trade actively in a certain stock, with the hope of driving the price upward and then liquidating their position at a profit. The term "pools" is also sometimes applied to simple poolings of funds for general investment purposes, without any specific trading objective.

Because of their nature, which tends to require centralization of management and often allows free transferability of interests, both syndicates and pools are frequently treated as corporations for federal tax purposes. When not so treated, however, they are partnerships.

*Joint ventures* also may be classified as partnerships or corporations. A joint venture simply requires the joining together of parties (who may be individuals, partnerships, or corporations) in a venture for their common benefit, with each contributing something (either property or services) and each having an interest in the profits. The term is most commonly employed in construction undertakings, but the joint venture can be used in almost any field of activity, including the operation of a business, the production of a play, the development of mineral properties, or strictly investment activities. The major distinction between the syndicate and the joint venture lies in the number of participants—the syndicate having a relatively large number and the joint venture normally a few.

For our purposes, it is of major importance to note that these are all treated as partnerships for tax purposes when their characteristics are more similar to the typical partnership than to the typical corporation.

## THE AGGREGATE CONCEPT OF THE PARTNERSHIP

The characteristics of a partnership (mutual agency, unlimited personal liability, termination upon any change in membership, and profit sharing) flow from a basic view of the nature of a partnership. The partnership is not a separate entity, in this view. It is simply an aggregation of the activities of the individual partners.

An individual engaged in a business would obviously be an agent of the business, capable of signing contracts without the approval of anyone else. Since his business would not be a legal entity separate and apart from the rest of himself, any business creditor would be able to proceed against nonbusiness assets if necessary to satisfy his claim. Death of the owner would terminate his legal existence and hence that of the business, even though the business might be carried on by another person (such as the decedent's son). And, of course, all profits would belong to the owner and all losses would be borne by him.

The aggregate approach to the partnership views it as essentially a multiple proprietorship. In accounting for a partnership, the owner's equity section of the partnership balance sheet illustrates the treatment, as you may recall from your accounting course and as you will see shortly when we prepare a partnership tax return.

## THE CONDUIT NATURE OF THE PARTNERSHIP RETURN

Viewing the partnership as simply a multiple proprietorship means, among other things, that we would not expect the partnership to pay an income tax. Nor does it. It is somewhat similar to the Small Business Corporation in this regard. The major difference is that certain types of income and expense are segregated into amounts allocable to each partner. On the Small Business Corporation return, tax-free income could not be passed tax free to the shareholders. Note that it will pass through tax free in the partnership. Our return will be based on the same facts as the Small Business Corporation return in Chapter 4, except that ownership of the business is now split evenly between John Doe and Richard Roe.

Take a look at Figures 4-1, page 80, and 4-4, page 83. This was how our Small Business Corporation return looked. The same data, except that we now have two partners instead of one stockholder, would appear on the partnership return as shown in Figures 5-1 and 5-2.

A separate schedule would be attached to the return, listing the $6,000 in contributions and showing that $3,000 each was attributable to Doe and Roe.

As we compare the two returns, the first thing that strikes us is the difference in the net income (called *taxable income* on the SBC return and *ordinary income* on the partnership return). The SBC has $77,900 of net income, whereas the partnership only shows $62,000. Why the difference?

| | |
|---|---|
| SBC net income | $77,900 |
| Add contribution deduction | 4,100 |
| | $82,000 |
| Deduct dividends received | 20,000 |
| Partnership net income | $62,000 |

The SBC is not a true conduit of income and deductions in the way that the aggregate theory requires that the partnership be. The contributions made by the SBC are deemed to be its own and are deducted (subject to the 5 percent limitation) in arriving at its net income. The contributions made by the partnership are deemed to be made by the partners. Thus, the $6,000 of contributions has the same effect on the partnership return as if Doe and Roe had withdrawn $6,000 and then had made their contributions personally. To facilitate their claiming a contribution deduction on their personal returns, however, an itemization of the partnership contributions is attached to the partnership return.

So too with the dividends received by the business. The dividend income of the SBC is deemed its own and is reported as such. No special dividends-received deduction is allowed the SBC as it is to regular corporations, because the SBC pays no tax on dividend income, and therefore there is no double taxation to be alleviated. (Dividends received by an individual, as we shall discover in a later chapter, are also given some slight relief from double taxation.) Under the aggregate theory, therefore, the dividends received by the partnership are deemed to be received by the partners and are so treated on the partnership return. They are shown on the return in line 3 of the distribution schedule, Schedule K, so that they may be properly reported on the individual returns of the partners.

We may, in fact, generalize on this point. Any item of income that is tax free, or that is specially taxed, will not be reflected in the computation of ordinary income on the partnership return. Any deduction that is limited in some manner, such as the contribution deduction, will similarly not be reflected in computing ordinary income. But all of these items will, in some manner,

Form **1065**
Department of the Treasury
Internal Revenue Service

**U.S. Partnership Return of Income**
FOR CALENDAR YEAR 19 or other taxable year beginning ........., 19 , and ending ........., 19....

| | | |
|---|---|---|
| A Principal business activity (See page 8 of instructions) Retailer | Name THE SIMPLE COMPANY | D Employer identification no. 306-3601434 |
| B Principal product or service (See page 8 of instructions) Dry Goods | Number and street 77 Sunset Boulevard | E Business code no. (See page 8 of instructions) 608 |
| C Enter total assets from line 13, column (D), Schedule L $ 511,000 | City or town, State, and ZIP code Valhalla, Arizona | F Date business commenced 1/1/54 |

IMPORTANT—Fill in all applicable lines and schedules. If the lines on the schedules are not sufficient, see Instruction Q. Enter any items specially allocated to the partners on Schedule K, line 15, instead of the numbered lines on this page or in Schedules D through J. (See General Instruction P.)

Check here ▶ ☐ if this is a final return.
☐ if this is a limited partnership. (See General Instruction S(3).)

| | | | | |
|---|---|---|---|---|
| INCOME | 1a Gross receipts or sales $ 534,000 1b Less returns and allowances $ 8,000 Balance ▶ | 1c | 526,000 | 00 |
| | 2 Less: Cost of goods sold and/or operations (line 34, Schedule A) | 2 | 359,000 | 00 |
| | 3 Gross profit | 3 | 167,000 | 00 |
| | 4 Ordinary income (loss) from other partnerships, syndicates, etc. (attach statement) | 4 | | |
| | 5 Nonqualifying dividends (attach list—see Instruction 5) | 5 | | |
| | 6 Interest | 6 | | |
| | 7 Rents (Schedule H) | 7 | | |
| | 8 Royalties (attach schedule) | 8 | | |
| | 9 Net farm profit (loss) (attach Schedule F (Form 1040)) | 9 | | |
| | 10 Net ordinary gain (loss) (Form 4797, line 9) | 10 | | |
| | 11 Other income (attach schedule) | 11 | | |
| | 12 TOTAL income (add lines 3 through 11) | 12 | 167,000 | 00 |
| DEDUCTIONS | 13 Salaries and wages (other than to partners) | 13 | 42,000 | 00 |
| | 14 Payments to partners—Salaries and interest | 14 | 20,000 | 00 |
| | 15 Rent | 15 | 8,000 | 00 |
| | 16 Interest (attach schedule) | 16 | | |
| | 17 Taxes (attach schedule) | 17 | 3,000 | 00 |
| | 18 Bad debts (Schedule I if you use reserve method) | 18 | 3,000 | 00 |
| | 19 Repairs | 19 | 1,000 | 00 |
| | 20 Depreciation (Schedule J) | 20 | 5,000 | 00 |
| | 21 Amortization (attach schedule) | 21 | | |
| | 22 Depletion (attach schedule—see Instruction 22) | 22 | | |
| | 23a Retirement plans, etc. (other than amounts for partners—see Instruction 23a). (Enter number of plans ▶.........) | 23a | | |
| | 23b Employee benefit programs (see Instruction 23b) | 23b | | |
| | 24 Other deductions (attach schedule) | 24 | 23,000 | 00 |
| | 25 TOTAL deductions (add lines 13 through 24) | 25 | 105,000 | 00 |
| | 26 Ordinary income (loss) (line 12 less line 25) (see General Instruction G) | 26 | 62,000 | 00 |

| Partnership's distributive share items | Total |
|---|---|
| 1 Salary, interest, and ordinary income (loss) (combine lines 14 and 26, page 1) | 82,000 |
| 2 Additional first-year depreciation (Schedule J, line 1) | |
| 3 Dividends qualifying for exclusion (attach list) | 20,000 |
| 4 Net short-term capital gain (loss) (Schedule D, line 3) | |
| 5 Net long-term capital gain (loss) (Schedule D, line 7) | |
| 6 Net section 1231 gain (loss) from involuntary conversions due to casualty and theft (Form 4797, line 2) | |
| 7 Net gain (loss) from sale or exchange of property used in trade or business and certain involuntary conversions under section 1231 (Form 4797, line 4) | |
| 8 Net earnings (loss) from self-employment (Schedule N, line 10) | 82,000 |
| 9 Contributions (attach list) | 6,000 |
| 10 Expense account allowance | 4,127 |
| 11 Foreign taxes (attach schedule) | |
| 12 Taxes paid by regulated investment companies on undistributed capital gains (attach schedule) | |

FIGURE 5-1
Partnership Return

appear on the partnership return. The function of the partnership return is, therefore, to act as a conduit. The transactions of the partnership are summarized on it and passed through, with their essential tax character unaltered, to be reported on the individual returns of the partners.

Form 1065 Page 4

**Schedule L—BALANCE SHEETS (See General Instruction K)**

| ASSETS | Beginning of taxable year (A) Amount | (B) Total | End of taxable year (C) Amount | (D) Total |
|---|---|---|---|---|
| 1 Cash | | 51,800 | | 60,000 |
| 2 Trade notes and accounts receivable | 43,000 | | 52,000 | |
| (a) Less allowance for bad debts | 7,500 | 35,500 | 9,000 | 43,000 |
| 3 Inventories | | 24,000 | | 31,000 |
| 4 Gov't obligations: (a) U.S. and instrumentalities | | | | |
| (b) State, subdivisions thereof, etc. | | | | |
| 5 Other current assets (attach schedule) | | | | |
| 6 Mortgage and real estate loans | | | | |
| 7 Other investments (attach schedule) | | 270,000 | | 350,000 |
| 8 Buildings and other fixed depreciable assets | 63,000 | | 63,000 | |
| (a) Less accumulated depreciation | 31,000 | 32,000 | 36,000 | 27,000 |
| 9 Depletable assets | | | | |
| (a) Less accumulated depletion | | | | |
| 10 Land (net of any amortization) | | | | |
| 11 Intangible assets (amortizable only) | | | | |
| (a) Less accumulated amortization | | | | |
| 12 Other assets (attach schedule) | | | | |
| 13 Total assets | | 413,300 | | 511,000 |
| **LIABILITIES AND CAPITAL** | | | | |
| 14 Accounts payable | | 22,000 | | 34,000 |
| 15 Mortgages, notes, and bonds payable in less than 1 year | | | | |
| 16 Other current liabilities (attach schedule) | | 4,000 | | 5,000 |
| 17 Mortgages, notes, and bonds payable in 1 year or more | | | | |
| 18 Other liabilities (attach schedule) | | | | |
| 19 Partners' capital accounts | | 387,300 | | 472,000 |
| 20 Total liabilities and capital | | 413,300 | | 511,000 |

**Schedule M—RECONCILIATION OF PARTNERS' CAPITAL ACCOUNTS (See Instruction for Schedule M)**
(Show reconciliation of each partner's capital account on Schedule K–1)

| Number of partners | a. Capital account at beginning of year | b. Capital contributed during year | c. Ordinary income (loss) from line 26, page 1 | d. Income not included in column c, plus non-taxable income | e. Losses not included in column c, plus unallowable deductions | f. Withdrawals and distributions | g. Capital account at end of year |
|---|---|---|---|---|---|---|---|
| 2 | 387,300 | | 62,000 | 41,000 | 6,000 | 12,300 | 472,000 |

**Schedule N—COMPUTATION OF NET EARNINGS FROM SELF-EMPLOYMENT (See Instruction for Schedule N)**

| | | |
|---|---|---|
| 1 Ordinary income (loss) (page 1, line 26) | | 62,000 |
| 2 Add: Payments to partners—salaries and interest (page 1, line 14) | 20,000 | |
| 3 Net rental loss from real estate (see instruction for Schedule N) | | |
| 4 Net ordinary loss (page 1, line 10) | | 20,000 |
| 5 Total | | 82,000 |
| 6 Less: Nonqualifying dividends (page 1, line 5) | | |
| 7 Interest (see instruction for Schedule N) | | |
| 8 Net rental income from real estate (see instruction for Schedule N) | | |
| 9 Net ordinary gain (page 1, line 10) | | |
| 10 Net earnings (loss) from self-employment. Enter on Schedule K, line 8 | | 82,000 |

FIGURE 5-2
Partnership Return (continued)

## THE RECONCILIATION SCHEDULE (SCHEDULE M, FIGURE 5-2)

Just as the distribution schedule on the partnership return is merely a facilitating device for passing items through to the partners, the reconciliation schedule functions to provide a net-worth type of reconciliation between the transactions reported on the return and their balance sheet effect. In the regular corporation, the reconciliation focuses on retained earnings, and in the SBC on the relationship between book income and taxable income.

But the owners' equity accounts in a partnership do not normally separate the original capital from the accretions through operations, so there is nothing comparable to retained earnings to reconcile. Partners can and do contribute additional capital to the firm and draw capital out, with no tax consequences attaching to these transactions. The significant factor in the partnership is the capital account balances of the partners.

Thus, in column d of Schedule M we find reflected the $20,000 of dividend income plus the $21,000 of tax-free interest. Column c shows the ordinary income of the partnership. Column e shows the charitable contributions. Column f shows the cash withdrawn during the year in excess of salaries drawn. By investigating the items shown in these columns, plus the balance-sheet accounts and selected income and expense accounts, a relatively thorough audit of a partnership return may be made in much the same manner as was done with the corporation in Chapter 3.

## PARTNERS' SALARIES AND INTEREST PAYMENTS

One of the more confusing aspects of the partnership return is the treatment of partners' salaries. They are recorded as a deduction. This may seem strange, because in accounting we normally treat such items as distributions of income rather than deductions in arriving at income, and so you may reason that there is some deep-seated tax peculiarity behind it. Could a partnership even reduce its partners' taxable income on their personal returns by paying them larger salaries?

Not so. What is taken away with one hand is given back with the other. The computation of self-employment income (Schedule N) is illustrative of the treatment of the salary item. It is added to the ordinary income in arriving at the amount of net income derived from the partnership. In fact, although labeled a salary, it is not treated as a salary for most tax purposes.

## SELF-EMPLOYMENT INCOME

As you may recall, the net income of the Small Business Corporation was treated as a dividend to the stockholders. Of course, salaries paid to those stockholders employed by the corporation were subject to Social Security taxes like any other salaries.

But salaries to partners are not subject to payroll taxes. Does this mean that partners pay no Social Security tax and get no Social Security benefits when they become old or disabled? Prior to 1951, it meant exactly that. Now, however, partnerships calculate the amount of the partnership's business income attributable to each partner. On his individual income tax return (see next chapter), each partner reports his share of the partnership business income and pays a Social Security tax.

The preceding paragraph referred to the "business income" of the partnership. Partnerships have many types of income, some of which are essentially passive investment types. These types of income are not subject to Social Security tax. Schedule N of the partnership return (at the bottom of Figure 5-2) shows how investment types of income are removed from business income, while salaries and interest paid partners are added back, to arrive at "net earnings from self-employment."

Rental income may or may not be passive investment income for this purpose. Operation of a motel produces rental income, but it is not passive and is subject to Social Security tax. Operation of an apartment house normally produces passive rental income that is not subject to self-employment tax. In general, the same types of rental income that—if they were more than 20 percent of gross receipts—would lead to loss of Small Business Corporation status will be excluded from partnership income in arriving at net earnings from self-employment.

## THE ENTITY CONCEPT OF THE PARTNERSHIP

Although the aggregate concept of the partnership dominates its income tax status, traces of the entity approach are still visible. These relate mainly to elections made in connection with the tax return, to transactions between the partners and the partnership, and to changes in the composition of the partnership.

Thus, the decision as to accounting methods must be made by the partnership, and not by the partners individually. You can visualize the impossible accounting situation that might result if each of the five partners in a partnership made his own choice of accounting methods (cash versus accrual, reserve method for bad debts versus specific write-off, and others that we shall discuss in a later chapter).

A partner may sell an asset to the partnership and have a gain or loss on the transaction. In spite of changes in the composition of the partnership, the partnership will not be deemed to have terminated for federal tax purposes unless there is a change within a 12-month period of 50 percent or more of the partnership interest.

## RELATIVE IMPORTANCE OF PARTNERSHIPS

There are over one million partnerships filing tax returns in the United States, as compared with almost two million corporate returns filed (regular plus SBC). These are impressive figures, even though partnerships involve much less economic activity than do corporations. Although the typical partnership is small, some partnerships have hundreds of partners, and gross revenues and net incomes that would compare favorably with those of the largest corporations.

Until relatively recently, member firms of the New York Stock Exchange could not be corporations, and most personal-service professions (law, medicine, public accounting, and so forth) could not be practiced in corporate form. In recent years, undoubtedly owing largely to the tax differential between corporations (with a maximum tax rate in 1977 of 48 percent) and partners (with individual rates running as high as 70 percent in 1977), the New York Stock Exchange has changed its rules, and most of the professions have reversed their historical positions on incorporation. In a majority of the states today, the professions can be practiced in corporate or quasi-corporate form. Because of the substantial tax savings involved in corporate practice of the professions, the Treasury Department was slow to recognize professional corporations as bona fide corporations, but finally gave in after numerous court defeats.

The advent of the Small Business Corporation in 1958 reduced the incentive toward partnership status of businesses that were under no legal or ethical restrictions governing use of the corporate form but that had simply avoided it because of its tax disadvantages. With many of these disadvantages eliminated by electing to be an SBC, many former partnerships proceeded to incorporate.

Even so, because of the relative ease of forming a partnership and operating as one, it can be anticipated that the partnership will continue to be a numerically important form of business organization for multiownership businesses for the indefinite future.

## CASE EXCERPTS

*Stanley C. Orrisch,* 55 TC 395 (1970) aff'd. (CA9-1973)
*D. G. Haley, et al.* v. *Commissioner* (CA5–1953) 43 AFTR 853

### *Stanley C. Orrisch*
55 TC 395 (1970) Partnership Special Allocation

> Under their 1963 partnership agreement, partners A and B were to share equally the gains and losses from the operation of two apartment houses as well as the proceeds of the sale thereof. In a 1969 amendment to the partnership agreement, the partners allocated to A all the deductions for depreciation allowable on the houses on the understanding that, in the event of a sale thereof, A would pay the tax on the gain attributable to the specially allocated depreciation.

Among the important innovations of the 1954 Code are limited provisions for flexibility in arrangements for the sharing of income, losses, and deductions arising from business activities conducted through partnerships. The authority for special allocations of such items appears in section 704(a), which provided that a partner's share of any item of income, gain, loss, deduction, or credit shall be determined by the partnership agreement. That rule is coupled with a limitation in section 704(b), however, which states that a special allocation of an item will be disregarded if its "principal purpose" is the avoidance or evasion of federal income tax. See *Smith* v. *Commissioner,* 311 F. 2d 298 (CA 7, 1964), affirming a Memorandum Opinion of this Court; *Jean V. Kresser,* 54 TC 1621 (1970). In case a special allocation is disregarded, the partner's share of the item is to be determined in accordance with the ratio by which the partners divide the general profits or losses of the partnership. Sec. 1.704-1(b)(2), Income Tax Regs.

In resolving the question whether the principal purpose of a provision in a partnership agreement is the avoidance or evasion of federal income tax, all the facts and circumstances in relation to the provision must be taken into account. Section 1.704-1(b)(2), Income Tax Regs., lists the following as relevant circumstances to be considered:

> Whether the partnership or a partner individually has a business purpose for the allocation; whether the allocation has "substantial economic effect,"* that is, whether the allocation may actually affect the dollar amount of the partners' shares of the total partnership income or loss independently of tax consequences; whether related items of income, gain, loss, deduction, or credit from the same source are subject to the same allocation; whether the allocation was made without recognition of normal business factors and only after the amount of the specially allocated item could reasonably be estimated; the duration of the allocation; and the overall tax consequences of the allocation. . . .

According to the regulations, an allocation has economic effect if it "may actually affect the dollar amount of the partners' shares of the total partnership income or loss independently of tax consequences." The agreement in this case provided not only for the allocation of depreciation to petitioners but also for gain on the sale of the partnership property to be "charged back" to them. The charge back would cause the gain, for tax purposes, to be allocated on the books entirely to petitioners to the extent of the special allocation of depreciation, and their capital account would be correspondingly increased. The remainder of the gain, if any, would be shared equally by the partners. If the gain on the sale were to equal or exceed the depreciation specially allocated to petitioners, the increase in their capital account caused by the charge back would exactly equal the depreciation deductions previously allowed to them, and the proceeds of the

*ED. NOTE: This term has been codified in IRC Sec. 704(b)(2). The regulations, when issued, will further clarify this concept.

sale of the property would be divided equally. In such circumstances, the only effect of the allocation would be a trade of tax consequences, i.e., the Crisafis would relinquish a current depreciation deduction in exchange for exoneration from all or part of the capital gains tax when the property is sold, and petitioners would enjoy a larger current depreciation deduction but would assume a larger ultimate capital gains tax liability. Quite clearly, if the property is sold at a gain, the special allocation will affect only the tax liabilities of the partners and will have no other economic effect.

Who is to bear the economic burden of the depreciation if the buildings should be sold for a sum less than their original cost? There is not one syllable of evidence bearing directly on this crucial point. We have noted, however, that when the buildings are fully depreciated, petitioners' capital account will have a deficit, or there will be a disparity in the capital accounts, approximately equal to the undepreciated bases of the buildings as of the beginning of 1966. Under normal accounting procedures, if the building were sold at a gain less than the amount of such disparity petitioners would either be required to contribute to the partnership a sum equal to the remaining deficit in their capital account after the gain on the sale had been added back or would be entitled to receive a proportionately smaller share of the partnership assets on liquidation. Based on the record as a whole, we do not think the partners ever agreed to such an arrangement. On dissolution, we think the partners contemplated an equal division of the partnership assets which would be adjusted only for disparities in cash contributions or withdrawals. Certainly there is no evidence to show otherwise. That being true, the special allocation does not "actually affect the dollar amount of the partners' shares of the total partnership income or loss independently of tax consequences" within the meaning of the regulation referred to above.

In the light of all the evidence we have found as an ultimate fact that the "principal purpose" of the special allocation agreement was tax avoidance within the meaning of section 704(b). Accordingly, the deduction for depreciation for 1966 and 1967 must be allocated between the parties in the same manner as other deductions.

*D. G. Haley, et al.* v. *Commissioner*
(CA5-1953) 43 AFTR 853
Partnership Agreement and Characterization of Organization

> Haley signed a lease with a corporation (River) whereunder Haley would grow gladioli spikes on River's land. River was to get 75 percent of any net income from the gladioli operation. The agreement specifically recited that it did not create a partnership or joint venture. Losses resulted rather than profits, and Haley gave River his personal note for his 25 percent of those losses. The Bureau of Internal Revenue (predecessor name of the I.R.S.) refused Haley any deduction for the losses. Its action was

upheld by the Tax Court. Haley then appealed successfully to the U.S. Court of Appeals for the Fifth Circuit.

The Tax Court, although conceding that "both River and the petitioner were involved in the operation of the business, regardless of what the operation is called," nevertheless refused to allow petitioner to deduct the alleged losses, mainly on the theory that under the agreements River Corporation sustained all of the losses and petitioner, being on the cash basis, had not suffered any deductible loss during the tax years involved, since he admittedly had never discharged his liability under the promissory notes.

It appears settled that neither local law nor the expressed intent of the parties as to the legal nature and effect of their written agreements are conclusive as to the existence or non-existence of a partnership or joint venture for federal tax purposes . . . Substance rather than form controls in applying the federal tax statutes, and "the realities of the taxpayer's economic interest rather than the niceties of the conveyancer's art should determine the power to tax." . . . Applying that principle here, even though it was expressly stated that the parties did not intend to enter into a joint venture or partnership, if the agreements and the conduct of the parties thereunder plainly show the existence of such relationship, and the intent to enter into it, it will nevertheless be held to exist for tax purposes. . . .

A joint venture has been defined as a "special combination of two or more persons, where in some specific venture a profit is jointly sought without any actual partnership or corporate designation," *Tompkins* v. *Commissioner,* 4 Cir., 97 F.2d 396, 398; *Aiken Mills* v. *United States,* 4 Cir., 144 F.2d 23; See also Mertens' *Law of Federal Income Taxation*, Vol. 6, Sec. 35.05, p. 118 . . .

The provisions of the Internal Revenue Code make it clear that for tax purposes a partnership, although a tax-computing unit, as a unit pays no tax, and individuals carrying on business in partnership are liable for income tax only in their individual capacities . . . . Consequently any gain or loss resulting from the operation of a partnership is that of the tax-computing entity, i.e., the partnership and is not directly attributable to the individual partners . . . . Even though an individual taxpayer is on a cash basis of accounting, if he is a member of a partnership on the accrual basis, consistency requires that he reflect in his individual return his distributive share of the net profits or losses of the partnership as shown on its return . . . . By the same token we think a taxpayer on the cash basis, such as petitioner here, is required to take deductions for losses resulting from his interest in a partnership or joint venture in the year they are legally sustained, even though liability for such losses is discharged with borrowed funds . . . .

Any other rule might well promote inconsistency in the annual reporting of profits and losses under the tax structure and enable taxpayers to manipulate their financial affairs so as to determine the most profitable year in which to claim losses, in violation of the Supreme Court's admonition that the liability of every taxpayer must be determined on the basis of the economic result to him of each year's experience, and that, "Only by such a system is it practicable to produce a regular flow of income and apply methods of accounting, assessment, and collection capable of practical operation." . . . Viewing the agreements here involved and the conduct of the parties in the light of the broad statutory definition of a partnership . . . and the avowed purpose of its adoption . . . we conclude that a partnership for tax purposes here existed and that petitioner is entitled to deduct his one-half distributive share of the losses sustained during 1944 and 1945.

## QUESTIONS AND PROBLEMS

1. What important characteristics of a corporation should an organization be without if it wants to be sure to be treated as a partnership for tax purposes?
2. What are the points of similarity and of difference between the tax return of the Small Business Corporation and that of the partnership?
3. The partnership return excludes a number of items of income and deductions in arriving at "ordinary income." What is the common characteristic all these items possess?
4. Contrast the structure and function of Schedule M of the partnership return with Schedule M of the ordinary corporate return and Schedule M of the Small Business Corporation return.
5. Describe the *aggregate* theory of the partnership and compare it with the *entity* theory of the corporation.
6. John Sadler and Horace Bach are the two equal partners in the Sadler Company (a partnership). At the beginning of the year, their capital accounts had balances of $62,500 each, and each withdrew, in addition to his salary of $27,500, the amount of $10,000. The financial statements of the concern are provided below. You are to prepare a partnership tax return on Form 1065, excluding supporting schedules, but not excluding Schedules K,L, and M.

SADLER COMPANY
Balance Sheet
December 31, 19X1

| | | |
|---|---|---|
| *Assets* | | |
| Cash | | $ 10,000 |
| Accounts receivable | $75,000 | |
| Less allowance for doubtful accounts | 5,000 | 70,000 |

| | | |
|---|---|---|
| Inventory, 12/31/X1 | | 95,000 |
| Land | | 3,500 |
| Building | 97,000 | |
| Less accumulated depreciation | 20,500 | 76,500 |
| Machinery & equipment | 83,000 | |
| Less accumulated depreciation | 42,000 | 41,000 |
| Other assets | | 4,000 |
| Total Assets | | $300,000 |
| *Liabilities* | | |
| Accounts payable | $ 37,000 | |
| Notes payable–due 12/31/X3 | 50,000 | $ 87,000 |
| *Equity* | | |
| Partners' capital accounts | | 213,000 |
| Total Liabilities and Equity | | $300,000 |

SADLER COMPANY
Income Statement
For Year Ended December 31, 19X1

| | | |
|---|---|---|
| Income: | | |
| Sales | $950,000 | |
| Dividends | $ 4,000 | $954,000 |
| Expenses: | | |
| Cost of goods sold | 585,800 | |
| Salaries (employees) | 90,000 | |
| Salaries (partners) | 55,000 | |
| Advertising | 34,000 | |
| Miscellaneous deductions | 28,000 | |
| Contributions | 23,000 | |
| Depreciation | 9,700 | |
| Local taxes | 8,000 | |
| Repairs | 6,000 | |
| Bad debts | 4,000 | |
| Interest | 2,500 | 846,000 |
| Net Income Before Taxes | | $108,000 |

You are given the following additional information: Inventory of 12/31/X0 was $87,000. The dividend income was received on stock purchased during the year as a temporary investment and sold for the exact amount for which purchased. (Compare your answer to this question with the answers you gave for the sixth question in the two preceding chapters.)

7. The Bravado Development Company, with Robert Gray and Donald Lusk as its equal partners, operates an amusement center named Bravado Park. Its

primary source of income is rent from concessionaires. The financial statements for the firm are shown below:

BRAVADO DEVELOPMENT COMPANY
Balance Sheet
December 31, 19X1

| | | |
|---|---|---|
| *Assets* | | |
| Cash | | $ 4,200 |
| Rent receivable | | 19,600 |
| Investments | | 256,000 |
| Land | | 528,000 |
| Building & equipment | $975,000 | |
| Less accumulated depreciation | 370,000 | 605,000 |
| Prepaid expenses | | 4,700 |
| Total Assets | | $1,417,500 |
| *Liabilities* | | |
| Accounts payable | $ 1,200 | |
| Notes payable—current | 249,000 | |
| Mortgage payable—noncurrent | 613,000 | $ 863,200 |
| *Equity* | | |
| Partners' capital accounts | | 554,300 |
| Total Liabilities & Equity | | $1,417,500 |

BRAVADO DEVELOPMENT COMPANY
Income Statement
For Year Ended December 31, 19X1

| | | |
|---|---|---|
| Income: | | |
| Rental income | $523,000 | |
| Municipal bond interest | 8,000 | |
| Other interest income | 1,100 | $532,100 |
| Expenses: | | |
| Depreciation | 170,000 | |
| Advertising | 167,300 | |
| Employees' wages | 67,000 | |
| Property taxes | 47,500 | |
| Repairs | 45,000 | |
| Interest | 33,000 | |
| Miscellaneous | 29,000 | |
| Partners' salaries | 20,000 | |
| Pension & profit sharing | 16,000 | 594,800 |
| Net Loss | | $ (62,700) |

The municipal bonds were originally purchased as a temporary investment of funds, but the bonds were not sold when cash was needed, because of the availability of a relatively low-interest loan for the amount needed. The interest paid to continue carrying the municipal bonds amounted to $3,000 of the total interest paid.

You are to prepare a partnership return for Bravado on Form 1065. (Compare your answer with the answer you gave for Problem 8, Chapter 3.)

8. The Coleman Company is an equal partnership among Peter Coleman, Charles Coleman, and Lefens Porter. The partners draw no salaries. Fill in Schedules K and M of the partnership return assuming the beginning-of-the-year capital account balances were $150,000 each. Consider the following information.

*Analysis of Partners' Capital Accounts*

| | *Dr.* | *Cr.* |
|---|---|---|
| Balance, 1/1/X1 | | $450,000 |
| Net earnings for 19X1, before taxes | | 110,000 |
| Additional Investments | | 50,000 |
| Withdrawals | $40,000 | |

A review of the partnership transactions for the year disclosed:

(a) The partnership received interest of $1,000 on City of Portland bonds.

(b) Contributions of $30,000 were deducted.

(c) The partnership paid interest of $800 on funds borrowed to purchase the City of Portland bonds.

(d) An amount of $900 was paid and expensed by the partnership on insurance policies covering the partners. There are buy-and-sell agreements which bind the surviving partners to acquire the interest of the deceased partner's share at a prearranged price. Because the proceeds of such insurance are not normally taxable, no tax deduction is allowed for premium payments on life insurance.

(e) During the year the partnership wrote off as an expense $5,000, representing a decline in value of certain land it held as an investment. At the beginning of the year, the land was worth $25,000; at the end of the year, only $20,000.

9. Fill in the summary of income and deductions and Schedules K and M of Form 1065 for the AB Company, the information on which is provided below. The two equal partners are Horace Abrams and the estate of Lester Barnes. The beginning-of-the-year capital account balances were $150,000 each. Their personal income taxes are assumed equal in amount, and the partnership actually pays the taxes. Thus, the refund checks on the 1976 refund were actually deposited in the partnership bank account, although each partner received a personal check for $6,500 from the I.R.S. Barnes

died during the year, and the partnership collected the proceeds of policies carried on his life. However, in accordance with the partnership agreement, his salary was continued until the end of the year. Five thousand dollars of it was received by Barnes' estate, and the balance by him during his lifetime. Under the partnership agreement, the partnership year was not closed by Barnes' death. Therefore, his share of the partnership earnings for the year will be nothing; his estate will report everything. There will thus be three partners shown on the return—Abrams, Barnes, and Barnes' estate. Assume that no withdrawals were made, other than salaries, until after Barnes' death. Show Barnes as having withdrawn all his capital on Schedule M, with the estate shown as having invested that amount, putting an asterisk after each of these two equal figures. At the bottom of Schedule M, explain the asterisk with the notation: "*Lester Barnes died on July 29, 19X1, and his partnership interest was succeeded to by the Estate of Lester Barnes."

Analysis of Partners' Capital

| | | |
|---|---|---|
| Balance, 1/1/X1 | | $300,000 |
| Net Profit per Books | | 152,000 |
| Cash Withdrawals | $75,000 | |
| Refund of 1976 Income Tax | | 13,000 |
| Balance, 12/31/X1 | 390,000 | |
| | $465,000 | $465,000 |

AB Company
Income Statement
For Year Ended December 31, 19X1

| | | | |
|---|---|---|---|
| Income: | | | |
| Sales | $1,940,000 | | |
| Less sales returns and allowances | 40,000 | $1,900,000 | |
| Miscellaneous income | | 26,000 | $1,926,000 |
| Expenses: | | | |
| Cost of goods sold | | 1,550,000 | |
| Depreciation | | 53,100 | |
| Officers' salaries | | 35,000 | |
| Other salaries | | 32,000 | |
| Local taxes | | 9,000 | |
| Contributions | | 5,500 | |
| Insurance premiums | | 3,000 | |
| Repairs | | 1,000 | |
| Interest expense | | 400 | 1,689,000 |
| Net Income before Taxes | | | $ 237,000 |

The Miscellaneous Income Account is made up of interest ($10,000) received from local banks and the tax refund, interest ($1,000) from the State of Ohio bonds, and the proceeds ($15,000) from a life insurance policy received on the death of a partner. The Charitable Contributions Account includes a $500 political contribution which is nondeductible for tax purposes. The interest expense was the cost of borrowing the money necessary to purchase the Ohio State bonds. The Insurance Premium Account reflects the cost of insurance policies on the partners under a buy-and-sell agreement. (See part d, Problem 8, for details on buy-and-sell insurance agreements.) The partners estimated their federal income tax for the year at $85,000 and had the company accountant send their payments in quarterly. The accountant deducted their total payments from the net income of the firm and transferred the balance to their capital accounts.

10. Taking into account the reasoning of both the *Haley* and *Orrisch* cases, what would have been the likely tax outcome if the facts in the *Haley* case were changed so that the agreement between Haley and River provided that River was to bear all losses (and thus Haley would not have given his promissory note to River)?
11. "The characteristics of an alleged partnership are to be determined under state law, but the characterization of the organization as a partnership for tax purposes must be determined without regard to the labels affixed by state statutes or by the agreement between the parties." Explain what this statement means with specific reference to the *Haley* case.
12. Suggest some language which, if inserted into the partnership agreement in *Orrisch* (see case excerpt at end of chapter), would have led the Tax Court judge to conclude that the special allocation of depreciation did have "substantial economic effect." Then write a brief argument explaining to an I.R.S. agent why the partnership agreement incorporating your language is sufficiently distinguishable from that used in *Orrisch* so that its special allocation ought to be allowed to stand.
13. Compare allocation of income and loss between a partnership and a Subchapter S corporation where ownership changes during the taxable year.

# 6

# The Individual Income Tax

## THE BUSINESS INCOME OF AN INDIVIDUAL

Over 80 million individual income tax returns are filed annually in this country. The most important source of individual income, "salaries and wages," accounts for over 80 percent of the income reported on individual returns. Proprietorship profit is the second largest category.

Let's take the data we've been using for The Simple Corporation and see how it looks when put on the "Profit from Business or Profession" schedule of the individual return. (See Figure 6-1.)

If you will look back at the corporation return on page 65, you will notice that net income, before the 85 percent special dividends-received deduction, amounted to $77,900. The proprietorship net income is $82,000. Why the difference of $4,100?

1. Dividends are not reported as "business" income on an individual return. They will be reported on a separate income schedule, as you will see later in this chapter.

2. The compensation, if any, paid the proprietor is not deductible. His profit covers his "salary," imputed interest on the capital he has invested, and "pure" profit—without distinguishing one of these factors from another.

3. The charitable contributions are not deductible as a business expense. They may be deductible on another part of the individual return, as we shall see.

Let us summarize these factors and see if they account for $4,100:

| | | |
|---|---|---|
| Dividends included elsewhere | | $20,000 |
| Less: | | |
| Salaries not deductible | $20,000 | |
| Contributions deducted elsewhere | 4,100 | 24,100 |
| Difference | | ($ 4,100) |

**SCHEDULE C (Form 1040)**
Department of the Treasury Internal Revenue Service

## Profit or (Loss) From Business or Profession

**(Sole Proprietorship)**
**Partnerships, Joint Ventures, etc., Must File Form 1065.**
► Attach to Form 1040. ► See Instructions for Schedule C (Form 1040).

Name of proprietor: JOHN M. DOE — Social security number: 360 | 14 | 3404

A Principal business activity (see Schedule C Instructions) ► Retailer; product ► Dry Goods
B Business name ► Simple Company — C Employer identification number ► 36-3601434
D Business address (number and street) ► 77 Sunset Boulevard
City, State and ZIP code ► Valhalla, Arizona 85291

| | Yes | No |
|---|---|---|
| E Indicate method of accounting: (1) ☐ Cash (2) ☒ Accrual (3) ☐ Other ► | | |
| F Were you required to file Form W-3 or Form 1096 for 1976 (see Schedule C Instructions)? | x | |
| If "Yes," where filed ► Ogden, Utah | | |
| G Was an Employer's Quarterly Federal Tax Return, Form 941, filed for this business for any quarter in 1976? | x | |
| H Method of inventory valuation ► Lower of cost or market. Was there any substantial change in the manner of determining quantities, costs, or valuations between the opening and closing inventories? (If "Yes," attach explanation) | | x |

**Income**

| | | |
|---|---|---|
| 1 Gross receipts or sales $534,000 Less: returns and allowances $8,000 Balance ► | 1 | 526,000 |
| 2 Less: Cost of goods sold and/or operations (Schedule C-1, line 8) | 2 | 359,000 |
| 3 Gross profit | 3 | 167,000 |
| 4 Other income (attach schedule) | 4 | |
| 5 **Total income** (add lines 3 and 4) | 5 | 167,000 |

**Deductions**

| | | | |
|---|---|---|---|
| 6 Depreciation (explain in Schedule C-3) | | 6 | 5,000 |
| 7 Taxes on business and business property (explain in Schedule C-2) | | 7 | 3,000 |
| 8 Rent on business property | | 8 | 8,000 |
| 9 Repairs (explain in Schedule C-2) | | 9 | 1,000 |
| 10 Salaries and wages not included on line 3, Schedule C-1 (exclude any paid to yourself) | | 10 | 42,000 |
| 11 Insurance | | 11 | 1,000 |
| 12 Legal and professional fees | | 12 | |
| 13 Commissions | | 13 | |
| 14 Amortization (attach statement) | | 14 | |
| 15 (a) Pension and profit-sharing plans (see Schedule C Instructions) | | 15(a) | |
| (b) Employee benefit programs (see Schedule C Instructions) | | (b) | |
| 16 Interest on business indebtedness | | 16 | 3,000 |
| 17 Bad debts arising from sales or services | | 17 | |
| 18 Depletion | | 18 | |
| 19 Other business expenses (specify): | | | |
| (a) Advertising | 16,000 | | |
| (b) Delivery expense | 2,500 | | |
| (c) Store supplies | 500 | | |
| (d) Miscellaneous | 3,000 | | |
| (e) | | | |
| (f) | | | |
| (g) | | | |
| (h) | | | |
| (i) | | | |
| (j) | | | |
| (k) Total other business expenses (add lines 19(a) through 19(j)) | | 19(k) | 22,000 |
| 20 **Total deductions** (add lines 6 through 19(k)) | | 20 | 85,000 |
| 21 Net profit or (loss) (subtract line 20 from line 5). Enter here and on Form 1040, line 29. **ALSO** enter on Schedule SE, line 5(a) | | 21 | 82,000 |

**SCHEDULE C-1.—Cost of Goods Sold and/or Operations** (See Schedule C Instructions for Line 2)

| | | |
|---|---|---|
| 1 Inventory at beginning of year (if different from last year's closing inventory, attach explanation) | 1 | 24,000 |
| 2 Purchases $........ Less: cost of items withdrawn for personal use $........ Balance ► | 2 | 366,000 |
| 3 Cost of labor (do not include salary paid to yourself) | 3 | |
| 4 Materials and supplies | 4 | |
| 5 Other costs (attach schedule) | 5 | |
| 6 Total of lines 1 through 5 | 6 | 390,000 |
| 7 Less: Inventory at end of year | 7 | 31,000 |
| 8 Cost of goods sold and/or operations. Enter here and on line 2 above | 8 | 359,000 |

**FIGURE 6-1**
**Profit from Business or Profession**

The treatment on the individual-return business schedule is similar to the one we used on the partnership return, with a slight exception in the treatment accorded owners' salaries. Since on the individual return, dividends and contributions are specially treated or are subject to limitations on deductibility, they are separately set forth rather than lumped into the computation of business profit.

The individual return contains no balance sheet. As a result, it contains no reconciliation schedule, either. However, the fact that the return form calls for no reconciliation does not mean that one should not be made by or for the taxpayer. The tax form merely recognizes the fact that many proprietorships tend to be quite small businesses, with only rudimentary accounting systems. Ordinary prudence dictates that the taxpayer should check his return for overall reasonableness through some sort of a rough net-worth test, even if his records do not do this for him automatically through preparation of a balance sheet as well as an income statement.

## SOCIAL SECURITY TAX ON THE SELF-EMPLOYED

Part of the self-employment return filled in by individuals constitutes a Social Security tax return. The Social Security tax of an employee is based upon his earnings, and his share is deducted from his paychecks. The self-employed person, the partner, and a limited number of other persons (such as ministers) calculate their Social Security taxes once a year. Based on the schedule of business profit we have just been looking at, John Doe's Social Security tax computation would look like Figure 6-2.

At first you may wonder why Doe has to pay Social Security tax at a higher rate than the one used in figuring an employee's payroll deduction. For 1977, an employee paid 4.85 percent plus 1.0 percent for Medicare, a total of 5.85 percent, and the employer matched this amount, making a total of 11.7 percent paid to the government. In 1977, self-employed persons paid 7 percent plus .9 percent for Medicare. Actually, therefore, the government collects less Social Security taxes on behalf of the self-employed than on account of employees. Because the benefits are the same for self-employed and employee alike, this provision acts as a slight inducement toward the noncorporate form of doing business. It dates back to the time when self-employed persons were not covered by Social Security at all. In the give-and-take that resulted in accepting them under Social Security, the setting of the tax at about three-fourths of the total collected for an employee (excluding Medicare, which was enacted at a later date) was one of the compromises made in order to gain the support of small business organizations and advocates who feared the additional tax burden that would be imposed.

Another partial explanation for the difference lies in a comparison of the after-tax cost to the employer and employee versus the after-tax cost to the self-employed person. The employer's half of the tax is deductible to the employer. Thus, for a corporation in a 48 percent tax bracket, the after-tax cost of its half in 1977 came to 3.042 percent. The employee could not take a tax deduction for his half, so that the total net revenue to the Treasury from employer and employee combined was 8.892 percent (3.042 + 5.85) as compared to the 7.9 percent collected from the self-employed person.

Employees' FICA and self-employment rates (including Medicare) have remained at 5.85 percent since 1973.

**SCHEDULE SE (Form 1040)**
Department of the Treasury
Internal Revenue Service

**Computation of Social Security Self-Employment Tax**

▶ Each self-employed person must file a Schedule SE. ▶ Attach to Form 1040.
▶ See Instructions for Schedule SE (Form 1040).

- If you had wages, including tips, of $15,300 or more that were subject to social security or railroad retirement taxes, do not fill in this schedule (unless you are eligible for the Earned Income Credit). See Instructions.
- If you had more than one business, combine profits and losses from all your businesses and farms on this Schedule SE.

**Important.**—The self-employment income reported below will be credited to your social security record and used in figuring social security benefits.

| NAME OF SELF-EMPLOYED PERSON (AS SHOWN ON SOCIAL SECURITY CARD) | Social security number of self-employed person ▶ |
|---|---|
| JOHN M. DOE | 360 ⁝ 14 ⁝ 3404 |

Business activities subject to self-employment tax (grocery store, restaurant, farm, etc.) ▶ Retail Dry Goods

- If you have only farm income complete Parts I and III. ● If you have only nonfarm income complete Parts II and III.
- If you have both farm and nonfarm income complete Parts I, II, and III.

**Part I** **Computation of Net Earnings from FARM Self-Employment**

**Part II** **Computation of Net Earnings from NONFARM Self-Employment**

| | | | |
|---|---|---|---|
| REGULAR METHOD 5 Net profit or (loss) from: a Schedule C, line 21. (Enter combined amount if more than one business.) | 5a | 82,000 | |
| b Partnerships, joint ventures, etc. (other than farming) | 5b | | |
| c Service as a minister, member of a religious order, or a Christian Science practitioner. (Include rental value of parsonage or rental allowance furnished.) If you filed Form 4361, check here ▶ ☐ and enter zero on this line | 5c | | |
| d Service with a foreign government or international organization | 5d | | |
| e Other (See Form 1040 instructions for line 36.) Specify ▶ | 5e | | |
| 6 Total (add lines 5a through e) | 6 | 82,000 | |
| 7 Enter adjustments if any (attach statement) | 7 | | |
| 8 Adjusted net earnings or (loss) from nonfarm self-employment (line 6, as adjusted by line 7) | 8 | 82,000 | |

If line 8 is $1,600 or more OR if you do not elect to use the Nonfarm Optional Method, omit lines 9 through 11 and enter amount from line 8 on line 12b, Part III.

*Note: You may use the nonfarm optional method (line 9 through line 11) only if line 8 is less than $1,600 and less than two-thirds of your gross nonfarm profits,[1] and you had actual net earnings from self-employment of*

**Part III** **Computation of Social Security Self-Employment Tax**

| | | | |
|---|---|---|---|
| 12 Net earnings or (loss): a From farming (from line 4) | 12a | | |
| b From nonfarm (from line 8, or line 11 if you elect to use the Nonfarm Optional Method) | 12b | 82,000 | |
| 13 Total net earnings or (loss) from self-employment reported on line 12. **(If line 13 is less than $400, you are not subject to self-employment tax. Do not fill in rest of schedule.)** | 13 | 82,000 | |
| 14 The largest amount of combined wages and self-employment earnings subject to social security or railroad retirement taxes for 1976 is | 14 | $16,500 | 00 |
| 15 a Total "FICA" wages and "RRTA" compensation — 15a | | | |
| b Unreported tips subject to FICA tax from Form 4137, line 9 or to RRTA — 15b | | | |
| c Total of lines 15a and b | 15c | | |
| 16 Balance (subtract line 15c from line 14) | 16 | 16,500 | |
| 17 Self-employment income—line 13 or 16, whichever is smaller | 17 | 16,500 | |
| 18 Self-employment tax. (If line 17 is $16,500.00; enter $1,303.50; if less, multiply the amount on line 17 by .079.) Enter here and on Form 1040, line 58 | 18 | 1,303 | 50 |

FIGURE 6-2
Social Security Tax Computation

These rates applied to a taxable wage or self-employment income base of $9,000 for 1971-72, $10,800 for 1973, $13,200 for 1974, $14,100 for 1975, $15,300 for 1976, and $16,500 for 1977. Congress often schedules FICA funding for years in advance. However, under the law the wage base rises to reflect inflation—in addition to increases mandated by Congress.

## THE INDIVIDUAL RETURN

On this first individual return, let's assume that John Doe is unmarried and has no dependents. His income consists of the business profit of $82,000 plus the dividends of $20,000. His only deductions are the $6,000 of contributions, which do not exceed the 50 percent general limit on individual charitable contributions; $500 of various other deductions; and a $750 exemption that every taxpayer was allowed for himself in 1976. (See Figures 6-3 and 6-4.)

The treatment of dividends on the individual return includes a gesture at compensating for the double taxation of corporate income. Doe gets to exclude the first $100 of dividend income and thus reports only $19,900 of the $20,000 he received.

Doe also gets to deduct the $6,000 in contributions made through the business. Contributions are one of a class of items called "itemized deductions" or "deductions from adjusted gross income." Other items in this group are interest paid, certain taxes paid (except federal), medical and dental expenses to the extent that they exceed certain minimums, losses through theft or accident, certain employee expenses, and expenses of producing income. Doe could have elected to take what is called the "standard deduction" or zero bracket amount instead of "itemizing" his deductions. The standard deduction for 1977 was $2,200. Because Doe is assumed to be seeking to minimize his taxes, he would itemize his deductions and claim the $6,500 of contributions and other deductions.

As an unmarried individual, Doe is in a relatively high tax bracket. His last dollar of income was taxed at a 69 percent rate, which we refer to as the marginal rate of tax to which he is subject. He paid an income tax of $49,219 (ignoring maximum tax considerations) on adjusted gross income of $101,900, making his average rate of tax approximately 48.3 percent. If Doe were incorporated, his tax picture would look different. (See Figures 6-5 and 6-6.)

The corporation would have had a tax of $15,732 for 1976 (see page 65) and Doe would have had an individual tax of $3,999. This would make a total of $19,731–a goodly sum but considerably less than the $49,219 in income tax Doe would pay as a sole proprietor.

Of course, Doe does not have to incorporate to reduce his tax. He can take unto himself a spouse. Assuming that she has no income and no deductions of her own, the return would look the same as the one on page 123 except that taxable income would be reduced by one more personal exemption and the tax computation would be different. On a joint return–that is a return filed jointly by husband and wife, and reporting all income of both–the 1976 tax on Doe would be $41,340, as contrasted with the $49,219 he would pay while enjoying single "bliss."

The above calculations will not be necessary under the new tax tables that will be based on "Tax table" income and the number of exemptions. For taxpayers using the standard deduction, "Tax table" income is adjusted gross income. The personal exemptions, the standard deduction, and the general tax credit will be built into the tax tables. The new look-up table will also be made available to taxpayers who itemize their deductions. They will have to subtract their itemized deductions in excess of the new standard deduction to obtain "tax table" income.

Form **1040** Department of the Treasury—Internal Revenue Service
**U.S. Individual Income Tax Return**

This space for IRS use only

For the year January 1–December 31, 197 , or other taxable year beginning , 197 ending , 19 .

Please print or type

| Name (If joint return, give first names and initials of both) | Last name | Your social security number |
|---|---|---|
| JOHN M. | DOE | 360 14 3404 |
| Present home address (Number and street, including apartment number, or rural route) | For Privacy Act Notification, see page 5 of Instructions. | Spouse's social security no. |
| 90 Miramonte | | |
| City, town or post office, State and ZIP code | Occupation: Yours ▶ Retailer | |
| Valhalla, Arizona 85291 | Spouse's ▶ | |

**Filing Status**

1 [x] Single (Check only ONE box)
2 [ ] Married filing joint return (even if only one had income)
3 [ ] Married filing separately. If spouse is also filing give spouse's social security number in designated space above and enter full name here ▶
4 [ ] Unmarried Head of Household. See page 7 of instructions to see if you qualify ▶
5 [ ] Qualifying widow(er) with dependent child (Year spouse died ▶ 19 ). See page 7 of Instructions.

**Exemptions**

6a Regular [x] Yourself [ ] Spouse — Enter number of boxes checked ▶ 1
b First names of your dependent children who lived with you — Enter number ▶
c Number of other dependents (from line 7) ▶
d Total (add lines 6a, b, and c) ▶ 1
e Age 65 or older . [ ] Yourself [ ] Spouse; Blind . . . . [ ] Yourself [ ] Spouse — Enter number of boxes checked ▶
f TOTAL (add lines 6d and e) ▶ 1

| 7 Other dependents: (a) Name | (b) Relationship | (c) Months lived in your home. If born or died during year, write B or D. | (d) Did dependent have income of $750 or more? | (e) Amount furnished for dependent's support: By YOU. If 100% write ALL. | By OTHERS including dependent. |
|---|---|---|---|---|---|
| | | | | $ | $ |

8 **Presidential Election Campaign Fund** . . ▶ Do you wish to designate $1 of your taxes for this fund? . . Yes / No. If joint return, does your spouse wish to designate $1? . . Yes / No. **Note:** If you check the "Yes" box(es) it will not increase your tax or reduce your refund.

Please attach Copy B of Forms W–2 here

**Income**

| | | | |
|---|---|---|---|
| 9 | Wages, salaries, tips, and other employee compensation (Attach Forms W–2. If unavailable, see page 6 of Instructions.) | 9 | |
| 10a | Dividends (See pages 9 and 16 of Instructions) 20,000, 10b less exclusion 100, Balance ▶ *(If gross dividends and other distributions are over $400, list in Part I of Schedule B.)* | 10c | 19,900 |
| 11 | Interest income. {If $400 or less, enter total without listing in Schedule B; If over $400, enter total and list in Part II of Schedule B} | 11 | |
| 12 | Income other than wages, dividends, and interest (from line 37) | 12 | 82,000 |
| 13 | Total (add lines 9, 10c, 11 and 12) | 13 | 101,900 |
| 14 | Adjustments to income (such as moving expense, etc. from line 42) | 14 | |
| 15a | Subtract line 14 from line 13 | 15a | |
| b | Disability income exclusion (sick pay) (attach Form 2440) | 15b | |
| c | **Adjusted gross income.** Subtract line 15b from line 15a, then complete Part III on back. (If less than $8,000, see page 2 of Instructions on "Earned Income Credit.") | 15c | 101,900 |

**Tax, Payments and Credits**

| | | | |
|---|---|---|---|
| 16 | Tax, check if from: [ ] Tax Table [ ] Schedule G [x] Tax Rate Schedule X, Y or Z [ ] Form 2555 OR [ ] Schedule D [ ] Form 4726 | 16 | 49,399 |
| 17a | Multiply $35.00 by the number of exemptions on line 6d — 17a: 35 | | |
| b | Enter 2% of line 47 but not more than $180 ($90 if box 3 is checked) — 17b: 180 — Enter larger of a or b *(If box on line 3 is checked see page 10 of Instructions)* | 17c | 180 |
| 18 | Balance. Subtract line 17c from line 16 and enter difference (but not less than zero) | 18 | 49,219 |
| 19 | Credits (from line 54) | 19 | |
| 20 | Balance. Subtract line 19 from line 18 and enter difference (but not less than zero) | 20 | 49,219 |
| 21 | Other taxes (from line 62) | 21 | 1,304 |
| 22 | Total (add lines 20 and 21) | 22 | 50,523 |
| 23a | Total Federal income tax withheld. (attach Forms W–2, or W–2P to front) — 23a | | |
| b | 1976 estimated tax payments (include amount allowed as credit from 1975 return) — 23b: 51,000 | | |
| c | Earned income credit. (from page 2 of Instructions) — 23c | | |
| d | Amount paid with Form 4868 — 23d | | |
| e | Other payments (from line 66) — 23e | | |
| 24 | **TOTAL** (add lines 23a through e) ▶ | 24 | 51,000 |

Pay amount on line 25 in full with this return. Write social security number on check or money order and make payable to Internal Revenue Service.

Please attach Check or Money Order here

**Due or Refund**

| | | | |
|---|---|---|---|
| 25 | If line 22 is larger than line 24, enter **BALANCE DUE IRS** ▶ (Check here ▶ [ ], if Form 2210 or Form 2210F is attached. See page 10 of instructions.) | 25 | |
| 26 | If line 24 is larger than line 22, enter amount **OVERPAID** ▶ | 26 | 477 |
| 27 | Amount of line 26 to be **REFUNDED TO YOU** ▶ | 27 | |
| 28 | Amount of line 26 to be credited on 1977 estimated tax ▶ 28: 477 | | |

Under penalties of perjury, I declare that I have examined this return, including accompanying schedules and statements, and to the best of my knowledge and belief it is true, correct, and complete. Declaration of preparer (other than taxpayer) is based on all information of which preparer has any knowledge.

**Sign here**

▶ Your signature — Date | ▶ Preparer's signature (and employer's name, if any) — Date

▶ Spouse's signature (if filing jointly, BOTH must sign even if only one had income) | ▶ Identifying number (see Instructions) — Address (and ZIP code)

FIGURE 6-3

Individual Income Tax Return

The tax advantages of the corporation appear superior, but other advantages of marriage might propel Doe in that direction, regardless of tax

**Part III Tax Computation**

| | | | |
|---|---|---|---|
| 43 | Adjusted gross income (from line 15c). If you have unearned income and can be claimed as a dependent on your parent's return, check here ▶ ☐ and see page 9 of Instructions | 43 | 101,900 |
| 44a | If you itemize deductions, check here ▶ ☐, and enter total from Schedule A, line 40, and attach Schedule A | | |
| b | Standard deduction—If you do not itemize deductions, check here ▶ ☐, and: If you checked the box on line . . . 2 or 5, enter the greater of $2,100 OR 16% of line 43—but not more than $2,800; 1 or 4, enter the greater of $1,700 OR 16% of line 43—but not more than $2,400; 3, enter the greater of $1,050 OR 16% of line 43—but not more than $1,400 | 44 | 6,500 |
| 45 | Subtract line 44 from line 43 and enter difference (but not less than zero) | 45 | 95,400 |
| 46 | Multiply total number of exemptions claimed on line 6f by $750 | 46 | 750 |
| 47 | Taxable income. Subtract line 46 from line 45 and enter difference (but not less than zero) | 47 | 94,650 |

- If line 47 is $20,000 or less and you did not average your income on Schedule G, or figure your tax on Form 2555, Exemption of Income Earned Abroad, find your tax in Tax Table. Enter tax on line 16 and check appropriate box.
- If line 47 is more than $20,000, figure your tax on the amount on line 47 by using Tax Rate Schedule X, Y, Z, or if applicable, the alternative tax from Schedule D, income averaging from Schedule G, tax from Form 2555 or maximum tax from Form 4726. Enter tax on line 16 and check appropriate box.

| | | | |
|---|---|---|---|
| 54 | Total (add lines 48 through 53). Enter here and on line 19 ▶ | 54 | |

**Part V Other Taxes**

| | | | |
|---|---|---|---|
| 55 | Tax from recomputing prior-year investment credit (attach Form 4255) | 55 | |
| 56 | Minimum tax. Check here ▶ ☐, and attach Form 4625 | 56 | |
| 57 | Tax on premature distributions from attached Form 5329, Part V | 57 | |
| 58 | Self-employment tax (attach Schedule SE) | 58 | 1,304 |
| 59 | Social security tax on tip income not reported to employer (attach Form 4137) | 59 | |
| 60 | Uncollected employee social security tax on tips (from Forms W-2) | 60 | |
| 61 | Excess contribution tax from attached Form 5329, Part IV | 61 | |
| 62 | Total (add lines 55 through 61). Enter here and on line 21 ▶ | 62 | 1,304 |

**Part VI Other Payments**

FIGURE 6-4
Tax Computation

benefits. Fortunately, the tax system is quite benign, so that Doe can, indeed, do both–get married *and* incorporate. As a single person, he had a combined corporate and individual tax of $19,731, but in his married state this will be cut to $18,631.

We now leave Mr. Doe, both married and incorporated as a result, at least in part, of the pressures exerted upon him by the tax structure.

## A JOINT RETURN VERSUS SEPARATE RETURNS

Married taxpayers may make a joint return and include all the exemptions, income, and deductions of both husband and wife, even though one of the two had no income; or each may file a separate return, including only his or her income, exemptions, and deductions. One thing to keep in mind, however, is that if the wife has any income at all, her husband may not claim an exemption for her on his separate return. On the other hand, if the wife has no income (and is not the dependent of another taxpayer), her husband may claim an exemption for her on his separate return.

### *Reasons for Filing a Joint Return*

If a married couple decides to file a joint return, they figure their tax under a special tax schedule that, in effect, "splits" their income and computes

Form **1040** Department of the Treasury—Internal Revenue Service
**U.S. Individual Income Tax Return**

This space for IRS use only

For the year January 1–December 31, 197 , or other taxable year beginning , 197 ending , 19 .

Please print or type

| Name (If joint return, give first names and initials of both) | Last name | Your social security number |
|---|---|---|
| JOHN M. | DOE | 360 14 3404 |
| Present home address (Number and street, including apartment number, or rural route) | For Privacy Act Notification, see page 5 of Instructions. | Spouse's social security no. |
| 90 Miramonte | | |
| City, town or post office, State and ZIP code | Occupation: Yours ▶ | |
| Valhalla, Arizona 85291 | Spouse's ▶ | |

**Filing Status**

1 ☒ Single (Check only ONE box)
2 ☐ Married filing joint return (even if only one had income)
3 ☐ Married filing separately. If spouse is also filing give spouse's social security number in designated space above and enter full name here ▶
4 ☐ Unmarried Head of Household. See page 7 of instructions to see if you qualify ▶
5 ☐ Qualifying widow(er) with dependent child (Year spouse died ▶ 19 ). See page 7 of Instructions.

**Exemptions**

6a Regular ☐ Yourself ☐ Spouse — Enter number of boxes checked ▶ 1
b First names of your dependent children who lived with you — Enter number ▶
c Number of other dependents (from line 7) ▶
d Total (add lines 6a, b, and c) ▶ 1
e Age 65 or older. ☐ Yourself ☐ Spouse — Enter number of boxes checked ▶
Blind . . . . ☐ Yourself ☐ Spouse
f TOTAL (add lines 6d and e) ▶ 1

7 Other dependents:

| (a) Name | (b) Relationship | (c) Months lived in your home. If born or died during year, write B or D. | (d) Did dependent have income of $750 or more? | (e) Amount furnished for dependent's support: By YOU. If 100% write ALL. | By OTHERS including dependent. |
|---|---|---|---|---|---|
| | | | | $ | $ |

8 **Presidential Election Campaign Fund** ▶ Do you wish to designate $1 of your taxes for this fund? Yes No — If joint return, does your spouse wish to designate $1? Yes No. Note: If you check the "Yes" box(es) it will not increase your tax or reduce your refund.

Please attach Copy B of Forms W-2 here

**Income**

| | | | |
|---|---|---|---|
| 9 | Wages, salaries, tips, and other employee compensation (Attach Forms W-2. If unavailable, see page 6 of Instructions.) | 9 | 20,000 |
| 10a | Dividends (See pages 9 and 16 of Instructions) ........, 10b less exclusion ........, Balance ▶ (If gross dividends and other distributions are over $400, list in Part I of Schedule B.) | 10c | |
| 11 | Interest income. {If $400 or less, enter total without listing in Schedule B; If over $400, enter total and list in Part II of Schedule B} | 11 | |
| 12 | Income other than wages, dividends, and interest (from line 37) | 12 | |
| 13 | Total (add lines 9, 10c, 11 and 12) | 13 | 20,000 |
| 14 | Adjustments to income (such as moving expense, etc. from line 42) | 14 | |
| 15a | Subtract line 14 from line 13 | 15a | |
| b | Disability income exclusion (sick pay) (attach Form 2440) | 15b | |
| c | Adjusted gross income. Subtract line 15b from line 15a, then complete Part III on back. (If less than $8,000, see page 2 of Instructions on "Earned Income Credit.") | 15c | 20,000 |

**Tax, Payments and Credits**

| | | | |
|---|---|---|---|
| 16 | Tax, check if from: ☒ Tax Table ☐ Schedule G ☐ Tax Rate Schedule X, Y or Z ☐ Form 2555 OR ☐ Schedule D ☐ Form 4726 | 16 | 4,179 |
| 17a | Multiply $35.00 by the number of exemptions on line 6d — 17a: 35 | | |
| b | Enter 2% of line 47 but not more than $180 ($90 if box 3 is checked) — 17b: 180 | 17c | 180 |
| | Enter larger of a or b (If box on line 3 is checked see page 10 of Instructions) | | |
| 18 | Balance. Subtract line 17c from line 16 and enter difference (but not less than zero) | 18 | 3,999 |
| 19 | Credits (from line 54) | 19 | |
| 20 | Balance. Subtract line 19 from line 18 and enter difference (but not less than zero) | 20 | |
| 21 | Other taxes (from line 62) | 21 | |
| 22 | Total (add lines 20 and 21) | 22 | 3,999 |
| 23a | Total Federal income tax withheld. (attach Forms W-2, or W-2P to front) — 23a: 5,000 | | |
| b | 1976 estimated tax payments (include amount allowed as credit from 1975 return) — 23b | | |
| c | Earned income credit. (from page 2 of Instructions) — 23c | | |
| d | Amount paid with Form 4868 — 23d | | |
| e | Other payments (from line 66) — 23e | | |
| 24 | TOTAL (add lines 23a through e) ▶ | 24 | 5,000 |

Pay amount on line 25 in full with this return. Write social security number on check or money order and make payable to Internal Revenue Service.

Please attach Check or Money Order here

**Due or Refund**

| | | | |
|---|---|---|---|
| 25 | If line 22 is larger than line 24, enter BALANCE DUE IRS ▶ (Check here ▶ ☐, if Form 2210 or Form 2210F is attached. See page 10 of instructions.) | 25 | |
| 26 | If line 24 is larger than line 22, enter amount OVERPAID ▶ | 26 | 1,001 |
| 27 | Amount of line 26 to be REFUNDED TO YOU ▶ | 27 | 1,001 |
| 28 | Amount of line 26 to be credited on 1977 estimated tax ▶ 28 | | |

Under penalties of perjury, I declare that I have examined this return, including accompanying schedules and statements, and to the best of my knowledge and belief it is true, correct, and complete. Declaration of preparer (other than taxpayer) is based on all information of which preparer has any knowledge.

**Sign here**

▶ Your signature — Date ▶ Preparer's signature (and employer's name, if any) — Date

▶ Spouse's signature (if filing jointly, BOTH must sign even if only one had income) ▶ Identifying number (see instructions) — Address (and ZIP code)

FIGURE 6-5
Individual Income Tax Return

the tax at the rate applicable to each half of the income. This is the major advantage of joint filing, particularly when one spouse has substantially more income than the other. Another advantage arises when both have income but the

| | *Single* | *Married* |
|---|---|---|
| Adjusted gross income (from line 15c) | $20,000 | $20,000 |
| Less: Zero bracket amount (standard deduction) | 2,200 | 3,200 |
| | 17,800 | 16,800 |
| Less: Exemptions | 750 | 1,500 |
| Taxable Income | $17,050 | $15,300 |
| Tax | $ 4,179 | $ 3,079 |
| Less: General tax credit | 180 | 180 |
| Individual tax | 3,999 | 2,899 |
| Corporate tax | 15,732 | 15,732 |
| Combined tax | $19,731 | $18,631 |

FIGURE 6-6
Tax Computation

income of one is less than the amount of the $750 personal exemption. When this happens, the other spouse benefits by the excess of the personal exemption over the small income. If separate returns are filed, the unused personal exemption is lost.

### *Reasons for Filing Separate Returns*

There is at least one situation in which separate returns may be to a married couple's advantage. This is when both have income but one has substantial medical expenses and the other has little or none. In this situation, combining the incomes will serve to reduce the medical expense deduction, because the couple must subtract 3 percent of their combined adjusted gross income from their total medical expenses and then deduct only the difference. In this connection, however, there is one important point to keep in mind: When a husband and wife file separate returns and one itemizes deductions, the other must also itemize deductions. If the taxpayer with substantial medical expense has a small income in comparison to the other spouse, the increased medical deduction may be of less value than the income-splitting benefits of a joint return.

In community property states, there may be no or little difference between the tax on separate returns and on a joint return if all the income is community income. Community income and deductions would be split equally between the taxpayers without regard to who earned such income.

### *Head of Household*

An unmarried person maintaining a household (i.e., who contributes more than 50 percent) gets a tax break in that he uses a tax rate scale that falls midway between that used for single individuals and the joint return rates. The taxpayer must maintain a home that is the principal place of abode for himself and his child or a descendant of his child (if this person is married, the taxpayer must be entitled to claim a dependency exemption), or any other related person whom the taxpayer is entitled to claim as a dependent. If the taxpayer maintains a separate home for his parents and he is entitled to a dependency exemption for one or both of them. he can claim head of household status.

## DEDUCTIONS: ITEMIZED VERSUS STANDARD

### *When You Should Itemize Deductions*

It will usually be advantageous to itemize deductions, whatever the income, if allowable deductions are more than the maximum standard deduction.

For many years, through 1970, the standard deduction was 10 percent of adjusted gross income, limited to $1,000 per return and further limited to a maximum of $500 per return in the case of a husband and wife filing separate returns. It is now a flat $3,200 on a joint return and for surviving spouses, $2,200 on a single return and for head of household, and $1,600 for the separate return of a married person.

Taxpayers who have itemized deductions that ordinarily approximate the allowable standard deduction may decrease their tax burden by accelerating or deferring payment of itemized deductions. Take, for example, a single taxpayer whose itemized deductions are ordinarily about $2,200. In December 1977, he might pay state income taxes, property taxes, and other items that would ordinarily be paid in 1978. If he is able to increase his itemized deductions to $3,200 for 1977, he would benefit from the additional $1,000 deduction and still be able to take the standard deduction of $2,200 in 1978. His acceleration of payments has increased his 1977 deductions without increasing his 1978 taxable income. In addition, payment of some deductible expenses ordinarily payable in December 1978 might be deferred to January 1979, since the standard deduction will be claimed in 1978 and deductions again itemized in 1979.

### *When You Must Use The Standard Deduction*

The standard deduction must be taken, regardless of the amount of income, if no record of deductions has been kept and their amount is not known or there is no way to prove them. In doubtful cases, the tax should always be figured both ways to see whether claiming the standard deduction is advantageous. For example, a person with an income of $4,000 will probably find that determining his tax by taking the standard deduction will be to his advantage. However, in a year in which that person has had unusually heavy medical expenses, it might well be to his advantage to itemize his deductions and compute his tax, even though his income for that year is no higher than before.

Statistics released by the Internal Revenue Service indicate that of the 80 million individual income tax returns filed in 1973, some 52 million showed standard deductions and 28 million reflected itemized deductions.

### *Dependent Care Expenses*

A 20 percent credit is allowed for certain dependent care expenses incurred to enable the taxpayer to be gainfully employed. The taxpayer must maintain a household for a dependent child under 15 years of age, or a dependent of the taxpayer or his spouse (regardless of age) who is physically or mentally incapable of caring for himself. Maximum credit is $400 if one dependent is being cared for and $800 if two or more.

## FILING REQUIREMENTS

1977 gross income levels requiring returns to be filed were:

| | |
|---|---|
| Single individual | $2,950 |
| Single individual over 65 | 3,700 |
| Married couple (filing jointly) | 4,700 |
| Married couple, one spouse over 65 | 5,450 |
| Married couple, both over 65 | 6,200 |
| Surviving spouse | 3,950 |

## TAX-LAW CONCEPTS FOR THE INDIVIDUAL INCOME TAX

By this time, you may have concluded that the individual income tax is quite confusing. Medical expenses that are deductible only to the extent that they exceed 3 percent of something called adjusted gross income! Charitable contributions that are deductible only to the extent that they don't exceed 50 percent of the same adjusted gross income! No tax on the first $100 of dividend income! Why are there all these little rules and exceptions? The corporate tax rules weren't nearly this bad!

The problem is, as we have noted before, that corporations and partnerships are not people. They act only as middlemen. Thus, their tax accounting proceeds from the starting point of net income for financial accounting purposes—a relatively clear concept. And there are few modifications that have to be made in translating accounting net income into taxable income.

But there is no one conceptual point of reference for the individual income tax. True, the business income of the individual follows a financial accounting approach, and related costs can generally be deducted against other types of investment and earned income.

Beyond that, you may be able to detect a hint that some concept of "disposable income" supports many of the tax-deduction provisions that apply to individuals. People with extra-large medical expenses, people who give a good deal to charities, people who pay high state and local taxes, people who suffer casualty losses (fire or theft, for example), people who have other people to support, people who are blind or getting on in years—all these people should get some sort of tax break.

The problem is that huge amounts of tax dollars are involved whenever an individual deduction or credit of general applicability is changed; so the rules are hedged in with restrictions, and the taxpayer needs to check a reference book to see whether a specific deduction or credit is available or not. Tax administrators, in turn, have to deal with the law as it is—which generally means that they will allow a deduction only when the law unmistakably grants it to the taxpayer and the taxpayer has clearly established the facts bringing him within the law.

The dependent care credit is an example. The original idea was simple. Working parents should be allowed a tax deduction for amounts spent to care for children when such care is necessary to enable the parent to work.

But hold on there! An increasing percentage of families have two working parents. We don't really want to give a deduction to *all* these people. So we will limit the deduction to women or widowers. But what if a man's wife is disabled, rather than dead? So we will allow the deduction to husbands with disabled wives. How do we handle the working wife? We provide that a married woman will have her deduction reduced by the amount, if any, that the combined income of her and her husband exceeds $6,000. (The same rule applied to husbands with incapacitated wives.) Then, to make sure that these deductions didn't get out of hand, a maximum deduction ceiling of $600 for one child and $900 for two or more was imposed.

Questions still came up. Why just children? What of other dependents? So the definition was broadened to cover not only children under 13 but also other dependents incapable of caring for themselves.

And who do we mean by married women? So the law got more specific and provided that a woman is not treated as married for this purpose if she was legally separated from her husband. Then what about deserted wives who don't have a legal separation? So a deserted wife who did not know the whereabouts of her husband at any time during the year was not to be considered as a married woman for this purpose. And so forth, on and on, with rules and exceptions to rules. And when we got all done, we still had not achieved absolute fairness. For example:

> A deserted wife could get the maximum child-care deduction, even though her income exceeded $6,000 for the year, if she did not know the whereabouts of her husband "at any time during the taxable year." This woman's husband was in jail during the early part of the year, thus providing no help in supporting the children. As soon as he was released, he took off for parts unknown. She argued that she should be able to deduct the amount that she paid to have her children cared for in order that she might be able to work, even though her income was too high to get a deduction if the $6,000 test applied.
>
> The Tax Court commented that "because of her unfortunate circumstances throughout the year, we would be happy to be able to extend benefits to her." But she did know where her husband was during part of the year (he was in jail—some help!), and thus did not meet the "standards specifically attached by Congress." The Court had to deny the deduction.

Then a male taxpayer who had never been married claimed the exclusion for expenses incurred for care of his invalid mother. On appeal from the Tax Court, the 10th Circuit held that the benefit must be extended to the taxpayer because the attempted limitation under the statute was unconstitutional insofar as it made an "invidious discrimination" premised on sex alone. So Congress made some more changes. Sex discrimination was eliminated. The allowable deduction went to $400 per month reduced by 50 percent of any adjusted gross income over $18,000 per year and subsequently increased to $35,000 per year. Age of an eligible dependent child was raised to 15.

Still there were problems. The 1976 Tax Reform Act changed the deduction to a credit, eliminated any reduction related to size of income, and even allowed payments to a grandparent to be eligible for the credit under limited circumstances.

This is just one provision affecting individuals. Similar trails could be traced for most of the others.

We'll return again to the subject of the tax law and how it changes, with particular reference to the individual income tax, in Chapter 23 on Tax Reform.

### *The Short Form*

An abbreviated version of Form 1040, called 1040A, may be filed by those whose income is from wages, salaries, tips, not over $400 of dividends, and not over $400 of interest. There is a limit on tips if they are not fully reported to the employer.

By filing the simplified form, the taxpayer gives up his rights to itemize his deductions and to claim such tax credits as retirement income credit, investment credit, and foreign tax credit. Neither would the taxpayer be able to claim sick-pay exclusion or moving expense deductions.

Therefore, the shorter return is ideally suited only for those taxpayers whose income consists mainly of wages and who have no special deductions or credits.

## HOW TO FILL IN DECLARATION OF ESTIMATED TAX

Employers must withhold, and pay to the government, income tax on compensation paid to their employees. This is called the "pay-as-you-go" system of paying income tax. This system also requires the self-employed as well as employees to pay-as-they-go on compensation and other income not subject to withholding and on compensation with respect to which not enough tax is withheld. A Declaration of Estimated Tax, Form 1040-ES, is filed for this purpose, and the tax estimated to be due may be paid in quarterly installments.

Taxpayers with estimated tax liability of $100 or more are required to file a Declaration of Estimated Tax if they fall into either of two groups. Group 1 consists of taxpayers whose estimated gross income includes over $500 of income from sources other than wages subject to withholding. The second group is subject to a gross income test. If, for a single person, head of a household, or married person whose spouse does not work, gross income is reasonably expected to exceed $20,000, an estimate is required. For a married individual whose spouse also works, the test is $10,000. For these purposes, estimated tax is net of estimated income tax withheld and allowable credits.

There are three ways to estimate. (1) A taxpayer may use last year's tax as his estimated tax for the current year. (2) He may use last year's income, adjust his exemptions, if necessary, for the conditions currently existing, and compute his tax on this amount, using current rates. (3) He may examine all his anticipated income and deductions for the current year and compute the tax on that amount.

Taxpayers who do not prepay at least 80 percent of their tax through withholding and estimated tax payments may be subject to penalty at the rate of 7 percent per annum on the amount by which their payments are less than the 80 percent. Taxpayers who estimate their tax using the first two methods outlined above, and who make timely payments, may avoid imposition of the penalty.

### *Tax Rates Compared*

From 1954 through 1963, tax rates remained unchanged, with the lowest rate of 20 percent applying to the first $2,000 of taxable income ($4,000 on a joint return), and the top rate of 91 percent applying to taxable income in excess of $200,000 ($400,000 on a joint return). The 1964 tax law changed the rates so that the range for 1964 was from 16 percent to 77 percent, and for 1965 and later years, from 14 percent to 70 percent. The Tax Reform Act of 1969 did not change the tax rates applicable to married taxpayers, whether filing separate or joint returns. However, for unmarried taxpayers there was a new tax-rate schedule, effective for 1971 and later years, in which the rate was never more than 20 percent higher than the joint-return rates for married couples with the same taxable income. In addition, the "Head of Household" rates for 1971 and later years were changed so that they were halfway between the rates for unmarried taxpayers and the rates for married couples filing jointly. See Figure 6-7 for tax-rate schedules for 1971 and later years.

Individual Tax Rates

| *Taxable Income* | *1963* | *1964* | *1965-1970* | **1971 and Later Years* |
|---|---|---|---|---|
| $ 0 - $ 500 | 20% | 16 % | 14% | 14% |
| 501 - 1,000 | 20 | 16.5 | 15 | 15 |
| 1,001 - 1,500 | 20 | 17.5 | 16 | 16 |
| 1,501 - 2,000 | 20 | 18 | 17 | 17 |
| 2,001 - 4,000 | 22 | 20 | 19 | 19 |
| 4,001 - 6,000 | 26 | 23.5 | 22 | 21 |
| 6,001 - 8,000 | 30 | 27 | 25 | 24 |
| 8,001 - 10,000 | 34 | 30.5 | 28 | 25 |
| 10,001 - 12,000 | 38 | 34 | 32 | 27 |
| 12,001 - 14,000 | 43 | 37.5 | 36 | 29 |
| 14,001 - 16,000 | 47 | 41 | 39 | 31 |
| 16,001 - 18,000 | 50 | 44.5 | 42 | 34 |
| 18,001 - 20,000 | 53 | 47.5 | 45 | 36 |

*Note that for years beginning after 1976 the new rates incorporate the standard deductions. However, the marginal rates are the same except that the taxable income column is to be increased by $2,200. For example, substitute $20,201 – 22,200 for $18,001 – 20,000.

## THE INDIVIDUAL INCOME TAX EVALUATED

In 1977, budgeted total receipts of the federal government (excluding $109 billion of social insurance taxes and contributions) were about $245 billion. The largest single source was the individual income tax:

| | *Billions* |
|---|---|
| Individual income tax | $153.1 |
| Corporation income tax | 56.6 |
| Estate and gift | 5.9 |
| Excise taxes | 17.9 |
| Misc. | 11.6 |

Obviously, the individual income tax is the main financial prop of our government.

When we looked at the corporation income tax, which is second in importance as a source of receipts, we noted that the bulk of the tax collected came from a small minority of the corporations. But on individual returns, better than 55 percent of the total income reported is on returns showing adjusted gross income of less than $15,000. Almost 90 percent is on returns showing adjusted gross income of under $100,000. As taxpayers get into higher tax brackets, they have an increasing incentive to seek sources of income that are tax sheltered, with the result that the sharply graduated rates of tax often represent more myth than reality. According to the rate tables, for instance, a person with an adjusted gross income in excess of $1 million should have been paying a tax of approximately 67 percent (with a marginal tax rate of 70 percent) of his adjusted gross income in 1968. In fact, for the handful of such persons filing returns, the effective rate of tax on the adjusted gross income reported was 44.9 percent, and the effective tax rate on taxable income was 57.7 percent. Furthermore, it is likely that these individuals had a substantial amount of income that never appeared on their tax returns because the resources of high-bracket taxpayers are often heavily invested in tax-free bond issues of states and their subdivisions. In later chapters, we shall discuss some of the techniques whereby these taxpayers were able to transmute an apparent 67 percent rate into an effective 44.9 percent.

Many critics of the income tax complain that the effect of high tax rates is to destroy work incentive. There are rebuttal arguments, however:

1. We have already seen that high tax rates stimulate the imagination to provide methods of circumventing them. Tax minimization may be criticized as nonproductive. And misallocation of energy, as compared with what would get attention in the absence of a tax system, is certainly an undesirable result. But this is a far different thing from the destruction of the incentive to work.

2. For the bulk of taxpayers, tax rates may not be of a height that would tend to destroy incentive. A married couple with net taxable income just under $20,000 was paying a marginal tax rate in 1977 of 28 percent. One study suggests that only when the marginal tax rate approaches 70 percent does the reduction in incentive to work exceed the increase in incentive to work caused by the tax. It is sometimes forgotten that a person who has been earning $12,000 per year after taxes has adjusted to a $12,000 standard of living. If the tax rate is now increased so that a few more hours of work a week is needed to

Income Tax Rates for 1977 and Later Years

*Married Individuals Filing Joint Returns and Surviving Spouses.*

| "If the taxable income is: | The tax is: |
|---|---|
| Not over $3,200 | No tax. |
| Over $3,200 but not over $4,200 | 14% of the excess over $3,200. |
| Over $4,200 but not over $5,200 | $140, plus 15% of excess over $4,200. |
| Over $5,200 but not over $6,200 | $290, plus 16% of excess over $5,200. |
| Over $6,200 but not over $7,200 | $450, plus 17% of excess over $6,200. |
| Over $7,200 but not over $11,200 | $620, plus 19% of excess over $7,200. |
| Over $11,200 but not over $15,200 | $1,380, plus 22% of excess over $11,200. |
| Over $15,200 but not over $19,200 | $2,260, plus 25% of excess over $15,200. |
| Over $19,200 but not over $23,200 | $3,260, plus 28% of excess over $19,200. |
| Over $23,200 but not over $27,200 | $4,380, plus 32% of excess over $23,200. |
| Over $27,200 but not over $31,200 | $5,660, plus 36% of excess over $27,200. |
| Over $31,200 but not over $35,200 | $7,100, plus 39% of excess over $31,200. |
| Over $35,200 but not over $39,200 | $8,660, plus 42% of excess over $35,200. |
| Over $39,200 but not over $43,200 | $10,340, plus 45% of excess over $39,200. |
| Over $43,200 but not over $47,200 | $12,140, plus 48% of excess over $43,200. |
| Over $47,200 but not over $55,200 | $14,060, plus 50% of excess over $47,200. |
| Over $55,200 but not over $67,200 | $18,060, plus 53% of excess over $55,200. |
| Over $67,200 but not over $79,200 | $24,420, plus 55% of excess over $67,200. |
| Over $79,200 but not over $91,200 | $31,020, plus 58% of excess over $79,200. |
| Over $91,200 but not over $103,200 | $37,980, plus 60% of excess over $91,200. |
| Over $103,200 but not over $123,200 | $45,180, plus 62% of excess over $103,200. |
| Over $123,200 but not over $143,200 | $57,580, plus 64% of excess over $123,200. |
| Over $143,200 but not over $163,200 | $70,380, plus 66% of excess over $143,200. |
| Over $163,200 but not over $183,200 | $83,580, plus 68% of excess over $163,200. |
| Over $183,200 but not over $203,200 | $97,180, plus 69% of excess over $183,200. |
| Over $203,200 | $110,980, plus 70% of excess over $203,200. |

*Heads of Households*

| "If the taxable income is: | The tax is: |
|---|---|
| Not over $2,200 | No tax. |
| Over $2,200 but not over $3,200 | 14% of the excess over $2,200. |
| Over $3,200 but not over $4,200 | $140, plus 16% of excess over $3,200. |

FIGURE 6-7
Income Tax Rates for 1977 and Later Years

FIGURE 6-7 (continued)

| **"If the taxable income is:** | **The tax is:** |
|---|---|
| **Over $4,200 but not over $6,200** | **$300, plus 18% of excess over $4,200.** |
| **Over $6,200 but not over $8,200** | **$660, plus 19% of excess over $6,200.** |
| **Over $8,200 but not over $10,200** | **$1,040, plus 22% of excess over $8,200.** |
| **Over $10,200 but not over $12,200** | **$1,480, plus 23% of excess over $10,200.** |
| **Over $12,200 but not over $14,200** | **$1,940, plus 25% of excess over $12,200.** |
| **Over $14,200 but not over $16,200** | **$2,440, plus 27% of excess over $14,200.** |
| **Over $16,200 but not over $18,200** | **$2,980, plus 28% of excess over $16,200.** |
| **Over $18,200 but not over $20,200** | **$3,540, plus 31% of excess over $18,200.** |
| **Over $20,200 but not over $22,200** | **$4,160, plus 32% of excess over $20,200.** |
| **Over $22,200 but not over $24,200** | **$4,800, plus 35% of excess over $22,200.** |
| **Over $24,200 but not over $26,200** | **$5,500, plus 36% of excess over $24,200.** |
| **Over $26,200 but not over $28,200** | **$6,220, plus 38% of excess over $26,200.** |
| **Over $28,200 but not over $30,200** | **$6,980, plus 41% of excess over $28,200.** |
| **Over $30,200 but not over $34,200** | **$7,800, plus 42% of excess over $30,200.** |
| **Over $34,200 but not over $38,200** | **$9,480, plus 45% of excess over $34,200.** |
| **Over $38,200 but not over $40,200** | **$11,280, plus 48% of excess over $38,200.** |
| **Over $40,200 but not over $42,200** | **$12,240, plus 51% of excess over $40,200.** |
| **Over $42,200 but not over $46,200** | **$13,260, plus 52% of excess over $42,200.** |
| **Over $46,200 but not over $52,200** | **$15,340, plus 55% of excess over $46,200.** |
| **Over $52,200 but not over $54,200** | **$18,640, plus 56% of excess over $52,200.** |
| **Over $54,200 but not over $66,200** | **$19,760, plus 58% of excess over $54,200.** |
| **Over $66,200 but not over $72,200** | **$26,720, plus 59% of excess over $66,200.** |
| **Over $72,200 but not over $78,200** | **$30,260, plus 61% of excess over $72,200.** |
| **Over $78,200 but not over $82,200** | **$33,920, plus 62% of excess over $78,200.** |
| **Over $82,200 but not over $90,200** | **$36,400, plus 63% of excess over $82,200.** |
| **Over $90,200 but not over $102,200** | **$41,440, plus 64% of excess over $90,200.** |
| **Over $102,200 but not over $122,200** | **$49,120, plus 66% of excess over $102,200.** |
| **Over $122,200 but not over $142,200** | **$62,320, plus 67% of excess over $122,200.** |
| **Over $142,200 but not over $162,200** | **$75,720, plus 68% of excess over $142,200.** |
| **Over $162,200 but not over $182,200** | **$89,320, plus 69% of excess over $162,200.** |
| **Over $182,200** | **$103,120, plus 70% of excess over $182,200.** |

*Unmarried Individuals (Other Than Surviving Spouses and Heads of Households).*

| **"If the taxable income is:** | **The tax is:** |
|---|---|
| Not over $2,200 | No tax. |
| Over $2,200 but not over $2,700 | 14% of the excess over $2,200. |

FIGURE 6-7 (continued)

| "If the taxable income is: | The tax is: |
|---|---|
| Over $2,700 but not over $3,200 | $70, plus 15% of excess over $2,700. |
| Over $3,200 but not over $3,700 | $145, plus 16% of excess over $3,200. |
| Over $3,700 but not over $4,200 | $225, plus 17% of excess over $3,700. |
| Over $4,200 but not over $6,200 | $310, plus 19% of excess over $4,200. |
| Over $6,200 but not over $8,200 | $690, plus 21% of excess over $6,200. |
| Over $8,200 but not over $10,200 | $1,110, plus 24% of excess over $8,200. |
| Over $10,200 but not over $12,200 | $1,590, plus 25% of excess over $10,200. |
| Over $12,200 but not over $14,200 | $2,090, plus 27% of excess over $12,200. |
| Over $14,200 but not over $16,200 | $2,630, plus 29% of excess over $14,200. |
| Over $16,200 but not over $18,200 | $3.210, plus 31% of excess over $16,200. |
| Over $18,200 but not over $20,200 | $3,830, plus 34% of excess over $18,200. |
| Over $20,200 but not over $22,200 | $4,510, plus 36% of excess over $20,200. |
| Over $22,200 but not over $24,200 | $5,230, plus 38% of excess over $22,200. |
| Over $24,200 but not over $28,200 | $5,990, plus 40% of excess over $24,200. |
| Over $28,200 but not over $34,200 | $7,590, plus 45% of excess over $28,200. |
| Over $34,200 but not over $40,200 | $10,290, plus 50% of excess over $34,200. |
| Over $40,200 but not over $46,200 | $13,290, plus 55% of excess over $40,200. |
| Over $46,200 but not over $52,200 | $16,590, plus 60% of excess over $46,200. |
| Over $52,200 but not over $62,200 | $20,190, plus 62% of excess over $52,200. |
| Over $62,200 but not over $72,200 | $26,390, plus 64% of excess over $62,200. |
| Over $72,200 but not over $82,200 | $32,790, plus 66% of excess over $72,200. |
| Over $82,200 but not over $92,200 | $39,390, plus 68% of excess over $82,200. |
| Over $92,200 but not over $102,200 | $46,190, plus 69% of excess over $92,200. |
| Over $102,200 | $53,090, plus 70% of excess over $102,200. |

*Married Individuals Filing Separate Returns.*

| "If the taxable income is: | The tax is: |
|---|---|
| Not over $1,600 | No tax. |
| Over $1,600 but not over $2,100 | 14% of the excess over $1,600. |
| Over $2,100 but not over $2,600 | $70, plus 15% of excess over $2,100. |
| Over $2,600 but not over $3,100 | $145, plus 16% of excess over $2,600. |
| Over $3,100 but not over $3,600 | $225, plus 17% of excess over $3,100. |
| Over $3,600 but not over $5,600 | $310, plus 19% of excess over $3,600. |
| Over $5,600 but not over $7,600 | $690, plus 22% of excess over $5,600. |
| Over $7,600 but not over $9,600 | $1,130, plus 25% of excess over $7,600. |
| Over $9,600 but not over $11,600 | $1,630, plus 28% of excess over $9,600. |

FIGURE 6-7 (continued)

| "If the taxable income is: | The tax is: |
|---|---|
| Over $11,600 but not over $13,600 | $2,190, plus 32% of excess over $11,600. |
| Over $13,600 but not over $15,600 | $2,830, plus 36% of excess over $13,600. |
| Over $15,600 but not over $17,600 | $3,550, plus 39% of excess over $15,600. |
| Over $17,600 but not over $19,600 | $4,330, plus 42% of excess over $17,600. |
| Over $19,600 but not over $21,600 | $5,170, plus 45% of excess over $19,600. |
| Over $21,600 but not over $23,600 | $6,070, plus 48% of excess over $21,600. |
| Over $23,600 but not over $27,600 | $7,030, plus 50% of excess over $23,600. |
| Over $27,600 but not over $33,600 | $9,030, plus 53% of excess over $27,600. |
| Over $33,600 but not over $39,600 | $12,210, plus 55% of excess over $33,600. |
| Over $39,600 but not over $45,600 | $15,510, plus 58% of excess over $39,600. |
| Over $45,600 but not over $51,600 | $18,990, plus 60% of excess over $45,600. |
| Over $51,600 but not over $61,600 | $22,590, plus 62% of excess over $51,600. |
| Over $61,600 but not over $71,600 | $28,790, plus 64% of excess over $61,600. |
| Over $71,600 but not over $81,600 | $35,190, plus 66% of excess over $71,600. |
| Over $81,600 but not over $91,600 | $41,790, plus 68% of excess over $81,600. |
| Over $91,600 but not over $101,600 | $48,590, plus 69% of excess over $91,600. |
| Over $101,600 | $55,490, plus 70% of excess over $101,600. |

*Estates and Trusts.*

| "If the taxable income is: | The tax is: |
|---|---|
| Not over $500 | 14% of the taxable income. |
| Over $500 but not over $1,000 | $70, plus 15% of excess over $500. |
| Over $1,000 but not over $1,500 | $145, plus 16% of excess over $1,000. |
| Over $1,500 but not over $2,000 | $225, plus 17% of excess over $1,500. |
| Over $2,000 but not over $4,000 | $310, plus 19% of excess over $2,000. |
| Over $4,000 but not over $6,000 | $690, plus 22% of excess over $4,000. |
| Over $6,000 but not over $8,000 | $1,130, plus 25% of excess over $6,000. |
| Over $8,000 but not over $10,000 | $1,630, plus 28% of excess over $8,000. |
| Over $10,000 but not over $12,000 | $2,190, plus 32% of excess over $10,000. |
| Over $12,000 but not over $14,000 | $2,830, plus 36% of excess over $12,000. |
| Over $14,000 but not over $16,000 | $3,550, plus 39% of excess over $14,000. |
| Over $16,000 but not over $18,000 | $4,330, plus 42% of excess over $16,000. |
| Over $18,000 but not over $20,000 | $5,170, plus 45% of excess over $18,000. |
| Over $20,000 but not over $22,000 | $6,070, plus 48% of excess over $20,000. |

FIGURE 6-7 (continued)

| **"If the taxable income is:** | **The tax is:** |
|---|---|
| Over $22,000 but not over $26,000 | $7,030, plus 50% of excess over $22,000. |
| Over $26,000 but not over $32,000 | $9,030, plus 53% of excess over $26,000. |
| Over $32,000 but not over $38,000 | $12,210, plus 55% of excess over $32,000. |
| Over $38,000 but not over $44,000 | $15,510, plus 58% of excess over $38,000. |
| Over $44,000 but not over $50,000 | $18,990, plus 60% of excess over $44,000. |
| Over $50,000 but not over $60,000 | $22,590, plus 62% of excess over $50,000. |
| Over $60,000 but not over $70,000 | $28,790, plus 64% of excess over $60,000. |
| Over $70,000 but not over $80,000 | $35,190, plus 66% of excess over $70,000. |
| Over $80,000 but not over $90,000 | $41,790, plus 68% of excess over $80,000. |
| Over $90,000 but not over $100,000 | $48,590, plus 69% of excess over $90,000. |
| Over $100,000 | $55,490, plus 70% of excess over $100,000." |

earn $12,000 after taxes, the average person is probably more likely to do that than to say, "Hang the whole thing!" and work less, thus cutting after-tax income still more.

3. Professional people, corporate executives, and similar persons have a great deal of discretionary control over how much they work. But their motives for working are highly complex. Few executives, for instance, appear to feel that tax considerations have major impact on the amount of effort they bring to their jobs. Such persons may, if anything, work harder as they try to achieve self-set goals of financial solvency or consumption—for example, as they try to keep up with the proverbial Joneses.

## CASE EXCERPTS

*W. Roland* and *Stella H. Cooper* v. *U.S.* (DC-Ala. 1975) 36 AFTR 2d 75-5419
*Adolph Posner,* Tax Court Memo 1976–216.

### *W. Roland* and *Stella H. Cooper* v. *U.S.* (DC-Ala. 1975) 36 AFTR 2d 75-5419

A state senator also was the sole proprietor of an auto dealership. Neither he nor his wife owned a car; rather they used dealership cars and the dealership claimed a tax deduction for the auto expense. The Coopers also claimed a tax deduction for gasoline taxes personally paid, and the I.R.S. did not challenge that deduction. The I.R.S. disallowed $4,800 per year as the business expenses attributed to the personal use of automobiles. The Coopers paid the deficiency and then sued for a refund.

In the instant case the plaintiffs did not offer direct evidence as to the deductible expenses attributable to the business expenses associated with the automobiles. Instead, the plaintiffs offered mileage estimates and a formula to be used by the court to compute the amount of nondeductible expenses attributable to their personal use of the automobiles.

The plaintiffs estimated the mileage associated with their personal use for the two years involved (2,000 miles for Mr. Cooper and 2,600 miles for Mrs. Cooper) and contended that the total of their mileage (4,600 miles) should be multiplied by 10 cents a mile and the result ($460.00) should then be deducted from the total expenses disallowed ($9,600.00) to arrive at the amount of deductible business related expenses ($9,140.00) improperly disallowed by the Commissioner.

*The plaintiffs' itemized deductions for the years involved include a deduction for state gasoline taxes in the amount of $65.00 for 1966 . . . . and $100.00 for 1967.*

*The deductions, computed by the plaintiffs on the basis of the gasoline tax imposed by this state, reflect mileage for personal use in excess of 12,000 miles in 1966 and 20,000 miles in 1967 by resort to the state gasoline tax tables prepared by the I.R.S. for the years involved.*

The court resolves the conflict between the plaintiffs' in-court estimate and their claim for gasoline tax deductions by finding that the plaintiffs' formula should be applied to the mileage estimates of 12,000 miles and 20,000 miles reflected by the tax tables for the years involved.

*Accordingly, $1,200.00 for 1966 and $2,000.00 for 1967 were properly disallowed as nondeductible expenses associated with the personal use of the automobiles and $3,600.00 and $2,800.00 for the respective years were deductible business expenses improperly disallowed by the Commissioner.*

*Adolph Posner,* Tax Court Memo 1976-216

What is the fair market value of something? While the income tax is not imposed on unrealized increases in value, questions of value arise both in ascertaining the amount of income and determining the amount of deductions. This case involves a charitable contribution deduction.

In 1969 petitioner donated a painting by Antonio Zanchi to the university art gallery of the State University of New York at Binghamton. Zanchi was a Venetian painter in the Baroque style. The gallery had the painting appraised by Mr. Clyde Newhouse, who valued it at $15,000. Petitioner thereupon claimed a charitable deduction for 1969 of $15,000, allowable under section 170(a)(1).

Respondent's Art Advisory Panel determined the value of the painting to be $5,000, whereupon respondent disallowed the deduction to the extent of $10,000. It is undisputed that a donation was made to an educational institution qualifying as a charitable organization for purposes of section 170. The only question for our determination is the amount of the deduction.

If a contribution is made in property other than money, the amount of the charitable deduction allowed is the fair market value of the property at the time of the contribution. The fair market value is the price at which the property would change hands between a willing buyer and a willing seller, where neither is under any compulsion to buy or sell and both are cognizant of the relevant facts. Section 1.170-1(c)(1), Income Tax Regs. The fair market value of the same property may vary, depending on the market in which the property is sold. Daniel S. McGuire, 44 T.C. 801, 806 (1965).

The Court is thus faced with an opinion by petitioner's expert, who placed a valuation of $15,000 on the painting, ostensibly prior to having made an in-depth study of the subject; the opinion of respondent's expert, who placed a value of $1,500 on the painting on the assumption that the subject was in poor condition and has been overpainted to the extent of 50 percent; and evidence that a painting by Zanchi entitled "The Holy Family" had been sold at auction for a price of $2,592 in 1971. In the face of such conflicting evidence, the Court is unable to find as a fact that the value of the painting exceeded $5,000.

## QUESTIONS AND PROBLEMS

1. If two otherwise identical businesses were, respectively, a sole proprietorship and a corporation, would you expect the taxable income of the corporation to be the same amount as the net profit (or loss) reported on Schedule C of the individual return? Why?
2. What sort of a net-worth reconciliation does the individual income tax return contain as contrasted to the partnership return or corporate return?
3. Some self-employed persons complain because they have to pay a higher rate of Social Security tax than do employees. Some critics of the Social Security law contend that it is inequitable because self-employed persons pay less tax than employees. What are the facts? Illustrate with a tax computation for a hypothetical individual as an employee and then as a self-employed person.
4. What is the difference between a marginal tax rate and an average tax rate? Which do you think has most impact on decisions?
5. At some taxable-income point, an individual would pay less income tax if he were married than if he were single. Assuming that the intended spouse has income exactly equal to her deductions and exemptions, how much taxable

income is necessary before this point is reached? How much taxable income is necessary before the single man finds it worth $2,000 per year to be married?

6. A married couple may find that from a tax viewpoint, they would be better off not being married if both have income. Construct an example of a situation where two people would be better off by living together without being married than they would be if married. Assuming that husband and wife earn equal incomes, what would their level of taxable income have to be before marriage was costing them $2,000 per year of income tax?

7. Visualize a married man, whose nonbusiness income exactly offsets his nonbusiness deductions and exemptions, and who would draw an annual salary of $25,000 per year if his business were incorporated. How much would his business have to be netting before he would save on the combined annual corporate and personal income tax by incorporating? How much would his business profit have to be before he would be saving $5,000 per year by incorporating?

8. An individual itemizes his deductions rather than taking the standard deduction. He is in a 60 percent marginal tax bracket. Collision insurance on his personal car is not deductible on his tax return, but damage to his car as the result of a collision is deductible to the extent it exceeds $100 per accident. Full collision coverage will cost $600 a year. A $500 deductible policy (that is, the policy will reimburse only for losses sustained to the extent they exceed $500) will cost only $250 a year. Which policy is he going to be better off getting, assuming that he has an accident every other year, and that each accident involves a loss of $1,500?

9. The Cooper case involved automobile expenses.
   (a) Describe the basic inconsistency reflected in the Cooper returns.
   (b) How heavy a burden of proof did the judge impose on the Coopers relative to the amount of expenses he allowed (e.g., any modicum of evidence, even though a self-serving statement; some corroboration other than the taxpayer's own statement; a burden of proving beyond the shadow of a doubt)?

10. Using the income and expenses on the trial balance of the Sadler Corporation (Problem 6, Chapter 3), assume that George Sadler is the proprietor of the Sadler Company. His capital account at the beginning of the year had a balance of $125,000. He took out of the business in addition to his $20,000 cash drawing in July, a salary of $55,000, which is listed as an expense. George is married to Martha Sadler. They have no income or deductions other than the data reflected on the books of Sadler Company and their own personal tax exemptions. Neither is over 65 or blind. Prepare their income tax return (Form 1040 plus Schedule C).

11. Rex Call is employed as sales manager by the C-D Manufacturing Company. During the year, he received an expense allowance from his employer of $24

per day for 100 days he spent away from home on business. In addition, he received an allowance of $50 per month for entertainment expenses, for which he was not required to make an accounting to his employer. His expenses for meals and lodging total $2,250 for the days away from home on business. He incurred entertainment expenses of $1,350 for which he has detailed records identifying salesmen, prospective salesmen, and customers entertained, and the place, nature, amount, and business reason for the incurrence of each item of expense. He wants to deduct the excess of his expenses over the amount reimbursed him. Prepare a Statement of Employee Business Expenses, Form 2106, to accompany Mr. Call's Form 1040.

12. Indicate whether each of the following statements is true or false, relative to an individual taxpayer's joint return:
    (a) Self-employed persons pay their Social Security (FICA) as a part of their income tax.
    (b) There are no situations where the taxpayers are worse-off filing a joint return than filing separate returns.
    *(c) If a child is under 19 or is a full-time student, his parents can claim an exemption for him regardless of how much he earns or how much of his support they provide.
    *(d) Pay received while absent from work due to injury or illness may be excluded from income, up to $100 a week, from the first day of absence. (Assume 1978 or later.)
    (e) Medical expenses are deductible only to the extent they exceed 3 percent of adjusted gross income.
    (f) Under the "pay-as-you-go" approach to the individual income tax, persons who receive wages, salaries, dividends, interest, or rents have tax withheld on these payments by the payors.
    (g) Persons receiving over $500 of income not subject to withholding, and whose estimated excess of actual tax liability over the taxes withheld will be $100 or more, are among the persons required to file declarations of estimated tax and pay their estimated tax in quarterly installments.

13. John Parket, who is unmarried and 66 years old, has the following items of income and deductions:

| Income: | |
|---|---|
| Dividends received from domestic manufacturing corporations | $ 950 |
| Interest income from corporations | 220 |
| Interest income on municipal bonds | 163 |
| Social Security benefits (not subject to tax) | 1,600 |
| Rental income | 1,800 |

| | | |
|---|---|---|
| Earnings from odd jobs (per W-2 forms, no income tax withheld) | $1,250 | |
| Deductions: | | |
| Depreciation on rental property | | $200 |
| Taxes and insurance on rental property | | 80 |
| Contributions: | | |
| First Presbyterian Church | | 900 |
| American Cancer Society | | 15 |
| Sheltering Arms Hospital | | 25 |
| Ohio University Fund | | 150 |
| State and local taxes | | 175 |
| Dr. I.X. Pensive, M.D. | | 315 |
| Interest paid Prudential Insurance Co. on home mortgage | | 212 |

Prepare Parket's income tax return making such additional assumptions as you wish regarding items not mentioned above (address, Social Security number, etc.).

*14. Leon Charles and his wife, Mary Lu, live at 1224 Skyline Drive, Inner City, Florida 33131. Leon is 52, Mary is 48. Their three children are Albert, 20, a full-time student at State University; Judith Ann, 16, a high school student; and George, 10. Mrs. Charles' mother, Luella Carsons, 67, also lives with them.

Albert worked during the summer and earned $900, which he used to buy a car. Judith earned $625, with which she purchased clothing. Mrs. Carsons had income of $810, consisting entirely of dividends on common stock in domestic corporations.

Estimated costs of supporting the Charles' dependents were:

| | |
|---|---|
| Albert | $2,500 |
| Judith | 1,600 |
| George | 1,200 |
| Mrs. Carsons | 4,265 |

The support furnished Mrs. Carsons included hospital and doctor bills of $3,265, with the other $1,000 being the estimated cost of room and board furnished.

Mrs. Charles, who has a B.S. degree in Home Economics, had no earnings during the year. However, she plans to teach in the local high school next year. To qualify for a teacher's certificate, she had to take several courses through the State University extension division. Tuition and books cost her $250. Her Social Security number is 987-68-7555.

Mr. Charles operates a cleaning plant, the A-1 Cleaners, 10102 Mannheim, Inner City. His personal Social Security number is 987-67-6138, and his employer identification number is 36-415473. His business records have been summarized for the year and show:

| | | |
|---|---|---|
| Receipts | | $80,400 |
| Expenses: | | |
| Cleaning supplies | $11,000 | |
| Net wages paid | 18,160 | |
| Payroll taxes withheld | 3,320 | |
| Employer's share of Social Security tax | 440 | |
| Mr. Charles' 1040-ES payments | 3,180 | |
| Repairs | 1,200 | |
| Burns Insurance Agency | 1,575 | |
| Auto expenses | 1,800 | |
| Utilities | 4,775 | |
| Real estate taxes | 400 | |
| Able Machine Company | 3,500 | |
| Rent expense | 1,500 | |
| Attorney's fees | 550 | |
| Interest on equipment | 600 | |
| Union health and welfare | 520 | |
| Miscellaneous (deductible) | 600 | 53,120 |
| Net profit | | $27,280 |

Included in receipts was a refund of federal income taxes. Of the $1,240 received, $1,150 was tax and the balance interest.

The Burns Insurance Agency expense included $125 on a policy covering the Charles' personal residence. The balance paid to Burns was for insurance on the business equipment.

During the year, Mr. Charles drove his auto 20,000 miles, of which 10,000 miles were for business. Auto expenses include state gasoline tax of $30.

The $4,775 paid for utilities includes $650 applicable to the Charles' personal residence. The real estate taxes relate entirely to the personal residence.

The $3,500 paid Able Machine Company was a down payment on a $12,000 cleaning machine purchased on June 30. The machine has an estimated life of ten years and will be depreciated on a straight-line basis with zero salvage value. Depreciation on the equipment owned at the start of the year will total $6,000.

The attorney received an annual retainer of $300 for handling customer claims. He was also paid $250 for preparing a will.

On June 30, $45 in interest was credited to a savings account at the First National Bank, and an additional $65 was credited on December 31. State sales taxes of $250 on personal purchases were paid during the year. State sales taxes on business purchases are included as part of the cost of the items purchased. Amounts paid by the Charleses to physicians, other than those paid for Mrs. Carsons, amounted to $350 for the year. In addition, $400 of medical insurance premiums were paid.

Mr. and Mrs. Charles made regular donations of $1,000 during the year to the First Christian Church and gave another $750 to the church building fund.

Prepare the individual income tax return of Mr. and Mrs. Charles.

*15. Mrs. Smith has been offered a job at a local advertising agency at $10,000 per year. Her husband makes $12,000 as a teacher. The Smiths have one child who is four years old and for whom they must provide care, if Mrs. Smith is to work. A local day care center will provide that service for $300 per month. What will be Mrs. Smith's after-tax contribution to the family income if we assume that commuting, lunches, clothing, etc., will represent an incremental cost of $900 per year?

*16. The Posner case deals with the valuation of a painting donated to an art gallery. Give three examples of other situations where the fair market value of something might be relevant to the determination of an individual's federal income tax? (Hint: Any income received other than in cash or any deductions claimed which were paid with other than cash might involve valuation questions.)

# 7

# Fiduciary Income Tax

We shall round out our survey of types of income tax returns by taking a superficial look at the fiduciary return. Let's call our old friend John M. Doe back into the picture. He has not married and/or incorporated after all. John has an emotional problem regarding his mother and his sister, who is 20 years younger than John. For this he probably needs a psychiatrist (fees paid to whom are deductible as a medical expense, subject, of course, to the 3 percent limitation). But instead, John talks to a tax practitioner and decides to set up a trust.

He transfers to the trust securities with a fair market value of $150,000, which are producing $20 000 a year in dividends—a high yield speculative promotional stock. For as long as she lives, John's mother is to receive the income from the trust; when she dies, the income will go to John's sister. Upon the sister's death, the trust will terminate and the assets will be distributed to her children or their descendants.

Gifts of property, whether outright or through a trust, have gift tax and estate tax implications and consequences over and above their income tax aspects. Chapter 19 will explore gift and estate taxes. John's gift through a trust may cost him some gift taxes, but it should remove any increases in value of the stock from being subject to estate tax when he dies. The gift taxes he pays now will, in effect, be recouped by the offset against the estate taxes due when he dies. If the stock does not increase in value, then John is paying $X now for the privilege of making a gift and avoiding paying the same $X at an indeterminate future time as well as the estate tax on the $X itself. It is unlikely that the dollars and cents of this make sense unless either: (1) his nontax motives are strong, or (2) he thinks that what he gives away will increase substantially in value so that his payment of $X now avoids his estate paying $X++ in tax in the future on the then much higher valuation of the property. More will be said of this in Chapter 19.

By transferring the property into a trust instead of giving it to his mother outright, John is assured that his mother will not squander the property and that his sister and her children will be taken care of.

## OPERATION OF THE TRUST

The stock is turned over to the trust department of the Mountain National Bank, together with a long document called a *trust agreement,* which sets forth exactly how the Mountain National Bank is to handle this trust. Once the trust agreement has been signed and the stock delivered to the bank, the deed is done. John cannot later recant and take his stock back. There are trusts in which it is possible for the grantor to get the trust assets back, but these create gift tax, estate tax, and income tax complications that go beyond the simple presentation that we want to limit ourselves to here.

The bank is now a *fiduciary,* which simply means that it has legal title to and possession of assets that it owns for somebody else. As a fiduciary, it collects the income of the trust and pays it over to John's mother. It must file an income tax return annually.

The term *fiduciary* includes executors, administrators, guardians, receivers for individuals, and conservators, as well as trustees. If a trust is created by a will, it is called a *testamentary* trust. All other trusts are called *inter vivos* trusts.

Income concepts are the same for a trust as for an individual, with gross income and deductions determined by the same rules. Deduction is allowed for reasonable trustees' fees and other expenses of administering the property of the trust, but no standard deduction is permitted. In lieu of the personal exemption, a *simple trust* is given a $300 exemption, and a *complex trust* a $100 exemption. (These terms are defined below.) Trusts are subject to the tax-rate schedule applicable to married persons filing separate returns and do not receive the benefit of the lower rate schedule for single persons.

### *A Simple Trust*

A *simple trust* is one that is required to distribute all its income currently, such as the trust John has set up. Figure 7-1 reflects a fiduciary return for John's simple trust. The fiduciary winds up with no income on which to pay tax, since all the income is distributed to Mrs. Doe. She will report her income from the trust as dividend income on her personal return.

Capital gains represent taxable income, but unless the trust instrument specifies otherwise, for trust accounting purposes they represent additions to principal, and thus are not distributable to the income beneficiary; accordingly, the trust is taxed on capital gains, against which the $300 exemption can be utilized.

Form **1041** — Department of the Treasury, Internal Revenue Service

**U.S. Fiduciary Income Tax Return**
for the year January 1–December 31, 197 or other taxable year
beginning ............, 197 and ending ............, 19....

**19**

Check whether:
☐ Estate
☒ Simple trust
☐ Complex-trust
If trust, check whether:
☐ Testamentary
☒ Inter vivos
☐ "Grantor type"
Also check if:
☐ Pooled income fund

Name of estate or trust ("Grantor type" trusts, see instruction O.)
DOE TRUST, #623

Name and title of fiduciary
MOUNTAIN NATIONAL BANK, TRUSTEE

Address of fiduciary (number and street)
20 CONGRESS STREET

City, State, and ZIP code
VALHALLA, ARIZONA

Employer identification number

Nonexempt charitable and split-interest trusts check applicable boxes (See Inst. U.):
☐ Described in section 4947(a)(1)
☐ Not treated as a private foundation by reason of sec. 509(a)(1), (2) or (3)
☐ Described in section 4947(a)(2)

Is this the first return? ☐ Yes ☐ No. If "No," has the fiduciary's address changed? ☐ Yes ☐ No.

| | | | | | |
|---|---|---|---|---|---|
| INCOME | 1 Dividends (Enter full amount before exclusion) | 1 | 20,000 | | |
| | 2 Interest | 2 | | | |
| | 3 Income from partnerships and other fiduciaries | 3 | | | |
| | 4 Gross rents and royalties | 4 | | | |
| | 5 Gross profit (loss) from trade or business | 5 | | | |
| | 6 Net gain (loss) from capital assets (Attach Schedule D (Form 1041)) | 6 | | | |
| | 7 Ordinary gains and (losses) (Attach Form 4797) | 7 | | | |
| | 8 Other income (State nature of income) | 8 | | | |
| | 9 Total income (lines 1 to 8, inclusive) | | | 9 | 20,000 |
| DEDUCTIONS | 10 Interest | 10 | | | |
| | 11 Taxes | 11 | | | |
| | 12 Fiduciary's portion of depreciation (Schedule A) and depletion. Explain depletion | 12 | | | |
| | 13 Charitable deduction (Schedule B, line 9) | 13 | | | |
| | 14 Other deductions (Itemize) Trust fee | 14 | 450 | | |
| | 15 Total (lines 10 to 14, inclusive) | | | 15 | 450 |
| | 16 Line 9 minus line 15 (Complex trusts and estates enter this amount in Schedule C, line 1 also) | | | 16 | 19,550 |
| | 17 Deduction for distributions to beneficiaries | 17 | 19,550 | | |
| | 18 Adjustment of dividend exclusion | 18 | | | |
| | 19 Federal estate tax attributable to income in respect of a decedent (Fiduciary's share) | 19 | | | |
| | 20 Long-term capital gain deduction. Enter 50% of Schedule D (Form 1041) line 17e | 20 | | | |
| | 21 Exemption (If final return, see General Instruction M.) | 21 | | | |
| | 22 Total (lines 17 to 21, inclusive) | | | 22 | 19,550 |
| | 23 Taxable income of fiduciary (line 16 minus line 22) | | | 23 | -0- |
| COMPUTATION OF TAX | 24 Tax on amount on line 23 (See tax rate schedule) | | | 24 | |
| | 25 If alternative tax is applicable, enter the tax from Schedule D (Form 1041) line 29 | | | 25 | |
| | 26 Fiduciary's share of foreign tax credit (Attach Form 1116) | 26 | | | |
| | 27 Fiduciary's share of investment credit (Attach Form 3468) | 27 | | | |
| | 28 Fiduciary's share of work incentive (WIN) program credit (Attach Form 4874) | 28 | | | |
| | 29 Total (lines 26 to 28, inclusive) | | | 29 | |
| | 30 Balance (line 24 or 25, whichever is applicable, less line 29) | | | 30 | |
| | 31 Tax from recomputing fiduciary's share of prior year investment credit (Attach Form 4255) | | | 31 | |
| | 32 Minimum tax (Attach Form 4626) | | | 32 | |
| | 33 Total (lines 30 to 32, inclusive) | | | 33 | |
| | 34 Fiduciary's share of credit for tax paid at source on tax-free convenant bond interest | 34 | | | |
| | 35 Credit for Federal tax on special fuels, nonhighway gas and lub. oil (Attach Form 4136) | 35 | | | |
| | 36 Credit from regulated investment companies (Attach Form 2439) | 36 | | | |
| | 37 Tax previously paid (See Instruction 37 and attach Form 2758) | 37 | | | |
| | 38 Federal income tax withheld (Attach Form W–2) | 38 | | | |
| | 39 Total (lines 34 to 38, inclusive) | | | 39 | |
| | 40 Balance of tax due (line 33 less line 39) | | | 40 | |
| | 41 Overpayment (line 39 less line 33) | | | 41 | |

Under penalties of perjury, I declare that I have examined this return, including accompanying schedules and statements, and to the best of my knowledge and belief it is true, correct, and complete. If prepared by a person other than taxpayer, this declaration is based on all information of which the preparer has any knowledge.

**Sign here** ▶ ............ Signature of fiduciary or officer representing fiduciary ............ Date

▶ ............ Signature of preparer other than fiduciary (and employer's name) ............ Date

............ Identifying number (see Instructions) ............ Address and ZIP code

FIGURE 7-1
Simple Trust Return

## *A Complex Trust*

Let's assume that John wanted only half the trust gross income to go to his mother, with the other half being accumulated so it would ultimately build up a tidy sum for his nieces and nephews. Such a trust, one not required to distribute all income currently, is a *complex trust.* The trust return would then look like Figure 7-2.

This trust return is rather an odd duck, compared with anything we have seen before. It operates on the conduit theory to the extent of the amount being distributed to Mrs. Doe (which, of course, she still picks up on her return as dividend income). But it is also treated as taxable entity in itself, taxable on income not distributed. This is accomplished by giving a deduction to the trust for amounts distributed. Because taxpayers, wishing the trust rather than a high-bracket beneficiary to be taxed, created trusts that accumulated income but distributed principal, the tax law now provides that principal as well as income distributions operate to shift income from the trust to the beneficiary. So if, in accordance with powers given the trustee in the trust agreement, the trustee were to distribute part of the principal of the trust to John's mother for emergency medical care or other needs, the distribution would be treated as an income distribution, deductible by the trust and taxable to John's mother, to the extent of any prior undistributed earnings of the trust.

## INCOME TAX SAVINGS

Let's see what happened to John Doe's total tax payment after he created the complex trust and how much total income tax the government is now collecting as compared with the tax collected before the trust was created:

| | | |
|---|---|---|
| Pre-trust tax on John Doe (exclusive of self-employment tax) using 1976 rates | | $49,219 |
| Post-trust tax: | | |
| On John Doe | $35,745 | |
| On Mrs. Doe (assuming no other income, over 65, and standard deduction) | 1,160 | |
| On the trust | 2,022 | 38,927 |
| Difference (saving to the family group) | | $10,292 |

The substantial tax savings result from the shifting of income from the high tax brackets of John Doe to the lower tax brackets of his mother and the trust. The optimum shift in income yielding the highest possible tax savings would result when all three taxpayers end up in the same top marginal bracket.

### *Throwback Rules*

Perceptive taxpayers had long utilized these concepts to reduce their overall tax burden, but after some particularly inventive taxpayers had conceived the idea of multiple trusts to create multiple taxpayers, taxing income in the lowest possible brackets, Congress reacted with a drastic legislative remedy—the *unlimited throwback rule.*

Form **1041**
Department of the Treasury
Internal Revenue Service

**U.S. Fiduciary Income Tax Return**
for the year January 1–December 31, 197 or other taxable year
beginning ............, 197 and ending ............, 19....

**19**

Check whether:
☐ Estate
☐ Simple trust
☒ Complex-trust
If trust, check whether:
☐ Testamentary
☒ Inter vivos
☐ "Grantor type"
Also check if:
☐ Pooled income fund

Name of estate or trust ("Grantor type" trusts, see instruction O.)
DOE TRUST, #623

Name and title of fiduciary
MOUNTAIN NATIONAL BANK, TRUSTEE

Address of fiduciary (number and street)
20 CONGRESS STREET

City, State, and ZIP code
VALHALLA, ARIZONA

Employer identification number

Nonexempt charitable and split-interest trusts check applicable boxes (See Inst. U.):
☐ Described in section 4947(a)(1)
☐ Not treated as a private foundation by reason of sec. 509(a) (1), (2) or (3)
☐ Described in section 4947(a)(2)

Is this the first return? ☐ Yes ☐ No. If "No," has the fiduciary's address changed? ☐ Yes ☐ No.

| | | | | | | |
|---|---|---|---|---|---|---|
| INCOME | 1 | Dividends (Enter full amount before exclusion) | 1 | 20,000 | | |
| | 2 | Interest | 2 | | | |
| | 3 | Income from partnerships and other fiduciaries | 3 | | | |
| | 4 | Gross rents and royalties | 4 | | | |
| | 5 | Gross profit (loss) from trade or business | 5 | | | |
| | 6 | Net gain (loss) from capital assets (Attach Schedule D (Form 1041)) | 6 | | | |
| | 7 | Ordinary gains and (losses) (Attach Form 4797) | 7 | | | |
| | 8 | Other income (State nature of income) | 8 | | | |
| | 9 | Total income (lines 1 to 8, inclusive) | | | 9 | 20,000 |
| DEDUCTIONS | 10 | Interest | 10 | | | |
| | 11 | Taxes | 11 | | | |
| | 12 | Fiduciary's portion of depreciation (Schedule A) and depletion. Explain depletion | 12 | | | |
| | 13 | Charitable deduction (Schedule B, line 9) | 13 | | | |
| | 14 | Other deductions (Itemize) Trust fee | 14 | 450 | | |
| | 15 | Total (lines 10 to 14, inclusive) | | | 15 | 450 |
| | 16 | Line 9 minus line 15 (Complex trusts and estates enter this amount in Schedule C, line 1 also) | | | 16 | 19,550 |
| | 17 | Deduction for distributions to beneficiaries | 17 | 10,000 | | |
| | 18 | Adjustment of dividend exclusion | 18 | 50 | | |
| | 19 | Federal estate tax attributable to income in respect of a decedent (Fiduciary's share) | 19 | | | |
| | 20 | Long-term capital gain deduction. Enter 50% of Schedule D (Form 1041) line 17e | 20 | | | |
| | 21 | Exemption (If final return, see General Instruction M.) | 21 | 100 | | |
| | 22 | Total (lines 17 to 21, inclusive) | | | 22 | 10,150 |
| | 23 | Taxable income of fiduciary (line 16 minus line 22) | | | 23 | 9,400 |
| COMPUTATION OF TAX | 24 | Tax on amount on line 23 (See tax rate schedule) | | | 24 | 2,022 |
| | 25 | If alternative tax is applicable, enter the tax from Schedule D (Form 1041) line 29 | | | 25 | |
| | 26 | Fiduciary's share of foreign tax credit (Attach Form 1116) | 26 | | | |
| | 27 | Fiduciary's share of investment credit (Attach Form 3468) | 27 | | | |
| | 28 | Fiduciary's share of work incentive (WIN) program credit (Attach Form 4874) | 28 | | | |
| | 29 | Total (lines 26 to 28, inclusive) | | | 29 | |
| | 30 | Balance (line 24 or 25, whichever is applicable, less line 29) | | | 30 | 2,022 |
| | 31 | Tax from recomputing fiduciary's share of prior year investment credit (Attach Form 4255) | | | 31 | |
| | 32 | Minimum tax (Attach Form 4626) | | | 32 | |
| | 33 | Total (lines 30 to 32, inclusive) | | | 33 | 2,022 |
| | 34 | Fiduciary's share of credit for tax paid at source on tax-free convenant bond interest | 34 | | | |
| | 35 | Credit for Federal tax on special fuels, nonhighway gas and lub. oil (Attach Form 4136) | 35 | | | |
| | 36 | Credit from regulated investment companies (Attach Form 2439) | 36 | | | |
| | 37 | Tax previously paid (See Instruction 37 and attach Form 2758) | 37 | | | |
| | 38 | Federal income tax withheld (Attach Form W–2) | 38 | | | |
| | 39 | Total (lines 34 to 38, inclusive) | | | 39 | |
| | 40 | Balance of tax due (line 33 less line 39) | | | 40 | 2,022 |
| | 41 | Overpayment (line 39 less line 33) | | | 41 | |

Under penalties of perjury, I declare that I have examined this return, including accompanying schedules and statements, and to the best of my knowledge and belief it is true, correct, and complete. If prepared by a person other than taxpayer, this declaration is based on all information of which the preparer has any knowledge.

**Sign here** ▶ ............ Signature of fiduciary or officer representing fiduciary ............ Date

▶ ............ Signature of preparer other than fiduciary (and employer's name) ............ Date

............ Identifying number (see Instructions) ............ Address and ZIP code

FIGURE 7-2
Complex Trust Return

Trusts are taxed, as before, on income accumulated. But when distributions are made in later years, the trust beneficiary must pay tax on such distributions based on the number of years during which the amount distributed by the trust was accumulated and the beneficiary's own taxable income during the five years immediately preceding the distribution. All other things being equal, the longer the period over which the trust accumulated the income, the lower the beneficiary's tax, since the amount of the distribution is divided by the number of years accumulated to arrive at the average annual accumulation on which tax will be calculated. Similarly, the lower the income of the beneficiary during the preceding five years, the less the tax, since the tax will be calculated by adding to his taxable income for three of those years (dropping the years of highest and lowest taxable income) the average accumulation represented in the distribution. The beneficiary receives a credit for taxes originally paid by the trust, so there is no duplication of tax paid.

John's nieces and nephews will eventually be taxed on the income accumulated by the trust, but they will receive credit for the taxes paid by the trust.

The complexities comprising our tax law, exemplified by the trust tax throwback provisions, result from ingenious "loopholes" fashioned by sophisticated taxpayers, closed by equally sophisticated remedial legislation, followed by still more ingenious "loopholes," followed by further legislative revision, and so on.

## TAX PROBLEMS OF A DECEDENT

Although the trust is a most interesting type of taxpayer, especially from the standpoint of tax planning, there are other types of fiduciaries. The estate of a dead person, during the period in which the wishes of the decedent are being carried out, is normally managed by a fiduciary (called an *executor* if appointed under the will, or an *administrator* if appointed by a court).

Everything belongs to someone. When a person dies, the title to all the things he owns ceases to be in him. Those things he held in joint tenancy now belong to the surviving joint tenant. Other things he owned become the property of an executor or an administrator. The executor is a fiduciary, holding the property only until the decedent's wishes can be ascertained and carried out. He will manage the property in the meantime and then finally turn it over to the decedent's heirs. One of the heirs may, of course, be a testamentary trust.

Let us for the last time recall our old friend, John M. Doe. He has never married and has decided against incorporation and against forming a trust for the benefit of his mother and sister. A number of years have gone by and he has now retired from business; his income now consists exclusively of consulting fees of \$500 per month and dividend income of \$60,000 per year. The year is 1981, and John is in good health. There is no reason he should die, except that we need a decedent in order to continue our discussion, and so with some gentle exercise of editorial license, we will permit him to pass away while sleeping on June 30, 1981.

Shortly before his death, John had received five months' consulting fees, or \$2,500, and he had earned an additional \$500 for the month of June, but he died before it could be paid to him, and so the executor of his estate received it. Of the $60,000 dividend income received in 1981, $40,000 was declared and paid prior to his death and $20,000 was declared after and paid to his executor. John paid $5,000 in state income taxes in April 1981, and interest payments on his home were made in the amounts of $500 before he died and of $400 after his death by his executor. The court permitted the fiduciary to pay himself a fee of $5,000, and other expenses of administering the property amounted to $2,000. Figures 7-3, 7-4, and 7-5 demonstrate what John's final tax return and the estate's first fiduciary return will look like.

An income tax return for John (on the regular Form 1040) must be filed by the executor of his estate; it must include the income John received while he was still alive and claim deductions for amounts he paid while still alive. The exemptions available to every taxpayer are allowed in full on the decedent's return for the year of his death. The executor will also file a fiduciary income tax return (on Form 1041, the same form as that used by a trust), which will include all income received by the executor after John's death. This will include as income all items that would have been income to John had he lived to receive them (termed *income in respect of a decedent*), and so the $500 consulting fee received by the executor for services performed by the decedent in June is taxable income to the estate.

A corresponding rule applies for any item that John could have deducted had he lived to pay the amount; such amounts are deductible in the fiduciary income tax return. It happens that the $500 consulting fee is also included in the assets subject to an estate tax upon John's death, and accordingly, double taxation has resulted, there being imposed upon this same item an estate tax and an income tax. For this reason there is allowed a deduction against the income tax in the fiduciary return for that amount of the estate tax that is applicable to the inclusion of the $500, which we will assume was $100. The fiduciary return will also, of course, include the dividends of $20,000 received by the executor after John's death, and the deduction for the $400 interest will be claimed. The estate is entitled to a $600 exemption, rather than the $100 or $300 allowed to simple or complex trusts.

The rule applicable to trusts that distributions of principal are treated as distributions of income is applicable to estates as well (with technical exceptions not discussed here). However, an estate is not subject to the throwback rules applicable to trusts.

When the decedent was married, if the surviving spouse and the executor wish, the decedent's final return may be a joint return. In that event, it will include the income of the surviving spouse for the entire year, even though the decedent's income covers only part of the year.

## SUMMARY

1. The term *fiduciary* includes executors, administrators, guardians, receivers for individuals, and conservators, as well as trustees. Where a trust is

Form **1040** Department of the Treasury—Internal Revenue Service
**U.S. Individual Income Tax Return** 19
This space for IRS use only

For the year January 1–December 31, 197?, or other taxable year beginning ending , 19

Please print or type

| Name (If joint return, give first names and initials of both) | Last name | Your social security number |
|---|---|---|
| JOHN M. | DOE (Deceased) | 360 14 3404 |
| Present home address (Number and street, including apartment number, or rural route) | For Privacy Act Notification, see page 5 of Instructions. | Spouse's social security no. |
| 90 Miramonte | | |
| City, town or post office, State and ZIP code | Occupation: Yours ▶ Consultant; Spouse's ▶ | |
| Valhalla, Arizona 85291 | | |

**Filing Status**

1 [X] Single **(Check only ONE box)**
2 [ ] Married filing joint return (even if only one had income)
3 [ ] Married filing separately. If spouse is also filing give spouse's social security number in designated space above and enter full name here ▶
4 [ ] Unmarried Head of Household. See page 7 of instructions to see if you qualify ▶
5 [ ] Qualifying widow(er) with dependent child (Year spouse died ▶ 19 ). See page 7 of Instructions.

**Exemptions**

6a Regular [X] Yourself [ ] Spouse Enter number of boxes checked ▶ 1
b First names of your dependent children who lived with you Enter number ▶
c Number of other dependents (from line 7) ▶
d Total (add lines 6a, b, and c) ▶ 1
e Age 65 or older. [ ] Yourself [ ] Spouse
Blind. [ ] Yourself [ ] Spouse Enter number of boxes checked ▶
f TOTAL (add lines 6d and e) ▶ 1

| 7 Other dependents: (a) Name | (b) Relationship | (c) Months lived in your home. If born or died during year, write B or D. | (d) Did dependent have income of $750 or more? | (e) Amount furnished for dependent's support: By YOU. If 100% write ALL. | By OTHERS including dependent. |
|---|---|---|---|---|---|
| | | | | $ | $ |

8 **Presidential Election Campaign Fund** ▶ Do you wish to designate $1 of your taxes for this fund? Yes No
If joint return, does your spouse wish to designate $1? Yes No
Note: If you check the "Yes" box(es) it will not increase your tax or reduce your refund.

Please attach Copy B of Forms W-2 here

**Income**

| | | | |
|---|---|---|---|
| 9 | Wages, salaries, tips, and other employee compensation (Attach Forms W-2. If unavailable, see page 6 of Instructions.) | 9 | |
| 10a | Dividends (See pages 9 and 16 of Instructions) 40,000, 10b less exclusion 100, Balance ▶ (If gross dividends and other distributions are over $400, list in Part I of Schedule B.) | 10c | 39,900 |
| 11 | Interest income. {If $400 or less, enter total without listing in Schedule B / If over $400, enter total and list in Part II of Schedule B} | 11 | |
| 12 | Income other than wages, dividends, and interest (from line 37) | 12 | 2,500 |
| 13 | Total (add lines 9, 10c, 11 and 12) | 13 | 42,400 |
| 14 | Adjustments to income (such as moving expense, etc. from line 42) | 14 | |
| 15a | Subtract line 14 from line 13 | 15a | |
| b | Disability income exclusion (sick pay) (attach Form 2440) | 15b | |
| c | **Adjusted gross income.** Subtract line 15b from line 15a, then complete Part III on back. (If less than $8,000, see page 2 of Instructions on "Earned Income Credit.") | 15c | 42,400 |

**Tax, Payments and Credits**

| | | | |
|---|---|---|---|
| 16 | Tax, check if from: [ ] Tax Table [X] Tax Rate Schedule X, Y or Z [ ] Schedule D [ ] Schedule G [ ] Form 2555 OR [ ] Form 4726 | 16 | 12,365 |
| 17a | Multiply $35.00 by the number of exemptions on line 6d — 17a: 35 | | |
| b | Enter 2% of line 47 but not more than $180 ($90 if box 3 is checked) — 17b: 180. Enter larger of a or b (If box on line 3 is checked see page 10 of Instructions) | 17c | 180 |
| 18 | Balance. Subtract line 17c from line 16 and enter difference (but not less than zero) | 18 | 12,185 |
| 19 | Credits (from line 54) | 19 | |
| 20 | Balance. Subtract line 19 from line 18 and enter difference (but not less than zero) | 20 | 12,185 |
| 21 | Other taxes (from line 62) | 21 | 198 |
| 22 | Total (add lines 20 and 21) | 22 | 12,383 |
| 23a | Total Federal income tax withheld (attach Forms W-2, or W-2P to front) | 23a | |
| b | 1976 estimated tax payments (include amount allowed as credit from 1975 return) | 23b | |
| c | Earned income credit (from page 2 of Instructions) | 23c | |
| d | Amount paid with Form 4868 | 23d | |
| e | Other payments (from line 66) | 23e | |
| 24 | TOTAL (add lines 23a through e) ▶ | 24 | |

Pay amount on line 25 in full with this return. Write social security number on check or money order and make payable to Internal Revenue Service.

Please attach Check or Money Order here

**Due or Refund**

| | | | |
|---|---|---|---|
| 25 | If line 22 is larger than line 24, enter **BALANCE DUE IRS** ▶ (Check here ▶ [ ], if Form 2210 or Form 2210F is attached. See page 10 of instructions.) | 25 | |
| 26 | If line 24 is larger than line 22, enter amount **OVERPAID** ▶ | 26 | |
| 27 | Amount of line 26 to be **REFUNDED TO YOU** ▶ | 27 | |
| 28 | Amount of line 26 to be credited on 1977 estimated tax ▶ | 28 | |

Under penalties of perjury, I declare that I have examined this return, including accompanying schedules and statements, and to the best of my knowledge and belief it is true, correct, and complete. Declaration of preparer (other than taxpayer) is based on all information of which preparer has any knowledge.

**Sign here**

▶ Your signature Date ▶ Preparer's signature (and employer's name, if any) Date

▶ Spouse's signature (if filing jointly, BOTH must sign even if only one had income) ▶ Identifying number (see Instructions) Address (and ZIP code)

FIGURE 7-3

Individual Income Tax Return

created by a will, it is called a *testamentary* trust. All other trusts are called *inter vivos* trusts.

2. The income of the fiduciary may be taxed entirely to the fiduciary, entirely to the beneficiaries, or partly to each, the beneficiaries being taxed on

| **Part I** Income other than Wages, Dividends and Interest | | |
|---|---|---|
| 29 Business income or (loss) (attach Schedule C) | 29 | |
| 30a Net gain or (loss) from sale or exchange of capital assets (attach Schedule D) | 30a | |
| b 50% of capital gain distributions (not reported on Schedule D—see page 10 of Instructions). | 30b | |
| 31 Net gain or (loss) from Supplemental Schedule of Gains and Losses (attach Form 4797) | 31 | |
| 32a Pensions, annuities, rents, royalties, partnerships, estates or trusts, etc. (attach Schedule E) | 32a | |
| b Fully taxable pensions and annuities (not reported on Schedule E—see page 10 of Instructions) | 32b | |
| 33 Farm income or (loss) (attach Schedule F) | 33 | |
| 34 State income tax refunds ( does not apply if refund is for year in which you took the standard deduction—others see page 10 of Instructions ) | 34 | |
| 35 Alimony received | 35 | |
| 36 Other (state nature and source—see page 11 of Instructions) ▶ Consulting fees | 36 | 2,500 |
| 37 Total (add lines 29 through 36). Enter here and on line 12 ▶ | 37 | 2,500 |

| Summary of Itemized Deductions **A** | |
|---|---|
| 34 Total medical and dental—line 10 | |
| 35 Total taxes—line 17 | 5,000 |
| 36 Total interest—line 20 | 500 |
| 37 Total contributions—line 24 | |
| 38 Casualty or theft loss(es)—line 29 | |
| 39 Total miscellaneous—line 33 | |
| 40 **Total deductions (add lines 34 through 39).** Enter here and on Form 1040, line 44 ▶ | 5,500 |

Part III Tax Computation

| | | |
|---|---|---|
| Adjusted gross income (from line 15c) | | $42,400 |
| Itemized deductions | $5,500 | |
| Less: Zero bracket amount | 2,200 | |
| Excess itemized deductions | | 3,300 |
| | | 39,100 |
| Less: Exemptions | | 750 |
| Taxable income | | $38,350 |

| | | |
|---|---|---|
| 54 Total (add lines 48 through 53). Enter here and on line 15 ▶ | 54 | |
| **Part V** Other Taxes | | |
| 55 Tax from recomputing prior-year investment credit (attach Form 4255) | 55 | |
| 56 Minimum tax. Check here ▶ ☐, and attach Form 4625 | 56 | |
| 57 Tax on premature distributions from attached Form 5329, Part V | 57 | |
| 58 Self-employment tax (attach Schedule SE) | 58 | 198 |
| 59 Social security tax on tip income not reported to employer (attach Form 4137) | 59 | |
| 60 Uncollected employee social security tax on tips (from Forms W-2) | 60 | |
| 61 Excess contribution tax from attached Form 5329, Part IV | 61 | |
| 62 Total (add lines 55 through 61). Enter here and on line 21 ▶ | 62 | 198 |
| **Part VI** Other Payments | | |

FIGURE 7-4
Tax Computations

income distributed. A *simple* trust is one that must distribute all its income currently to beneficiaries. A *complex* trust is one in which all or part of the trust income is accumulated for future distribution.

3. Income concepts are the same for a fiduciary as for an individual, but trusts and estates must use the tax rates for trusts and estates.

4. Deductions for a fiduciary are generally the same as for an individual. Deductible expenses include those for preservation and management of the estate.

Form **1041** — **U.S. Fiduciary Income Tax Return**

Department of the Treasury
Internal Revenue Service

| Check whether: | |
|---|---|
| ☒ Estate | Name of estate or trust ("Grantor type" trusts, see instruction O.): ESTATE OF JOHN DOE |
| ☐ Simple trust | Employer Identification Number: |
| ☐ Complex trust | Name and title of fiduciary: MOUNTAIN NATIONAL BANK, EXECUTOR |
| If trust, check whether: ☐ Testamentary ☐ Inter vivos | Address of fiduciary (number and street): 20 CONGRESS STREET |
| Also check whether: ☐ Pooled income fund | City, State, and ZIP code: VALHALLA, ARIZONA |

| | | | | |
|---|---|---|---|---|
| INCOME | 1 | Dividends (Enter full amount before exclusion) | 20,000 | |
| | 2 | Interest | | |
| | 3 | Income from partnerships and other fiduciaries | | |
| | 4 | Gross rents and royalties | | |
| | 5 | Gross profit (loss) from trade or business | | |
| | 6 | Net gain (loss) from capital assets (line 12, column 3, Schedule D, Form 1041) | | |
| | 7 | Ordinary gains and losses (line 15, Schedule D, Form 1041) | | |
| | 8 | Other income (State nature of income) Consulting fee (Income in re decedent) | 500 | |
| | 9 | Total income (lines 1 to 8, inclusive) | | 20,500 |
| DEDUCTIONS | 10 | Interest | 400 | |
| | 11 | Taxes | | |
| | 12 | Fiduciary's portion of depreciation (Schedule A) and depletion. Explain depletion | | |
| | 13 | Charitable deduction (line 9, Schedule B) | | |
| | 14 | Other deductions (Itemize) Fiduciary fee | 5,000 | |
| | | Administration expenses | 2,000 | |
| | 15 | Total (lines 10 to 14, inclusive) | | 7,400 |
| | 16 | Line 9 minus line 15 (Complex trusts and estates enter this amount on line 1 in Schedule C also) | | 13,100 |
| | 17 | Deduction for distributions to beneficiaries | -0- | |
| | 18 | Adjustment of dividend exclusion | 100 | |
| | 19 | Federal estate tax attributable to income in respect of a decedent (Fiduciary's share) | 100 | |
| | 20 | Long-term capital gain deduction. Enter 50% of line 13(e), Schedule D, Form 1041 | | |
| | 21 | Exemption | 600 | |
| | 22 | Total (lines 17 to 21, inclusive) | | 800 |
| | 23 | Taxable income of fiduciary (line 16 minus line 22) | | 12,300 |
| COMPUTATION OF TAX | 24 | Tax on amount on line 23 (See tax rate schedule) | | 2,938 |
| | 25 | If alternative tax is applicable, enter the tax from line 21 (or 42 if applicable), Schedule D, Form 1041 | | |
| | 26 | Tax surcharge (See instruction 26) | | |
| | 27 | Total (line 24 or line 25, whichever is applicable, and line 26) | | 2,938 |
| | 28 | Fiduciary's share of foreign tax credit (Attach Form 1116) | | |
| | 29 | Fiduciary's share of investment credit (Attach Form 3468) | | |
| | 30 | Total (lines 28 and 29) | | |
| | 31 | Balance (line 27 less line 30) | | 2,938 |
| | 32 | Tax from recomputing fiduciary's share of prior year investment credit (Attach Form 4255) | | |
| | 33 | Minimum tax (Attach Form 4626) | | |
| | 34 | Total (lines 31 to 33, inclusive) | | 2,938 |
| | 35 | Fiduciary's share of credit for tax paid at source on tax-free covenant bond interest | | |
| | 36 | Credit for special fuels, nonhighway Fed. gas. tax and Lub. oil (Attach Form 4136) | | |
| | 37 | Credit from regulated investment companies (Attach Form 2439) | | |
| | 38 | Tax previously paid (Attach Form 2758) | | |
| | 39 | Tax withheld (Attach Form W–2) | | |
| | 40 | Total (lines 35 to 39, inclusive) | | |
| | 41 | Balance of tax due (line 34 less line 40) | | 2,938 |
| | 42 | Overpayment (line 40 less line 34) | | |

Under penalties of perjury, I declare that I have examined this return, including accompanying schedules and statements, and to the best of my knowledge and belief it is true, correct, and complete. If prepared by a person other than taxpayer, his declaration is based on all information of which he has any knowledge.

**Sign here** ▶ ______ Signature of fiduciary or officer representing fiduciary ______ Date

▶ ______ Signature of preparer other than fiduciary ______ Address ______ Date

16—81177-1

FIGURE 7-5

Fiduciary Income Tax Return

5. When a person dies, a personal income tax return is filed including his income and deductions for the period prior to his death. Income received and deductions paid by an executor after the decedent's death must be reported on a fiduciary return.

## CASE EXCERPTS

*Estelle Morris Trusts,* 51 TC 20(1968)
*Nilssen Estate* v. *U.S.* (DC Minn.–1971) 27 AFTR 2d 71-1318

### *Estelle Morris Trusts*
51 TC 20(1968)

> In 1953 grantors E. S. and Etty Morris each executed ten irrevocable declarations of trust, each of which directed the trustee, subject to certain discretionary distributions, to accumulate the income for the life of each of two primary beneficiaries and, upon the death of both of them, to distribute the principal and accumulated income to trusts to be created for their surviving issue. The ten instruments were similar in form except for differing periods for income accumulation and distribution, and differing termination dates.

Finding that the grantors created multiple trusts rather than a single trust for tax-avoidance reasons, respondent determined that the ten purported B. R. Morris Trusts constitute a single trust for Federal income tax purposes and that the ten purported Estelle Morris Trusts constitute a single trust for Federal income tax purposes. By amended answer, respondent asserted that all 20 purported trusts constitute a single trust for Federal income tax purposes, and alleged increased deficiencies . . . . Respondent apparently concedes that two or more trusts may be created by one instrument in an undivided *res* by the same grantor for different beneficiaries and that such trusts would be entitled to independent recognition for tax purposes. See *U.S. Trust Co.* v. *Commissioner*, 296 U.S. 481 (1936). He contends, however, that these trust instruments failed to establish separate trusts for Barney R. Morris and Estelle Morris, but created a single trust having two shares.

The question is a factual one. We are not concerned with the reason why the grantors desired to create two trusts by one instrument; rather we must determine whether the language they used was sufficient to accomplish this intent.

We need not rely solely on the cold language of the trust instruments, however, for here the grantors, acting in their capacities as trustees, have established a basis for our interpretation by meticulously administering the several trusts as separate entities and by filing 20 separate Federal income tax returns for each year. Cf. *Helfrich's Estate* v. *Commissioner,* 143 F. 2d 43, 46 (C.A. 7, 1944), affirming 1 T.C.590(1943); *Estate of Marvin L. Pardee,* 49 T.C. 140, 148 (1967). While this may have been done to avoid taxes, it by no means alters the fact that it was done. Cf. *U.S. Trust Co.* v. *Commissioner, supra.* We conclude, therefore, that by each "Declaration of Trust" the grantors intended to create, and in fact created, two separate trusts.

The second issue for determination is whether E. S. and Etty Morris created the multiple trusts, as respondent contends, principally, "if not solely, for tax avoidance." The burden of proof on this issue rests with petitioners. While recognizing that the burden is particularly onerous because of the lapse of time between the creation of the trusts and the attack by respondent, we are reminded nevertheless that difficulty or even impossibility of proof does not relieve petitioner of the burden.

Having determined that the Morris Trusts were created primarily for tax-avoidance purposes, and that this purpose continues to "taint" the trusts' income, we must now decide the final and most difficult question presented, i.e., the legal consequences of our determinations. We must decide whether each of the several trusts for the same beneficiary should be accorded independent significance as a taxable entity, or whether, as a matter of law, all of these trusts should be consolidated for purposes of Federal income taxation.

Proper consideration of respondent's arguments must begin with the realization that the Internal Revenue Code, by recognizing even one trust for tax purposes, sanctions to some degree income splitting and the resulting lessening of taxes. Many of the advantages of multiple trusts–including accumulation of income at a lower tax rate–may be accomplished to a lesser extent by a single trust. We are concerned here only with a quantitative extension of the advantages of a single trust, a difference in degree; and not with a qualitatively distinct phenomenon, that is, a difference in kind.

After careful consideration, we are constrained to reach the conclusion that a finding of tax avoidance is simply not enough to invalidate multiple trusts. Evidence of tax avoidance does not invalidate family partnerships. *Commissioner* v. *Tower,* 327 U.S. 280 (1946); *Commissioner* v. *Culbertson,* 337 U.S. 733, 744 fn. 13 (1949). Corporations are not invalidated if the creator's aim is tax reduction, but are recognized for tax purposes if they engage in business activity. See, e.g., *Moline Properties* v. *Commissioner,* 319 U.S. 436 (1943); *Jackson* v. *Commissioner,* 233 F. 2d 289, 290 (C.A. 2, 1956), affirming 24 T.C. 1 (1955); *National Investors Corp.* v. *Hoey,* 144 F. 2d 466 (C.A. 2, 1944). We see no reason why the result should be different here.

*Nilssen Estate* v. *U.S.*
(DC Minn.–1971) 27 AFTR 2d 71-1318

On January 28, 1959, Haakon K. Nilssen entered into an employment contract with George A. Clark and Son, Inc. (Clark), under the terms of which Clark agreed to pay Mr. Nilssen not less than $54,000 annually during the term of his active employment with the company. If he remained with the company until retirement and rendered certain services after retirement he was to be paid $4,500 a month for the remainder of his life. If his wife survived him, she was to receive monthly payments of $2,250 for the remainder of her life, provided that in the event of her remarriage the payments would cease three months thereafter. The agreement to make these payments was stated to be an inducement for Mr. Nilssen to continue in Clark's employ in light of his past and potential value to the employing corporation. . . .

The court concludes that the payments represent section 691 income to the surviving widow. . . . Although section 691 does not provide a definition of "income in respect of a decedent" the scope of its coverage may fairly be delimited by reference to the purpose for which it was enacted. That purpose was, and is, to avoid the "bunching" effect on the incomes of cash basis taxpayers whose final returns were placed on an accrual basis pursuant to section 42 of the Revenue Act of 1934. 48 Stat. 680. Thus the essential inquiry here is whether the payments represent income which may be said to have accrued to the deceased husband prior to his death. See S. Rep. No. 1631, 77th Cong., 2d Sess., 100-05 (1942). In finding section 691 applicable to post-death payments made pursuant to a substantially similar employment contract, the court in *Bernard* v. *United States,* 215 F. Supp. 256 (S.D.N.Y. 1963), stated at page 260:

> The critical question that must be answered is, who did the work or performed the services that give rise to the income. If it is the decedent then such payments fall within Section 691 and are taxed to the recipient in the way that they would have been taxed to the decedent.

Plaintiffs however contend that although the payments were made in recognition of the deceased husband's "economic activities," the income may not be said to have accrued to him because he was not sufficiently "entitled" to the income prior to his death. This contention is based upon the fact that under the employment contract the deceased husband would never receive the payment in issue, such being conditioned upon the widow's surviving his death. The principal upon which plaintiffs rely is not disputed. It is clear that a taxpayer must be entitled to income prior to its accrual at date of death, free from contingencies. *Keck* v. *Commissioner,* 415 F. 2d 533 (6th Cir. 1969); *Trust Company of Georgia* v. *Ross,* 392 F. 2d 694, 695 (8th Cir. 1967); *Lacomble* v. *United States,* 177 F.Supp. 373 (N.D. Cal. 1959).

However, this is not to suggest that such taxpayer must at any time have an absolute contractual right to its physical receipt. Rather, in the case of post-death payments solely attributable to the personal services of the decedent, the right to the income is fully created by the decedent during his life, and the right in someone surviving to receive the money has certainly matured without conditions precedent or contingencies at the time of his death. Under such circumstances the question of the decedent's "entitlement" to the payments in the sense of actually receiving them in hand prior to his death is simply not relevant to a determination of whether the income may be said to be income in respect of a decedent. . . .

. . . Were the income tax not to be assessed on such payments, the widow would receive money on which no income tax has been or would be paid.

## QUESTIONS AND PROBLEMS

1. Mike Rabbit is married and has seven sons, ages 5 through 12. Mike wishes to set aside money to permit each of his sons to go into business or to help them buy homes when they marry. Suggest a good way this can be accomplished and explain your choice.
2. "The return of a simple trust is always a conduit, funneling items of income and expense to the individual returns of the beneficiaries in exactly the same fashion that a partnership funnels such items to the partners." Would you agree?
3. Distinguish between the tax status of an agent and that of a fiduciary.
4. Howard Morgan set up a trust for his nine-year-old daughter Emilie at the beginning of the taxable year. He gave to the American National Bank, as trustee, 1,200 shares of Campbell Soup Company common stock, which pays a dividend of $1.10 per share per year. The trust provides that income is to be accumulated until Emilie reaches age 30, and at that time both the corpus of the trust and the accumulated income are to be distributed to her. The trust duly collected the $1,320 in dividends and charged a $50 trust fee. No other expenses were incurred during the year, but $35 interest was received on the temporary investment of the dividend money pending accumulation of a larger amount and the making of a more permanent investment. Prepare a fiduciary income tax return on Form 1041. Make any necessary assumptions.
5. When Emilie, in Problem 4, reaches the age of 30, to what extent, if at all, will the distribution of accumulated income be taxed to her? Discuss generally.
6. Edward Orens set up an irrevocable trust with the City Bank as trustee for the benefit of his sister and her daughter. His sister is to receive $200 per month from the trust for the balance of her life, and upon the sister's death the entire income of the trust is to go to her daughter. Upon the daughter's death, the trust shall terminate and be distributed among the daughter's children or their issue. The trust income for the year consisted of dividends of $3,000, interest of $980, rental income of $12,000, and refunds of prior-year insurance premiums of $120. Expenses included real estate taxes of $2,700, interest of $4,100 on the mortgage on the rental property, depreciation on the rental property of $3,600, and a trust fee of $1,000. Prepare the fiduciary income tax return on Form 1041.
7. Pete Peters died on October 2. His residence, stocks, and savings accounts were held in joint tenancy with his wife. He left a wife and two children as the beneficiaries of his will. Pete received a salary of $15,000 up to the time he died, and his executor received $1,000 salary due but not paid until after Pete died. The estate tax paid, applicable to inclusion of the $1,000 salary

receivable in computing the estate tax, amounted to $200. Pete's wife also worked, and during the year she earned $5,000. Interest income of $4,000 was earned during the year, credited in equal amounts, quarterly. Dividends in the amount of $2,000 each were received in June and in December. Interest payments on the Peters' home were $150 a month, paid on the tenth of each month. Medical expenses paid prior to October 2 amounted to $1,400. Prepare Pete's and his wife's joint return for the year.

8. Using the facts in Problem 7, prepare the first fiduciary return for Pete's estate. The executor incurred $300 in administration expenses. No distributions were made to beneficiaries during the year.

*9. Construct an example to show how the Morris Trusts (case excerpt) might save taxes for the Morris family. Then discuss how the throwback rules now in effect would, or would not, dissipate any advantages of multiple trusts.

# 3

# A CLOSER LOOK AT THE DETAILS

*Now that you have seen something of who the taxpayers are and how the income tax generally applies to them, you are ready to explore more fully some of the topics that we have not mentioned or that we have lightly passed over. In this Part, we shall discuss such things as capital gains, coping with fluctuating incomes, depreciation, income and expenses related to natural resources, dollar-value LIFO, employee benefits, retirement income, corporate capital transactions, tax aspects of various types of investments, estate taxes, gift taxes, and foreign tax matters.*

# 8

# Capital Gains

At first glance, the capital gains provisions of the tax law seem relatively unimportant. Less than 10 percent of the individual income tax returns filed report net capital gains and only about 4 percent of the total income tax is derived from taxing capital gains. However, the capital gains provisions of the tax law are unimportant in the same sense that the safety valve on a steam boiler is unimportant—and, in a way, both fulfill about the same function.

More than 60 percent of individual-taxpayer net capital gains are reported on returns that have adjusted gross income, including one-half the net long-term capital gains, of over $20,000. Through their extensive use of the capital gains provisions, upper-bracket taxpayers are able to pay an effective rate of income tax that is substantially lower than the structure of the individual tax rates would lead one to expect. According to the tax-rate structure in effect during 1977, a single taxpayer with taxable income of $100,000 would (except for "earned income") be paying an effective rate of at least 53 percent, the maximum rate being 70 percent. Married taxpayers with over $100,000 of taxable income would be paying an effective rate of at least 45 percent, and marginal rates from 62 to 70 percent. However, for 1977 the effective tax rate actually paid by individual taxpayers with income of $100,000 or more would more probably be in the range of 35 to 40 percent.

As we explore the capital gains provisions, we shall see that a highly graduated structure of individual tax rates, coupled with the individual inequities resulting when such rates are actually applied to a given individual, has resulted in many types of income being classified as "capital gains." In Chapter 17, relating to problems of the investor, we shall return to this theme and tentatively conclude that a taxpayer with high income has a variety of ways to avoid being affected by the upper brackets of the individual income-tax-rate structure.

## CAPITAL GAINS IN THE U.S. TAX LAW

In the United States prior to 1922, all capital gains were taxed in the same manner as any other items of income. From 1922 to 1942, preferential treatment was accorded to capital gains of individuals, but corporate gains were still taxed in the same manner as any other income. Since 1942, both individuals and corporations have had special tax treatment accorded their capital gains.

Ordinary income arises from some sort of economic activity on the part of the taxpayer, whereas capital gains arise from changes in the market value of property. In abstract tax theory, if a taxpayer owns a citrus grove, the income he derives from the sale of fruit is ordinary income. If, however, he sells the grove, any resulting gain on the sale would be a capital gain. Other examples of pure capital gains would be purchase and sale of securities; the sale of property used in a trade or business, such as machinery and livestock; and purchase and sale of such personal assets as a residence, an automobile, a yacht, a coin collection, and so forth.

The United States income tax law adopts a slightly different approach. Capital assets are defined negatively. They encompass all assets except:

1. Stock in trade or other inventory property
2. Property held primarily for sale to customers in the ordinary course of business
3. Depreciable or real property used in a trade or business
4. The normal notes or accounts receivable derived from the sale of goods or services
5. A copyright, a literary, musical, or artistic composition, a letter or memorandum, or similar property in the hands of the author, composer, or someone whose basis is determined by reference to the author
6. Governmental non-interest-bearing discount obligations maturing in one year or less.

But many types of assets that are not capital assets can still produce capital gains upon their sale or exchange, as will become clearer later in this chapter when we discuss the tax treatment of depreciable and real property used in a business (item 3 above).

The operational result is that some gains on "pure" capital assets do not get capital gains treatment, while other gains that are compensatory in nature are categorized as capital gains. Generally, if a "capital asset" is held for more than one year, the capital gain is considered long term and receives preferential tax treatment.

When livestock qualifies for capital gains treatment, the minimum holding period is generally 12 months, but for horses and cattle it is 24 months.

Gains on "capital assets" not held for the minimum holding period are considered either ordinary income or short-term capital gains, which are treated in most respects as ordinary income.

Losses are netted against gains, and only the excess of long-term gains over long-term losses and net short-term losses gets special tax treatment.

### *Individuals*

Long-term capital gains of individual taxpayers are taxed in the following manner:

Step 1. For the first $50,000 of gain, the tax is the smaller of:
- a. The tax resulting from including one-half the capital gain with all other income and applying regular tax rates; or
- b. Twenty-five percent of the full amount of the gain up to $50,000.

Step 2. The tax on the gain in excess of $50,000 is computed by taxing one-half the excess at the normal tax rates.

For married persons filing separate returns, substitute $25,000 for $50,000 in the explanation above.

The maximum effective tax on any excess long-term capital gains is limited to 35 percent—that is the top marginal tax rate of 70 percent applied to one-half the excess gains included in taxable income. This maximum effective tax of 35 percent does not reflect either the minimum tax on tax preferences or the impact of capital gain on the maximum tax on earned income, which will be discussed in Chapter 13.

*Example 1:*

Assume that a married taxpayer has long-term capital gains amounting to $10,000 and ordinary income of $13,200. Tax on his ordinary income for 1977 would be $1,820. If he includes one-half the capital gains in ordinary income, as in Step la, his tax would be based on taxable income of $18,200 and would amount to $3,010. Thus the tax on the capital gain would be $1,190, which is an effective rate of 11.9 percent. The tax as computed is lower than 25 percent of the full gain as permitted by Step 1b, which would produce a total tax of $4,320. He would thus compute his tax by including half the capital gain with his ordinary income rather than making the alternative computation. The general tax credit was ignored.

*Example 2:*

Assume, instead, that the same taxpayer has $103,200 of taxable income from other sources and $50,000 long-term capital gains. His tax on the $103,200 would be $45,180. Including one-half the capital gains with his other income would raise his taxable income to $128,200, resulting in a tax of $60,780. The incremental tax caused by the capital gains would thus be $15,600, or 31.2 percent. However, Step 1b, the alternative tax computation, allows the gains of $50,000 to be taxed at a flat 25 percent, which results in a total tax of $57,680, as follows:

| | |
|---|---|
| Tax on $103,200 of ordinary income | $45,180 |
| 25% of $50,000 capital gain | 12,500 |
| Total tax before general tax credit | $57,680 |

In the preceding examples, the amount of capital gains did not exceed $50,000, and consequently Step 2 of the formula on page 165 was not necessary. However, assume the following for 1978:

| | |
|---|---|
| Ordinary income | $103,200 |
| Long-term capital gains | 150,000 |
| Capital gains deduction (½ of $150,000) | ( 75,000) |
| Taxable income | $178,200 |

The tax would be computed as follows:

| | | |
|---|---|---|
| 1. On $103,200 ordinary income at regular rates | | $45,180 |
| 2. On $50,000 of long-term gain (Step 1b) | | 12,500 |
| 3. On $178,200 taxable income | $93,780 | |
| *Less* tax on $128,200 (ordinary income plus ½ of the amount taxed at 25 percent) at regular rates | 60,780 | 33,000 |
| | | $90,680 |

The tax computed at line 3 results in an effective rate of 33 percent on the long-term capital gains in excess of $50,000.

In general, ignoring the minimum tax on tax preferences and the maximum tax on earned income, individuals will pay tax on their long-term capital gains at rates ranging from less than 10 percent to a maximum of 35 percent.

### *Corporations*

Corporations include their full capital gains with their other income but have the benefit of an alternative tax computation at a 30 percent rate.

A corporation with other income of $50,000 and long-term capital gains of $10,000 would pay a tax of $3,000 on the capital gains. On the other hand, assume a corporation that, disregarding capital gains, has a net operating loss for 1978 of $20,000 and long-term capital gains of $100,000. If capital gains are offset against the operating loss, the resulting tax will be on $80,000 at regular corporate rates, or $24,900. The corporation is not allowed to net its long-term gains against its operating loss and then take the alternative tax on the difference. If it could, its alternative tax would be $24,000–but since it can't, the alternative tax would otherwise be $30,000. Thus, when a corporation has a capital gain and an operating loss, the effective tax on its capital gain may exceed 30 percent, although it will never quite reach the maximum corporate rate of 48 percent. In our example, the tax is $24,900 on capital gains (net of operating losses) of $80,000, resulting in an effective rate of approximately 31.1 percent.

***Other Taxpayers***

Partnerships and Small Business Corporations, with one exception, act as conduits, passing their capital gains through to their owners. The owners report the gains on their individual returns. Capital losses of Small Business Corporations, however, are not passed through, even though losses of partnerships are. Fiduciaries pay tax on any capital gains that are not passed through to their beneficiaries in the same fashion as do individuals, and cannot pass through capital losses, except upon termination of the estate or trust.

The one exception to the conduit characteristic of the Small Business Corporation on capital gains occurs when such a corporation incurs a large capital gain. If the capital gain (1) exceeds $25,000 and (2) represents more than half the taxable income of (3) a corporation that has not been an electing Small Business Corporation during the 3 preceding years or since its inception–then the gain in excess of $25,000 is taxable to the corporation. This provision was put into the law to eliminate the "one-shot" election of Small Business Corporation status, which would otherwise allow a pass-through and distribution of a substantial capital gain while avoiding a tax at the corporate level. (The phrase "one-shot election" refers to a corporation that has been a regular corporation and that makes a Small Business Corporation election for only one taxable year and then terminates it.)

Even though the tax price appears high, the Small Business Corporation election may still prove less costly to the stockholders than to have a regular corporation realize the capital gains, pay tax on all the gain rather than just the excess over $25,000, and then distribute the proceeds to the stockholders, who would normally be taxed on dividend income at ordinary rates. The following example illustrates the saving still resulting from such a one-shot election:

| | *Small Business Corporation* | *Regular Corporation* |
|---|---|---|
| Capital gain | $100,000 | $100,000 |
| Less amount not taxed at corporate level | ( 25,000) | |
| Taxable gain | 75,000 | 100,000 |
| Corporate tax @ 30% | ( 22,500) | ( 30,000) |
| Net gain | 52,500 | 70,000 |

| | *Small Business Corporation* | *Regular Corporation* |
|---|---|---|
| Capital gain not taxed | 25,000 | |
| Distributed one-third to each of three stockholders | 77,500 | 70,000 |
| Tax to stockholders on capital gain @ 25% | 19,375 | |
| Ordinary income @ 60% assumed rate | | 42,000 |
| Total stockholder tax | 19,375 | 42,000 |
| After-tax cash | $ 58,125 | $ 28,000 |

Although some of the original value of a "one-shot" election has been eliminated, the example demonstrates that it can still save tax dollars.

## CAPITAL LOSSES

### *Noncorporate Taxpayers*

Capital losses of a given year may be offset against capital gains of that year. If there is an excess of *short-term* capital loss, such excess may be used to offset up to $3,000 of ordinary income for taxable years beginning after 1977. However, it takes $6,000 of *long-term* capital losses to offset $3,000 of ordinary income, since, in an attempt to make the treatment of long-term gains and losses parallel, the law requires that long-term losses offset only 50 percent of their equivalent in ordinary income.

Unused losses may be carried forward for an unlimited period of time as either short-term or long-term capital loss of the year to which carried, depending on the original status of the loss.

### *Corporate Taxpayers*

Just like noncorporate taxpayers, corporations may offset current capital losses against capital gains arising during the year, but net corporate capital losses can never be used to offset ordinary income and cannot result in increasing a net operating loss for the year to which carried. Unlike the case with noncorporate taxpayers, corporations' capital losses in excess of gains may be carried back to the earliest of the three taxable years preceding the year of the loss and then carried forward for five years. Corporate capital losses are treated as short-term capital losses in the year to which carried.

Capital losses, however, may not be carried back to a year in which the corporation was a regulated investment company, a real estate investment trust, or a foreign personal holding company. The carryback provisions also do not apply to a Small Business Corporation if a Form 1120S was filed for either the year of loss or the year to which the loss could otherwise be carried back. However, the five-year carryover provisions apply even when the carryback is barred.

*Example:*

A corporation sustained a $50,000 capital loss during 1978. It had had a long-term capital gain of $100,000 and taxable income (including the capital gain) of $30,000 for 1975.

The capital loss is carried back to 1975 as a short-term loss (regardless of what it actually was in 1978). Only $30,000 of it is absorbed in 1975, so the remaining $20,000 is available to be carried over to 1976 and 1977. If there were no capital gains in those years, the $20,000 would still remain available to offset $20,000 of capital gains during the five-year period from 1979 through 1983.

## DEPRECIABLE PROPERTY

Chief among the "pure" capital gains not entitled to capital gains treatment would be the gains on sale of depreciable personal property. Such gains, to the extent of the depreciation allowed for tax purposes since January 1, 1962, result in ordinary income. This provision is aimed at closing a tax loophole. Since depreciation is deductible as an offset against ordinary income, and since the methods of accelerated depreciation in use since 1954 (see Chapter 10) make it likely that many assets will be overdepreciated in the early years of life, treating gains on sale of such assets as capital gains would represent a tax windfall to the taxpayer.

For example, take the extreme instance of a landlord in a 70 percent marginal tax bracket, who used his car entirely for business. He drove a $5,000 car, which he would prove had a useful life to him of three years. In the first year, he claimed depreciation on the car of $3,333 (declining-balance depreciation at twice the straight-line rate of 33 1/3 percent, or 66 2/3 percent). His basis for computing gain or loss was now $1,667. He sold the car for $4,333, realizing a gain of $2,666.

The depreciation deduction reduced the landlord's tax by $2,333. The gains, taxed as a capital gain, cost only $667 in tax. And look at the cash flow:

| | *Cash Outflow* | | *Cash Inflow* |
|---|---|---|---|
| Car purchase | $5,000 | Car sale | $4,333 |
| Tax on gain | 667 | Tax saved | 2,333 |
| Total | $5,667 | Total | $6,666 |

In other words, from this example, the more expensive the car that the landlord drove, the more profitable it was for him. This example is, of course, deliberately extreme. Actually, the Internal Revenue Service, on audit, would have been able to challenge the depreciation deduction claimed by the landlord on the ground that depreciation below salvage value was not permissible. Also, I.R.S. could have challenged the useful-life estimate if the experience of the landlord did not support the three-year life used.

The prevalence of this type of result, mainly in forms less extreme than this example, led to a change in the law in 1962. Gains on the sale of depreciable assets (except buildings) are not capital gains to the extent of depreciation deductions taken after January 1, 1962.

The 1964 tax law, the 1969 Tax Reform Act, and the 1976 Tax Reform Act treat part of the gain on the sale of real estate (excluding land) as ordinary income. Regardless of the depreciation method, gain on disposition is ordinary income if the property is held one year or less.

Ordinary income results after 12 months of ownership when the real estate is being depreciated using an accelerated rate, but only to the extent that cumulative depreciation exceeds depreciation computed by the straight-line method. However, with respect to depreciation taken prior to 1970 and depreciation on residential property taken from 1969 to 1975, such recapture is reduced by 1 percent for each month over 20 months and 100 months, respectively, that the property is held. Thus, as to pre-1970 depreciation on any realty, there will be no recapture after it has been held for ten years (120 months). For 1970–1975 depreciation, there will be no recapture on residential realty after it has been held 16 2/3 years (200 months). Except for low-income housing, all post-1975 depreciation in excess of straight-line is recaptured as ordinary income. Low-income housing, as narrowly defined in the tax law, stays on the 1970–1975 residential realty recapture rules–i.e., recapture drops by one percentage point for each month held in excess of 100 months (8 1/3 years), so that there is no recapture as to such housing if it is held for 16 2/3 years.

For any asset being depreciated on an accelerated basis, the second half of its estimated life normally involves taking less annual depreciation than by the straight-line method. The result is that gains representing straight-line depreciation will be taxed as capital gains, and that absolutely no recapture will occur if real estate is sold at the end of its originally estimated useful life, and relatively little recapture if the end of that estimated life is near.

## "SPECIAL" CAPITAL GAINS PROVISIONS

Many assets get capital gains treatment even though they are not "pure" capital assets or are specifically excluded from the capital asset category under the tax law. Usually, one or more of three reasons underlie their favored treatment:

1. It is felt that certain types of income cannot bear the full burden of income taxation.
2. It is deemed inequitable to tax in one year, under a graduated rate structure, gains that have actually been built up over a period of years.
3. It is desired to provide an incentive for certain types of transactions.

The discussion that follows covers some of these items that get capital gains treatment even though they are not capital assets.

### *Property Used in a Trade or Business*

Gains on the sale of property used in a trade or business are ordinary income to the extent of the depreciation deductions taken, as previously noted. Otherwise, they are capital gains. Although these assets fit our concept of "pure" capital assets, they are excluded from the tax definition of capital assets for a rather pragmatic reason. The losses from the sale of such assets are ordinary losses and fully deductible, if they exceed the gains during a given year from the sale of such assets.

Therefore, it is common tax-planning strategy, where both gains and losses are expected to be realized on such assets, to attempt to put the gains into one year and the losses into another. If gains and losses go into the same year, the losses offset the gains dollar for dollar. If the gains go into one year and the losses into another, the gains are taxed at the favorable capital gains rates, although the losses are fully deductible.

Assume that a corporation in a 48 percent tax bracket owns two buildings. Sale of Building A will result in a gain of $1,000,000. Sale of Building B will result in a loss of $1,000,000. If both buildings are sold in the same year, the loss on B will exactly offset the gain on A. But if B is sold in the first year, the result will be a tax benefit of $480,000, since the loss is fully deductible against other income. Building A can then be sold in the second year. The gain on its sale will be taxed as a capital gain, assuming that no depreciation recapture is involved, thus incurring a $300,000 tax. By splitting the transactions into separate years, the corporation has saved $180,000 in Federal income taxes!

### *Timber*

We noted in an example earlier in this chapter that the sale of a citrus grove would result in a capital gain, even though sale of the citrus fruit would produce ordinary income. If land is used to raise timber, then the timber that is cut and sold is analogous to the citrus fruit in that it is a crop rather than the capital asset itself. But timber as a crop differs from citrus in one crucial respect. It takes a long time before a sapling matures to the point where it is marketable. It was thus felt that it was unfair to tax the gain from cutting timber as ordinary income all in one year.

Further, it seemed quite unfair to allow capital gains on the sale of standing timber while treating the proceeds of the sale of cut timber as ordinary income. A timber owner could merely sell a section of land containing standing timber and then buy back the land after the timber had been cut, leaving him in roughly the same economic position as if he had contracted to have the timber cut for him (with some differential in his expenses).

As a result, income from the cutting of timber is entitled to long-term capital gains treatment. As with property used in a trade or business, losses from the cutting of timber are ordinary losses.

### *Livestock*

Livestock has some of the aspects of property used in a trade or business and some of the aspects of property held for sale to customers. After many years of controversy and uncertainty, the tax rules are now relatively clear-cut. Livestock (excluding poultry) held for draft, breeding, dairy, or sporting purposes may receive favored capital gains treatment if the minimum holding-period requirements are met. In the case of depreciable livestock, purchased rather than raised, gains representing prior depreciation are taxed as ordinary income, since the depreciation-recapture rules applying to personal property also apply to livestock.

### *Coal and Iron Ore Royalties*

Royalties received on coal and iron ore leases are treated as capital gains. Two main arguments are discernible underlying this particular tax peculiarity. One argument is that, because timber owners are allowed to get capital gains, owners of coal and iron deposits should receive equal treatment. To the extent that there is logic in this type of "me-too" argument, it may explain to you how each exception put into the tax law helps lay the groundwork for the next exception.

The strongest argument for capital gains treatment for coal and iron ore royalties appears to be the economic one. Owners of coal and iron lands are in a relatively bad way, and this is a way of helping them with a modest amount of tax relief.

### *Patents*

The proceeds from the sale of a patent, whether paid in a lump sum or through royalties, constitute capital gains to the inventor or to the financial backer of an inventor. It matters not whether the inventor is a professional or an amateur. This provision for converting earned income into capital gains stems from the desirability of encouraging the development of inventions.

But note the difference in the case of copyrights in literary, musical, or artistic works. When General Eisenhower sold his rights to his book, *Crusade in*

*Europe,* he was able to obtain capital gains treatment for the proceeds on the ground that he was an amateur writer. Since 1950, however, this would be impossible. Neither amateurs nor professionals can get capital gains treatment on disposal of the works they have created. The contrast between these rules and the ease of obtaining capital gains treatment on patents could probably be viewed by a cynic as a trenchant comment on our national system of values.

### *Brief Historical Review*

The handling of capital gains and losses in the United States has varied over the years. Early in the life of the Tax Law, capital gains were given the same treatment as other income. Later the capital gains were separated into long-term (two years) and short-term, with the long-term capital gains subject to a maximum rate of 12½ percent while short-term were included as other income. Next, the law was changed so that a percentage of the capital gain, depending upon how long the asset had been held, was treated as regular income. The handling of capital gains, as set forth in this chapter, began to develop about 1938 and has been continuously modified over the years. The treatment of capital losses has gone from non-recognition, to full allowance against any income regardless of classification, to limitations upon the amount of loss which can be deducted.

This brief review of the past indicates that many of the proposals being made today for changes in the capital gains section of the Code are not new but have been tried before. The fact that they have been tried before is in itself neither a recommendation nor a condemnation. But the fact that they were tried, and replaced with something else, may at least cause us to wonder why they were abandoned before we too enthusiastically embrace them.

In addition, the great concern over the taxation of capital gains, as represented by the various approaches that have been tried and the emotion with which many commentators approach the subject, may help to underscore the crucial role played by investors in maintaining the vigor of the economy from which we all draw our sustenance.

## CAPITAL GAINS AND DECISIONS

Any tax, even a reduced tax, acts as a barrier to the transactions on which it is imposed. Thus, the existence of a tax on capital gains tends to lower the relative attractiveness of many alternative investments.

Assume that you own 100 shares of ABC common stock, which you purchased for $1 a share. It is now selling for $100 per share. If you sell ABC and pay a 25 percent tax on your gain, you will have $7,525 to invest in XYZ common stock. The question that faces you, then, can be phrased in this fashion: Is $7,525 of XYZ common equal in value to $10,000 of ABC common? Obviously, XYZ will have to be substantially more attractive than ABC before you can answer "Yes" to that question.

Those situations in which gains are capital and losses ordinary should appear relatively more attractive than situations in which gains and losses are treated the same. We will see in connection with our discussion of Small Business Investment Corporations in Chapter 14, that under these circumstances it is possible to have a net loss before taxes and yet still have a net profit after taxes. If the world were more mathematically ordered, and if one's returns were always proportionate to the risk involved, such investments would be as close to being a "sure thing" as would tax-free ownership of a slot machine set to pay out only $95 for each $100 put in.

The desire to convert what would otherwise be ordinary income into capital gains can dictate casting one's income-producing activities into a corporate form. Jack Benny incorporated his radio show many years ago. He was then able to sell the corporate stock to a network and report the proceeds of the sale as a capital gain. Changes in the tax law since then have made such sales more hazardous, although not impossible. The same business result could have been achieved with a production contract with the network, but with ordinary income rather than capital gains effects.

At a less "gimmicky" level, a highly talented, productive-individual may be motivated to start his own business through hopes of realizing capital gains rather than ordinary income. Even though, as an employee, he may be fully compensated for the value of his services, the marginal tax rate applicable to a person of relatively high income may prove discouraging. But if he can merely produce the same amount of income within the framework of a corporate entity, and ultimately realize the capitalized value of those earnings at capital gains rates, he may perceive that he will be substantially ahead.

On a broader scale, it may be argued that the capital gain and loss provisions appear to stimulate certain types of excesses. During periods of rising values, investors will tend to hold securities off the market because of the tax they would incur upon their sale. This decrease in supply in the face of rising demand combines with the other factors that tend to push security prices to unrealistic heights. On the other hand, during periods of declining values, the fact that some tax benefit may be obtainable by realizing losses provides an incentive to sell and thus increases supply, helping to drive prices further down. Because there were market excesses when there was no income tax in the United States, it should be obvious that the tax provisions are probably a minor contributory factor and that investor psychology is far more important. Certainly, however, the tax provisions have some effect—probably on the movement of individual securities even more than on the market as a whole.

The use of a tax to discourage certain types of activity has the sanction of tradition behind it. The currency issued by state banks right after the Civil War was driven off the market by imposing a tax on its circulation. In mid-1963, to help stop the outflow of gold from the United States, President Kennedy proposed that a tax (the Interest Equalization Tax) be imposed on American purchases of foreign securities. There are taxes on narcotics, on sawed-off shotguns, and on persons engaged in the gambling business. If the effect of the capital gains tax were to be assessed from this point of view, its message might be: "Hold those things on which you have unrealized gains; sell those on which you have losses."

## SUMMARY

The definition of capital assets and the type of gains eligible for special capital gains treatment have changed over the years and probably will continue to change. It is possible to argue that capital gains should not be subject to tax at all, at least to the extent that the sales proceeds are invested in another capital asset. To a limited extent, this treatment is already accorded such transactions as:

1. Gain on sale of a personal residence, which is not taxed to the extent that sales proceeds are reinvested in another residence
2. Gains on involuntary conversions (through fire, condemnation, and so forth) of business or investment assets, to the extent that the proceeds are reinvested in similar property
3. Gains on the "trade-in" of depreciable business property on similar property
4. Gain on the trade of any business or investment property (except such things as stocks, bonds, notes, and so forth) for similar property
5. Certain exchanges of stock for stock (Chapter 17).

It is also possible to argue, with equal plausibility, that our tax system deals with completed transactions, and that it is inequitable to give preferential tax treatment to a type of income typically realized by a small minority of upper-bracket taxpayers while subjecting to full taxation the income of the large majority of taxpayers who have no opportunity to convert their normal sources of income from ordinary-income status to capital gains status.

## CASE EXCERPTS

*Chartier Real Estate Co., Inc.* 52 TC 346 Aff'd (CA1 1970)
*Carl E. Mathena* v. *U.S.* (CA9 1971) 28 AFTR 2d 71-5402

### *Chartier Real Estate Co., Inc.*
### 52 TC 346 Aff'd. (CA1 1970)

Why can't a corporation apply the alternative tax rate to its net taxable income when that amount is less than its net long-term capital gains?

Petitioner seeks to demonstrate the alleged inequity by pointing out that a taxpayer (whose capital gain is so large as to make the "alternative" method of computing taxes more advantageous than the "regular" method) with a deficit in ordinary income will pay the same amount of tax regardless of the size of the deficit. Petitioner argues that the *Weil* doctrine creates an artificially separate tax on capital gains which ignores ordinary income and deductions, and which Congress did not intend to create. The short answer is that the legislative history demonstrates that Congress did intend to make such a distinction between the two elements of the "alternative" tax, at least to the extent of the *Weil* doctrine, and that result is required by the plain words of the statute.

*Carl E. Mathena* v. *U.S.*
(CA9 1971) 28 AFTR 2d 71-5402

> Mathena, once an employee of Akron Savings & Loan, managed to get capital gain treatment on what in many respects was a payment to terminate a consulting contract.

An arrangement was made under which Mathena could "eat his cake and keep it, too." He drew his retirement benefits out of the retirement fund of Akron. He had been drawing a salary of $19,000 a year.

On July 1, 1963, he turned up with a new arrangement. He went on the payroll of Akron at a salary of $10,000 a year as a consultant—obviously an attempt at a "fee" setup. Also, simultaneously, he was newly hired at a price of $10,000 a year to work for Automated Business Services and Systems, Inc. (Automated), a "services" company of which he was the controlling stockholder. Automated had two customers: Akron and Bankers. A contract was signed between Akron and Automated, terminable on one year's notice, for "services." A monthly contract was drawn with Bankers, which was never signed, but the parties seem to have operated under it.

By December, 1963, Akron and Bankers wanted to get rid of Mathena.

No formal contract to terminate was ever drawn up. A price of $25,160 was agreed upon. Bankers paid Mathena $2,160 and took Mathena's controlling stock in Automated. Akron treated the transaction as a severance pay deal and paid Mathena $25,000. Mathena treated the whole transaction as a sale of his stock in Automated and only as a capital gain on his stock.

The district court thought the parties' subjective intents were important and liked Mathena's version better. We arrive at the same result in a different way.

Our reasoning is this: At the time Mathena "sold out" he had no tenure with Akron. Akron only had to pay him for the current month to release him. This was done two weeks before the sale. Strictly, Mathena had no tenure with Automated, but he was assured a job with Automated as long as he had a controlling interest in the stock. And Automated had a right to work for a year for Akron before a termination would be effective. Thus Mathena's stock in Mathena's hands had two elements of value: some market value and a lot of nuisance value. That was all that Mathena sold. So it was a stock sale.

We cannot rightly censure Akron and Bankers, because they are not before us. (If they were, they might have an opportunity to be heard.) But on our record, as between Akron and Mathena, Akron itself bought nothing for its $25,000. Under Ohio state law, Akron could not buy Automated stock. Bankers could. It paid $2,160 and got the stock. Having given up nothing directly to Akron, Mathena may treat the deal as a sale of stock, the only thing he directly gave up.

## QUESTIONS AND PROBLEMS

1. What is a capital asset as distinguished from other assets?
2. In theory, how would a capital gain differ from ordinary income?
3. "In tax matters, we are like a juror who believes in capital punishment as a general proposition, but cannot bring himself to vote for execution of a specific murderer. We believe in a highly graduated, almost confiscatory at the upper levels, pattern of individual income taxation, so long as the high rates don't apply to anyone we know." Does the structure of our tax law, especially relative to capital gains, support or conflict with the point of view expressed in the quotation?
4. Assume that a certain unmarried individual with $35,000 of other net taxable income can receive increments of capital gain in $100 amounts. Other income equals deductions plus exemptions. What is the maximum percentage of tax on long-term capital gains that this particular individual will pay on any $100 increment if we increase his capital gains by $100 steps until the alternative tax computation (25 percent of the first $50,000) produces a lesser tax than results from including 50 percent of the long-term capital gains as ordinary income?
5. Machinery and equipment used in a trade or business would seem to constitute capital assets in the nontax usage of the term. Are they deemed to be capital assets for tax purposes? Why?
6. Explain, with an example of your own construction, why it may be undesirable to have both gains and losses on the sale of real property used in a trade or business fall into the same tax year.
7. Contrast the tax treatment of the professional inventor with that of the professional author.

8. List four types of assets that are not capital assets under the tax law, but that may produce capital gains on disposition.

9. "Tax law provisions for taxing real estate gains and losses are contributing factors to the periodic real estate booms, followed by busts, which this country has seen recurrently." What are some of the provisions to which the quotation may be referring?

10. Black, Inc., a manufacturing company, sold the plant and property at one of its operating facilities on January 2, 1978. Based on the sales agreement, the land was valued at $200,000, the building at $2,000,000, and the operating machinery and equipment at $500,000. The land, building, and machinery and equipment had been purchased new on January 2, 1973, for $150,000, $1,800,000 and $1,500,000, respectively. Black, Inc., depreciated both the building and he machinery and equipment using declining-balance depreciation at 150 and 200 percent respectively of the straight-line, with lives of 40 years and 10 years, respectively. All assets were depreciated for the full years of 1973 through 1978, and the accumulated depreciation at the date of sale was $368,876 for the building and $1,008,480 for the machinery and equipment. Assume that the corporate tax rate on ordinary income is 48 percent; the alternative tax rate on capital gains is 30 percent; and that Black, Inc., had $100,000 of ordinary income, disregarding the sale. What is Black, Inc.'s total tax liability for 1978? What is the effective tax rate on the gain resulting from the sale of the plant, property, and equipment?

*11. Short-term capital gains "are treated in most respects as ordinary income." Explain how the treatment of short-term capital gains differs from that accorded ordinary income, constructing an example of a situation in which the taxpayer would pay less tax if a particular transaction resulted in a short-term capital gain than if it resulted in ordinary income.

*12. Does a motel qualify as residential realty for depreciation recapture purposes? What difference would such qualification make to a taxpayer using accelerated depreciation and a 33 1/3-year life on a motel he intends to resell after 17 years?

*13. Christmas trees are timber. Is it possible for a producer of Christmas trees to get capital gains treatment accorded his profits? (Maybe there is a Santa Claus after all, if he can.)

14. Mr. Jones has a large tract of land which he has held for four years and for which he has received an offer of $225,000. His tax basis for the land is $75,000. He is presently in the 70 percent tax bracket and has no other capital gains or losses. Mr. Jones is a lawyer by profession and purchased the land as an investment three years ago. He estimated his federal tax as follows:

| | |
|---|---:|
| Sales price | $225,000 |
| Tax basis | 75,000 |

| | |
|---|---|
| Taxable gain | 150,000 |
| Tax (25% of $250,000) | 37,500 |
| Net income | $112,500 |

The cash in his pocket after the sale would be ($225,000 − $37,500) $187,500. However, his son returned from college for the weekend and suggested that his father develop the land and sell the lots. A call to a local contractor provided them with an estimate of $65,000 for the development of the land. The tract would yield about 70 lots with an average price of $5,000 per lot. From this information, the son figured the net income and the after-tax cash flow:

| | | |
|---|---|---|
| Sales price ($5,000 x 70) | | $350,000 |
| Land | $75,000 | |
| Development | 65,000 | 140,000 |
| Taxable income | | 210,000 |
| Tax (25% of $210,000) | | 52,500 |
| Net income | | $157,500 |

The cash in his pocket would be [$350,000 − ($65,000 + $52,500)] $232,500, or an increase of $45,000. Mr. Smith has come to you for advice. What comments would you make?

15. The Rackter Tractor Company has net taxable income from operations of $75,000. In addition, it had the following four transactions which had not been included in the determination of taxable ordinary income. Determine the amount of tax the Rackter Tractor Company will have to pay for the current year.
    (a) A bulk loader purchased for $30,000 was sold for $12,000. Depreciation of $1,000 per year has been taken for eight years.
    (b) A delivery truck, purchased five years ago, which had been fully depreciated, was traded on a new truck. The dealer allowed a trade-in of $400 on the old truck. Depreciation taken on the old truck amounted to $2,100.
    (c) A scale purchased three years ago at a cost of $700 was sold for $800. The accumulated depreciation account reflected $375 of depreciation taken on this asset.
    (d) A platform loader purchased last year for $1,200 was damaged beyond repair and scrapped. Book value of the asset was $950 at the time it was scrapped.
16. Mr. Smith had $13,000 of taxable income before consideration of capital asset transactions. His net capital asset transaction balance was a long-term

loss of $9,000. How should this be handled? What would Mr. Smith's taxable income be for the year?

(a) During the following year Mr. Smith had ordinary income of $6,000 and a long-term capital gain of $2,000. Determine Mr. Smith's taxable income for the year.

(b) Would your answers to the above questions change if the original net balance had been a short-term loss of $9,000?

17. Mr. Higbe built a new factory for $500,000 with a life of 50 years and an estimated salvage value of $100,000. He elected to take depreciation on the accelerated basis using 150 percent declining balance. Listed below are the depreciation charges for each year. The building is going to be sold January 1, 1985, for $600,000 and Mr. Higbe wants you to determine his net after taxes on the transaction. Mr. Higbe is in the 70 percent tax bracket and he has no other capital gains or losses to report for the year.

| *Year* | *Depreciation Charge* |
|---|---|
| 1976 | $15,000 |
| 1977 | 14,553 |
| 1978 | 14,114 |
| 1979 | 13,690 |
| 1980 | 13,280 |
| 1981 | 12,880 |
| 1982 | 12,494 |
| 1983 | 12,120 |
| 1984 | 11,756 |
| | $119,887 |

18. Mr. Wren had taxable ordinary income of $90,000; he files a separate return and had the following security investment transactions:

| *Security* | *Date Acquired* | *Date Sold* | *Cost* | *Selling Price* |
|---|---|---|---|---|
| ABC Corporation | 6/7/X1 | 3/9/X9 | $1,500 | $8,500 |
| Jones, Inc. | 12/3/X8 | 12/3/X9 | 400 | 1,000 |
| IRS Corporation | 4/9/X5 | 6/14/X9 | 2,500 | 3,600 |
| XYZ Corporation | 8/10/X7 | 1/15/X9 | 1,200 | 2,000 |

(a) Assuming X9 is the current year, determine the amount of tax Mr. Wren would have to pay for the current year.

(b) Same as (a) except that capital gains are treated as follows: those held two years or less will be treated as short-term and taxed at the ordinary income rates, while those held in excess of two years will have the gain reduced by 15 percent for each full year held, but not below 25 percent.

(c) Same as (a) except that capital gains are treated as follows: Include all gains subject to the capital gain treatment as regular income and tax it the same as regular income.

(d) Same as (a) except that capital gains should be averaged over the years each asset was held and that average should be treated as ordinary income. For instance, a capital asset held five years would be taxed at one-fifth of the gain.

(e) Evaluate the various alternatives. What would you suggest? What value judgments and/or assumptions are implicit in your evaluation?

# 9

# The Timing of Income

The U.S. income tax contains a great number of provisions that affect the timing of the recognition of income or the taking of deductions. It also contains many provisions that apply, directly or indirectly, different tax rates to some types of income than they do to other types of income. Most of this book is concerned with these differences, but in this chapter we focus on certain key provisions in which the taxpayer has options as to the timing of his income.

Timing differences may have two possibilities:

1. The tax rates applicable will be the same in any of the taxable periods in which the income might be reported; or
2. The applicable tax rates are expected to be different in different periods.

In the first situation, timing differences can be analyzed in terms of their cash-flow effect. Normally, the decision will be to adopt the alternative that produces the smallest amount of current tax.

In arriving at a decision in the second situation, the present value of the future cash outflow for taxes should be balanced against the amount of the current tax saving. Thus, an exclusion may cost too much in a year in which the corporation pays a 22 percent tax if it will have to be reported as ordinary income three years hence when it is anticipated that the corporation will be paying tax at a 48 percent marginal rate:

| | |
|---|---|
| Tax benefit of $10,000 exclusion at 22% | $2,200 |
| Tax cost of $10,000 of income at 48% | 4,800 |
| Effective annual nondeductible simple interest rate if $2,200 borrowed now is repaid as $4,800 in three years | 30% |

And, of course, in the reverse situation, a 30 percent after-tax profit will result from postponing the year in which the income will be reported.

## INSTALLMENT SALES

Taxation, as we are by now aware, is not based solely on the receipt of money. It is based on transactions. A sale of property will normally result in income based on the fair market value of the consideration received. The unfairness of taxing a taxpayer before the transaction had produced enough cash even to pay the tax led to the early adoption of special rules governing those sales in which only a part of the selling price is received in cash.

### *Dealers*

A business that normally sells merchandise on the installment basis may elect to report its gross profit on a sale as payments are received from the customer during that period. This installment method of reporting is widely used by furniture stores, appliance dealers, automobile dealers, and a host of other retail merchants. Assume that an installment dealer operated with a gross profit margin of 30 percent. Then 30 percent of the amounts collected from its installment customers would constitute its realized gross profit for the year on installment sales. Also, 30 percent of its installment receivables would constitute unrealized income.

Acme Appliances started business on January 1. During its first year, sales (all on an installment basis) totaled $1,000,000. Cost of goods sold totaled $700,000. Other expenses came to $210,000. Collections on receivables amounted to $700,000. Income could be computed on either basis:

| | *Accrual* | *Installment* |
|---|---|---|
| Sales | $1,000,000 | |
| Cost of goods sold | 700,000 | |
| Gross profit | $ 300,000 | $210,000 (0.3 × $700,000) |
| Expenses | 210,000 | 210,000 |
| Net profit, before tax | $ 90,000 | 0 |

Using the installment method of reporting, Acme defers the tax on the unrealized profit in its year-end receivables. We can check this result. If sales were $1,000,000 and collections were $700,000, the year-end receivables (ignoring bad accounts) would be $300,000. The unrealized gross profit in these receivables is 30 percent of $300,000, or $90,000.

### *Casual Sellers*

The installment sale provisions are available to persons who are not dealers. They may be invoked for any sales of real estate and for casual sales of personal property (that is, property that is not real property) excluding inventory of $1,000 or more. For a nondealer to utilize the installment method of reporting a specific transaction, the amount of the cash payments received in the year of sale cannot exceed 30 percent of the selling price. Where real estate is involved, the computations sometimes become complicated by the fact that mortgages may be assumed by the buyer or given by the buyer to the seller. In fact, the handling of the mortgage may be varied to make a realty sale qualify under the installment sales provisions even though more than 30 percent cash is obtained by the seller in the year of sale.

Assume that Jones plans on selling a piece of real estate. At present it is free of any mortgage. He finds a buyer willing to pay $100,000 for the property. The buyer plans on obtaining a $60,000 loan on the property and paying an additional $10,000 cash in the year of sale with notes for $30,000 covering the balance. If the buyer does obtain the $60,000 loan and pays the proceeds, plus $10,000 to Jones, the installment sales provisions will not be available, because Jones has received $70,000, or 70 percent of the selling price, in the year of sale.

Instead, suppose that Jones himself borrows $60,000 against the property. No income tax consequences result from borrowing. Now he sells the property, with the buyer assuming the mortgage and paying an additional $10,000 and giving him notes to cover the balance. Under the installment sales provisions of the tax law, only $10,000 will be deemed to have been paid, and thus the sale will qualify for installment sales treatment. If we further assume that Jones has a tax basis of $70,000 for the property, here is the way he will report his gain:

| | |
|---|---|
| Selling price | $100,000 |
| Tax basis | 70,000 |
| Profit ultimately to be reported | 30,000 |
| To be received from buyer | 40,000 |
| Profit as a percentage of amount to be received | 75% |
| Payments received in year of sale | $ 10,000 |
| Profit to be reported in year of sale | 7,500 |
| Profit to be reported in future years, based on 75% of payments received, as received | 22,500 |

Notice that where a mortgage assumption is involved, the percentage that is used to determine what portion of each payment is profit is *not* the profit percentage, but rather the percentage that the profit is to the total cash payments to be received from the buyer.

Thus, by slightly reordering the transaction, Jones can arrange to have only $7,500 of profit on which to pay tax in the year of sale, rather than the $30,000 on which he would have had to pay tax. Yet he has received exactly the same amount of cash under both methods. He has a contingent liability on the mortgage, using the tax-deferral method, but he can eliminate even this by having in the mortgage note a contractual provision stating that his liability ceases when the mortgage is assumed by a responsible individual satisfactory to the lender.

Often, with a little imagination, the installment sales provisions may be made applicable in cases where it seems at first they are not. For example, a corporation decided to sell off a division of its business. The accounts receivable and inventory relating to that division were to be sold for $1,000,000 cash, whereas the fixed assets were to be sold to the same buyer for $700,000, with a down payment of $200,000. As originally contemplated, the sales contract called for a total price of $1,700,000, with cash of $1,200,000 being paid at the time of sale and the balance covered by a contract secured by the pledge of the fixed assets. After review of the transaction by the seller's tax advisers, two separate transactions and contracts were employed–one covering the receivables and inventory, and the other covering the fixed assets. The result was the utilization of the installment sales provisions to defer taxability of the gain on the sale of the fixed assets. Because the sale of the receivables resulted in a loss and that of the inventory in neither gain nor loss, the net effect in the year of sale was actually a generation of cash, through having a net loss to report for tax purposes rather than a substantial net profit.

The installment sale election on the sale of a capital asset may reduce the total tax on the gain realized. There can be a saving of as much as $5,000 for each $50,000 of gain that can be deferred to separate future years, since the first $50,000 of net long-term capital gains in a year is subject to a maximum tax of 25 percent, and the balance to a maximum tax of 35 percent. Similarly, the minimum tax on tax preferences may be avoided or reduced because of the minimum annual exclusion of $10,000 for tax preferences.

### *Financial Accounting*

Under generally accepted accounting principles, the accrual method is normally used for reporting sales for financial purposes. When the installment method is used for tax reporting purposes, the use of the accrual method for financial statements results in a deferred income tax credit representing the portion of the tax to be paid as future collections are received.

## COST RECOVERY

When the seller receives obligations of the buyer, such as a contract for deed, that do not have an ascertainable fair market value, an alternative method of reporting gain may be utilized. This involves treating all payments received as tax-free recoveries of investment until the tax basis of the property sold has been received, and then reporting the entire amounts received thereafter as profit. If Mr. Jones, in our previous example, had been able to utilize this method, no taxable profit would have been reported in the year of sale, but all payments received from the buyer thereafter would have been 100 percent taxable. The

Internal Revenue Service, however, generally takes the position that it is only in a rather unusual situation that the promise of the buyer has *no* fair market value. If the I.R.S. is successful in establishing that the promise of the buyer has any value at all, the result may be a tax boomerang. What might have been capital gain to the seller may be, in part at least, converted to ordinary income.

This conversion of capital gain to ordinary income results from collections on the contract not being treated as being from sale or exchange of the contract. If the contract has no fair market value when received, the theory is that the transaction is a continuing one, with payments received all being part of the selling price. If the contract has a value, however, then the transaction is a closed one, with the fair market value of the contract deemed as both the sales price for determining gain or loss, and the purchase price of the contract. The payments received on the contract are not, then, from the sale of the property; they are simply collections on a contract and, as such, normally result in ordinary income. The exception would occur when the obligor on the note or contract is a corporation. A specific provision of the tax law provides that payments received on corporate indebtedness shall be deemed to be on a sale or exchange therefor.

## RESTRICTED PROPERTY

As a general rule, of course, property received for services is includible in taxable income at its fair market value. But it is possible to arrange the transfer of property so that tax incidence is postponed. This can be accomplished by making the property forfeitable if substantial future services are not performed by the person receiving it.

The tax effect is then to tax the person receiving the property when there is no longer a substantial risk of forfeiture. The person paying for the services with property does not get a tax deduction until the payee has to report income.

While this tactic is most often used in connection with transfers of stock to employees, the timing of income can be controlled in other situations as well. For example, an attorney is going to take common stock as part payment of his fees for organizing a new corporation. The corporation will get no benefit from a current tax deduction since it anticipates initial losses, while the attorney prefers not having to pay out cash currently for income taxes. If his stock will be forfeited in the event he declines to render services as general counsel to the corporation during the next five years, pursuant to a retainer fee arrangement calling for a substantial part of his time, then he probably can postpone recognizing income from receipt of the stock until the end of the five-year period.

But there is a price. If he realizes income at the beginning, then subsequent increases in value of the stock ultimately will be realized as capital gain. If he postpones recognition until the end of the fifth year, the fair market value of the stock at that time will be the basis for recognizing ordinary income. Thus, the decision-making trade-off of the payee will compare the present value of the increased future tax (resulting from having ordinary income rather than capital gain) with the tax that would otherwise have to be paid currently. To the payer, the trade-off is the present value of a potentially greater future tax deduction (greater because the value of the property will presumably increase with time) compared to the current tax deduction foregone.

For both payer and payee, there is also the real business effect of the forfeitability provision, which may be more important to either than the tax benefits or detriments.

## CONTRACTORS

Building and other construction contractors have a peculiar income-determination problem because of the length of their contracts and the uncertainties as to total cost until the contract is fully completed.

Normal accounting procedures impose serious practical problems. Costs are being incurred, of course, but these costs will build up as work-in-process inventory until the contract is completed. They are not expenses. At the same time, the contractor is making progress billings to his customers and receiving payments (less, perhaps, a percentage that is held back until the job is finally finished). Yet these billings are not sales in the normal accounting meaning of "sales," because they usually do not integrate with any specific determinable amount of costs that have been used up.

The result is that income on long-term contracts (generally, more than one year from start to finish) can be determined as for any other business taxpayers, but it can also be determined by either of two other approaches:

1. The percentage-of-completion method, in which the percentage of the total contract completed is estimated, costs incurred to date are deducted, and the result is the profit or loss to date.
2. The completed-contract method, in which no profit or loss is estimated until the contract is entirely finished.

Assume that a contractor is engaged in building a $3,000,000 hospital. Construction covers a three-year period:

| | *Year 1* | *Year 2* | *Year 3* |
|---|---|---|---|
| Percentage completed at end of year | 15 | 70 | 100 |
| Costs incurred during year | $440,000 | $1,560,000 | $700,000 |

By the percentage-of-completion method, which is analogous to the accrual method, the profit calculation would be:

| | *Year 1* | *Year 2* | *Year 3* |
|---|---|---|---|
| Percentage completed | 15 | 55 | 30 |
| Revenue earned (% X $3 million) | $450,000 | $1,650,000 | $900,000 |
| Costs of earning revenue | 440,000 | 1,560,000 | 700,000 |
| Net profit | $ 10,000 | $ 90,000 | $200,000 |

Using the completed-contract method, the entire profit of $300,000 would be reported in the third year.

Which method to use depends on a number of factors, including the requirement that, once one of these methods is adopted, it must be used consistently. Many contractors are small corporations, and they find the percentage-of-completion method preferable because it keeps all their income in the lowest corporate tax bracket by keeping it flowing smoothly. Others find that they prefer the temporary "loan" of the taxes they defer by using the completed-contract method.

## INCOME AVERAGING

The basic theory of tax accounting is that income will be reported on a yearly basis. However, because of the possible hardship that unusual fluctuations of income can work on an individual, an averaging device may be used to lessen the burden. The income-averaging provision can be used only if the income of the current year is at least $3,000 more than 120 percent of the average income for the prior four years. Thus, if average income for the years 1974 through 1977 was $7,200, averaging would be available to the taxpayer only if his 1978 income exceeded $11,640 ($7,200 X 1.2 = $8,640; $8,640 + $3,000 = $11,640).

Assuming that the 1978 income is actually $20,200, the tax computation will result in limiting the tax on the last $11,560 of income (that is, on the excess over 120 percent of the average income) to five times the tax attributable to 1/5 of the $11,560. The actual computation, using the tax rates for a single individual, would go like this:

| | |
|---|---|
| Nonaverageable income | $ 8,640 |
| 1/5 of averageable income ($11,560) | 2,312 |
| Total | $10,952 |
| Tax on $10,952 | $ 1,778 |
| Tax on $8,640 | 1,216 |
| Tax attributable to last $2,400 | $ 562 |
| Multiplied by 5—tax on averageable income | $ 2,810 |
| Tax on $8,640 (as above) | 1,216 |
| Total tax | $ 4,026 |

The tax on $20,200 without income averaging would be $4,510; accordingly, income averaging results in a saving of $484.

The user of income averaging may not use the limited exclusion of income earned abroad alternative tax for capital gains nor the 50 percent maximum tax-rate limitation on personal service income (which will be discussed in Chapter 13).

All categories of income, except premature distributions to an owner-employee from a retirement plan and certain amounts received from a trust as an accumulation distribution ("throwback"), are averageable.

## OPERATING LOSSES

A man on a salary is not apt to have a loss on his tax return, but many a business or an individual with business interests may have some years of profit and some of loss. A new business may take several years before it gets operating profitably. It would be unfair to tax the profits without first allowing the business to at least replace the capital depleted through the losses of other years.

The tax law thus provides for a pattern of business-loss carrybacks and carryovers covering a period of 11 years. A net operating loss is first carried back to the third year prior to the loss year unless taxpayer irrevocably elects not to carry back such loss. To the extent of the profit for that year, the loss carryback is treated as a special deduction in that year, thus reducing the taxable income of that year and giving rise to a refund of part of the taxes previously paid for that year. To the extent not absorbed by the profit for the third prior year, the loss is then carried as a special deduction to the second prior year. If the profit for that year fails to absorb the remaining loss, the balance is carried to the year preceding the loss year. Any balance not used up against the profits of the three prior years can then be carried over to the seven years after the loss year, in sequence, until used up. A dollar of loss can never be used twice, nor does a dollar of profit ever absorb a dollar of loss more than once.

However, some deductions affected by the amount of net income are recalculated for the various years to which the loss is carried. Also, on noncorporate returns, the nonbusiness deductions of the taxpayer will be eliminated in computing the net profit absorbed by the loss, except to the extent of nonbusiness income.

Assume that the tax returns of the Bruder Corporation showed the following amounts of net taxable income before reflecting any net operating-loss carrybacks or carryovers:

| *Tax Year* | | *Net Taxable Income* | *Losses Applied of 1976* | *Losses Applied of 1979* |
|---|---|---|---|---|
| 1973 | | $125,000 | $125,000 | |
| 1974 | | 75,000 | 75,000 | |
| 1975 | | 25,000 | 25,000 | |
| 1976 | Loss | (260,000) | | |

| Tax Year | | Net Taxable Income | Losses Applied of 1976 | of 1979 |
|---|---|---|---|---|
| 1977 | | 10,000 | 10,000 | |
| 1978 | | 40,000 | 25,000 | $15,000 |
| 1979 | Loss | (35,000) | | |
| 1980 | | 5,000 | | 5,000 |
| 1981 | | 20,000 | | 15,000 |
| | | | $260,000 | $35,000 |

The 1976 net operating loss of $260,000 would first be carried back to 1973, and then carried over to 1974 and 1975. Refunds would be obtained of the income taxes paid in each of those years. But the income of those 3 years would absorb only $225,000 of the $260,000 loss. The remaining $35,000 would be carried over and shown on the 1977 return as a special deduction. In 1977, $10,000 of that would be soaked up by that year's profit, resulting in no income tax for that year. The remaining $25,000 would be carried over to 1978 as a special deduction. The return for that year would show taxable income of $15,000 ($40,000 – $25,000) on which tax would be paid. If not absorbed sooner, the 1976 net operating loss could be carried over through 1983—but it would expire if not used up by 1983.

The 1979 loss can be carried back to the third prior year, but that year of 1976 has no net taxable income against which it can be used. It is then carried over undiminished to 1977. But 1977 no longer has any net taxable income to be absorbed. In 1978, however, there still remains $15,000 of net taxable income. The loss is therefore used to soak up that income, resulting in a refund of the tax paid for 1978. The $35,000 loss, reduced by the $15,000 use made of it in 1978, now becomes a carryover to 1980. It soaks up the $5,000 of 1980 income and results in no tax being paid for that year. It is now a carryover to 1981 of $15,000, and is applied to reduce the $20,000 income of that year, leaving $5,000 subject to tax.

The general rule for individuals (or fiduciaries, for that matter) is the same as for corporations. Losses can be carried back three years and forward seven. But whereas a corporation, by definition, has no items of income or deduction that are nonbusiness, an individual does. The purpose of the net-operating-loss provisions is to allow a tax benefit for (1) only business losses sustained, and (2) only a net economic loss from taxable transactions for the year.

Thus, an individual is allowed to deduct his nonbusiness deductions only to the extent of his nonbusiness income. However, certain items that are actually nonbusiness are treated as business deductions for net-operating-loss purposes. Among these are nonbusiness casualty and theft losses, and losses on the stock of Ordinary Loss Small Business Corporations and Small Business Investment Corporations.

The objective of allowing only a net economic loss means, for instance, that no deduction will be allowed for the 50 percent of net long-term capital gains that may be excluded in arriving at adjusted gross income. This item represents merely a technical deduction allowed for the purpose of taxing capital gains less heavily than other income, and therefore represents no actual expense.

Assume that Austin Clanton's 1978 tax return shows the following:

| | |
|---|---|
| Dividends | $ 3,000 |
| Business income (loss) | (10,000) |
| Capital gains (after 50% reduction) | 2,000 |
| Itemized deductions | 1,200 |
| Exemptions | 1,800 |

The capital gains were all long term.

In figuring Clanton's net operating loss, which can be carried back to 1975, we must add back the capital gains deduction, thus increasing the capital gains to $4,000. The itemized deductions will be allowed to the extent of the nonbusiness income. In this instance, it means that they will be allowed in full, because nonbusiness income is $7,000 versus deductions of only $1,200. The exemptions are eliminated.

| | | |
|---|---|---|
| Business loss | | $10,000 |
| Reduced by: | | |
| Capital gains | $4,000 | |
| Dividends | 3,000 | |
| Total | 7,000 | |
| Less deductions | 1,200 | 5,800 |
| Net operating loss carryback to 1975 | | $ 4,200 |

A similar adjustment would take place in the year to which the loss is carried in arriving at the amount to be carried over to the next year, if the loss were not fully absorbed in the first year.

A partnership, as such, has no net operating loss, nor does an Electing Small Business Corporation. Instead, the partners and stockholders, respectively, pick up the losses and treat them, if appropriate, as business losses in computing their personal net-operating-loss carrybacks and carryovers.

A net operating loss's value depends on the effective tax bracket in the year to which it will be carried. The right to take a carryback can be waived by an election filed with the tax return of the loss year. Such a waiver may be a good gamble when the carryback year is, for instance, one where the corporation paid a 22 percent tax while it is anticipated that as a carryover the loss will be utilized at a 48 percent rate.

To a business with an unused net-operating-loss carryover, profits are peculiarly valuable. The loss carryover can be viewed as a contingent asset. A corporation with a $1 million net-operating-loss carryover, therefore, has a contingent asset worth potentially as much as $480,000. A profitable operation can convert this contingent asset into an actual asset. Otherwise, it is lost. As we shall see in Chapter 17, this often leads such corporations to acquire profitable businesses and makes them willing to pay a higher price than others might pay for the promise of immediate profitability. The net-operating-loss provisions of the tax law, therefore, can be a substantial factor in the decision to rehabilitate an ailing business rather than to abandon it.

## MULTIPLE ENTITIES

Another approach to counteracting fluctuating incomes and/or graduated tax rates is the use of the corporation as a business vehicle, particularly the use of several corporations. In Chapter 4 we saw an example of how the Electing Small Business Corporation could accomplish such an equalization of an essentially uneven flow of income.

A married individual with a business income that fluctuates from $12,000 to $62,000, instead of having some income taxed at 53 percent, can equalize his current tax rate at a maximum of 22 percent by using a corporation. The corporation pays him a salary of $12,000 (marginal tax bracket, 22 percent) and itself has net income of from $0 to $50,000–taxed at a maximum of 22 percent.

At one time, one individual could own 100 percent of as many separate corporate entities as good business reasons could justify, and thus he could obtain the benefit of lower tax brackets for both himself and each individual corporation. Using 1977 tax rates, one corporation with $500,000 of taxable income would pay $226,500 of federal income tax, while ten unaffiliated corporations with $50,000 each of taxable income would pay $10,500 each, for a total of $105,000–or $121,500 less income tax. With the multiple corporations, the after-tax net income would be over 44 percent greater than with one corporation.

As will be discussed in Chapter 18, which deals with foreign taxes, advantages still remain in handling foreign business through separate corporate entities, and there may be state income tax advantages to using separate corporations. For federal income tax purposes, tax rate advantages can only be obtained if ownership of corporations under common control is diffused enough to meet either level of this two-layer test:

1. No five or fewer individuals own 80 percent or more of each of the corporations in the group. (Note that it is not necessary that all of the five own stock in all of the corporations constituting the test group.) Or
2. The same individuals as in (1) do not own more than 50 percent of each corporation in the test group (counting for this test the least amount of stock each individual owns in any of the test corporations).

Assume, for example, that Jones and Smith each own 50 percent of ten corporations. They meet both tests. They own 80 percent or more of all ten, and they also own more than 50 percent.

Now assume that Jones owns 50 percent of five of the corporations, with the other 50 percent owned by a different person in each of the five; and similarly Smith owns 50 percent of the other five, with the other 50 percent in each owned by the same people who own the other 50 percent of Jones' corporations. Call these other five people Alpha, Beta, Gamma, Delta, and Sigma. Let us chart the ownership:

| *Corporation* | *Jones* % | *Smith* % | *Alpha* % | *Beta* % | *Gamma* % | *Delta* % | *Sigma* % |
|---|---|---|---|---|---|---|---|
| 1 | 50 | | 50 | | | | |
| 2 | 50 | | | 50 | | | |
| 3 | 50 | | | | 50 | | |
| 4 | 50 | | | | | 50 | |
| 5 | 50 | | | | | | 50 |
| 6 | | 50 | 50 | | | | |
| 7 | | 50 | | 50 | | | |
| 8 | | 50 | | | 50 | | |
| 9 | | 50 | | | | 50 | |
| 10 | | 50 | | | | | 50 |

On the 80 percent test, all kinds of combinations of four of the corporations fail. For instance, if Jones, Alpha, Beta, Gamma, and Delta are used as the five test shareholders, then corporations 1 through 4 fail the test. The same is true for Jones with any four of the five or Smith with any four of the five.

However, the "over" 50 percent test is another story. No two corporations fail that test. For example, take corporations 1 and 2. Alpha owns 0 percent of the stock of 2 and Beta owns 0 percent of the stock of 1. Thus, counting the least amount of stock owned by a shareholder in any of the corporations in the test group, Jones owns 50 percent but Alpha and Beta each own 0 percent, and hence the total is 50 percent which is not "over" 50 percent!

If Jones or Smith were corporations, they might still be able to consolidate the results of the five corporations for financial statement purposes; and, as a minimum, would be able to reflect in the "parent" corporation financials the current earnings of all five.

As an example of ownership that would pass the first test, but would fail the second, consider a group of corporations in which the stock is owned equally by seven unrelated individuals. While any five would own more than 50 percent of the stock in every corporation in the group, no five would own 80 percent or more. Hence, if the corporations were actually separate businesses, each corporation would be treated separately for income tax purposes.

## CASH BASIS

Normal accounting practices can be described as "accrual basis" accounting. Taxpayers who do not have substantial amounts of inventory have the right to use another basis of accounting, called the "cash basis." The same items are income or are deductible under either basis, but the timing differs. On the accrual basis, the transaction's occurrence requires recognition of income or allows a deduction. Thus, if merchandise is delivered to a customer, a sales transaction has taken place even though the customer may not pay for 60 days.

On the cash basis, income is not deemed realized until cash is actually or constructively received. Deductions cannot be taken until the expenses are actually paid. This method of accounting, available to and widely used by farmers, professional men, and a wide variety of service businesses, allows the building up of substantial assets without imposition of an income tax. It is available to almost any taxpaying entity for which inventories are not a material income-determining factor.

For instance, a three-man medical partnership might have $120,000 of accounts receivable on its books, of which $80,000 might be collectible. In a sense, at least, the doctors have been allowed to build up these assets tax free. The fact that expenses are deducted only as paid poses little problem to the average cash-basis taxpayer, because his major expenses are normally paid as incurred anyway.

By postponing collection efforts, or even delaying billing, it is quite easy to shift the income of a cash-basis business from one year to the next, thereby attempting to equalize income.

However, it should be realized that the cash-basis taxpayer often faces a day of reckoning. The receivables of the medical partnership in the example above will all be collected when the partnership is wound up, and this will constitute ordinary income even if collected by the heirs of the doctors. If the cash-basis business is a corporation, the day of reckoning may never come directly for its shareholders and may be realized as long-term capital gain by their heirs.

### CASE EXCERPTS

*Warren Jones Co.* v. *Commissioner* (CA9 1975) 36 AFTR 2d 75-5954
*Woodward* v. *U.S.* (DC Va.–1971) 27 AFTR 2d 71-702
*Fetzer Refrigerator Co.* (CA6–1971) 27 AFTR 2d 71-613

*Warren Jones Co.* v. *Commissioner*
(CA9 1975) 36 AFTR 2d 75-5954

A cash basis seller of an apartment building attempted to report the transaction on a "cost recovery" basis. The Tax Court agreed, but the Appeals Court did not.

. . . the Tax Court held that the taxpayer's contract, which had a face value of $133,000, was not the "equivalent of cash" since it had a fair market value of only $76,980. Had the taxpayer sold the contract, the discount from the face value, approximately 42 percent, would have been "substantially greater than the generally prevailing premium for the use of money."

The Tax Court observed that requiring the taxpayer to realize the fair market value of the contract in the year of the sale could subject the taxpayer to substantial hardships. The taxpayer would be taxed in the initial year on a substantial portion of its gain from the sale of the property, even though it had received, in cash, only a small fraction of the purchase price. To raise funds to pay its taxes, the taxpayer might be forced to sell the contract at the contract's fair market value, even though such a sale might not otherwise be necessary or advantageous. Most importantly in the Tax Court's view, if the taxpayer were required to realize the fair market value of the contract in the year of the sale, the sale transaction would be closed for tax purposes in that year; hence, the taxpayer's capital gain on the transaction would be permanently limited to the difference between its adjusted basis and the contract's fair market value plus the cash payments received in the year of sale. If the taxpayer did retain the contract, so as to collect its face value, the amounts received in excess of the contract's fair market value would constitute ordinary income. The Tax Court also noted that requiring the cash basis taxpayer to realize the fair market value of the real estate contract would tend to obscure the differences between the cash and accrual methods of reporting . . . .

On several occasions, we have held that if the fair market value of a deferred payment obligation received in a sale or other exchange can be ascertained, that fair market value must be included as an amount realized under section 1001 (b). Most recently, in *In re Steen* [75-1 USTC ¶9199], 509 F. 2d 1398, 1404-05 (9th Cir. 1975), we held that the fair market value of an installment payment contract received in exchange for shares of stock was ascertainable and that, consequently, that fair market value was an amount realized in the year of the sale. In *Heller Trust* v. *Commissioner* [67-2 USTC ¶9626], 382 F. 2d 675, 681 (9th Cir. 1967), our court affirmed a Tax Court decision requiring a taxpayer to include the fair market value of real estate contracts as an amount realized in the year of a sale, even though the fair market value of the contracts there involved was only 50 percent of their face value. See also *Clodfelter* v. *Commissioner* [70-1 USTC ¶9413], 426 F. 2d 1391 (9th Cir. 1970); *Tombari* v. *Commissioner* [62-1 USTC ¶9261], 299 F. 2d 889, 892-93

(9th Cir. 1962); *Gersten* v. *Commissioner* [59-1 USTC ¶9303], 267 F. 2d 195 (9th Cir. 1959).

There are, of course, "rare and extraordinary" situations in which it is impossible to ascertain the fair market value of a deferred payment obligation in the year of sale . . . .

The Tax Court found, as a fact, that the taxpayer's real estate contract with the Storeys had a fair market value of $76,980 in the taxable year of sale. Consequently, the taxpayer must include $76,980 in determining the amount realized under section 1001 (b) . . . .

*Woodward* v. *U.S.*
(DC Va.–1971) 27 AFTR 2d 71-702

> Taxpayers who reported 1960 income on the accrual basis tried to report 1960 income under the installment method on an amended return that was filed after the statutory deadline for filing returns.

. . . The claim was formally disallowed, . . . the District Director of Internal Revenue advising plaintiffs that they had made a valid election on their original return to report income from 1960 sales on the accrual accounting basis, and that their election by way of amended return to report such income under the installment method was not timely made. . . .

The single issue for determination is whether, having reported income from sales under the accrual method on their original return for 1960, plaintiffs thereby made an election as to accounting methods which precluded change to an installment basis of reporting such income in an amended return filed after the statutory deadline for filing returns. Plaintiffs urge that, at the time their amended return was filed, nothing in either §453 or the applicable regulations precluded such a change.

. . . Until some 21 months after plaintiffs had filed their amended return, the regulations promulgated under §453 did not expressly require that an election, in order to be timely, be made on or before the filing deadline for returns. . . .

Present sections 453 (a) and (b) of the Internal Revenue Code (see n. 1, *supra*) are derived materially unchanged from sections 44 (a) and (b), respectively, of the Internal Revenue Act of 1928, 45 Stat. 791. In *Pacific National Company* v. *Welch, supra,* the Supreme Court considered the question of whether a taxpayer, having filed a return reporting income from installment sales under the deferred payment method, was entitled to have such income recomputed under §44 (installment method) after the time for filing returns had expired. The claim was there urged that installment sales had been "erroneously" reported as cash sales on the taxpayer's original return. As here, the taxpayer in *Welch* could have reported income on his original return under either of two accounting methods. Having chosen one, the Court ruled, the taxpayer thereby made an election which became binding upon expiration of the time allowed for filing returns. . . .

At the time *Welch* was decided, regulations promulgated under the installment method provision made no mention of elections. . . .

Plaintiffs' reliance on decisions which have distinguished *Welch* is misplaced. In *Bayley* v. *C.I.R.*, 35 T.C. 288 (1960), taxpayers who had reported a gain from the sale of their residence on their original return but who had failed to include it as income thereon were allowed to compute such income on the installment basis in an amended return filed after the statutory period for filing had expired. In *Hornberger* v. *C.I.R.*, 289 F.2d 602 (5th Cir. 1961), taxpayers were allowed, by way of a late amended return, to report on the installment method income from the sale of their house, where they had failed to report the sale at all on their original return. To the same effect as *Hornberger* is *Bookwalter* v. *Mayer,* 345 F.2d 476 (8th Cir. 1965); and see *Rev. Rul.* 65-297, 1965-2 Cum. Bull. 152.

The foregoing cases stand only for the proposition that, in appropriate circumstances, an election to report income under the installment method of accounting may be made after expiration of the time allowed for filing where that income has not been previously reported under an inconsistent method.

In summary, there is neither factual nor statutory basis for excepting plaintiffs from the rule announced in *Welch.* By reporting their income from calendar 1960 sales on an accrual basis in their original return, plaintiffs elected an accounting method as to the income from those sales, which election became binding upon expiration of the statutory period for filing returns.

*Fetzer Refrigerator Co.*
(CA6–1971) 27 AFTR 2d 71-613

> Can a corporation on the accrual method be entitled to deductions for yearly rent paid to a controlling shareholder who has authority to draw checks on the corporation—even though, reporting under the cash method, he did not report rents in the year in which they accrued and the corporation did not segregate rents in a separate account—on the ground that he "constructively received" rents?

In order for Section 267(a)(2) to apply, each of its requirements must first be satisfied. *Geiger & Peters, Inc.,* 27 T.C. 911, 918 (1957). Such satisfaction as to only one requirement is in dispute. Paraphrased, this requirement provides that the amounts involved be includable in the gross income of the person to whom the payment is to be made within the taxable year of the taxpayer or two and one-half months after the close thereof. Int. Rev. Code of 1954, §267(a)(2)(A). To determine whether the amounts are includible in the gross income of such person, the Regulations for Section 267 refer to the rules of constructive receipt which are found in the Regulations under Section 451 of the Code. Treas. Reg. §1.267(a)-1 (b) 1 (iii) (1958).

Regulations Section 1.451-2(a) gives the following definition of constructive receipt of income:

> . . . Income although not actually reduced to a taxpayer's possession is constructively received by him in the taxable year during which it is credited to his account, set apart for him, or otherwise made available so that he may draw upon it at any time, or so that he could have drawn upon it during the taxable year if notice of intention to withdraw had been given. . . .

As has been pointed out in *Hyland* v. *Commissioner,* 175 F.2d 422 (2d Cir. 1949), "[c]onstructive receipt of income by a taxpayer on the cash receipts basis is a creature of the Regulations; they prescribe the conditions which make the doctrine applicable." 175 F.2d at 423.

Thus, our purpose here is to determine whether the facts of this case permit a finding of constructive receipt within the language of Section 1.451-2(a) above.

In *Ross* v. *Commissioner,* 169 F.2d 483 (1st Cir. 1948), Justice Frankfurter described the coverage of the doctrine of constructive receipt of income in the following manner: "The doctrine of constructive receipt treats as taxable income which is unqualifiedly subject to the demand of a taxpayer on the cash receipts and disbursements method of accounting, whether or not such income has actually been received in cash. . . ." There was no evidence presented in this case to negate the conclusion that the rents due Mr. Fetzer were subject to his unqualified demand. See *O. H. Kruse Grain & Milling,* 28 T.C.M. 419 (1959).

## QUESTIONS AND PROBLEMS

1. The income of a lawyer, Harry Comes, fluctuates violently. Looking back over recent years, Harry notes that his net taxable income has been:

| | |
|---|---|
| 1971 | $10,000 |
| 1972 | 50,000 |
| 1973 | 20,000 |
| 1974 | 4,000 |
| 1975 | 40,000 |
| 1976 | 20,000 |
| 1977 | 60,000 |
| 1978 | 10,000 |

Harry expects this pattern to continue. He is single and is contemplating taking a job as legal counsel for a corporation. This job would pay a flat salary. Harry has annual itemized deductions of $3,000 and has only the one exemption—for himself. Assuming that the future will be pretty much like the past, and ignoring fringe benefits available to an employee, what is the minimum salary that Harry could accept and still wind up after taxes in approximately the same financial position as his average after taxes for the years 1971-1978? Assume that the tax rates for all years are the tax rates now in effect.

2. The De Haven Appliance Company operates on a gross-profit margin of 22 percent. For tax purposes, it reports its income on the installment method. For financial accounting purposes, it uses the same treatment, employing an account called "Deferred Profit on Installment Sales," which it deducts from the account "Installment Notes and Contracts Receivable" in arriving at the book value of the latter. On the 12/31/x2 balance sheet, the book value of the installment receivables is $1,560,000.
   (a) How much profit on installment sale is being deferred?
   (b) Assuming an applicable 48 percent rate, how much tax is being deferred?
   (c) Is the company's accounting presentation proper?
3. Which of the following transactions can be reported on the installment method?
   (a) Sale of a personal residence for $20,000, with the buyer assuming a mortgage of $12,000, paying $4,000 cash in the year of sale, and giving the seller a note for $4,000.
   (b) Sale of a residential lot for $900, with the buyer giving the seller a used car (valued at $250), cash of $300, and a note of $350.
   (c) Sale of common stock in the X Corporation for $980 by Mr. Jones to Mr. Smith, with Mr. Jones receiving $100 in the year of sale, plus a note of $880.
   (d) Sale by a corporation of a warehouse building, for $1,000,000. The corporation received in the year of sale $300,000 in cash, stock in the purchaser with a fair market value of $200,000 at the time of receipt, plus a note for $500,000.
4. In each of the situations in Problem 3, what would be the tax effect on the seller of a payment by the buyer of all the balance due in the year following the year of sale?
5. John Decker sold his stock in the Decker Corporation on the installment basis, receiving $30,000 down in the year of sale, plus a note of the buyer for $70,000. Cost of the stock had been $10,000. Payments of $10,000 a year have subsequently been made for five years. Due to a pressing need for cash, Decker sells the note for $15,000. Bearing in mind that the transactions themselves determine the amount of gain, whereas all that the installment-sales provisions really do is to determine the timing for reporting

gain, what is the logical tax result to Decker of his sale (that is, the amount of gain or loss realized)?

6. Distinguish between the installment sale and the cost recovery sale.
7. Joe Deese, who is in a 60 percent tax bracket, sold unimproved realty to Anderson Dean. He received a down payment of $5,000, plus a contract for $95,000. Cost of the land had been $20,000. Dean had no personal liability under the contract, and under its terms the actual title to the land would be transferred only when all payments had been made. Deese considers that the contract has no fair market value, and he is planning to report his gain on the cost-recovery basis. The gain will be long-term capital gain. What advantage is there to Deese in using the cost-recovery method as contrasted with the installment-sales method? What risk does he run?
8. The Deerland Building Corporation has a construction contract to build a new hospital. It anticipates that its disbursements and cumulative percentages of the total contract completed will be:

| | *Disbursements* | *% Completed* |
|---|---|---|
| 19x1 | $ 450,000 | 10 |
| 19x2 | 2,325,000 | 90 |
| 19x3 | 225,000 | 100 |

The total contract price is $3,600,000. Deerland estimates that its net taxable income from other work will be about $50,000 per year. It has a tight cash-flow situation. What are the alternative ways in which it can report income on this contract, and which one will most help its cash flow?

9. Barry Richards had $4,000 of dividend and interest income during the year. His net business loss was $15,000. Nonbusiness deductions amount to $5,000. In addition, Richards paid $10,000 to a "finder" in a futile attempt to obtain long-term financing for his business. In previous years, he has paid substantial amounts of income tax. What difference will it make to Richards whether the $10,000 is classifiable as a business expense or is allowable as a deduction from adjusted gross income (that is, is an "itemized deduction") in arriving at net income?
10. The Kay Company, Inc., is desperately short of cash as the result of a too-rapid expansion of the corporation business. In 19x1, it had taxable income of $500,000; in 19x2, of $750,000; and 19x3, of $1,000,000. It has no dividend income. In 19x4, sales volume is up, but it appears that the corporation will only break even. It is contemplating raising cash by selling either of two pieces of property, retaining use of the property by leasing it back for 10 years. The lease arrangement would be the same for either property, as would the selling price. Only the tax basis differs between the two:

| | *Sales Price* | *Tax Basis* |
|---|---|---|
| Plant #1 | $1,200,000 | $1,500,000 |
| Plant #2 | 1,200,000 | 800,000 |

Which plant would you recommend they sell, and why? Comment on the financial-statement effects of your recommended course of action. Do the financial statements seem to be saying that the action that looked best to you was inferior to the other course of action?

11. Fred and Bradley Jones are identical twins. Fred owns 100 percent of the stock of Federico, Inc., which in turn owns 50 percent of the stock of Ex, Why, and Zee. Bradley Jones personally owns the other 50 percent of the stock of Ex, while Mrs. Bradley Jones and her father, respectively, own the other 50 percent of Why and Zee. Bradley is a full-time employee of Ex, but has no involvement whatsoever in Why or Zee. His wife is a full-time employee of Why, but has no involvement whatsoever in Ex or Zee. There are no restrictions, options, or side agreements covering any of the stock. All four companies are merchandising companies. Each of the four corporations earned $50,000 of taxable income during the current year. What will be their combined federal income tax? Would your answer change if Bradley were an employee of Why or his wife an employee of Ex? Why?
12. A corporate executive has purchased stock for $8 per share which has a fair market value of $10 per share, subject to a substantial risk of forfeiture which will expire in ten years. He expects the value of the stock to be $12 at the end of the ten years, and anticipates that he will sell the stock at that time. Assume that he will pay tax on ordinary income at a 40 percent rate and on capital gain at a 20 percent rate. Under IRC 83, he can elect to report $2 per share as ordinary income now, which will mean that he will have $2 of long-term capital gain ten years from now. If he does not elect to report the spread between the $8 price and $10 value as income now, the difference between $8 and the $12 selling price ten years from now will be ordinary income. He can earn 6 percent after taxes on any amounts he has available to invest. Prepare an analysis both with and without reflecting the time-value of money that would help him decide whether or not to make the election. Then change the expectation as to the value of the stock ten years hence to make it $30 per share and see whether or not he should make the election.

# 10

# Depreciation

In 1947, the United States Steel Corporation precipitated a battle of depreciation ideologies by computing depreciation on its financial statements, including the income statement, on the basis of estimated replacement costs. Its independent C.P.A.'s refused to accept the financial statements as so prepared. U. S. Steel finally had to back down.

The position of U.S. Steel was one shared by many businessmen and financial analysts. From the businessman's point of view, the purpose of depreciation to an ongoing corporation is sometimes felt to be the provision of sufficient assets from the current revenue to replace assets as they wear out. If depreciation is to properly perform its function in computation of income, they argue, then at the end of the useful life of an asset, the total accumulated depreciation attributable to that asset should be an amount sufficient to replace it with a new asset. If the original asset cost \$1,000,000, but the replacement asset would cost \$1,500,000, owing to price-level or technological changes, then the depreciation allowance should be based on the \$1,500,000.

When depreciation allowed for tax purposes is based only on the original cost rather than the replacement value, then, it is argued, the income tax is actually taxing capital. The basic proposition is that income can exist only after a reasonable provision (in terms of current price levels and conditions) for maintaining the productive capacity of the organization. To the extent that the depreciation allowed is less than this amount, the income tax is actually acting to expropriate capital.

## DEPRECIATION IN TAX ACCOUNTING

The word *depreciation* means different things to different people. To the businessman, it may mean provision for replacement. To the man in the street, it may mean "decline in value." But in taxes it means an arbitrary allocation of part of the original cost (or other tax basis) of an asset to a particular year.

The basic idea of tax depreciation stems from the nature of accounting "income." If I lend Jones $10,000 without interest, I realize no income when Jones repays me any part or all of my $10,000. This is a recovery of my investment. If Jones pays me my $10,000 plus $600 of interest, I have $600 of income. If, at the end of the first year of the loan, Jones pays me only $5,000 on the principal of the note, plus $600 interest, I still have income of $600.

If I buy for $10,000 a piece of equipment that will be of use in producing income during this year and the following year, my income for this two-year period can be fairly determined only if I am first allowed to recoup my $10,000 investment. The same principle applies whether the investment is made in something with a useful life of two years or of twenty years. Practically all the significant tax problems involving depreciation stem from the basic problem of how to allocate a given amount of investment to the tax years over which that investment will be producing income.

Two basic rules are thus immediately apparent:

1. No matter what method of depreciation is used, the total amount of cost that will be written off will be the same.

2. Depreciation can be taken only on something whose utility can be thought of as being consumed over the passage of time or with use, and that is used, directly or indirectly, in attempting to produce income. Thus, even though the value of a personal residence may decline with the passage of time, depreciation deductions cannot be taken for it on an income tax return if it is used as the taxpayer's personal residence. The same house held for production of rental income will depreciate for tax purposes. The land on which the house stands, however, because it does not decrease in value with either use or the passage of time, will not be depreciable, regardless of the use of the house.

The second of these two rules—that the property must be used in a trade or business—requires no elaboration for our purposes. But the first rule immediately raises the question, "If the total written off will always be the same, then how can depreciation be of any importance in making decisions?"

If we assume that tax rates remain constant and that a dollar today means no more and no less than a dollar ten years from now, then the ways in which depreciation is allocated to different tax years would be of interest only to technicians. So we have to ask ourselves. "Is there a difference between a dollar in the hand today and the promise of a dollar ten years from now?"

What can I do with a dollar that I have today? I can consume it! But businesses, as such, consume nothing. A corporation cannot eat, drink, or make merry. It must, willy-nilly, either distribute this dollar as a dividend to its shareholders, who may consume it, or it must invest it in some manner. If the corporation has exceptionally profitable investment opportunities open to it, it might be able to invest the dollar in something that would produce an after-tax rate of return of, say, 20 percent. If the 20 cents earned in the first year could in turn be invested at 20 percent, and similarly with the 24 cents earned in the second year, and so forth, at the end of ten years that one dollar will have grown to $6.19!

If one dollar today can be invested so as to amount to $6.19 in ten years, then certainly one dollar today is worth more than one dollar ten years from now. Assuming that we are talking only about dollars that will be invested, and that we further assume that these dollars can be put to work at a known after-tax rate of return, we can compute what the value is today of a dollar to be received at some point in the future. Using the 20 percent rate of return of the preceding paragraph as an illustration, won't the value to us today of the prospect of receiving a dollar ten years from now be the amount we would have to invest today in order to have a dollar ten years from now? Look at what I shall have if I invest 16 cents today at 20 percent per year (with the earnings all being received as of the end of the year):

| *End of Year* | *Amount (1.2 × Previous Amount)* |
|---|---|
| 1 | $0.19 |
| 2 | 0.23 |
| 3 | 0.28 |
| 4 | 0.33 |
| 5 | 0.40 |
| 6 | 0.48 |
| 7 | 0.58 |
| 8 | 0.69 |
| 9 | 0.83 |
| 10 | 1.00 |

My 16 cents will have grown to a dollar! Of course, if the investment opportunities open to me offer a return of only 7 percent after taxes then I shall have to invest 51 cents today in order for it to grow to a dollar ten years from now. If the best that I can do is 4 percent after taxes on my investments, then I must invest $.68 now if I hope to have a dollar ten years from now.

What does all this have to do with depreciation? If a taxpayer in a 40 percent tax bracket can take one dollar of depreciation now rather than ten years from now, he has the use of 40 cents for ten years. If he can earn 20 percent on money invested in his business, that 40 cents will have grown to $2.48 by the end of ten years. As long as the depreciation deduction reduces his tax bill, and tax rates remain relatively constant, a dollar of deduction will always be considered more valuable now than at some future date.

## SOME IMPLICATIONS OF COST DEPRECIATION

Let us look again at the replacement position adopted by U.S. Steel and see whether it is really as sharply opposed to cost depreciation as it appears to be.

When U.S. Steel found itself unable to take depreciation on replacement cost, it switched to figuring depreciation on the basis of original cost. The method it adopted allocated the original cost over the period of useful life based on the percentage of capacity at which its properties were operating. The result, for 1947, was that U.S. Steel was able to deduct more depreciation for financial statement purposes than it had attempted to take on the replacement-cost basis.[1] In a static physical situation, of course, where the only changes in the physical plant were the results of inflation, there would ultimately come a day of reckoning when cost depreciation would inevitably fall below replacement-cost depreciation. In a growing company in an expanding economy, such a day of reckoning may be indefinitely postponed. (We shall shortly return to this topic and see the types of accelerated depreciation now in use, and also attempt to evaluate their effects.)

But there are other aspects of cost depreciation. If a company is operating profitably, it is generating working capital available for general use in the amount of its depreciation expense. Let us visualize a one-asset company. Its one asset cost $1,000,000 and has a ten-year useful life. The company operates in an industry in which its prices are regulated by law to allow it 6 percent return after taxes on the original cost of its asset. At the beginning of year 1, total assets are $1,000,000. During the year, the company charges off $100,000 of depreciation and earns a profit of $60,000. At the end of year 1, its total assets consist of:

| | | |
|---|---|---|
| Cash | | $ 160,000 |
| Fixed assets | $1,000,000 | |
| Less: Depreciation | 100,000 | 900,000 |
| Total | | $1,060,000 |

Assume that the company pays out its $60,000 operating profit as a dividend. At the start of year 2, however, it still has available for investment the $100,000 represented by the depreciation. If we assume that the company can make investments that will produce 6 percent per year after taxes, we can figure out how much this $100,000 will amount to at the end of the tenth year.

The same thing will happen in the second year. There will be generated $160,000 of working capital, of which $60,000 will represent profit and $100,000 will be available for investment for 8 years at 6 percent per year.

This pattern will be repeated for the full ten years. At the end of the tenth year, the amount available to replace the company's one asset will *not* be a mere $1,000,000. No, indeed! It will be the sum of $1,318,079, representing the accumulation, at 6 percent compound interest, of the $100,000 made available to the company each year over and above its operating profit.

[1] An analysis by Prof. Lee J. Seidler (as reported in *Business Week*, June 7, 1976, page 53) of the 1974 U.S. Steel figures indicates, however, that with all balance sheet items converted to a replacement cost basis, and expenses calculated accordingly, reported net income of $691 million would have shrunk to $3.1 million.

Thus, when we ask ourselves whether cost depreciation is adequate to provide for replacement of an asset, we need really to mount a much more searching inquiry than simply the adding up of the dollars of cost depreciation. We must inquire into the long-run and short-run impacts of depreciation on pricing policy for the company and the industry. We also need to know something about the rate of return that the company can earn on its internal and external investments.

Even then, we have not fully exhausted our analysis of the implications of cost depreciation. Most businesses are not, in fact, one-asset organizations. They are multi-asset organizations. In any given year, some assets are being retired and new assets are being added. If we view depreciation as a method of financing the replacement of assets, we must also look into this matter of timing.

Take, for example, a mature corporation, growing at a modest rate. Its total depreciable assets have an original cost of $30,000,000, of which $14,000,000 has already been written off. They have an average useful life of eight years. Each year, $4,000,000 of fixed assets is added, including both replacements and additions. Let us see how inadequate this corporation's depreciation, based on cost, will be if a declining-balance method (at 200 percent of the straight-line rate) is used. We shall assume that all assets are added at the start of the year involved.

| *Year* | *Depreciation* | *Additions* | *End-of-Year Book Value* |
|---|---|---|---|
| 1 | $4,000,000 | $4,000,000 | $16,000,000 |
| 2 | 4,000,000 | 4,000,000 | 16,000,000 |
| | and so on | | |

In our example, we have postulated a situation in which the annual depreciation on a cost basis is sufficient, at least initially, to provide for the replacement of assets and—barring extreme inflation—some expansion of plant. Assuming no inflation or expansion, annual depreciation of $3,750,000 (1/8 of $30 million) would initially allow for maintaining the plant in a constant condition. Thus, our example allows $250,000 in year 1 for the combination of inflation and physical expansion. To the extent that we view a corporation as an ongoing entity, as long as it is both expanding its physical plant in dollar terms (as the result of either physical expansion or inflation, or both) and using accelerated methods of depreciation, there is a tendency for cost-based depreciation to generate for many years sufficient working capital to provide for plant replacements.

This is just an example. We started out with accumulated depreciation of $14,000,000; but the lesson our example teaches is a valid one, if properly generalized. With a "young" physical plant, a company will be taking more depreciation annually than the amount necessary to provide, on a current basis, funds sufficient to replace assets requiring replacement. At some point, however, as the physical plant "ages," a condition is reached in which the annual depreciation tends to provide only a sufficient number of dollars to replace the original cost of the plant being retired. At this point, merely to maintain the status quo will require either that current earnings be withheld from shareholders or that outside financing be resorted to, or perhaps a combination of both.

Important: Making a book entry to record depreciation does not itself generate any assets. But if prices are set to recover costs plus a profit, and if depreciation is one of the costs, then assets are being generated indirectly. And depreciation deducted for tax purposes does reduce the cash outflow for taxes.

## PATTERNS OF DEPRECIATION

For tax purposes, as we have said, the function of depreciation is merely to allocate the original cost of the asset over the period of its useful life. The major techniques for doing this are the straight-line and the so-called accelerated-depreciation methods. Other methods, such as the units-of-production method, are also permitted, if they can be shown to be reasonable. The two most common forms of accelerated depreciation are the declining-balance and the sum-of-the-years'-digits methods.

The most customary form of declining-balance depreciation is the 200 percent declining-balance method, which is more usually referred to as double-declining-balance depreciation. This method can best be described by an illustrative example. Assume that we purchase a $10,000 machine with a useful life of ten years. Since the salvage value of the machine at the end of the ten-year period is anticipated to be only $900, it would be ignored in the computation of straight-line depreciation (salvage value to the extent of 10 percent of cost may generally be ignored for this type of asset). Straight-line depreciation would therefore result in ten annual depreciation deductions of $1,000 each. The double-declining-balance depreciation method will, in contrast, permit a deduction of $2,000 in the first year, because we may take a deduction at double the straight-line rate—that is, 20 percent instead of 10 percent. The deduction is, however, based upon 20 percent of the undepreciated cost (original cost less prior depreciation) rather than 10 percent of the original cost. Thus, while in the first year the deduction is $2,000, in the second year it drops to $1,600 (20 percent of $8,000), in the third year it is $1,280 (20 percent of $6,400), and so on. It will eventually be necessary to switch to the straight-line method, because a declining-balance method will never result in full recovery of cost. In the illustration, the switch would take place in the seventh year, and the undepreciated balance would be written off over the four remaining years at $655 per year. Incidentally, while salvage value is not considered in calculating declining-balance depreciation, the asset may not be depreciated below this value—except that to the extent of 10 percent of cost, salvage value may, even here, be ignored.

Depending upon the nature of the asset and the date of acquisition, the fastest permitted rate of declining-balance depreciation may be the 200 percent method illustrated above, the 150 percent method (which in the example would result in an annual deduction of 15 percent of the undepreciated cost), or the 125 percent method.

The other commonly used method of accelerated depreciation, the sum-of-the-years'-digits method, involves totaling the numbers of the years of useful life. Again using the example of the 10 year machine, the total of the numbers 1, 2, 3, 4, . . ., 10 is 55. Annual depreciation is taken on the basis of a fraction with a constant denominator of 55 but an annually declining numerator. Thus, in the first year the depreciation deduction is 10/55 of the $10,000 cost, or $1,818; in year 2 it is 9/55 of $10,000, or $1,636; and so forth, until the tenth year, when it is 1/55, or $182.

The following table compares two of the accelerated methods of depreciation to the straight-line method.

| *Year* | *Straight-Line* | | *200 Percent Declining-Balance* | | *Sum-of-the-Years-Digits* | |
|---|---|---|---|---|---|---|
| | *Annual Charge* | *Cumulative Charges* | *Annual Charge* | *Cumulative Charge* | *Annual Charge* | *Cumulative Charges* |
| 1 | $1,000 | $1,000 | $2,000 | $2,000 | $1,818 | $1,818 |
| 2 | 1,000 | 2,000 | 1,600 | 3,600 | 1,636 | 3,454 |
| 3 | 1,000 | 3,000 | 1,280 | 4,880 | 1,455 | 4,909 |
| 4 | 1,000 | 4,000 | 1,024 | 5,904 | 1,273 | 6,182 |
| 5 | 1,000 | 5,000 | 819 | 6,723 | 1,091 | 7,273 |
| 6 | 1,000 | 6,000 | 655 | 7,378 | 909 | 8,182 |
| 7 | 1,000 | 7,000 | 655 | 8,033 | 727 | 8,909 |
| 8 | 1,000 | 8,000 | 655 | 8,688 | 545 | 9,454 |
| 9 | 1,000 | 9,000 | 655 | 9,343 | 364 | 9,818 |
| 10 | 1,000 | 10,000 | 657 | 10,000 | 182 | 10,000 |

As we will soon see, the method of depreciation may have a substantial effect upon the cash flow of a business. It is therefore important from a budgeting and investment viewpoint to know what assets may be depreciated at accelerated rates. Congress, in placing various limitations upon the permissible methods, was well aware of the effect that the privilege of using accelerated depreciation could have upon an investment decision. By combining permissible depreciation methods with depreciation "recapture" provisions, Congress has attempted to channel investment funds into certain areas (for example, residential housing instead of office buildings).

The 200 percent declining-balance method and the sum-of-the-years-digits method were not permitted until the enactment of the 1954 Internal Revenue

Code. As originally enacted, the 1954 code permitted these methods to be used for tangible assets acquired after 1953, provided that the asset was new (that is, had had no previous use) and had a life of three years or more. The 1969 Tax Reform Act placed further limitations on use of these methods; they can now be used only for personal property (generally, assets other than buildings) and for residential rental real property (buildings used for housing). Other new real property is limited to methods not exceeding 150 percent declining balance.

Property acquired prior to 1954 and used property could formerly generally be depreciated by the 150 percent declining-balance method. Here again, the 1969 act placed limitations on the use of this method. The 150 percent declining-balance method may still be applied to used personal property. Buildings, however, if they are not new, may be depreciated only by use of the straight-line method, with the one exception of a used residential building having a remaining life of 20 years or more when acquired, in which case a 125 percent declining-balance method may be used.

Also, a special additional first-year depreciation allowance is available for tangible personal property (as distinguished from buildings, for instance, which are tangible real property) with a useful life of six years or more. Twenty percent of the cost of the property may be written off as additional depreciation in the year of acquisition—but the amount that can be so deducted is limited to $2,000 on a corporate or an individual return and to $4,000 on an individual joint return. Where the 20 percent first-year depreciation is claimed, the cost of the asset for other depreciation purposes is reduced by the first-year depreciation.

In addition, those taxpayers adopting the Asset Depreciation Range (ADR) system of depreciation (discussed later in this chapter) have the option of taking depreciation in the year of acquisition under special assumptions. Any asset acquired in the first 6 months of a year can be depreciated for a full year; any asset acquired during the last 6 months of the year can be depreciated for half a year.

## DEPRECIATION RECAPTURE

It was once "fashionable" to depreciate an asset using an accelerated rate and a short life so as to obtain an "ordinary" deduction and a subsequent capital gain. The depreciation deductions reduced the amount of income subject to tax at "ordinary" rates. A subsequent sale of the asset, however, could result in income that was subject to tax at a capital gains rate.

Congress did not believe it was proper that a capital gain should be realized upon the sale of an asset when the gain resulted solely from the fact that the cost was reduced by ordinary deductions. It was thus decided that, to the extent that gain on personal property resulted from depreciation deductions taken after

1962, the gain would be taxed as ordinary income. This rule, however, did not originally apply to buildings, and so it generally affected only gain upon the sale of machinery, automobiles, trucks, and similar items of personal property.

This change left what was considered a huge "loophole" for real estate investors. Mr. A purchases a new building for $1,000,000 and uses double-declining-balance depreciation. The building has a 40-year life, and his depreciation deduction in the first year is $50,000 (5 percent of $1,000,000). In the second year the deduction is $47,500. At the beginning of the third year, Mr. A sells the building for $950,000. If Mr. A was in a 70 percent bracket, he would save $68,250 in taxes as the result of the depreciation deductions, but he would pay only $11,875 of tax on the gain—$1,000,000 cost less $97,500 of depreciation, or $902,500 adjusted cost from the $950,000 sales price resulting in a $47,500 gain taxed at the old maximum rate of 25 percent. His before-tax cost of owning the building was $50,000 ($1,000,000 cost less $950,000 selling price), but he made $56,375 on taxes ($68,250 tax savings less the capital gains tax of $11,875). Assuming that all other factors are equal—that is, that the building earned as much as it cost to maintain—our friend Mr. A made a profit of $6,375, resulting solely from the fact that the depreciation is an ordinary deduction and the gain can be taxed at capital gains rates.

The Treasury Department kept pushing to close this loophole, and Congress finally decided that the recapture provisions should be extended to real estate. The recapture rules are discussed in Chapter 8, dealing with capital gains.

## USEFUL LIFE

The life expectancy of a depreciable asset will vary from taxpayer to taxpayer. Useful life, for tax purposes, means useful life to the particular taxpayer involved. It is usually shorter than the physical life of the asset involved. The useful life of an automobile to a traveling salesman who trades autos every 2 years is 2 years; to the cab company that uses an auto for 4 years before trading it off, the useful life is 4 years; and to the corporation that uses the same auto for 6 years for light messenger service around town, the useful life is 6 years.

Therefore, useful life for tax purposes cannot be determined by an engineering study. It is a product of taxpayer intent. Of course, when the taxpayer's past experience furnishes no clue as to probable useful life and it is impossible to determine useful life to the taxpayer in any other way, the physical life of the asset may be relevant for purposes of computing depreciation.

Taxpayers also have the right to utilize the Asset Depreciation Range (ADR) system promulgated in 1971 by the Treasury Department. Under this approach, the taxpayer elects to keep his asset records and compute depreciation either on an item basis or using accounts that keep together all acquisitions in a given year (called "vintage" accounts). He can adopt any life for the asset acquisitions of a given year, as long as it is in a range prescribed by the Treasury.

This range runs from a life 20 percent less than the guideline life for the asset involved to 20 percent more than the guideline life. Once adopted for the acquisitions of a given year, the life figure can be changed for those acquisitions only if the taxpayer requests the I.R.S. to change it and the I.R.S. okays the change.

The purpose of the ADR system was to give the economy a "shot in the arm" by allowing American industry to take faster depreciation than was previously permitted, and to take it under a system by which controversy would be reduced to a minimum.

## TAX DEPRECIATION AND CAPITAL BUDGETING

Some variant of the return-on-investment concept is utilized in most sophisticated capital-budgeting evaluation techniques, focusing on estimated cash flows and giving consideration to the fact that a dollar today is considered to be more valuable than a dollar sometime in the future. Following are some examples of this technique wherein there is calculated a ratio of the present value of the cash inflows, discounted at an appropriate rate of return, to the investment in the property. This ratio of return to investment we will call the "profitability index of the project."

*Example 1:*

Purchase of machine A is contemplated at a cost of $29,800. Annual cash savings of $14,040 per year for 5 years will be generated. Tax rate is 50 percent. Removal costs will equal resale value at the end of 5 years.

| *Year* | *Before-tax Saving* | *Depreciation* | *Taxable Saving* | *Tax (50%)* | *After-tax Saving* | *Present Value @ 10%* | *Present Value* |
|---|---|---|---|---|---|---|---|
| 1 | $14,040 | $5,960 | $8,080 | $4,040 | $10,000 | 0.91 | $ 9,100 |
| 2 | 14,040 | 5,960 | 8,080 | 4,040 | 10,000 | .83 | 8,300 |
| 3 | 14,040 | 5,960 | 8,080 | 4,040 | 10,000 | .75 | 7,500 |
| 4 | 14,040 | 5,960 | 8,080 | 4,040 | 10,000 | .68 | 6,800 |
| 5 | 14,040 | 5,960 | 8,080 | 4,040 | 10,000 | .62 | 6,200 |
| | $70,200 | | | | | | $37,900 |

Our profitability index will give us $37,900/$29,800, or 1.27.

Now let us take the identical situation and shift our pattern of depreciation to 200 percent declining-balance depreciation (with a shift to straight-line for the fourth and fifth years):

| Year | Before-tax Saving | Depreciation | Taxable Saving | Tax (50%) | After-tax Saving | Present Value @ 10% | Present Value |
|---|---|---|---|---|---|---|---|
| 1 | $14,040 | $11,920 | $ 2,120 | $1,060 | $12,980 | 0.91 | $11,800 |
| 2 | 14,040 | 7,150 | 6,890 | 3,445 | 10,595 | .83 | 8,800 |
| 3 | 14,040 | 4,290 | 9,750 | 4,875 | 9,165 | .75 | 6,900 |
| 4 | 14,040 | 3,220 | 10,820 | 5,410 | 8,630 | .68 | 5,900 |
| 5 | 14,040 | 3,220 | 10,820 | 5,410 | 8,630 | .62 | 5,300 |
| | | | | | $50,000 | | $38,700 |

Our profitability index is now $38,700/$29,800, or 1.30. As between two investment alternatives otherwise equally attractive, the one with the faster depreciation write-off would presumably get the nod. And because we are dealing with a compound-interest situation, the longer-lived the asset, the more pronounced the effect of the shift in pattern.

Shorter lives for calculating depreciation, especially coupled with accelerated depreciation, improve the attractiveness of capital investment by shifting the outflow of cash for taxes from earlier years to later years.

Also relevant in the capital-budgeting situation is the unrecovered cost of the asset to be replaced *if* gain or loss will be recognized on the retirement for tax purposes. If the disposition of the old asset is at a loss, then the tax benefit of that loss has the effect of reducing the incremental investment required for the new asset that is replacing the old. Availability of the investment credit similarly reduces the investment in the new asset, the recapture of investment credit taken on the old increases it.

*Example 2:*

The new asset costs $29,800, as in our previous example, but is replacing an asset with an unrecovered cost of $10,000. Expenses of removing the old asset will equal the salvage value derived from its sale as scrap. The $10,000 loss deduction will reduce the cash outflow for taxes by $5,000, and this tax reduction is a direct consequence of the purchase of the new machine. Thus, our investment in the new machine is reduced by $5,000, to $24,800. The result is that our profitability-index calculation is now $38,700/$24,800, or 1.56.

Here we encounter a vast difference between the thought process involved in contemplating a proposed investment and the manner in which the performance of the company will tend to be evaluated. Because capital budgeting is concerned with cash flows, it treats the $5,000 tax reduction generated by the $10,000 of unrecovered investment as a positive aspect of the investment alternative. From the standpoint of net earnings per share, however, in the year that the new asset is purchased the accounting records will show a loss on the retirement of the old asset, and thus earnings per share will be reduced. Decision making concerns itself only with those aspects of the situation that are affected by the decision. "Sunk costs" are irrelevant except as they may have an effect on tax liability. Accounting concerns itself with allocation of costs, regardless of when incurred. Decision making deals with the dynamic, whereas financial accounting deals with the historical.

Let us hasten to add that the accounting aspects of depreciation are not irrelevant. It is probably true that, in a perfectly competitive situation, if all decisions were rationally made, neither tax nor book depreciation (because the two may differ, and often do) would exert any effect on decisions made by the company. Indirectly, they would affect the capacity of the industry, because the decision to invest or not to invest in new plant would be affected by tax depreciation, in the manner we have seen. But the determination of whether a given market price justified operation of a particular facility would relate only to the incremental costs of such operation. Only the actual decline in value of the plant as the result of such operation would therefore be relevant, and this would have no relation to either tax or book depreciation.

## DEPRECIATION AND SELLING PRICES

In an area where some form of imperfect competition exists, as it does for most business in the United States today, accounting depreciation may well exert more influence on decisions than in the situation of perfect competition. If selling prices, for instance, respond to what sellers conceive costs to be, the fact that the unit costs produced by the cost accounting system may be thought to be the relevant costs for decision making will have the same impact on the decision reached as if these costs were, in fact, relevant. Furthermore, where prices are set with one eye on the probable effects on earnings per share, another eye on labor relations, and a consciousness of possible antitrust action or of charges of price discrimination under the Robinson-Patman Act, it would be naive to assume that accounting depreciation has no influence on selling prices.

Also, with regard to selling prices, it should be remembered that government is a big customer of many industries. If government contracts are involved, the Armed Services Procurement Regulations relate allowable depreciation to tax basis and methods, although not specifically to depreciation claimed for tax purposes. However, as a practical matter, depreciation taken for tax purposes is the easiest figure to use and is therefore commonly used. If the taxpayer is subject to the Renegotiation Act, his allowable costs under that act normally include the depreciation allowable for tax purposes.

Before leaving the subject of depreciation, we had better comment on one of the major tax "gimmicks" in which depreciation has been involved.

## SALE AND LEASEBACK

Assume that the Jennings Corporation owns a large manufacturing facility. It was erected during World War II. Now it is fully depreciated, even though the buildings have a fair market value of $20 million. The land has a fair market value of $300,000 and an original cost of $200,000. Jennings is in a 50 percent tax bracket. It figures that its internal investments return at least 9 percent after taxes.

An insurance company is willing to buy the facility for $20 million if Jennings will sign a 20-year lease calling for the payment of $2.2 million a year rental. At first blush, this looks ridiculous. The company will get $20 million but will obligate itself to pay back $44 million.

The company will pay a capital gains tax of $5,940,000 on the sale, leaving it with funds available for investment of $14,060,000. Invested at 9 percent this will generate, after taxes, $1,265,400 per year. The $2.2 million a year rent being paid, to a taxpayer in a 50 percent tax bracket, generates a reduction of $1.1 million in taxes, and therefore has an after-tax cost of $1.1 million. Thus, of $1,265,400 being earned, $1,100,000 will be paid to the insurance company and $165,400 will be invested internally. A total of $165,400 per year for 20 years, compounded at 9 percent, will amount to over $9 million at the end of the 20 years.

The company in this example has found the sale and leaseback a profitable strategy. The profit arises from the ability of the company to put its capital to work at 9 percent after taxes. If the company had investment opportunities offering it only 6 percent after taxes, there would be a profit potential only if the rent was less and/or the lease allowed the company to repurchase the property after the 20 years at a price less than its anticipated fair market value.

The sale and leaseback is a type of transaction whose tax attractiveness flows largely from the ability to pick up certain types of gains as tax-sheltered capital gains and from the deductibility of depreciation and/or rental payments at ordinary rates. When the lease is coupled with an option to repurchase, the transaction becomes essentially a financing device wherein the annual payments being made on the "obligation" are fully deductible. Where the option is at a nominal price, there is a real possibility that the entire transaction may be characterized as a sham, and the purported rental payments may be treated simply as installment payments on an obligation. Note, too, the effect that the "recapture" of depreciation provisions may have. Some of the gain may be taxed as ordinary income, thus substantially reducing the cash available for investment.

In addition, as will be discussed in Chapter 13, the capital gain will be a "tax preference" and so may result in an additional "minimum tax."

## ACCOUNTING PROBLEMS AND DEPRECIATION

Tax accounting objectives differ from financial accounting objectives, and thus their techniques often differ, too. When an item is handled one way for tax purposes and another way for financial statement purposes, problems of what is known as "tax allocation" arise. These problems have been peculiarly acute in the area of depreciation, and especially so since 1954.

Prior to 1954, with the exception of emergency legislation during World War II and the Korean War, it was generally assumed that the amount of depreciation claimed on the tax return should probably agree with that claimed on the financial statements. The 1954 tax law authorized the use of the accelerated methods of depreciation that we have already discussed (double-declining-balance and sum-of-the-years'-digits). Many taxpayers took advantage of these more rapid depreciation write-offs for tax purposes, although they continued using their old straight-line method for financial statement purposes. Unlike many other countries, the United States has no provision that depreciation for tax purposes cannot exceed depreciation taken on the books.

The effect of taking accelerated depreciation this year is that the taxpayer will have smaller depreciation deductions in some future year. If the income tax expense on the financial statements is only the amount shown on the current-year return, then the reader of the financial statements is unaware that part of the economic utility of the depreciable assets—their deductibility for tax purposes—has been used up at a faster rate than is indicated in the depreciation expense shown on the income statement. Generally accepted accounting practice requires that, in a situation such as this, the excess of tax depreciation over book depreciation multiplied by the applicable tax rate shall be set up as a liability under the caption "Deferred federal income taxes" and the income tax expense be correspondingly increased. In those future years when book depreciation will exceed tax depreciation, the income tax expense shown on the financial statements will be less than the amount shown on the tax return.

In general, the concept of tax allocation indicates that differences between book income and taxable income in the current year that will be offset by differences in the other direction in another year shall be adjusted for by adjusting the income tax expense and the liability for deferred federal income taxes.

Transactions like sale/leasebacks are also part of this tax allocation discussion. Many transactions that are treated as purchases of property for financial reporting, for example, can be considered as leases for federal income tax purposes. For financial reporting purposes, the "purchaser" has depreciation and interest expense, while for tax purposes, he has rental payments. To the extent that these amounts differ, tax allocation may be required.

## CASE EXCERPTS

*Massey Motors, Inc.* v. *U.S.*, 5 AFTR 2d 1780 (80 S. Ct. 1411) (1960)
*Commissioner* v. *Seaboard Finance Company* (CA9–1966) 18 AFTR 2d 5803
*The Merchants National Bank of Topeka*, T.C. Memo 1975–238

### *Massey Motors, Inc.* v. *U.S.*
### 5 AFTR 2d 1780 (80 S. Ct. 1411)(1960)

> What is the purpose of depreciation in the tax law? Does "useful life" refer to the physical life inherent in the asset or to something else?

The automobiles involved here are, for tax purposes, depreciable assets rather than ordinary stock in trade. Such assets, employed from day to day in business, generally decrease in utility and value as they are used. It was the design of the Congress to permit the taxpayer to recover, tax free, the total cost to him of such capital assets; hence it recognized that this decrease in value—depreciation—was a legitimate tax deduction as business expense. It was the purpose of Sec. 23(1) and the regulations to make a meaningful allocation of this cost to the tax periods benefited by the use of the asset. In practical life, however, business concerns do not usually know how long an asset will be of profitable use to them or how long it may be utilized until no longer capable of functioning. But, for the most part, such assets are used for their entire economic life, and the depreciation base in such cases has long been recognized as the number of years the asset is expected to function profitably in use. The asset being of no further use at the end of such period, its salvage value, if anything, is only as scrap.

It is the primary purpose of depreciation accounting to further the integrity of periodic income statements by making a meaningful allocation of the cost entailed in the use (excluding maintenance expense) of the asset to the periods to which it contributes. This accounting system has had the approval of this Court since *United States* v. *Ludey*, 274 U.S. 295, 301, 6 AFTR 6754 (1927), when MR. JUSTICE BRANDEIS said, "The theory underlying this allowance for depreciation is that by using up the plant, a gradual sale is made of it." The analogy applies equally to automobiles. . . .

We therefore conclude that the Congress intended that the taxpayer should, under the allowance for depreciation, recover only the cost of the asset less the estimated salvage, resale or second-hand value. This requires that the useful life of the asset be related to the period for which it may reasonably be expected to be employed in the taxpayer's business. Likewise salvage value must include estimated resale or second-hand value.

*Commissioner* v. *Seaboard Finance Company*
(CA9–1966) 18 AFTR 2d 5803

The Tax Court had the problem of determining how much, if any, of the amount paid by Seaboard in acquiring other small loan businesses was attributable to good will or other elements of value for which depreciation deductions are not allowed. . . .

During the tax years in question, Seaboard's program of rapid growth resulted in the purchase of fifty-five small loan businesses. In connection with each purchase the company paid an amount in excess of the face value of the loans outstanding and the fixed assets acquired. Seaboard treated the excess purchase price, referred to herein as the "premium," as part of the depreciable cost of acquiring the loan accounts. Accordingly, it sought to depreciate the premium over the average useful lives of the loan accounts, namely, three years for secured loans and five years for unsecured loans.

The Commissioner asserts that the customer structure should be treated as an indivisible asset with an indeterminate useful life (and hence, not depreciable) because although its value may fluctuate from time to time as contracts expire and are replaced by new ones, this should not be regarded as a process of exhaustion, but as a process by which a continually existing asset is kept intact.

The rationale and purpose of the "indivisible asset" rule is to prevent taxpayers from increasing the value of depreciable property to offset the amount paid in excess of book value of assets purchased. This doctrine makes it possible to strike down depreciation deductions for amounts which should properly be allocated to goodwill.

In this case, Seaboard apparently made an honest attempt to value the premium paid, under the impression that a depreciation deduction would be allowed. Each contract was individually analyzed to determine its ultimate worth. Although part of the premium was correctly held by the Tax Court to be goodwill, it does not appear that the remaining portion of the premium should be declared nondepreciable on the basis of the "indivisible asset" rule.

. . . The "indivisible asset" rule is inapplicable where the purchase price was derived by appraising the value of each individual asset. . . .

The Commissioner contends that the premium which Seaboard is seeking to depreciate is not "for a 'determinable amount of income' over an 'ascertainable period.' " He contends that since no contract could run over thirty-six months under any state law, these amounts could not be depreciated over a three- to five-year period.

Experience had indicated, however, that secured loans ran off the books on the average of three years whereas unsecured loans, where possibilities for renewal are greater, remained on the books an average of five years. These figures apparently comply with the Treasury Regulations on depreciation. Treas. Reg. § 1.167(a)-3 (1956). These regulations permit a depreciation deduction for the cost of intangible assets if the life of the intangible can be estimated with reasonable accuracy.

Not only the courts, but also the Commissioner, have agreed that a contract right with a limited useful life is the proper subject of an amortization deduction. 1954-1 Cum. Bul. 6, acquiescing in *Stewart Title Guar. Co.*, 20 T.C. 630 (1953). It is unnecessary that such a contract be limited to its duration on paper when taxpayer can demonstrate, as he did here, that the contract will be extended over a longer period of time.

*The Merchants National Bank of Topeka* v. *Commissioner,* T.C. Memo 1975–238

> Instead of using one composite life for a building, the taxpayer separately depreciated the building's various components (e.g., the basic structure, the plumbing fixtures, the electrical transformers and panels, etc.). The I.R.S. objected to the lives used, apparently at least in part on the ground that the depreciation should produce about the same dollars either way. Thus, where the taxpayer had claimed a 50-year life on the building structure and a 30-year life on the sprinkler system, I.R.S. found a 65-year life on both. In arriving at lives somewhere between the taxpayer and the I.R.S. figures (e.g., a 55-year life on both building structure and sprinklers), the Tax Court made the following observations:

Respondent does not dispute that petitioner was entitled to utilize the component method of depreciation. See *Herbert Shainberg* [Dec. 23, 838], 33 T.C. 241, 254 (1959), acq. 1960-1 C. B. 5: sec. 1.167(a)-7(a), Income Tax Regs.; Rev. Rul. 68-4, 1968-1 C. B. 77. That petitioner would have been entitled to a greater or lesser annual depreciation deduction in the year before us had it decided to avail itself of the composite method of depreciation and had it chosen one useful life for its entire building from the guideline useful lives presented in Rev. Proc. 62-21, 1962-2 C. B. 418, is not significant in the instant case because we are convinced that the record before us establishes the proper useful lives for purposes of the component method and that a "reasonable allowance for exhaustion, wear and tear" (sec. 167(a)) is calculable therefrom. Any such difference in the annual amounts of depreciation to which petitioner would have been entitled only suggests to us that respondent's guidelines in Rev. Proc. 62-21 might not be entirely accurate for the instant case . . .

This Court professes no special expertise in the areas in which we are called upon to render a decision in the instant case. *As we noted at trial, agreement between the parties would have been a far more satisfactory method for settling the issues now before us, issues which are simply not susceptible to any precise formula treatment.* (Emphasis added.) On the basis of all the facts in the record before us, including the testimony of the expert witnesses called by both parties, we hold that the useful lives of those components of petitioner's building as to which the parties were unable to reach agreement are as follows: (omitted) . . . .

## QUESTIONS AND PROBLEMS

1. Contrast a businessman's view of depreciation (as being for the purpose of providing an amount sufficient to replace an asset) with the tax view of depreciation.
2. If, over the life of a particular asset, the total amount of depreciation that can be written off is the same regardless of the method used, what difference does it make whether the dollars of deduction fall into one year or another?
3. Assuming that a corporation has opportunities for profitable internal investment, what is the rationale of arguing that even cost depreciation may generate sufficient funds to replace assets during a period of inflation? Does depreciation really generate cash?
4. On January 1, 19X1, the Maragon Corporation acquired a new factory building at a cost of $500,000. What is the maximum amount of depreciation that may be taken on this new factory building during 19x1? Indicate the method used, and show your calculations, using a 45-year life.
5. On January 1, 19x1, Maragon, which manufactures electrical equipment, acquired machine tools costing $70,000. What is the maximum amount of depreciation that can be claimed on these in 19x1 if they have an ADR guideline life of 12 years?
6. What is the rationale of permitting up to 200 percent declining-balance depreciation for machinery, equipment, etc., but not in excess of 150 percent declining-balance depreciation for commercial real estate, such as a factory building?
7. Is the determination of useful life for tax depreciation purposes primarily one that calls for the services of an engineer? What is the definition of "useful life"?
8. Can depreciation be taken on intangibles as well as tangibles? If not, why not? If "yes," what does the taxpayer have to establish in order to obtain a deduction? (Hint: See the *Seaboard* case excerpt.)
9. The Sebastian Lathe Company is contemplating purchase of a new piece of equipment. The piece of equipment that it is replacing had an original cost of $37,000, and $12,000 of depreciation has been taken on it. Only $10,000 will be received for it when it is sold. The invoice price of the replacement machine is $42,000, but in figuring the return on the proposed investment, the assistant to the production manager had deducted 48 percent of the $15,000 loss on the old piece of equipment from the $42,000. The applicable corporate tax rate is 48 percent. The corporation uses the profitability-index method of evaluating investments, and a 10 percent target rate of return. Useful life of the proposed piece of equipment

is 10 years, and annual savings after taxes (as compared to costs of operating the old machine) will be $5,800.

(a) The company treasurer complains that the $15,000 loss should be added to the $42,000 cost of the new machine, and that on that basis the $5,800 per year will just barely return the investment in the new piece of equipment. Evaluate his argument.

(b) What profitability index will the assistant to the production manager come up with? What would be the P.I. if the investment was deemed to be $42,000?

(c) Which is the most fruitful approach to measuring the profitability of the new machine in attempting to reach a decision on whether to retain the old machine or buy the new one?

10. In what ways is it possible that depreciation may affect selling prices?
11. Having heard of the advantages of sale and leaseback transactions, William Aloysius Webster decides to climb on the bandwagon. He owns a luxury apartment building in a resort area. The lack of depreciability of the land on which the building stands has long bothered him. The land is worth $200,000, although its tax basis is only $20,000. Webster sells the land to the Mutual Insurance Company for $200,000 and then leases it back on a 30-year lease at an annual rental of $13,000. The lease contains an option to buy the land back at the end of the 30 years for $1. Assume that Webster is in a 60 percent bracket.

    (a) What tax benefits is Webster trying to achieve? Show specific amounts that he will pay out and receive back.

    (b) As the sale is between unrelated parties, and title is actually transferred to the insurance company, on what basis might the I.R.S. try to deny Webster the tax benefit of his sale and leaseback?
12. "Accelerated depreciation makes possible the conversion of ordinary income into capital gain." Construct an example to support this statement. For what types of property would your example be valid?
13. "The problems created by using accrual accounting for financial statements and installment accounting for tax purposes is similar to the problem created by using accelerated depreciation for tax purposes and straight-line depreciation for book purposes." What are the similarities and dissimilarities in the two situations? Are the two problems solved in the same way in terms of financial-statement presentation?
14. Assuming that neutrality in a tax system is defined to mean that the same choices will be rationally made with the tax system as would be made without it, what type of depreciation policy would theoretically provide neutrality in capital investment decisions?
15. What was the taxpayer trying to accomplish by using component rather than composite depreciation in *The Merchants Bank* case? Construct an example to illustrate your point.

# 11

# Investment Credit

## INTRODUCTION

Capital investments will be made only when potential after-tax return on such investment seems attractive. Tax policy affects the investment climate in two ways: (1) To the extent that tax policies directly affect consumer demand, they will indirectly affect capital-investment decisions; (2) The timing of tax deductions for capital investments affects profitability index approach to measuring rate of return.

## CREDIT VERSUS DEDUCTION

The anticipated rate of return on a proposed capital outlay is the product of the outlay itself and the income anticipated from it. It can be improved by reducing the investment as well as by increasing the income. We have already seen that the after-tax income is improved, in terms of its present value, by accelerating the timing of depreciation deductions. At one extreme, assuming a 50 percent tax rate, we would find the after-tax rate of return equal to half the before-tax if none of the capital outlay were deductible for income tax purposes (e.g., interest earned on an industrial bond). At the other extreme, the after-tax rate of return would equal the before-tax if the investment were 100 percent deductible in the year made.

The investment credit works the other side of the street. At the extreme, with a 100 percent investment credit, and no restrictions on its use, the after-tax cost of an investment would be zero and any anticipated after-tax income would offer an infinite rate of return. But the rate is not 100 percent and there are limitations on use of the credit.

## EFFECTIVENESS OF INVESTMENT CREDIT

There are many opinions as to the effectiveness of the investment credit in stimulating capital expenditures. One economist stated that his studies show that 24½ percent of those he surveyed indicated that a 7 percent investment credit caused them to increase their capital expenditures.[1] Those responding to the survey accounted for more than 50 percent of total U.S. private capital spending.[2]

In an investigation of 66 large companies in 1967, Gay Halvorson[3] found that, during the investment review of a proposed capital expenditure, the following weight was given the 7 percent investment credit:

TABLE 1

Weight Given Investment Credit

| | *Number* | *Percent* |
|---|---|---|
| None | 8 | 12 |
| Minor consideration | 24 | 36 |
| Cash flow considered, but not considered critical | 28 | 43 |
| Material consideration | 6 | 9 |
| Totals | 66 | 100 |

The firms felt that the investment credit was small in comparison with other figures used in analyzing a capital expenditure, that competitive necessities played a major role in capital decisions, and that much uncertainty surrounded the availability of the investment credit. During a suspension of the investment credit, Halvorson inquired into the impact of the suspension upon investment decisions and found the following:

[1] Statement of Dr. Pierre A. Rinfret made to the Committee on Ways and Means, House of Representatives, 93rd Congress on the Subject of General Tax Reform (Part 3 of 11–February 7, 1973), p. 428.

[2] *Ibid.*

[3] Gay Halvorson, *Can Taxes Condition the Economy? Executive Viewpoints.* Research Report Number 6, Bureau of Business Research, Graduate School of Business, Indiana University, 1969.

TABLE 2

Impact of Investment Credit Suspension

| | *Number* | *Percent* |
|---|---|---|
| Equipment purchased earlier anticipating suspension | 20 | 30 |
| Capital Investment policy modified by suspension | 15 | 23 |
| Deviations from capital budget after suspension | 6 | 9 |
| Change in capital investment policy after suspension repeal | 5 | 8 |
| Shifts in capital expenditures caused by suspension | 4 | 6 |

The Halvorson study indicates that large businesses regarded the investment credit as of primary importance for its impact on cash flow, and that a suspension of the credit had no substantial impact on capital expenditures.

Another study[4] supports the findings of Halvorson. Edwards studied 44 large companies in the summer of 1965 and found that 22 gave explicit consideration to the use of the 7 percent investment credit in their formal analysis of alternative capital expenditure proposals. He also cited two secondary reasons given for not using the investment credit in such analyses: "A firm cannot earn income merely by buying assets . . ." and "The uncertainty of a provision that can be 'repealed at any time by the Congress.' "[5] The primary reason given Edwards for not using the credit was its relative insignificance. Edwards reported that "even the firms explicitly recognizing it in the evaluation process generally indicated that only marginal projects could possibly have been affected thus far by the credit."[6]

What does the investment credit do to the profitability index, for instance? This index is the present value of the earnings anticipated from the asset, discounted at the corporation's own rate of return (which may be a historical cost of capital rate or a target rate), then divided by the size of the required investment. Assume that in our project the discounted present value of the earnings would be $920,000, while the investment would be $1,000,000. Thus, the profitability index would be 0.92—and the project presumably would not be

[4] James Wyatt Edwards, *The Effects of Federal Income Taxes on Capital Budgeting,* Unpublished Ph.D. dissertation, Department of Accounting and Financial Administration, Michigan State University, 1966, p. 77.

[5] *Ibid.,* p. 78.

[6] *Ibid.,* p. 79.

undertaken since a P.I. of 1.00 normally would be the cut-off point. If, however, the investment is reduced by $100,000 as the result of an available 10 percent investment credit, the P.I. is then $920,000/$900,000, or 1.02, which is a viable project, if only barely so.

We can hypothesize that where companies ration capital to projects offering rates of return well in excess of the cost of capital, whatever that may be, and where they find the availability of funds to be their major constraint, the investment credit will have a positive impact on the availability of funds through reducing the cash flow for income taxes. Companies operating without serious capital constraints will find the investment credit offering some improvement in perceived profitability of proposed projects. But the investment credit will not make attractive projects that do not offer earnings, nor, at least so long as there are limits on its use, will it provide a stimulus to businesses lacking sufficient profits to fully use it.

## INVESTMENT CREDIT DESCRIPTION

The Kennedy Administration succeeded in adding the 7 percent investment-credit provision to the United States tax law in 1962. Initially, the credit proposed had been 8 percent, with no adjustment of depreciation resulting from taking the credit. As finally enacted, however, the credit was reduced to 7 percent, and the amount of the credit reduced the depreciation otherwise allowable dollar for dollar.

The 1964 tax law removed the requirement that the basis for depreciation had to be reduced by the amount of the investment credit. The credit was twice suspended: the first time in 1966-67 and the second time in 1969-71. The credit was restored in 1971 and had risen 10 percent by 1977. The specific details in the discussion that follows relate, unless otherwise indicated, to the 1977 rules.

Actually, the credit applies only to certain types of property and can be used only to a limited extent. It applies to business machinery and equipment whether new or used. However, only a percentage of property with useful lives under seven years is eligible for the credit. The same lives must be used for investment credit as for depreciation. In a given year, not over $100,000 of used property can be included. For most taxpayers, the credit can offset the tax liability only up to $25,000, plus 50 percent of the tax liability in excess of $25,000. Unused credits can be carried back three years and carried over seven.

The general manner of operation of the investment credit is illustrated on the following Form 3468, which is the form used in computing the investment credit. An illustrative figure for a simple situation has been inserted. The reverse side of the form explains the rules governing the investment credit.

Form **3468**
Department of the Treasury
Internal Revenue Service

## Computation of Investment Credit

▶ **Attach to your tax return.**

Name | **Identifying number as shown on page 1 of your tax return**

1 Use schedule below to list qualified investment in new and used property acquired or constructed and placed in service during the taxable year; and also list qualified progress expenditures made during the 1976 taxable year and qualified progress expenditures made in 1974 and 1975 taxable years providing a proper election as prescribed in section 46(d)(6) was made for such prior years. If progress expenditure property is placed in service during the taxable year, do not list qualified progress expenditures for this property. See Specific Instruction for line 1.
If 100% investment credit is being claimed on certain ships, check this block. ▶ ☐ See Instruction K for details.

**Note:** *Include your share of investment in property made by a partnership, estate, trust, small business corporation, or lessor.*

| Type of property | | Line | (1) Life years | (2) Cost or basis (See instruction G) | (3) Applicable percentage | (4) Qualified investment (Column 2 x column 3) |
|---|---|---|---|---|---|---|
| New property | | (a) | 3 or more but less than 5 | 15,000 | 33⅓ | 5,000 |
| | | (b) | 5 or more but less than 7 | 9,000 | 66⅔ | 6,000 |
| | | (c) | 7 or more | 10,000 | 100 | 10,000 |
| Qualified progress expenditures | 1974 and 1975 | (d) | 7 or more | | 20 | |
| | 1976 | (e) | 7 or more | | 40 | |
| Used property (See instructions for dollar limitation) | | (f) | 3 or more but less than 5 | 12,000 | 33⅓ | 4,000 |
| | | (g) | 5 or more but less than 7 | | 66⅔ | |
| | | (h) | 7 or more | | 100 | |

| Line | | Amount |
|---|---|---|
| 2 | Qualified investment—add lines 1(a) thru (h) | 25,000 |
| 3 | 10% of line 2 | 2,500 |
| 4 | 7% (4% for public utility property) of certain property (see Instruction for line 1) | |
| 5 | Electing corporations with qualifying stock ownership plans—Enter 1% of line 2 (see Instruction I). (Attach election statement.) | |
| 6 | Carryback and carryover of unused credit(s). See instruction F—attach computation | |
| 7 | Tentative investment credit—Add lines 3, 4, 5 and 6 | 2,500 |

**Limitation**

| Line | | | Amount |
|---|---|---|---|
| 8 | (a) Individuals—Enter amount from line 18, page 1, Form 1040<br>(b) Estates and trusts—Enter amount from line 24 or 25, page 1, Form 1041<br>(c) Corporations—Enter amount from line 9, Schedule J, page 3, Form 1120 | | 20,000 |
| 9 | Less: (a) Credit for the elderly (individuals only) | | |
| | (b) Foreign tax credit | | |
| | (c) Tax on lump-sum distributions (see instruction for line 9(c)) | | |
| | (d) Possession Tax Credit (corporations only) | | |
| 10 | Total—Add lines 9(a), (b), (c) and (d) | | |
| 11 | Line 8 less line 10 | | 20,000 |
| 12 | (a) Enter amount on line 11 or $25,000, whichever is lesser. (Married persons filing separately, controlled corporate groups, estates, and trusts, see instruction for line 12.) | | 20,000 |
| | (b) If line 11 exceeds line 12(a), enter 50% of the excess. (Public utilities, railroads, and airlines see instruction J.) | | |
| 13 | Total—Add lines 12(a) and (b) | | 20,000 |
| 14 | Investment credit—Amount from line 7 or line 13, whichever is lesser. Enter here and on line 50, Form 1040; line 10(b), Schedule J, page 3, Form 1120; or the appropriate line on other returns | | 2,500 |

**Schedule A** **If any part of your investment in line 1 or 4 above was made by a partnership, estate, trust, small business corporation, or lessor, complete the following statement and identify property qualifying for the 7% or 10% investment credit.**

| Name (Partnership, estate, trust, etc.) | Address | Property: Progress expenditures | Property: New | Property: Used | Life years |
|---|---|---|---|---|---|
| | | $ | $ | $ | |
| | | | | | |
| | | | | | |

*If property is disposed of prior to the life years used in computing the investment credit, see instruction E.*

FIGURE 11-1
Computation of Investment Credit

## ACCOUNTING FOR THE INVESTMENT CREDIT

The investment credit illustrates rather dramatically the great pressures that can be involved in financial accounting. The original investment credit of 1962 was the subject of several pronouncements in the early days of the Accounting Principles Board. While the board ultimately concluded that the investment credit should be amortized over the useful life of the property under consideration, the Securities and Exchange Commission refused to adopt this restrictive viewpoint, and the APB was forced to accept either immediate utilization of the credit as an increase in earnings through its effect as a reduction in income tax expense (flow-though), or the deferral over the useful life of the property.

For illustrative purposes, assume a corporation with a net profit before taxes (and before the investment credit) of $100,000. It is entitled to an investment credit of $10,000 and is in a 50 percent tax bracket. Let us compare the two extreme alternatives of (1) treating the credit as a reduction of basis and (2) treating the credit as current income (flow-through):

| | *Basis Reduction (Deferral)* | *Current Income (Flow-through)* |
|---|---|---|
| Acquisition year: | | |
| Profit before tax and credit | $100,000 | $100,000 |
| Income tax expense | 50,000 | 40,000 (tax minus credit) |
| Net income | $ 50,000 | $ 60,000 |
| Subsequent years (10-year life): | | |
| Profit before tax | $100,000 | $100,000 |
| Income tax expense | 49,000* | 50,000 |
| Net income | $ 51,000 | $ 50,000 |

*Credit amortized over the ten-year period.

Obviously, over the life of the asset, the reported income will be the same. The question is one of timing.

When the investment credit was being restored in 1971, the APB informally ascertained from the SEC that the SEC would back it up if it took a strong position requiring that the credit be amortized over the life of the property and prohibiting the use of flow-through. After the APB had released an exposure draft of an opinion embodying this approach, the Senate Finance Committee, in its report accompanying the 1971 tax law revision, expressed its feeling that the benefit of the investment credit should not be restricted and that no one method of accounting should be required. Rather, the Senate Finance Committee felt that either the flow-through or the deferral methods should be allowed and that the financial statements should disclose which approach was used. The language of the committee report was then embodied in an amendment made to the bill on the floor of the Senate. The amendment survived the Conference Committee, and was part of the final bill enacted into law. The APB, by statute, was forced to back down and to continue to accept flow-through even though it was not, in the opinion of the board, a fair presentation of income. Moral? Determination of income is not just a process involving abstract reasoning applied to economic events, but is a rather controversial subject which can become involved in the political forum as well.

This situation may help to illustrate one of the problems involved in obtaining conformity between financial and tax accounting. Tax provisions frequently are inserted for reasons other than the raising of revenue. They are interpreted by courts which do not approach them as economists or accountants might, but as lawyers do. Thus, it is probably futile to expect that there would ever be complete conformity between financial accounting and tax accounting unless financial accounting were to capitulate and become a creature of statute rather than a part of the interpretive function of the accounting profession itself. This alternative, of course, is not outside the bounds of possibility in the years ahead.

## DETAILS OF THE INVESTMENT CREDIT

Property qualifying for the investment credit includes depreciable tangible personal property; elevators and escalators, but only when acquired new; and all other tangible depreciable property (except buildings and their structural components) used in qualified activities such as manufacturing, production, extraction, and the furnishing of utilities. The credit also applies to livestock other than horses. Property amortized under any of the 60-month provisions providing for rapid write-off is not eligible for the credit.

Qualified property with a life of seven years or more is entitled to the full credit of 10 percent, while property with a shorter life is entitled to a reduced credit as follows: five to seven years, two-thirds credit; three to five years, one-third credit; and no credit for property with a life of less than three years. The credit is allowed when the property is placed in service. This means that property purchased at the end of the year is entitled to the full credit.

The maximum credit allowed is $25,000 plus 50 percent of taxpayer's tax liability in excess of $25,000. Assume the taxpayer had a tax liability of $65,000 and an investment credit of $48,000; the maximum amount of usable credit during the current year would be figured as follows:

$$\$25,000 + \tfrac{1}{2}(\$65,000 - \$25,000) = \$45,000$$

In the above illustration, the unused portion of the credit could be carried back three years, and, if not used up, carried forward for seven years.

## COMPLEXITIES OF THE INVESTMENT CREDIT

The credit is not simply a special tax benefit for "purchasing" a piece of equipment with a given estimated life. The chapter on depreciation mentioned that useful life is a meaningful concept only as it applies to a particular taxpayer, his intentions, and his experience. Useful life does *not* mean physical life. In a real sense, therefore, the useful life of an asset can be determined only after the asset has been disposed of, even though it must be estimated at the time of the acquisition. For investment credit purposes, if the asset on which the credit is based is disposed of at an earlier point than the original useful life estimate would indicate, the credit must be recomputed based on this after-the-fact useful life.

Thus, if an asset costing $30,000 were purchased at a time when its useful life was estimated to be seven years, a credit of $3,000 would be available. If this piece of property were disposed of after only four years, the credit would be recomputed based on an estimated life of four years and would amount to only $1,000 (one-third of the full 10 percent). At the time of disposition, the "recapture" of $2,000 of the credit originally taken acts to increase the tax in the year of disposition by that amount.

Note that this recomputation of useful life does not work in reverse. If an asset originally had an estimated life of four years but actually was used for seven years, no increase would be allowed in the investment credit originally claimed. There is, thus, a certain amount of incentive as a result of the investment credit to estimate useful life somewhat on the long side, thus partially counterbalancing the tax desirability of estimating shorter lives for depreciation purposes.

On used property, the credit is not allowed to the extent that the newly acquired used property replaces old property within 60 days before or after disposition of the old property. Where this is the situation, the investment credit is allowed only on the excess of the cost of the newly acquired used property over the tax basis (reduced by depreciation) of the old property. Thus, if a used machine cost $30,000 but replaced an old machine which had a tax basis of $10,000, the investment credit would be based only on the $20,000 "additional" investment. On the other hand, if the replacement machine was acquired 61 days prior to disposition of the old machine, the credit would be allowable on the full $30,000! And the full credit will be allowed if the disposition of the old property resulted in recapture of investment credit because of early disposition.

The noncorporate lessor is entitled to the credit in only two instances: (1) where he manufactured or produced the property subject to the lease in the ordinary course of his business, or (2) the life of the lease is less than 50 percent of the useful life of the leased property *and* certain expenses assigned to the property during the first 12 months of the lease exceed 15 percent of the rental income produced by the property. However, leased property may create a situation in which the lessor (owner) and the lessee (tenant) can agree to pass the credit on to the lessee. Who gets the investment credit in this type of situation is, of course, a matter for bargaining between lessor and lessee. If the lessee gets the credit, the lease will likely provide for a greater rental than if the lessor gets the credit. This can benefit both lessor and lessee.

Assume that the lessor depreciates the property under an accelerated method of depreciation, such as the sum of the year's-digits. The lessee gets the investment credit, and the amount of the rent is increased by the amount of the credit. In this situation, the lessor collects more rent, which is sheltered from tax in the earlier years of the lease by the accelerated depreciation. The lessee, in effect, gets an interest-free loan of the amount of the investment credit, repayable ratably over the period of the lease. Depending upon relative tax brackets and ability to use the credit, the lessee may be able to pay something less than the entire amount of the investment credit in the form of increased rent.

## SOME SAMPLE EFFECTS ON DECISIONS

We have already considered the relatively straightforward effect of the investment credit on investment alternatives. We have also pointed out that the timing of disposal of equipment being replaced by used equipment will be affected by the 60-day rule, that the question of disposing of any item of equipment which has been subject to the credit will be affected by the recapture provisions, and that leases will be substantially affected by the option of letting either lessor or lessee claim the credit. There are other peculiar results of the credit.

Where equipment is purchased and a service contract is separately entered into, an increased credit may be available if the service contract is changed to a complete warranty of the product for whatever period the service contract would have covered. This, of course, may have excise tax implications which counterbalance the investment-credit advantages. If a manufacturer's excise tax is imposed on the equipment, but not on the service contract, then the excise tax will be incurred in exchange for receiving the investment credit.

Reconditioning a piece of equipment is counted as an investment in a new piece of equipment. Since there are limits on getting the credit on used equipment (for example, the $100,000 limit and the replacement limit), certain types of transactions will generate more investment-credit benefit than will others. Thus, if a reconditioned machine is purchased for $200,000, a *used* piece of equipment costing $200,000 has been purchased, and only $10,000 of that $200,000 can be used for investment credit purposes. If, instead, an unreconditioned machine costing $50,000 had been purchased, and then $150,000 had been spent having it reconditioned, the economic and physical result would be the same, but the tax result would differ. For investment-credit purposes, $50,000 of *used* equipment and $150,000 of *new* equipment would have been purchased, and the investment credit would be obtainable on $200,000 rather than only $100,000!

## NEW JOBS CREDIT

The Tax Reduction and Simplification Act of 1977 adds a "New Jobs" credit for 1977 and 1978. The objective is to provide an incentive to create employment comparable to the incentive to acquire equipment provided by the investment credit. Maximum credit for each new employee will range from $630 to $1,806, depending on the employer's tax bracket, since the credit is offset by a reduction of the deduction for wages paid. For smaller corporations it will be $1,638 to $1,680 per new employee, while it will come to only $1,092 for higher income corporations. The credit for a given year can't exceed $100,000.

## CONCLUSION

We have discussed the investment credit at some length because of the general point it illustrates, as much as because of its specific importance. With the understandable intent of creating a more attractive investment climate, the administration proposed a simple 8 percent credit in 1962. In the process of legislative give-and-take, what emerged was something that *seemed* quite close to what went in. In fact, however, the direct benefits had been almost halved, whereas the specific rules and exceptions that had been grafted onto the original proposal produced a provision that has been criticized by some of its supposed beneficiaries as being so expensive to administer that its advantages were largely negated. Thus, little more than a year after its initial passage, we find amendment of the provision both to expand its benefits (roughly, doubling them as to larger corporations) and to simplify some of the consequent accounting problems.

We have touched on this type of situation before, and shall do so several times again. It is an important point. Tax legislation is a focal point for a myriad of interests and pressures. Therefore, it is usually a compromise and it is seldom simple. Furthermore, most major legislation has implications and repercussions that are usually little understood at the time of its passage. We shall see an extreme example of this sort of thing in the inventory chapter when we discuss a concept of inventory never dreamed of when the legislation that spawned it was moving through Congress.

The effect of tax provisions on capital expenditures is only dimly understood. We have tried in this, in other chapters, and in the appendix, at least to explore what this impact may be. But we should also bear in mind that the complexity of tax-law provisions leads to uncertainty as to their effects. Uncertainty, in business decisions, tends to inhibit action. And it seems plausible that there is some level of tax law complexity which will result in either widespread disregard of the tax provisions or a gradual stagnation of the economic machine.

## CASE EXCERPTS

*The Kramertown Co., Inc.* v. *Commissioner,* (CA5) 33 AFTR 2d 74-599
*Marineland of the Pacific, Inc.,* T.C. Memo 1975–288

*Kramertown Co., Inc.* v. *Commissioner*
(CA5) 74–1 USTC 9196

Taxpayer is the owner of a seven store shopping center. It provides rooftop heating and air conditioning units to six of the center's store tenants pursuant to negotiated leases. The eleven units provided for these six stores cost the taxpayer 69,021.71 dollars. These dual energy units are supplied with natural gas and electric energy from the interior of the stores. The gas lines run through an exterior cutoff valve before reaching the point of connection to the units which is a pipe coupling. The electric lines run through an exterior weather-proof disconnect switch box before the ultimate point of connection to the units. The units themselves rest upon wood runners or steel beams laid upon the finished surface of the roof and are not directly attached to the building. However, the units are connected to permanent ducts which lead through the roof surface into the store they service. These same ducts distribute treated air throughout the inside of the store.

Section 38(a) of the Internal Revenue Code of 1954 provides for a credit against income tax for investment in certain depreciable property. Section 48 of the Code defines "Section 38 property" as tangible property but "not including a building and its structural components." Since these heating and air conditioning units are clearly tangible property, the issue presented by this appeal turns upon whether the units are structural components of a building for purposes of Section 48 . . . .

The taxpayer argues that the effect of Treas. Reg. 1.48(e)(2) and the interpretive revenue rulings is contrary to the intent of Congress in two respects: (1) they fail to adequately distinguish between individual air conditioning units and a central air conditioning system as required by the legislative history of Section 38; (2) they fail to accord enough significance to state fixtures law and employ a test contrary to the Eighth Circuit's decision in *Minot Federal Savings and Loan* v. *United States* [71-1 USTC ¶9131], 435 F.2d 1368 (1970) . . . .

Section 38(b) provides: "[t]he Secretary or his delegate shall prescribe such regulations as may be necessary to carry out the purposes of this section and subpart B." The reason for this statutory grant of power in Section 38 is obvious. Congress deemed it more appropriate to rely upon the administrative flexibility of the Treasury Department for those nice distinctions which must be drawn as to eligibility of various types of property for the investment credit. Regulations issued pursuant to the express statutory authorization in Section 38(b) are legislative in character and as binding upon a court as a statute if they are (a) within the granted power (b) issued pursuant to proper procedure and (c) reasonable, K. Davis, Administrative Law, Section 5.03 at 299.

The taxpayer's second contention asserts that under Mississippi law these combination units are considered personal property and that this determination should be given some weight. Taxpayer gleans from the Committee Report an intention to permit the term tangible personal property to be given a broader meaning than that term is given under state law, but without in any sense permitting it to have a more restrictive meaning. We think a more reasonable reading of the cited Committee Report language is that state law is irrelevant. See *Watson* v. *Commissioner* [53-1 USTC ¶9391], 345 U.S. 544, 73 S. Ct. 848, 97 L. Ed. 2d 1232 (1953). Additionally taxpayer's argument taken to its logical conclusion would result in creating investment credit rights which would vary from state to state. For instance, if State X defined detachable components of a central air conditioning system to be personal property and the law of State Y considered such components to be real property, an investment credit for like property would be allowable in State X but not in State Y.

Finally, the taxpayer argues that to hold these units to be structural components of a building is necessarily inconsistent with *Minot Federal Savings and Loan Association* v. *United States*, 435 F. 2d 1368 (8th Cir. 1970). In *Minot* the Commissioner argued that movable partitions used as room dividers in a building owned by the taxpayer-lessor served the function of walls and were thus structural components of the leased building not eligible for the investment credit. This argument was rejected by the court as contrary to the legislative history of Section 48, the intent of the investment credit, and to the Treasury Department's regulations. The court held that since these dividers were not *permanent* in nature and could be easily detached and moved, they were tangible personal property, eligible for the investment credit.

The taxpayer asserts that these rooftop air conditioning units similarly cannot pass a permanency test because they too can be detached. Taxpayer concedes that the air ducts and the gas and electric lines which make the unit functional are structural components. However, it argues that since the units themselves are designed and installed so that they can be removed from the building for service or replacement and since no unit services more than one store tenant, they are "individual" units. We disagree. The motors and compressors of most central air conditioning units are capable of being removed and replaced by relatively simple mechanical methods. Thus, the quality of removability is not the sole determinant of whether a piece of machinery is a structural component. The weight, location and capacity of these storewide rooftop units are all indications of the reasonableness of classifying these machines as structural components of the buildings they serve under either a functional test or a permanency test. The decision of the tax court is

Affirmed.

*Marineland of the Pacific, Inc.*
T.C. Memo 1975–288

The I.R.S. refused to allow an investment credit for part of the cost of certain steel towers upon which observation gondolas ascend and descend. Petitioner contends the towers constitute "tangible personal property" under section 48(a)(1)(A), and that consequently petitioner is entitled to an investment credit for all the costs incurred by it in acquiring and erecting the towers. Alternatively, petitioner contends the towers are "elevators" within the meaning of section 48(a)(1)(C). Respondent disallowed the investment credit insofar as it related to the cost of acquiring and erecting the steel towers themselves (including their foundations), but allowed the credit for the remaining costs of the "Sky Towers." Respondent maintains that the steel towers are not tangible personal property within the meaning of section 48(a)(1)(A) or elevators within the meaning of section 48(a)(1)(C), but are "inherently permanent structures which are not items of machinery and that the credit is therefore not allowable . . . .

Respondent points out that the steel towers are inherently permanent structures because they were solidly constructed to support the gondolas in all weather conditions and affixed to the ground either in a foundation of poured concrete (in the case of the California tower) or by 52 pilings 85 feet deep (in the case of the New Jersey lower). Petitioner offered evidence to show that the towers can be moved. On one occasion a similar tower was moved. We do not think their possible mobility alone is sufficent to warrant our holding that the towers are not inherently permanent structures. *C. C. Everhart* [Dec. 32,241], 61 T.C. 328 (1973).

The real issue in this case is whether the steel towers were items of machinery inseparable from or forming an integral mechanism with the rest of the "Sky Towers," which the respondent has conceded is machinery and equipment and therefore section of property. Earlier, in *Beverly R. Roberts* [Dec. 32,121], 60 T.C. 861 (1973), respondent had taken the position that under section 1.48-1(c), Income Tax Regs., "tangible personal property" excluded "inherently permanent structures" even if in the nature of machinery. Later, in *Joseph*

*B. Weirick* [Dec. 32,668], 62 T.C. 446 (1974), respondent changed his position and contended that if an inherently permanent structure were determined to be property in the nature of machinery, and otherwise qualified as an item of personal property, it would qualify as section 38 property. We hold that the steel towers in this case are property in the nature of machinery because they are an integral part of the "Sky Towers" machinery, and that they therefore constitute section 38 property.

## QUESTIONS AND PROBLEMS

1. How does tax policy affect the investment "climate"?
2. Contrast the decision-making impact of a 25 percent investment credit with that of allowing 100 percent of the depreciation in the year of acquisition to (1) a corporation in a 50 percent income tax bracket and (2) an individual in a 20 percent tax bracket.
3. Discuss the reasons why one might use each of the two different methods available for accounting for the investment credit.
4. If the purpose of the investment credit is to stimulate the purchase of new equipment, how can one explain, or justify, allowing the credit for up to $100,000 per year of used equipment?
5. On January 1, 19X2, the Clearing Corporation purchased a new automatic milling machine for $50,000. Engineering estimates indicated a useful life of at least 12 years on the machine. On January 1, 19X4, however, due to substantial technological changes, Clearing sold the machine. Depreciation of $14,000 had been taken during 19X2 and 19X3. What investment-credit results did this series of transactions have? What was the tax basis (for purposes of computing gain or loss) of the machine on an accounting basis? If the machine sold for $46,000, how was the gain or loss treated for tax purposes?
6. The complexities of the investment credit introduce technicalities into a number of fairly common transactions, including:
   (a) Purchase of used equipment to replace other equipment;
   (b) Sale of any equipment which originally was subject to the investment credit;
   (c) Leases of personal property;
   (d) Selling service contracts separately from equipment;
   (e) Purchasing reconditioned equipment or purchasing unreconditioned equipment and then having it reconditioned.
   (f) Deciding whether to build in lighting as part of an office building or integrate it into the office furniture.

For each of these transactions, explain how the investment credit alters the strategy of a rational decisionmaker.

7. The Smith Corporation has a tax liability of $75,000 for 19X3. During 19X3 it purchased the following fixed assets:

| *Asset* | *Cost* | *Useful Life (in years)* |
|---|---|---|
| Equipment | $ 10,000 | 4 |
| Land | 45,000 | 15 |
| Used elevator | 25,000 | 10 |
| Equipment | 60,000 | 10 |
| New escalator | 15,000 | 10 |
| Building | 250,000 | 40 |
| Equipment | 15,000 | 5 |
| | $420,000 | |

The Smith Corporation has investment-credit carryovers totaling $8,000. What is the maximum investment credit that can be used this year and how much, if any, will be carried over to 19X4?

8. By buying assets subject to the investment credit and using the investment credit to reduce expenses (namely taxes), can a firm create income? Construct an example to illustrate your answer.

9. Mr. Jones owns a machine with an adjusted basis of $900 which he trades for a new machine with a market value of $2,100. He is given $1,100 for a trade-in and pays $1,000 cash. Assuming that the equipment is subject to investment credit and that the old machine had been held over seven years, what, if any, investment credit is Mr. Jones entitled to on this transaction?

10. Would your answer to the preceding question change if the machine acquired had been a used one?

11. The Higbe Corporation has purchased $80,000 of used equipment subject to the investment credit this year. They now are debating whether to purchase another piece of used equipment costing $50,000 which has been completely reconditioned, or to buy the same type of equipment, but a unit which they must recondition themselves, for $16,000, with estimated reconditioning costs of $34,000. What would you recommend and why? What factors other than taxes would you consider in this decision?

*12. Mr. Charles proposes to acquire a resort hotel in the Poconos. Land, improved with a golf course, tennis courts, driveways, and a parking lot, will cost him $1,300,000. The buildings will cost $500,000, while the building furnishings and equipment will cost $250,000. In order to upgrade the property into the type of establishment he wants, Mr. Charles will have to spend $100,000 on the buildings and $200,000 on new furniture and equipment. Analyze for him the degree to which his investment will be eligible for the investment credit. Will that eligibility be affected if he finances the acquisition and the upgrading with borrowed money? Will it be affected if he uses a Subchapter S (Small Business) Corporation to make the investment? If he uses a regular corporation?

13. In *Kramertown*, the Court distinguishes between interpretative regulations and legislative regulations. Explain this distinction, especially as it relates to regulations issued under the tax law sections dealing with the investment credit.
14. Reconcile the holding in *Kramertown* that air conditioning units not physically attached to the building are not eligible for the investment credit with the holding in *Marineland* that steel towers affixed to the ground in a foundation of poured concrete are eligible.

# 12

# Depletion and the Costs of Exploration and Development

## DEPRECIATION VERSUS DEPLETION

A basic accounting objective is to properly match revenue earned with the costs used up in earning the revenue. If we pay $1,000,000 for 1,000,000 units of X, then the cost of each unit of X we sell is $1. This basic idea is applied, with variations, to determine the cost of merchandise sold, as we shall discuss in Chapter 16. It is applied to the determination of depreciation, as we saw in Chapter 10. If we are dealing with natural resources, the application of this basic idea produces what is known as "cost depletion."

### *Cost Depletion*

Each year, a new computation of cost depletion is made. The approach is to divide the beginning-of-the-year unrecovered cost of the natural resource by the estimated number of mineral units remaining as of the beginning of the year. This gives a cost per unit. This cost is multiplied by the number of units sold to get the total depletion deduction by the cost method.

### *Percentage Depletion*

The actual depletion deduction allowable may exceed the cost-depletion deduction, however. Another way of computing depletion is the "percentage-depletion" technique. This allows a deduction that is a percentage of gross income (but limited to not more than 50 percent of net income from the particular property, before depletion).

Thus, even though we paid $1,000,000 for 1,000,000 units of X and sold 200,000 units (at $10 per unit) in the current year, our depletion deduction could exceed the $200,000 of cost depletion. If the percentage-depletion rate applicable was 20 percent, then our percentage-depletion deduction would be 20 percent of the $2,000,000 of sales, or $400,000.

The percentages in use range from 22 percent (for some producers of oil and gas, uranium, clay, and a range of other items) down to 5 percent (such things as clay used for tile, gravel, sand, and stone). The taxpayer uses cost depletion or percentage depletion, whichever is larger. If he uses percentage depletion, he must reduce the amount of his unrecovered cost for calculating cost depletion for subsequent years by the amount of the depletion taken, even though it was not cost depletion. However, the taxpayer can continue taking percentage depletion even after he has recovered all his cost.

Going back to our example with 20 percent depletion, if our cost was $1,000,000, our cost depletion for the year $200,000, and our percentage depletion $400,000, then our tax basis at the beginning of the next year would be $600,000 ($1,000,000 cost less $400,000 depletion taken). The remaining units would be 800,000, and thus cost depletion per unit would be reduced to 75 cents. If during each of the next two years we sold 200,000 units at $10 per unit, we would be able to claim percentage depletion at the same 20 percent of the $2,000,000 gross income—or percentage depletion of $400,000 per year. At the end of three years, we would have deducted $1,200,000 of percentage depletion, even though the property cost us only $1,000,000. Our tax basis in the property, and hence our cost depletion, would be reduced to zero.

Percentage depletion is thus unique in our tax law, in that taxpayers are allowed to deduct amounts that represent no investment or expenditure by them.

How did this peculiar concept, this percentage depletion, arrive in our tax law? As with most tax concepts, it did not spring full-blown upon the world. It started out as a laudable attempt to achieve equity, matured into an administrative problem of some complexity, and was finally converted into a major political issue.

As you may remember, the first income tax law after the Sixteenth Amendment provided that, for purposes of measuring gain or loss, the fair market value of property as of March 1, 1913 (if greater than its pre-March 1, 1913, cost) was to be deemed its tax basis. This was also to be the basis for depreciation and for depletion.

If Ring discovered an oil well on February 27, 1913, he was able to take cost depletion on the basis of the fair market value of his well on March 1, 1913. But if his friend Peal discovered a well on March 2, 1913, his cost depletion was based on the relatively minor amount of investment he had in the property. Because the value of a well, a mine, or anything similar increases enormously over its cost once a discovery has been made on the property, the use as a depletion basis of fair market value for one taxpayer and cost for another appeared discriminatory and inequitable.

In 1918, therefore, Congress inserted in the law a provision aimed at curing this inequity and also at encouraging the discovery and development of natural resources within the United States. The country, you should remember, was quite conscious of the dangers of being dependent upon foreign sources of supply, after the World War I experience with German submarines.

The new provision allowed depletion to be computed on the fair market value of the mineral property at the date of the discovery or within 30 days of discovery, if such fair market value was materially disproportionate to the cost of the property. This new legislation created problems, especially with oil and gas. Fair market value was normally established through the testimony of engineers, geologists, and other experts. Frequently, the taxpayer's experts and the government's experts would be unable to agree, and time-consuming and expensive litigation would result.

By 1924, the Treasury Department was able to secure the enactment of a provision limiting the discovery depletion deduction to 50 percent of the net income from the property before deducting depletion. Now, at least, discovery depletion could not be used as a complete offset to income from natural resources. A taxpayer with $60,000 of discovery depletion to deduct could use only $5,000 of it if his net income before depletion was only $10,000 from a particular property.

To get away from the administrative difficulties involved in determining the value of oil and gas wells, Congress finally switched to percentage depletion in 1926. It was a substitute for discovery-value depletion and was based on the idea that the market value of an oil well was simply the present value of all the oil to be extracted from that well in the future, net of expenses and discounted at a reasonable discount rate. Market value of the property, in other words, bore a relationship to future sales of oil. How better to solve the problem than to forget about valuing the property now, and to simply substitute a depletion deduction that would be a flat percentage of all the oil sold from the property.

And this was what they did for oil and gas in 1926. The rate of percentage depletion proposed by the House was 25 percent. After Senate consideration and a House-Senate conference, the rate of 27½ percent, which stayed through 1969, was adopted.

Other minerals were less of a valuation problem than oil and gas had been. But over the years, depletion rules concerning all the others were changed, until by 1954 the concept of discovery-value depletion was entirely eliminated from the Internal Revenue Code and percentage depletion covered all wells and mines.

## OIL AND GAS DEPLETION

The desirability of percentage depletion, its economic effects, and its effects on the morale of taxpayers not in extractive industries have all been stridently debated over the years—and are being debated today. Most of the discussion centers on oil and gas and the depletion allowance of 22 percent of gross income. Proponents of percentage depletion make much of the greater uncertainty involved in making investments in the oil industry as compared with other industries. They also point out that the recent substantial elimination of percentage depletion for all except very small producers merely encourages sale of the oil in place (as real estate, while still in the ground) at capital gains rates and produces far less tax revenue than many commentators had estimated.

Opponents center their attack on the misallocation of resources caused by using the tax system to encourage investment in oil and gas beyond the level dictated by the market mechanism. They argue that *percentage depletion* is simply another expression for *subsidy,* even though the industry being subsidized can actually operate profitably without a subsidy. As to risks involved, they point out that more than 70 percent of the more than $5 billion of depletion claimed on corporate tax returns was taken on returns of corporations with assets of over $100 million, and that almost 97 percent was claimed by companies with total assets of at least $1 million. In firms of this size, the tax structure already allows for tax benefits through the offsetting of losses on dry holes and unproductive properties against the income from producing properties in computing tax. It is only the taxpayer who has no other sources of income against which to offset his losses who really faces an uninsured risk. Because percentage depletion is limited to 50 percent of net income from the property, it cannot be of much benefit to this taxpayer. Fifty percent of a loss is nothing.

The Tax Reduction Act of 1975 was a victory for the opponents of oil and gas depletion. It repealed the percentage depletion allowance for oil and gas, with two exceptions. The exception of most interest to us here is that for small producers. For 1978, percentage depletion is allowed to small producers for an average of 1400 barrels per day (or its equivalent in cubic feet of gas). This phases down to an average of 1,000 barrels per day (or its equivalent in cubic feet of gas) for 1980 and thereafter. The percentage depletion rate stays at 22 percent through 1980, and then gradually lessens until it reaches 15 percent for 1984 and thereafter.

In addition, the percentage depletion attributable to the small producer exemption can't exceed 65 percent of the taxpayer's taxable income. Generally, the taxpayer is not entitled to the small producer exemption if he acquired an interest in an oil or gas property after 1974 and the property was "proven" at the time, since the purpose of this exemption was to encourage the development of new wells and not merely the acquisition of established properties.

## EXPLORATION AND DEVELOPMENT

### *Oil and Gas*

The intangible drilling and development costs of oil or gas wells may be deducted in the year incurred, rather than being treated as part of the cost of acquiring a producing well. If these expenses were capitalized, they would be of relatively little advantage in any situation where percentage depletion exceeded cost depletion, because they would be recovered as a part of the cost depletion.

These intangible drilling and development costs include wages paid, fuel, repairs, hauling, and supplies. They do not include items essentially related to the production of the oil, such as pumping equipment, flow lines, storage tanks, or even the well casing. However, post-1975 intangible drilling and development costs may be "recaptured," in a manner similar to depreciation on realty, and thus convert into ordinary income part of what would otherwise be capital gain on sale of an oil or gas property.

### *Other Natural Deposits*

Exploration costs of other mines may be deducted when incurred. If the project proves successful, the amount deducted will be "recaptured." The taxpayer can either report the amount as income in the year in which the mine reaches the producing stage, or he can offset it against the depletion to which he would otherwise be entitled. To the extent not deducted, these costs become part of the cost of the property and are thus subject to cost depletion. If the exploration project proves unsuccessful, such capitalized costs are, of course, then deductible as a part of the loss on the property.

Development expenses are expenses incurred after it has been established that a mine contains commercially marketable quantities of the ore or mineral. These expenses are deductible as incurred and need not be capitalized, although the taxpayer may, if he wishes, elect to capitalize them and defer the time of deduction until the ore or mineral is sold. Development expenses include the depreciation on equipment and other depreciable assets but do not include the cost of the assets themselves.

## OIL AND GAS, AND THE INVESTORS

The tax-law provisions dealing with oil and gas depletion and the expensing of intangible drilling and development costs have helped spawn millionaires who pay little or no income taxes on their way up the financial ladder. Undoubtedly, they have also helped induce many a naive investor to lose his shirt on speculative oil and gas ventures.

Let us trace through a hypothetical illustration of how expensing intangibles can work. Wood has $50,000 of capital. In year 1, he invests his $50,000 in acquiring a one-fourth interest in an oil venture. Of the $50,000, $30,000 goes to intangible drilling and development costs. Very little oil is produced in this first year, and Wood receives only about $30,000 as his share of the sales proceeds. In year 2, production booms. Wood receives $200,000. But in year 2 he borrows against the security of his well an additional $200,000. He sinks $400,000 into a second well, of which $295,000 is intangible drilling and development cost. The second well comes in and produces $95,000 worth of oil that year.

In two years, let us see what has happened:

| *Year* | *Income* | *Deductions* | *Tax* |
|---|---|---|---|
| 1 | $ 30,000 | $ 30,000 | 0 |
| 2 | 295,000 | 295,000 | 0 |

If the value of his interest in the first well is about $400,000 and the value of his interest in the second well is about $800,000, Wood has gone from a net worth of $50,000 to a net worth of $1,000,000 in two years without paying one cent in income taxes.

Many people who object violently to percentage depletion, on the ground that tax deductions are allowed for more than the amount invested except for oil and gas exploration or exploitation, are far less antagonistic to expensing intangible drilling and development costs for oil and gas wells and exploration and development costs for other properties. After all, they point out, the taxpayer gets to deduct no more than the amount of his investment.

As implied in the chapter on depreciation, an argument can be made for allowing capital investment to be deducted on a cash-flow rather than an accrual-accounting basis. If this were universally done for such investments, the before-tax and the after-tax profitability index would produce the same result, and hence the income tax structure would presumably be neutral in capital investment alternative-choice situations.

Of course, where such cash-flow expensing is allowed for some types of investment (such as those we are discussing here in the natural resources area, or research and development intangible costs in the industrial area), the types of investment so tax-favored do become more attractive to investors having other income against which these deductions can be offset. They become even more attractive when the investment deduction is an ordinary deduction but recovery of the investment upon disposition of the property is treated in part or in whole as a capital gain.

## CASE EXCERPTS

*John W. Meyers, Jr.,* 66 T.C. 235
*U.S.* v. *Marvin Shurbet, et. ux.,* (CA5) 15 AFTR 2d 1149

*John W. Meyers, Jr.*
66 T.C. 235

The sole issue for our decision is whether petitioner, who is engaged in the business of planting and cultivating sod for sale, is entitled to a deduction for the depletion of the topsoil removed and sold with the sod.

Under section 611(a), there is allowed a deduction in computing taxable income for depletion in the case of "natural deposits." This allowance is designed to permit the owner of a capital interest in an exhaustible natural resource in place to make a tax-free recovery of his depleting capital asset. *Parsons* v. *Smith,* 359 U.S. 215 (1959). Fundamental in such an allowance is the ultimate exhaustibility of the natural resource on which depletion is claimed.

... In this case petitioner's topsoil will be exhausted in 16 cuttings. Respondent, however, contends that topsoil removed in conjunction with the sale of sod ought not to be classified as a "natural deposit." Rather, it is his position that petitioner's operations are more properly characterized as a farming activity in which there is a foreseen diminution of the capacity of the land to produce crops with each planting. Owners of farmland are specifically denied a deduction for exhaustion and wear and tear due to erosion, wind, or privation of soil nutrients, and respondent would have us treat this case similarly. See secs. 1.167(a)-6(b) and 1.612-1(b)(1), Income Tax Regs.

This issue was expressly left open by us in *Benedict O. Warren, Jr.,* 40 T.C. 991, 996-997 (1963). In that case, however, we did express doubt concerning the analogy between the diminution in land value resulting from the physical removal of topsoil with sod and the diminution in land value resulting from the exhaustion of soil nutrients with the planting of crops, the analogy upon which respondent relies. We believe that it would be unnecessary overgeneralization to treat the cultivation and sale of sod as we would a purely farming activity and prefer to follow our earlier suggestion.

It is conceded that if petitioner were engaged in the severance and sale of topsoil per se, such soil in place would be considered a "natural deposit," the proceeds from the sale of which would be subject to a cost depletion allowance. See Rev. Rul. 78, 1953-1 C.B. 18. In this regard, we can see no distinction between the sale of topsoil per se and the sale of sod. Perhaps the fundamental differences on this point originate in differing conceptions of sod. Respondent, it seems, would have us define sod as grass to which a certain amount of topsoil adheres. Webster's, on the other hand, defines sod as "the upper stratum of the soil or humus that is filled with the roots of grass or other herbs." (Webster's Third New International Dictionary (1971)).

Since sod is by definition a combination of soil and plantlife, the loss of topsoil suffered in a sale of sod cannot be considered minimal, as respondent argues. Such a sale would involve losing more than a few incidental morsels of topsoil. In each case some topsoil is being physically removed, so that after 16 cuttings the layer of topsoil on petitioner's land would be totally exhausted.

Hence, there is an actual loss of soil which results in eventual exhaustion of petitioner's capital investment in a natural resource, precisely the circumstances in which a depletion allowance was intended. *United States* v. *Shurbet, supra;* see also *Don C. Day,* 54 T.C. 1417, 1425 (1970).

Respondent, after distinguishing sod from topsoil, maintains that petitioner's sod operations are in the nature of farming and therefore governed by Rev. Rul. 54-241, 1954-1 C.B. 63. In that ruling respondent determined that sod and balled nursery stock were not assets subject to a depletion allowance because, after removal of such items, it was possible to restore the productivity of the land. Thus, the farmer would instead be able to deduct the cost of land productivity maintenance as a business expense.

In *Flona Corp.* v. *United States,* 218 F.Supp. 354 (S.D. Fla. 1963), the District Court rejected the application of Rev. Rul. 54-241, *supra,* where the taxpayer showed that after the removal of sod, his land could not be restored "except at costs which [were] totally prohibitory." On this point *Flona Corp.* is indistinguishable from the facts found herein that, upon the exhaustion of topsoil, it would not be economically feasible to replenish the soil.

Accordingly, despite respondent's argument to the contrary, we choose to follow our earlier inclination in *Benedict O. Warren, Jr.*, and the reasoning of the District Court in *Flona Corp.* We therefore hold that the sod sold by this petitioner was a "natural deposit" subject to the depletion allowance under section 611.

*U.S.* v. *Marvin Shurbet, et. ux.*
(CA5) 15 AFTR 2d 1149

The case was carefully and elaborately tried as a test case for the irrigation farmers in the Southern High Plains of Texas and New Mexico. It comes to this Court on a printed record of more than 1,700 pages plus many voluminous exhibits . . . .

The Southern High Plains is a plateau about 150 miles wide from east to west and 200 miles wide from north to south, with an area of approximately 35,000 square miles, situated in Texas and New Mexico. Underlying the Southern High Plains is the Ogallala formation, a geologic formation composed of interbedded layers of quartz, sand, pebbles, silt, gravel, water, clay, rocks, and other similar materials. Water suitable for human consumption, for stock watering and for irrigation purposes occurs in the voids between the mineral particles which compose the formation. The formation is permeable, that is, water can move through the materials. There has been water in the formation since it was deposited millions of years ago.

During Pliocene times, from one to ten million years ago, streams flowing eastward from the Rocky Mountains deposited the materials and water which make up the Ogallala formation. Later some of the formation was eroded away;

the Canadian River carved out a valley to the north; the Pecos River turned south and carved out a valley to the west. The present boundaries on three sides of the Southern High Plains and of the Ogallala formation are: the escarpment, or steep cliff, cut by the Canadian River on the north, and escarpment cut by the Pecos River on the west, and an escarpment on the east. On the south the Ogallala formation slopes southeastward into older formations which lie at a lower elevation. The thickness of the Ogallala formation in the Southern High Plains ranges from a few feet to several hundred feet. The top of the Ogallala water table ranges from 50 to 250 feet below the surface of the land. Both the land surface and the bottom of the Ogallala formation in the Southern High Plains slope from northwest to southeast at an average rate of about 10 feet per mile.

Underlying the entire Ogallala formation in the Southern High Plains are the "red beds" several thousand feet thick and relatively impermeable, so that water does not percolate downwards to any appreciable degree. The general direction of movement of water through the Ogallala reservoir is from the northwest to the southeast at the rate of approximately 60 to 200 feet per year.

The only source from which new water of any kind can move into the Ogallala formation in the Southern High Plains is from precipitation upon the surface of the ground. Under natural conditions, prior to pumping the Ogallala reservoir was in a state of dynamic equilibrium; that is, the average annual natural recharge was approximately equal to the average annual natural discharge.

The advent of irrigation farming on the Southern High Plains occurred since 1934, at which time there were only 620 wells pumping water from the entire Ogallala reservoir. By 1948 that number had increased to 8,000 and by 1958 to 47,000.

The recoverable water in storage in the entire Ogallala formation in the Southern High Plains in 1938, 1958 and 1962 was approximately as follows:

| *Year* | *Recoverable Water in the Ogallala Reservoir* |
|---|---|
| 1938 . . . . . | 250 million acre-feet |
| 1958 . . . . . | 220 million acre-feet |
| 1962 . . . . . | 210 million acre-feet |

. . . In Texas the common law rule prevails that the owner of the land owns the soil and the percolating water which is a part of the soil. *Houston & Texas Ry. Co.* v. *East*, Tex. 1904, 81 S. W. 279. More specifically, a Texas statute has recognized that the ownership of underground water in the Ogallala formation is vested in the owners of the land. Vernon's Texas Civil Statutes, Art. 7880-3c . . . .

The main thrust of the government's argument is that ordinary ground water is not a "natural deposit" for cost depletion purposes. In that connection, we would confine the holding in this case to the water extracted by taxpayers from the Ogallala formation in the Southern High Plains. We agree with the finding of the district court that:

> "Ground water in the Ogallala formation of the Southern High Plains is a mineral and natural deposit within the meaning of the federal tax statutes and regulations governing deductions for cost depletion."

The government insists that throughout the years since 1913, the natural deposits on which depletion was allowed have been consistently equated with mineral deposits from which income is derived through severance and sale of the mineral as a mineral. We think that argument applies with greater force to percentage depletion now allowed as an alternative basis for computing depletion allowance in the case of nearly all minerals.

Percentage depletion looks to the gross income from the production of the mineral and may well apply only to minerals which are commercially exploited by sale. Even percentage depletion has been applied to a taxpayer who mines a mineral which it owns and processes it into a product which it sells. *United States* v. *Cannelton Sewer Pipe Company,* 1960, 364 U.S. 76, 89; *United States* v. *Henderson Clay Products,* 5 Cir. 1963, 324 F. 2d 7; *United States* v. *Longhorn Portland Cement Co.*, 5 Cir. 1964, 328 F. 2d 491. The present case, however, is based entirely upon cost depletion.

The term "natural deposits" must, of course, be interpreted consistently with the policy and purpose of Congress in allowing the depletion deduction. The Income Tax Law of 1913, c. 16, 38 Stat. 114, 166, sec. II provided the first specific depletion deduction based on cost or March 1, 1913 value, "not to exceed, in the case of mines, 5 per centum of the gross value at the mine of the output for the year for which the computation is made." Of course, in the usual case, "the gross value at the mine of the output" would be established by the market price or sale price of the output. The statute did not, however, require a sale or deny depletion in the unusual case where value might be established by means other than sale or market price . . . .

As we read the legislative history, it means no more than that Congress intended depletion as a means of allowing an annual deduction to represent the capital exhausted in the taxpayer's business operations. In cost depletion, we do not agree with the government that "natural deposits" have been equated to "mineral deposits" from which income is derived through severance and sale of the mineral. The language of the cost depletion provisions, sections 611 and 612 of the Internal Revenue Code of 1954, does not convey any such meaning, and it seems to us inconsistent with the purpose and rationale of cost depletion.

The government argues, however, that the exclusion of water from "other minerals" in section 613(b)(6) of the 1954 Internal Revenue Code, applicable to percentage depletion, furnishes strong evidence that water was never intended to be included in "natural deposits" in section 611, applicable to cost depletion. That argument would be more impressive if water had been classed as one of the "inexhaustible resources" in subsection (B) of section 613(b)(6) along with "minerals from sea water" and "the air." The exclusion of water from "other minerals" allowed percentage depletion occurs, however, in subsection (A) along with "soil, sod, dirt, turf, *water*, or mosses." (Italics added.) The same contention as applicable to "sod" was ruled against the government in *Flona Corporation* v. *United States*, S. D. Fla. 1963, [63-2 USTC ¶9544] 218 F. Supp. 354, 356. The appeal in that case was docketed in this Court as No. 20981, and was disposed of on April 17, 1964 by an unpublished order quoted in the margin.

Section 1.611-1(d) (5) of the Treasury Regulations on Income Tax (1954 Code) also strongly implies, if indeed it does not definitely recognize, that some minerals may be subject to cost depletion which are not subject to percentage depletion.

> "(5) 'Minerals' includes ores of the metals, coal, oil, gas, and all other natural metallic and nonmetallic deposits, except minerals derived from sea water, the air, or from similar inexhaustible sources. *It includes but is not limited to* all of the minerals and other natural deposits subject to depletion based upon a percentage of gross income from the property under section 613 and the regulations thereunder." (Italics supplied.)

The Court concluded that the taxpayer was entitled to cost depletion.

## QUESTIONS AND PROBLEMS

1. If a corporation takes more depreciation for tax purposes than for financial accounting purposes, accounting practice requires that a provision for deferred federal income tax be set up. If a corporation takes more depletion for tax purposes, through using percentage depletion, than it takes for financial accounting purposes, for which it uses cost depletion, is a provision for deferred federal income tax also logically required?
2. What was discovery depletion, and what administrative problems did it create?
3. What was the rationale of percentage depletion relative to discovery depletion?

*4. Hurlbut Number One is an oil well, owned and operated by Winthrop Sargent. Mr. Sargent has $40,000 per year of taxable interest income, is unmarried, used the standard deduction, and has only himself as a dependent. His transactions relative to Hurlbut Number One were:

| | | |
|---|---|---|
| 1974 | Intangible drilling and development costs | $ 15,000 |
| | Production equipment (10-year life, no salvage) | 5,000 |
| 1975 | Oil sales | 20,000 |
| | Out-of-pocket operating expenses | 10,000 |

| | | |
|---|---|---|
| 1976 | Oil sales | 40,000 |
| | Out-of-pocket operating expenses | 15,000 |
| 1977 | Sold entire interest in Hurlbut Number One | 200,000 |

Show the effect of the oil transactions for each year on Sargent's tax liability, and indicate the average effective tax rate at which his oil income was assessed for the period 1974–1977.

5. Distinguish between the tax treatments accorded exploration costs of oil and gas wells and exploration costs of other mineral properties.
6. Does a purchase of an interest in an oil or gas well inevitably provide the investor with special tax benefits? Explain.

*7. Contrast the depreciation recapture rules applicable to post-75 depreciation on commercial buildings with the recapture rules relating to post-75 intangible drilling and development costs of oil and gas wells. Which do you think allows the greatest conversion of ordinary deduction into capital gain?

8. George Lane owns Alice Number 4. Annual operating results for each of the next five years are expected to be:

| | |
|---|---|
| Gross revenue | $100,000 |
| Operating expenses | 30,000 |
| Depreciation | 15,000 |
| Cost depletion | 10,000 |

Lane is in a 50 percent tax bracket. At the end of five years, the well will have a resale value of $20,000, but Lane will have written off his entire investment in the well through the depreciation and depletion deductions claimed. Lane is contemplating selling his interest in the well. What is the minimum amount he can sell out for and still be as well off after taxes as if he continued to operate the well, ignoring the time value of money?

9. The facts here are the same as for Problem 8. What is the maximum amount a buyer could pay Lane for Alice Number 4, ignoring the time value of money, without actually sustaining a loss on the investment?
10. Assuming that both buyer and seller would have available to them a source of income that, after taxes, would return them 10 percent per annum on all amounts invested, what would be the answers to Questions 8 and 9?
11. Ross drilled Advance No. 1 in 1977 at a cost of $76,000, of which $60,000 was deductible as intangible drilling and development cost. He expects to sell 400,000 barrels of oil in 1978 at $10 per barrel. His costs of operating the well for the year will be $630,000. His net taxable income, other than for this, his only oil or gas venture, will be $225,000. What amount can Ross deduct for percentage depletion in 1978?
12. Explain whether the *Shurbet* case appears to stand for the proposition that water will generally be viewed as depletable for federal income tax purposes.

# 13

# Minimum and Maximum Tax

The Tax Reform Act of 1969 introduced the minimum and maximum taxes, both aimed at closing so-called "tax loopholes" which developed over the years. In this chapter we will examine the background of these taxes and some of the details involved in computing them.

## MINIMUM TAX

### *Introduction*

In considering tax reform proposals in 1969, Congress detected a ground swell of opposition to special tax shelters for high income taxpayers. These provisions allowed some taxpayers to avoid paying taxes entirely, and others to greatly reduce their tax bills.

The Congressional reaction was not to eliminate the tax shelters, although some were modified then and in the later 1976 Tax Reform Act. One result was the introduction of a new tax concept—the minimum tax on tax preferences. While the 1969 version had relatively little "bite," the 1976 Tax Reform Act broadened the items of tax preference to which the tax applies, raised the tax rate to 15 percent, and reduced the amount of tax preference triggering the tax.

The items of tax preference do not include tax-exempt interest income, but they do include many of the special deductions which have been cited as tax loopholes. The tax preferences are:

1. Excess itemized deduction—itemized deductions of individuals (except medical expense and casualty losses) that exceed 60 percent of the taxpayer's adjusted gross income;
2. Excess accelerated depreciation on real property and on leased personal property over what straight-line depreciation would be;

3. Excess fast amortization of certified pollution-control facilities, railroad-rolling stock and on-the-job training and child-care facilities over what their depreciation deductions would have been;

4. Depletion deductions in excess of the tax basis for cost depletion;

5. Excess current year intangible drilling and development costs over the amount of amortization that would have been allowable if they had been capitalized;

6. The 50 percent long-term capital gain deduction allowed individuals (and a corresponding item for the capital gains of corporations);

7. Excess bad-debt expense deductions allowed banks and savings and loan associations over the bad-debt deduction they could have taken based on their actual experience; and

8. The amount by which the fair-market value of stock acquired through a qualified option plan exceeds the option price.

### *Details of the Minimum Tax*

While the list of tax preference items appears rather easy to follow, it might be worthwhile to consider a few of the items in more detail. Accelerated depreciation on leased personal property is not merely the excess of depreciation taken over straight-line depreciation for the useful life involved. Under ADR, lives up to 20 percent less than the actual guideline lives are frequently used. In such cases, the amount of preference is the excess of what was taken over what the straight-line would have been if the actual guideline life had been used.

Proper calculation of the intangible drilling and development tax preference item is still not settled. Whereas accelerated depreciation and depletion are calculated separately for each property rather than aggregated for all properties, the intangible drilling item is an aggregate. The I.R.S. position is that the proper amount to be subtracted from the current year intangible drilling expense of successful wells is only the amortization that would have been allowed for the current year for only those wells if the expenses on those wells had been capitalized. Some practititoners contend that the preference item should be calculated by subtracting the amount of amortization that would have been available if all intangible drilling for all relevant years had been capitalized and amortized. (In any event, intangible drilling costs of "dry" holes are not a preference item.)

Depletion based on the percentage method is considered a tax preference item when the percentage depletion exceeds the basis of the property remaining at the end of the year without regard to depletion taken for the current year. Assume that the basis of your property is $100,000, while cost depletion would be $15,000 and percentage depletion amounts to $35,000. Since percentage depletion is not in excess of the basis of $100,000, there is no tax preference. However, changing the facts to assume that the basis of the property is $50,000, cost depletion is $5,000, and percentage depletion is $60,000 would mean that $10,000 of the percentage depletion would be considered a tax preference item. Since the basis of property is reduced by any depletion taken ($50,000 - $60,000), all of the percentage depletion taken the following year will be considered a tax preference because the basis of the property will be zero.

The amount subject to the minimum tax rate of 15 percent is the excess of tax preference items over the greater of a $10,000 exclusion ($5,000 if married and filing separately), or half the regular tax computed on income for the current year.

Individuals, corporations, estates, and trusts are subject to the minimum tax. However, corporations have special rules. Their exemption is the greater of $10,000 or 100 percent of their regular tax; and excess itemized deductions, accelerated depreciation on leased personal property, and intangible drilling costs are not preference items. In addition, only 18/48, or 37½ percent of their long-term capital gains are a preference item as compared to 50 percent for an individual. When preparing an estimate of tax to be paid in the following year, the minimum tax does not have to be included in the estimate. While both the investment credit and the foreign tax credit reduce the amount of regular tax to be paid, they cannot be used to reduce the minimum tax.

## MINIMUM TAX AND RECAPTURE

What is the effect of the minimum tax on depreciation policy? Should the taxpayer adopt or change to straight-line depreciation and thus avoid having a tax preference amount? Or should he go with accelerated depreciation and risk the minimum tax? Prior to the minimum tax, accelerated depreciation involved taking an ordinary deduction now and having income at some future time. If effective tax rates did not climb sharply, the effect at worst was an interest-free borrowing of tax money. The advent of the 15 percent minimum tax had the effect of imposing an "interest" charge.

*Example:*

A taxpayer can take $5,000 of excess depreciation in 1978 on a property that he plans to sell at its original cost in 1983. He is and will be in a 70 percent bracket. The full $5,000 will be subject to the minimum tax in 1978, and he anticipates he will be subject to the minimum tax in 1983.

The taxpayer is, in effect, borrowing $2,487 for five years ($3,500 in 1978 tax savings less $1,013 in 1978 minimum tax). Here is how $1,013 is calculated:

| | |
|---|---|
| Increase in preference items (accelerated depreciation) | $5,000 |
| *Add:* One-half of decrease in regular income tax which tax is a preference exclusion | 1,750 |
| Total increase in preference income | $6,750 |
| 15% preference tax | $1,013 |

At the end of five years, he has to pay back $3,237. Although he will have to pay $3,500 in tax for 1983, this will reduce the amount subject to the preference tax, to the extent of $1,750, thus saving him $263 in 1983 minimum tax, resulting in a net incremental cash outflow of $3,237 for taxes as the result of recapture of the 1978 accelerated depreciation.

Our problem then is simple. What is the effective rate of interest if the cost of borrowing $2,487 today is a payback of $3,237 in five years? Will a taxpayer borrow at this 5¼ percent rate? Bear in mind that his "interest" is nondeductible.

Of course, the assumptions are crucial, but the problem is straightforward. Change the assumptions and the calculations change. If it is not anticipated that the taxpayer will pay a minimum tax for 1983 then he pays back $3,500, and the cost of borrowing $2,487 is increased with a corresponding increase in the interest rate being paid.

Generally, the lower the marginal tax bracket, the greater will be the effective rate of interest. Given the same facts, a taxpayer who is and will be in a 22 percent marginal tax bracket (e.g., a small corporation) would obtain a $185 loan with a "payback" of $935 and pay "interest" at a rate of almost 40 percent (nondeductible).

### *Effective Rate of Minimum Tax on Capital Gains (Individuals)*

In some cases where there are substantial capital gains the marginal rate of minimum tax on capital gains of individuals could approach 7½ percent. However, it should not normally exceed 4.875 percent at the margin after the tax on the capital gain passes $20,000 because of the interplay between the regular tax and the minimum tax.

*Example 1:*

Marginal rate on regular income = 0%
Tax on long-term capital gain = $0–$20,000
Minimum tax = 15% of (50% of capital gain − ½ of tax on capital gain if ½ exceeds $10,000)
= .15 (.50 – .00) = .075 marginal minimum tax rate on capital gain over $20,000 up to point where regular tax on capital gain exceeds $20,000.

*Example 2:*

Marginal rate = 70%
Tax on long-term capital gain = 35%
Minimum tax = 15% of (50% of capital gain −½ of tax on capital gain)
= .15 (.50 – .175) = .04875 marginal minimum tax rate

Calculating the marginal minimum tax for the long-term capital gain of a corporation is somewhat easier. The minimum tax (0.15) applies to the excess of 0.375 of the capital gain over the regular tax of 0.30 of the capital gain already being paid:

0.15 (0.375CG – 0.30 CG) = 0.1125 CG

Thus, the marginal rate of minimum tax to a corporation will normally be only 1.125 percent of its long-term capital gain.

***Figuring the Minimum Tax***

Assume that Mr. Higbe, unmarried, had taxable income of $32,000 upon which the regular tax was $10,290. His taxable income was a result of many factors, including a net long-term capital gain of $5,000, $2,000 of "excess" depreciation from a lease on equipment, percentage depletion of $21,000 on an oil well which had a basis of $3,000, and double-declining balance depreciation of $36,000 in excess of the straight-line method on apartment buildings. His minimum tax would be computed as follows:

| | | |
|---|---|---|
| Tax Preference Items: | | |
| One-half net long-term gain | | $ 2,500 |
| Lease excess depreciation | | 2,000 |
| Depletion in excess of base | | 18,000 |
| Realty excess depreciation | | 36,000 |
| Total Tax Preference Items | | $58,500 |
| Less: Exemption | $10,000 | |
| or ½ of Regular Tax | 5,145 | 10,000 |
| Subject to Minimum Tax | | $48,500 |
| Regular Tax | | $10,290 |
| Minimum Tax .15 X $ 48,500 | | 7,275 |
| Total Tax | | $17,565 |

Taking the information that was supplied for Mr. Higbe and assuming that it was for the Higbe Corporation instead of the individual, the minimum tax would be computed as follows:

| Tax Preference Items | | |
|---|---|---|
| 37½ percent of the net long-term capital gain | | $ 1,875 |
| Depletion in excess of base | | 18,000 |
| Excess depreciation on realty | | 36,000 |
| Total Tax Preference Items | | $55,875 |
| Less: Exemption | $10,000 | |
| or Regular tax | 6,540 | 10,000 |
| Subject to Minimum Tax | | $45,875 |
| Regular tax | | $ 6,540 |
| Minimum tax | | 6,881 |
| Total Tax | | $13,421 |

**SUMMARY**

The minimum tax rate of 15 percent is charged against all tax preference items in excess of the greater of the $10,000 exclusion or half the regular tax (100 percent for a corporation). However, even with the minimum tax, the preference items may protect income which otherwise might be subject to 50 to 70 percent tax, thus providing a saving of at least 35 to 55 percent even with the minimum tax. And there are still tax shelters available, such as tax-exempt bonds and research and development expenses of new ventures, which are not presently listed as tax preference items.

## MAXIMUM TAX ON PERSONAL SERVICE INCOME

### *Introduction*

The House Ways and Means Committee Report covering the 1969 Tax Reform Act provided for a maximum tax on earned income, because the Committee felt that existing high tax rates were unrealistic and caused serious distortions in our tax system. Because of the revenue loss, they felt they could not reduce tax rates across the board, but they did want to adopt some measures applicable to earned income in order to discourage the use of tax loopholes. The Committee Report pointed out:

> A major motivation for tax avoidance is to protect earned income from the top bracket rates by engaging in activities which create artificial losses or convert what would otherwise be earned income into capital gains. Under present law, the avoidance of a 70 percent rate on earned income provides a substantial incentive to engage in what otherwise would be unprofitable activities.

### *The Maximum Tax Provisions*

The maximum tax (available only to individuals) is 50 percent and takes effect when the taxable personal service income goes beyond $55,200 on a joint return; for a single taxpayer or head of household, the cutoff point is reduced to $40,200. The 50 percent maximum is available only for personal service income, which is, in turn, reduced by tax preference items. Generally speaking, personal service income is wages, salaries, and professional fees received as compensation for personal services performed. The professional fees received by doctors and lawyers, even when the services are performed by their assistants, are treated as personal service income. In the case of a taxpayer such as an artist or author whose personal efforts create property, the gain upon the sale or other use of the property is treated as personal service income unless the tax law allows the transaction capital gain treatment (e.g., special capital gain provisions available to inventors).

However, for those engaged in a trade or business (other than through a corporation) involving both personal services and capital as material income-producing factors, there is a restriction on how much of the income can be treated as personal service income. A reasonable amount of the income can be considered personal service, but not in excess of 30 percent of the taxpayer's share of the profits. Under normal partnership arrangements, the 30 percent rule would apply. However, it may be possible (although I.R.S. disagrees) to use a guaranteed salary to avoid the 30 percent rule. The amount of the salary plus 30 percent of the share of profit may then be the ceiling.

There are several approaches to determining whether or not capital is a material income-producing factor: Is the capital investment necessary to the successful operation of the business? Why is the capital used? Does the capital produce a substantial portion of the income reported?

Items which are not considered personal service income include the following: rents (30 percent rule if personal services are involved), dividends, interest, gambling gains, capital gains, alimony, mineral royalties, and some payments from retirement plans such as lump sum distributions.

The taxpayer has the choice of using either the maximum tax or income averaging, but he cannot use both. Therefore, in a situation in which it appears that both of these tax opportunities are present, both methods should be considered before making a decision.

### *Figuring the Tax*

Mr. Jones is married and files a joint return with his wife. Their taxable income this year is $103,200, which comes from professional fees. Under normal circumstances their tax would be $45,180. Using the maximum tax approach, their tax would be as follows:

| | *Income* | *Tax* |
|---|---|---|
| Regular computation up to and including 50 percent bracket | $55,200 | $18,060 |
| Maximum tax on balance | 48,000 | 24,000 |
| | $103,200 | $42,060 |

The maximum tax provisions provided a tax saving of $3,120.

Now let us complicate Mr. Jones' income picture and say that he has $103,200 of taxable income which comes from various sources. Personal service income accounts for $75,000, and the balance derives from rents, royalties, dividends, interest, etc. Let us assume that the current year's tax preference items come to $3,920, and Mr. Jones' adjusted gross income is $125,000. The formula to determine what amount of income is subject to the maximum tax is:

$$\left(\frac{\text{Personal Service Income}}{\text{Adjusted Gross Income}} \times \text{Taxable Income}\right) - \left(\text{Current year's tax preference items}\right) = \text{Amount Subject to Maximum Tax}$$

$$\left(\frac{\$75{,}000}{\$125{,}000} \times \$103{,}200\right) - \$3{,}920 = \$58{,}000$$

Tax on the income subject to the maximum tax rules would be:

| | *Income* | *Tax* |
|---|---|---|
| Regular computation up to and including 50 percent bracket | $55,200 | $18,060 |
| Maximum tax rules on balance | 2,800 | 1,400 |
| | $58,000 | $19,460 |

The formula for determining tax on other income not subject to maximum tax is:

$$\left(\text{Regular Tax Rates} \times \text{All Income}\right) - \left(\text{Regular Tax Rates} \times \text{Personal Service Income Subject to Maximum Tax}\right) = \text{Tax on Income not Subject to Maximum Tax}$$

$$\$45{,}180 - \$19{,}544 = \$25{,}636$$

Mr. Jones' total tax would be $19,460 plus $25,636 or $45,096. This is only a net saving of $84 from using the maximum tax. As might be anticipated, the really dramatic savings from using the maximum tax involve individuals with relatively high personal service income—and little else, including no tax preferences. A single individual with taxable income of $102,200 would pay $53,090 on income other than personal service income, but only $44,290 on personal service income.

Figure 13-1 shows the step process and how the income over and above that subjected to the maximum tax is taxed. Notice that the income not subjected to the maximum tax rates is taxed at the same rates that would normally apply to that income if there were no special rates for personal service income.

(Regular Tax Rates X All Income) — (Regular Tax Rates X Personal Service Income Subject to Maximum Tax) = Tax on Income not Subject to Maximum Tax

$110,980 — $83,580 = $27,400

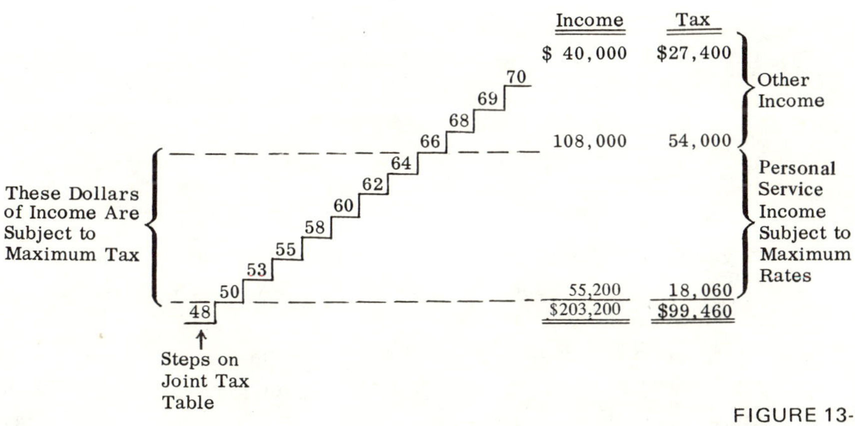


FIGURE 13-1

Taxation of Income Not Subject to Maximum Tax

## IMPACT OF MINIMUM AND MAXIMUM TAX

The interplay between the minimum tax on tax preferences and the maximum tax on personal service income can increase the effective tax rate on capital gains substantially above the apparent 35 percent maximum rate—

Follow the reasoning:

(1) The basic tax on the capital gain, at the margin, is 35 percent.

(2) The minimum tax, at the margin, is 4.875 percent.

(3) For a high-income individual, shifting a dollar from personal service income results in shifting that dollar from a 50 percent to a 70 percent bracket–and at the margin 50 percent of the capital gain makes that 20 point shift, an additional 10 percent (less the reduction in minimum tax of 15 percent of ½ of the increase in regular tax) for the current year. Notice that part of the reason for this hefty impact is that the regular income tax plays no role in calculating preference income for maximum tax purposes. 10 percent – 15 percent (½ of 10 percent) = 9.25 percent.

Steps one through three justify saying that given a high bracket individual and a large enough capital gain, it is quite possible for the effective rate of tax to almost reach 50 percent on the capital gain–35 + 4.875 + 9.25 = 49.125.

## SUMMARY

The maximum tax rate of 50 percent is available for personal service income subject to a deduction for tax preference items. A married couple must file a joint return to use the maximum rate, and, if the maximum rate is used, the taxpayer cannot also claim the use of the income averaging provision.

## QUESTIONS AND PROBLEMS

1. Would you have included any items as tax preference that Congress did not? Why? Would you have eliminated any of the tax preference items which Congress did include? Why?
2. Should a taxpayer attempt to avoid tax preference items so that he can protect himself against the minimum tax? Is there any advantage to tax preference items if they are going to be subject to the minimum tax? Construct an example to illustrate your point.
3. What advantage does the maximum tax have in attempting to encourage taxpayers to avoid tax preference items?
4. Compute the minimum tax for each year.

| *Year* | *Regular Tax* | *Tax Preference Items* |
|---|---|---|
| 19x1 | $42,000 | $61,000 |
| 19x2 | 28,000 | 87,000 |
| 19x3 | 36,000 | 63,000 |
| 19x4 | 41,000 | 72,000 |
| 19x5 | 43,000 | 84,000 |

5. Mr. Higbe is the sole proprietor of a small laundry and dry cleaning chain. His net income from his business this year was $80,000; he is single and has no other income. Of what advantage will the maximum tax be to Mr Higbe?
6. Assume in Problem 5 that a large corporation wished to acquire Mr. Higbe's business and agreed to pay him $75,000 a year to operate it for them along with other options and fringe benefits. Considering only the salary, will Mr. Higbe be better off with the $75,000 salary or the $80,000 from his business?
7. Mr. Jones had income of $115,000, including $45,000 of salary, $30,000 of net long-term capital gain, and $10,000 of interest from state bonds. His expenses included $20,000 of excess depreciation on an apartment complex and $13,000 of depletion from a well which has a zero basis. His total deduction, including his personal exemptions, were $80,000. What will Mr. Jones owe the government for taxes if he files a joint return with his wife, who had no income or deductions of her own?
8. Mr. Smity is already at the point where his tax preference items will cause him to pay the minimum tax. He has been approached by an individual who wants to go into a real estate partnership with him and who explained that they could protect their earnings plus other income with the excess depreciation from the buildings. Mr. Smity feels that this is not a wise investment because he will be subject to the minimum tax. Mr. Smity has come to you for advice; what would you tell him?
9. A friend has averaged $47,000 of taxable income over the last four years. This year, however, he switched jobs, and his earnings were $74,000. All of his current income is from his salary as president of a local company. Of what benefit will the maximum tax be to your friend?
10. Mary Smith is married and receives $400,000 in salary and $50,000 in other adjusted gross income in 19x5. Her itemized deductions and personal exemptions are $90,000. Her husband has no income or deductions of his own. Mary has $150,000 of tax preferences in 19x5. Determine their tax liability on a joint return.
11. Bob Avels is a successful salesman, unmarried, earning $150,000 a year of taxable income. His only investments up to the present have been tax-exempt municipal bonds. He has been offered a chance to invest in a partnership which will generate $50,000 a year of tax losses (and $50,000 of tax preferences) to him for five years. However, in the sixth year, he will realize $250,000 of ordinary income which will not be personal service income. Avels actually will have to put up $50,000 of cash each year for the five years, and will get back $250,000 cash in the sixth year. Assuming Avels can earn 6 percent on investments in tax-free municipals, prepare an analysis to help Avels decide whether or not to go into the partnership.

*12. "The minimum tax is not an income tax," argues one tax commentator, "but rather an excise tax. As an excise tax on certain types of business activity (e.g., oil and gas), it should be deductible by those paying it as a trade or business expense—just as the highway use tax, a federal excise tax, is deductible as a trade or business expense." List some of the arguments that might support this point of view as well as some of the arguments that rebut it.

# 14

# How the Tax Law Affects the Investor

## REAL ESTATE

An unsung wit once likened taxpaying to golf playing, "In both," he said, "you drive as hard as you can to reach the green, but you always wind up in a hole." It may have been the same wag who commented that if high tax rates continued for another generation, it might become impossible to find a man with more money than brains. So the name of the game for investors is not just "Making Maximum Dollars," but is rather "Making Maximum After-Tax Dollars."

The objectives of investors vary widely. At one end of the spectrum is the investor who is solely concerned about certainty of income, with no regard for appreciation in the value of his investment. At the other extreme we find the out-and-out speculator, contemptuous of current income but seeking the possibility of a big gain. Somewhere in between is the mythical "average" investor. His choice of investment is influenced by the favorable tax advantages to be derived from what are popularly known as "tax-shelter" investments.

We have already covered much material dealing with the impact of the tax laws on all these people. We know that the investor seeking income alone may find corporate bonds attractive. We know that the gains of the speculator may often be taxed as capital gains, leaving to the financial adventurer a greater portion of his earnings after taxes than the same amount flowing to a salaried person.

In this chapter we shall explore different types of investments and different ways of taxing the investments. In Chapter 19, we shall look at the impact of estate and gift taxes on persons who have managed to accumulate wealth that they want to pass on to succeeding generations.

### *Unimproved Land*

Real estate has been the basis for many an American fortune. Because land is relatively fixed in amount but population tends to expand, the value of land increases with the growth of the community. There are several ways to try to make money out of real estate; the tax consequences are equally varied.

The investor who buys undeveloped land and then passively sits back and waits for it to increase in value is able to deduct the interest and taxes, which constitute his main carrying costs, against other income. His ultimate gain, if the land is sold at a profit, will be taxed as a capital gain. However, the Tax Reform Act of 1976, by limiting deductibility of net investment interest exceeding $10,000 per year, reduces the advantages of carrying substantial amounts of non-income-producing investment assets.

Complete passivity, of course, is far from the rule. The investor may seek to enhance the value of the land by getting its zoning changed—which may increase its value by making it suitable for additional uses—or by dividing up one big piece into several smaller pieces. As he takes steps to enhance the value of the land through his own efforts rather than passively allowing community development to do it for him, he comes closer and closer to a vaguely defined area in which the land he owns is deemed to be held primarily for sale to customers in the ordinary course of a trade or business. Once the taxpayer aggressively engages in buying and selling real estate, so that his transactions are frequent and the sales he makes are solicited, his gains will definitely be classified as ordinary income rather than capital gains. Since it is a question of fact whether property is held primarily for sale to customers in the ordinary course of a trade or business, the courts are often called upon to make such determinations.

### *Rental Property*

Real estate may, of course, be held for the production of current income as well as for appreciation in value. Like any business income, the net profit from the real estate rentals (after deducting expenses, including depreciation) will be taxed as ordinary income. Gain on disposition of the property will normally be considered capital gain, except to the extent of accelerated depreciation required to be recaptured as ordinary income. Because depreciation acts as a reduction of ordinary income, depreciation of buildings below their fair market value may result in having the depreciation, in excess of straight line taken, recovered at capital gains rates. How this works is illustrated in the chapter on depreciation. Its effect is to render investment in new buildings, on which accelerated depreciation may be claimed, relatively more attractive than investment in used buildings. Since depreciation is based on total cost, regardless of method of financing, the use of the maximum amount of borrowed funds consistent with safety is also encouraged. Through maximum use of debt instruments, much larger depreciation deductions are obtainable.

Visualize, for instance, an investor with $200,000 of available funds. He is in a 70 percent tax bracket. He can buy either of two improved properties on which residential rental housing has been newly constructed. The land value of each property is $100,000. The first property will cost him $400,000, of which $300,000 will be for the building. He will have to get a $200,000, 8 percent mortgage. The second property will cost $1,000,000, of which $900,000 is for the building. He will have to get an $800,000, 8 percent mortgage. Useful life of both buildings is 25 years. Our investor estimates that he can obtain rentals, net of all expenses except interest and depreciation, of 8 percent of the total cost of each property per year. He estimates that at the end of five years, he can sell the properties for exactly what they cost him. To simplify our illustration, (1) we shall assume that he need not make any payments on the mortgage principal during the five years, and (2) we will ignore the effect of the minimum tax. Here is the cash-flow picture:

| | *Building No. 1* | *Building No. 2* |
|---|---|---|
| Per year: | | |
| Rent income | $32,000 | $80,000 |
| Interest expense | 16,000 | 64,000 |
| Net cash inflow, before tax reduction | $16,000 | $16,000 |

Taking declining-balance depreciation on residential rental housing at twice the straight-line rate results in writing off 34.09 percent of the original cost of a building in the first five years. On building No. 1, this means that the cash inflow of $80,000 during the first five years is more than offset by $102,270 of depreciation deductions. Thus, the building shows a tax loss, which is deductible at a 70 percent tax rate, producing a further cash inflow of $15,589 (70 percent of $22,270). When this first property is sold, the gain on the sale will be the full amount of the $102,270 depreciation, part of which will be ordinary income and part of which will be capital gains. This will result in tax on the gain of $46,670 (income tax of $45,589 plus minimum tax of $1,081), assuming no other gains are realized during the year. Our total cash-flow picture on building No. 1 will then reveal:

| | | |
|---|---|---|
| Cash outflow at time of purchase | | $200,000 |
| Inflow from net income during 5 years | $ 80,000 | |
| Inflow from tax reduction | 15,589 | |
| Proceeds of sale, net of $200,000 mortgage and $46,670 income tax | 153,330 | 248,919 |
| Excess of inflow over outflow | | $ 48,919 |

The effect is different for building No. 2. During the five years, net income before depreciation is also $80,000. But depreciation is based on a cost of $900,000 for the building, and over the five years it will amount to $306,810! Thus, a tax loss of $226,810, deductible at the assumed 70 percent rate, will produce cash savings of $158,767. The gain on the sale will result in a tax of $149,260 (income tax of $146,767 plus minimum tax of $2,493), assuming no other gains are realized during the year. Look at our cash-flow picture on building No. 2:

| | | |
|---|---|---|
| Cash outflow at time of purchase | | $200,000 |
| Inflow from net income during 5 years | $ 80,000 | |
| Inflow from tax reduction | 158,767 | |
| Proceeds of sale, net of $800,000 mortgage and $149,260 income tax | 50,740 | 289,507 |
| Excess of inflow over outflow | | $ 89,507 |

By keeping the return equal to the interest rate, we eliminated the effect of leverage on the net income. Nevertheless, because of the greater depreciation base and the interaction of depreciation's deductibility as an ordinary expense with the taxation of a portion of the gain on the building as a capital gain, we almost double the cash return on our investment, using dollars that were not time-adjusted or discounted.

In a real-life situation, of course, the return on the property would probably exceed the interest rate being paid on the mortgage; otherwise, the prospective purchaser might be unwilling to incur the added risk that the additional indebtedness entails.

The income tax on the gain in both alternatives exceeds the maximum capital gains rates (25 percent on the first $50,000 of gain and 35 percent on the balance) because a portion of the gain is taxed as ordinary income. The portion taxed as ordinary income in the illustrations above is the excess of the accelerated depreciation taken during the five years over the depreciation that would have been taken on the straight-line basis using the same life.

Rental real estate also poses the problem of whether it is being held primarily for sale, and therefore, whether gain on its sale over and above the excess depreciation should be ordinary income. A person who builds apartment houses, operates them for a period of a year or two, and then sells them, might well wind up with any gains treated as ordinary income once he had done this three or four times.

### *Syndicates*

Because of the large dollar amounts involved and the high risk inherent in many real estate investments, investors frequently acquire fractional interests in a piece of property. In this way, the small investor can participate in a big deal, and the larger investor can achieve some degree of diversification. Perhaps you would like to invest in a medium-sized downtown office building in Boston. Instead of putting up $5 million to acquire the entire equity interest, you might acquire as little as a 1 percent interest in a syndicate for, say, $50,000.

There is no such tax animal as a syndicate. Therefore, the tax aspects of your investment will depend on whether your syndicate is, for tax purposes, a partnership, a limited partnership, a corporation, or a real estate investment trust. If what you have acquired is an interest in a general partnership, or a limited partnership that has general partners with substantial assets outside the partnership, then your tax treatment will be that of any other partner. But if your syndicate has more corporate than noncorporate characteristics under its agreement, as determined by state law, it will be taxed as a corporation. These corporate characteristics include continuity of life of the organization regardless of the death, bankruptcy, or withdrawal of any participant; centralization of management; limitation of liability for syndicate debts to syndicate assets; and free transferability of ownership interests. There are two other characteristics common to all syndicates—a profit motive and associates.

Taxation of the syndicate as a corporation is usually quite onerous. Real estate syndicates tend to pay out substantially all their cash flow to the various participants in the syndicate. Hence, a syndicate that generated taxable income and was taxed as a corporation would get no deduction for its distributions in computing its federal income tax, although its participants would be taxed on the amounts they received as dividends. If the syndicate had capital gains, these would still wind up being taxed as ordinary dividend income to the recipients.

If the newly organized syndicate showed tax losses and was treated as a corporation, none of the losses could be deducted by the syndicate participants on their personal tax returns. Payments received from the syndicate would, however, be tax-free recoveries of the investment in the syndicate until the participant had recovered his entire investment. After that, the payments would generally be capital gains.

As a partnership for tax purposes, on the other hand, the syndicate could offer its participants projected tax-free cash distributions, plus an increment to cash flow in the form of participant deductibility of syndicate losses on personal income tax returns. In addition to avoiding double taxation of all income, the partnership is also able to pass through its capital gains income as capital gains to its participants. Therefore, a high-bracket taxpayer, if he is sure that annual losses can be passed through to him, may find a partnership syndicate investment in a new piece of rental property quite worthwhile. If the syndicate were to be treated as a corporation, the investment would probably lose its attractiveness.

### *Real Estate Investment Trusts (REIT)*

Because of the inhibiting effect on investors of classifying syndicates as corporations, a 1960 tax-law created a conduit type of entity called a *real estate investment trust.* The trust can be an actual corporation or a trust that would be taxable as a corporation. If a trust, it is centrally managed by a group of trustees, similar to a board of directors and its ownership interests consist of transferable shares much like stock. However, if a REIT distributes at least 90 percent of its ordinary income (95 percent after 1979), it can deduct the amounts distributed to its owners in computing its own corporate income tax. In addition, capital gains can be then passed through to, and retain their capital gains identity on, the individual returns of the owners. Losses, however, do not pass through to the owners, and the REIT is denied the right to carry its operating losses back. For purposes of the minimum tax on tax preferences, the owners must take into account on their individual returns the capital gains and all other items of tax preference (except accelerated depreciation on realty) deemed to be distributed by the REIT.

To qualify, a REIT must have at least 100 owners, and the five largest owners cannot own more than 50 percent of its total equity. A REIT cannot hold any property primarily for sale to customers in the ordinary course of its trade or business. It therefore faces the same problem as does an individual in determining how much activity in enhancing property values, and how many transactions, will result in its being deemed to be in the real estate business. Each year, at least 90 percent (95 percent after 1979) of the REIT's gross income must be derived from:

1. Real estate rentals
2. Interest on real estate mortgages
3. Gains from sale of realty
4. Dividends on, and gains from sale of, other real estate investment trust shares.
5. Other dividends, interest, and gains from sale of stock or securities

The first four categories must also comprise at least 75 percent of the REIT's annual gross income. Furthermore, it must be more of an investor than a speculator, because short-term capital gains plus gains on realty held less than 4 years cannot exceed 30 percent of its income. Finally, the value of the REIT's assets must fall within certain categories (primarily real estate and cash items) at the close of each quarter of the year.

Thus, the real estate investment trust is a type of tax entity available to investors that combines some of the advantages of a corporation with some of the tax advantages of a partnership. However, it does not have all the tax attributes of a partnership–and, particularly in the area of losses, actually has certain disadvantages when compared with both a corporation and a partnership. Unlike the case with a partnership, losses of the REIT are not passed through to the actual owners. Unlike a regular corporation, the real estate investment trust has no net-operating-loss carryback deduction available to it, although it can carry losses forward for eight years.

### *Mortgaging versus Selling*

As improved property increases in value, the investor is faced with the problem of putting the increased value to income-producing use. One obvious solution is to sell the appreciated property once the outlook for further increase in value seems less bright. This is the conservative approach. The more speculative investor finds sale of the property unattractive because of the tax bite that he will incur. This is especially true of the active speculator, who may face a problem of having his real estate gains taxed as ordinary income.

A speculator in the 70 percent tax bracket with a piece of rental property having a depreciated cost of $40,000 and a present value of $140,000 could incur an ordinary income tax expense of $70,000 upon sale of the property. He would lose the income from the property and yet have only $70,000 to reinvest. By borrowing against his encumbered property, he can possibly raise $100,000 with a first mortgage, without relinquishing the property itself and without incurring any tax. Because the cash he receives from the bank is balanced by an obligation to repay, there is no exchange transaction to produce an income tax at the time money is borrowed. The interest rate on the first mortgage is normally lower than the return that the rental property is producing, so the property will still be profitable to the speculator; and he can then use the $100,000 as a down payment to purchase another piece of rental property. In time, as the properties appreciate in value, the remortgaging process can be repeated, and additional property can be purchased, without incurring any income tax.

### *Trading versus Selling*

It is extremely difficult to borrow against unimproved realty. Also, the investor may not want to hang onto a particular piece of property, improved or unimproved. He wants to invest in another piece of realty. Fortunately for the real estate investor, real property held either for investment or for the production of income can be traded, tax-free, for other real property.

Thus, the owner of a motel in Massachusetts decides that now would be a good time to sell out and go to Florida. He could obtain $200,000 for his motel—but the sale would create a sizeable income tax liability because his tax basis (unrecovered cost) for the property is low. He plans on buying an apartment building in Miami with the proceeds. Instead of selling, therefore, he works out a swap whereby he receives an apartment building in Miami in exchange for his motel. There are realtors who specialize in this type of three-way deal. Such a realtor might buy the apartment building in Miami for his own account, then trade it off for the motel, and finally turn around and sell off the motel, in order to facilitate the swap transaction.

The situation in which the two properties involved are equal in value is unusual, of course. This does not eliminate the possibility of achieving a tax-free trade, but simply requires that the investor take advantage of the fact that borrowing money against a piece of property is not a transaction with an income tax effect, nor is paying down a mortgage on such property.

Assume that we want to acquire a piece of property with a fair market value of $1,000,000 against which there is a mortgage of $400,000, leaving an equity of $600,000. Our present piece of property is owned free and clear and has a fair market value of $700,000. Our tax basis is only $100,000, so we are anxious to keep the transaction tax-free if we can. Certainly, we would not trade our $700,000 equity for the seller's $600,000 equity. We could have him pay us cash "boot" of $100,000 to equalize things. This, however, would result in our gain on the exchange being taxable to the extent of that cash "boot." The same result can be accomplished by having him pay $100,000 to reduce the debt against his property. Both properties now have an owner's equity of $700,000, so that a swap is fair. If we would like to get the $100,000 in cash ourselves, we may be able to wait until after we own the new property, and then borrow another $100,000 against it.

We have seen that as long as the investor continues to hold onto a parcel of real estate, an increase or decrease in the mortgage liability to which such property is subject has no effect upon his tax basis, nor upon his tax liability at that time. When the property is sold, however, the amount of any outstanding debt that is transferred to the buyer along with the property is added to the money or other property received when computing the investor's gain realized on the sale. In turn, the purchaser's tax basis for the parcel will be equal to the money and other property paid, plus the amount of indebtedness on the property. Thus, where property is purchased or sold, debt will affect the tax cost to the buyer as well as the amount realized by the seller.

Imaginative juggling of debt can produce interesting tax results in realty trades. One trap to watch out for, however, is the situation in which your indebtedness on your property exceeds the other party's indebtedness on his. Where such a situation exists, the excess will be treated as money received by you, and will be taxable. Thus, if I have a piece of property with a value of $500,000 but subject to an indebtedness of $300,000, which I plan on trading for a piece of property with a value of $350,000 but subject to an indebtedness of $150,000, I will be deemed to have received cash "boot" of $150,000 (my debt of $300,000 less the other debt of $150,000), and my gain will therefore be taxable to that extent.

If the tax basis of my $500,000 piece of property was $100,000, the same amount would be my basis for figuring gain or loss on the $350,000 piece of property I acquired. In this instance, the computed tax basis of the new property is equal to the tax basis of the old property; however, such will not necessarily be the case in every tax-free exchange transaction.

You should realize that what has been accomplished through a tax-free exchange is not so much an avoidance of tax as a deferral or postponement of the time of taxability.

### *Dividing Up the Fee*

The ownership of all the property rights in a particular piece of land is often called the ownership of a fee simple title. Hence the expressions, "dividing up the fee," or "slicing up the fee." Possibly the most famous deal of this type was the sale of New York's Yankee Stadium some years back. The Yankees sold the land and building to a Mr. Johnson for cash of $3.5 million plus a mortgage contract for an additional $3 million—a total price of $6.5 million. Then they leased the land and stadium back from the buyer for $500,000 a year. Mr. Johnson, in turn, sold the land to the Knights of Columbus for $2.5 million and then leased it back for $200,000 per year.

The Yankees obtained cash, at the cost of paying a capital gains tax, still retaining the use of the property they had before. They exchanged their fee simple interest for a leasehold interest. Johnson put up $3.5 million for the fee simple title, but immediately sold off the land (but not the stadium itself) for $2.5 million, leaving him with a net investment of only $1 million. He needed to lease back the land, of course, for his ownership of the stadium would be meaningless without some sort of interest in the land. His annual rental income from the Yankees is $500,000, while his rent payments are $200,000. He has annual net income of $300,000, less amortization of his investment in the stadium and less his federal income tax.

The important thing to some people is having a steady source of rental income; to others, it is having the use of the buildings or other improvements that stand on the land; and to still others, it is the appreciation potential inherent in the land itself. It is sound business, and it often offers tax advantages, to set up a deal so that everyone gets what he wants. This sometimes means that the ownership of land will be separated from that of the buildings situated on it.

### *A Paradox?*

In our discussion of realty, you may have noted a paradox of sorts. In the folklore of America, we pay great homage to the men who build and improve our cities. On the other hand, we have precious little use for the greedy land speculator who gobbles up land while it is cheap, sits idly by while others build around him and increase the value of his holdings, and then finally sells out in one fell swoop at an enormous profit.

Or maybe it's the other way around! If our tax laws mirror our national standards, then as a people we seem to say that we would like to encourage the speculator. We allow him to deduct against his ordinary income most of the carrying costs of his idle land. When he finally sells the land, we generally permit him to report his gain as a capital gain. He can convert his land in one location to land at another location free of any tax. On the other hand, the businessman who takes raw land, improves it, puts in roads, sewers, and streets—this man's gain is taxed as ordinary income. Since he holds his land for sale to customers, he cannot exchange it tax-free for more raw land that he may also improve.

Of course, the federal income tax is not alone in encouraging the speculator. Local property taxes do about the same thing in most states and cities. Unimproved land tends to be taxed quite lightly, and improved land is heavily taxed. Many observers feel that this type of taxation encourages slums and discourages new building, encourages speculation and discourages productivity.

## SECURITIES

### *Corporate Stocks*

Some investors buy stocks in order to obtain income. However, when most blue-chip stocks are paying dividends that run no more than 5 or 6 percent of their market price, investors are certainly seeking something more than current income. They are seeking capital appreciation; and most of them are seeking protection against inflation.

The big tax advantage to the individual investor lies with the corporation that plows its earnings back into the business. In effect, the corporation is reinvesting the stockholder's dollars, untouched by any income tax at the shareholder level, in order to improve the corporate earnings, thereby increasing the market value of the shareholder's stock. This increment can be realized by the shareholder at any time upon sale of his stock. His profit on such a sale will be long-term capital gains, not ordinary income, if he has held the stock for over one year. Whereas frequent transactions in real estate can jeopardize your right to report your profits as capital gains, no question will be raised as to the capital gains status of security profits.

## SBIC's and SBC's

Not the least among the possible sources of confusion awaiting anyone embarked on a study of taxes is the use of the same words and phrases to cover different meanings. We have had occasion to discuss Small Business Corporations before, when we were talking about corporations that are taxed in a manner quite similar to the way partnerships are taxed. Now, however, we are going to meet a corporation with the same name but a far different appearance—although, to complicate matters further, it is possible for one corporation to be both types of Small Business Corporations simultaneously.

The tax law allows a taxpayer to treat the loss on the sale of stock in a Small Business Corporation as an ordinary loss rather than a capital loss, up to a maximum of $25,000 per year ($50,000 on a joint return). The stockholder must have acquired the stock directly from the corporation. The corporation must have had no more than $1 million of equity capital at the time the stock was acquired, including stock being offered pursuant to the plan under which the stock is acquired. Total amounts of capital raised since June 30, 1958, must not have exceeded $500,000. Furthermore, during the five years immediately preceding the loss year, more than half the corporation's gross receipts must have come from operating income, as distinguished from such items of income as royalties, rents, dividends, interest, annuities, and sales of securities.

Contrast these requirements with those of our other Small Business Corporation, which could elect to have its income taxed to its shareholders. It could generally have no more than ten shareholders, no more than one class of stock, and no more than 20 percent of its gross receipts from nonoperating sources. These, then, are two types of Small Business Corporations. From now on, when we have to distinguish between the two, we shall call the one that is taxed much like a partnership an Electing Small Business Corporation and the other an Ordinary Loss Small Business Corporation.

There is another type of corporation, called a "Small Business Investment Corporation," that is of tax interest to us at this point. Loss on the stock of an SBIC is an ordinary loss, without limit. The corporations that qualify are those operating under the Small Business Investment Act of 1958; a list of them can be obtained from the Small Business Administration, Washington, D.C. It matters not where or how the taxpayer acquired his SBIC stock, so that these provisions are more favorable than those governing Ordinary Loss Small Business Corporations on two points: (1) no limit on the amount of loss deductible in any given year, and (2) no restriction of benefits to stock acquired directly from the corporation. Because some of these stocks are traded on stock exchanges, and many in the over-the-counter market, they constitute interesting trading vehicles for almost any taxpayer.

Whenever gain is capital, although loss is ordinary, it follows that the taxpayer need not so much as break even before taxes in order to show an after-tax profit. Take, for example, a taxpayer in a marginal tax bracket of 40 percent. He has $10,000 of gain on SBIC stock held for more than one year, and $11,000 of loss. Not a good year, you would say. But his $10,000 of gain is subject to tax at only 20 percent (one-half of the gain is included in income at his regular rate of 40 percent), thus incurring tax of $2,000. His loss is fully deductible, providing a tax benefit of $4,400. His net profit is $1,400!

| | | |
|---|---|---|
| After-tax gain | ($10,000–$2,000) | $8,000 |
| After-benefit loss | ($11,000–$4,400) | 6,600 |
| After-tax net gain | | $1,400 |

### *United States Bonds*

Certain types of United States bonds (Series E, F, and J) are sold on a discount basis: for example, a $25 bond will cost $18.75. Cash-basis taxpayers owning such bonds can elect to report each year's increase in value as income of that year, or they can wait until the maturity of the bond and report the entire increase in value as interest income at that time. Series E and J bonds, and some Series F bonds, can be exchanged for Series H bonds with no tax incurred on the exchange. Although these provisions allow deferral of the time of taxation, they do not allow a taxpayer to escape taxation altogether, even by dying. The person who ultimately receives the value increment will be considered to have interest income, even if he acquired the bonds from a deceased taxpayer.

The United States bonds traded in the over-the-counter market are of more interest as investment vehicles with tax overtones. Since the Federal Reserve System terminated its support of the United States bond market in 1951, these bonds have sold at varying percentages of their redemption value. As United States obligations, the only difference between them and money is that they are interest bearing and not due for some period of time, whereas money bears no interest and is a demand obligation. (Take a look at your paper money and you will see that it is actually a demand note payable by a federal reserve bank! This is why some people argue that it is not real money at all, since they define "real" money as silver or gold, or something redeemable in silver or gold.)

The price at which the already outstanding United States bond sells tends to equalize the difference between its interest rate and the current interest rate on United States obligations. If newly issued United States obligations are being sold to yield 6 percent, then an already outstanding United States obligation paying 4 percent and maturing in 1985 will be selling at only about 85 percent of its maturity value. The taxpayer buying the already outstanding bond will receive taxable interest each year. On his $85,000 investment, he will receive $4,000 of fully taxable interest. On maturity of the bond in 1985, he will receive $100,000 back, and the $15,000 increment will be taxed as a capital gain. He may thus be better off after taxes than if he had purchased the newly issued bond, because part of his return is capital gains rather than all being ordinary income.

This capital gains feature has also made it seem quite advantageous, from a tax standpoint, to borrow to purchase such bonds selling at a discount. United States bonds are regarded as excellent collateral, and a high percentage of their cost can usually be borrowed at low interest rates. Assume that you are a married taxpayer in the 70 percent tax bracket. You are offered the opportunity of purchasing $10,000,000 worth of 4.25 percent United States bonds, maturing in two years, at a price of $9,750,000. You can borrow $9,651,500 of this at 6 percent, using the bonds as collateral. How would this transaction look to you?

*Before Tax*

| | | |
|---|---|---|
| Actual cash outlay | | $ 98,500 |
| Interest expense | $ 1,158,180 | |
| Interest income | 850,000 | 308,180 |
| Total cash outflow | | $406,680 |
| Cash inflow at maturity | $10,000,000 | |
| Less: Loan repayment | 9,651,500 | 348,500 |
| Net loss | | $ 58,180 |

This would not appear too appetizing. But before you turn it down, take a look at the same transaction after taxes are reflected.

*After Tax*

| | | |
|---|---|---|
| Actual cash outlay | | $ 98,500 |
| Interest expense | $ 1,158,180 | |
| Interest income | 850,000 | |
| Net expense, before tax reduction | 308,180 | |
| Tax reduction (70%) | 215,726 | 92,454 |
| Total cash outflow | | $190,954 |
| Cash inflow, net of loan repayment | 348,500 | |
| Tax on $250,000 capital gain | 95,062 | 253,438 |
| Net gain | | $ 62,484 |

(The tax computation assumes that the taxpayer has substantial investment income from other sources, thereby enabling him to avoid the limitation on deduction of investment interest expense.)

This represents a rate of return of about 32 percent on the $98,500 equity investment, with absolutely no risk attached to anything except the tax effect. Unfortunately for high-bracket taxpayers, the courts have adopted the attitude that if a transaction possesses no true economic profit potential at all, except for its tax benefits, the tax benefits will be denied on the ground that the transaction is all form and no substance.

### *Regulated Investment Companies*

The tax treatment accorded real estate investment trusts drew its inspiration from almost two decades of experience with the taxation of regulated investment companies. Commonly known as "mutual funds" or "investment trusts," these corporations receive a deduction for the dividends paid their shareholders if at least 90 percent of their investment income is paid out as dividends. Such dividend distributions retain their character in the hands of the shareholders, who may thus take advantage of the long-term capital gains rates for the part of the distributions that represent capital gains and of the $100 dividend exclusion with respect to the distributions treated as qualifying dividends. For all practical purposes, these corporations sidestep the problem of double taxation of corporate earnings as to their own earnings. (Of course, such corporations do not get a dividends-received deduction, as ordinary corporations do, but this is hardly necessary under the circumstances.) This favorable tax treatment allows the investor to obtain the diversification and management benefits involved in owning a small fraction of a carefully selected and professionally managed portfolio without paying any tax penalty for the privilege.

### *Municipal Bonds*

Income tax exemption for interest income received on the obligations of states and their subdivisions has been a part of the tax law since 1913. At one time, the weight of authority was that it would be unconstitutional for the federal government to attempt to tax these obligations, because it would be, in effect, levying a tax against the states themselves. With states' rights no longer so broadly interpreted and fiercely protected by the Supreme Court, the prevailing opinion would seem to hold that such interest income could be taxed. Congress, however, has not found it politically expedient to eliminate the statutory exception of such interest from income taxation.

Billions of dollars of such bonds are outstanding, and several billion dollars per year in interest is collected on them. This interest is not subject to federal income tax at all, nor does it generally enter into calculations of the effective rates of taxation of individuals and corporations. If an individual is in a 60 percent tax bracket, a tax-exempt bond paying 5 percent interest is the equivalent to him of a taxable security paying almost 13 percent interest. Thus, an investor can effectively control the portion of his annual income that flows out in income tax payments simply by varying the portion of his investment portfolio that is held in municipal bonds. By putting it all into municipal bonds, he may escape income taxes entirely.

A cute little tax gimmick may now suggest itself to you if you are imaginative. Why not borrow in order to buy municipal bonds, just as we talked about doing to buy United States bonds? The tax consequences would appear to be even more attractive. Unfortunately for your creative planning, there is a specific provision in the tax law disallowing any deduction for interest paid on indebtedness incurred to buy or carry such tax-exempt securities.

Banks are probably the most obvious breakers of this rule. In the normal course of its business, a bank is borrowing money from its depositors. But banks are also major holders of municipal bonds. For many years, no question was raised as to the propriety of a bank's deducting the interest paid to its depositors even though a substantial part of its investment portfolio was in bonds producing tax-free interest. When the question was finally raised in the early 1960's the bankers were successful in getting the Internal Revenue Service to abandon its attempt to disallow some of the interest being paid, on the ground that deposits in banks are not considered debt incurred to buy or carry tax-exempt securities.

Whereas there are advantages in buying a United States bond that is already outstanding and is selling at a discount, there are disadvantages in buying an outstanding municipal bond at a discount. Although the interest received on the bond may be tax-free, the gain on its redemption will be taxable (albeit as a capital gain). On the other hand, the discount on a bond at the time of its original issue is considered under the tax law to constitute additional interest and, as such, gives rise to a tax-free income upon redemption.

The 1976 Tax Reform Act broadened the availability of municipal bonds to smaller investors and those seeking diversification by allowing mutual funds, if set up primarily to invest in tax-exempts, to pass through to their investors the tax-free income characteristics of their own income just as mutual funds in other securities, and REIT's, had been able to do for some time.

### Short Sales

Investors who buy securities presumably anticipate that they will rise rather than fall in value. An investor who holds a security is said to be "long" in that security, or to have taken a "long position." It should be obvious that there are investors who may from time to time think that certain securities will decline in value. These people may sell a security they do not have and thus take a "short position" in the security. A short sale is a sale of a security that the seller does not own but that he has to borrow in order to deliver. The borrowing, incidentally, is normally done by his broker rather than by the investor himself.

Thus, if an investor decided that at a price of $90 a share, College Education common stock was too high, he might instruct his broker to sell 100 shares of the stock at $90. He is now "short" 100 shares of College Education. Sure enough, the price of the stock drops from 90 to 80 to 70. At that point, the investor tells his broker to close out his short position. The broker does this by buying 100 shares at 70 in order to return the stock he had borrowed on behalf of the investor. The investor thereby realizes a profit of $2,000.

In the normal transaction, the investor buys his stock and then sells it. If he holds his stock for over one year, he has a long-term capital gain. In a normal short sale, however, the investor sells the stock and then buys it. His holding period is zero days. His gain will therefore be short-term capital gain.

### *Wash Sales*

Frequently, a taxpayer has unrealized losses in a security. Perhaps he bought College Education at 90 and it is now selling at 70. He still has great faith in College Education—but understandably, he would like to get some tax benefit from this $20 per share unrealized loss if he could. If he could sell the stock and then buy it back at the same price, he could establish his loss and yet retain his position in College Education. But he cannot do this.

The purpose of the wash-sales provisions of the tax law is to prevent a taxpayer from establishing a loss and yet maintaining his position. If substantially identical stock is purchased within 30 days before or after the loss sale, the loss will be disallowed. This rule applies to stock and other securities. "Substantially identical" means, normally, the same security, or one convertible into it. Thus, a sale of General Motors at a loss would not be disallowed even though American Motors was purchased within the 30-day period.

### *Puts and Calls*

Puts and calls are merely options to buy or to sell. An investor who owns a substantial number of shares of College Education may not care too much whether he disposes of 100 shares at 105 (it is selling at 90) or retains them. Thus, he may be willing, for $15 a share, to sell someone the right to buy 100 shares of College Education from him at any time during the next 12 months and 10 days at a price of 90.

The amount he receives for the option is not income to him until the option is exercised or is allowed to lapse. If the option is exercised, then the option fee is simply a part of his selling price, which is actually 105 per share. If the option lapses, the fee constitutes ordinary income.

Why would anyone want to buy an option? Some people use them for leverage. A given dollar can control more shares of stock by being invested in an option than in the stock itself. A man wishing to speculate on the movement of College Education would have to invest $9,000 in order to control 100 shares of College Education outright; and he would run a potential risk of losing the $9,000, as well. For $1,500, he can purchase an option controlling 100 shares of College Education. The most that can be lost will be $1,500. There is no limit to the possible gain. If College Education soars to $180 per share, our option buyer will have turned a profit of $7,500 on his $1,500 investment! Incidentally, it should be pointed out that, although specific individuals have made substantial sums speculating in options, the only ones who consistently make a good profit out of them are the people who sell them and the brokers who act as middlemen.

Another use of option contracts is to provide insurance. A man sells 100 shares of College Education short. He will have a gain if College Education moves down, but he stands to incur a substantial loss if it moves up. Such a person might buy a contract guaranteeing that he could purchase 100 shares of College Education at 90 (or some other price) simply to protect himself against a potential loss when he covers his short sale.

The options we have been talking about are "call" options. The holder of the option contract has the right to call on the writer of the contract to sell certain securities at a certain price. A "put" option works similarly, but the holder of a put option has the right to force the writer of the contract to *buy* from him certain securities at a certain price.

Options have specific tax uses. Thus, a person who buys a security has to maintain his "long" position over 12 months to obtain long-term capital gains treatment. Yet he may be unwilling to face the market uncertainties for that long a period. He can buy insurance against a market decline through purchase of a put option on the same day he buys the stock. If the taxpayer is in the 70 percent tax bracket, and equal chances of a $100,000 gain or loss might be involved, failure to hold the stock for 12 months could make a difference of approximately $35,000 in income tax. A prudent man might well feel that investing $15,000 in an option was reasonable if it would protect against the $100,000 loss without jeopardizing the chance to get long-term capital gains treatment.

Thus, options are of use in eliminating or reducing risk while meeting holding-period requirements for long-term capital-gains treatment, or just for shifting a gain from one year to another. A man who would like to sell his stock on December 15, for instance, can postpone payment of tax on his gain by obtaining a put option that will run through January 2 so that he does not actually realize his gain until that date.

In dealing with call options, the investor usually finds it desirable to sell the option rather than exercise it. If the option is exercised, the holding period of the stock acquired starts with the date of exercise. If the stock is sold the same day to nail down the gain, the gain is bound to be short term. On the other hand, if the option has been held over 12 months, sale of the option itself will produce long-term capital gains. Your broker can handle the option transaction either way—it makes no economic difference, but it does make a substantial tax difference.

### *Discount Mortgages*

The purchase of mortgages, second mortgages and contracts-for-deed at a discount is a profitable investment opportunity for many individuals and institutions. These contracts and mortgages tend to offer rates of return that are handsome compensation for the risks assumed, although the handsomeness relative to the risk tends to be greater during periods when home values are rapidly increasing. Interest income received from such investments is taxed the same as any other income. The discount is another matter.

Assume that you buy a 9 percent, $10,000, 10-year contract for $6,000. Each month you will receive a payment that is partly interest and partly a payment on principal. At some point, assuming that the contract pays off, you will realize $4,000 of discount income. Is a part of this $4,000 included in each monthly payment? Or can you apply the principal part of each monthly payment to your $6,000 investment and only report discount income when you have fully recovered your investment?

The Internal Revenue Service argues that part of each monthly payment is discount income. However, some courts hold that if you are a cash-basis taxpayer, you can put off reporting the discount as income until you have recovered your $6,000 investment if ultimate realization of the discount income is uncertain.

If reporting the discount as income can be deferred, then a possibility exists for obtaining some capital gains on the transaction. Holding the contract and collecting on it will not produce capital gains, because merely collecting a noncorporate obligation is not deemed to be a sale or exchange, and there must be a sale or exchange for the gain to be capital. As the contract is paid down, its value will normally rise and a part of the discount will disappear. By selling the contract after the cost has been recovered tax-free but before any part of the discount has been included in income, part of the discount is, in effect, converted into capital gain.

*Example:*

Bartlett buys a $10,000, 10 percent second mortgage, for $6,500. He reports the interest received as income. When $6,500 has been received on principal and $3,500 still remains due, the value of the contract has risen to $3,000.

This results from the fact that the first mortgage has been paid down substantially whereas the property has not declined in value, and from the added fact that a history of prompt payment in the early years of a mortgage gives some assurance that the entire mortgage will be paid off. If Bartlett holds the mortgage to maturity, because he is in a 70 percent tax bracket, he will net after taxes only 30 percent of $3,500, or $1,050, and this over a period of time. Sale of the mortgage for $3,000 will net him $2,250, and give it to him *now.*

Although this result may be achieved in an isolated transaction, if the taxpayer's transactions in contracts are such as to transform such contracts into property held for sale to customers in the course of a trade or business, his gain would be treated as ordinary income under the same rationale as we discussed previously relative to real estate.

## NATURAL RESOURCES

Investment in natural resources can be accomplished by investing in companies active in this field, which presumably will have improved earnings as a result of the tax benefits available to them. Frequently, however, investors acquire interests in natural resources more directly. The most common vehicle is through acquisition of a limited partnership interest or of an undivided interest in, say, an oil well. In the oil venture, the investor will get an immediate deduction for his share of the intangible drilling and development expenses incidental to bringing in the well, but limited to his investment at risk. He may be able to take percentage depletion. We discussed these matters in Chapter 12 and shall not repeat that discussion here.

We will point out, however, that the investor in natural resources may be a speculator or he may be extremely conservative. The speculator tends to go for the wildcat venture, with its prospect of a big return. The more conservative investor will buy an interest in a producing property, with almost as much predictability and as little risk to his investment as if he were investing in industrial bonds and generally with no more tax benefits, either.

The investor of advancing years who has never been covered by Social Security may find a peculiar advantage in a noncorporate working-interest investment in an oil or gas well. His income will be considered self-employment income for Social Security purposes, and he will thus be able to qualify for Social Security benefits. The benefits tend to be quite generous relative to the dollars of contribution involved. Although Social Security coverage can be obtained through investment in other types of partnerships, the relative lack of risk and the ease of marketability of many oil and gas investments make them particularly well adapted to this particular purpose.

## AT RISK

Tax shelters were a major concern of Congress when it enacted the 1976 Tax Reform Act. It was concerned not so much for the revenue lost as for the damage done to the morale of the "average" taxpayer, who felt that others were getting an unfair advantage and who resented it; and for the misallocation of investment dollars that might result through unsound or unproductive projects being able to obtain financing solely because of their promised tax benefits.

The most significant remedy for all this was to limit deductions generally available to investors to the amounts which they had "at risk." Real estate investments were exempted from the "at risk" rules, as were any investments made by regular corporations.

The general rule treats debt as part of an investor's investment for tax purposes. Thus, depreciation can be taken on the cost of a computer regardless of whether it was purchased for cash, paid for with a note on which the purchaser is fully liable, or paid for with a note on which the purchaser has no personal liability. The "at risk" rule does not change this, but limits the deductible loss for any year to the cash which the investor has put up plus the debt on which he is personally liable.

*Example:*

Howard purchases a small computer, which he leases to Essec Corporation. He pays $20,000 in cash, and he signs a note promising to pay $230,000. However, the note contains an exculpatory clause stating that the holder can look only to the equipment itself for payment, and cannot hold Howard personally responsible. In 1978, the deductions attributable to the computer exceed its income by $28,000. Howard can only deduct $20,000 of the $28,000, since he is "at risk" to only that extent. The other $8,000 is carried forward to 1979. When Howard puts up additional cash in 1979 to make the first principal payment on the note, the amount of that principal payment will increase what he has "at risk." Assuming that for 1979 the rental income from the computer exactly equalled deductions attributable to the computer (including, of course, the interest on the note), and that Howard paid at least $8,000 on the note principal, he would get a 1979 deduction for the unusable portion of the 1978 loss.

(The interest Howard paid may have separate limits on its deductibility if the computer lease is classifiable as a "net lease" for investment interest purposes.)

The "at risk" rules can be thought of as applying to any individual investment in a partnership, except a real estate partnership, plus any direct investment in:

1. Holding, producing, or distributing motion picture films or video tapes;
2. Farming (except timber operations);
3. Leasing of personal property; or
4. Exploring for, or explointing, oil and gas resources.

## HOLDING COMPANIES

Some people can save taxes by having their corporations receive income rather than receiving it themselves. It depends on how much income and what types of income they have. An example would be an individual with an operating business. If he can shift $50,000 of taxable income over to a corporation where it will be taxed at 20 and 22 percent, and out of his own personal return, where the average rate of tax on it might be 50 percent, he will have an immediate cash advantage of $14,500 per year.

Of course, this results in the individual's controlling wealth he cannot consume, to the extent that the corporation has assets that are excessive for its business needs. But the corporation can act as an investment vehicle. The minimum tax on tax preferences does not hit it as heavily, and other tax restrictions, such as the "at risk" and investment interest limits on deductibility, don't affect it. For certain types of investment income, such as dividends on domestic corporation stocks, it has a preferred tax-status over an individual.

Thus, a corporation in a 22 percent tax bracket will pay only 3.3 cents of tax on $1 of dividend income, whereas an individual receiving the same dollar might be paying out 35 or 40 or 70 cents in tax.

Two restrictions constrain the abuse of the corporation as an investment vehicle. If a corporation accumulates earnings beyond the reasonable needs of the business, or $150,000, whichever is greater, then it may be subject to a penalty surtax. This penalty is 27½ percent of the amount unreasonably accumulated (38½ percent of the amount in excess of $100,000) in any one year. This provision encourages closely held corporations to pay dividends to their shareholders. However, the imposition of this penalty tax is uncertain, and in many instances it is still more economical to pay the tax than to pay dividends.

Let us say that an individual in a 60 percent tax bracket, by creating a corporation, removed $50,000 from his taxable income. He thus saves, between the corporation and himself, $19,500 in tax per year. The corporation unreasonably accumulates its earnings. The penalty surtax is imposed on the corporate net income, after tax. The penalty surtax is 27½ percent of $39,500, or $10,862.50. Obviously, there is still some immediate saving, even by paying the tax—and the tax, remember, may not even be imposed—and will not be imposed until accumulated earnings exceed $150,000.

The second restriction on the abuse of the corporation as an investment vehicle is the provision for taxing personal holding companies. A personal holding company is one that derives more than 60 percent of its ordinary gross income from investment sources, including income from rent as personal-holding-company income only if the net rent is not more than 50 percent of its adjusted ordinary gross income. Half or more of its stock must be owned by five or fewer individuals. Because the tax on its income not paid out in dividends is almost confiscatory (70 percent of undistributed income, as adjusted), no investor would normally want to create a personal holding company as an investment vehicle.

Yet a holding company that just skirts the definition of a personal holding company without quite being one has been an extremely useful capital builder for many a person, including taxpayers somewhat below the maximum tax brackets.

Visualize a physician who has reached the point where he can start making investments. A dollar of income may cost him 40 cents in taxes, leaving only 60 cents to reinvest. If he creates a corporation as a personal investment vehicle, putting into that corporation rental property generating taxable income, he can cut the tax on that income to 20 percent of the first $25,000, leaving 80 cents of each dollar to reinvest. Such a corporation need not worry about the penalty surtax on unreasonable accumulations of earnings until it has accumulated at least $150,000. At that point, the corporation stock may be cashed in, perhaps through liquidation, but also perhaps by being exchanged in a tax-free merger for readily marketable securities of an investment company.

The corporation may be used to shelter income from a working interest (as opposed to royalty income) in natural resources, as well as certain types of investment income (other than interest, dividends, and royalties), such as income from partnerships that are engaged in operating businesses. As long as the operating income (not including rent) accounts for over 40 percent of ordinary gross income, the corporation can be used to tax-shelter strictly investment-type income. Since only 15 percent of dividends received by the corporation will be subject to tax, the use of the corporation can cut the tax on $1 of dividend income to as little as 3 cents. This is in rather sharp contrast to the 40 cents in tax that our hypothetical physician would have to pay on $1 of dividend income if he did not use the corporation. Or, to put it another way, through use of the corporation, 97 cents per dollar of dividend income is available for reinvestment, instead of only 60 cents.

Assuming that the corporation has surmounted or sidestepped the traps of unreasonable accumulation of earnings and personal holding-company status, just how does the stockholder cash in on the assets that have been building up for him within his corporate tax shelter? He has four basic routes:

1. Liquidate the corporation. He will have a capital gain, measured by the difference between his original investment in the corporation and the fair market value of the assets he received at the time of liquidation. A variant on this to sell the corporate stock, in part or in whole, to insiders or outsiders.
2. Merge the corporation, tax-free, into a corporation whose securities are readily marketable. This will be explored in Chapter 17.
3. Pay himself a salary for managing the corporate affairs, subject to the limitation that the salary must be reasonable compensation for current or past services to be deductible. As the corporate assets build up, looking after those assets can become a demanding job and justify a meaningful level of compensation. Upon his death, whoever inherits his stock can also step into his shoes as a corporate officer.
4. Use the corporate stock as collateral security for bank loans, which might even be guaranteed by the corporation. Stockholders of closely-held corporations have been known to borrow from the corporation, then borrow from the bank to pay off the amount owed the corporation, then borrow from the corporation to pay off the bank, etc., for extended periods of time.

## CATTLE INVESTMENTS

The three broad categories of cattle operation are often described as breeding operations, stocker operations, and feeder operations. A cattleman may be involved in all three at the same time; or he may be engaged in just one type or a combination of two.

A breeding operation involves owning a herd of cows and usually some bulls (although artificial insemination is becoming more and more common). Most of the offspring are then sold. Typically, the bull (male) calves that are to be sold are castrated shortly after birth, after which they are called steers. Usually some of the heifer (female) and bull calves are kept to be raised for replacement of the older breeding stock. The exact number kept depends on the particular breeder's culling practices.

Stocker operations usually involve purchasing calves that weigh 400 to 600 pounds and then providing them grazing or pasture. When they weigh from 550 to 800 pounds, they are sold to the feeders.

Feeder operations are those that "finish" the animals by feeding high-energy rations (a high ratio of grains to other ingredients). Typically, the feeder cattle are kept in enclosed pens and fed from troughs. At between 900 and 1,200 pounds, the animals are sold to be butchered.

Inventory methods are the key to this tax shelter. Ranchers (cattlemen), despite what some of them may think of the word, are labeled "farmers" from a tax standpoint. Farmers may elect one of three accounting methods when they file their first tax return for a new venture: (1) the cash basis: (2) a cash basis with the use of either the farm-price method or the unit-livestock method of valuing inventories; or (3) the accrual method with inventories kept on the cost basis, the lower of cost or market, the farm-price method, or the unit-livestock method. One of the latter two methods of accounting may be elected by one who prefers to have the income from cattle operations remain as steady as possible to offset large fluctuations in income from other sources. However, in most cases, the advantages of the cash basis of accounting far outweigh the disadvantages of fluctuating income that can result when it is used. For this reason, the rest of this discussion assumes use of the cash basis.

The principal advantages to a cattleman of the cash basis are these:

1. The increase in value of the livestock on hand at the end of the year is not taken into income as it is with the other two methods.
2. The money spent to feed and care for all classes of cattle is a current deduction from income. None of the current expenses need be capitalized.
3. Ranching operations typically require the purchase of large inventories, such as feedstuffs that will be fed in current and future years. Supplies on hand do not have to be taken into consideration in computing taxable income, since purchases are deductible in the year of purchase

if cash is expended for them. This prepayment of certain expenses can be used at the end of the year to lower taxes if the profit appears to be more than desired.

4. Since income is not recognized until cash is received, cash is usually available to pay any taxes that may be due. In addition to leaving cash available, this allows for selective selling to influence the amount of taxes that will ultimately be paid. If some calves are ready to be sold and year-end analysis reveals high profits for the year, the sale can be delayed till the next year. If, on the other hand, profits are low, the sale can be made before the year has ended.
5. Capital gains income is maximized, since Section 1231 assets (that is, breeding cattle) typically have a zero tax basis.

The 1976 Tax Reform Act did impose some limitations on cattle as well as other farming operations. The individual investing in cattle may find himself able to deduct feed costs only as the feed is consumed unless he actively participates in the management of the cattle operation. To the extent that he finances his cattle activities with loans, or is given guarantees against loss, he may find his deductions limited by the "at risk" rules previously discussed. To the extent that his cattle activities are carried out through a non-Subchapter S or family corporation in which his family owns less than a 50 percent interest, or which has gross receipts of over $1 million, he may find his corporation forced onto the accrual basis of accounting.

### *Capital Gains*

The entire cash costs of maintaining the breeding herd are deductible in the year the expenditures are made. However, the big income from the breeding herd itself does not come in until a few years later when the breeding stock is sold. If proper planning has occurred, this income is treated in large part as a long-term capital gain when it is finally received. However, if breeding stock is sold at a loss, the loss is fully deductible.

To qualify as Section 1231 property and thus be eligible for treatment as described above, cattle (heifers and bulls only) must be held for 24 months or more. In addition, they must be held for breeding purposes.

A cattle operator in the breeding business is even in a position to routinely produce long-term capital gains income from his operations. Raised breeding stock can qualify as Section 1231 assets. Since raised stock have no tax basis, their entire sales proceeds are taxed as long-term capital gains. Thus, by originally purchasing breeding stock, depreciating them to the extent allowed, deducting the expenses of feeding and maintaining them, replacing them with raised breeding stock, developing a regular pattern of culling less-desirable stock, and selling the culls and older stock, a circular operation is established that regularly produces long-term capital gains.

Stocker and feeding operations offer no long-term capital gains prospects. They are widely used as tax shelters, however, in the sense that they can defer income. A taxpayer who would otherwise have $100,000 of taxable income for a year might go into a feeding operation that would produce sufficient deductible expenses to cut that taxable income substantially, even though the amount he had spent was represented in unrealized income in the form of cattle that he owned at year-end. Of course, these would be sold the following year, thus throwing additional income into that year. Then, either tax would have to be paid or tax shelter again sought—again, perhaps, through feeder cattle.

Since cattle operations are a business, and the income derived is operating income, throwing such operations into a corporation can often eliminate certain types of tax problems—such as the problem of being categorized as a personal holding company, or the problem of unreasonably accumulating earnings.

Finally, it should be noted that cattle operations can easily be handled on an absentee or even a fractional basis. A number of organizations specialize in servicing cattle investors, with the result that the investor can invest the amount of money he wants to in the type of operation he wants without even seeing, hearing, or smelling a cow.

## CASE EXCERPTS

*Earl A. Phillips* v. *Frank* (CA9) 8 AFTR 2d 5654
*Lazarus* v. *U.S.*, 3 AFTR 2d 1079 (172 F. Supp. 421) (Ct. Cl. 1959)
*Alderson* v. *Commissioner* (CA9-1963) 11 AFTR 2d 1529
*Estate of Charles T. Franklin* (CA9) 38 AFTR 2d 76-6164

### *Earl A. Phillips* v. *Frank*
(CA9) 8 AFTR 2d 5654

> Earl Phillips purchased real estate contracts at a discount. He argued that none of the discount should be reported as taxable income until the principal payments he had received on a given contract equalled his investment in the contract.

While one of the admitted facts stated in the pretrial order is that the contracts involved in the instant case are of a type bought and sold by investors, the uncontradicted testimony before the district court is that there is no open market for the sale of the contracts in question; and that they were difficult to sell and that it took considerable time—two or three years—to dispose of them. It is further uncontradicted in the record that a large portion of the contracts purchased by the taxpayer were "highly speculative," consisting of second, and in some instances third liens, on the real properties which were the subject of the contracts, which prior liens taxpayer was required to keep "in order" so as to be able to convey title upon payment in full of the contract price. In some instances, taxpayer suffered losses due to defaults by vendees which resulted in repossessions and sales of the properties. Each contract was purchased by taxpayer on an individually negotiated basis in light of such factors as the value of the real property involved, the existence of prior liens, the burdens and responsibilities of the taxpayer, and the financial ability and credit standing of the vendee.

In the instant case, taxpayer purchased for cash (no loans being involved) from vendors thereof executory contracts entered into between such vendors and other persons covering the sale and purchase of real properties. None of such vendors agreed to pay or return to taxpayer any sum, either principal or interest. The contracts were acquired by taxpayer unconditionally, not by way of security for loans. All taxpayer received from the vendors as consideration for the purchase money paid to them were assignments of executory contracts. The district court found as a fact that such contracts were purchased by taxpayer. Clearly, the transactions between the taxpayer and the several vendors were sales and purchases. Under the facts of this case it would be a great distortion to hold that any part of the contract payments received by taxpayer for the periods under review from the several vendees constitutes "discount income" and therefore equivalent of interest. . . The taxpayer recognizes that when periodic payments on each contract equal the purchase price of such contract, payments received by taxpayer in each year subsequent thereto must be treated as ordinary income in the year of receipt. Such is the law. *Lee* v. *Commissioner of Internal Revenue,* (7 Cir. 1941) 119 F. 2d 946. The simple question presented on this appeal is: Did the cash basis taxpayer receive during the years under review any payments of which a portion should be allocated to and considered for tax purposes as payment of a portion of the profit which the taxpayer hopes to realize? Taxpayer received for his capital invested the right to receive the unpaid balances due on such contract. What were such rights worth when purchased?

There is no evidence in the record that such rights had any market value, fair or unfair, or any other value in excess of taxpayer's costs. There is no evidence in the record that taxpayer at any time could have sold such contracts at a profit. The only source from which he might reasonably expect to realize any part of his profit is from periodic payments subsequent to the return to him of his invested capital. The fact that the likelihood of realizing a profit might increase as the amount of his investment decreases from receipt of periodic payments does not convert any part of such payments into payments on the hoped for or expected profit. Clearly, the payments received by taxpayer during the period under review aggregating less than his costs constitute a return of capital. A return of capital is not income.

*Lazarus* v. *U.S.*
3 AFTR 2d 1079 (172 F. Supp. 421) (Ct. Cl. 1959)

In situations where taxpayers acquired sizeable tracts of land and subsequently decided to offer the property for sale to the public as subdivided acreage, the courts have frequently been called upon to determine whether profits derived from such sales constituted ordinary income or capital gains. . . . Every case of the type mentioned must be decided on the basis of its own facts, there being no single test that can be applied to all such cases with decisive results. . . . There are, however, several factors that courts have considered in disposing of such cases.

One of the factors regarded by courts as pertinent is the purpose for which the land was originally acquired–i.e., whether it was originally purchased for the purpose of resale or was acquired for some other purpose. . . . The motive of the taxpayer in selling the property as subdivided acreage. . . . The extent of the time and effort devoted by the taxpayer to selling the parcels of land or to other sales-related activities. . . . The frequency of sales and the continuity of sales-related activities. . . .

An additional criterion that courts have applied in dealing with this problem is the extent of the improvements made in subdividing the property and preparing it for sale to the public. . . .

Courts have also considered the relation of the taxpayer's profits from the sale of his subdivided acreage to the taxpayer's total income. . . .

The various criteria that have been previously mentioned are merely aids to be used in determining the basic question of whether a taxpayer, in selling subdivided acreage, was or was not engaged in the business of selling realty.

When the present case is considered in the light of the statutory standard, it must be concluded. . . that the plaintiffs in 1950 were not engaged in the business of selling lots. Carrying on such a business ordinarily involves holding oneself out to others as engaged in it. . . . This was never done by the plaintiffs. Rather they turned over to an independent real estate broker the task of liquidating an investment in land that the plaintiffs had made some years earlier for the purpose of establishing a farm. The fact that the farm was sold in the form of small parcels rather than as a single tract was not sufficient to change what was essentially the liquidation of a capital investment by the plaintiffs into the conduct of a real estate business by the plaintiffs. . . .

*Alderson* v. *Commissioner*
(CA9-1963) 11 AFTR 2d 1529

Taxpayers had entered an escrow agreement to sell farm property to a corporation. When they found other like kind property they wanted in exchange, they amended the agreement, so that the corporation deposited

> the amount it had agreed to pay for taxpayers' property and taxpayers paid into the escrow the difference between the price of their land and the higher price of the land they wanted. Under taxpayers' instructions, the escrow agent purchased the like kind property and transferred title to it to the corporation. Thereafter, in simultaneous transactions, taxpayers and the corporation transferred their respective titles to each other.

It is the position of respondent that from the facts and circumstances outlined above it must be concluded the Buena Park property was sold by petitioners to Alloy and the Salinas property was purchased by petitioners, not Alloy. However, it does not appear from the terms of the amended Orange escrow (August 19, 1957) that there was ever any obligation on the part of Alloy to pay cash for the Buena Park property or for the petitioners to receive cash for said property as provided in the May 21, 1957, escrow, by reason of the fact that *prior* to September 11, 1957, Alloy did deposit with Orange a deed to the Salinas property conveying same to petitioners. Neither liability of Alloy to petitioners for payment of cash for the Buena Park property nor liability of petitioners to sell the said property to Alloy for money ever matured because under no conditions was there to be a sale of the Buena Park property for cash until September 11, 1957, and *then only* if the Salinas property *was not* acquired by Alloy and exchanged for the Buena Park property as of that date (R. 21). Deed of Alloy to petitioners conveying the Salinas property and deed of petitioners to Alloy conveying the Buena Park property were exchanged and recorded September 4, 1957. Consequently, an agreement on the part of petitioners to sell to Alloy the Buena Park property for money did not come into being.

Respondent argues the Tax Court found only that petitioners from the outset "desired" to exchange their Buena Park property and not that from the outset they "intended" to do so. This would appear in the circumstances to be a distinction without a difference since it does not seem logical that one would intentionally take steps to accomplish a result not desired, and that, therefore, all acts of the petitioners may be considered as having been performed with the intent to accomplish their desired result, to wit, "exchange their Buena Park property for other property of a like kind."

The court further concludes that there was no sale by petitioners of the Buena Park property to Alloy, but that the pertinent transactions resulted in an exchange of the Buena Park property for property of like kind to be held either for productive use in trade or for investment, and that by reason thereof there was no gain or loss from said exchange which should be recognized for income tax purposes.

*Estate of Charles T. Franklin*
(CA9) 38 AFTR 2d 76-6164

Eight doctors, of whom this taxpayer was one, were limited partners in a tax shelter deal involving the purchase and lease back of an Arizona motel.

Under a document entitled "Sales Agreement," the Romneys agreed to "sell" the Thunderbird Inn to Associates for $1,224,000. The property would be paid for over a period of ten years, with interest on any unpaid balance of seven and one-half percent per annum. "Prepaid interest" in the amount of $75,000 was payable immediately; monthly principal and interest installments of $9,045.36 would be paid for approximately the first ten years, with Associates required to make a balloon payment at the end of the ten years of the difference between the remaining purchase price, forecast as $975,000, and any mortgages then outstanding against the property.

The purchase obligation of Associates to the Romneys was nonrecourse; the Romneys' only remedy in the event of default would be forfeiture of the parntership's interest. The sales agreement was recorded in the local county. A warranty deed was placed in an escrow account, along with a quitclaim deed from Associates to the Romneys, both documents to be delivered either to Associates upon full payment of the purchase price, or to the Romneys upon default.

The sale was combined with a leaseback of the property by Associates to the Romneys; Associates therefore never took physical possession. The lease payments were designed to approximate closely the principal and interest payments with the consequence that with the exception of the $75,000 prepaid interest payment no cash would cross between Associates and Romneys until the balloon payment. The lease was on a net basis; thus, the Romneys were responsible for all of the typical expenses of owning the motel property including all utility costs, taxes, assessments, rents, charges, and levies of "every name, nature and kind whatsoever." The Romneys also were to continue to be responsible for the first and second mortgages until the final purchase installment was made; the Romneys could, and indeed did, place additional mortgages on the property without the permission of Associates. Finally, the Romneys were allowed to propose new capital improvements which Associates would be required to either build themselves or allow the Romneys to construct with compensating modifications in rent or purchase price.

. . . We believe the characteristics set out above can exist in a situation in which the sale imposes upon the purchaser a genuine indebtedness within the meaning of section 167(a), Internal Revenue Code of 1954, which will support both interest and depreciation deductions. . . .

In none of these cases, however, did the taxpayer fail to demonstrate that the purchase price was at least approximately equivalent to the fair market value of the property. The Tax Court explicitly found that on the basis of the facts before it the value of the property could not be estimated. 64 T. C. at 767-768. In our view this defect in the taxpayer's proof is fatal.

Such evidence of fair market value as was relied upon by the appellants, *viz.* two appraisals, one completed in 1968 and a second in 1971, even if fully admissible as evidence of the truth of the estimates of value appearing therein does not require us to set aside the Tax Court's finding. As the Tax Court found, the 1968 appraisal was "error-filled, sketchy" and "obviously suspect." 64 T. C.

at 767 n. 13. The 1971 appraisal had little relevancy as to 1968 values. On the other side, there existed cogent evidence indicating that the fair market value was substantially less than the purchase price. This evidence included (i) the Romney's purchase of the stock of two corporations, one of which wholly-owned the motel, for approximately $800,000 in the year preceding the "sale" to Associates ($660,000 of which was allocable to the sale property, according to Mr. Romney's estimate), and (ii) insurance policies on the property from 1967 through 1974 of only $583,200, $700,000, and $614,000. 64 T. C. at 767-768.

Given that it was the appellants' burden to present evidence showing that the purchase price did not exceed the fair market value and that he had a fair opportunity to do so, we see no reason to remand this case for further proceedings.

Reason supports our perception. An acquisition such as that of Associates if at a price approximately equal to the fair market value of the property under ordinary circumstances would rather quickly yield an equity in the property which the purchaser could not prudently abandon. This is the stuff of substance. It meshes with the form of the transaction and constitutes a sale.

No such meshing occurs when the purchase price exceeds a demonstrably reasonable estimate of the fair market value. Payments on the principal of the purchase price yield no equity so long as the unpaid balance of the purchase price exceeds the then existing fair market value. Under these circumstances the purchaser by abandoning the transaction can lose no more than a mere chance to acquire an equity in the future should the value of the acquired property increase. While this chance undoubtedly influenced the Tax Court's determination that the transaction before us constitutes an option, we need only point out that its existence fails to supply the substance necessary to justify treating the transaction as a sale *ab initio*. It is not necessary to the disposition of this case to decide the tax consequences of a transaction such as that before us if in a subsequent year the fair market value of the property increases to an extent that permits the purchaser to acquire an equity.

Authority also supports our perception. It is fundamental that "depreciation is not predicated upon ownership of property *but rather upon an investment in property, Gladding Dry Goods Co.*, 2 BTA 336 (1925)." *Mayerson, supra* at 350. (italics added). No such investment exists when payments of the purchase price in accordance with the design of the parties yield no equity to the purchaser. *Cf. Decon Corp.*, 65 T. C. 71 (1976); *David F. Bolger*, 59 T. C. 760 (1973); *Edna Morris*, 59 T. C. 21 (1972). In the transaction before us and during the taxable years in question the purchase price payments by Associates have not been shown to constitute an *investment in the property*. Depreciation was properly disallowed. Only the Romneys had an investment in the property.

Authority also supports disallowance of the interest deductions. This is said even though it has long been recognized that the absence of personal liability for the purchase money debt secured by a mortgage on the acquired property does not deprive the debt of its character as a bona fide debt obligation able to support an interest deduction. *Mayerson, supra* at 352. However, this is no longer true when it appears that the debt has economic significance only if the property substantially appreciates in value prior to the date at which a very large portion of the purchase price is to be discharged. Under these circumstances the purchaser has not secured "the use or forbearance of money." See *Norton* v. *Commissioner,* 474 F. 2d 608, 610 (9th Cir. 1973). Nor has the seller advanced money or forborne its use. See *Bornstein* v. *Commissioner,* 334 F. 2d 779, 780 (1st Cir. 1964); *Lynch* v. *Commissioner,* 273 F. 2d 867, 871-872 (2d Cir. 1959). Prior to the date at which the balloon payment on the purchase price is required, and assuming no substantial increase in the fair market value of the property, the absence of personal liability on the debt reduces the transaction in economic terms to a mere chance that a genuine debt obligation may arise. This is not enough to justify an interest deduction. To justify the deduction the debt must exist; potential existence will not do. For debt to exist, the purchaser, in the absence of personal liability, must confront a situation in which it is presently reasonable from an economic point of view for him to make a capital investment in the amount of the unpaid purchase price. See *Mayerson, supra* at 352. Associates, during the taxable years in question, confronted no such situation. Compare *Crane* v. *Commissioner,* 331 U.S. 1, 11-12 (1947).

Our focus on the relationship of the fair market value of the property to the unpaid purchase price should not be read as premised upon the belief that a sale is not a sale if the purchaser pays too much. Bad bargains from the buyer's point of view–as well as sensible bargains from buyer's, but exceptionally good from the seller's point of view–do not thereby cease to be sales. See *Commissioner* v. *Brown* 380 U.S. 563 (1965); *Union Bank* v. *United States* 285 F. 2d 126, 128 (Ct. Cl. 1961). We intend our holding and explanation thereof to be understood as limited to transactions substantially similar to that now before us.

## QUESTIONS AND PROBLEMS

1. Explain how one taxpayer may derive capital gains from his sales of real estate, whereas another taxpayer may find his realty gains taxed as ordinary income.
*2. The *Lazarus* decision covered the taxable year 1950. As part of the Internal Revenue Code of 1954, a new section was enacted dealing with the tax treatment of real property subdivided for sale (Section 1237). Would the outcome of the *Lazarus* case have differed if the taxable year under consideration by the court had been 1978 instead of 1950? What is the purpose of the code section dealing with the subdivision of real estate?

3. Richard Scott has $50,000 available for investment purposes. He is in a 40 percent tax bracket. Three opportunities are available to him:
   (a) New apartment building. Price $200,000, financed by a down payment of $50,000, plus an 8 percent mortgage for $150,000. Payments on the mortgage are $10,000 per year, plus interest. Land is on a 99-year lease, with annual rental of $2,000. Gross rental income is estimated to run $30,000, and cash operating expenses (taxes, insurance, maintenance, management fees, etc.) will total $7,000. Property value at the end of 15 years: $150,000.
   (b) Cash purchase of a gas station site. Land will cost $15,000; improvements will cost $35,000. A major oil company will pay $5,000 per year on a 15-year lease, plus an override on gallons that should produce an average of $1,000 per year more. The oil company will pay all taxes, insurance, etc., so that the amount Scott gets will be free and clear. Property value at the end of 15 years: $30,000.
   (c) Purchase of an interest in Steckel Number 1, an oil well, for $50,000. The well will produce gross income of $13,000 per year, against which there will be cash expenses of $4,000. Production is limited by the state, so that this flow can be anticipated for an indefinite period into the future. However, reserves are being depleted, so estimated value of the well at the end of 15 years would be only $27,000.

   Ignore the return on any cash that these investments would throw off annually. With which investment will Scott be best off at the end of 15 years, after taxes, assuming that whichever investment he makes he liquidates after 15 years?
4. The Overbrook Realty Syndicate erected a high-rise apartment building for $3,000,000. A 30-year useful life is being used for tax purposes, and depreciation is being taken at twice the straight-line rate on a declining-balance method. Net income before depreciation is $150,000 annually—all of which is distributed to the 115 syndicate participants. Assume that this is the first year of syndicate operation and that the building was completed on January 1. You are an individual taxpayer in a 40 percent tax bracket, owning a 5 percent interest in the syndicate. What are the tax consequences to the syndicate and to you if the syndicate is, for tax purposes, each of the following:
   (a) Partnership
   (b) Corporation
   (c) Real estate investment trust
5. In the situation described in Problem 4, state the characteristics that would have to be present for the syndicate to be treated as each one of the three types of tax entities.

6. Because of the frequency of his realty transactions and the substantial portion of his total income represented by realty profits, upon audit of Edward Grey's 1976 income tax return, the Internal Revenue agent treated his gains on the sale of realty as ordinary income instead of long-term capital gains. Grey owns 27 different rental properties, mainly duplexes, and the buying, selling, and operation of these constitute his full-time occupation. Grey's rental properties have an aggregate cost of $500,000, against which he has taken $210,000 of depreciation. The present fair market value of the properties, due to excellent maintenance and land appreciation, is approximately $550,000. Lending agencies in the area will loan up to 80 percent of the value of improved realty at 8 percent interest. Grey wants to purchase several additional units with an aggregate cost of $80,000. He is contemplating raising the cash required by selling two of his older, substantially appreciated units. The selling price of these units would be $81,000; their tax basis is $20,000. Grey is in a 40 percent tax bracket. Contrast the effect on Grey of selling units to raise cash versus borrowing to raise cash.
7. Herman Craig, a real estate investor, owns an industrial building site in Brooklyn, New York, which he has held for 10 years. Cost: $10,000. Value: $500,000. He wants to trade it for a hotel in Florida. Indicate what the tax results will be to Craig if the trade takes place with each property mortgaged as indicated below:
   (a) Site, nothing; Hotel $300,000
   (b) Site, $200,000; Hotel $200,000
   (c) Site, $300,000; Hotel, nothing
8. Assume that after acquiring the hotel, Herman Craig takes $20,000 of depreciation deductions. He pays down the mortgage 10 percent. He then sells the hotel for $400,000 cash. What will be his tax gain or loss in each of the three mortgage situations in Problem 7?
9. Leonard Marlboro is in a 40 percent tax bracket. His long-term capital gains are thus taxed at 20 percent, and his ordinary losses are deductible at 40 percent. He has decided to speculate in the stocks of SBIC's, reasoning that his losses should not exceed his gains by more than 25 percent before taxes. Will he break even after taxes if he achieves such a result? If not, by how much can his losses exceed his gains before taxes and still allow him to break even? Assume that all gains are on stock held for 12 months and 1 day.
10. On November 1, 1978, a U.S. bond paying 3 percent interest and maturing on November 1, 1979, is selling for 98: It appears that Al Albert, a stock market investor, will have an excess of long-term capital losses over short-term capital gains in 1978 of $56,000. Of this amount $6,000 will be used to offset ordinary income on his 1978 income tax return and $50,000

will become a carryover to 1979. Albert does not expect to realize any capital gains from his stock market activities in 1979. What are the tax advantages to Albert of his purchasing a quantity of the U.S. bonds and holding them to maturity? How many bonds should he buy? Would it make any difference, from a tax standpoint, if he purchased the bonds with funds borrowed at 5.75 percent interest per annum?

11. Indicate the equivalent interest rate that would have to be obtained from a fully taxable security to equate it with a municipal bond paying 4 percent for each of the following taxpayers:
    (a) Corporation in a 48 percent tax bracket
    (b) Individual in a 20 percent tax bracket
    (c) Tax-exempt pension trust
12. Explain why an investor cannot get long-term capital gains treatment on a short sale.

*13. Charles Gilbert, a high-bracket taxpayer, purchased 1,000 shares of Datatronics Computer Corp. on January 27, 1978, at 18. By December 26, 1978, Datatronics was selling at 42, but the chart pattern of the stock indicated to the taxpayer that it was about to start sliding. Since he was in a 70 percent tax bracket, Gilbert was reluctant to take a short-term capital gain, since it would be taxed at ordinary income rates. Is there any way he could nail down his gain, or at least most of it, and still get long-term capital gains treatment?

*14. Ex Corporation's stock is all owned by Mr. Lax. For the first half of the calendar year 1978, the corporation's income is as follows:

| | |
|---|---|
| Dividends | $70,000 |
| Interest | 63,000 |
| Rents (net) | 18,000 |

It is anticipated that this pattern will continue for the balance of 1978. An operating business will be acquired in March 1979. Mr. Lax has heard that cattle feeding might solve his personal holding-company problem for 1978. Explain to him how this might work.

*15. Y Corporation is a Subchapter S corporation that sold its operating business during 1978. During 1979, it will receive payments on that sales contract. Total payments of $100,000 will be received, of which $35,000 will be interest and $65,000 principal. Could a cattle operation help Y Corporation retain its Subchapter S status?

16. George Ortiz owns an old office building that he inherited from his father. The land on which the building stands is not owned by George, but is used under terms of a 50-year lease. The lease expires in five years. The profit-and-loss statement for the building for last year is as follows:

| | | |
|---|---|---|
| Gross rentals | | $700,000 |
| Deductions: | | |
| Utilities | $ 50,000 | |
| Repairs and maintenance | 100,000 | |
| Depreciation (straight-line) | 200,000 | |
| Wages and salaries | 20,000 | |
| Other expenses | 15,000 | 385,000 |
| Net income | | $315,000 |

No change is anticipated in the pattern of income over the next five years. The depreciation deduction is sufficient to exactly amortize Ortiz' unrecovered tax basis over the remaining term of the land lease. Ortiz is married, files a joint return with his wife, and has an excess of other income of $40,000 per year over his other deductions and exemptions. George inherited the building about a year ago and has no particular desire to retain it. He would like to have you figure out for him what minimum cash selling price he could afford to accept to be just as well off after taxes as if he continued to operate the building. At the same time, he would like to know the maximum amount that a corporate buyer could afford to pay for the building without sustaining an after-tax loss.

*17. In which of the following transactions would gain be recognized?

Exchange of stock in General Motors for stock in American Motors

Sale of a personal residence for $35,000, followed by purchase of another personal residence for $60,000

Exchange of a New York business building for a Texas ranch

Exchange of an old truck, plus cash, for a new truck

Sale of land to the state for highway use for $35,000, under threat of taking by right of eminent domain, followed by purchase of land for a similar use for $20,000

18. Kramer is a physician in a small city. He would like to retire in about 10 years but has had little success in accumulating a retirement nest egg. He owns some stock and some rental property. Dividend income runs about $2,000 per year, and net rental income is $10,000 on gross rentals of $30,000. Assume that he is in a personal tax bracket of 45 percent. Cash available in a corporation would be reinvested in rental industrial real estate offering a before-tax return of 10 percent per annum on Kramer's equity. Assume that as long as more than 90 percent of the corporation's gross income is from real estate rentals, it will not be a personal holding company. Contrast the amount that Kramer could accumulate over the next ten years by using a corporation with the amount he would otherwise accumulate.

19. Assume that Dr. Kramer in Problem 18 decided to go ahead with a corporation. What would be the tax consequences he might encounter when he decided to retire ten years hence and draw upon the corporate assets?

# 15

# Taxation of Employee Benefits and Retirement Income

Old Mother Hubbard went to the cupboard. . . .
But when she got there, the cupboard was bare. . . .

Undoubtedly, Old Mother Hubbard had worked for a company that didn't have any sort of pension, profit-sharing, stock-bonus, or employee-annuity plan. And her Social Security just wasn't enough. As of March 1970, the median income of those persons over 62 who had money income was $1,732. There are lots of Mother Hubbards. But there are probably fewer than there would be if it weren't for certain favorable provisions in our tax laws that encourage employers to create employee-benefit plans.

## TRUSTEED BENEFIT PLANS

The key tax feature of the trusteed benefit plans (pension plans, profit-sharing plans, and stock-bonus plans) is that the employer gets a current tax deduction for his contribution to the plan, whereas the employee has no tax to pay until he actually draws amounts from the plan. An added tax benefit is that the earnings of the plan can accumulate free of any income tax. The latter feature can make more difference than is generally realized. Say that the trust can earn 6 percent per year on its investments. After taxes, this would amount to 4.8 percent per year to an individual in the 20 percent tax bracket. Over a 30-year period, $1 invested at 4.8 percent would amount to $4.11, while $1 at 6 percent would amount to $5.14.

The fact that the employee has no current tax to pay means that more can be invested through the plan than if tax first had to be paid on the same amount as salary and then what was left was invested. In addition, the fact that the trust pays no tax means the amounts in the plan will increase more rapidly.

Ignoring the time value of money, these benefit plans involve no tax subsidy but only a deferral of tax imposition. In most instances, the employer should theoretically be indifferent to whether he pays out $1 in wages or $1 in benefit-plan contributions. Both dollars are equally deductible, and what restrictions exist on deductibility apply to the benefit plan rather than to the wage payment. The employee, on the other hand, should be far from indifferent. Through the benefit plan, he can obtain both a tax deferral on amounts invested and an increase in his effective rate of return through deferral of income tax on the plan's earnings.

Where employees are barely existing at low wage rates, the attractiveness of benefit plans in lieu of wage increases may be questioned. But as the affluence level of an employee rises, and he starts thinking in terms of investing part of his income, the payment of dollars to the plan rather than as taxable wages should gain in attractiveness.

### *Pension Plans*

A pension plan provides for payment to employees, after retirement, of specific amounts (so much per month) or determinable amounts (for example, a certain percentage of your earnings for the 5 years immediately preceding retirement). In many such plans the employee is required also to contribute to the plan, whereas in others, the employee may increase his benefits by contributing, but such contributions are voluntary and usually limited. The employee gets no tax deduction for his direct contribution to the trust. However, the amounts earned by his contribution through the trust's investments are free of current tax, so that the trust is capable of earning a higher rate of return than the employee can earn for himself in comparable investments.

The general limit on the amount that the employer can deduct for his contributions to a pension plan is the amount necessary to fund the ultimate benefits. Since employees already on the payroll at the time a plan is adopted are usually entitled to retirement benefits based on their total service and not just on their employment from the date the plan is adopted, an additional deduction is allowed to fund this past-service credit. Generally, no employee can receive an annual retirement benefit of more than $75,000 (adjusted for cost of living changes after 1974) or his average compensation for his three highest years, whichever is least.

Since 1974, the law has also required a minimum funding of the past service credits. Pension plans in existence on January 1, 1974, have to fund the balance of their past service credits in equal annual amounts over not more than 40 years, while new plans generally have to fund over not less than 30 years.

Between the minimum that has to be paid to the plan trustee, and the maximum that can be deducted, there is a wide area where individual employers have discretion as to the policy they will follow. There is also a fair degree of discretion as to the permissible financial accounting for pension plans.

The cost of a plan for financial accounting purposes should be based upon a consistent method of computation that reflects both the current and the past-service credit, but some latitude is allowed in the amortization of the past-service credit as long as a consistent method is followed from year to year. The minimum annual provision should be not less than the total of the normal cost, an amount equivalent to the interest on "prior" service cost, and a provision for vested benefits. In order to prevent unreasonably large charges to income, the maximum annual provision should not exceed the total of the normal cost and 10 percent of the past-service costs (with certain additional adjustments).

### *Profit-Sharing Plan*

A profit-sharing plan's benefits will depend upon the employer's earnings as well as the plan's income from investment. No set benefits are given in the plan, although various optional ways of receiving benefits may be provided. The employer cannot deduct more than 15 percent of the aggregate compensation of the employees covered under a profit-sharing plan. Special provisions, however, allow the employer to contribute and deduct up to 25 percent of covered compensation in a specific year as a result of contributing less than 15 percent in prior years. No one employee can have added to his profit-sharing account in any year more than 25 percent of his compensation, or $25,000 (adjusted for changes in the cost of living after 1974), whichever is least.

### *Stock-Bonus Plan*

A stock-bonus plan is similar to a profit-sharing plan. Instead of investing in the securities of other companies, the plan will invest in the securities of the employer. The same 15 percent limit that applies to profit-sharing plans applies to stock-bonus plans.

Relatively little use has been made of the stock-bonus-plan provisions. Yet these provisions may, in effect, allow the corporation to print its own money. This results from the fact that in one type of stock-bonus plan the trust acquires the stock directly from the employer. Thus, the employer is enabled to generate cash in the amount of the tax rate times the fair market value of the stock turned over to the trust. However, a price is being paid in order to obtain the income tax deduction. That price is the dilution in the ownership interests of the stockholders. That dilution will, in turn, vary to the extent that stockholders are also employees, and thus beneficiaries of the stock bonus trust. At the extreme, if all beneficiaries are shareholders, and compensation is proportionate to stock ownership, then no dilution will take place—and any tax deduction is without cost.

## EMPLOYEE STOCK OWNERSHIP PLANS (ESOPs)

An ESOP is a stock bonus trust that has been given certain special tax benefits, can engage in some transactions barred to a regular stock bonus trust, and is subject to certain special restrictions. The special status of ESOPs reflects objectives other than employee compensation or retirement. ESOPs are encouraged because of a belief that employee ownership of U.S. industry, or at least of major interests therein, would be desirable for the Amerian economy. While many employee benefit plans do invest in stocks and bonds of U.S. companies, the ESOP supporters seek to have specific companies set up programs for the employees of those companies to acquire stock in them.

At times, employers have been able to get investment credits, in addition to their regular tax deductions, for contributions to ESOPs. On a few occasions, nontax legislation has made loan money available to ESOPs on extremely favorable terms. Some of the interesting ways in which ESOPs have been used include:

1. A corporate division was going to be discontinued, throwing several thousand people out of work. Instead, the corporation set up an ESOP for the employees of that division. The ESOP borrowed money at low interest and with a long repayment period. The money was used to buy the division from the corporation. The former division annually will contribute to the ESOP trust the amount needed to pay off the loan. The employees of the former division are now, through the ESOP trust, its owners.
2. The controlling stockholder of a corporation was willing to sell 50 percent of his stock to the employees. However, such a purchase did not seem feasible to the key employees if it had to be made out of after-tax income. An ESOP trust was created, and the stock was sold to that trust on an installment basis. The corporation gets a tax deduction for the amounts it contributes to the trust. These amounts are used to pay off the installments due the shareholder, but the employees have no taxable income at that time.
3. Three shareholder-officers disagreed on company policy. For the company to continue, one of the three had to go. He was willing to sell out—but only for cash. Neither the other two stockholders, nor the corporation, had the cash, but the corporation's projected cash flow indicated that it could pay off a loan of the amount needed if only it could take a tax deduction for the principal payments. The corporation's attorney further opined that it would be illegal under state law for the corporation to redeem the shareholder's stock because it lacked sufficient retained earnings. An ESOP was created, borrowed the needed money from a bank (backed by the guarantee of the corporation and the two shareholders), and purchased the third shareholder's stock. The corporation gets a tax deduction for the annual payments it makes to the trust, even though the trust turns around and uses those same dollars to pay the debt.

### *Nondiscrimination*

The plan can define "employees" somewhat narrowly. It can, for example, under some circumstances exclude persons with less than three years of employment and persons who put in less than 1,000 hours per year. Neither the contributions under the plan nor the benefits can be designed to especially favor officers, employees who are shareholders, or highly paid employees.

### *Operation of a Benefit Plan*

The corporation makes out a check, or transfers property, to a trust. The trustees receive the funds, keep an account for each covered employee (the employees being the beneficiaries of this trust), and invest and reinvest the funds entrusted to them. They may buy stocks, bonds, mortgages, real estate, or even annuities. The trust files an information return, but since it is a tax-exempt organization, normally pays no income tax.

At the time provided in the plan, an employee will file a request with the trustees for the amounts he has coming. The trustees will then start making disbursements to him, according to the provisions of the plan.

## ANNUITIES

Instead of using a trust, an employer may buy annuities directly from an insurance company for his employees. Such annuity plans must generally meet the same nondiscrimination tests as trusteed plans. The limit on the amount deductible is the amount needed to provide the benefits promised.

## TAX TREATMENT OF EMPLOYEE DISTRIBUTIONS

### *Payment in One Year*

If the employee receives the total balance due him all in one taxable year, owing to death or to termination of employment, then a portion of his gain may be treated as a capital gain. His gain will be the excess of what he receives over any amounts he contributed to the plan himself. The portion of his gain represented by total benefits accrued during plan years beginning before 1974 will be treated as capital gain. The balance of the gain will be treated as ordinary income, subject to special averaging rules that serve to reduce the tax impact of a large amount of ordinary income in one year.

If part of what he receives is securities in the employer corporation, then his gain will be figured on the amount the trust paid for those securities rather than on their current fair market value. Of course, his tax basis for subsequent gain or loss will also be the amount the trust paid for the securities.

Since a lump-sum distribution in one year offers the employee favored income tax treatment, one of the purposes of the special tax provisions governing pension and profit-sharing plans thereby tends to be frustrated. A major purpose of such plans is to provide the employee with retirement income. This purpose is hardly furthered by encouraging the employee to take a lump-sum settlement rather than a life annuity. Annuity-type payouts to beneficiaries of a deceased employee *are* encouraged by an estate-tax provision allowing exclusion of such payment rights from the taxable estate.

### *Payment in More Than One Year*

The employee's tax basis for the amounts he receives is the amount of the contributions he made to the plan. If the benefits he will receive are large enough so that he will recover within three years the amounts he contributed, he treats the amounts he receives from the plan as tax-free recoveries of an investment until he has recovered his contribution. After that, the amounts are fully taxable. If he will not receive back his contributions within three years, then he allocates the amount he has invested over the period during which he expects to receive payments.

Thus, if the employee's contributions amounted to $10,000 and he was to receive $3,000 per year for 20 years, he would allocate his $10,000 over 20 years, giving him $500 per year. This $500 would be tax-free, whereas the balance of $2,500 would be fully taxable. If the same employee was instead to receive an annuity of $3,000 per year for life, we would refer to actuarial tables to determine his life expectancy. His $10,000 investment divided by his life expectancy would give us the amount of his annual exclusion. If the life expectancy were 20 years, the result would be the same as in our previous example.

### *Quantitative Aspects*

The magnitude of pension and profit-sharing plans is impressive, however they are measured. As of 1977, private pension and profit-sharing trusts were estimated to have assets of over $220 billion, with an annual growth of $16 billion. By 1980, the total assets of private and government plans is expected to approach $600 billion. Approximately half the work force was covered under private plans as of 1977.

## PENSION PLANS FOR THE SELF-EMPLOYED AND THE PROFESSIONAL

For over a decade prior to 1962, a concerted drive had been aimed at Congress to obtain for self-employed persons, particularly professional men who then could not operate in corporate form, the pension and profit-sharing benefits available to employees. The complaint was simple. Most proprietorships and partnerships could conduct their businesses in corporate form. Since 1958 and the advent of the Small Business Corporation, these people could obtain the benefits of being corporate employees without even incurring the disadvantage of having to face the corporate income tax.

Not so for the poor psychiatrist, physician, dentist, lawyer, C.P.A., and so on. State law and/or the standards of their professional bodies prohibited practice in corporate form. As proprietors or as partners in a partnership, they could set up employee-benefit plans for their employees. But they, who were in relatively high tax brackets, could obtain no aid in the form of tax concessions to help provide for eventual retirement. Compared to their colleagues employed by corporations, universities, and foundations, they felt that they were being discriminated against.

The Treasury Department fought the proposal tooth and nail, and the bill got through the House many times only to flounder in the Senate. Finally, in 1962, a much watered-down bill passed. Sometimes referred to as the Keogh or H.R. 10 Bill, it allows self-employed persons to set up retirement plans for themselves. However, they must also cover all regular full-time employees with more than three years of service. The maximum amount that the self-employed person can take as an annual tax deduction for himself is limited to $7,500.

While legislation was struggling along, however, another line of attack was being pursued, spearheaded by the doctors. In a series of court cases, they established the proposition that a medical clinic could be a partnership under state law but a corporation for federal income tax purposes. Although they achieved success in specific cases, the doctors found that the Internal Revenue Service was unwilling to concede. Unable to obtain favorable administrative rulings and faced with recurrent and expensive court battles, the doctors tried a new approach. They tackled the state legislatures. In most states, they were joined by the other professions. By 1970, 48 of the states had enacted some sort of bill that at least purported to set up professional corporations for the practice of one or more professions.

The Internal Revenue Service continued to force taxpayers into court, even though the courts, without exception, upheld the validity of professional corporations. The finale came on March 2, 1970, when the Internal Revenue Service ruled that "in light of recent court decisions, professional service organizations formed under state professional association or corporation statutes will generally be treated as corporations for tax purposes."

### *Present Status*

Businessmen who continue to operate in proprietorship or partnership form may still obtain the limited benefits of a self-employed pension plan. Many professionals, however, have incorporated their practices to obtain the more liberal benefits of a corporate pension or profit-sharing plan.

## ANNUITIES FOR EMPLOYEES OF TAX-EXEMPT ORGANIZATIONS

Before 1958, some employees of tax-exempt religious educational and charitable organizations had a tax gimmick. Instead of taking all their salary as salary, they had the organization buy them annuities. Physicians and dentists serving nonprofit institutions on a part-time basis were particularly conscious of the tax advantages resulting from taking compensation as an annuity and thereby having no immediate taxable income in that compensation.

The Internal Revenue Service did not, of course, concede that these annuities were tax-free when taken in lieu of present compensation. They went to court and ultimately proved successful.

While the I.R.S. was making its point in court, however, Congress at its urging was changing the rules of the game.

Why Congress did exactly what it did is difficult to say. Why the I.R.S. has gone along with what Congress did is a little easier to see. Between them, they have now engrafted a rather unique concept into the area of personal compensation.

Briefly, employees of churches, hospitals, schools, and certain other tax-exempt organizations are allowed, as long as they agree to such an arrangement for a minimum period of one year and agree to it in advance of earning anything under the contract for that year, to direct their employer to take part of their compensation and pay it directly to a designated insurance carrier to apply to the purchase of a nonforfeitable annuity or to pay it to a mutual fund. The amounts so handled, which may even be treated by the employer as a payroll deduction, are excludable from the employee's income.

Unlike pension or profit-sharing plans of for-profit corporations, there is no requirement for a formal plan or agreement, nor is I.R.S. approval required. Also, such arrangements may be made arbitrarily, without concern for discrimination. The essential requirement is that the employer must be approved as a tax-exempt organization.

The regulations prior to the law change had tried to distinguish between an annuity that was being purchased *as a supplement* to current compensation and an annuity that was being purchased *in lieu of* compensation. Among the tests set up were that it would be considered in lieu of compensation and taxable if the contract was purchased as a result of an agreement for a reduction of the employee's salary or if it was purchased at his request in place of an increase in current compensation to which he might otherwise be entitled. The Senate Finance Committee, in its report on the 1958 changes, stated, "Your committee intends the objective 20 percent rule set forth above as a complete substitute for these rules in the regulations."

The 20 percent rule provides that the maximum amount the employee can exclude from compensation in any given year is to be determined by multiplying his years of service by 20 percent of his current compensation, and then deducting all amounts previously excludable that were used to purchase retirement benefits for him. This exclusion cannot exceed the overall limitation on contributions to a qualified defined contribution plan.

The employee begins to pay tax at the time he starts receiving the annuity proceeds. At his death, as much as $5,000 of the proceeds to his survivor may be excludable as a death benefit. Any amounts guaranteed to the survivor are excluded from the employee's gross estate for estate tax purposes.

Thus, a professor employed by a college or university, or any other employee of a charitable, religious, scientific, or educational nonprofit organization, can simply arrange to have a substantial part of his compensation excluded from his income by directing his employer to purchase annuities or mutual funds on his behalf.

A cynic might point out that the 1958 legislation was designed as a loophole-closing measure. The court cases, it turned out, would have resulted in the loophole being quite adequately closed, without any legislation. And the legislation, as it turned out, simply froze the loophole into the tax structure and established its dimensions, rather than closing it. Perhaps it even set a precedent for new loopholes.

## LIFE, HEALTH, AND ACCIDENT INSURANCE

Premiums paid on life insurance policies are generally nondeductible. Thus, if a corporation carries insurance on an employee, and the corporation is the beneficiary, the premiums paid by the corporation are nondeductible. If the corporation pays the premiums on an individual policy on which the employee names the beneficiaries, the premiums will be deductible to the corporation as additional compensation to the employee but will be taxable income to the employee. However, if the corporation carries group term life insurance on its employees, the employees normally realize no income from the premiums paid thereon even though they name the beneficiaries and the corporation gets a deduction.

A type of life insurance benefit provided by some employers is known as "split-dollar" insurance. Under such a plan, the employer loans the employee, interest-free, the amount of the annual increase in cash value of the life insurance policy. The advantage to the employee is that he is enabled to obtain larger amounts of insurance than he would otherwise be able to finance. The disadvantage is that the employee must report in his income the value of the insurance protection received, but not paid for, by him.

An employer can also cover his employees through a plan of health and accident insurance. The premiums paid by the employer constitute deductions to him but are not considered to be income to the employee.

Occasionally, there are comments that the various employer-financed benefit plans really cost the employer nothing because of the fact that payments to the plan are deductible for tax purposes. Since tax rates do not go as high as 100 percent, this is obviously not true. Nor is it any more true for employee-benefit-plan payments than for any other expense. On the other hand, there is a distinct advantage to having the employer furnish the benefits through a group plan rather than increasing the employee's pay and letting the employee buy the benefits himself. A man of 45 will find that $50,000 in term life insurance will cost about $1,000 per year. If he is in a 30 percent tax bracket, he will have to have his salary increased by $1,430 per year to cover both the 30 percent tax and the $1,000 of premium. His employer can furnish him with the same coverage at a cost of about $500 through a group life insurance policy or can use the $1,000 to give him a package of broader group-plan coverages. In fact, both the employer and the employee can benefit.

## COMMERCIAL ANNUITIES

The tax treatment of annuities is particularly well adapted to economic reality. The pure annuity provides a definite amount per year for the balance of the annuitant's life. If the annuitant fails to live out his life expectancy, he never recovers the amount he has invested in the contract. If he lives beyond his life expectancy, the annuity contract proves increasingly profitable for him. Obviously, he would not feel too keenly the financial loss resulting from his premature death. If he lives a long time, he can enjoy the satisfaction of an advantageous investment. Of course, the insurance company is playing the averages. It knows that some annuitants will die before they recover their capital and others will more than recover theirs, but the insurance company also knows that its overall rates are set so that the company will come out fairly well in the long run.

The system works like a roulette table in Las Vegas, where there are 35 numbers, plus "0" and "00," or 37 possible results of any spin. The house pays 35 to 1 if you bet on the correct number. If $37,000 is wagered in the course of the evening, the house should come out with a gross take of approximately $2,000. A little old lady from Des Moines may walk up to the table, plunk down $10, and walk off with $350. A man from Atlanta may sit all evening, playing $1 at a time, and pour in $250 while never winning once. The house could not care less. If enough is wagered, by the law of averages the house will profit.

The tax treatment of annuities follows the same general pattern. A taxpayer is entitled to recover his investment in the annuity over the period of his life expectancy. If this investment is divided by the life expectancy, an "annual exclusion" amount is arrived at. Of the annual payments received under the annuity, the taxpayer is entitled to exclude this much, reporting only the balance as ordinary income, no matter how long he may live.

Thus, a taxpayer who has a life expectancy of 25 more years has invested $75,000 in an annuity paying him $5,000 per year. Each year, for the rest of his life, he will be entitled to exclude $3,000 ($75,000/25) of the $5,000 payment he receives.

Unfortunately for the cause of keeping things simple, annuities are marketed in a wide variety of packages. Some annuities provide a guaranteed-payment feature (for example, even if you die before you have recovered your investment, your estate or heirs will get back the difference between your investment and the amounts drawn by you as an annuity); others are written on a joint-and-survivorship basis (for example, annual payments of $5,000 will be made to you and/or your wife as long as either of you live). Although the same basic theory of an exclusion allowance based upon investment and life expectancy still applies, adjustments must be made to reflect the multiple lives involved or the nonannuity features that the premium is also purchasing.

## CREDIT FOR THE ELDERLY

Retirement benefits received under either Social Security or the Railroad Retirement System are exempt from income tax. Nor has the person receiving these benefits ever had to pay any tax on the employer's contribution on his behalf, which is equal to the amount withheld from the employee's wages. On the other hand, persons who provide for their own retirement without the benefit of Social Security find their retirement income (rents, dividends, interest, and the includable portion of pensions and annuities) fully subject to income tax.

To put these self-providers on a tax basis more comparable with Social Security annuitants, Congress could simply have taxed Social Security payments on the same basis as other pensions (that is, allowed the annuitant a tax-free recovery of his contribution to the plan). Instead, Congress provides a tax credit for the self-providers.

As of 1976, the credit was 15 percent of not more than $2,500 of retirement income received during the year by a person over 65, or $3,750 if both spouses on a joint return are over 65. The $2,500 (or $3,750) is reduced dollar for dollar by any Social Security or Railroad Retirement benefits received. It is also reduced by half of adjusted gross income in excess of $7,500 for a single person and in excess of $10,000 for a married couple filing jointly. Thus, the credit is of no benefit to persons age 65 or over receiving Social Security in excess of $2,500 (or $3,750 for a couple filing jointly if both are age 65 or older), nor is it of any benefit to an unmarried individual with adjusted gross incomes in excess of $15,000 (or $20,000 for a couple over 65).

Eligibility requirements for the credit are:

1. The taxpayer must be over 65, or retired under a public retirement plan. The rules are slightly different in the latter situation.
2. He must not be a nonresident alien.

## BENEFIT PLANS AND THE SMALL BUSINESS

The thought is frequently encountered that the widespread use of various sorts of pension, profit-sharing, stock-bonus, life insurance, health and accident coverage, and similar plans by large businesses has put the small business at a disadvantage in securing employees. If we look at the small business that exists mainly because it pays low wages, then this is probably true. Any factor that would increase labor costs, whether an increase in the minimum wage law to $5.00 an hour or whatever, would jeopardize continuation of such a business.

For the new small business that exists because it does things better than its bigger competitors, in regard to either costs or products, these benefit plans can actually be a help. Such a business can package its benefit plans to fit the needs and wants of its prospective employees, thus offering them something that will seem more attractive to them than the plan of a less flexible employer. Where the employer is not large enough to offer group plans because he has too few employees to constitute a "group" under the insurance company's standards, he may be able, through a trade association, to join with other smaller employers in forming a group.

To the extent that benefit plans require continued employment in order to "cash in" on values built up over a period of years, they do have a tendency to lock people in their jobs and thus reduce job mobility. This may be detrimental in its effect on new employers seeking experienced personnel. But it also has an effect on the employers of such senior personnel—they probably wind up with a certain amount of dead weight in the organization in the form of people who are hanging around only until retirement day.

It is probable that retirement plans and group insurance plans have increased the reluctance of many employers to hire older workers. Certainly, premiums will be higher with a work force composed of older persons. But premiums are only one element of employee expense. Many companies have discovered that the increased dependability of the older employee more than balances the benefit-plan disadvantages. To the extent that larger companies are more inclined to have inflexible policies discriminating against older workers, the competitive advantage of the smaller concerns would again seem to be improved, since more, better, and more experienced workers are thus made available to them.

## CASE EXCERPTS

*Commissioner* v. *Pepsi-Cola Niagara Bottling Corp.* (CA2–1968) 22 AFTR 2d 5051

### *Commissioner* v. *Pepsi-Cola Niagara Bottling Corp.* (CA2–1968) 22 AFTR 2d 5051

> The profit-sharing plan covered only salaried employees and none of the hourly employees. Almost all the salaried employees earned more than any hourly employees.

Congress adopted a twofold approach. Plans would qualify if a sufficient proportion of the firm's employees were eligible or participated. If, however, a plan's coverage provisions were not so broad as to include the minimum percentage of employees prescribed in §401 (a) (3) (A), they were to be subjected to a more intensive scrutiny by the Treasury Department whose nature the legislature could prescribe only in a more generalized way. Restrictive plans were to qualify only if the Secretary or his delegate were to find that the eligibility requirements were not "discriminatory" in favor of officers, shareholders, supervisors, or "highly paid employees." The legislative history suggests that Congress did not believe itself equipped to give more content to the two phrases we have quoted. The original House Bill sought to define more precisely the characteristics of plans that discriminated in favor of the "highly paid," at least with regard to a companion provision, §401 (a) (4), which guarded against the danger that highly paid employees would gain a disproportionate share of pension benefits despite the fact that eligibility requirements were not found discriminatory under §401 (a) (3). It stated that the "benefits or contributions" required under the plan shall "not have the effect of discriminating in favor of *any* employee whose compensation is greater than that of *other* employees." H.R. 7378, §144 (a) (4), 77th Cong. 2d Sess. (1942) (emphasis supplied). A literal reading of this provision would unequivocally have made fairness to the lowest-paid employee covered by the plan the test of qualification. This formulation, however, was apparently believed to be unduly rigid, for when the tax bill was returned from the Ways and Means Committee to which it had been referred for reconsideration, §401 (a) (4) had been amended to correspond with the more general language of §401 (a) (3) (B), simply banning discrimination in favor of the "highly paid."

The Commissioner found himself confronted with problems in administering the statute similar to those that Congress had encountered in drafting it. While there are attractions in the idea that a plan can be rejected under §§401 (a) (3) and (4) only if it discriminates in favor of employees who would generally be regarded as "highly paid," it poses difficulties of administration which the Tax Court did nothing to resolve. Words like "high" and "highly" clamor for a referent. A 500-foot hill would look high in Central Park but not among the Grand Tetons or even at Lake Placid. Apparently the Tax Court regarded the president of the Bottling Corporation with a \$28,000-\$30,000 salary as "highly paid," and we assume he would be so considered in Niagara Falls, but he hardly would be in Hollywood. More to the point, while we would not regard Bernard J. Riggs, with a salary of \$7595-\$8580 from the Bottling Corporation as "highly paid," that might not be the view of Helen Kendall whose wages ranged from \$3969 to \$4420 in the same period. Considerations such as these led the Commissioner to rule in 1956:

> In order for the plan to meet the coverage requirements, there must be sufficient participation by the lower-paid employees to demonstrate that in practice the plan does not discriminate in favor of the high-paid employees. . . . The terms "highly compensated" and "lower-compensated" are relative, and the distinction between them must be based upon the circumstances of each case. [Rev. Rul. 56-497, 1956-2 Cum. Bull. 284, 286.]

We cannot say that in thus reading "highly" as "more highly" and taking the compensation of noncovered employees as the standard, the Commissioner went beyond the powers Congress conferred upon him by §401 (a) (3). When Congress has used a general term and has empowered an administrator to define it, the courts must respect his construction if this is within the range of reason. *Gray* v. *Powell,* 314 U.S. 402, 411-13 (1941); *NLRB* v. *Hearst Publications, Inc.,* 322 U.S. 111, 130-32 (1944). That requirement was met here and it was not for the Tax Court to substitute its reading for that of the administrator on the firing line. . . .

## QUESTIONS AND PROBLEMS

1. Your employer is considering adopting either a pension or a profit-sharing plan. How would your preference for one or the other be apt to differ depending on your age? If you were 24, which would you prefer? If 48? If 68?
2. Briefly discuss the discrimination and coverage requirements of pension and profit-sharing plans.

*3. On July 6, 1978, the Ajax Company instituted a qualified pension plan for its employees. Of $245,000 in total wages paid to all employees during 1978, $150,000 was paid to employees covered under the plan. Since this was the first experience the corporation's officers had had with a pension plan, they were somewhat unsure of themselves when the time came to compute the contribution to the pension trust. During 1978, they paid $12,700 to the trustees ($6,000 of this amount was to fund the past-service liability), and an additional contribution of $3,000 was made on March 14, 1979, to pay the balance that was accrued on December 31, 1978. The corporation's actuary delivered a report after the end of the year stating that the total amount necessary to pay retirement benefits on behalf of employee services rendered prior to July 6 was $55,000, and the normal cost for 1978 should be $6,700. Compute the allowable deduction on Ajax Company's 1978 federal income tax return. What would your answer be if Ajax was on the cash basis of accounting and the $3,000 was paid on March 19, 1979?

*4. Referring to Problem 3, in 1979 Ajax paid to the trustees, in addition to the March 14, 1979, contribution, an amount of $5,000. The next payment was made on September 1, 1980. The normal cost for 1979 was the same as for 1978. What amount is deductible on the 1979 federal income tax return? What is the amount of the contribution carryover to 1980? (Assume accrual method of accounting.)

*5. Assume the same facts as in Problem 3 except that the Ajax Company has a profit-sharing plan providing for a contribution of 20 percent of its net income before the contribution deduction, and after federal and state income taxes at a combined rate of 50 percent. For 1978, the net income for this purpose was $143,000. How much will the corporation contribute to the profit-sharing trust? What amount is deductible on the 1978 federal income tax return? What is the amount of the contribution carryover? What is the amount of the credit carryover?

*6. Referring to Problem 5, in 1979 Ajax paid to the trustees after March 14, 1979, an amount of $5,000. No payments were made in 1980 until September 1. Assuming the same income and tax rates in 1979 as in 1978, what amount is deductible on the 1979 federal income tax return? How much excess contribution, if any, will carry over to 1980? How much is the credit carryover to 1980?

*7. On June 1, 1978, Jerry Smith retired at the age of 65, after having been employed by Apex Engineering for 25 years. He received a lump sum payment of $76,500 from Apex's profit-sharing fund, computed as follows:

| Contribution made by Apex | |
|---|---|
| Prior to January 1, 1974 | $40,000 |
| During 1974-1978 | 5,000 |

| | |
|---|---|
| Forfeitures and earnings credited to Jerry's account | |
| Prior to January 1, 1974 | 3,500 |
| During 1974-1978 | 28,000 |
| Total of Jerry's account | $76,500 |

How would Jerry report this distribution on his 1978 tax return?

8. Assume that in Problem 7 Jerry contributed $5,000 of the $40,000 pre-1974 contribution and $500 of the $5,000 post-1973 contribution. Now, how will Jerry report the distribution on his tax return?

*9. Assume that Apex (in Problem 7) in 1971 issued its 8 percent cumulative preferred stock as part of its contribution to the profit-sharing trust fund. Fifty shares of this contribution were credited to Jerry's account, for which Apex deducted $5,000 on its 1971 corporation income tax return. The stock had a fair market value of $6,000 at the time it, together with the cash, was distributed to Jerry in 1978. Will your conclusion in Problem 7 change? What is Jerry's basis in the stock? Would your answer be different if the shares were contributed by Apex in 1977?

*10. Instead of contributing the Apex preferred stock (in Problem 9), the corporation contributed I.B.M. 8 percent debentures worth $5,000. These debentures had appreciated to $6,000 at the time they were distributed to Jerry. How will Jerry treat the distribution of these debentures on his tax return?

11. Adam, an employee of Beta Manufacturing Co. for 35 years, retired January 1, 1978, at the age of 65. Beta has an annuity pension plan that will pay Adam $3,000 per year for life. Adam did not contribute to the fund. How much will he report on Schedule E of his 1978 federal income tax return?

12. In Problem 11, if Adam contributed $5,000 to the fund, how much would be taxable in 1978? In 1979? Will he report ordinary or capital gains income?

13. In Problem 11, if Adam contributed $15,000 toward the annuity, how much would be taxable in 1978? In 1979?

*14. Arthur is self-employed. He has an HR 10 (Keogh) plan to which he contributes the maximum deductible per year. In 1977, his net income from his proprietorship was $20,000. In 1978, it was $27,000. How much did he deduct for his contribution to his plan?

*15. Alvin is the sole stockholder of a Subchapter S corporation that has a pension plan for all its employees. Alvin received a salary of $20,000 in 1977 and $27,000 in 1978, and in addition, the corporation contributed $3,000 in each year on his behalf to the pension trust. What was the tax effect of this contribution to the corporation? To Alvin?

*16. Professor Bannister of Ohio University signs an agreement with the university in the summer of 1978 that $4,000 of his $22,000 annual salary for the period 1978-1979 will be used to purchase an annuity for the professor from the College Insurance Company. The university thereupon reduces the professor's salary from $22,000 to $18,000 for tax purposes, paying the $4,000 to the insurance company in monthly payments of $400 each over the ten pay periods of the school year. Assume that no other payments have been or are being made by or for retirement benefits. What will be the tax effect if:

(a) This is the professor's first year at Ohio University?

(b) This is the professor's fifth year at Ohio University?

17. Through a plan of group life, accident, and hospitalization insurance, the Claremont Company can obtain coverage for its employees at a cost that is approximately 80 percent of what the average employee would have to pay for the same contractual coverage. Total annual cost will run $250 per person. To finance the plan, Claremont proposes to reduce raises that employees would otherwise be receiving by this amount. As an average employee, in a 20 percent marginal tax bracket, assuming that you would purchase an equivalent amount of insurance coverage anyway and that the premiums paid would not provide you with any tax benefits, would you evaluate Claremont's proposal as being in your best interest?

18. In the third example in the ESOP discussion, the trust borrowed money which it then used to redeem the shareholder's stock. Suppose the corporation could, itself, have legally redeemed the stock. Compare the way the transaction was handled in the example with an alternative approach in which the corporation directly borrowed the money, and then contributed stock to the trust each year in an amount equal to the principal payments it was making on the loan:

(a) As to the after-tax cash flow available to service the corporation's debt;

(b) As to the point at which the deduction limitation of 15 percent of the compensation of the covered employees might limit feasibility of the redemption; and

(c) As to the dilution effect on the other two shareholders (assuming that as employees they will be 25 percent beneficiaries of the trust, and assuming further that the per-share value of the stock increases 10 percent per year).

19. A corporate pension plan provides that an employee can retire at age 60 at a pension based upon the highest average annual income he has earned during any period of five consecutive years. Joe Tightwad, a member of the Board of Directors, is arguing that the pension plan should be changed to a "money purchase" plan where the pension paid to an employee is whatever

amount is produced by the sums that have been accumulated to his credit through employer contributions that are a flat percentage of salary. "We can pay the same percentage of salary we pay now, almost 10 percent," argues Joe, "but we will eliminate the twin devils of forcing the corporation to make up investment losses of the trust and of accelerating costs to the corporation when high salary increases are caused by inflation." Contrast these two approaches to providing benefits (i.e., making whatever contribution is needed to provide a formula-determined benefit, and making a formula-determined contribution with the accumulated fund determining the amount of the benefit) in a period of inflation:

(a) From the viewpoint of the employee; and

(b) From the viewpoint of the employer.

*20. Frank Solomon first became a participant in his employer's Profit-Sharing Plan on January 1, 1947. He died on December 31, 1977. At the time of his death, his interest in the plan amounted to $117,000, all of which was payable to his wife. Under the plan, she can take her distribution in cash, in stock of the employer corporation, or in some combination of stock and cash. The employer stock that would be distributed would have a cost basis to the profit-sharing trust of $35.00 per share even though its fair market value at the time of distribution would be $65.00 per share. If Mrs. Solomon took all stock, she would thus receive 1,800 shares. She would anticipate selling the stock within three years if she did take stock. No estate tax will be due from Mr. Solomon's estate. For purposes of any calculations, assume that Mrs. Solomon has $10,000 of other ordinary income, net of all exemptions and deductions, for any relevant years, and has no preference income.

(a) Should Mrs. Solomon elect to take stock or cash?

(b) Should Mrs. Solomon elect not to treat any part of the distribution received as capital gain?

# 16

# Inventory—Especially LIFO

## HOW INVENTORY AFFECTS INCOME

Have you ever heard of Macy's department store in New York? R.H. Macy & Company is quite a large department-store chain. In 1942, like many another taxpayer, Macy was struggling with the problems of high costs, rising prices, and 80 percent marginal wartime tax rates.

Macy, along with many other retailers and the National Retail Dry Goods Association, felt that part of the solution to their problem lay in a law Congress had passed in 1939. This law dealt with the method of valuing business inventories—that is, merchandise ultimately destined for sale to customers. The 1939 law allowed all taxpayers to adopt what is called the LIFO (for *last-in, first-out*) method of determining inventory cost. What difference does inventory cost make?

In computing taxable income, a business that has merchandise on hand at the end of its tax year is required to exclude from its expenses the cost of this unsold merchandise. From the sales of the current year are deducted the costs of the merchandise sold, but not the costs of merchandise still on hand.

If a business has available for sale 150 gizmos, but actually sells only 100, its profit will be the revenue derived from the sale less the cost of the 100 gizmos sold. It would make little sense to allow a deduction for the cost of all of the 150 gizmos, since the unsold 50 really represent an investment to be carried over to the next year.

If gizmos always cost the same amount, the problem of determining the cost of the 100 gizmos sold and the 50 unsold would be minor. But if we assume that, as was the case in 1942, the cost of gizmos is moving steadily higher, then the problem of valuation becomes greater. We can say to ourselves, as many people did after 1939, that we must have gizmos to stay in business. If we sell a gizmo, we must buy a gizmo to replace the one sold. Therefore, the cost of the gizmos sold during, say, 1942, is logically the cost of the gizmos bought during that year to replace the gizmos sold.

Or we can be "realists" and say that the gizmos on hand are obviously the gizmos we purchased most recently, so therefore the gizmos we sold in 1942 must have been, first, the gizmos we had at the *beginning* of 1942. Only after these were all gone could we sell the gizmos bought *during* 1942.

Gizmo Inventory Data

| | | | | *Total $* | |
|---|---|---|---|---|---|
| 1/1/42 | Inventory | 50 | @ $10 | $ 500 | |
| 1942 | Purchases | 100 | @ $15 | 1,500 | |
| | Available for sale | 150 | | 2,000 | |
| 12/31/42 | Inventory | 50 | | ? | $ 500 or $ 750 |
| | Sold | 100 | | ? | $1,500 or $1,250 |

Assume that the 100 gizmos sold realized $2,000. If these 100 were the 100 purchased in 1942, the profit would be calculated by deducting $1,500 from $2,000, and would be $500. If the gizmos sold consisted of 50 from the January 1, 1942, inventory and 50 from the 1942 purchases, then the cost of the gizmos sold would be $1,250 and the profit would be $750.

The 1939 law change permitted a taxpayer to assume that the 100 gizmos sold were the 100 gizmos bought during 1942. But retailers do not handle one kind of gizmo. They handle thousands and thousands of gizmos. They do not keep track of them in the same manner that auto dealers keep track of the cars in their inventory. The auto dealer keeps a record on each car. But the retailer's accounting records are frequently set up only on a dollar basis.

And so it was with Macy.

## HOW MACY TRIED TO USE LIFO

To figure the cost of its inventory, Macy would take the inventory in terms of the marked selling price on the merchandise. Then, using the percentage of markup maintained for the year, the inventory would be reduced to cost. Thus, if the inventory at retail price was $2,000, and the maintained markup percentage (expressed as a percentage of selling price) was 40, then the cost of the inventory would be $2,000 less 40 percent of $2,000 ($800), or $1,200.

Macy and other retailers had figured out that if they applied price indexes to their retail-method inventories, they could wind up with just as valid an application of the LIFO principle as if they were dealing with physical quantities of specific items. Their reasoning was that, under the retail method as they employed it, they were charging to cost of goods sold the cost of the goods on hand at the beginning of the year, plus some part of the goods purchased during the year. To charge to cost of goods sold only the cost of goods purchased during the year (assuming that the total inventory did not decrease), all they had to do was to remove from the ending inventory the dollar values that were in the beginning inventory and restate them in terms of the kind of dollars that were in the beginning inventory.

| | | |
|---|---|---|
| Beginning inventory retail | 1941 $ | $ 25,000 |
| Markup percentage | | 40 |
| Beginning inventory cost | 1941 $ | $ 15,000 |
| Purchases | 1942 $ | $100,000 |
| Ratio of 1942 $ to 1941 $ | | 110% |
| Ending inventory retail | 1942 $ | $ 40,000 |
| Markup percentage | | 40 |
| Ending inventory cost | 1942 | $ 24,000 |

Looking at this from the way Macy had been doing things, the cost of goods available for sale would have been $115,000, the ending inventory would have been $24,000, and the cost of goods sold $91,000. On the LIFO basis, the cost of goods available for sale would still have been $115,000, but the ending inventory would have been only $22,500, and hence the cost of goods sold would have been $92,500 instead of $91,000. Here is the computation:

| | |
|---|---|
| Ending inventory–retail 1941 $ ($40,000/1.10) | $36,363.63 |
| Increase over opening inventory of $25,000 | $11,363.63 |
| Increase converted into 1942 $ ($11,363 X 1.10) | $12,500.00 |
| Ending inventory at retail: | |
| Inventory in 1941 $ | $25,000 |
| Inventory increase in 1942 $ | $12,500 |
| Total | $37,500 |
| Ending inventory at cost ($37,500 X 0.6) | $22,500 |

The retailers got the National Industrial Conference Board to develop price indexes for each of the departments of a department store so that this type of conversion of a retail inventory to a LIFO inventory could be made. But the Bureau of Internal Revenue (now the Internal Revenue Service) turned thumbs down on this use of LIFO. The Bureau felt that LIFO could be applied only to inventories expressed in quantity terms, not to inventories expressed in dollar terms.

Macy filed its 1942 return in a peculiar fashion. The inventory was computed on a LIFO basis. But then an adjustment was made so that the amount of taxable income was arrived at without the use of LIFO. As company officials later explained, Macy did this to put the company on record as wanting to use LIFO, but made the adjustment to comply with the regulations of the Bureau of Internal Revenue.

Other retailers computed their taxable income on the LIFO inventory basis. The bureau denied their right do do so. In 1947, the Tax Court was called upon to decide whether the Bureau or the retailers were right. The retailers won!

Based upon the Tax Court decision, which was accepted by the Bureau, Macy filed claims in 1948 asking for refunds of taxes for 1942 and subsequent years. The company argued that its taxable income should have been computed on the LIFO basis, and would have been if the Bureau of Internal Revenue had not forbidden LIFO to retailers. Normally, a refund claim could not be filed in 1948 for a 1942 tax, the statute of limitations running three years after the return was due, but Macy had foresightedly entered into agreements with the government to extend the statute of limitations until a court decision could be reached in the LIFO cases that were pending.

A revenue agent audited Macy's 1942 return. He recommended a refund of part of the 1942 tax. But this recommendation was overturned in Washington. The refund claims were denied. Why? Macy had not filed a proper election to use LIFO, said the Bureau!

Macy sued for a refund in district court. The judge commented, ". . . for its failure to join . . . in contesting the validity of the Commissioner's interpretation of the statute, the defendant [the government] would visit upon Macy a denial of the Congressional grant of the right to adopt the elective method [LIFO] for all years antecedent to the decision in [1947]. The pervasive theme of the defendant's brief is that '. . . erroneous interpretation of the act by the Treasury Department does not estop the government from asserting the tax, even though the taxpayer may have been misled by such interpretation.' " Judge Bicks therefore concluded, ". . . to deny relief to Macy would be to permit the Commissioner to benefit by his own non-feasance."

But the Second Circuit Court of Appeals reversed the district court decision and denied Macy its tax refund! Said the court, "It is no excuse that this failure [to file a timely election] occurred because the Commissioner [of Internal Revenue] opposed Macy's exercise of its statutory right. . . . Not thus is the United States of America to be estopped in the collection of its revenue."

Although Macy lost, the principle that LIFO could be applied to dollar aggregates rather than to specific quantities had won out. This principle was broader than simply its application to retailers. Wholesalers, manufacturers, and other taxpayers with inventories (yes, even new car dealers) could all seize on the rationale of the retailer decisions to justify using index numbers to compute LIFO inventories, thus eliminating most of the clerical expense of employing LIFO. Even then, it took 13 years–from 1948 to 1961–before the Internal Revenue Service managed to issue regulations explaining how taxpayers not using the retail method of inventory were to employ LIFO on what became known as the "dollar-value" method.

Possibly the simplest way to grasp this type of dollar-value LIFO is to illustrate its use. Assume that a small manufacturer decided to adopt LIFO in 1978. His inventory at the start of 1978 would naturally have been expressed in terms of December 31, 1977, prices. He would have taken a physical inventory, showing quantities, descriptions, prices, and value (quantity times price) for each item, and totaled all the inventory items he owned . . . let's say a total of $14,000.

At December 31, 1978, he would again take a physical inventory. Again he would show for each item the quantity on hand, the description, and the price per unit. But instead of showing only one price per unit, he would show the January 1, 1978, price per unit and the December 31, 1978, price per unit. He would also show two value extensions (quantity times price) for each item. Thus, the December 31, 1978, inventory would have been priced at two price levels—January 1, 1978, and December 31, 1978:

| | *Price Level* | |
|---|---|---|
| | *1/1/78* | *12/31/78* |
| 12/31/78 inventory | $20,000 | $24,250 |

Given the assumed figures above, we could determine that the December 31, 1978, price level for this taxpayer's merchandise was 121.25 percent of the January 1, 1978, price level by dividing $24,250 by $20,000. We could then proceed to value the inventory of December 31, 1978, on the LIFO basis as follows:

| | *1/1/78* | | *12/31/78* |
|---|---|---|---|
| | *Dollars* | *Factor* | *Dollars* |
| 1/1/78-inventory | $14,000 | 100.00 | $14,000 |
| 1978 inventory increase | 6,000 | 121.25 | 7,275 |
| Total LIFO inventory at 12/31/78 | $20,000 | | $21,275 |

On the dollar-value LIFO basis, then, the value of the December 31, 1978, inventory would be $21,275. At December 31, 1979, the inventory would again be taken on the double-extension dollar-value basis, with all items being priced at both their January 1, 1978, prices and their December 31, 1979, prices. Now our inventory data would look like this:

| | *Price Level* | | |
|---|---|---|---|
| | *1/1/78* | *12/31/78* | *12/31/79* |
| 1/1/78 inventory | $14,000 | | |
| 12/31/78 inventory | 20,000 | $24,250 | |
| 12/31/79 inventory | 18,000 | | $27,000 |

This time, the relation between the current price level and the January 1, 1978, prices is meaningless for our purpose because, in terms of January 1, 1978, prices, there has been a decline in the inventory. In terms of January 1, 1978, prices, in other words, there is no inventory increase in 1979. Instead, we have used up some, but not all, of the 1978 increment. Our valuation would therefore be:

| | *1/1/78* | | *12/31/79* |
|---|---|---|---|
| | *Dollars* | *Factor* | *Dollars* |
| 1/1/78 inventory | $14,000 | 100.0 | $14,000 |
| Balance of 1978 inventory increase ($18,000 – $14,000) | 4,000 | 121.25 | 4,850 |
| Total LIFO inventory at 12/31/79 | $18,000 | | $18,850 |

On December 31, 1980, the inventory is again taken, and again priced on a double basis. Our inventory data now looks like this:

| | *Price Level* | | | |
|---|---|---|---|---|
| | *1/1/78* | *12/31/78* | *12/31/79* | *12/31/80* |
| 1/1/78 | $14,000 | | | |
| 12/31/78 | 20,000 | $24,250 | | |
| 12/31/79 | 18,000 | | $27,000 | |
| 12/31/80 | 25,000 | | | $30,000 |

In terms of January 1, 1978, prices, there has been an inventory increment of $7,000; 1980 prices are 120 percent ($30,000/$25,000) of January 1, 1978, prices, so that the valuation of the increment is $8,400. Our inventory at December 31, 1980, contains three LIFO layers, totaling $27,250:

| | |
|---|---|
| $ 8,400 | 1980 dollars |
| $ 4,850 | 1978 dollars |
| $14,000 | 1/1/78 dollars |

Inventory decreases will dip into the most recently added layers, whereas inventory increases will add new layers at the price level of the year of increase.

## TAX LIFO AND ACCOUNTING LIFO

From an accounting viewpoint, LIFO is a method of determining cost. If market is below cost, then presently accepted accounting practice would be to show the inventory at market rather than at cost. But the inventory valuation of the preceding period becomes cost, for accounting purposes, of the current period. Accounting LIFO, then, has the tendency to show inventory valuations of LIFO users at the lowest prices that have prevailed since the adoption of LIFO. Tax LIFO, on the other hand, cannot be used in conjunction with a lower-of-cost-or-market approach.

Thus, in adopting tax LIFO, management should be satisfied that price levels of the pertinent inventory items are at a low point relative to the future, rather than at a high point. Depending on the nature of the business, of course, price drops can be compensated for by year-end inventory liquidations, followed by restocking at the new and lower price level, which will then become a new LIFO layer.

If LIFO is adopted for tax purposes, the tax law requires that no other basis be used in calculating income for reports to shareholders, credit grantors, and so forth.

This is the only place in the entire tax law where a specific rule requires financial accounting to conform to tax accounting. At the time that LIFO first became generally available to taxpayers in 1939, the weight of accounting thought was that LIFO was not suitable for most businesses–that it was appropriate only where it tended to correspond to physical flow of inventory of where raw materials were involved. The idea of applying LIFO to a department store would have as readily horrified a conservative C.P.A. of 1939 as it did the Bureau of Internal Revenue in 1942. Thus the Treasury Department had the requirement inserted in the law that LIFO must be used for reporting purposes as well as for tax purposes, confident that its use would then be limited by the C.P.A.'s to those situations where it was appropriate.

As we shall see from time to time in this book, accounting theory has in the past adapted itself (too readily, some critics say) to changes in tax rules. In a few years, LIFO became accepted as a way of handling cost for any business, under the rationale that it was the flow of economic utility that was being costed and not specific inventory items.

## WHY ISN'T EVERYONE ON LIFO?

For many taxpayers, it doesn't matter much what inventory method they use. Inventory just is not significant. The slight advantages to them of adopting LIFO are more than outweighed by its inconvenience. If inventories are $10,000 at year-end, and cost of goods sold is $500,000 a year, with price-level changes of only 2 or 3 percent a year, how much difference can $200 or $300 more in cost of goods sold make?

Many taxpayers have felt that prices in their particular line would be more likely to decline than to rise. Suppose you were a television wholesaler in 1950. Television prices have tended to fall between then and now–and rather substantially. LIFO would have cost you more tax dollars rather than less.

Other taxpayers simply have not understood how dollar-value LIFO operated, and with the absence of official guidelines, they were reluctant to get involved in what seemed to them a risky business. Until 1961, for example, the Internal Revenue Service did not allow the application of dollar-value LIFO on a business-entity basis, but instead required that the inventory be broken up into homogeneous pools. Thus, the Klein Chocolate Company (see case excerpt) was originally required to have ten different inventory pools. The more inventory pools, the more danger of a substantial reduction taking place during the year in one of these pools, resulting in cost of goods sold being charged with low-cost merchandise purchased many years before. Some of the ambiguity has been eliminated and the matter of pools clarified, much to the taxpayer's advantage, but inventory pools still are a murky area.

Taxpayers have been concerned over the resulting financial statements if they adopted LIFO. Would stockholders understand why profits were lower? Would credit grantors understand that the LIFO inventory shown as a current asset was actually worth a great deal more? Conservatism of accountants and of the SEC has prevented use of such presentations as FIFO under current assets (balanced by a noncurrent liability) and of LIFO on the income statement.

It is interesting to project the long-term effect of adopting LIFO. Imagine a corporation that can earn, after taxes, 7 percent on each dollar available to it, and that has an effective income tax rate of 50 percent. It has an inventory of $1,000,000 at the time it adopts LIFO. Prices increase in a straight line, so that the inventory at the end of year 1 is valued at $1,100,000 under FIFO but still $1,000,000 under LIFO; at the end of year 2 it is valued at $1,200,000 under FIFO but still $1,000,000 under LIFO; and so forth. After 20 years the inventory would have shown $3,000,000 on FIFO, but it is still being carried at $1,000,000 on LIFO. But does this mean that assets are actually shown as $2,000,000 less under LIFO?

Quite the contrary! The corporation has generated from tax savings a cash flow of $50,000 per year, invested to yield 7 percent after taxes and compounding annually. This has been going on for 20 years. It now has somewhere near $2,049,750 more assets under LIFO than it would have had under FIFO. Assuming that the corporation will continue for an indefinite period into the future, it is in almost any real sense $2,049,750 better off.

In fact, close to one-half of the larger corporations are probably using LIFO for some part of their inventories. The 1975 edition of *Accounting Trends and Techniques* (published by the American Institute of C.P.A.'s) reports that 238 of their sample 600 companies were clearly using LIFO at the beginning of 1974. The prevalence of LIFO varies substantially from one line of business to another. Two out of 11 companies engaged in manufacturing meat products used LIFO, although no dairy product company did. [Prices of livestock (the raw material used by a meat packer) have tended to rise over the past few decades, and so the meat packers were among the earliest users of LIFO. In fact, they used LIFO (in the form of the base-stock method) before it was permissible for tax purposes, because it was the opinion of many of their managements that it produced a more meaningful measurement of income in a business where prices fluctuated violently, where inventories were heavy, and where selling prices tended to move up and down with buying prices.] Ten of the 12 department store chains covered used LIFO (shades of Macy's!), but only one of the variety store chains; 22 of 27 petroleum companies used LIFO, but no auto manufacturer.

## MISCELLANEOUS LIFO EFFECTS

One of the little-noticed effects of taxation on inventory decisions is that it encourages a company to recognize obsolescence and value declines in inventories, and thereby it presumably facilitates pruning of the inventory. This results from the tax deductibility of the cost of the item in the year in which it declines in value or is sold or scrapped. If the lower-of-cost-or-market approach is used (mandatory from an accounting standpoint except for dealers in precious metals who may use market, but optional from a tax standpoint if any inventory method other than LIFO is used, and prohibited from a tax standpoint if LIFO is used), the tax benefit is obtained without the disposition of the item. Otherwise, the item must be sold or scrapped in order for the cost to provide a tax deduction.

When LIFO is used, the management of the company acquires substantial control over the amount of profits it will earn and report, both for tax and for accounting purposes. In a year of relatively poor profits, assuming that price levels have generally been rising, management could allow the year-end inventory to decline to a substantial extent. This would have the effect of increasing profits by charging into cost of sales for the current year merchandise carried at costs based on price levels of previous years. On the other hand, if profits appear too high, they can in some LIFO applications be reduced by substantial purchases of inventory right at year-end.

Of course, a management that does not have good control over its inventory levels may find that allowing inventories to run down may have an unexpected impact on profits and, to a lesser extent, that allowing inventories to increase beyond a reasonable level may unexpectedly reduce profits.

*Example:*

Assume that the begining-of-the-year inventory consists of the following LIFO layers:

| | *1975 $* | *Factor* | *LIFO Inventory* |
|---|---|---|---|
| 1975 | $ 30,000 | 100 | $ 30,000 |
| 1976 | 50,000 | 105 | 52,500 |
| 1977 | 20,000 | 120 | 24,000 |
| 1980 | 20,000 | 150 | 30,000 |
| Totals | $120,000 | | $136,500 |

The price level at the end of 1981 is 200 percent of the 1975 price level as to the particular items in this inventory. In terms of 1975 dollars, the inventory shows $120,000 (that is, LIFO cost is still $136,500), and the net profit before tax comes to $100,000.

If management anticipated this year-end situation and wanted to increase this profit, they could allow the inventory at year-end to run down (probably replacing it a few days later). If the inventory was cut in half, the result would be a change in profit of $46,000, or 46 percent before taxes.

Cutting the inventory in half is accomplished by reducing purchasing at year-end. Purchases are, of course, being made in current (1981) dollars. Assume that, if the inventory remained at the level at which the pre-tax profit is $100,000, the "Cost of goods sold" section of the income statement would look like this:

| | |
|---|---|
| Beginning inventory | $ 136,500 |
| Purchases | 2,000,000 |
| Available for sale | $2,136,500 |
| Ending inventory | 136,500 |
| Cost of goods sold | $2,000,000 |

Reducing cost of goods sold increases net profit. Purchases are reduced $120,000 (in 1981 dollars). What happens? Ending inventory is reduced by peeling off the most recently added LIFO layers.

| | *1975 $* | *Factor* | *LIFO Cost* | *1981 $* |
|---|---|---|---|---|
| 1975 | $ 30,000 | 100 | $ 30,000 | $ 60,000 |
| 1976 | 50,000 | 105 | 52,500 | 100,000 |
| 1977 | 20,000 | 120 | 24,000 | 40,000 |
| 1980 | 20,000 | 150 | 30,000 | 40,000 |
| | $120,000 | | $136,500 | $240,000 |

We remove the 1980 and 1977 layers and 40 percent of the 1976 layer:

| | LIFO Cost |
|---|---|
| 1980 | $30,000 |
| 1977 | 24,000 |
| 1976 (40%) | 21,000 |
| | $75,000 |

We have left, in ending inventory, all of the 1975 layer and 60 percent of the 1976 layer:

| | LIFO Cost |
|---|---|
| 1975 | $30,000 |
| 1976 (60%) | 31,500 |
| | $61,500 |

Now look at our cost of goods sold:

| | Old | New |
|---|---|---|
| Beginning inventory | $ 136,500 | $ 136,500 |
| Purchases | 2,000,000 | 1,880,000 |
| Available for sale | $2,136,500 | $2,016,500 |
| Ending inventory | 136,500 | 61,500 |
| Cost of goods sold | $2,000,000 | $1,955,000 |

Our cost of goods sold is now $45,000 less ($2,000,000 – $1,955,000). Our profit, before tax, is $45,000 more. Our $120,000 reduction in purchases reduced the ending inventory (because of the different types of dollars involved) by only $75,000. Our $45,000 profit increase is the result.

## CASE EXCERPTS

The basic "dollar-value" LIFO case–*Hutzler Bros.*, 8 TC 14 (1947)
LIFO pools–*Klein Chocolate Co.*, 36 TC 142 (1961)
What overhead goes into inventory?–*All-Steel Equipment Inc.*, 54 TC 176 (1970)
Is good accounting good taxes? *Thor Power Tool Co.*, 64 TC 154 (1975)

*Hutzler Brothers Company* v. *Commissioner*
8 TC 14 (1947)

Refined to its simplest terms, the fundamental question is whether the identification of specific articles in an inventory is the prerequisite for application of the last-in, first-out method. Respondent's contention that it is seems supported neither by logic nor by legislative intent. His principal reliance, the interpretative regulations, will not withstand examination. Those provisions most nearly dealing with the present question were inserted long after the tax year and, in fact, after the present proceeding had been brought to hearing. Their retroactive application seems unwarranted. All of the regulations are as consistent with petitioner's position as they are with that of respondent. It is simpler and more rewarding to seek the meaning of the statute itself than of ambiguous and largely irrelevant administrative interpretations.

As to the language of the statute, it is urged that the term "goods" is used advisedly and "in the common and ordinary sense." But the dictionary gives as synonyms "wares and merchandise." Wares may have a slightly archaic flavor, but merchandise is a term in the day-to-day vernacular, and it is difficult to conjure up one more accurately describing in the generic sense the stock in trade of a typical department store.

It is true that the legislative history indicates agitation for the amendment which became section 22(d) as having its origin among certain groups of producers for whose special problem the LIFO solution would be particularly appropriate. It is also indicated that in these instances taxpayers followed generally an inventory system which dealt with specific articles, and that they were faced also with the problem of attributing a cost to the articles so ascertained. But it does not follow from this that, when the statute was amended to acquire its present all-embracing character, it was designed to cover only the industries which originally sought its enactment. The conclusion is rather to be drawn that, like all revenue legislation, particularly of a relief character, the purpose of the lawmakers was to have it apply in general terms to all those coming within its provisions.

We have already had occasion to note that the primary characteristic of inventories maintained under the retail method is the use of dollars as the measure of quantity. In a period of radically and rapidly changing price levels, the dollars so attributed to an inventory will be neither the current cost of replacement nor the presumptive level at which the inventory will be diminished by sales. But this is precisely the basic problem faced by the industries to which the legislation was concededly directed. The method of its application in those cases is simple, while with respect to such taxpayers as petitioner it is relatively complex. But, since the fundamental situation to which the provision is directed is identical, and since no portion of its operation or language is inherently inapplicable, it should, if possible, be given effect in all cases presenting the problem with which it deals. It remains to be considered whether the practical impediments to its application are so great as to eliminate the possibility of its use in such situations as that now before us.

The process envisaged by LIFO involves not so much the ascertainment of cost as the ascertainment of what it is of which we are to discover the cost. The last-in, first-out formula assumes that the merchandise remaining in the inventory is that which was first purchased. When that assumption is made, the process of ascertainment becomes difficult in the case of a retail merchant primarily because of the complications of the retail method itself.

If we were dealing with a fabricator or manufacturer, the first step would be to determine which merchandise it is to which a cost is to be attributed, and the second, to determine that cost. The corresponding process engaged in by petitioner is to reduce the price level of the retail stock to that prevailing as of the opening inventory, and thereby to identify the merchandise remaining in inventory at the close of the year as that constituting inventory at the beginning of the year to the extent of the size of the opening inventory. That this is done by dealing with the merchandise stated in terms of dollars rather than of numbers of quantities is a requisite of the aspect of department store accounting which relies for its inventory volume on a statement in dollars alone.

But it will not do to say that this method does not truly reflect a taxpayer's inventory or that the use of dollars instead of other measures of quantity has the effect of distorting the inventory content. The retail method has been used with respondent's complete approval for too long a time for the assumption to be permissible that the contents of an inventory cannot be satisfactorily represented for all purposes by its expression in dollars only; or for the result, to be acceptable, unless entirely necessary, that the use of that method for the statement of an inventory forecloses the user from other benefits.

It is difficult to see that in either . . . the selection of the merchandise constituting the inventory, or the assignment to that merchandise of a cost figure, such violence is done to recognized principles of retail inventory practice as to demonstrate either from principle or application that Congress intended the LIFO provisions to be inapplicable to the accounting procedure of retail merchants. The computations involved may be somewhat extensive, but they lack neither adequate clarity nor logic, and they cannot be discarded as unduly burdensome in the light of the permissive character of the statutory option. We conclude that adaptation of the LIFO theory to inventories maintained in terms of dollars through the approach generally employed by the present petitioner is permissible and proper within the provisions of section 22(d).

## DISSENTING OPINION

In my opinion, the method prescribed contemplates some physical matching of goods on hand at the end of the year with goods on hand at the beginning of the year, and, as near as I am able to determine, the majority opinion does not deny that such is the intendment of the statute, the conclusion being, however, that a matching of dollars as of the beginning and the end of the year constitutes compliance with the statute even though there is no attempt to show any matching of goods and the number of dollars matched is arrived at by indulging in assumptions on assumptions which "may, and generally do," vary from the facts. Such assumptions are indulged in both as to cost and as to the goods themselves. To illustrate: The retail method of inventory itself assumes the cost of goods on hand to be the listed retail price reduced by the use of a factor which represents the average "mark-on" made on goods during the year but without regard to the actual cost of the specific goods which constitute the closing inventory. Next, for the purposes of applying section 22(d), it is assumed that the goods are fungible and that those on hand at the end of the year are of the same type and quality as the goods on hand at the beginning of the year, while admitting that they "may, and generally do, differ considerably as to type, quality, and price." By this method, which the majority opinion approves, the petitioner arrives at a "cost" for the goods in his closing inventory which, though it may not even approximate, is assumed to have been, the cost of such goods on hand at the beginning of the year, and this, even though in fact there may not have been any such goods on hand at the beginning of the year. Such indulging in assumption on assumption, or piling of fiction on fiction, does not in my opinion result in an inventory reflecting facts or actualities, and the use of such a method does not offer any assurance that there will be anything approximating a clear reflection of income. The fact that inventory by the last-in, first-out method permits the indulgence in one assumption, namely, that goods in the closing inventory may be listed at the cost price of the first of such goods on hand during the taxable year, is not, in my opinion, to be regarded as a license to indulge in fiction to the extent here approved.

*Klein Chocolate Company* v. *Commissioner*
36 TC 142 (1961)

> In its 1942 return, the petitioner elected to change its method of pricing goods for inventory purposes from the first-in, first-out method to the dollar-value last-in, first-out method, using a single pool or classification for the goods covered. It consistently adhered to that method for pricing its inventories beginning with 1942 and through the years 1946 and 1947, the taxable years herein. The respondent examined petitioner's returns for 1942, 1943, and 1944. He was fully advised as to the method by which the inventories were reported and approved them without change.

...We are persuaded that the respondent's determination is more an expression of preference for the use of 10 pools or classifications of goods, particularly for the years herein, over the single pool consistently used by petitioner and heretofore approved by him than a determination that petitioner's consistent use of a single pool or classification will not reasonably reflect income in the long run. We find nothing in the regulations relating to the change to and use of the last-in, first-out method of taking inventory to indicate that there was any intention on the part of the respondent that the said regulation should be regarded as changing or modifying the long-standing rule that greater weight is to be given to consistency than to any particular method of taking inventory or basis of valuation. Since in the case of this petitioner the use of the single pool or classification has been approved by the respondent as proper and as clearly reflecting income and it has consistently been used by the petitioner in the pricing of his goods for inventory purposes, we conclude and hold that the respondent was in error in determining the deficiencies herein through the use of multiple pools or classifications.

A motion was filed on January 23, 1961, for entry for decision for petitioner on the ground that the respondent in T. D. 6539, approved January 16, 1961, 1961-1 C. B. 167, has accepted and approved the proposition that the use of a single pool or classification for inventory purposes by a taxpayer engaged in a manufacturing business such as that of this petitioner is correct and proper and will clearly reflect income. For the purposes here, it is sufficient to say that the Treasury decision in question was promulgated under and pursuant to section 472 of the Internal Revenue Code of 1954 and by its terms it is limited to "taxable years beginning after December 31, 1953, and ending after August 16, 1954, except where otherwise provided." We find nothing in the portion of the Treasury decision relied upon to indicate that it was to be applicable to any taxable year prior to the earliest year specified. We accordingly leave the question of applicability of T. D. 6539 in cases such as this for consideration in a case for a year to which by its terms it is applicable.

*All-Steel Equipment Inc.* v. *Commissioner*
54 TC 176 (1970)

> The [taxpayer] consistently valued its inventory by use of the prime cost method, including in inventory only the cost of direct labor and materials. The I.R.S. determined that such method did not clearly reflect . . . income and that inventory should be valued by use of the full absorption method.

When the question of the use of the prime cost method has come before the courts, its use has been disapproved. *Photo-Sonics, Inc.,* v. *Commissioner,* 357 F.2d 656 [17 AFTR 2d 582] (C.A. 9, 1966), affg. 42 T.C. 926 (1964); *Dearborn Gage Co.,* 48 T.C. 190 (1967); *Frank G. Wikstrom & Sons, Inc.,* 20 T.C. 359 (1953). See also *Fort Howard Paper Co., supra.* Thus, in the light of the unequivocal position of the AICPA, the regulations, and the court precedents, prime costing, in the abstract, must be recognized as an erroneous method for valuing inventories.

Next, we turn to the argument on which the petitioner relies heavily. It argues that as a practical matter, the prime cost method clearly reflects its income since it has consistently used such method over many years and its taxable income computed under such method does not materially differ from its taxable income resulting from the use of the method proposed by the respondent. In support of such argument, the petitioner has produced certain accountants' reports and has called expert witnesses whose professional stature is impressive and who testified that under the circumstances of this case the petitioner's method would clearly reflect its income for purposes of commercial accounting. In addition, the petitioner argues that its position is supported by the income tax regulations and the legal precedents. The case has been thoroughly and exceptionally well prepared, but after considerable deliberation, we have concluded that the petitioner's position is unacceptable.

The petitioner relies on the fact that since 1933, it has been audited yearly by independent public accounting firms. So far as we can tell, none of the reports resulting from such audits has taken serious exception to the petitioner's method of costing inventories. Most of the reports state unqualifiedly that the financial statements of the petitioner fairly reflect its financial condition and the results of the operations, in conformity with generally accepted accounting principles. Some of the reports, which state the same general conclusion, specifically note the conservative method by which the petitioner valued inventory, but state that such valuation did not materially affect income. Other reports indicate that the petitioner's method of valuing inventory was not in accordance with generally accepted accounting prinicples. However, such reports do not specifically disapprove the petitioner's valuation method and we have concluded that the accountants believed that even though the petitioner departed from generally accepted accounting principles, such departure did not prevent the petitioner's financial statement from fairly reflecting the results of operations. All of the reports available to us for examination disclose in some way that the petitioner included only direct labor and materials in inventory cost.

In addition to the accountants' reports, the petitioner's expert witnesses testified that its method of accounting clearly reflected income. None of these witnesses, however, stated that prime costing was a generally accepted accounting procedure. Rather, their testimony was posited on the belief that no material distortion of income resulted from prime costing in the facts of this case.

Although we accept the fact that the petitioner's method of accounting fairly reflected the results of its operations for commercial accounting purposes, we do not think its departure from applicable generally accepted accounting principles and tax regulations can be justified for tax purposes on the argument that the errors were not material. Since it is clear that prime costing is not a generally accepted accounting procedure, the opinions of public accountants adduced in favor of the petitioner's position must rest on the accounting doctrine of materiality. Such doctrine finds broad application in commercial accounting, but we do not think it may appropriately be extended to the law of taxation in cases in which the taxpayer's method of accounting is clearly erroneous.

The objective of the method of valuing inventories is to assign to such inventories the cost of their production; thus, in a later year when the inventories are sold, the income resulting therefrom may be offset by the costs of producing such goods. The use of an improper method for valuing inventories involves the risk of distorting income by failing to offset against the income from the sale of the inventories the expenses properly attributable thereto. For a year in which the inventory expands, the use of the prime cost method results in an understatement of income; whereas, its use causes an overstatement of income when there is a decrease in the inventory. For example, according to the table presented by the petitioner, the use of the prime cost method caused an understatement of income for 10 of the 14 years and an overstatement of income in only 4 of the years. That table also shows that, even though the prime cost method was used consistently, the errors resulting from its use were not eliminated. What is more, the continued use of an erroneous method involves the risk that it will produce a much greater error in a later year, especially if the petitioner's business should increase significantly.

We have already stated our reasons for concluding that the accountants' attitude toward mistakes considered immaterial by them is not acceptable for tax purposes. Furthermore, there is no legal basis for permitting the petitioner to continue to use an erroneous method merely because of the smallness of the amounts of income not reported in the years before us; and there is surely no basis for holding that the petitioner may continue to use such method until a year in which it does result in the underreporting of larger amounts of income.

*Thor Power Tool Co.*
64 TC 154 (1975)

The adjustments to 1964 ending inventory. . . . consist of the following:

(1) A downward valuation of $744,030 due to excess items computed by petitioner based primarily on 1964 usage of the items;

(2) A downward valuation of $160,832 due to excess items based upon flat percentages applied to inventories at the LaGrange Park and Cincinnati plants where usage information was not available; and

(3) A downward valuation of $22,090 to reflect amortization of parts and accessories stocked for tools no longer manufactured by petitioner.

All three of the above-described procedures were employed by petitioner to reduce the value of the 1964 ending inventory to what petitioner considered to be the net realizable value. All three of the procedures were designed to write down the value because there were units on hand which management deemed to be in excess of the *future* needs of petitioner's business. There was no segregation of the inventory which management determined to be excessive.

. . . Petitioner contends that there is no specific statutory authority contrary to the general requirements of sections 446 and 471 of the Code which require the valuation of inventory to be in accordance with generally accepted accounting principles and to clearly reflect income. Petitioner produced distinguished members of the accounting profession who testified that the inventory valuation methods employed by petitioner were in accordance with generally accepted accounting principles and thoroughly convinced us that such was the case. A write-down of inventory for excessive stock in this case was not merely desirable for accounting purposes, it was required in order to produce a certified balance sheet. Petitioner has, therefore, amply demonstrated that the write-down of inventory was in accordance with generally accepted accounting principles and within the term, "best accounting practice," as that term is used in section 471 of the Code and the regulations promulgated under that section. However, petitioner must also show that the method clearly reflects taxable income. . . .

Two sections of the Code are involved: section 446 because the valuation of inventory constitutes a method of accounting and section 471 because that section grants authority to the Commissioner to prescribe the method for taking inventories. The sections will be discussed together because both contain the requirement that the inventory method must clearly reflect income.

Sections 446 and 471 impose a heavy burden of proof on petitioner. We described that burden as follows in *All-Steel Equipment Co.,* 54 T.C. 1749, 1761 (1970), affd. on this issue 467 F. 2d 1184 (7th Cir. 1972):

> The wording of sections 446(b) and 471 makes clear that, in matters of accounting methods, the respondent is invested with broad discretion. If a taxpayer's method of accounting does not clearly reflect income, the respondent may compute income "under such method as, in *** [his] opinion *** does clearly reflect income." Sec. 446(b). More specifically, section 471 provides that "inventories shall be taken *** on such basis *as the Secretary or his delegate may prescribe* as conforming as nearly as may be to the best accounting practice in the trade or business and as most clearly reflecting the income." These provisions have been a part of our tax law for many years, and they have been interpreted as imposing an extremely heavy burden of proof on taxpayers challenging the respondent's determinations–the Supreme Court has gone so far as to require a showing that such determinations are "plainly arbitrary." *Lucas* v. *Structural Steel Co.,* 281 U.S. 264 (1930). See also *Photo-Sonics, Inc.* v. *Commissioner, supra; Finance & Guaranty Co.* v. *Commissioner,* 50 F.2d 1061 (C.A. 4, 1931), affirming 19 B.T.A. 1313 (1930); *Commissioner* v. *Joseph E. Seagram & Sons, Inc.* 394 F.2d 738 (C.A. 2, 1968), reversing 46 T.C. 698 (1966). *** [Emphasis supplied.]

Proof that the method is in accordance with generally accepted accounting principles does not also prove that the method clearly reflects income under the income tax law. . . . We hold that the adjustments of $926,952 to ending inventory on December 31, 1964, did not result in a clear reflection of taxable income for petitioner's taxable year 1964. . . .

## QUESTIONS AND PROBLEMS

1. A condensed income statement of the Nite Corporation which uses the same accounting procedures for financial accounting as it does for tax accounting, shows:

| | | |
|---|---|---|
| Sales | | $5,000,000 |
| Cost of goods sold: | | |
| Beginning inventory | $ 400,000 | |
| Purchases | 6,000,000 | |
| Available for sale | 6,400,000 | |
| Ending inventory | 2,400,000 | 4,000,000 |
| Gross margin | | $1,000,000 |
| Operating expenses | $ 900,000 | |
| Federal income tax | 48,000 | 948,000 |
| Net profit | | $ 52,000 |

How much will ending inventory have to be changed, and in which direction for there to be no net profit?

*2. The Brill Department Store's records show the following:

| | Cost | Retail |
|---|---|---|
| Sales | | $1,550,000 |
| Opening inventory | $ 400,000 | 600,000 |
| Purchases | 1,050,000 | 1,400,000 |
| Ending inventory | | 450,000 |

Using the retail method of inventory, what is Brill's closing inventory at cost?

3. The Specialty Store has decided to adopt LIFO as of January 1, 1978. A mark-up of 33 1/3 percent on selling price is consistently maintained. The December 31, 1978, price level is 110 percent of that of January 1, 1978, according to data furnished for this purpose by the Bureau of Labor Statistics (BLS). The January 1, 1978, inventory, at retail, was $60,000. The December 31, 1978, inventory, at retail, was $99,000. Compute the LIFO inventory at January 1, 1978, and December 31, 1978. If the tax rate

is 48 percent, how much tax will the Specialty Store save by adopting LIFO?

*4. The Gizmo Manufacturing Company adopted LIFO as of January 1, 1978, using the double-extension method. Its January 1, 1978, inventory was $20,000. The December 31, 1978, inventory was $30,000 in terms of January 1, 1978, prices and $40,000 in terms of December 31, 1978, prices. Compute the December 31, 1978, LIFO inventory. At a 48 percent tax rate how much tax will Gizmo save by being on LIFO?

5. A company anticipates that it is able to earn 10 percent after taxes on all capital it can obtain. It is in a 50 percent tax bracket and is contemplating adopting LIFO. Assume that inventories will remain constant in physical terms, but that prices will advance a constant percentage of the price level in the starting year (that is, in an arithmetic progression and not in a geometric progression). What rate of price rise per year would be necessary for the company's balance sheet to show the same total assets 10 years after adopting LIFO as it would show if it stayed on FIFO?

6. The Ward Manufacturing Company is a family-owned corporation whose financial statements are mainly for bank credit purposes. It uses LIFO for inventory purposes. At December 31, 1978, some of the pertinent information concerning its inventory would include:

| | |
|---|---|
| Cost, 12/31/78 price levels | $2,425,000 |
| Cost, if on FIFO | 2,410,000 |
| LIFO cost | 1,635,000 |
| Value in a forced liquidation (which is a highly unlikely event) | 1,900,000 |

The Ward Manufacturing Company is in a 50 percent tax bracket. Show some of the alternative balance-sheet presentations that could be made of the inventory, indicating for each its acceptability for accounting and for tax purposes as well as its utility in communicating the pertinent information to the statement reader. For each, indicate the cost concept that would be used in computing income.

7. "Accounting LIFO tends to show inventory valuations at the lowest prices that have been experienced since LIFO was adopted, whereas tax LIFO perpetuates the prices in effect at the time LIFO is adopted." Why does this difference result?

8. In which of the following businesses would you think that methods of inventory valuation would be most important and least important?

   (a) A manufacturer who produces only to order and has a production cycle of approximately 1 week. Raw materials are ordered only for specific customer orders.

(b) A meat packer who must maintain a constant flow of inventory, from animals headed for slaughter through finished goods in storage in large warehouses.

(c) A wholesaler of fresh fruit and produce, whose inventory turns over on the average, every 4 days.

(d) A wholesaler of eggs who sometimes has the equivalent of 3 or 4 months of sales in cold storage waiting for the next phase in the seasonal market, and who sometimes has nothing in storage.

(e) A manufacturer of standardized heavy equipment, whose manufacturing process requires over a year from start to finish, and who may take an additional year to sell the equipment.

9. Why would an increase in the number of inventory pools decrease the utility of LIFO to a taxpayer? Construct an example to illustrate your answer.
10. The financial statements, and particularly the reported earnings, constitute yardsticks for measuring management achievement. Achievement may be measured against past performance, against budgeted targets, or against industry ratios. Assume that during a period of prosperity, management is inspired to more intensive effort when company profits fail to grow as rapidly as the level of economic activity, and that during periods of business decline the ability to maintain a better-than-average earnings structure reassures management and prevents it from losing faith in its own judgment and the inherent soundness of the economy. Which method of inventory valuation–FIFO, average cost, or LIFO–would be most inclined to lead to optimum management performance?
11. You are director of industrial relations for a firm that has a profit-sharing plan covering all employees. The company is contemplating changing from FIFO to LIFO. Would you have any valid interest in discussing this proposed change with the controller?
12. Contrast the views of tax LIFO expressed in the majority and dissenting opinions in the Tax Court's *Hutzler Brothers* decision (excerpt at end of chapter).
13. What is the single most important factor in accounting for inventories for tax purposes, according to the *Klein Chocolate Company* decision (excerpt at end of chapter)?
14. Hercules Manufacturing Company has just completed the bargain purchase of the Apollo Manufacturing Company which had become insolvent because its inventory was allowed to expand beyond its financial capabilities. Apollo will be continued as a manufacturing division of Hercules. The inventory purchased cost $200,000, although its replacement cost would be nearer $700,000. Much of the material involved is relatively slow-moving, and there are few companies that utilize exactly the sizes and shapes used by

Apollo–hence the extreme discrepancy between cost and ultimate value. The Hercules controller is concerned that within the next 2 years, as the materials purchased are processed and sold, Hercules will have to report for tax purposes $500,000 of profit that he would like to avoid paying taxes on, if possible. Can LIFO offer any help to Hercules in this situation?

15. Contrast the weight accorded consistency in *Klein Chocolate* with the weight given it in *All-Steel.* Why the difference?
16. Is absorption costing necessarily the same thing in valuing inventories for tax as it is for accounting purposes, per *All-Steel*?
17. Looking at the *Thor* and *All-Steel* cases, would you say that the same standards are to be applied for tax as for financial reporting purposes in determining inventory valuations? Explain.
18. Construct an example to illustrate that a company on LIFO may be able to cut its taxable income by making year-end purchases.

# 17

# Corporate Organizations, Reorganizations, Distributions, and Liquidations

The life of a corporation is in some respects similar to the life of an individual. If we wanted to know about the life of a person who lived in a culture alien to ours, we could gain a certain amount of insight by merely studying the experiences of one individual, picked at random, in that culture.

We are going to study the things that happen to a hypothetical corporation and thereby glean some idea of the tax-law provisions that affect certain key areas of corporate life. The areas that we are interested in have relatively little to do with the business of the corporation; they are concerned with the business of *being* a corporation.

## BIRTH OF A CORPORATION

On October 5, 1969, Tom Warren and Jim McCall met with their lawyer and their C.P.A. Warren and McCall were partners in a small construction operation and had heard that if they incorporated, they might save some taxes. Their 1969 income was already so large that the size of the tax bill they would face had them scared. But they were equally afraid of the complexities of corporate life.

"A small corporation operates much like a partnership," their lawyer assured them. "Things are a little more formal, but your day-by-day business operations are no different. Even your name can be the same as it is now–the W & M Construction Company."

"Pretty expensive, ain't it?" grunted McCall.

"You know better than I that cost is relative," said the C.P.A. "You'll pay maybe \$600 to get the corporation formed and the initial paperwork done. Your annual fee to the state will run \$100. It may cost you \$200 to \$400 more a year for accounting services. But if you keep on the way you're going, the income tax saving through the corporation will run you $10,000 to $15,000 a year, which will help you expand your business much more rapidly."

And so the W & M Construction Corporation was born—with taxes for its father and red tape for its mother. The partnership transferred all its assets to the new corporation. The C.P.A. prepared a listing of these assets:

| | *Tax Basis* | *Market Value* |
|---|---|---|
| Cash | $ 1,000 | $ 1,000 |
| Contracts receivable | 25,000 | 25,000 |
| Work in process | 10,000 | 20,000 |
| Machinery and equipment | 5,000 | 50,000 |
| Total assets | $ 41,000 | $ 96,000 |
| Note payable to bank | 20,000 | 20,000 |
| Stockholders' investment | $ 21,000 | $ 76,000 |

"Does this mean we're each getting $38,000 worth of stock?" asked Warren, quite impressed. The partnership balance sheet, prepared from the tax return, showed he had a net worth of only $10,500.

"That's right," said the C.P.A.

Warren pondered this for a minute. "Is my gain capital gain or something?"

"Your gain isn't recognized for tax purposes," explained the C.P.A. "There's a provision in the tax law that if property is transferred to a corporation solely for stock or other securities, and immediately after the transfer the people who transferred the property own 80 percent or more of the corporate stock, then the tax law will treat you as though you had simply taken something from one pocket and put it into another. There will be no tax right then. However, the corporation will ultimately have to pay the tax. If the corporation sold that equipment right now for $50,000, there would be a gain of $45,000 on the corporate tax return. If the corporation hangs onto the equipment, it will have to base its depreciation on a cost of $5,000. Either way, the government doesn't lose anything; and you're able to shift your business over to a corporation without their trying to tax you as though you had sold your business, since all you've really done is to change its legal form."

## ACQUISITION OF A SUBSIDIARY

During the next two years, the W & M Construction Corporation far surpassed its owners' hopes. The corporation was able to acquire a brick building of its own and build up a small but capable headquarters staff. When large contracts were under way, cash sometimes became a little tight but the company had good bank contacts and was always able to borrow whatever it needed to keep on a current basis with the various subcontractors and suppliers it dealt with.

One of these suppliers was the Humphrey Lumber Company. Humphrey operated a retail lumberyard but depended primarily on contractors for its business. Pushed by competition to offer substantial discounts from retail prices and to extend liberal credit terms, Humphrey was in bad financial trouble. Some of its sources were shipping to it only on a C.O.D. (cash on delivery) basis.

McCall knew old Mr. Humphrey, who still controlled most of the corporate stock even though his son ran the business. McCall felt that W & M would be in an advantageous position with its own lumberyard, particularly in view of the steady increase in prefabrication of sections in much of the mass-residential construction that W & M was getting into. A firm hand at the credit helm, a little more backbone when it came to holding the line on price, and sharper buying practices could turn Humphrey into a strong operation, McCall felt.

After talking to Warren, he sounded out old Mr. Humphrey. W & M could not come up with much cash, but cash wasn't what Humphrey wanted, anyway. First, he was anxious not to have to pay any income tax on the sale. Although the book value of his stock in the lumber company was over $1 million, his original investment in the stock 50 years before had been only $5,000. Next, he wanted to have a steady income of around $50,000 per year coming in to his family. Then he wanted some assurance that his son would continue to have a job.

McCall had lunch the next day with the C.P.A. and spread the situation out for him to look at.

"Sort of like a midget wanting to marry a six-foot beauty queen," said the C.P.A. "You guys have a net worth of $600,000 and you're trying to swallow Humphrey with his million dollars!"

"Don't give me that," said McCall. "You know better than me that it's not net worth that counts at all. It's what you can earn. We can earn $400,000 next year. Humphrey would give his lower plate just to break even. Besides, he's stuck with slow-turning inventory and dead-beat receivables."

"You have all the answers," said the C.P.A. "What do you want from me?"

"We can make a deal if it costs the old man nothing in taxes, but he has to be sure he'll get $50,000 a year and a job for his boy. You tell me–what kind of a deal can I make him?"

The C.P.A. pursed his lips. "This is pretty complicated, you know. I'm just talking off the top of my head. Whatever I say, I'll have to get back to the office and check out pretty carefully." McCall nodded.

"First thing," the C.P.A. said, "for this to be tax-free to Humphrey, he has to get stock in W & M, and nothing else. We could set it up as a merger and make it nonvoting preferred stock."

"No." said McCall, "I'm sure the old boy would insist on having his say."

"Okay, then, let's make it voting preferred, and put a high enough basic dividend rate on it to give him his $50,000. You guys between you now have 7,600 shares of $10-par stock. This gives you 7,600 votes. We could make Humphrey's preferred a $100-par stock, paying, say, $10 a share in cumulative preferred dividends and then participating with the common on any dividends on common. He would get 5,000 shares. This would give him stock with a par value of $500,000, which might make him happy. We could increase the stock you have through a tax-free stock dividend of common on common. A 100 percent stock dividend would give you another 7,600 shares and a total of 15,200 votes to Humphrey's 5,000."

"You work it up as a proposal and give it to me in nice, neat form," said McCall. "I suppose we simply agree to take care of the son."

"Something like that," said the C.P.A. "Key thing on this tax-free bit is to think through what you want to do. You can go ahead and get his stock from old man Humphrey, and keep operating the lumberyard as a separate corporation, a subsidiary of W & M. Or you could swap your preferred with the corporation itself, getting its assets and leaving it with the stock. Then the corporation would liquidate and distribute the W & M stock to Humphrey. Or an even simpler way would be to just merge Humphrey into W & M, with W & M being the surviving corporation and the old man getting his preferred."

"Better keep it operating separately," McCall said. "In fact, it'd probably be best for both the lumberyard and the construction business if it wasn't smarted around about our being connected. There's some guys we bid against might not feel like doing business at the lumberyard if they knew they were really doing business with W & M."

The plan for acquisition of the Humphrey stock was easy enough to lay out over a luncheon table. But the W & M lawyer had to draft five versions of the exchange agreement before everyone was satisfied. Humphrey made the whole deal contingent on getting a ruling from the Internal Revenue Service that the exchange of his Humphrey common for the W & M preferred would be tax-free. The ruling took three months to get. Finally, all the paperwork was done. W & M owned its first subsidiary! And the son, whose job old Mr. Humphrey had fought so hard to preserve, resigned the day after the exchange.

"I just hung around here because I figured the old man needed me," he told an astounded Warren—then headed for New York, where he shipped out as a radioman on a British merchant ship.

## THE CONSOLIDATED-RETURN QUESTION

The W & M fiscal year ended June 30, whereas Humphrey's fiscal year ended March 31. The acquisition of the Humphrey stock took place on January 10.

"The way that operation's been going, and the amount of business you've been doing with them, I think we ought to close their year right now," said the C.P.A., "and plan on having them switch to a June 30 year and file a consolidated return with you."

"I don't follow you," complained Warren.

"They're operating at a loss," explained the C.P.A. "Unfortunately, this isn't their first loss year. We can't get any benefits from carrying their loss back, since there aren't any profitable years open that haven't already had their profits soaked up by losses. They'll probably continue operating at a loss for at least a while. W & M gets no tax benefit out of even these current losses unless it files a return that combines the income and expenses of both W & M and Humphrey. Then, Humphrey's losses can be used to absorb part of W & M's profits."

McCall asked, "How about the old Humphrey losses? Are those just wasted?"

"That's up to you. Humphrey's losses can be carried over against any profits Humphrey may earn after your acquisition."

Warren spoke up again. "This filing a consolidated return, is this something that we can do just this year and then drop next year if it doesn't work out?"

The C.P.A. shook his head. "No. An election to file a consolidated return is purely voluntary; the government can't force you to compute your income on a consolidated basis. But once you make the election, it will be very tough to break it. You must get permission from the Treasury Department to change the election, and they won't grant permission unless there's a change in the tax law making it more expensive to file on a consolidated basis."

"What if we get some more companies?"

"A new company won't help break the consolidated election. It could have before the law changed, but now any new company would be included in the consolidated return, together with W & M and all the other corporations in which it owns 80 percent or more of the stock. This group is what actually files the consolidated return, with the return being prepared in the name of the parent corporation of the group." The C.P.A. paused to see if they followed his explanation.

"One other thing," he finally went on. "The consolidated return doesn't reflect any profit on transactions between members of the group. This means that if you buy as much from Humphrey as you have in the past, and if your June 30 work-in-process inventory is as high as it seems it's going to be, a consolidated return will result in quite a lot of intercompany profit being eliminated."

A comparison showed that on a separate-return basis, W & M would have $450,000 of taxable income and Humphrey would have a post-acquisition loss of $3,000. However, the W & M work-in-process of $1,050,000 included $350,000 worth of material purchased from Humphrey since the acquisition, on which the average gross-profit margin to Humphrey was 18 percent; and so a consolidated return would result in W & M's having a taxable income of only $384,000. With a corporate tax rate of 48 percent on income over $50,000, this meant a saving in taxes of $31,680 for the year. Therefore, a consolidated return was filed.

## A STOCK REDEMPTION

In the aftermath of President Nixon's 1972 election victory, McCall was asked to take a major post in the Department of Housing and Urban Development. Frustrated by wage and price controls, environmental impact reports, and endless mountains of paper work as well as by miles of red tape, he decided to accept. "Better to give the ulcers than to get them," he explained.

Warren hired a young C.P.A. named Carlson as a full-time controller to cope with all the complexities. Then the mortgage money started to dry up, even while skyrocketing prices were driving prospective home buyers out of the single family market in which W & M had done so well.

Back in town on a speaking tour, McCall and Warren had a meeting on future plans. It became clear that Warren would be happier if McCall didn't come back. McCall was willing to bow out of the company–but only at a price.

"How much?" asked Warren.

The price McCall came up with, $750,000, stunned him. "In my tax bracket, I couldn't hardly live long enough to get that much together."

"Take it from the corporation," McCall suggested. "It has plenty of cash right now. I'll take $250,000 cash, and the balance in a note payable $100,000 a year for 5 years."

The controller, Carlson, suggested that instead of Warren's buying the stock, the corporation actually be the purchaser. "With 15,200 shares of common out, plus 5,000 shares of preferred, even half the common still represents control."

"Furthermore, if we lower the cash payment to $220,000, you should be able to report this as an installment sale, since the down payment will then be less than 30 percent of the redemption price. Under the installment method, you need pay a tax only when the notes are paid on the amount of the installment that represents the pro rata portion of the profit."

But Carlson was afraid the Internal Revenue Service might argue that Warren had received a constructive dividend when the corporation redeemed McCall's stock. "Actually," he pointed out, "we get almost the same effect as if you got a cash dividend from the corporation, which would be fully taxable to you, and then you used it to buy the stock. Either way, you wind up owning 100 percent of the common stock." Carlson also wanted reassurance that McCall could get capital gains treatment and also use the installment method.

Carlson and the company's lawyer huddled on this question and finally decided that the risk was too great unless they first obtained an advance ruling from the Internal Revenue Service.

"And service is what we got!" exclaimed the lawyer jubilantly, as he showed Warren the ruling approving capital gains and installment treatment for McCall and no taxability at all for Warren.

"If this is a sample of tax planning," said Warren, "I'm all for it."

## A PROPERTY DIVIDEND

Now that he owned 100 percent of the common stock, Warren's attitude toward the corporation started subtly to change. Before, he had viewed it as being entirely separate and apart from himself. Even when he had used his secretary and corporate envelopes and stamps for personal correspondence, he had felt a twinge of guilt. Now, however, it was all his.

Carlson rode herd on him, trying to separate personal items charged to the corporation from business items. Sometimes this amused Warren, but after a few months it started to get under his skin. The big blow-up came over the Wisconsin resort property.

"You told me this was for corporate use when we bought it last year," complained Carlson. "It's on our books, but it seems to me that all you use it for is your family and friends. How can I justify taking depreciation on the building?"

"I said it'd be a good investment for the corporation," said Warren icily. "We paid $12,000 for it, and it's worth $25,000 today. I call that a good investment, even if you don't." Seeing that Carlson was unmoved by his argument, he stood up and leaned over the desk toward him. "Take it off the corporate books. Transfer the title over to me personally. And while you're transferring things, you might even start thinking about transferring jobs. You're getting so particular, I swear I'm afraid to take a drink at the water cooler if I've worked up a sweat that wasn't on company time!"

So W & M paid a property dividend to Warren, and Carlson found a job that paid $5,000 a year more. The property had a tax basis of $11,260 to the corporation, and the dividend reduced the corporation's retained earnings by this amount. Even though the fair market value of the property was estimated to be $25,000, no corporate income resulted from its distribution. Of course, Warren had $25,000 of dividend income to report on his personal income tax return.

"Blowing up like that sure was expensive," he told his C.P.A. at tax-return preparation time.

"You won't really know how expensive until you start missing Carlson," grunted the C.P.A.

## PUBLIC UNDERWRITING

By 1976, Warren's need for cash from the corporation had reached the point where his salary of $75,000 was inadequate. He seemed to be attracted to bad investments like steel filings to a magnet. He started out small, but with each loss he grew a little more frantic and thus plunged more heavily on the next get-rich-quick scheme that came along. It wasn't the money; he wanted mainly to vindicate his judgment.

"I've heard of deals where guys get money out of their corporations at capital gains rates," he told the lawyer. "They pay a dividend of preferred on common, sell the preferred to an insurance company, and then have their corporation redeem the preferred."

The lawyer checked into this with the C.P.A. and reported back that this particular loophole had been closed by the 1954 tax law.

Ultimately, Warren was back. This time he had a complete deal all worked out for a public underwriting.

"This is what is known as a secondary," he told the lawyer, who listened politely and diplomatically failed to tell Warren that he had been on the legal staff of the Securities and Exchange Commission for four years in his earlier career. "They take part of my stock," said Warren, "and sell it to investors all over the country. I get a check, and my gain is capital gain. Also, with a market for W & M stock, I can sell off any of the rest of my stock any time I want to raise more cash. And with a stock that has a market, we'll be able to pick up smaller companies by trading them our marketable stock, tax free, for their locked-in stock."

"In order to get enough shares, we can capitalize all our retained earnings and issue a common-stock dividend to you," the lawyer said. "There is only one thing that bothers me. I heard there might be some new rules that make a common-stock dividend taxable."

After checking with the C.P.A., the lawyer reported back that there could be a tax on dividends of common stock issued to common stockholders when such dividends increased the proportionate interest of the common stockholders, if at the same time another class of stock was paid cash dividends. "In our case," said the lawyer, "since the preferred stock will have to get its share of the dividend, the interest of the common stockholders will not be increased by the stock dividend. Accordingly, a stock dividend to you would not be taxable."

So the corporation capitalized all its retained earnings through a common stock dividend. Warren sold 60 percent of his stock to the underwriting syndicate, and soon he was able to look in *The Wall Street Journal* and see price quotations for W & M. The C.P.A. groused a bit about the fact that the high expenses of registering the stock were not deductible to the corporation. He thought that maybe these should actually have been paid by Warren and was afraid that the Internal Revenue Service might consider them to be a dividend to Warren. But he decided to worry about that if and when the problem arose.

## LOSSES AND NEW MANAGEMENT

Warren was now a financier, engaged in manipulating capital structures and investigating proposed acquisitions. The business of W & M was left to fend for itself. Volume stayed up, but somehow profits disappeared and losses took their place.

"We have to shade our bids to get the work," the construction estimators reported at one of Warren's infrequent staff meetings. Warren had to admit the justice of that observation.

"When you face low bids and high costs like we've been facing them," groused the construction supervisors, "you simply can't come out."

The Humphrey Lumber Company reported a nice profit. "Made mainly from their sales to us," complained the W & M purchasing agent.

1977 proved worse than 1976; 1978 was a shambles; 1979, a catastrophe. The W & M stock started skidding, then dived almost straight down, while Warren tried to tighten up operations. He retained an industrial psychologist to review his key men and make recommendations for changes. The key recommendation was to promote Warren to chairman of the board and get in a hard-nosed professional manager as president!

This was easier said than done. The man they finally hired, Cliff Englewood, drove a hard bargain. Warren was to get out of the office and show up only for board meetings. Englewood got a salary, a profit-sharing bonus, and a bargain stock purchase deal that would make him independently wealthy if he could get the W & M stock back up to where it had once been.

During the first 6 months, he shook up the purchasing department at W & M. Firm bids were obtained from suppliers as the basis for W & M's bids; but now, once W & M had a contract in hand, it went back to its bidders and started playing them off against one another until a rock-bottom price was reached. "If you can't skin 4 percent off the low bid once you have a contract, you don't belong around here!"

Anguished phone calls besieged Warren. But when he called Englewood, he was bluntly told to go fishing and stop listening to anything except the quarterly financial statements.

Englewood also went out and purchased a profit-making electronics manufacturer. "We've got to give this thing glamor," he said. "Besides, we have those operating-loss carryovers to soak up. The sooner we do it, the better." The corporate name was changed to Mid-American Industries.

In the meantime, old Mr. Humphrey continued to draw his $50,000 a year in dividends on his preferred stock. The corporate losses only made him smile. When the corporation had neither current earnings nor retained earnings left from prior years, his $50,000 a year would become a tax-free recovery of capital to the extent of his basis. Whatever happened there was a silver lining.

At his desk in Washington, James McCall pored over the PERT schedules for the low-cost housing project he was developing. Later in the evening, he would work over the monthly report from his stockbroker. The $750,000 from his W & M stock had all been invested in solid growth stocks that now had a market value of over $1,000,000. He felt sort of sorry for Tom Warren. He'd heard things were going poorly with him. Running a business was a rough grind, all right.

His musing was interrupted by the arrival of the German economist, the British geologist, the Chinese wholesaler, the Indonesian lawyer, and the retired Dutch Merchant Marine captain who made up his weekly poker group.

## LOSSES AND MERGER

Englewood's driving tactics paid off in the construction business, but the electronics company proved to be a lemon of the first magnitude. Renegotiations with the government on contracts reaching back into prior years resulted in substantial government refunds, but a huge backlog of fixed-price contracts turned out to consist mainly of profitless assembly work. Key engineers left to go to work for one of the industry giants. Englewood sold off the electronics operation at a loss of $3 million after a desk-pounding board meeting at which Warren discovered that he no longer controlled the board of directors.

Warren contemplated forcing liquidation of the corporation, but this would probably entail a proxy fight.

"There's no percentage in liquidating a corporation of this sort," the lawyer explained. "Reorganize it, yes. Merge it, yes. But liquidate it? Never. There would be too much of a tax to pay. If the corporation owned mainly real estate that had increased in value, we could liquidate it tax free, but since Mid-American is not a real estate corporation, you would have to pay a large capital gains tax on the liquidation. If you wanted to keep on operating the business as a partnership or proprietorship, we could set up the liquidation in such a fashion that the corporation would realize no taxable gain even though some of its property has appreciated—and you would get capital gains.

"Here, with only a substantial minority interest, your best bet seems to be to let this guy Englewood keep on running the construction business. Get it understood that he can't mix in on acquisitions or things like that. If he can keep the construction business profitable, this thing will get back on its feet."

"In the meantime, you can be looking for a corporation that might want to merge with yours. As long as the Mid-American stockholders get at least 40 percent* of the stock in the surviving corporation or the new corporation created by the merger, and if you can establish a strong business reason for the merger, all your corporation's tax attributes, including your operating loss, should carry over to the buyer unabated."

No longer trusting Englewood's judgment, and disliking the man personally, Warren searched for a larger corporation that might want to take over Mid-American Industries. To his surprise, Englewood proved receptive to the

*In a further exploration of the rules governing loss carryovers, see page 348.

merger proposal that Warren finally came up with. And the W & M Construction Corporation, renamed Mid-American Industries, was fused into the massive and robust corporate structure of the North American Manufacturing and Investment Corporation. Thus did W & M finally disappear as a separate corporate entity, although for tax purposes it bequeathed to North American its net operating-loss carryovers, its accumulated earnings and profits, and certain of its accounting methods.

Few there were who even knew that W & M (or rather Mid-American) had ceased to be. And none there were to mourn. Business continued as usual, Warren now watched the market quotations on North American as he had watched those on Mid-American and W & M before, and Englewood still rode the purchasing department to beat down subcontractor bids even as he kept alive the hope that his restricted bargain stock, now North American stock, might some day set him financially free—for what, he knew not. And old Mr. Humphrey, receiving his $50,000 a year in dividends on his preferred stock (now North American preferred), grumbled mildly over the fact that they were still taxable.

## SUMMARY

The act of forming a corporation in itself entails no tax. The transfer of property to a corporation is normally a taxable transaction, with gain or loss measured by the difference between the fair market value of the consideration received from the corporation and the tax basis of the property transferred. However, if property is transferred to a corporation solely in exchange for stock or securities (short-term notes are not, for this purpose, deemed to be securities), then no gain or loss will be recognized to the transferors if immediately after the transfer they own 80 percent or more of all the stock of the corporation.

The logic of this tax-free transfer of property to a corporation is that a change in form only, and not a change in substance, has taken place. There is a continuity of ownership.

This tends to be true in the area of corporate reorganizations as well. Usually, a reorganization involves the giving up of securities and the receiving of securities by the shareholders. Unless such an exchange of securities is rendered tax free by the reorganization provisions of the tax law, it will normally be taxable. A reorganization, to be tax-free, must have a legitimate business purpose.

The most common type of reorganization is the acquisition by one corporation of stock of another corporation in exchange for its own stock. For such an acquisition to be tax free, the acquiring corporation must own at least 80 percent of the acquired corporation's stock immediately after the transaction. A variant of the same pattern is the acquisition of the other corporation's properties, or substantially all of them, for a consideration consisting only of the voting stock of the acquiring corporation. If there is "boot" (that is, nonvoting-stock or other consideration) given in these types of reorganization, then the entire transaction will be taxable.

Another type of reorganization is the statutory merger of one corporation into another. In such a reorganization, the selling corporation disappears and its stock is automatically converted into stock of the acquiring corporation. In a statutory merger, if there is "boot," then gain will be recognized, but only to the extent of such "boot." It is not the entire transaction that will be taxable.

Cash dividends paid a shareholder are fully taxable to him as long as they are from either current or accumulated earnings. Otherwise, they are considered a recovery of investment until the shareholder's tax basis has thus been recovered tax free. After that, they are capital gains. Property dividends paid to an individual shareholder are taxable to the shareholder at fair market value. Generally, the paying corporation is not deemed to have any gain as the result of distributing appreciated property in the form of a dividend.

Shareholders, especially of closely held corporations, frequently seek to get earnings out of a corporation at capital gains rates rather than as ordinary dividend income. If a shareholder's stock is redeemed in an amount that substantially reduces his proportionate interest in the corporation, capital gains treatment can be obtained. A complete redemption, of course, will have such an effect.

Corporations, unlike individuals, can have perpetual life; but in spite of this legal potential, many are liquidated each year. If a corporation adopts a plan of liquidation and then sells its assets at a profit and liquidates, it can usually avoid any corporate tax on those profits. The shareholder will usually have a capital gains tax to pay on the gain he receives in liquidation of a corporation, just as though it were gain on any other sale of his stock.

One exception to this general rule of capital gains on stock sales or in liquidation is in the area of what are known as "collapsible corporations." These are corporations that are used to attempt to convert what would otherwise be ordinary income into capital gains and yet avoid the corporate tax on the gain. Thus, a builder transfers raw land to a corporation in 1975. The corporation plots the land for a subdivision, installs streets, sewers, water, and gutters, and grades the property. The market value of the property has now been considerably enhanced. Then, in 1978, before the corporation has sold any or many of the lots, it liquidates. The lots are distributed to the shareholder as a liquidating dividend. Under our general rule, the stockholder would have a capital gain based upon the difference between the fair market value of what he received in liquidation of the corporation and the amount he had invested in the first place. This excess, as you can see, is essentially the unrealized increase in value of the improved land. When the builder then turned around and sold the lots, his tax basis would be the value at the time he got the lots from the corporation. Thus, income that should be ordinary income would become capital gains.

The collapsible-corporation provisions of the law provide that, in a situation of this sort, the shareholder's gain on liquidation shall be ordinary income.

## DOES THE TAX LAW INDUCE MERGERS?

In many specific situations, some sort of merger is a logical solution to a tax problem—if we use the word *merger* in the loose sense of acquisition of control of one corporation by another, even though neither a statutory merger nor a consolidation may be involved. A corporation with loss carryovers that might otherwise be of no use to it may find itself either eager to go out and acquire profitable subsidiaries (for example, Textron and Studebaker) as a way of using up the carryovers, or may allow itself to be acquired. In the former situation, where the loss corporation seeks acquisitions, it can afford to pay somewhat more for earning power than could a corporation not possessed of the contingent asset of tax-loss carryovers.

Thus, a corporation with operating-loss carryovers of $1 million, which it can utilize only if it acquires a company with the ability to earn a profit, has a contingent asset of $500,000, if the corporate tax rate is a flat 50 percent. This contingent asset can be made actual only through earning profit. Theoretically, this loss corporation could afford to pay up to $500,000 more to acquire a company that could allow it to use this loss than could someone not so situated.

However, both the acquisition of a profitable corporation by a loss corporation and that of a loss corporation by a profitable corporation are transactions that may be uncertain in their effects. The Internal Revenue Service can challenge any such acquisitions where the acquiring corporation is unable to show that its principal purpose is not tax minimization.

Traffic in loss corporations is also controlled by some specific rules. For the loss carryover of a loss corporation that is involved in a statutory merger to be available to the surviving corporation, the stockholders of the loss corporation must wind up owning at least 40 percent of the participating stock of the new or surviving corporation. To the extent that they get less than 40 percent, the loss carryover is scaled down. If the potential loss carryover was $200,000, and stockholders of the loss corporation received only 30 percent of the stock of the surviving corporation, the loss carryover would be scaled down to $130,000.*

Another situation in which a merger has tax advantages is the collapsible corporation. Assume that the taxpayer is the sole stockholder of a corporation

*The 40 percent rule is scheduled to apply to reorganizations adopted on or after January 1, 1978. Prior to the effective date of the new law, loss carryovers were allowed in full if the former owners of the loss company received at least a 20 percent stock interest in the surviving company. A lesser ownership interest would result in a proportional reduction in the loss carryover.

that has just completed construction of a shopping center. He has done this before, and so for tax purposes, he is considered a dealer in shopping centers. Long-term leases from responsible tenants have been obtained, and the value of the shopping center is now considerably more than its cost, based on capitalizing the anticipated rental income. The stockholder would like to sell out and go on to more remunerative pastures. By merging his corporation into a corporation whose stock is marketable, he incurs no tax. The securities that he acquires are no longer securities in a collapsible corporation, so he can presumably dispose of them at capital gains rates after a decent waiting period and with due regard to SEC rules. Note that, because the specific securities being issued in such a reorganization are frequently not registered with the SEC, the issuing corporation will, in such cases, normally require a letter affirming that the stockholder is acquiring these securities for investment and not for resale. Subsequent sale of these securities is subject to limitations based on SEC rules.

Perhaps the most frequent tax fact influencing mergers is the estate tax. Although the estate tax itself will be discussed in Chapter 19, it should be noted here that the owner of stock in a closely held corporation faces a dual estate-tax problem. First, there is great uncertainty as to the value that will be put on his stock for estate-tax purposes. The fair market value of something for which there is no market becomes a highly subjective concept. Yet the optimum tactics in estate planning will differ substantially, depending on whether the taxpayer's stock in the X Corporation will be valued at $600,000, or $1,600,000.

Added to this is the difficulty of raising the money to meet the estate tax. The corporate stock may have value, but when there is no market, just how is that value to be turned into cash? The Internal Revenue Service does not accept stock certificates in payment of taxes.

By merging his corporation with a corporation whose stock is actively traded, the stockholder solves both problems. There is now an ascertainable market price for the stock. He may argue successfully that it is worth less than the market indicated, but at least he will not be stuck with a valuation that is more. Furthermore, since there is a market, enough stock can usually be sold on that market to raise the cash necessary to pay the taxes.

Nontax reasons for mergers are undoubtedly of great importance. The final decision to merge, though, like most decisions, results from the cumulative effect of all the forces impinging on the shareholder. Among these, taxes certainly are not ignored.

## ACCOUNTING FOR BUSINESS COMBINATIONS

Some business combinations involve one company's acquiring control of the assets of another company via the route of purchasing its stock. Money, bonds, or the stock of the purchasing company may be the consideration given the sellers. The proper accounting for the transaction would require the buyer to set up the assets acquired at their cost—meaning the cost to the buyer, which would normally approximate the value of the assets at the time purchased.

When the assets are acquired through the use of stock rather than cash or debt, it often happens that the seller wants the transaction to be tax-free and that it will be tax-free. This means that the tax basis of the assets acquired by the buyer will be the tax basis of the assets to the seller, and not the fair market value of the assets as determined by the values exchanged at the time of purchase.

Since the early 1950's, there had been an increased tendency for the accounting for combinations that were tax-free to follow the tax treatment. Other factors were involved, of course, but certainly the substantial differences between financial income and tax income that would inevitably result encouraged the spread of what is called the "pooling-of-interest" concept. Under this concept the transaction is viewed as being a marriage of the two corporations with their accounts being combined, rather than a purchase by one of the other. However, in the 1960's there had been abuse of the concept, and in 1970 the AICPA revised the rules of accounting for business combinations and placed some limitations on the use of pooling-of-interest accounting.

Assume that the Alvernon Corporation has decided to acquire the assets of the Speedway Company and has issued 100,000 shares of its stock for them. The balance sheets of the two corporations on the date of acquisition show:

| | *Alvernon Corp.* | *Speedway Co.* |
|---|---|---|
| *Assets:* | | |
| Current assets | $ 2,000,000 | $ 100,000 |
| Fixed assets | 20,000,000 | 1,000,000 |
| Total | $22,000,000 | $1,100,000 |
| *Equities:* | | |
| Current liabilities | $ 1,000,000 | $ 150,000 |
| Capital stock | 3,000,000 | 100,000 |
| Retained earnings | 18,000,000 | 850,000 |
| Total | $22,000,000 | $1,100,000 |

The fair market value of Alvernon stock is $50 per share. Thus, Alvernon is issuing stock with a fair market value of $5,000,000 to acquire the $950,000 book value that is Speedway. If this is a purchase, then the $4,050,000 of excess over book value should be assigned to specific assets. To the extent that this excess can be assigned to assets that are depreciable, such as buildings or equipment, or amortizable, such as patents, the earnings of Alvernon should reflect as expense each year a proper amortization of such cost. To the extent that such excess is allocable to "goodwill," this goodwill must also be amortized over a period not to exceed 40 years.

On the other hand, because the acquisition is only for stock, it will probably be tax free. Depreciation and amortization for tax purposes will therefore be based on the tax basis of the two corporations prior to the combination, thereby creating a possible difference between accounting net income and taxable net income.

In the situation in which the transaction is a purchase for accounting purposes and a tax free transaction for tax purposes, the question may arise as to what impact the tax-free character has on the accounting for the purchase. Obviously, if the transaction had been taxable, then the tax basis (for depreciation and for gain or loss on disposition) would be the same as for financial accounting. But in this situation, fixed assets that are being purchased for $2 million have a tax basis of $400,000. Should this be reflected in the financial statements?

Some accountants would answer "Yes." They would do one of two things.

One approach would be to reflect in deferred taxes the amount of tax estimated to be attributable to the difference, setting up each year as income tax expense only the amount that would be payable if the assets had a tax basis equal to their price. The other approach would be to reflect the lack of tax deductibility in valuing the assets on the financial statements—for example, if a 50 percent tax rate applied, the equipment would be carried not at $2 million but at $1.2 million, to reflect the fact that the tax basis was only $400,000.

If the transaction is accounted for as a "pooling," the fact that $5,000,000 of Alvernon stock has been issued for $950,000 of net book-value assets is not even noted in the accounting records. Future earnings will reflect in expense only the write-off of $1,000,000 of fixed-asset cost. Look at the differences in the resulting Alvernon Corporation consolidated balance sheets:

| | *Purchase* | *Pooling* |
|---|---|---|
| *Assets:* | | |
| Current assets | $ 2,100,000 | $ 2,100,000 |
| Fixed assets | 25,050,000 | 21,000,000 |
| Total | $27,150,000 | $23,100,000 |
| *Equities:* | | |
| Current liabilities | $ 1,150,000 | $ 1,150,000 |
| Capital stock | 8,000,000 | 3,100,000 |
| Retained earnings | 18,000,000 | 18,850,000 |
| Total | $27,150,000 | $23,100,000 |

Obviously, one advantage of a pooling is that it will not be necessary to amortize the $4,050,000 excess purchase price against future earnings.

When a combination occurs in which no substantial change takes place in stockholder positions, such as the merger of a subsidiary into a parent, the pooling approach seems quite defensible. If two firms of approximately equal size combine, and the former stockholders of both continue as stockholders in the new entity, some type of pooling approach may be justified—although it can also be argued that an entirely new accounting entity has been created and that this new entity should start out with no retained earnings and with all assets shown at fair market value.

But when a giant swallows a pygmy, pooling seems hardly calculated to lead to meaningful balance-sheet presentation or meaningful income measurement, even where the transaction is viewed for tax purposes as a tax-free reorganization. Nevertheless, the accounting rules for business combinations do not incorporate a relative-size test, so that giants and pygmies still qualify for pooling.

## CONCLUSION

As long as corporations and their shareholders are separate entities for income tax purposes, and as long as capital gains are taxed less heavily than ordinary income, the area of corporate organizations, reorganizations, distributions, and liquidations will probably prove complex. The tax law attempts to reconcile the irreconcilable. It tries to be specific, so that both government and taxpayer may know where they stand in a proposed transaction. At the same time, it tries to be flexible, so that changes may be made in relationships without tax effect when these changes are desirable for business purposes and are essentially changes in form rather than substance. The provisions so inserted may, in turn, prove burdensome or may open loopholes.

This chapter has grossly oversimplified the problems and technicalities involved, in the interest of achieving some degree of insight on the part of the reader. The actual complexity may be suggested by merely reproducing one sentence from one of the many Internal Revenue Code sections dealing with aspects of this problem. (See Figure 17-1.)

## CASE EXCERPTS

*Wilford E. Thatcher* v. *Commissioner,* (CA9) 37 AFTR 2d 76-1068
*Gregory* v. *Helvering,* 14 AFTR 1191 (55 S.Ct. 266)(1935)

### *Wilford E. Thatcher* v. *Commissioner* (CA9) 37 AFTR 2d 76-1068

A cash basis partnership transferred its assets, as well as its liabilities, to a newly-formed cash-basis corporation.

Because the liabilities assumed (including accounts payable) exceeded by some $102,367.73 the partnership's adjusted basis in the assets transferred to the corporation, the Commissioner took the position that the excess was taxable under §357(c) as a gain to the partners in the year their partnership debts were assumed.

**(1) Sales or exchanges of stock.**—For purposes of subsection (a)(1), a corporation shall not be considered to be a collapsible corporation with respect to any sale or exchange of stock of the corporation by a shareholder, if, at the time of such sale or exchange, the sum of—

(A) the net unrealized appreciation in subsection (e) assets of the corporation (as defined in paragraph (5)(A)), plus

(B) if the shareholder owns more than 5 percent in value of the outstanding stock of the corporation, the net unrealized appreciation in assets of the corporation (other than assets described in subparagraph (A)) which would be subsection (e) assets under clauses (i) and (iii) of paragraph (5)(A) if the shareholder owned more than 20 percent in value of such stock, plus

(C) if the shareholder owns more than 20 percent in value of the outstanding stock of the corporation and owns, or at any time during the preceding 3-year period owned, more than 20 percent in value of the outstanding stock of any other corporation more than 70 percent in value of the assets of which are, or were at any time during which such shareholder owned during such 3-year period more than 20 percent in value of the outstanding stock, assets similar or related in service or use to assets comprising more than 70 percent in value of the assets of the corporation, the net unrealized appreciation in assets of the corporation (other than assets described in subparagraph (A)) which would be subsection (e) assets under clauses (i) and (iii) of paragraph (5)(A) if the determination whether the property, in the hands of such shareholder, would be property gain from the sale or exchange of which would under any provision of this chapter be considered in whole or in part as gain from the sale or exchange of property which is neither a capital asset nor property described in section 1231(b), were made—

(i) by treating any sale or exchange by such shareholder of stock in such other corporation within the preceding 3-year period (but only if at the time of such sale or exchange the shareholder owned more than 20 percent in value of the outstanding stock in such other corporation) as a sale or exchange by such shareholder of his proportionate share of the assets of such other corporation, and

(ii) by treating any sale or exchange of property by such other corporation within such 3-year period (but only if at the time of such sale or exchange the shareholder owned more than 20 percent in value of the outstanding stock in such other corporation), gain or loss on which was not recognized to such other corporation under section 337(a), as a sale or exchange by such shareholder of his proportionate share of the property sold or exchanged,

does not exceed an amount equal to 15 percent of the net worth of the corporation.

FIGURE 17-1
One Sentence from the Internal Revenue Code

. . . We believe that the integrity of the standard meaning of liability can be retained while giving vitality to the purposes of both §351 (tax-free exchange) and §357 (closing the escape of taxes by borrowing against assets before transferring them to the new corporation, and blocking the creation of a "negative" basis.)

Judge Hall, dissenting in the present case when it was before the Tax Court, did not undertake to redefine "liability", but advanced a theory that would permit a constructive "wash" narrowly limited to this kind of case. 61 T.C. at 42-44. While the wash, or setoff, solution is not without its own doctrinal difficulty it is consistent with the spirit of §351, as it prevents wholly unwarranted tax windfalls in favor of the government. It is equally consistent with §351, as it prevents wholly unwarranted tax windfalls in favor of the government. It is equally consistent with §357 (c) so long as its employment is limited as Judge Hall suggests.

Under Judge Hall's proposal, accounts payable are considered liabilities and §357(c) gain is recognized when the sum of the liabilities assumed exceeds the basis of the assets transferred. Under the statute, assumption of debt supplants the usual requirement of actual payment for recognition of gain by cash-basis taxpayers. If no trade receivables are surrendered, recognition of the §357(c) gain completes the income analysis of the incorporation exchange.

However, if receivables are transferred, Judge Hall believes the cash-basis transferor has in effect sold those accounts to the transferee-corporation. The consideration to be received is extinguishment of the transferor's payables. When the transferee-corporation provides that consideration, the cash-basis transferor should be able to recognize the now-completed sale of receivables. He can do so through a setoff to the §357(c) gain. Since there is no statutory recognition rule for this sale, the cash-basis transferor can invoke the setoff only upon actual payment of the allocable and deductible trade payments by the transferee-corporation. If the sum of the receivables transferred equals or exceeds in amount the §357(c) gain, and the "purchase" of those receivables is completed in the year of the transfer, the setoff will completely wash out the §357(c) gain.

Such a setoff is realistic. It prevents treatment as gain of something that was not in fact a gain, but only appeared to enhance the partners' balance-sheet position because of the cash-basis accounting method. The setoff thus avoids the Draconian effects of the Raich formula in this case without opening for exploration the kind of "borrowing-out" and other manipulations of credit and depreciation which, prior to enactment of §357 and its predecessor (§112(k) of the 1939 code), may have permitted massive escapes from taxation in §351 transfers.

We hold, therefore, that the taxpayers were entitled to set off the deductible and paid trade accounts which are allocable to the purchase of the receivables. On the facts of this case the §357(c) gain is met by the setoff.

*Gregory* v. *Helvering*
14 AFTR 1191 (55 S.Ct. 266) (1935)

The existence of a tax motive for casting a transaction into a particular form will not thereby make the form ineffective. However, if there is no business purpose for the transaction at all, then the existence of a tax avoidance motive will result in disregard of the form adopted for tax purposes. This is especially true in reorganizations, where absence of a business purpose is fatal. . . .

> (1) The term 'reorganization' means . . . (B) a transfer by a corporation of all or a part of its assets to another corporation if immediately after the transfer the transferor or its stockholders or both are in control of the corporation to which the assets are transferred. . . .

It is earnestly contended on behalf of the taxpayer that since every element required by the foregoing subdivision (B) is to be found in what was done, a statutory reorganization was effected; and that the motive of the taxpayer thereby to escape payment of a tax will not alter the result or make unlawful what the statute allows. It is quite true that if a reorganization in reality was effected within the meaning of subdivision (B), the ulterior purpose mentioned will be disregarded. The legal right of a taxpayer to decrease the amount of what otherwise would be his taxes, or altogether avoid them, by means which the law permits, cannot be doubted. But the question for determination is whether what was done, apart from the tax motive, was the thing which the statute intended.

When subdivision (B) speaks of a transfer of assets by one corporation to another, it means a transfer made "in pursuance of a plan of reorganization" (section 112[g]) of a corporate business; and not a transfer of assets by one corporation to another in pursuance of a plan having no relation to the business of either, as plainly is the case here. Putting aside, then, the question of motive in respect of taxation altogether, and fixing the character of the proceeding by what actually occurred, what do we find? Simply an operation having no business or corporate purpose—a mere device which put on the form of a corporate reorganization as a disguise for concealing its real character, and the sole object and accomplishment of which was the consummation of a preconceived plan, not to reorganize a business or any part of a business, but to transfer a parcel of corporate shares to the petitioner. No doubt, a new and valid corporation was created. But that corporation was nothing more than a contrivance to the end last described. It was brought into existence for no other purpose; it performed, as it was intended from the beginning it should perform, no other function. When that limited function had been exercised, it immediately was put to death.

In these circumstances, the facts speak for themselves and are susceptible of but one interpretation. The whole undertaking, though conducted according to the terms of subdivision (B), was in fact an elaborate and devious form of conveyance masquerading as a corporate reorganization, and nothing else. The rule which excludes from consideration the motive of tax avoidance is not pertinent to the situation, because the transaction upon its face lies outside the plain intent of the statute. To hold otherwise would be to exalt artifice above reality and to deprive the statutory provision in question of all serious purpose.

## QUESTIONS AND PROBLEMS

1. The Clinchfield Manufacturing Company was formed October 1, 1978. George Clinchfield transferred the following assets to the corporation:

| | *Tax Basis* | *Value* |
|---|---|---|
| Cash | $2,000 | $ 2,000 |
| Accounts receivable | 0 | 10,000 |
| Inventory | 0 | 1,000 |
| Machinery and equipment | 5,000 | 15,000 |

George received $28,000 of common stock in Clinchfield. At the same time, Don Daum and Edward Ekco each invested cash of $14,000, and each received $14,000 worth of common stock.

(a) Did George Clinchfield recognize any taxable gain on this transaction?

(b) What is the Clinchfield Manufacturing Company's tax basis for the various assets it acquired?

(c) Prepare a balance sheet as of October 1, 1978, after the stock was issued, showing the tax basis in one column and the accounting basis of the assets in another.

(d) Assuming that they had no intention of paying any premium for goodwill, and that the corporation will operate profitably, did Daum and Ekco pay too much for their stock? If you think they did, show what you would consider a fair price, assuming a corporate tax rate of 48 percent.

2. Dunn Manufacturing Company is an existing corporation. Flavius Flato, a sole proprietor, transfers his business to Dunn in exchange for 10,000 shares of Dunn common stock. The assets of Flato's business have a tax basis of $38,000 and a fair market value of $78,000, the difference being entirely attributable to appreciation in real estate used in the business, which he has

owned for 5 years. Dunn already has outstanding 100,000 shares of common stock, all owned by George Dunn.

(a) Does Flato have any taxable gain on this transaction?

(b) What is Dunn's tax basis for the assets acquired?

3. In Problem 2, what difference would it make to your answers if Dunn had acquired for its stock all the stock of Flato Corporation?

*4. Lucien Hacker controls all the stock of four corporations. Hacker Manufacturing is extremely prosperous. Hacker Furniture just about breaks even. Hacker Investment Company earns a good profit, but owing to its oil investments seldom has any taxable income. Hacker Realty, a new enterprise, owns several apartment buildings on which tax losses are anticipated for several years, because of accelerated depreciation and large interest payments. Hacker would like to take advantage of the realty losses in some fashion. He has thought of having Hacker Realty elect to be an Electing Small Business Corporation, and he has also considered filing a consolidated return for all four corporations. Is either of these alternatives open to him? If not, what rearrangements could he make, tax-free, in order to gain some current tax benefit from the realty company's tax losses?

*5. Duval Corporation has net operating-loss carryovers of $500,000. It operates a small sand and gravel operation, having discontinued the concrete contracting business that resulted in the losses. Louis Duval has been the 100 percent stockholder of the company all along. He is now negotiating for the purchase, for 30 percent of Duval stock, of a prosperous cement-block plant. Does Duval run any risk of losing the use of its net-operating-loss carryovers?

*6. Haddock Discount Stores has a net-operating-loss carryover of $1 million. Mr. Haddock, owner of 70 percent of the stock, sells all his stock to John Denton. Denton immediately eliminates ten of the stores' fifteen units by selling them, and puts Haddock into the shopping center development business. Profits are substantial. Can Haddock take advantage of its net-operating-loss carryover?

*7. Assume in Problem 6 that instead of selling the store units, Denton had Haddock merge with Gigantic Discount Stores, Inc. The former Haddock stockholders received 1,000,000 out of a total of 6,000,000 post-merger shares of common stock outstanding. Can Gigantic Discount Stores take advantage of the Haddock net-operating-loss carryover?

*8. In Problem 7, would it make any difference to your answer if Gigantic Discount Stores merged into Haddock?

9. Distinguish between a tax-free reorganization that might be accounted for as a purchase and a tax-free reorganization that might be treated as a "pooling" for financial accounting purposes. Which method of financial account-

ing corresponds most closely to the tax accounting for a tax-free reorganization?

10. Gwinn Bros., Inc., owns a piece of real estate that cost it $10,000 and that now has a fair market value of $18,000.
    (a) It distributes this real estate to its individual shareholders as a dividend. How much gain is recognized to the corporation? How much dividend income do the shareholders have?
    *(b) Gwinn transfers the land to an individual shareholder in redemption of all his stock (10 percent of the total). The stock had cost the shareholder $6,000 but had a fair market value of $18,000 at the time of the redemption. How much gain, if any, is recognized to the corporation? How much gain is recognized to the shareholder? Will the gain be treated as a dividend? What is the shareholder's basis for gain or loss if and when he sells the land?
    *(c) Gwinn takes the stock it acquired in (b) and sells it a year later for $23,500. How much gain does it realize?
11. Hitchcock owns stock in the Mosby Realty Corporation. Because of high depreciation charges on the new rental properties that are its major assets, Mosby operates at a tax loss. Because the depreciation charges are not a cash drain, Mosby is able to pay dividends to its shareholders. Hitchcock originally invested $10,000 in Mosby stock in June 1962. He has received tax-free dividends totaling $4,000 to date. Mosby stock is now selling at a price whereby Hitchcock could get $9,000 for his stock. What will be his taxable gain or loss if he sells on June 30, 1978?
12. Hudson Manufacturing Co. and Bogart Enterprises are consolidated into Hudson-Bogart, Inc., pursuant to the provisions of the corporation law of the state of Arizona. Fred Hudson surrenders his 5,000 shares of Hudson Manufacturing, for which he has a tax basis of $25,000, and receives 5,000 shares of Hudson-Bogart having a fair market value of $975,000. Does Hudson have any gain on the exchange? What is Hudson's basis for gain or loss if and when he sells the Hudson-Bogart shares?
13. In the example in the text, when W & M Construction Corporation acquired all the stock of Humphrey Lumber in exchange for its preferred stock, what would have been the advantages from W & M's point of view of issuing a debenture bond paying the same interest rate as the rate of the preferred-stock dividend? What would have been the disadvantages to W & M? What would have been the disadvantages from the point of view of Mr. Humphrey?

*14. Bonbon Corporation acquired all the stock of Sweetooth, Inc., from George Sweetooth, its sole shareholder. Mr. Sweetooth received 10,000 shares of Bonbon voting common stock and an old pickup truck that Bonbon no longer needed. Will Sweetooth have any tax to report? Was there any better way to set this up?

15. The *Thatcher* case deals with an inequity created by a provision [IRC 357(c)] inserted into the tax law to close a loophole. Describe what that loophole was, and give an example of how it might work and how 357(c) would eliminate it. Then explain how the Court rationalized its failure to apply 357(c) in *Thatcher.*

# 18

# Foreign Tax Matters

## U.S. CITIZENS ABROAD

Prior to 1942, a U.S. citizen who was a nonresident for more than six months of the taxable year did not have to pay any U.S. income tax on his "earned income" from outside the United States. This was similar to what other countries did and still do.

From 1942 until 1963, the United States allowed a U.S. citizen who was a bona-fide foreign resident to exclude income earned abroad when calculating his U.S. tax. In 1951, the law was amended to provide that the citizen who was out of the U.S. for 17 out of 18 months (actually 510 days out of an 18-month period) could also get an exclusion, but in 1953 a $20,000 per year limit was put on that exclusion. The big exception from these Section 911 exclusion rules was income received from the U.S. government itself, or any of its agencies or instrumentalities. That income was subject to U.S. tax. But the government worker had something that partially compensated for this tax disadvantage–he received a tax-free cost-of-living allowance. Tax exemption of that allowance was conferred by Section 912 of the Internal Revenue Code.

After 1962, the rules changed. A limit was put on the amount of foreign income that a U.S. citizen who is a bona-fide foreign resident could exclude from U.S. tax. The exclusion is also available, by treaty, to resident aliens who are citizens of certain countries. That limit was $20,000 per year for the first three years of bona-fide foreign residence, and then $35,000 per year. (The $35,000 was dropped to $25,000 in 1964.)

Before 1962, of course, the bona-fide foreign resident paid no U.S. income tax on allowances and other fringe benefits. To the extent that his income, including fringes, exceeded the dollar limits, after 1962 he found these items subject to taxation. The exclusion of the government employee's cost-of-living allowance was not disturbed, however.

Thus, prior to the 1976 Tax Reform Act, the pattern had been one of a gradually narrowing area of tax exemption for employees of the private sector. Government employees abroad, on the other hand, had seen cost-of-living allowances rising with inflation, so that the area of their tax exemption, small though it was, was broadening rather than contracting.

## THE 1976 TAX REFORM ACT

The 1976 Tax Reform Act cut the excludible amount to $15,000 (except for employees of nonprofit organizations, whose amount stayed at $20,000), and changed the method of determining the $15,000 exclusion. The old exclusions had come off the top of the individual's income, thus saving tax at his highest brackets, while the $15,000 now comes off the bottom (i.e., the tax is calculated on the total income, including the $15,000, and then the tax on $15,000 is deducted).

The Act also provided that the foreign taxes attributable to the $15,000 cannot be claimed as a foreign tax credit. The value of the $15,000 exclusion was thus further reduced.

*Example:*

Assume a single individual with $50,000 of foreign salary income. Ignore deductions and the personal exemption, since these are close to being constants and complicate the example. Assume the foreign country imposes a flat 18 percent tax.

| | *Pre-1976* *$* | *1976 TRA* *$* |
|---|---|---|
| U.S. tax on $30,000 ($50,000 – 20,000 exclusion) | 9,390 | |
| U.S. tax on $50,000 | | 19,290 |
| Less: U.S. tax on $15,000 | | 3,520 |
| U.S. tax on $35,000 | | 15,770 |
| Foreign tax credit | 9,000 | 6,300 |
| Net U.S. tax payable | 390 | 9,470 |

Thus, what looks like merely a 25 percent reduction in an exclusion turns out to be better than a 25-fold increase in the size of the tax check someone has to write to the United States. Recognizing the reduced use of the exclusion, and also recognizing that taxpayers taking advantage of the exclusion may suffer an added tax detriment by forfeiting deductibility of some of their relocation expenses, the new law allows a taxpayer to elect not to take the $15,000 exclusion. Once foregone, however, the exclusion can only be used in a future year after obtaining I.R.S. permission.

## WHO PAYS THE BILL?

Almost all U.S. companies employing U.S. citizens abroad have some policy whereby the employer shares or absorbs the extra tax paid as the result of the foreign assignment. Usually, the employee is expected to absorb the estimated U.S. tax that he would pay on his base salary—with the manner of computing this estimated tax varying from company to company. The employer then reimburses the employee for the excess of his actual taxes over this hypothetical figure.

Since the 1976 Tax Reform Act contained no corresponding increase in the taxation of U.S. taxpayers generally, application of any of these "tax equalization" policies will not increase what the employee's tax would have been "if . . .," but it will increase the tax actually due. Ergo, it will increase the amount the employer will pay to the employee. This payment is itself taxable to the employee. Thus, an algebraic formula must be used to compute the tax on the tax so as to fully "gross-up" the tax reimbursement. The cost to the employer is estimated at from $3,000 to $6,000 per overseas employee pre-gross-up, and perhaps double that when the tax reimbursement is considered.

What kinds of corporate decisions do such costs influence? One decision is whether to use U.S. citizens or another country's nationals. If a multinational corporation can employ someone from Canada, France, or almost anywhere else in lieu of a U.S. citizen, it will be that much cheaper to employ that someone else, all other things being equal. The 1976 Tax Reform Act change did not create this discriminatory bias, incidentally, for it was grafted onto the international business scene in 1962. But the 1976 Tax Reform Act exacerbated it. The message Congress seems to be communicating to the multinational corporation by its actions is to discriminate against U.S. citizens in giving its people the type of worldwide exposure and experience that is vital to managerial and professional success in a multinational environment. Phrased that way, this is indeed a strange national policy for a people who abhor discrimination based on race, sex, religion, or country of origin. Abhor it, apparently, unless the discrimination is directed against U.S. citizens.

Who pays the bill? The employer writes the check to the employee to reimburse him for the increased tax. Unless that cost increase is passed on to customers in the form of higher product or service prices, corporate profits drop.

If corporate profits drop, then one result is that less income tax is due to the foreign country and the United States. A second result is that less money is available for internal investment or for distribution to stockholders. Corporations, even multinationals, are only conduits; they cannot consume even a toasted cheese sandwich. And the employee, who *can* consume a toasted cheese sandwich, initially is not the one who normally pays the bill.

If employment opportunities abroad are curtailed for U.S. citizens, though, some of those employees will re-enter the U.S. labor market. Thus, the long-run effect of tax discrimination against U.S. citizens working abroad may well be to swell the supply side of the labor market, thus contributing to the unemployment that, with inflation, is a perennial key national problem. The unemployed person may not be the U.S. citizen no longer employed abroad, but rather the person he displaces. So, indeed, who pays?

### *Earned Income*

The definition of "earned income" is the same for foreign resident tax purposes as it is for the 50 percent maximum tax on personal service income. Wages, salaries, and professional fees all qualify as earned income, whereas interest, rents, dividends, and royalties would not be considered "earned." If capital is a material income-producing factor in a business, then earned income would be "a reasonable allowance" for the personal services rendered by the individual in the business–but not more than 30 percent of the taxpayer's share of the business profits.

Here we see how technical provisions in the tax law, otherwise inexplicable, do make some sort of sense. One would think that some taxpayers doing business abroad could bypass the 30 percent-of-profits rule and take maximum advantage of the earned-income exclusion by utilizing an Electing Small Business Corporation.

*Example:*

Smith's wholesale business involves a substantial capital investment. Profit is about $20,000 per year. Without a corporation, Smith can't exclude more than $6,000 per year and must pay U.S. tax on $14,000. If he could use an Electing SBC, he could pay himself a $15,000 salary that would be free of U.S. tax and have tax to pay on only $5,000 of "dividend" income from the SBC.

But Smith cannot do this, because having more than 80 percent of gross receipts from foreign sources terminates the SBC election.

Of course, Smith can use a corporation to create salary income that can be excluded–and, as we will discuss later in this chapter, can even defer U.S. taxation of the $5,000 profit remaining in the corporation after his salary.

The business or professional man abroad, whether a solo practitioner or in a partnership, faces an added complication. The exclusion applies to income, but it carries with it the corollary that the expenses of earning the excluded income are nondeductible. Thus, an architect practicing alone and grossing $50,000 in fees while netting $25,000 could not exclude $15,000 of that $25,000 from his income. Since 30 percent of his income was excludable ($15,000/$50,000), 30 percent of his expenses (or $7,500) would be nondeductible. He would thus have to pay tax on $17,500 rather than $10,000.

If it is otherwise feasible, a corporation can provide the solution to that problem as well.

The same type of problem arises in a partnership, such as an international law firm, that has partners living abroad but has income from both foreign and domestic sources. The partner residing abroad will be deemed to have foreign income of the same percentage of his share of the partnership income as the total foreign-source income is of the total partnership income. If the partnership's foreign-source income is $100,000 while total income is $1,000,000, then only 10 percent of the foreign-resident partner's $40,000 share of partnership income will be deemed earned abroad and eligible for exclusion.

The solution to the partnership problem is quite straightforward. If the partnership gives the foreign-resident partner a salary, determined without regard to partnership income, then the entire salary will be deemed to be foreign income. A $15,000 or more salary for the partner in this example would raise the amount he could exclude from income from $4,000 to $15,000. This, of course, may require that all partners be given salaries in order not to upset the pattern of income distribution. (While paying a partner a salary generally has no tax effect, this is one situation where the salary provision produces tax differences.)

### *Bona Fide Residence and 510-Day Test*

Residence is a matter of intent. The question comes up in many contexts but is most frequently involved with U.S. citizens abroad and foreign nationals present (but not necessarily resident) in the United States. Living somewhere, with no definite intentions as to length of stay and no specific place to which one will return, makes one a resident of that somewhere. By contrast, someone who goes to another country to carry out a specific project or assignment that has a definite life, and who continues to maintain a residence in his "home" country to which he expects to return, is not a bona fide foreign resident.

Various criteria are employed in arriving at the taxpayer's intent. While taxation of income by the foreign country is not a prerequisite to excluding income for U.S. purposes, if a person makes a statement to the authorities of a foreign country that he is not a resident of that country and the authorities accept his statement and hold him not subject to the taxes ordinarily paid by residents of that country, this statement is taken as conclusive evidence that the individual is not a bona fide resident of that country.

Subjective determinations create controversy, and the anticipation of controversy inhibits action. Mobility of U.S. citizens is in the public interest, so the 510-day test was devised to provide a quantitative rather than a subjective test. If a U.S. citizen is physically present in one or more foreign countries for at least 510 days during any period of 18 consecutive months (that is, 510 days out of approximately 548 days), then he can exclude up to $15,000 a year of his income earned during that period ($20,000 if he works for a nonprofit organization), even though he is not a bona fide foreign resident. The income must not, however, be from the U.S. government (or any agency or instrumentality thereof).

The 18-month period is arbitrarily selected by the taxpayer. It does not have to begin on the first day of a month, nor does it have to coincide with any physical event such as the taxpayer's arrival in a foreign country. Periods of less than 24 hours on the high seas (which are not a "foreign country" for this purpose) are disregarded; an airline pilot will not lose qualifying days even though he spent some time over the high seas on almost every day of his qualifying period, but a seaman will usually be unable to qualify under the 510-day rule because he will have spent much of his time at sea.

Income earned abroad does not include compensation for services rendered in the United States. Employees traveling to the United States on business have to allocate their compensation between services rendered in the U.S. and those rendered abroad, based on the number of working days spent in each country. Vacation pay is attributable to the country where services are rendered. Although it is thus immaterial where the employee spent his vacation in determining how much income was earned abroad, where he spent the vacation may be important relative to the 510-day test.

The amount excluded is determined for each year separately, and no carry-over is allowed for the unused portion of the exclusion. However, in determining the amount excluded, compensation received for past and future years' services is applied against the exclusion of the respective years; an individual may be able to exclude more than $15,000 in one year if he receives compensation applicable to several years in one taxable year and he has unused exclusion available for several of the years involved. However no amount can be excluded unless it is paid within the taxable year subsequent to the year of its accrual; exception is made for certain deferred-compensation items accrued in or before 1962.

In the first and last years of his bona fide residence in a foreign country, a taxpayer will usually not be a resident of that foreign country for the entire year. In such cases, the exclusion is limited to a fraction of the basic amount, determined by the period he was a bona fide resident of a foreign country during the taxable year. Similarly, the exclusion available under the 510-day rule is prorated based on the number of days of the taxable year that were included in an 18-month period chosen by the taxpayer to qualify foɪ the 510-day rule. Sometimes this rule results in a higher exclusion in the first year of foreign residence than the "bona fide residence" rule. A taxpayer who qualifies for the use of both methods is entitled to choose the method more advantageous to him. It is also permissible to have various parts of the year included in different 18-month periods, and the 18-month periods may overlap.

*Example:*

During 1977, Frazer spent 6 months working as an accountant in South America. The first 3-month period was part of an 18-month period ending March 31, 1977, during which he was outside the United States more than 510 days. The last 3 months was part of an 18-month period commencing October 1, 1977, during which he will be outside the United States for 510 days. Income earned during the 6 months abroad can be excluded up to 50 percent of the $15,000 figure.

In the first year that a taxpayer qualifies for the exclusion of income earned abroad, he faces a practical problem. His return becomes due long before he is able to ascertain whether he will qualify under the bona fide residence rule (which requires an entire taxable year) or under the physical presence rule (which involves an 18-month period). In this situation the taxpayer has two options. He may file his tax return without claiming the exclusion and eventually file an amended return when he qualifies under either rule. This method will benefit him only if he expects substantial refunds even without the use of the exclusion. As an alternative, by filing Form 2350 he may obtain an extension until a date 30 days past the end of his "qualifying period." (The "qualifying period" is the first full taxable year spent as a bona fide resident of a foreign country, in the case of a taxpayer claiming the benefit of the bona fide residence rule; or the 18-month period chosen, in the case of a taxpayer claiming the benefit of the 510-day rule.)

The exclusion is obviously of most value to the U.S. taxpayer when the foreign country taxes his earned income lightly or not at all. It becomes of less and less practical value as the foreign tax rises toward the amount of U.S. tax that would be imposed on the same income. If the foreign country is taxing the income, then the rules relating to deduction or credit for foreign taxes paid become significant.

## FOREIGN-TAX CREDIT

With some exceptions (notably Subchapter S corporations and certain nonresident aliens), taxpayers are allowed to claim foreign income taxes paid or accrued as a credit against U.S. income tax rather than as a deduction in computing taxable income. Claiming the foreign taxes as a credit is optional, and the election may be made either on the original return or at any later time, as long as the statute of limitations has not run out for filing a refund claim.

Three kinds of taxes qualify for the foreign tax credit treatment:

1. Income taxes
2. Excess profit taxes
3. "In lieu" taxes

An "in lieu" tax is a tax that is an integral part of a foreign income tax system and that, for purposes of administrative convenience, is imposed upon the taxpayer in lieu of the income taxes imposed by the same law. For example, if a foreign country imposes an income tax and provides that in lieu of computing their net taxable income, farmers may pay an income tax based on 5 percent of their gross product, this tax will qualify as an in lieu tax.

In determining what constitutes an income tax, the language of the foreign law is frequently disregarded in order to obtain some uniformity of criteria. If the tax is imposed on an item that is income under U.S. standards, the tax will be considered an income tax. Accordingly, the social security taxes of several countries do qualify, even though the foreign law does not give them the classification of "tax." However, a tax imposed on the fair rental value of an owner-occupied residence would not be an income tax because the fair rental value of the residence does not constitute income under U.S. standards, even though several European tax systems consider it the equivalent of income received.

Accrual-basis taxpayers have to claim foreign tax credit on an accrual basis. Cash-basis taxpayers have a choice of claiming the foreign tax credit on a cash or on an accrual basis. If they convert to the accrual basis, in the year of conversion they may deduct both taxes paid and those accrued, but they may not change their method back to cash thereafter without permission of the Internal Revenue Service.

When the foreign tax credit was first introduced into the U.S. income tax system, the purpose was to avoid double taxation of income. If the same income was taxed by both the United States and the foreign country, and the U.S. tax rate was higher, the taxpayer would pay the foreign tax and claim credit for it on his U.S. tax return, limiting his actual U.S. tax to the difference between the U.S. tax rate and the foreign tax actually paid. If the two tax rates were equal, the foreign tax would exactly offset the U.S. tax, and the taxpayer would pay tax to the foreign country but none to the United States. If the foreign tax rate was higher than the U.S. tax, the taxpayer would pay the foreign tax and no U.S. tax; in this case, although his total tax burden would be heavier than that of a taxpayer operating exclusively in the United States, this would occur not because of the operation of the U.S. tax law, but because of his own decision to operate in a high-tax foreign country.

This arrangement looks simple enough in theory, but endless problems were caused by differing concepts of taxable income and by the inability of the various countries to agree what income was attributable to what country.

Prior to 1961, a per-country limitation had to be used in computing all foreign tax credits. Under this rule, if, for example, 5 percent of your taxable income was attributable to Germany and 15 percent to Canada, your credit for German taxes was limited to 5 percent of the U.S. tax and the credit for Canadian taxes to 15 percent. If both foreign countries had very high or fairly low tax rates, this caused no problems. But problems arose when one of the foreign countries had a very high tax rate and the other a low one. Suppose that in the example above you actually paid German taxes equaling 15 percent, and Canadian taxes totaling 5 percent of your U.S. tax. Your foreign tax credit would be limited to 10 percent of the U.S. tax, composed of the Canadian taxes actually paid and the German taxes limited to 5 percent.

To give some relief to the taxpayers faced with this problem, Congress introduced the so-called overall limitation, beginning with 1961. Under the overall limitation, taxable incomes and taxes attributable to all foreign countries are added together, and the limitation is determined on the overall amount. In the preceding example, this limitation results in a foreign tax credit of 20 percent, twice the amount allowable under the per-country limitation. Unfortunately, the opposite effect results if the taxpayer has a net loss from one or more of the foreign countries involved. If, for example, the taxpayer had $10,000 of net taxable income from Germany and a $10,000 net loss from Canada, under the overall limitation his foreign-tax credit would be limited to zero, since he has no net taxable income from foreign sources.

Through 1975, the taxpayer could elect the limitation to be used in computing the foreign tax credit. The 1976 Tax Reform Act eliminated use of the per country limitation.

What is "taxable income from a foreign country" for purposes of computing the limitation on foreign tax credit? Compensation from services is attributable to the country where the services were performed. Excluded income is obviously not "taxable income." (Foreign tax paid on such income is not available to offset U.S. taxes payable on other foreign-source income.) Dividends from U.S. corporations are U.S.-source income. However, dividends from certain U.S. corporations operating almost exclusively abroad (such as Creole Petroleum) are foreign-source income; these companies can be identified in published dividend-record publications by the note "Withholding of U.S. income tax from nonresident aliens is not required." Dividends from foreign corporations are foreign-source income (and corporations in Puerto Rico and U.S. possessions are considered "foreign").

In computing both foreign and total taxable income, personal exemptions are disregarded. However, itemized deductions are to be divided between foreign and U.S. income.

1. Expenses directly attributable to U.S. income (employee business expenses connected with services performed in the United States, interest on money borrowed to purchase U.S. securities, state income taxes paid on exclusively domestic income, etc.) are to be deducted from U.S.-source income.
2. Expenses directly attributable to foreign-source income (employee business expenses attributable to services performed abroad, interest on money borrowed to purchase foreign securities, etc.) are to be deducted from foreign-source income.
3. Expenses attributable to several classes of income (state income taxes paid on several types of income, interest on amounts borrowed to purchase both U.S. and foreign securities, etc.) are to be apportioned among the types of income they are related to.
4. Expenses not directly identifiable with any type of income (contributions, medical expenses, property taxes, interest on money borrowed for personal purposes, etc.) are to be allocated to various countries in proportion to the income derived from each country.

Virtually all tax returns involving a foreign tax credit will contain such an allocation of deductions, and the allocation will occasionally result in the complete elimination of the foreign tax credit.

Foreign taxes in excess of the current year's limitation are available as a foreign tax credit carryback to the two preceding years and as a carryover for the five subsequent years. In each year to which foreign taxes are carried back or forward, they are subject to the same computation of limitation as in the year in which they were paid. The taxpayer may be unable to use any of the carrybacks or carryovers if he has no foreign income in the carryback or carryover years. Furthermore, the unused credit is not available as a deduction.

The foreign tax credit lends itself to endless planning opportunities. Take the case of the $15,000-a-year U.S. employee working abroad for several years as a bona fide resident of a foreign country. None of his salary is taxable for U.S. income tax purposes, but he will have paid thousands of dollars in income taxes to the foreign country of which he is a resident. Is he going to derive any benefit from these foreign taxes? Without careful planning, probably not. But if he is sufficiently sophisticated in the matter of taxes and not too eager to throw away the benefit of a few thousand dollars, he may arrange a few opportunities to benefit from this foreign tax credit. To begin with, he might concentrate his investments in those U.S. stocks the income from which is considered to be foreign-source income, as explained above, or maybe a few Puerto Rican stocks ("foreign" for U.S. income tax purposes), as long as his dividends are not high enough to subject him to Puerto Rican income tax. By selling his securities in the foreign country of his residence (even to a U.S. broker acting as a principal), he can realize "foreign-source" capital gains. The U.S. income tax on these capital gains may be entirely offset by his excess foreign tax credit. It should be noted that the net effect of this planning is the offsetting of foreign taxes paid on his salary against U.S. taxes payable on his capital gains. This result may be a little far from the original purpose of the foreign tax credit, which was to eliminate double taxation of the same item by two nations. Congress has seen fit to narrow but not entirely eliminate this loophole.

The taxpayer can elect, of course, to claim his foreign taxes (except those on excluded income) as a deduction instead of as a credit. This is an all-or-nothing proposition—the foreign taxes for a given year cannot be taken partially as a deduction and partially as a credit.

## THE NONRESIDENT ALIEN AND U. S. TAXES

Nonresident aliens are subject to two independent and parallel systems of income taxation in the United States.

1. On income "effectively connected with the conduct of a trade or business in the United States," they are taxed at the rates applicable to U.S. citizens and resident aliens. However, nonresident aliens are not permitted to file joint returns or to claim head-of-household status; with a few exceptions established by law or treaty, they are limited to one personal exemption for themselves and no exemptions for dependents. They are entitled to claim neither the standard deduction nor most of the itemized deductions available to U.S. citizens and residents.

2. On income not "effectively connected with the conduct of a trade or business in the United States," nonresident aliens are taxed at a flat 30 percent rate, with no deductions or personal exemptions allowed. The 30 percent rate is replaced by a lower rate through many tax treaties.

Interest received on a U.S. bank account is not considered to be U.S. source income for this purpose and, accordingly, it is not taxable to a nonresident alien.

Nonresident aliens are subject to separate low rates of estate tax. Moreover, the taxable estate of a nonresident alien includes only property situated in the United States at the time of death. Thus, nonresident aliens will face possible U.S. estate tax on real estate located in the United States, securities of U.S. corporations or governmental bodies regardless of location of the certificates, and other tangible property (for example, jewelry) physically located in the United States. The rates for nonresident aliens are as follows:

| *If the taxable estate is:* | *U.S. Estate Tax* |
|---|---|
| Not over $100,000 | 6% |
| Over $100,000 but not over $500,000 | $ 6,000 plus 12% of excess |
| Over $500,000 but not over $1,000,000 | $ 54,000 plus 18% of excess |

| *If the taxable estate is:* | *U.S. Estate Tax* |
|---|---|
| Over $1,000,000 but not over $2,000,000 | $144,000 plus 24% of excess |
| Over $2,000,000 | $384,000 plus 30% of excess |

In arriving at the taxable estate, a nonresident alien is allowed a credit of $3,600 (as compared to $47,000 for a U.S. resident).

Gifts are not taxed if the property donated is property situated outside the United States or intangible property situated within the United States—for example, stocks. But if they are subject to gift tax, the gifts of a nonresident alien are taxed in the same manner and at the same rates as those of a U.S. citizen or a resident alien.

## FOREIGN OPERATIONS OF U.S. CORPORATIONS AND SUBSIDIARIES

The U.S. taxes its citizens and aliens who retain their U.S. resident status on their worldwide income. The same is true for the taxation of U.S. corporations. The result is that a U.S. corporation operating in a foreign country has not only the taxes of that foreign country to pay but also U.S. income taxes.

U.S. corporations thus frequently find it convenient to operate through foreign subsidiaries, since a U.S. corporation with its heavier tax burden seldom proves to be competitive. U.S. oil companies are an exception to this rule: through a combination of special tax benefits granted by the United States to oil companies (intangible drilling-expense deduction, percentage-depletion allowances, foreign tax credit), these companies have found it advantageous to operate abroad as U.S. corporations, even though their special benefits have been sharply curtailed by recent tax law changes. As a consequence, virtually all U.S. oil companies operate abroad through U.S. subsidiaries, but most other U.S. corporations prefer to use foreign subsidiaries for their foreign operations. These foreign subsidiaries are subject to no U.S. tax, unless they do business in the United States.

There is little objection to bona fide subsidiaries conducting bona fide foreign operations. But situations developed in which foreign corporations were used principally for tax avoidance. One of these situations was eliminated long ago through the introduction of the foreign-personal-holding-company provisions, which taxed the shareholders on the foreign corporation's undistributed income. But the foreign-personal-holding-company rules failed to reach many situations that were felt to involve tax avoidance. To deal with this problem, the Revenue Act of 1962 created what is known as Subpart F (Sections 951 to 964) of the Internal Revenue Code.

The law provides that U.S. persons who own 10 percent or more of a "controlled foreign corporation" have to include in their taxable income their ratable share of the corporation's "Subpart F income."

"Subpart F income" includes:

1. The income derived from the insurance of United States risks.
2. Foreign-personal-holding-company income (for example, interest, dividends, capital gains).
3. "Foreign-base-company sales income"—that is, the income from sales that either are made *to* a related person or entity or involve a product originally purchased *from* such a related person or entity; but only if the property is produced outside the country in which the controlled foreign corporation is organized, and is sold for use, consumption, or disposition outside such foreign country.
4. "Foreign-base-company-services income"—that is, income from the performance of services for or on behalf of any related person, performed outside the country under the laws of which the foreign controlled corporation is created or organized.

The last three items are grouped under the common name of "foreign-base-company income." If foreign-base-company income is less than 10 percent of gross income, it is disregarded; if it exceeds 70 percent of gross income, the entire gross income is treated as foreign-base-company income.

If a controlled foreign corporation invests any of its earnings in a U.S. property, the U.S. shareholders realize a constructive dividend to the extent of their ratable share of the net increase in U.S. properties during the taxable year. What is U.S. property is determined under special rules. Bank deposits in the United States are not "United States property" if they do not exceed the amount that is ordinary and necessary to carry on the trade or business. Stock of a U.S. corporation is not "United States property," unless the investee either owns 10 percent or more of the controlled foreign corporation or is 25 percent or more owned by the shareholders of the controlled foreign corporation. However, there is no prohibition against investment in stocks of Puerto Rican corporations, since these corporations are considered to be "foreign" under the Internal Revenue Code.

It should be realized that while Subpart F has a much broader scope than the foreign-personal-holding-company legislation, it reaches a fairly limited number of special situations that were considered by the legislators to be especially conceived for tax avoidance purposes. But the Internal Revenue Service, in addition, has a powerful all-purpose tool in Section 482 of the Internal Revenue Code, which can reach situations not reached by Subpart F. Section 482 authorizes the Internal Revenue Service to distribute, apportion, or allocate income, deductions, credits, or allowances among related businesses if such allocation is necessary in order to prevent evasion of taxes or clearly to reflect the income of any such entity. While this weapon is widely used even within the United States, its principal use is in situations involving a foreign entity.

Typically, the situation that comes under I.R.S. attack under the authority granted by Section 482 involves an intercompany transaction that is not an arms-length deal. Take the case of a foreign subsidiary in a low-tax country that sells merchandise to its parent in the United States. It charges exorbitant prices for the merchandise in order to siphon off most of the combined profit of the affiliated group into a country where it is subject to low taxes. Under the authority of Section 482, the Internal Revenue Service can modify this transaction, treating it for tax purposes as if the subsidiary had charged the parent the prevailing arms-length price for the merchandise.

And with all this, what happens to our friend the wholesaler who earlier in this chapter was going to let $5,000 per year of his earnings accumulate tax free in his foreign corporation? What happens when he finally decides to get the money out of his foreign corporation and return to the United States?

Ordinary income.

With the exception of pre-1976 accumulated earnings of stock held for over ten years in less-developed-country corporations, U.S. persons owning 10 percent or more of the stock of a foreign corporation will realize ordinary income upon sale of the stock or liquidation of the corporation, up to the amount of the accumulated earnings and profits of the corporation. So, in reality, the ability to tax-shelter the income of a foreign corporation is usually merely an ability to defer the time when tax will have to be paid.

The appropriateness of allowing U.S. individuals and corporations to defer taxation of their foreign income by using foreign corporations depends on your point of view. Proponents of tax deferral emphasize that it creates an equitable (and competitively neutral) situation vis-a-vis foreign persons. Opponents contend that it is unfair to allow some U.S. taxpayers to avoid current taxation of current income when other U.S. taxpayers are denied that privilege. Proponents of deferral argue that its elimination would make U.S. business uncompetitive with foreign business in every country of the world with lower income tax rates than the United States. They point out that removing the U.S. business presence from these lower-income-tax countries, which are mainly underdeveloped or emerging economies, in effect, abandons them to foreign businesses and may have substantial long-run detrimental effects on the global balance of power. Opponents of deferral respond that multinational corporations operate in many countries, and that their effective worldwide tax rates are not so much below U.S. rates as to render ineffective the erasure of double taxation that is performed by the foreign tax credit.

## FOREIGN TAX CREDITS OF CORPORATIONS

Corporations are entitled to foreign-tax credits under the same rules applicable to noncorporate taxpayers. In addition to this, a domestic corporation that owns at least 10 percent of the voting stock of a foreign corporation from which it receives dividends is entitled to a foreign-tax credit for its ratable share of the foreign taxes paid by the foreign corporation if all the earnings of the foreign corporation are distributed as a dividend. If the foreign corporation distributes only part of its earnings as a dividend, the credit available to the parent is reduced according to the percentage of earnings retained by the foreign corporation. If the foreign corporation owns 10 percent or more of another foreign corporation, a ratable share of the taxes paid by this second-tier foreign corporation is attributed to the first-tier foreign corporation and then to the U.S. parent and if a second-tier foreign subsidiary owns at least 10 percent of a third-tier foreign subsidiary, the U.S. corporation may also be entitled to a credit.

It should be noted that the U.S. corporation realizes a constructive dividend in the amount of the foreign tax credit made available by the foreign corporation.

In recent years, the competitive position of U.S. companies and their foreign affiliates has been deteriorating, owing to the increased reliance on the so-called "value-added tax" instead of an income tax in many European tax systems. The value-added tax is somewhat similar in concept to the manufacturers' excise taxes in the U.S. tax system. However, the tax is not levied upon the entire manufacturer's sales price, but upon the value added to the product by each step in manufacturing. A mining company would pay value-added tax on mining the iron ore; a steel company would pay value-added tax on transforming it to steel; a car manufacturer would pay the tax on transforming the steel into the end product, a car. Every one of these companies will pass on the value-added tax to the purchaser of its products. Ultimately, the final consumer of the product pays all value-added taxes included in the cost of the merchandise.

One reason for the popularity of the value-added tax in Europe is the widespread tax cheating that takes place among businesses, and especially among smaller businesses. The nature of the value-added tax is such that the returns required put a premium on substantiating the amounts paid to suppliers and employees—for these are deductions. But one business's deductions are the next business's income, and so the V.A.T. provides an automatic internal administrative cross-check on both income and deductions. Knowledge of that cross-check makes the V.A.T. returns more reliable. The same information can also be used to check the validity of reported income and deductions on income tax returns, and thus the returns are also made more honest.

The value-added tax creates severe problems for U.S. companies because it is not an income tax. American taxpayers operating abroad don't get a foreign tax credit for value-added taxes they pay in certain foreign countries, nor do U.S. parent corporations get a foreign tax credit for value-added taxes paid by the foreign subsidiaries. To the extent that the value-added tax partially or completely replaces the income tax in the foreign country, this results in the type of double taxation the foreign tax credit tried to prevent. The U.S. corporation still bears the burden of both the U.S. income tax and the value-added tax imposed by the foreign country, the latter being available as a deduction, not as a foreign tax credit. Even though foreign subsidiaries of U.S. corporations are not subject to such double taxation, the value-added tax keeps them from making the foreign taxes they pay available to their parent corporations for the purpose of offsetting the U.S. tax due on their dividend distributions.

Some people argue that the United States should introduce a value-added tax similar to the European system. Part of the motivation for adoption of such a tax would be to make U.S. companies more competitive abroad and at home. Agreements on international trade make it difficult to subject to U.S. income tax the merchandise being imported to the United States; they also make it awkward to selectively exempt from income tax any merchandise from the United States ultimately destined for export. A U.S. value-added tax would easily and acceptably allow both results to be achieved.

But since the V.A.T. is really a type of sales tax, it has a regressive effect (as compared to the progressive nature of the income tax). Thus, opponents of the V.A.T. argue that part of the problem can be better solved by a more liberal definition of foreign taxes eligible for the foreign tax credit.

### *Domestic International Sales Corporations*

A corporation engaged in manufacturing or distributing a product sold in foreign markets may want to consider the use of a separate corporation to handle its foreign sales operation. In addition to the possibility of forming a foreign corporation, the U.S. firm would have to consider the Domestic International Sales Corporation (DISC).

A DISC, much like the Small Business Corporation, is not subject to federal taxes on any of its income. Whatever income is subject to tax, the shareholders report and pay tax on. Shareholders pay tax on as little as one-half of the DISC's taxable income. However, the untaxed portion of the profits are taxed if and when they are distributed.

The amount of income the DISC can defer depends in part on when it was started, in part on its net profit, and may depend in part on the ratio of its current gross receipts to its gross receipts for the period 1972-1975 (or a four year base period which moves forward one year for each year after 1979). For a

DISC formed after 1975, the deferral for 1978 and 1979 will be the full 50 percent of taxable income so long as the DISC does not have interest income on producer's loans, or gain on noninventory sales or on military sales. Regardless of when formed, a DISC with taxable income of $100,000 or less, and none of the income sources referred to in the previous sentence, likewise can defer the full 50 percent of its profit.

But a DISC that was in existence during part or all of the period 1972-1975 has a more involved calculation. An example may be the best explanation:

Gross receipts for the base period years–

| | |
|---|---|
| 1972 | $ 200,000 |
| 1973 | 400,000 |
| 1974 | 600,000 |
| 1975 | 800,000 |
| Total | $2,000,000 |
| Average | $ 500,000 |
| Adjusted average (x 0.67) | $ 335,000 |

1978 gross receipts total $1,000,000, with adjusted taxable income thereon of $200,000. The same percentage of that $200,000 as the $335,000 is of the $1,000,000 (33½ percent) is taxable to the shareholders. They are also taxed on half of the remaining 66½ percent, leaving 33¼ percent of the 1978 profit (i.e., 33¼ percent of $200,000 or $66,500) as the amount of DISC income for 1978 on which tax can be deferred.

The tax-deferred income retained by the DISC may be used in expansion of its business, for purchase of certain Export-Import Bank obligations, and for the making of producer's loans to provide suppliers with funds for financing facilities, inventory, and so on used in export production. These latter loans must be evidenced by a note, with interest, and a stated maturity date not to exceed five years.

The DISC, organized as a U.S. corporation, must elect within 90 days of beginning of the tax year to be so taxed. In addition, the DISC must meet the following requirements: one class of stock; equity capital of at least $2,500; 95 percent of its assets in the form of qualified export assets; 95 percent of its receipts from qualified export receipts.

Qualified export assets would include such items as inventory and property held for lease in foreign markets, assets used in connection with export sales (storage, handling, etc.), trade receivables from foreign trading, producer's loans and Export-Import Bank obligations. Qualified export receipts would include sale of export inventory, leasing of exported property, services rendered in relationship to a qualified sale of exported property, and gains from the sale of qualified export assets.

In addition to the ability to defer U.S. taxation on half of the DISC's income, the implementation of the DISC statute through liberal regulations has resulted in an ability to shift income to a DISC without risking I.R.S. challenge in a manner not available with any other type of export entity. This is mainly accomplished through liberal intercompany pricing rules.

Thus, almost any U.S. corporation engaged in the manufacture or distribution of products sold abroad will usually find it a profitable tax move to set up a DISC to handle its export operations—even though the same operations conducted through a foreign corporation subsidiary might have saved little or no taxes because little or no profit would have been lodged in the foreign subsidiary after I.R.S. finished allocating income and expense between the U.S. parent and the foreign subsidiary.

## TAX TREATIES

Tax treaties with foreign countries may supersede any provisions of the Internal Revenue Code. The right to modify tax law through international treaties has been used widely by the U.S. government. As applicable to the residents of certain foreign countries, tax treaties concluded with those countries modify the provisions of the Internal Revenue Code as to what is includable in taxable income, what deductions and personal exemptions are allowable, and what tax rate applies to the taxpayers. In any foreign tax matter, it should therefore be ascertained whether the United States has a tax treaty with the country involved. If such a treaty exists, its provisions should be carefully checked to determine the extent to which they affect the taxpayer.

## INTERNATIONAL TAX PLANNING

Like all business planning, and certainly all tax planning, international tax planning starts with a description or forecast of what is expected or desired. A U.S. corporation intends to start selling its products in South America. It has conducted market studies, has created cost analyses, and has a fair idea of how it would like to go about this new venture and the expected amount and timing of its earnings.

At the same time, the tax planner must be aware of the ways in which the plan can be changed. Does a major warehouse have to be established in Caracas, or could it be in some country other than Venezuela? Must earnings be repatriated back to the United States or can they be used for expansion into other parts of the world?

With this preliminary information, the tax planner can then start rearranging what can be changed and can look at the tax consequences that would ensue. At the same time, he can get feedback as to the nontax consequences so that his alternative suggestions are realistic. For example, establishing a Panamanian subsidiary may make good tax sense, but it may create operating problems because of the tensions between Panama and the major country in which marketing activities will be conducted.

We will discuss tax planning at some length in Chapter 22. International Tax Planning is tax planning, but tax planning complicated to an almost untold degree by not only the need to reflect U.S. tax information and business practices and conditions, but the need to encompass literally all the countries of the world.

## CASE EXCERPTS

*Grunebaum* v. *Commissioner* (CA2-1970) 25 AFTR 2d 70-380
*Eli Lilly & Co.* v. *U.S.* (Ct. Cl. 1967) 19 AFTR 2d 712
*PPG Industries, Inc.*, TC Memo 1970-354

*Grunebaum* v. *Commissioner*
(CA2-1970) 25 AFTR 2d 70-380

In 1961 all four of the taxpayers were citizens and residents of the United States, they had sizable income from salary and investments in this country, and they also had substantial income from West Germany and paid West German taxes on the West German income. Section 901 of the Code permits taxpayers to credit foreign taxes so paid upon foreign income directly against the United States tax they would otherwise owe on their entire income, subject, however, to various applicable limitations set forth in Section 904, including the overall maximum limitation, the proper computation of which is at issue on this appeal.

Section 904 limits the credit for foreign taxes to a sum no larger than the United States tax which would otherwise be payable on the income received from the foreign sources. Thus the ratio between the foreign tax credit and the total tax from which it is subtracted may not exceed the ratio between the taxpayer's foreign source income and his total income both domestic and foreign. The maximum foreign tax credit, or foreign tax credit limitation, can thus be calculated by the following formula:

$$\frac{\text{Taxable income from foreign sources}}{\text{Taxable income from foreign and United States sources combined}} \times \text{United States tax on total taxable income from both United States foreign sources, before foreign tax credit} = \text{Maximum amount allowable as foreign tax credit under overall limitation}$$

The question before us for decision concerns the way in which certain deductions from income should be allocated between foreign source income and total income in calculating the numerator and denominator of the fraction above. The resident citizen taxpayers had deductions for charitable contributions, interest, state and local taxes, accounting fees, and casualty losses due to storm damage. On their 1961 returns they allocated these properly deductible items entirely to total income—the denominator of the fraction in the formula—and did not allocate any of the deductions to the numerator, or foreign source income. The Commissioner, however, held that since these deductions did not relate specifically to income from any particular source, they should be divided pro rata between United States income and foreign source income. Accordingly, the Commissioner applied part of the deductions to the foreign source income, which constitutes the numerator of the fraction. As a result the numerator was smaller, and therefore the foreign tax credit limitation was also smaller, than the equivalent figures produced by the taxpayers' method.

. . . Section 862(b) of the Code, which defines the method for calculating taxable foreign source income, states that there shall be subtracted from gross foreign source income "the expenses, losses, and other deductions properly apportioned or allocated thereto, *and a ratable part of any expenses, losses, or other deductions which cannot definitely be allocated to some item or class of gross income.*" (Emphasis supplied.) This language is quite explicit in compelling the method of computation used by the Commissioner. Taxpayers and the *amicus curiae* argue that the deductions referred to in the quoted section comprehend business deductions only and do not include the personal deductions involved here. We do not find any support whatsoever in the language of the statute that would justify such a construction of it.

The *amicus* argues that the Commissioner's method is unfair in that it gives the taxpayer with foreign income only part of his personal deductions. We do not follow this argument, for the tax on income from all sources, from which the taxpayer subtracts his foreign tax credit, reflects these deductions in full. The *amicus* further points out that the resident citizen with both domestic and foreign income is placed in a less advantageous position than the nonresident alien with both United States and foreign income. This is undeniably true, but irrelevant, since the Code clearly indicates that under appropriate conditions resident citizens will be taxed on their foreign income whereas nonresident aliens will not. One of the very last places in the whole encyclopedic compilation of federal statutes to expect to find equality of treatment in all particulars is the Internal Revenue Code of 1954.

*Eli Lilly & Co.* v. *U.S.*
(Ct. Cl. 1967) 19 AFTR 2d 712

The I.R.S. reallocated income from a subsidiary to the parent, even though the taxpayer showed that business rather than tax considerations motivated its pricing policies.

. . . It is obvious, of course, that one result of the above-described inter-company pricing method was to assemble in Pan-American nearly all the taxable income derived from sales of Lilly products in foreign countries within the Western Hemisphere. . . . The resulting tax advantage flowing to the affiliated corporate group from such pricing method is equally obvious.

But, says Eli Lilly, there is nothing wrong in this. It vigorously asserts, and on this record has satisfactorily proved, that sound business reasons primarily motivated its pricing policy on goods destined for foreign markets. Accordingly, it insists that any resulting tax advantage is nothing more than was intended by Congress. . . .

The Government disagrees. It does not dispute Eli Lilly's right to organize internally in any way company management may desire, nor does it question Pan-American's status. . . . But for tax purposes, says the Government, section 482, *supra,* and the regulations issued thereunder, require it to intervene and determine the "true taxable income" of each of the controlled group.

During the course of his audits covering the 1952 through 1957 tax returns of Eli Lilly, International, and Pan-American, an Internal Revenue agent became convinced that Eli Lilly's intercompany pricing arrangements did not clearly reflect the respective taxable incomes of the related organizations and resulted in unwarranted tax avoidance.

. . . On the basic assumption that the same profit earned by Eli Lilly on its domestic expense dollars should be earned by it on its foreign trade expense dollars, he first computed the percentage figure which Eli Lilly's net income from domestic sales bore to its expenses on those sales. He reasoned that, if International's cost of goods purchased from Eli Lilly were increased by such percentage figure, the results under the intercompany agreements would be (1) to increase Eli Lilly's sales (and thereby its taxable income) in a like amount and (2) to increase Pan-American's cost of goods purchased from International (thereby decreasing Pan-American's taxable income) in a like amount.

However, in discussing the matter with Eli Lilly's representatives, the agent became aware of certain flaws in his basic assumption that Eli Lilly should earn the same profit on its sales to International as it earned on its domestic sales to wholesale distributors. It became apparent to him that the sales were not entirely comparable, the major difference being that International was one large customer to whom Eli Lilly could be expected to sell its goods in quantity at a lower profit than to its numerous domestic wholesalers.

In an effort to take this difference into account, the agent did something to which Eli Lilly points, among other things, as clear proof of arbitrary and unreasonable action. He simply applied one-half of Eli Lilly's profit percentage for domestic sales to the cost of goods sold to International. However, he applied the full percentage to the allocated expenses. . . . Whatever criticism may be directed to the agent's methodology, Eli Lilly has failed, in my judgment, to prove that he arrived at an unreasonable result. As the Tax Court has said in analyzing a section 482 (then section 45) allocation:

> Although the method of allocation used by the respondent, based on the gross income of each company, might appear to be arbitrary, we cannot say, on any evidence before us, that it led to arbitrary and unreasonable results. Our concern is more with the ultimate results arrived at by the Commissioner than the methods which he uses. [*Leedy-Glover Realty and Insurance Co.,* 13 T. C. 95, 107 (1949)]

The reasonableness of the result of the reallocation in this case seems to me apparent from a comparison of total book profits enjoyed by the three companies on sales of Lilly products in the Western Hemisphere both before and after the reallocation.

. . . It shows that, during the six years involved, prior to the reallocation, Pan-American received a share of the total profits from Western sales ranging from 92.84 percent to 97.68 percent; Eli Lilly's share of such profits ranged from 0.61 percent to 5.65 percent; and International's share ranged from 0.70 percent to 2.08 percent. After the reallocation, Pan-American's share of such profits was still high and ranged from 62.07 percent to 74.56 percent, while Eli Lilly's share had increased to a range of from 22.90 percent to 28.30 percent, and International's share ranged from 0.53 percent to 9.63 percent.

Hence, the lion's share of the profits from Western Hemisphere sales remained in Pan-American even after the reallocation, and to this extent it continues to enjoy (as it properly should) the tax benefits . . . . To accept Eli Lilly's contention that this is not enough, and that its cost-oriented pricing policy must be accepted, would require the court to ignore the provisions of Treas. Reg. 1.482-1, *supra,* which states that the standard to be applied in a section 482 allocation is that of "an uncontrolled taxpayer dealing at arm's-length with another uncontrolled taxpayer." It must surely be obvious that, if International were an "uncontrolled" purchaser from Eli Lilly, it would not have been able to buy Lilly products for the prices paid by it in this case. It is equally obvious that, being a large volume purchaser, an "uncontrolled" International could expect to buy Lilly products at prices somewhat less than the suggested retail price minus 15 percent paid by Lilly's domestic wholesale distributors. But, how much less? The revenue agent roughly split the difference, and Eli Lilly justifiably complained of such subjectivity. Yet, in electing simply to defend its cost-oriented pricing policy to its subsidiary, Eli Lilly has failed to meet its admittedly difficult burden of proving what it would have charged a volume purchaser, such as International, if it were an "uncontrolled" purchaser. In a refund suit such as this, the taxpayer in order to prevail must go further than proving arbitrary action by the Commissioner of Internal Revenue. In addition, the taxpayer must prove the correct amount of the tax and resulting overpayment.

In its briefs Eli Lilly places great emphasis on the importance of the many business reasons which motivated its intercompany pricing policies. There is no doubt that the record here clearly establishes the existence of sound and well-considered business reasons for the pricing policies adopted. . . . There is also no doubt that serious consideration was given to the "continuing tax problem" under section 45, now section 482, and surely management would have been considered derelict in its duties if it had not considered such an important problem. Nonetheless, there is ample credible testimony that the predominant reasons for Eli Lilly's pricing policies were those connected with its management's efforts to expand and develop the foreign market.

Eli Lilly's eminent counsel argue, in effect, that this should be the end of the matter, that a finding of business motivation effectively removes section 482 from the Government's arsenal. Consequently, they say, Eli Lilly's "position is and has always been that no amount should be reallocated." Reply Brief, p. 129.

I am unable to agree that the existence of valid and sound business purposes for intercompany arrangements will thus devitalize section 482. . . .

It will be recalled that section 482 states that its purposes are twofold. First, the Commissioner may resort to it "in order to prevent evasion of taxes." Secondly, he may resort to it whenever he deems it necessary "clearly to reflect the income" of the related organizations. Here, the facts show that Eli Lilly's shift to its subsidiaries of a part of the income which it had earned from its manufacturing operations was done predominantly for business reasons. Hence, the applicability of the first purpose mentioned above is dubious. However, the shift resulted in a failure to reflect clearly Eli Lilly's income from manufacturing, and this is enough to warrant an allocation under section 482. . . .

*PPG Industries, Inc.*
TC Memo 1970-354

PPGI is the wholly-owned foreign subsidiary of the petitioner. The first issue involves the correctness of the respondent's allocation under section 482 of the Internal Revenue Code of 1954 of a portion of PPGI's gross income to the petitioner in 1960 and 1961. Section 482 authorizes the allocation of income and deductions between related entities to prevent the evasion of taxes by shifting of profits, the making of fictitious sales, and other methods usually used to "milk" a taxable entity. *Ballentine Motor Co.,* 39 T.C. 348 (1962), aff'd. 321 F. 2d 796 [12 AFTR 2d 5448] (C.A. 4, 1963). Respondent has considerable discretion in applying section 482 and his determination must be sustained unless that discretion has been abused. *Grenada Industries, Inc.,* 17 T.C. 231 (1951).

One of the difficulties encountered in this case is the episodic unveiling of new positions by the respondent at various stages in the proceedings. In the statutory notice of deficiency, respondent originally made allocations of gross income from PPGI to petitioner in 1960 and 1961 in the respective amounts of $1,032,999 and $866,749. In making these allocations, the respondent relied upon the Source Book of Statistics of Income compiled by the United States

Treasury Department for 1960 and 1961. The statistics were based upon corporation income tax returns in the following category: "Returns with Net Income–Wholesale and Retail Trade: Wholesale Trade: Other Wholesalers: Drugs, Chemicals, and Allied Products." Using the statistics in the corporate category of 10 to 25 million assets, the respondent computed a net profit of 3.59 percent of gross sales in 1960 and 2.43 percent of gross sales in 1961. He then applied these percentages to gross sales figures for PPGI for 1960 and 1961 in the respective amounts of $17,793,900 and $12,989,000 and obtained the amounts of $638,801 and $315,632, which respondent regarded as appropriate net profits for PPGI in the years 1960 and 1961. Subtracting $638,801 from PPGI's income of $1,671,800 for 1960, the respondent determined that the difference, or $1,032,999, was allocable under section 482 to the petitioner in 1960. Similarly, the respondent subtracted $315,632 from PPGI's income of $1,182,381 for 1961 and determined that the difference, or $866,749, was allocable under section 482 to the petitioner in 1961.

At the trial, respondent announced a new position to the effect that (1) PPGI's activities were comparable to those of a combination export manager (CEM) with a nominal net profit margin of 2 percent of sales, and (2) PPGI's sales of petitioner's glass products to petitioner's two Canadian subsidiaries (CPI and Duplate) were merely "paper shuffling" and in effect sham transactions. The net result of this new position was that *all* of PPGI's income from the Canadian sales would be allocated to petitioner and that any earnings of PPGI in excess of 2 percent on its remaining sales would also be allocated to the petitioner. .

To reflect his new position, the respondent amended his answer to show an allocation of gross income from PPGI to petitioner in 1960 and 1961 in the respective amounts of approximately $1,470,500 and $1,490,200, or a total allocation of $2,960,700.

We are convinced that respondent's original allocation of income based upon the Source Book of Statistics of Income was arbitrary and unreasonable. There is no indication in the record to show that the operations of the unnamed corporations in the 10 to 25 million dollar asset category were in any way comparable to the operations of PPGI and, in fact, the evidence that does appear in the record emphasizes this lack of comparability. Moreover, it appears that the revenue agent resorted to these statistics only "because this was the best available source to me at the time of the examination." The revenue agent admitted he had no idea of the nature of the operations of the corporation in the asset category used by him. It also appeared at the trial that in computing the 3.59 percent and the 2.43 percent as the proper return on gross sales in 1960 and 1961 he misapplied the statistical information appearing in the compilation so that the lack of comparability with PPGI, both as to its operations and to its capital structure, was aggravated.

We find, on the basis of the entire record, that the operations of PPGI in 1960 and 1961 were not comparable to those of a CEM and we also find that

PPGI did in fact earn the net profits it realized on the sale of petitioner's products to the Canadian subsidiaries. As we have indicated earlier in this opinion, the petitioner has established to our satisfaction that its pricing policies with regard to the sales of its prodicts to PPGI were arm's-length prices and that the profits earned by PPGI and petitioner were reasonable. Therefore, no justification exists on this record for any reallocation of the profits of PPGI to petitioner in the years 1960 and 1961. We hold for the petitioner on this issue.

## QUESTIONS AND PROBLEMS

1. An individual, assigned by his employer to a branch in a foreign country, spends the month of July every year in the United States on vacation. He also spends all of every January at company headquarters in the United States working on planning operations for the company. Will these facts alone prevent him from excluding his income under the 510-day "physical presence" rules?
2. Will the same facts alone prevent him from excluding his income under the "bona fide residence" rule?
3. Assuming that the same individual does not qualify for the foreign-income exclusion, how much of his salary is foreign-source income for tax credit purposes?
4. Three U.S. citizens qualify for the foreign-income exclusion as bona fide foreign residents. What will be the taxable portion of:
   (a) A salary of $25,000?
   (b) An attorney's fee of $25,000 (no allocable expenses in the current year)?
   (c) A farmer's net income of $25,000?
5. An individual, resident of California, shows the following items on his return:

| | |
|---|---|
| Salary (all earned in California) | $20,000 |
| Dividends (all from Canadian sources) | 10,000 |
| Total income | $30,000 |
| Contributions (all to U.S. charities) | $ 2,000 |
| Medical expenses (net, all incurred in the U.S.) | 1,000 |
| California income tax | 900 |
| California sales tax | 600 |
| Employee business expenses | 800 |
| Interest on amounts borrowed in U.S. to purchase Canadian stocks | 3,000 |
| California disability insurance tax, de-deducted from salary | 74 |

| | |
|---|---|
| Total deductions | $ 8,374 |
| Personal exemption | $ 750 |

Canadian income tax of $1,000 was withheld from the dividends. Since the taxpayer intends to claim this as a foreign tax credit, compute his taxable income from Canadian sources.

6. Are the following items taxable if received by a nonresident alien?
   (a) Interest on a U. S. savings account
   (b) Dividends from General Motors
   *(c) Dividends from Creole Petroleum (U. S. corporation operating exclusively in Venezuela)
   *(d) Professional fee of $2,000 earned during his 6-week stay in the United States for services rendered to a foreign employer
7. Subject to the 10 percent and 70 percent rules, which of the following items are Subpart F income for a wholly owned subsidiary (incorporated in Hong Kong) of a domestic corporation?
   (a) Dividends received from an unrelated corporation
   (b) Interest received on trade notes
   (c) Capital gain on sale of stock
   (d) Profit on the sale of merchandise manufactured in Hong Kong and sold to the parent corporation for use in the United States
   (e) Profit on the sale of merchandise manufactured in Macao and sold to the parent corporation for use in the United States
   (f) Income from engineering services rendered to another subsidiary of the U.S. parent in Singapore
   (g) Income from engineering services rendered to an outsider in Singapore
8. A nonresident alien individual dies owning the following assets:

| | |
|---|---|
| U.S. bank account | $ 25,000 |
| Foreign real estate | 100,000 |
| Stock in U.S. corporations | 125,000 |
| Stock in foreign corporations | 65,000 |

Calculate his estate tax.

*9. Which of the following countries are "less-developed" countries for U. S. tax purposes?
   (a) Poland
   (b) Hong Kong
   (c) Puerto Rico

(d) Mexico

(e) Spain

*10. Describe each of the following in terms of the consolidated tax effect on a U.S. parent corporation:

(a) U.S. corporation subsidiary

(b) DISC subsidiary

(c) Foreign corporation subsidiary

11. A parent corporation's consolidated financial statements reflect the assets and earnings of a foreign subsidiary. Earnings of the foreign subsidiary have not been subjected to U.S. tax, but would be taxed to the parent corporation as, if, and when remitted to the parent. How, if at all, should this possible future tax liability be reflected in the consolidated financial statements?

12. Discuss the effect on the foreign tax credit of an "income tax" imposed by a foreign country on companies engaged in purchasing raw materials within such country, when the raw materials are processed in the United States.

*13. Allowance of a credit against the federal estate tax for state estate taxes up to a certain level resulted in all states adopting some sort of death transfer taxes. Assume you are the finance minister of a foreign country with no income tax. How might existence of the U. S. foreign tax credit offer you a way of taxing some U. S. corporations without really costing them any money?

*14. A U. S. corporation is planning a foreign operation that will not produce Subpart F-income. It is anticipated that operations for the first few years will produce a loss. Discuss the different tax effects on the U. S. corporation of setting up the foreign operation in a U. S. corporation subsidiary or in a foreign corporation subsidiary.

15. Contrast the approach to reallocation of income adopted by the I.R.S. in the *Lilly* case (see excerpt) with that adopted by the I.R.S. in the PPG case (see excerpt), and explain why a court could adopt the I.R.S. approach in one while rejecting it in the other.

16. Comment on the logic of the following argument, advanced by the taxpayers in the *Grunebaum* case (see excerpt):

> The deductions at issue have already been taken into account in the computation of the taxable income from foreign and domestic sources combined (the denominator in the calculation formula). To consider them again elsewhere in the formula would be to count them twice.

17. The RI Corporation had sales of 2 million fudangles at $15 each this year, of which 500,000 were sold in foreign markets. The manufacturing cost of the fudangles was $8, with selling and miscellaneous costs amounting to $2 per unit. What could the RI Corporation save if it created a DISC and sold

the units to the DISC at $9 per unit and had the DISC absorb the costs of selling and miscellaneous expenses associated with those units?

*18. Under FASB 8, gains and losses of U.S. corporations from foreign currency fluctuations are credited to earnings every quarter whether or not realized. Such unrealized gains or losses often tend to overshadow the operating performance of the company involved during such a short period as three months. What impact do currency fluctuations have on the calculation of taxable income of U.S. companies doing business abroad?

# 19

# Estate Taxes, Gift Taxes, Trusts, and Insurance

## TRANSFER TAX

The U.S. tax law integrates the estate tax and the gift tax through the use of one tax table (see page 389). The law treats lifetime gifts and transfers at death as part of one unified computation with no particular *direct* tax advantage to making a transfer during life instead of a transfer as a result of death so as not to give the wealthy a tax benefit by making lifetime transfers.

*Example:*

Jones dies in 1981, a widower, leaving an estate of $500,000 and having made lifetime gifts (after 1976) of $100,000 on which no gift taxes have been paid because of credits allowed.

| | |
|---|---|
| Estate | $500,000 |
| Gifts | 100,000 |
| Total transfers | $600,000 |
| Tax on $600,000 | $192,800 |
| Credit | 47,000 |
| Estate tax due | $145,800 |

The credit is $34,000 in 1978, $38,000 in 1979, $42,500 in 1980, and $47,000 for 1981 and thereafter.

The $47,000 credit (after 1980) means that no transfer tax is due until total transfers exceed $175,625. This, in turn, means that fewer than two percent of the estates of people dying in any given year even need to file a federal estate tax return. A third of those filing, in turn, show no tax due as the result of special deductions (mainly the marital and charitable bequest deductions). The 5 percent of filed returns showing estates of over $1 million wind up paying half of the total $3 billion a year of estate tax collected.

## ESTATE TAXES

For that small minority of persons with sufficient assets to have an estate-tax problem, planning for the minimization of the estate tax and of other expenses associated with transfer of an estate is often a major undertaking. The costs of administering an estate, getting it through probate, and so forth, are often more substantial than the estate tax, running about 8 percent of the total estate and not subject to any credit.

Planning for minimum transfer tax usually involves:

1. Taking maximum advantage of the marital deduction
2. Disposing of property during life (*inter vivos* gifts)
3. Imaginative use of charitable beneficiaries
4. Using trust devices to prevent transfer taxes from depleting capital in each generation

Let us take a look at each of these four planning devices.

(c) Rate Schedule.—

| If the amount with respect to which the tentative tax to be computed is: | The tentative tax is: |
|---|---|
| Not over $10,000 | 18 percent of such amount. |
| Over $10,000 but not over $20,000 | $1,800, plus 20 percent of the excess of such amount over $10,000. |
| Over $20,000 but not over $40,000 | $3,800, plus 22 percent of the excess of such amount over $20,000. |
| Over $40,000 but not over $60,000 | $8,200 plus 24 percent of the excess of such amount over $40,000. |
| Over $60,000 but not over $80,000 | $13,000, plus 26 percent of the excess of such amount over $60,000. |
| Over $80,000 but not over $100,000 | $18,200, plus 28 percent of the excess of such amount over $80,000. |
| Over $100,000 but not over $150,000 | $23,800, plus 30 percent of the excess of such amount over $100,000. |
| Over $150,000 but not over $250,000 | $38,800, plus 32 percent of the excess of such amount over $150,000. |
| Over $250,000 but not over $500,000 | $70,800, plus 34 percent of the excess of such amount over $250,000. |
| Over $500,000 but not over $750,000 | $155,800, plus 37 percent of the excess of such amount over $500,000. |
| Over $750,000 but not over $1,000,000 | $248,300, plus 39 percent of the excess of such amount over $750,000. |
| Over $1,000,000 but not over $1,250,000 | $345,800, plus 41 percent of the excess of such amount over $1,000,000. |
| Over $1,250,000 but not over $1,500,000 | $448,300, plus 43 percent of the excess of such amount over $1,250,000. |
| Over $1,500,000 but not over $2,000,000 | $555,800, plus 45 percent of the excess of such amount over $1,500,000. |
| Over $2,000,000 but not over $2,500,000 | $780,800, plus 49 percent of the excess of such amount over $2,000,000. |
| Over $2,500,000 but not over $3,000,000 | $1,025,800, plus 53 percent of the excess of such amount over $2,500,000. |

| If the amount with respect to which the tentative tax to be computed is: | The tentative tax is: |
|---|---|
| Over $3,000,000 but not over $3,500,000 . . | $1,290,800, plus 57 percent of the excess of such amount over $3,000,000. |
| Over $3,500,000 but not over $4,000,000 . . | $1,575,800, plus 61 percent of the excess of such amount over $3,500,000. |
| Over $4,000,000 but not over $4,500,000 . . | $1,880,800, plus 65 percent of the excess of such amount over $4,000,000. |
| Over $4,500,000 but not over $5,000,000 . . | $2,205,800, plus 69 percent of the excess of such amount over $4,500,000. |
| Over $5,000,000 . . . . . . . . . . . . . . . . . . . . . | $2,550,800, plus 70 percent of the excess of such amount over $5,000,000. |

### *Marital Deduction*

A minority of states (Louisiana, Texas, New Mexico, Arizona, Nevada, California, Washington, and Idaho) are community-property states. Prior to 1948, residents of those states had certain tax advantages flowing from the fact that under state law, one half of earned property acquired by either husband or wife during marriage belonged to the other. In a community-property state, to the extent of the community property involved, the estate of a deceased spouse would include only his or her half of the property owned by the marital community. Thus, if a man who owned with his wife $500,000 of community property were to die, only $250,000 would be includable in his estate for federal estate-tax purposes. There were such definite income, estate, and gift tax advantages to being a resident of a community-property state that many states to whose legal tradition community property was foreign began to adopt community-property laws in the years 1947 and 1948. Congress was thus forced to do something about the special advantage available to persons living under community-property laws. It provided for a separate rate calculation on joint income tax returns, which had the effect of splitting the income between husband and wife regardless of state law, and provided for the marital-deduction approach to the estate tax and gift tax.

The estate tax marital deduction is a reduction allowed in figuring the amount of the estate subject to tax. The deduction is the amount of property bequeathed to the surviving spouse—but not more than half the adjusted gross estate (that is, the gross estate reduced by debts and expenses). Thus, if the man who died owning, with his wife, $500,000 of property lived in a state such as Illinois, which is not a community-property state, all the property could be included in his gross estate unless some of it had actually originated with his wife or unless he had made a completed gift of it to her. However, if he left at least $250,000 of it to her, his executor would be able to deduct $250,000, leaving the estate in the same tax position as that of the man from the community-property state.

As a special break for "smaller" estates the rule that the marital deduction can't exceed half of the estate has an exception: The marital deduction will be the amount of property going to the surviving spouse, if that amount is not over $250,000, without regard to the 50 percent rule.

Thus, in planning for the disposition of an estate, it is common practice to make sure that maximum advantage is taken of the marital deduction.

### Inter Vivos *Gifts*

The main transfer tax advantage of making lifetime gifts is that increases in the value of the property given will be removed from the taxable estate. The income tax advantage of lifetime gifts is that the person receiving the gift (the donee) may be in a lower tax bracket than the donor—and hence may have less income tax to pay on the income that the property throws off. Many people also find nontax satisfactions in passing their wealth on to the persons for whom they ultimately intend it while the donor is still around to observe the effects of the gift.

Gifts to one's spouse, however, offer a unique transfer tax saving potential, because of the gift tax marital deduction. The first $100,000 of otherwise taxable gifts to a spouse are excluded from the gift tax. The next $100,000 of gifts are fully taxable, as if they had not been made to a spouse. Gifts over $200,000 are 50 percent excludible.

*Example:*

Jones, who has never previously made any taxable gifts, gives his wife $356,000 in 1981. He can exclude from gift tax consideration half of that as a marital deduction. He can also exclude $3,000 (which will be discussed in a moment).

| | | |
|---|---|---|
| Gift | | $356,000 |
| Exclusions— | | |
| Marital | $178,000 | |
| Annual | 3,000 | 181,000 |
| Taxable | | $175,000 |
| Tax | | $ 46,800 |
| Credit | | 47,000 |
| Tax due | | $ –0– |

In calculating the estate tax upon death, the amount of Jones' gift that will be added to the calculation is only the $175,000, even though he has removed $356,000 from his taxable estate, assuming that he lives more than three years from the date of the gift.

What's the $3,000 used in the example? An annual exclusion for gifts is allowed. This is $3,000 per donor, per donee.

*Example:*

A married couple, both 45, have four married children. They can give each child, and the spouse of each child, $6,000 per year ($3,000 for each parent). With four children, this means that they can give away $48,000 per year (2 *donors* X 8 donees X $3,000). Over 25 years, they can thus give away, completely free of any transfer tax problems, $1,200,000! Assuming that these dollars were invested and compounded at an after-tax return of only 5 percent, about $1,785,000 would thus have been removed from the taxable estates of the parents at no tax cost, thus saving some $684,000 or more in estate taxes.

There are thus two straight-forward ways of reducing the transfer tax impact for people of moderate wealth—gift programs, utilizing the $3,000 annual exclusion, carried out over a period of years, and maximum use of in-family gifts and the marital deduction. An example may help focus the previous discussion on how the second method can work:

*Example:*

Mr. Jones has a net worth of $606,000. He is 60, and while he will probably live at least three or four more years, his health is not good. Mrs. Jones is 45 and is in robust health. He gives her $356,000, which uses up his transfer tax credit but does not require him to write a check. His will leaves to her the rest of what he owns, $250,000, which is also not subject to tax because of the estate tax minimum marital deduction.

If they had, say, a daughter, and felt comfortable having her get such a substantial sum, either outright or in trust, Mr. Jones could avoid any tax and still dispose of $656,000. They would jointly give the daughter $356,000, thus using up both of their transfer tax credits. Mr. Jones would give Mrs. Jones $100,000, which is excludable under the gift tax marital deduction, and leave her $200,000 (which is not taxable due to the minimum marital deduction).

Both of these examples present one problem. What about the death of Mrs. Jones? Assuming she does not remarry and does not use up her property, she will face a substantial estate tax problem. In the first example, she will have $606,000 when she dies, which will mean an estate tax of $148,020 (net of the $47,000 credit). In the second example, she will have only $300,000, but the computation will include $175,000 of the gift to the daughter deemed to come from her, so tax will be calculated on $475,000. This (net of the $47,000 credit) would be $100,300.

We can generalize and say that some of the planning that can be done to save taxes in the estate of the first of a married couple to die can lead to estate tax problems when the survivor dies. Thus, tax planning in this area often focuses on achieving the minimum transfer taxes for an entire family group and not just for one person.

## BYPASSING AN ESTATE

What happens to the property of a decedent in excess of the amount that qualifies for the estate tax marital deduction? With modest estates, the primary interest of the deceased spouse is often that everything go to the survivor. But every dollar that goes to the survivor builds up the tax problem that will exist in the estate of the survivor. Amounts over and above the marital deduction are fully taxed in the decedent's estate, and can then be again fully taxed when the surviving spouse dies.

The solution is often to use a bypass trust. The amount of property needed to get the maximum marital deduction is left to the surviving spouse, with the balance of the property being left in a trust for the benefit of the surviving spouse. Such a trust might provide that all of its income would go to the survivor, that the survivor could obtain any amounts of principal needed to maintain his or her standard of living in the event other resources were insufficient, and that upon the survivor's death the assets remaining in the trust would be divided up as the survivor might have directed (but with the limitation that the survivor could not direct that any amounts be paid to his or her estate or creditors). The property in the trust, while available to the surviving spouse, normally would not be included in the survivor's estate due to the above limitation.

Does this sound like a good idea? It is. But the thought might then occur to the survivor that leaving the trust property to his or her children, who are now well-to-do, could only aggravate their own tax problems, so why not do with them what his or her dead spouse did. That would be to give them a right to get at the trust assets if they needed them, but to pass the property down to their children, his or her grandchildren. This can be done, but only up to $250,000 per child. Thus, if the surviving spouse has two children, he or she could bypass their generation as to transfer taxes on up to $500,000 of trust assets.

Leaving the surviving spouse the maximum marital deduction possible may not always be good planning. Assume Mr. Jones will have an estate of $350,000. His will leaves $250,000 outright to Mrs. Jones (all eligible for the marital deduction) and leaves the other $100,000 to a bypass trust to be used for her benefit. If Mrs. Jones still has the $250,000 when she dies, her estate will have to write a tax check for $23,800, but Mr. Jones' estate has avoided all tax.

But the $23,800 can be saved. He makes a $100,000 gift to Mrs. Jones. In his will, he provides only $75,000 for her (which, of course, qualifies as a marital deduction) and leaves the other $175,000 in the bypass trust. His estate incurs no tax, because the credit soaks up the tax on $175,000 transfer, and the $100,000 gift qualified for the gift tax marital deduction and hence used none of the credit. Now her estate will be $175,000, and the credit will avoid any tax when she dies.

Even if the surviving spouse will have assets that might create an estate tax problem, she can do things to cut down that problem. Annual gifts under the

$3,000 per donee exclusion are often utilized. Annuities can provide an assured income and yet leave nothing to be subject to estate tax. Remarriage may either dissipate the inheritance or provide another crack at the marital deduction with a new spouse.

### *Charitable Beneficiaries*

The estate tax is imposed on the property itself, regardless of who the beneficiary may be. However, there are two exceptions to this rule. One is the allowance of the marital deduction, already discussed. The other exception allows a deduction in computing the estate subject to tax for bequests to religious, charitable, scientific, literary, or educational purposes.

Let us illustrate how this works with an extreme example. Tracy owns 70 percent of the stock of the Tracy Manufacturing Company. Other members of his family own the remaining 30 percent. The fair market value of Tracy's stock is approximately $20 million. The corporation is engaged in a vigorous expansion, and Tracy hopes that this can be carried through without diluting the family's control. Borrowing power is already strained to the limit.

Tracy's tax advisers suggest that he leave stock to the University of Arizona Foundation, which is organized and operated exclusively for scientific and educational purposes. Because Tracy's wife is already dead, and the 30 percent of the stock not owned by Tracy is distributed in the proportions in which Tracy desires to see control maintained, the suggestion is made that the corporate charter be amended to authorize a class of 6 percent cumulative nonvoting preferred stock. Tracy's will then provides that the stock he owns shall be exchanged upon his death for the preferred stock, and the preferred stock all be distributed to the foundation. This effectively eliminates *all* estate tax, while leaving control within the family. In the absence of such a program, or some alternative, the estate tax on Tracy's $20 million estate would have been over $13 million. To raise this sum, family control of the corporation would almost certainly have had to be relinquished—or, at best, seriously weakened. The basic plan can be made more attractive by having Tracy start during his lifetime to donate stock to the foundation, thus gaining for himself the income tax benefit of a charitable contribution and also participating in setting up the foundation's *modus operandi* relative to the corporation.

## THE TRANSFER TAX CREDIT

How should the transfer tax credit ($47,000 after 1980) be reflected in an analysis of the costs of making gifts? One approach is to look at cash flows. Using the credit involves no present cash flow, and thus the appropriate measure for the cost of the gift is only the check that has to be written now.

The opposite approach would be to ignore differences in timing, and, in a situation where it seemed almost certain that a credit not used now would be usable in full at some later date either against gifts or upon the taxpayer's death, consider the gift tax before deduction of the credit as the appropriate measure of cost.

The most precise approach would be to look at the probable life expectancy of the taxpayer, recognizing that to the extent that gift tax is not currently paid because of the credit, more estate tax will ultimately be due. The amount of credit being utilized, discounted at an appropriate rate for the taxpayer's life expectancy, would then be the amount to be added to the gift tax actually being paid.

*Example:*

Jones has a life expectancy of 22 years. Because of his expectations as to inflation, he believes 10 percent is an appropriate discount rate to use. The present value of $47,000 due in 22 years, discounted at 10 percent, is $5,774—and this is the amount to be used in an analysis prepared for him.

The examples in this chapter use the cash flow method, however, because it makes them a little easier to follow.

### Gifts, Death, and Tax Basis

Gifts can be used to shift gains, but not losses, around within a family group. Assume that Dad, who is widowed, is so active in real estate that his gains are ordinary income. He owns a piece of property that cost him only $100,000, but for which he has had an offer of $1,000,000 cash. He wants to sell, and yet his tax will be so substantial if the gain is ordinary income that he is much better off not selling. A gift of the property to his three children, followed by a sale of the property by them, may prove much less expensive.

Dad's sale of the property would produce a tax of $611,460. His gift of the property (assuming that he has made no prior taxable gifts) will produce a gift tax of $345,800, at a cash cost of $298,800 after the $47,000 credit.

The children would take as their basis of the property the $100,000 tax basis of Dad, plus the gift tax paid attributable to the $900,000 of gift tax value in excess of Dad's tax basis, which would be $268,920, for a total basis of $368,920 for figuring gain. Their gain, assumedly taxed to them as capital gain if, in fact, the property is theirs and the sale is made by them, will be $631,080, on which their tax would be $219,453. The gain is deemed to be long term, because their holding period of the property is deemed to start when their Dad acquired it. The total taxes involved would thus be $518,253 instead of $611,460—and, in addition, the property would be out of Dad's estate.

Our rule for the basis of gift property is, therefore, that it is the donor's basis (if less than fair market value) increased (but not above fair market value) by a part of any gift tax paid on the transfer. But what if the fair market value of the property is less than the donor's tax basis at the time of the gift? Here the rule becomes more complex. The objective is to prevent taxpayers from shifting losses around within a family group. So the rule where fair market value is less than donor's basis is that, if the property is subsequently sold for less than its fair market value, the amount of tax loss is measured by the difference between the fair market value and the selling price. If the property is sold for more than the donor's basis, then gain is measured by the difference between the donor's basis and the selling price. And if the property is sold for more than fair market value but less than donor's basis, then there is neither gain nor loss.

Father gives Son property with a tax basis of $50,000 but a fair market value of $40,000. The gift tax paid obviously does not increase the basis, since fair market value is the upper limit of such an increase. If Son subsequently sells the property for $35,000, he sustains a $5,000 tax loss ($40,000 - $35,000). If he sells the property for $55,000, he has a gain of $5,000 ($55,000 - $50,000). If he sells the property for any amount from $40,000 to $50,000, he has neither gain nor loss!

In selecting property for gifts, therefore, it is important to bear the tax basis and fair market value of the property in mind. Giving away property that has depreciated in value may result in no one's ever getting any tax benefit from the unrealized loss. Giving away property that has appreciated in value may result in the donee's having tax to pay when he disposes of it, as we saw earlier. If the purpose of the gift is to reduce the taxable estate, then the ideal gift property is property that is worth approximately its tax basis. If the property has depreciated in value, it makes more sense to sell it, get the tax benefit of the loss, and give away the proceeds. In a large estate, there is usually enough variety in the types of assets held to allow for reasonable choice in constructing a gift program.

Note that the minimum tax on tax preferences adds to the attractiveness of gifts within the family, because each family member (except one's spouse) can have up to $10,000 (or half his regular tax) of preference income without paying preference tax. When the head of the family has large amounts of earned income, gifts of property that would produce preference income can save substantial income taxes by preventing the shifting of earned income (subject to a maximum tax of 50 percent) into tax brackets ranging to 70 percent.

Property inherited after 1976 has tax basis rules similar to property acquired by gift. The decedent's tax basis is increased by federal and state death taxes attributable to the appreciation in value of the property (i.e., attributable to the excess of the fair market value for estate tax purposes over the decedent's tax basis).

*Example:*

Jones, Jr. inherited unimproved real estate upon his father's death in 1984. The real estate had been purchased in 1977 for $20,000, but had a fair market value of $80,000 when Jones, Sr. died. The estate tax attributable to the unrealized $60,000 gain was $15,000. Jones, Jr. will calculate any gain on sale of the realty by using $35,000 as his tax basis.

However, such was not always the rule. The changeover date for this system of determining the tax basis of inherited property was December 31, 1976. Thus, the general rule has a major exception—property which the decedent owned on December 31, 1976. And, to avoid extensive record-keeping in small estates, there are two minor exceptions.

First, the minor exceptions. Estates under $60,000 will result in heirs having as their tax basis the fair market value of the property inherited. This results from allowing a minimum amount of tax basis of $60,000 for each estate (but not more than the estate's fair market value). Additionally, fair market value can be used as tax basis for up to $10,000 of household and personal items, at the same time providing that in the event of a sale of household or personal items at a loss, tax basis can't exceed what fair market value was when the decedent died.

Marketable securities owned by the decedent at December 31, 1976 take their value as of that date as the tax basis to the heirs, if that value is greater than the decedent's tax basis adjusted for death taxes under the general rule.

All other property falls under a rule which assumes, without any opportunity for rebuttal, that increases in value occurred ratably during the ownership. To calculate basis, you need to know the decedent's basis, date of acquisition, estate tax value, and date of death.

*Example:*

Jones died in 1984 owning real estate then worth $400,000, which he had purchased in 1964 and which had a tax basis of $100,000 when he died. Of the 7,200 days between his purchase and his death, 4,200 came before 1977. His heirs will have a tax basis that will include:

| | |
|---|---:|
| Jones' basis | $100,000 |
| 42/72 X $300,000 | 175,000 |
| | $275,000 |

The tax basis will thus be $275,000 plus the death taxes attributable to the $125,000 of estate tax value that will not be part of the income tax basis.

## EXTENSION OF TIME FOR PAYMENT OF ESTATE TAX

An executor can elect to pay over a ten-year period the portion of the estate tax attributable to the inclusion in the estate of an interest in a closely-held business, if the value of the interest exceeds 35 percent of the value of the gross estate or 50 percent of the taxable estate.

Alternatively, a 15-year extension may be elected. The executor can then defer the payment of the tax for a period of five years and pay it in equal installments over the next 10 years. To qualify for the 15-year rule:

1. The value of the closely-held business must be at least 65 percent of the adjusted gross estate.
2. It must be a proprietorship; or at least a 20 percent interest in a partnership or corporation; or an enterprise which has no more than 15 partners or shareholders.

A special 4 percent interest rate is charged on approximately the first $300,000 of tax attributable to the closely-held business. Interest at the current rate is charged on the balance.

Any estate will be eligible for a discretionary extension of up to ten years to pay the estate tax upon a showing of "reasonable cause."

## REDEMPTION OF STOCK TO PAY ESTATE TAXES

Capital gain treatment of a redemption of stock by a corporation to a shareholder to pay death taxes is permitted if the value of the stock exceeds 50 percent of the decedent's adjusted gross estate. This treatment is available only to those shareholders whose interests in the estate are reduced by payment of funeral and administration expenses or death taxes of the estate, and only to the extent so reduced.

## STATE-LAW CAUTION

All the states impose some sort of death taxes, and many of them also impose gift taxes. The variances among the states are so great that any attempt to generalize would be meaningless, and any attempt to be specific would require too much space. Adequate tax planning requires that state law and its effects be carefully looked into. Taxpayers have been known to change their state of legal residence because tax laws in one state were more favorable than in another, especially if some time were spent in both states. Of course, taxpayers have been known even to change their country of residence because of tax laws. A most notable example was probably Sir Harry Oakes, who left Canada for the Bahamas for tax reasons, and later was the victim in a celebrated murder mystery that has never been solved.

## CHARITABLE CONTRIBUTIONS

One of the traditional responsibilities of wealth has been to generously support religious and charitable institutions. In a relatively wealthy nation, this responsibility is presumably shared by a substantial portion of the population. Just as basis problems require careful choice of the property to be given to individuals as part of a gift program, so do these problems affect charitable contributions.

Assume that a taxpayer owns stock that is worth $60,000 but that cost him $10,000. He can sell the stock, pay $12,500 capital gains tax, and donate the remaining cash—$47,500—to, say, his church. If he is in a 50 percent tax bracket, he will obtain a $23,750 tax benefit from this donation.

The church got $47,500, and the taxpayer saved $23,750. If, instead, the stock itself had been contributed to the church, which in turn would sell it, the church would get $60,000, instead of $47,500; the taxpayer would get a $60,000 charitable contribution deduction, and a tax benefit of $30,000 instead of $23,750. The basic reason for this result is that a contribution is not deemed to be a transaction in which any gain can be recognized, in spite of the fact that the statutory measure of a charitable-contribution deduction of property that would produce capital gains on its sale is fair market value of the contributed property. Thus, the increment between tax basis and fair market value escapes income taxation while producing a tax benefit.

This same result does not follow if the property would produce ordinary income upon sale. The statute limits the deduction, in such a situation, to the tax basis of the property.

## SHORT-TERM TRUSTS

Many gifts have reduction of estate taxes as their tax objective. Others, however, have income tax reduction purposes. Typical of these is the so-called Clifford trust (named after the landmark Supreme Court decision in *Helvering* v. *Clifford,* 23 AFTR 1077). As a general proposition, a taxpayer cannot assign to another his right to receive income and thereby shift the income tax impact to that other person. I can inform a corporation in which I own stock that future dividends are to be paid to my mother for the balance of her life, but doing this will not relieve me of reporting these dividends as income and paying income tax on them.

Yet if I am in a relatively high tax bracket, it takes a substantial amount of pretax income for me to come up with the, say, $4,000 per year that my mother needs. In a 60 percent bracket, I need almost $10,000 of dividends before taxes to produce $4,000 after taxes. My only tax solace is a $750 exemption that I will get only if my mother doesn't herself have taxable gross income over $750.

The short-term trust offers me an alternative. Assume that Mother will incur an income tax of $400 on $4,400 of dividend income, and that the fee of a trustee will run $100 per year. I transfer to a trust sufficient securities to produce $4,500 per year in dividend income. The trust is to terminate, and my securities revert to me, once Mother dies. I now have no income to report from these securities, while Mother is being adequately taken care of. I save over $5,000 per year.

The short-term trust will be effective only if the property either cannot come back to the grantor of the trust until after the death of the income beneficiary, or cannot come back to the grantor in less than 10 years. Transfer of property to the trust is a gift of a future interest to the extent of the present value of the income rights being transferred. If the mother in the example above was 78 years old, and securities with a fair market value of $100,000 were transferred to the trust, the value of the gift would be $33,546. No $3,000-per-donor-per-donee annual exemption could be used here to offset the gift taxes that might be due, but the credit would more than soak up the gift tax unless large gifts had previously been made.

Needless to say, the transfer of property to a Clifford trust does not remove it from the grantor's estate, so that there are limited estate tax advantages to such a gift.

## INSURANCE

Life insurance deals with both protection and investment. Term life insurance, for instance, offers pure protection and no investment. An endowment offers little insurance and much investment. The average life insurance policy offers substantial amounts of both—and thus differs from other sorts of investments. Our concern here is not with the failure of insurance to protect against inflation or with its ability to provide certainty that a specific sum will be available to meet a known need. Our concern here is with the tax aspects of insurance to the investor.

First, the cash-value provisions in insurance policies result in a tax-free buildup. An insurance contract that is based on 5.4 percent interest offers the equivalent of a 9 percent taxable investment to an individual in a 40 percent tax bracket, assuming that the protection aspect of the policy is worthwhile in itself.

Second, in figuring gain on the cashing in of a life insurance policy during the insured's life, all the premiums paid are figured into the tax basis of the policy, even though part of these premiums actually provided insurance coverage. Thus, in a way, the taxpayer may get a tax benefit from the cost of his life insurance coverage.

Third, the proceeds of life insurance are normally free of income tax, and the policies can be set up, through the use of such devices as the insurance trust, so that the proceeds escape estate tax as well.

Like the trust device, with which it is often combined, life insurance imaginatively used can play a substantial role in both income and estate planning. The possibilities are almost endless, but let us be content with two or three examples.

Assume that our taxpayer has a wife, a daughter, and an interest in his alma mater, Ohio University. He would like to take care of all of them. His earning power is high, even though his liquid assets are few. One plan might be to take out a $300,000 life insurance policy. The proceeds would be payable to a trust, under which the taxpayer's wife and then his daughter will receive an annuity of $15,000 per year until they die. After the death of the last of the two to survive, Ohio University receives the remaining corpus of the trust and any undistributed income. No right would be given the trustee or the wife or daughter to invade corpus or accumulated income for any reason whatever.

These provisions would satisfy the requirements of the tax law relating to charitable-remainder trusts. Accordingly, at the time of the taxpayer's death, the present value of the university's right to receive the funds remaining in the trust after the death of the wife and daughter will be a deduction in figuring the estate tax.

That part of each premium paid that represents the university's share of the insurance is a current income tax deduction as a contribution if an irrevocable trust is set up during life and if the trust is made the irrevocable beneficiary of the life insurance policy. However, that part of each premium paid that represents the share of the wife and daughter will represent a gift by the taxpayer, against which the $3,000 annual exclusion may not be applied, since the gift is one of a future interest. Thus, such premiums will result in gifts subject to tax once the transfer tax credit has been utilized.

Another approach to using insurance to both build an estate and achieve tax savings is for the taxpayer to give a policy on himself to, say, his children. The taxpayer will then pay the annual premiums. Since the policy has been given outright, the annual $3,000 per-donor-per-donee gift-tax exclusion will be allowed and no gift tax will be incurred. The taxpayer is assured that his children will receive a certain minimum number of dollars from him, regardless of what may happen to his financial affairs.

A variant on this is to take out insurance on the children, with them naming the beneficiary. Again, the annual premium will usually be too small to be subject to gift tax. Unlike other gifts, which may be dissipated, a gift of life insurance provides the child with security for his family at a time when it costs the least but is usually the most difficult to finance.

A taxpayer in a high enough tax bracket may find it well worth his while to buy large amounts of life insurance, borrowing against the cash values of policies in order to pay the premiums. If a taxpayer in the 70 percent tax bracket borrows the cash value of his policies and pays 5 percent interest, his after-tax interest cost is really only 1½ percent. If, at the same time, the cash value of the policy is increasing on the basis of compounding the premiums paid at only 3 percent per year, the interest he is paying is being more than offset by the increase in the value of his insurance. In an extreme (and therefore exaggerated) example, if the policy were solely investment and all the premium paid was being treated as invested and compounded, our investor would actually be generating cash:

| *Year* | *Premium* | *Loan* | *Interest Paid* | *Tax Benefit* | *Net Interest* | *Policy Increment* |
|---|---|---|---|---|---|---|
| 1 | $11,000 | $11,000 | $550 | $385 | $165 | $330 |
| 2 | 11,000 | 11,330 | 567 | 397 | 170 | 670 |
| 3 | 11,000 | 11,670 | | | | |

Thus, the taxpayer would have paid out $33,000 in premiums, plus $335 in after-tax interest, and would have received back cash of $34,000. In this caricature of reality, he is getting no insurance coverage, but he is generating current cash. Ultimately, when he cashes the policy in, he will have a tax to pay. However, he may well be in a much lower tax bracket by that time. Besides, with this type of a deal, why would he ever want to cash the policy in?

In recent years, the courts have tended to adopt the position that, where it is impossible to realize gain in an insurance (or annuity) situation except for the current interest-deductibility and the nontaxability of the interest element in the policy loan value, then the transaction will not be recognized for federal tax purposes. The tax law itself denies an interest deduction in some circumstances when insurance is taken out in contemplation of systematic loans against the policy. This illustrates an old tax-planning maxim: Don't kill a good thing. With discretion, an idea can be useful; but carried too far, it provokes remedial administrative and/or legislative action.

## CASE EXCERPTS

*Helvering* v. *Clifford,* 23 AFTR 1077, 60 S. Ct. 554 (1940)
*Guynn* v. *U.S.* (CA4–1971) 27 AFTR 2d 71-1653
*Fred A. Berzon*, 63 T.C. 601 (1975)
*Est. of Edward Tully, Sr.* v. *U.S.* (Ct.Cl.) 37 AFTR 2d 76-1529

### *Helvering* v. *Clifford*
23 AFTR 1077, 60 S.Ct. 554 (1940)

Mr. Clifford made a gift of property, but retained substantial control over its management. The gift was in trust, Mr. Clifford was trustee, and the beneficiary of the trust was Mrs. Clifford. At the end of the term of the trust, the property would revert to Mr. Clifford. The thinking enunciated in this case was subsequently made more precise through statutory enactments and regulations.

Technical considerations, niceties of the law of trusts or conveyances, or the legal paraphernalia which inventive genius may construct as a refuge from surtaxes should not obscure the basic issue. That issue is whether the grantor after the trust has been established may still be treated, under this statutory scheme, as the owner of the corpus. See *Blair* v. *Commissioner,* 300 U.S. 5, 12, 57 S. Ct. 330, 81 L. Ed. 465. In absence of more precise standards or guides supplied by statute or appropriate regulations, the answer to that question must depend on an analysis of the terms of the trust and all the circumstances attendant on its creation and operation. And where the grantor is the trustee and the beneficiaries are members of his family group, special scrutiny of the arrangement is necessary lest what is in reality but one economic unit be multiplied into two or more by devices which, though valid under state law, are not conclusive so far as Sec. 22(a) is concerned.

In this case we cannot conclude as a matter of law that respondent ceased to be the owner of the corpus after the trust was created. Rather, the short duration of the trust, the fact that the wife was the beneficiary, and the retention of control over the corpus by respondent all lead irresistibly to the conclusion that respondent continued to be the owner for purposes of Sec. 22(a).

No one fact is normally decisive but all considerations and circumstances are relevant to the question of ownership and are appropriate foundations for findings on that issue. Thus, where, as in this case, the benefits directly or indirectly retained blend so imperceptibly with the normal concepts of full ownership, we cannot say that the triers of fact committed reversible error when they found that the husband was the owner of the corpus for the purposes of Sec. 22(a). To hold otherwise would be to treat the wife as a complete stranger; to let mere formalism obscure the normal consequences of family solidarity; and to force concepts of ownership to be fashioned out of legal niceties which may have little or no significance in such household arrangements.

The bundle of rights which he retained was so substantial that respondent cannot be heard to complain that he is the "victim of despotic power when for the purpose of taxation he is treated as owner altogether."

*Guynn* v. *U.S.*
(CA4–1971) 27 AFTR 2d 71-1653

> Mrs. Calvert bought a home less than two years before her death and conveyed it to her daughter, Mrs. Guynn, four months after its purchase. Mrs. Calvert continued to live there until her death.

Section 2036 describes a broad scheme of inclusion in the gross estate, not limited by the form of the transaction, but concerned with all *inter vivos* transfers where outright disposition of the property is delayed until the transferor's death. *Estate of Linderme,* 52 T.C. 305 (1969); cf. *C.I.R.* v. *Estate of Church,*

335 U.S. 632, 645 (1959). The donor's interest need not be reserved by the instrument of transfer, nor need it be legally enforceable. *McNichol's Estate* v. *C.I.R.,* 265 F. 2d 667 (3d Cir.), *cert. denied,* 361 U.S. 829 (1959). An interest retained pursuant to an understanding or arrangement comes within §2036. *Skinner's Estate.* v. *United States,* 316 F. 2d 517 (3d Cir. 1963). The understanding need not be express. It may be implied from all the circumstances surrounding the transfer. *Estate of Linderme,* 52 T.C. 305 (1969); Treas. Reg. §20.2036-1, T.C. 6296 (1958), as amended, T.C. 6501 (1960).

Both mother and daughter expected Mrs. Calvert to live in the house indefinitely. Indeed, that expectation underlay Mrs. Guynn's selection of a house close to her own: "It would be more feasible with her advanced years to have her permanently located where I could look after her a little better." Mrs. Guynn stated that her mother never discussed the possibility of moving out of the house once she moved in.

. . . Mrs. Calvert retained all the attributes of ownership except bare legal title. She remained in exclusive possession, paid the taxes, made improvements out of her own funds, and paid no rent. From every outward indication, Mrs. Calvert's relationship to the property was no different after the transfer to her daughter than before. Conversely, Mrs. Guynn's possession and economic enjoyment of the property was totally postponed until her mother's death. We hold, therefore, that the testimony of Mrs. Guynn and the actions of the parties establish an implied understanding that Mrs. Calvert would retain the possession and enjoyment of the property within the meaning of §2036. (The home was included in Mrs. Calvert's estate.)

*Fred A. Berzon*
63 T.C. 601 (1975)

> What constitutes a gift of a "present interest," the classification which is necessary to get the $3,000 per donee per donor annual exclusion?

For gift tax purposes the term "future interest in property" refers to "any interest or estate, whether vested or contingent, limited to commence in possession or enjoyment at a future date." * * * Section 25.2503-3(b), Gift Tax Regs., defines a "present interest in property" as "[a]n unrestricted right to the immediate use, possession, or enjoyment of property or the income from property (such as a life estate or term capital)."

Therefore, the determination of the question at hand requires the inquiry of whether, at the date of each gift, the interest received by a beneficiary was a present or future interest. * * * Petitioners have the burden to show that their claims to the annual exclusions fall within the rule of law allowing those exclusions. * * * In resolving the question at hand we must consider the provisions of the trust indentures involved and the surrounding circumstances in order to decide the case on its own particular facts. * * *

It is well settled that a gift may be separated into its component parts, one of which may qualify as a present interest under section 2503(b). * * * We think it clear that as of the dates of the gifts, under paragraphs (C) and (D) of Article I of the trust indentures, the rights of all the beneficiaries herein to the distribution of the corpora of the trusts were deferred and thus their interests in the corpora of the trusts are future interests for which annual exclusions under the provisions of section 2503(b), apart from (c), are not available. * * *

Clearly the use, possession or enjoyment of the corpus of each trust by any beneficiary was postponed until the happening of one of a number of future events of uncertain date (i.e., the redemption of the Simons Co. stock, the passing of 20 years from the date of execution of each trust indenture, the death of a beneficiary, or a minor's reaching age 21 if the Simons Co. stock placed in trust for him had been previously sold). Petitioners also cannot employ section 2503(c) in order to qualify the gifts of the principal interests in the Simons Co. stock as present interests with respect to the minor beneficiaries since there is no provision in the trust indentures for the expenditures of any of the trusts' corpora for the benefit of any minor beneficiary before his attaining the age of 21 as required by section 2503(c)(1). * * *

The question of whether the income interests qualify for the exclusion, or any part thereof, under section 2303(b) and (c) presents a more complex problem. It is clear that the two adult beneficiaries had the right to receive the income of their respective trusts at least quarterly under paragraph (A) of Article I of their trust indenture.

Under paragraphs (A), (B), (C) and (D) of Article I of the trust indentures, the minor beneficiaries were to have the income of their respective trusts accumulated until age 21. The trustees had the power to distribute the accumulated income for the support or maintenance of the beneficiary for whom the income was to be accumulated. Any undistributed accumulated income was to be distributed to the beneficiary upon his reaching the age of 21 and, if he died before age 21, the entire trust estate, including accumulated income, was to be paid to his estate. After reaching age 21, a beneficiary had the right to receive the income of his respective trust at least quarterly.

It is clear that, without use of section 2503(c), the income interest given to each minor beneficiary does not qualify as a present interest under section 2503(b). * * * However, it is also clear that under our decision in Arlean I. Herr, 35 T.C. 732 (1961), affd. 303 F.2d 780 (3d Cir. 1962), the minor beneficiaries' income interests up to age 21 in this case can and do meet the literal requirements of section 2503(c) and that under our decision in Estate of Levine, 63 T.C. (1974), the minor beneficiaries' rights to income after age 21 in this case can and do, in conjunction with their income interests prior to age 21 under section 2503(c), meet the literal requirements of section 2503(b). Since the rights to income of the eight beneficiaries come within the literal requirements of section 2503(b) and (c), respectively, we will assume, without deciding, that the gifts of the income interests were gifts of present interests. * * *

A crucial inquiry involved in the issue at hand is whether the income interests herein are subject to valuation. "Since the statutory exclusion provided by Section 1003(b)(3) [the predecessor under the 1939 Code to section 2503(b)] applies to the first $3,000 of a gift to each beneficiary, it is axiomatic that the interests transferred must have a determinable value." * * *

We realize that in the trust indentures the trustees, who were both stockholders in Simons Co., did have the power to sell the Simons Co. stock and to reinvest the proceeds in income-producing property (as well as in non-income-producing property). However, there is no indication in the record that they intended to do so or that they would in fact reinvest in income-producing property. Moreover, the stockholders' agreement, to which the trust indentures are subservient, appears to prohibit any transfer, except by gift, of the Simons Co. stock by a donee of a stockholder. In such case, where the sole asset of the trust is Simons Co. stock, the power of the trustee (donee) to sell and reinvest would not be a factor to consider in valuing the income interest.

After considering the entire record, we conclude that, as of the time each gift of stock was made in the years 1965 through 1968, the income interests in question were insusceptible to valuation.

. . .The third issue for decision is whether the $3,000 annual exclusions for the years 1962 through 1964 claimed by petitioners under the provisions of section 2503 for gifts in trust of Simons Co. stock under the terms of the aforementioned 1962 trust indenture may be disregarded in determining the aggregate sum of taxable gifts made by each petitioner for computation of his and her gift tax due during the years 1965 through 1968. It is well settled that exclusions under section 2503, which have been erroneously allowed in prior years, may be disregarded in determining the gift tax due in a year under review even though the statute of limitations for those prior years has run. Based upon our above reasoning for the years 1965 through 1968, we think the claimed $3,000 annual exclusions for the years 1962 through 1964 were erroneously allowed and must be disregarded in determining the correct gift tax due for the years 1965 through 1968.

*Estate of Edward A. Tully, Sr.* v. *U.S.*
(Ct.Cl.) 37 AFTR 2d 76-1529

Defendant's contentions, specifically its argument that sections 2038(a)(1) and 2033 must be treated as virtually identical, suggest at the outset that we consider the basic philosophy of estate tax law. As enacted by Congress, the primary purpose of the estate tax is to tax "the transfer of property at death." C. Lowndes & R. Kramer, Federal Estate and Gift Taxes §2.2 (3d Ed. 1974). If sufficient incidents of ownership in an item of property are given away before death, no tax will be imposed. Since all estate tax statutes are directed at taxing property transferred at death, it can become easy to confuse their operation or to apply them in an overlapping fashion.

Within this context, the two estate tax sections involved in the instant case, 2038(a)(1) and 2033, both impose a tax on property transferred at death. However, they are directed at two different situations. Section 2038(a)(1) is specific in its terms. It taxes property which an individual has given away while retaining enough "strings" to change or revoke the gift. Section 2033 is more general in its approach, and taxes property which has never really been given away at all.

Certain of defendant's arguments misconstrue this basic difference between section 2038(a)(1) and section 2033. By suggesting that the same "controls" over property which might represent a section 2038(a)(1) "power" can also be viewed as a section 2033 "interest," the Government attempts to turn section 2033 into an estate tax "catch all." This was not the intent of Congress in enacting section 2033. Congress has provided a "catch all" in the income tax statutes. It has not done so in the estate tax area. *Estate of Spiegel* v. *Commission* [49-1 USTC ¶10,703], 335 U.S. 701, 714 (1949). *Cf. Helvering* v. *Safe Deposit & Trust Co.* [42-1 USTC ¶10,167], 316 U.S. 56 (1942); *United States* v. *Field* [1 USTC ¶40], 255 U.S. 257 (1921). Therefore, defendant's efforts to treat the two sections as virtually identical by the "catch all" method are misplaced.

In accordance with this analysis, our inquiry takes two avenues. First, did Tully transfer the death benefits but keep a power to change or revoke them until the time of his death? If so, section 2038(a)(1) applies. Second, did Tully have an "interest" in the benefits at his death? If he had an "interest," section 2033 applies.

Finally, Tully did not retain a section 2038(a)(1) "power" to revoke or terminate the transfer to his wife by virtue of the *possibility* that he could have divorced her. The contract called for T & D to make the death benefit payments to Tully's *widow.* It might be argued that Tully could have divorced his wife to terminate her interest in the death benefits, but again such an argument ignores practicalities, reduces the term "power" to the speculative realm, and is not in accord with prior cases. In reality, a man might divorce his wife, but to assume that he would fight through an entire divorce process merely to alter employee death benefits approaches the absurd. Further, in various cases, death benefits payable to the "widow," *Estate of Porter v. Commissioner* [71-1 USTC ¶12,778], 442 F. 2d 915 (1st Cir. 1971), or "wife," *Estate of Kramer v. United States,* 186 Ct. Cl. 684, [69-1 USTC ¶12,585] 406 F. 2d 1363 (1969), were not thereby held includable in the gross estate. The possibility of divorce in the instant situation is so *de minimis* and so speculative rather than *demonstrative, real, apparent,* and *evident* that it cannot rise to the level of a section 2038(a)(1) "power." *Harris, supra; Hinze, supra.* Thus the use of "widow" in the death benefit contract did not give Tully a real power to revoke or terminate the death benefit transfer to his wife.

. . . "Interest" as used in section 2033 connotes a stronger control than "power" as used in section 2038(a)(1). If controls over property cannot rise to the dignity of section 2038(a)(1) "powers" they equally cannot create section 2033 "interests." In the instant case, having failed to establish that corporate stock ownership, "pegging" the benefits to Tully's salary and naming the "widow" as beneficiary created section 2038(a)(1) "powers," defendant equally fails to demonstrate that the same facts create section 2033 "interests."

We find that Tully effectively transferred his interests in the death benefits before his death, determine that he did not keep any significant powers to "alter, amend, revoke or terminate" the transfer and conclude that he had no "interest" in the benefits at the time of his death. We, therefore, hold that the death benefits at issue here were not includable in Tully's gross estate.

## QUESTIONS AND PROBLEMS

1. Harold Lamb has a net worth of $1,200,000. His present will leaves his property in equal amounts to his wife, Mary, and his four sons. The sons are all well fixed already, each having a taxable estate of $500,000, and have no need for any of the capital that would be represented by the legacy, although they could probably use the additional income that they could earn on the additional funds. Ignore administration and probate costs, and assume state inheritance taxes are nonexistent. What would be the estate tax payable upon Lamb's death?
2. Give at least two specific suggestions for reducing the Lamb family estate taxes while still leaving all of Lamb's property within the family group. Rule out any lifetime gifts, for Lamb is simply not disposed to make any. Compute the estate tax that would be payable if your suggestions were followed. Note that a credit for prior estate taxes paid is allowed where a person inheriting property dies less than 10 years after the death of the person from whom the property was inherited, so assume that Mrs. Lamb and the sons all outlive Lamb by at least 10 years. Compare the total family estate taxes under your suggestions with those that would be payable without your suggestions.
3. Morris Rand has never made any taxable gifts. His wife is dead. His will leaves all that he has, an estate of $700,000, to his daughter. If he felt that by giving her part of this property now, it would increase the aggregate amount she would ultimately receive, he would be quite eager to make substantial gifts to her. Suggest a plan for lifetime gifts for Mr. Rand, including the amount thereof, that will minimize the transfer tax on his property.

4. Helen Oslow, the widow of William Oslow, owns all the capital stock of the Oslow Stores, Inc., a chain of retail shoe stores. Her stock has an estimated fair market value of $5,000,000. She plans on leaving it to her three children–two girls and a boy. However, because of the competitive situation in Oslow's industry, Mrs. Oslow is worried over the estate tax consequences of her death–particularly how much cash the corporation would have to make available to the estate, and at what times. Her other assets beside the stock are approximately $175,000. How much estate tax will Mrs. Oslow's estate owe, and when can it be paid?
5. Mrs. Oslow (Problem 4) is quite interested in cancer research because her husband died of cancer and she has herself undergone a successful operation for the removal of a malignancy. She wants you to investigate the possible income and/or estate tax benefits she might be able to derive by having the corporation create a class of nonvoting preferred stock, paying a cumulative dividend, which she could use to donate to the Cancer Foundation. She is in a 60 percent personal income tax bracket. Show her, with examples, what a donation of stock might be able to do to her taxes.

*6. Mr. and Mrs. Murray Sears made the following gifts, all of which were of a present interest, divided equally among their four children:

| | |
|---|---|
| 1974 | $ 80,000 |
| 1975 | 111,000 |
| 1976 | 24,000 |
| 1977 | 40,000 |
| 1978 | 70,000 |
| 1979 | 215,000 |
| 1980 | 30,000 |

Compute their gift tax liability for each year.

7. Mrs. Reinhart is dying. She owns $700,000 of separate property, which upon her death will pass to her husband according to her will. Would she be better off, in reference to only the estate and gift taxes involved, to give her husband the property now?
8. Oswald Hess gave his son Robert 100 shares of the Otis Company as a birthday gift. The stock had cost Oswald $50 a share 5 years before. At the time of the gift, the market value of the stock was $30 a share. It was the only gift Mr. Hess made to Robert that year.
   (a) How much gift tax will Mr. Hess have to pay on the gift?
   (b) Robert later sold the stock. On how much profit will he have to pay tax if the selling price is:
      (1) $20 a share?
      (2) $30 a share?

(3) $40 a share?

(4) $60 a share?

9. Paul Noble is contemplating a $50,000 contribution to the Ohio University Fund. He owns some stock in Sky-High Enterprises, which originally cost him $5,000 but now has a market value of $50,000. Assume that he is in a 50 percent tax bracket and that his capital gains are taxed at 25 percent. Compute the difference in tax effect on Mr. Noble if he sells the stock and donates the proceeds, or simply donates the stock.

*10. On its highest-priced line of shoes, the Exclusive Shoe Salon, Inc., has a gross profit margin of 50 percent. It is in a tax bracket of 55 percent when city, state, and federal income taxes are all considered. State and city income tax laws follow the federal rules. Mr. Charles, the manager of Exclusive, receives a bonus based on after-tax profits. He is contemplating having Exclusive donate substantial amounts of shoes to the various charitable organizations in the community. His theory is that every time he donates a pair of his highest-priced shoes without cutting into his normal market, he increases the after-tax profit. Is he correct?

11. Russell Rouse would like to start each of his three children off in their adult lives with a substantial gift. As he is in the 70 percent bracket, Rouse finds it hard to accumulate property in substantial amounts, so he would prefer that the tax collector provide most of the dowries. The children are now 9, 10, and 13. Mr. Rouse is considering putting into each of three trusts enough property to produce sufficient income (at 8 percent per year pretax) so that the accumulated income at age 21 for each child will amount to $200,000. At that time, the corpus of each trust would revert to Mr. Rouse.

(a) Is what Mr. Rouse wants to do feasible?

(b) How much would Mr. Rouse have to put into the trust for the 9-year-old to achieve his objective of $200,000 of accumulated income in the trust 12 years from now?

12. Paul McNeill, age 34, has a wife, two children, and itemized deductions of $4,000 per year. His salary is $32,000 as a tax specialist with a C.P.A. firm. He is planning his retirement estate, on the assumption that he will retire at age 65. He figures, based on mortality tables, that he faces a .65 probability of living to 65, and would have a 15-year life expectancy thereafter. His house is mortgaged and his savings to date are modest. He estimates that he can put aside $3,000 per year.

(a) He can invest the $3,000 in stocks paying a 5 percent dividend per year, reinvest the dividend, and watch the value of the stocks increase by approximately another 4 percent per year.

(b) He can invest in interest-paying securities returning 8 percent per year of taxable income.

(c) He can buy tax-exempt municipals paying 5 percent per year.

(d) He can buy $130,000 worth of life insurance. The cash value of the policy at age 65, assuming that all dividends and interest amounts are accumulated, will be $118,000.

Project McNeill's probable financial position at age 65 for each of these alternatives. Which would you recommend?

13. Paul McNeill, Problem 12, decided to purchase the insurance. Now, at age 65, he is faced with the choice of taking the cash of $118,000 or taking a monthly annuity of $800 for life. The other investment alternatives are still open to him. Show the tax effects of taking the lump sum and the annuity, and discuss the pros and cons of the annuity settlement versus the cash settlement.
14. What was the tax benefit sought by Mrs. Calvert's estate (see *Guynn* case excerpt), and under what different circumstances might it be achievable?
15. Indicate two situations in which a gift in trust can nevertheless qualify for the $3,000 annual exclusion (see *Berzon* case excerpt).

*16. In the last paragraph of *Berzon*, the judge is deciding an issue that relates gifts excluded in years barred by the statute of limitations to the calculation of gift tax in the years before the Court. What is the problem that he is discussing, and what is his conclusion?

*17. Grandpa, with a net worth of $1 million, leaves the $1 million in trust, with the income to be divided among his four sons, then the survivors among them, and upon the death of the last son the trust to terminate and be divided among his grandchildren. Discuss the income and transfer tax consequences to the sons and the grandchildren, and contrast these consequences with what would have happened if he had left the $1 million outright to the sons (assuming that each son had a net worth of $600,000 at the time he died).

# 4

# A LOOK AT TAX PRACTICE AND POLICY

*In Chapter 1, we reviewed superficially the environment of tax practice. Some parts of that environment deserve a more careful scrutiny–and that is the purpose of the chapters in Part Four.*

# 20

# Handling the Tax Audit

The procedural steps involved in negotiating and settling tax cases are sketched in Chapter 1 and are well developed in official Treasury Department rulings, I.R.S. procedures, and so on. However, the subjective factors producing successful tax settlements cannot be found in these sources. Once the taxpayer or tax practitioner is fully aware of his procedural alternatives, he must acquire, either empirically or through experience, some of the skills of the professional negotiator. If he acquires these skills, the tax audit can be a financially and psychologically rewarding experience.

This chapter will both summarize the procedural aspects of the tax audit and attempt to convey some of the intangibles involved. Since office audits (audits in which the examination is conducted in the local Internal Revenue Service office) are concerned generally with less sophisticated matters and with issues of less materiality than those developed by field audits, our attention will be directed to field audits of business returns.

We shall assume that, as the accountants for the taxpayer, we prepared the return from our audit workpapers. The client, having informed us that his return is to be examined, requests us to handle the audit.

## THE FIELD AUDIT

Generally, the client will have received notice that his return is to be examined, accompanied by the suggestion that either the taxpayer or his representative call to schedule the time, date, and place of the audit. The notice will designate the year or years to be examined.

Although most tax audits are conducted at the taxpayer's place of business, a request to conduct the audit at the office of taxpayer's representative will often be honored.

The representative's office is generally preferable for several reasons:

1. It is generally more comfortable, and an empty office can usually be found.
2. The tax-return workpapers are, in most cases, in the possession of the representative.
3. It prevents the agent from meeting with company personnel, who through inadvertence or ignorance may create unnecessary problems.

Another, and possibly the most important, reason why most tax practitioners prefer to have the audit take place in their own offices is the psychological advantage it offers. The representative, sitting comfortably behind his desk, is better able to set the tone for the audit, and possibly a future advantageous settlement.

If the examination is to be conducted in the client's office, the client should make available some responsible employee as liaison with the revenue agent. The employee should be instructed that he is not to answer technical questions but should be able to explain the flow of information into the books of entry. The agent should be requested to prepare a list of any questions he might have or a list of supporting documentation he wishes to see. Furthermore, the agent should be requested not to raise questions, except those that are obviously routine, with the client or his employees, but to save them for the representative.

Both in preparation for the examination and as guidelines for future meetings with the agent, the following rules should be followed by the taxpayer's representative:

1. Review thoroughly the tax return and supporting workpapers for accuracy and possible areas of exposure.
2. Keep the client informed at all stages of the audit.
3. Make a summary of all material discussions with the agent, with copies supplied to the agent and preferably to the client as well.
4. When the agent requests documentary support, make and give him copies that he can retain.
5. The agent should generally be given access to office machines, typing, duplicating, or secretarial services of the client or his representative, as needed.
6. Keep a record of everything the agent looks at, everyone he talks to and the gist of the conversation, and everything he is given.
7. At all meetings with the agent, attempt to evaluate his personal and technical strong points or weaknesses.
8. Generally, permit the agent to complete his examination before discussing the technical aspects of any particular issue. However, at times, a quick response to a casual question raised by the agent may prevent a detailed review at a later time.
9. Avoid volunteering information. You may be raising questions the agent has not yet even considered.

### *Negotiating with the Field Agent*

Once the agent has concluded his examination, he will give the taxpayer and/or his representative the opportunity to discuss his findings.

While agents are basically fact finders, like other professionals they pride themselves on having acquired sufficient technical understanding of the subject matter to reach reasonable conclusions based upon not only the facts but also the law. Although the representative should direct his attack principally at proving the facts that favor the taxpayer, subtle conclusory remarks about the applicable law may prove helpful, in that the agent may find it necessary to do extensive research before he can discuss the issue properly. Rather than engage in this additional work, he may drop the issue entirely.

If the agent has not modified his position after oral argument, but you believe he can yet be convinced, suggest your submitting a written memorandum. Many times the agent ends up adopting in his report the strong arguments made by the representative. If the representative prepared the return under examination, he possibly foresaw questions that the agent might raise and was prepared for them. Remember, the agent is judged in part by his ability to support his recommendations.

### *Requests for Technical Advice*

In many instances, part of the problem with the agent lies in the fact that you and he simply do not see eye to eye on the facts and the issues, let alone on what their interpretation should be. Here Rev. Proc. 73-8 can be of great advantage.

Either during an examination or at an informal conference, the taxpayer has the right to request that an issue be referred to the National Office of the Treasury Department for technical advice. One of three reasons should be given when the request is made:

1. Within the Treasury Department, lack of uniformity exists as to disposition of the issue;
2. The issue is unusual; or
3. The issue is complex.

This type of appeal will generally be used only in situations where there is a question as to how the law applies to a particular factual situation. But it also has value where the practitioner knows of an unpublished position that the agent will not apply to his client.

While the district office does not have to grant the request, relatively few such requests appear to be denied. If the request is denied, the taxpayer may appeal to the District Chief, Audit Division, within ten days. An adverse decision here cannot be appealed. The National Office, however, will, if the taxpayer requests, review the file. It may disapprove of denial and authorize the request for technical advice.

If technical advice is to be requested, an attempt is made to prepare a statement of facts and issues on which the agent and the taxpayer can agree. In the process of trying to reach agreement on such a statement, it is often the case that the taxpayer and the agent come to see their positions more clearly and find they have a basis for a settlement of the dispute without recourse to the National Office. If agreement on the statement cannot be reached, then separate statements may be filed with the National Office.

In either event, the taxpayer may submit a statement to the National Office explaining his position on the issues involved. He can also request an oral conference, if it appears that the National Office position will be adverse to the taxpayer, but this request must be made when the matter is first being referred to the National Office.

The National Office reply will be given the same weight as a private ruling. Normally, the taxpayer can obtain a copy of the reply upon request, but he has no right to such a copy.

Once National Office advice has been obtained, the likelihood of settling the case in a manner contrary to that advice is fairly remote, short of docketing the case with the Tax Court. Therefore, requests for advice should be a last resort, when you feel reasonably sure that all basis for compromise is gone. However, in some types of cases, the preparation of a statement of facts and issues creates a climate in which compromise is possible. And, of course, there are rare occasions when the agent is taking an untenable position and a request for technical advice has the effect of sobering him up.

### *Settling with the Agent*

When the agent has prepared his report, he will send the taxpayer a copy, together with a Form 870, Waiver of Restrictions on Assessment of the agreed deficiency.

A Form 870 is the method by which the taxpayer notifies the district director that he agrees to the findings of the agent. The signing of a Form 870 is not, however, binding on the Internal Revenue Service or on the taxpayer. The taxpayer signing the 870 is waiving his right to any further hearings before paying the tax. See page 422 for a discussion on the 90 day letter.

A taxpayer signing an unconditional waiver of assessment will stop the running of interest on the deficiency on the 30th day after the waiver is filed with the I.R.S. and assessment may be made at such time. A taxpayer signing a conditional waiver of assessment will stop the running of interest on the 30th day after the waiver becomes effective—when signed by an authorized I.R.S. officer at which time the assessment may be made.

The Internal Revenue Service may reopen the case even after the deficiency has been paid, when there has been fraud, malfeasance, collusion, concealment, misrepresentation, or substantial error, or where failure to reopen would be a serious administrative omission. Furthermore, cases closed by the use of Form 870 or by a letter sent to the taxpayer informing him the case is closed ("agreed cases") may be reopened by post-review made in Washington. Cases in which a refund or credit (not due to overpayment of estimated tax or where foreign tax credits or investment credits are allowed) in excess of $200,000 is allowed are automatically post-reviewed in Washington.

The taxpayer may (after executing the Form 870 and paying the tax deficiency) file a refund claim or sue for a refund. In a hardship case, even before paying the tax, he can offer to pay a lesser sum in compromise of the deficiency. If the taxpayer intends to contest the deficiency before paying, he does not sign the Form 870.

Although most representatives are given authority by the client through a Power of Attorney to execute settlement agreements, it is good practice to have the taxpayer actually sign the agreement. Occasionally, however, where a favorable settlement seems to require immediate action, a phone call authorization may have to be relied upon. A written note of the phone conversation should be made by the representative so that no question as to his authority will be raised at a later date.

At any stage of the proceeding, the taxpayer may be requested by the Treasury Department to execute a Form 872, Consent Fixing Period of Limitation Upon Assessment of Income and Profits Tax. The request to sign the Form 872 will usually be made when the expiration of the statutory period of assessment appears imminent. Normally, a request for the execution of a Form 872 will be made within 6 months of the expiration of the statute of limitations, in order to give both the government and the taxpayer time to arrive at a proper conclusion.

Should the taxpayer refuse to execute the Form 872, the Treasury will issue a statutory 90-day letter (discussed below) almost immediately. Generally, a Form 872 is freely signed by the taxpayer in order to prevent a jeopardy assessment and to leave the avenues of appeal open, but reasons for possibly not signing the Form 872 may be:

1. The taxpayer feels settlement is impossible at the agent, district-conference, or appellate-division levels.
2. Negotiation could best be conducted after the issuance of a 90-day letter.
3. There is insufficient time for the Treasury to conduct an examination, as the statute of limitations is about to expire. (Note that it is possible to grant a selective extension of the statute of limitations, so that only certain types of issues may later be raised.)

In cases in which it appears the agent is obviously in error, and in the rare case in which he refuses to adjust his position or is prolonging the audit unnecessarily, a request to speak to his supervisor is proper. This procedure is virtually worthless, however, if a technical point is involved. The agent's supervisor is usually thoroughly familiar with the technical issues, having discussed them with the agent as the audit proceeded, and it is doubtful that the agent has taken a position different from that of his supervisor.

## THE DISTRICT CONFERENCE

The district conference represents the first true level of appeal from the findings of the agent. The district conferee's conclusion, unlike the agent's determination, is not subject to review by the district review staff. It is especially worth considering this potential settlement level if basically factual questions and/or relatively small amounts are involved. Generally, 60 to 70 percent of all district conferences result in settlement.

The district conferee's settlement authority is limited; it is considered only slightly broader than the agent's. Since the litigation aspects of a case are not a material consideration in the district conferee's determination in cases involving more than $2,500, many practitioners have made a rule of bypassing the district conference whenever a material amount of tax is involved.

When it appears that an advantageous settlement at the district conference is possible and a protest is to be prepared, it should be written as if it were to be used at appellate division. If settlement is not reached at the district conference, the protest will be forwarded by the conferee to the appellate division.

To secure a district conference if less than $2,500 is in dispute, the taxpayer need only send a letter, within 30 days of the date on which the 30-day letter (see below) is mailed, to the attention of the "Chief, Conference and Review Staff," requesting the conference. If the dispute concerns more than $2,500, a written protest must be filed.

The district conference is conducted in a rather informal atmosphere. The agent will not usually be present. Witnesses may be brought to the conference, but this is seldom done, as written affidavits are usually sufficient. Furthermore, the client's inexperience with matters of this type may hamper what should be a rather simple method of disposing of the controversy, so he should not be present. If the issues are extremely complex and do not lend themselves to easy settlement, the district conference probably should not be used.

The Internal Revenue Service has taken the position that taxpayers are not entitled to a district conference (nor, for that matter, an appellate-division conference) as a matter of judicial or legislative right. For example, where failure or refusal to comply with the tax laws is due to moral, religious, political, constitutional, conscientious, or similar grounds, a conference will not be granted.

### *The 30-Day Letter*

The 30-day letter is an administrative letter advising the taxpayer, after review is completed, that the agent has proposed a deficiency and that the taxpayer must either pay the deficiency or take certain administrative steps to have the proposed deficiency abated. If he fails to take either step within the 30-day period, a statutory 90-day letter will be issued.

At least three types of 30-day letters are used by the Treasury:

*Form L-191 30-day letter,* if the amount in dispute is less than $2,500. This letter advises that the taxpayer may have a district conference if he wishes, and he may submit a memorandum of his position. Furthermore, the taxpayer is advised that he can bypass the district conference and go directly to the appellate division if he wishes, but a written protest must be filed.

*Form L-191A 30-day letter,* if the amount in dispute is more than $2,500 and the reviewer believes the case can be settled at the district conference. This letter suggests that the taxpayer seek a district conference but advises that a written protest is required. Again, the taxpayer is informed that he may bypass the district conference by filing a protest with the appellate division.

*Form L-191B 30-day letter* is used when the review staff believes the case cannot be settled at the district-conference level. In this letter, the taxpayer is advised to go directly to the appellate division by filing a written protest with the regional commissioner.

The taxpayer should follow the instructions of the 30-day letter. To seek a district conference when not so advised will only result in wasted effort on the part of the taxpayer and his representative.

## THE APPELLATE-DIVISION CONFERENCE

The last level within the Internal Revenue Service at which a case can be settled is the appellate division of the regional commissioner's office. The first two levels (agent and district conference) are within the local district director's office. In the eyes of the I.R.S., the appellate division is the only Internal Revenue Service organization that has true settlement authority.

After you have carefully evaluated the basic issues in your case, you may decide that the case can best be settled by considering the "hazards of litigation" as opposed to only the factual matters involved. If a Revenue Ruling or regulation precludes a favorable determination at the agent level, it may be advisable to go directly to the appellate division, bypassing the district conference.

In order to proceed to the appellate division, a written protest must be filed in duplicate, specifically identifying the issues to which the taxpayer takes exception. No particular form is required, but it should contain the information required by the instructions in the 30-day letter. A properly drafted protest will represent a major plus in settlement negotiations. After presenting the facts, it should analyze the issues raised by the agent in his report, citing cases, rulings, and so on, favoring the taxpayer's position. The taxpayer should not address the brief to issues not raised by the agent or the district conference. If new issues are brought up, the appellate conferee will request supplementary memoranda.

One does not proceed to the appellate division without some risk. The conferees are experienced I.R.S. personnel and will raise more sophisticated arguments or even, on occasion, bring up new issues.

A careful evaluation of issues must thus be made prior to the appellate conference. Timing items (such as asset-depreciation lives and overaccruals) are generally far less significant than permanent items (such as capital gains versus ordinary income). Those issues that are material and that warrant litigation in court should be segregated. The ability to trade issues in a manner most beneficial to your client is a major factor in these negotiations.

The preparation of a protest for the appellate division and the overall preparation necessary for the conference will probably represent a substantial investment in professional time. The client should therefore be encouraged to view the situation from a dollars-and-cents standpoint. The fee he is being charged has to be measured against the amount of tax in controversy.

If appellate-division settlement does not look possible, thought should be given to having legal counsel brought into the picture. Getting the client's lawyer involved with the appellate-division protest will ensure his familiarity with the issues and permit him to act as devil's advocate to insure complete preparation for the conference. He will then be in a much better position to help the client decide whether to go the Tax Court route or pay the tax and sue for a refund.

Settlement at the appellate division is usually executed on a Form 870AD. The conferee will send the appropriate form along with instructions for its execution. The settlement agreed upon at the appellate division will not be upset by I.R.S. post-review unless there has been fraud, malfeasance, or a material misrepresentation of fact. However, the legal effect of an 870AD remains to some degree unclear. The I.R.S. position is generally that the taxpayer is barred from later filing a refund claim.

### *The 90-Day Letter*

A taxpayer can request a 90-day letter at any time after the agent has rendered his report. The 90-day letter is the statutory notice of deficiency that is required, under Sections 6212 and 6213 of the Internal Revenue Code, before a deficiency can be assessed and collected. Whereas the assessment itself is merely the recording of the deficiency on the summary record of assessment maintained by the district director or the director of a regional service center, this step initiates the collection process.

The 90-day letter states that if within 90 days (150 days if the letter is mailed to a taxpayer outside the United States) the taxpayer does not file a petition with the Tax Court, the tax will be assessed.

A 90-day letter is issued either:

1. At the request of the taxpayer who desires to file a petition with the Tax Court.
2. By the district director when the taxpayer has failed to file a protest from a 30-day letter.
3. By the appellate division upon failure to reach a settlement. The office of the regional counsel of the Internal Revenue Service will be requested to concur in the issuance of a 90-day letter at this level, as that office will have to fight the case should it go to Tax Court.

When he has received the 90-day letter, the taxpayer can:

1. File a petition with the Tax Court.
2. Pay the deficiency, file a claim, and then sue for refund in either district court or the Court of Claims.
3. Allow the Treasury to assess the deficiency, at which time the normal collection procedures will begin.

## THE COURT BATTLE

In reviewing the judicial authorities applicable to your case, you should be mindful that a forum must be chosen if settlement cannot be achieved within the Internal Revenue Service (including the appellate division). The immediate avenues of appeal are the Tax Court, the district court, and the Court of Claims. The district court and the Court of Claims, however, are available only if the deficiency is paid and a refund action instituted.

Figure 20-1, on page 424, shows the organization of appeals available to the taxpayer.

More cases go to the Tax Court than go the refund-claim route. Decisions of the Tax Court or of the district court can be appealed to the appropriate circuit court of appeals. Since there are eleven circuit courts of appeal, the taxpayer must carefully review the decisions in similar cases of the specific circuit court to which he must appeal if the Tax Court or district court renders an adverse decision.

It might be mentioned again at this point that the Tax Court has a small-tax-disputes procedure for cases where the amounts involved are less than $1,500. Decisions in these small cases cannot be appealed. While the district court is bound by the decisions of the circuit court in which it sits, the Tax Court has not always been so restricted. After taking a position on a particular issue, the Tax Court, until 1970, applied its rule to all taxpayers on a national

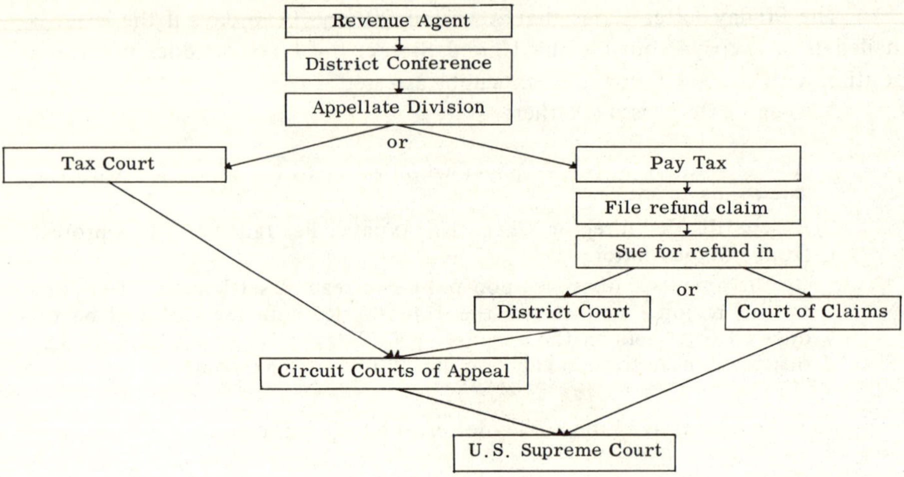


FIGURE 20-1
Organization of Appeals Procedure

basis. The taxpayer would then have to appeal to the circuit court in order to have the decision reversed. A reversal by the circuit court of appeals was then not binding in the Tax Court, which in subsequent cases would again render a decision based upon its own position, forcing the taxpayer to appeal.

The Tax Court now has a different policy. It will follow decisions of a court of appeals for cases arising in that court's jurisdiction even if the Tax Court disagrees. When it does disagree, it will hand down a decision based on the appellate court's rule and will state its own disagreement. If a similar case arises in the jurisdiction of another appeals court that hasn't ruled on the problem, the Tax Court will follow its own view despite its earlier decision that followed a contrary circuit court view.

By resorting to the Tax Court, the taxpayer forgoes the possibility of a district-court refund suit, which might have been based on facts that become known after the Tax Court decision, so that he cannot look back to bemoan "if only I had gone to district court instead of Tax Court" or of having a jury act as fact-finder. If a refund suit is brought in the Court of Claims, a switch cannot later be made by filing a refund suit with the district court.

It is not the purpose of this chapter to detail the procedural and/or theoretical problems involved in choosing one of these forums. What should be clear is that the decision is not an easy one and is not one that can be reversed at the whim of the taxpayer or his representative. It is little consolation to the distraught taxpayer who has lost his case in the Tax Court that, had he paid the deficiency, the district court or the Court of Claims would have reached a more favorable conclusion. Nor is it any consolation to discover too late that the Tax Court would have been the more favorable forum. The decision as to which route to go should be made by the taxpayer only after considering the views of both his accountant and his attorney. However, there are situations–for instance, when he cannot pay the proposed deficiency–when the taxpayer has no choice but to go the Tax Court route; and other situations, such as payroll and excise tax matters, where he cannot go to the Tax Court.

## CASE EXCERPTS

*Joseph B. Ferguson* 47 TC 11 (1966)
*U.S. et. al.* v. *Coopers & Lybrand* 39 AFTR 2d 77-809

*Joseph B. Ferguson* v. *Commissioner*
47 TC 11 (1966)

> The taxpayer can win the battle and lose the war! Mr. Ferguson went to the Tax Court to argue that the alimony he paid was deductible. And look what happened to Mr. Ferguson.

In the course of preparing for their defense in this Court of a deficiency of less than $1,200 resulting from disallowance of an alimony deduction, [the I.R.S.] attorneys found themselves swept along on a voyage of discovery which in its own way came to rival Carter's exploration of the tomb of Tutankhamen; the wonders and tax treasures ultimately unearthed from beneath an unobtrusive surface were so great that respondent has now conceded the original alimony adjustment which prompted his voyage and has amended his pleadings to allege new deficiencies totaling in excess of $300,000. Petitioner, whose tax return showed a modest salary as his only income, was discovered to have had control of three parcels of valuable real estate and to have been enmeshed in a complicated series of transactions involving, *inter alia,* payments during 1959 of $132,592.57 to a mysterious "experimental department." And the taxable income represented by these payments, like the Fergus automobile, appears to have vanished from the American scene.

. . . Since we have held that the experimental department was owned by petitioner, the entire [amount] paid to it is also income to petitioner. We agree with respondent that the payments were in substance rent income to 444; 444's earnings and profits would be increased by the amount thereof, thus supporting constructive dividend treatment in the same amount within the limitations of section 316(a) (2), Internal Revenue Code of 1954. Accordingly, we hold that petitioner realized unreported taxable income from constructive dividends in the total amount of $130,712.09 in 1959 as a result of the payments by Imported under the terms of the 1958 agreement. . . .

In an amendment to the pleadings herein petitioner made the alternative allegation that if he is chargeable with any gross income by reason of payments made by Imported to the experimental department, then he is entitled to offsetting deductions for ordinary and necessary expenses in connection with a trade or business. As to this allegation, petitioner bears the burden of proof, and he has wholly failed to establish that he is entitled to any such deductions.

*U.S. et. al.* v. *Coopers & Lybrand* 39 AFTR 2d 77-809

> The I.R.S. attempted to obtain a C.P.A. firm's tax working papers (called "tax pool" papers in the case).

In the instant case, the I.R.S. has not challenged respondents' argument that the tax pool does not contain records of transactions. The evidence is clear that the Tax Pool was not prepared in connection with the preparation and filing of J-M's tax returns. The I.R.S. here does not seek records of corporate transactions or the data which are customarily maintained in support of company transactions, instead it seeks private thoughts and theories of the taxpayer.

Consolidated financial statements are prepared annually by Johns-Manville for inclusion in reports to stockholders and certain mandatory filings with the Securities and Exchange Commission. Coopers and Lybrand examines and reports on these consolidated financial statements (and utilizes the tax pool analysis file to that end).

* * *

. . . The uncontradicted evidence establishes to our satisfaction that the Tax Pool Analysis file and related papers were not issued or compiled in connection with the preparation or filing of J-M's income tax returns. Coopers & Lybrand has no responsibility in regard to determining or reporting on J-M's tax liability. The limited purpose for which the Tax Pool was created by J-M and communicated to C&L was unrelated and distinct from J-M's tax liability or the preparation of J-M's tax returns. . .

I.R.S. contends that the file comes within a §7602 summons because it *might* show tax fraud, because it *might* show substantial tax liability, and because it would be relevant to show and establish the state of mind of employees at the time the returns were filed. I.R.S. acknowledges it has no direct or precedential substantive authority supportive of its position.

The general cases cited by I.R.S. all deal, for the most part, with summonses issued for the production of materials utilized in the preparation and filing of tax returns. However, extending I.R.S. contentions herein to their logical conclusion, it is hard to determine what corporate records would not fall under a §7602 summonses if the standard endorsed the production of *any* records which *might* show tax fraud or tax liability. I.R.S. does not, as it appears to assume on this appeal, have *carte blanche* discovery. . . .

One of the limitations which may be properly imposed upon a judicial summons was noted in *United States* v. *Matras* [73-2 USTC ¶9801], 487 F. 2d 1271 (8th Cir. 1973):

> . . . Obviously, that issue must be determined on an ad hoc basis. Certainly, a taxpayer should not erect roadblocks for the purpose of frustrating or preventing the IRS from a full-scale inquiry of the liability of the taxpayer. By the same token, the government should not, for the mere sake of its convenience, impose unnecessary burdens on a taxpayer in conducting an audit or investigation for tax liability, particularly where, as here, there is no indication of a purpose to escape any tax liability. The term "relevant" connotes and encompasses more than "convenience." Consequently, we are not persuaded to fault the district judge for concluding that government failed to sustain its burden of proof by alleging a general need for a "road map." If we were to accede to the government's view, it is difficult to imagine corporate materials that might not contribute to a more comprehensive understanding of the workings of the corporation, and thus, according to the government, be deemed relevant to the tax investigation. . . .

Applying these standards, we hold that the court properly found that the tax pool analysis file was not relevant and therefore not subject to production under the summons. In this respect we deem it worthy of repeating that it was uncontroverted that the tax pool analysis file was not prepared in connection with or used to facilitate the preparation and filing of J-M's tax returns and that C&L has no responsibility for any J-M tax matters.

## QUESTIONS AND PROBLEMS

1. Technical advice may be requested by the taxpayer during the examination. Describe the procedure for securing technical advice and the impact the request has upon settlement at the agent level.
2. Differentiate between a 30-day letter and a 90-day letter. Give an example of when a 90-day letter may be requested by a taxpayer.
3. Describe the function of the appellate division in the settlement process.
4. The Tax Court has recently changed its procedure in regard to following decisions of a court of appeals. Describe this change.
5. (a) Explain why many practitioners prefer to handle the tax audit in the privacy of their own offices rather than at the client's place of business.
   (b) What instructions should be given to client personnel when they are told they are to assist the agent in his review of the books?

*6. Contrast the finality, in terms of filing a refund claim, of signing a Form 870 as against signing an 870AD. What significance could this difference have in regard to a taxpayer's willingness to "trade off" issues at the agent level as opposed to trading issues at the appellate-division level?

7. An individual taxpayer claimed a deduction for an unusually large amount of sales tax on his income tax return. The explanation he gave, in a statement attached to the return, was that he had built an addition onto his house. The I.R.S. agent asked for proof. The taxpayer produced some bills (marked "Cash" in many instances) and some cancelled checks made out to various hardware and lumber-supply stores. The agent takes the position that this is not sufficient proof–that the taxpayer has to prove that the sales tickets showing the customer as "Cash" were actually paid by the taxpayer, and has to negate the possibility that the checks to lumber yards, etc., were not merely cashed for cash. Is the agent imposing an undue burden of proof on the taxpayer? What recourse does the taxpayer have against such an attitude by the agent?

8. A revenue agent has challenged the deductibility of the compensation paid to the president of a corporation. The president owns all the stock of the corporation, and the corporation has never paid any dividends. What would be the approach you would use in trying to persuade the agent that the entire amount paid to the president was reasonable compensation for services rendered? In your answer, set forth some of the types of proof you might furnish the agent.

9. A revenue agent, auditing a 1040 prepared by you, proposes to disallow a claimed deduction. Your notes (filed with your retained copy of the return) cite a Court of Claims 1950 decision as to the authority for the deduction. In the 30-day letter, the agent cites no cases, but your discussions with him have brought out the fact that he is relying, at least in part on a BTA 1932 decision. The pertinent facts involved in both the BTA and Court of Claims cases are similar, while the decisions are in exact conflict with each other. Neither decision has ever been cited by any court, and there are no other court decisions or administrative rulings on this point. What would be the possible strength of your position at district conference, in the appellate division, in Tax Court, in district court, or in Court of Claims?

10. An I.R.S. agent is auditing the 1974, 1975, and 1976 federal income tax returns of Fast Food, Inc., which has filed its federal income tax returns on the cash basis since it started in business, but has always maintained its books and records, and prepared its financial reports for creditors and stockholders, on the accrual basis. The agent claims that under IRC 446, taxable income should be computed using the method of accounting employed in keeping the books and records–namely, the accrual method. He has not yet proposed the deficiency formally, and may yet come up with

additional issues, but he seems adamant on the accrual versus cash basis question. The potential deficiency on this issue is approximately $500,000. The consolidated after-tax net income, ignoring these possible tax adjustments, is about $700,000; total assets amount to $2,500,000; stockholders' equity is $1,300,000. The tax partner of the C.P.A. firm that audits Fast Food estimates that the issue will most likely be settled at the appellate-division level of the I.R.S. by Fast Food's paying about 45 to 50 percent of the proposed deficiency. The lawyer for Fast Food feels that the position of Fast Food is defensible and that the deficiency will certainly be contested. How should this situation be disclosed in the Fast Food 1978 financial statements?

11. The revenue agent in Problem 10 has decided that he could like to look at anything in the C.P.A. firm's audit working papers having to do with the Fast Food income tax liability or expense. The C.P.A. firm has already made available to the agent what they call the "Tax Return Assembly Workpapers," which contain everything they have that entered into the preparation of the income tax return, including working papers showing the adjustments made to the trial balance for tax purposes, the reclassifications involved, etc. The other working papers they have, which played no role in the preparation or the tax return (in fact, were not prepared until after the tax return had been completed) reflect the possible tax issues that might be raised, and the C.P.A.'s evaluation of them. They were prepared to help the C.P.A.s decide what a reasonable tax liability provision might be and what additional footnote disclosures might be needed on the annual financial statements. Using the *Coopers & Lybrand* excerpt as your reference point, discuss whether you think the agent has a right to these latter tax working papers and what position you think the C.P.A. firm should take relative to his request.

# 21

# Tax Fraud

The man in the street reads in the evening newspaper that a prominent professional man has been convicted of tax evasion, sentenced to 2 years in prison, and fined $5,000. The next morning, he gets a form letter from the I.R.S. telling him that his 1977 income tax return is being examined and additional detail, plus receipts and canceled checks, is wanted to support the amounts he has claimed as charitable contributions and medical expenses. He gets a funny feeling in his stomach. What did he do on that 1977 return? He digs it out, looks it over. What if he can't prove the $300 that he claimed as a deduction for used clothing, old furniture, and similar items given to his church? Is he also on the way to being a newspaper headline?

Not a chance! His deduction may be disallowed or scaled down, but Mr. Taxpayer is not going to be prosecuted for an honest difference of opinion. A deficiency may well result, which is the case in some 60 percent of the 3 million income tax returns audited annually by the I.R.S. A deficiency may indicate that a taxpayer made a mistake or was unable to prove something, but it is not in itself an indication of tax fraud.

Tax fraud, in fact, is a relatively rare thing. Few accountants, few businessmen, and few lawyers actually get involved with tax fraud cases. The primary job of the I.R.S. is to collect taxes, and its fraud activities tend to be aimed heavily at the underworld. Its concern with the average taxpayer is mainly one of providing a deterrent, so that the voluntary compliance so unique in the U.S. tax system will continue.

Fraud involves "willfulness," and the existence of fraud must be quite clear to the I.R.S. before a recommendation for criminal prosecution will be made. (There is also something called "civil fraud," where the only penalty is a monetary one—50 percent of the total tax deficiency shown on the return. We will mention civil fraud again.)

Unlike other tax cases, which generally can wind up being taken to the Tax Court, to the Court of Claims, or to a U. S. district court, at the taxpayer's option, a criminal tax fraud case is always tried in a U. S. district court. Thus either the taxpayer or the government can ask for a jury trial, and thus, also, the case is apt to be tried before a judge who handles a wide variety of civil and criminal matters and only rarely gets involved in tax cases.

## HOW FRAUD CASES COME ABOUT

The Audit Division of the I.R.S. selects income tax returns for examination, and examines them for the purpose of determining whether or not the taxpayer should be prosecuted criminally. In the course of such an examination, the revenue agent may have reason to suspect that fraud is involved. He may have come across a bank account owned by the taxpayer and reflecting substantial deposits, the source of which was not disclosed to the agent. Or the agent may become aware that the amount of personal living expenditures of the taxpayer appears to be inconsistent with the income reported.

The agent will prepare a report describing the situation observed and will forward the report through channels to the Intelligence Division. He will take this action at the earliest possible moment that he can provide the Intelligence Division with sufficient information upon which to consider the case; this early referral is because of the complexities involved in a criminal case, which are out of the bailiwick of the revenue agent. The Intelligence Division specializes in the handling of investigations of criminal violations.

Upon receipt of the agent's report, the Intelligence Division personnel (designated "special agents"), after consideration of the file, will either reject the case for lack of apparent criminal violations or accept the case for criminal investigation. In some instances, where fraud is indicated but not clearly enough to warrant acceptance of the case for a full-scale investigation, the case is accepted for preliminary investigation.

Once the case is accepted for either preliminary or full-scale investigation, the special agent becomes the focal point of the examination and to a large extent may direct the subsequent actions of the revenue agent with respect to the taxpayer. On the other hand, the special agent may rely heavily upon the revenue agent for assistance in interpreting and applying the tax law applicable to any nonfraud aspects of the case.

Some fraud cases arise through the type of investigations initiated by the Intelligence Division after receipt of specific information about a taxpayer that suggests the desirability of criminal investigation. Special agents are never assigned to a random canvass of taxpayers at large. You may hear comments that special agents will "stake out" a doctor's office for a period of time to get an idea of the number of patients seen over a normal span of office hours. This type of surveillance does not take place, however, without specific cause for suspicion of the taxpayer. That specific cause may be information received from an informant—perhaps seeking revenge, perhaps seeking the "fee" of up to 10 percent of the tax deficiencies involved, which the I.R.S. may pay for information.

## THE CRUCIAL MOMENT

Having accepted a case for investigation, the special agent goes into action. In some instances, the special agent will visit the taxpayer with the revenue agent. Whenever the revenue agent confronts the taxpayer with another person, the taxpayer should inquire the name and role of such other person, or ask to see his credentials.

In other instances, the special agent will begin his investigation by canvassing savings institutions, stockbrokerage firms, real estate firms, and the like, and word will get back to the taxpayer of such inquiries. At the moment the interest of a special agent is ascertained, the taxpayer should get in touch with an attorney having experience in tax fraud matters.

Immediate decisions must be made: If he is guilty should the taxpayer cooperate nevertheless to create an aura of good faith? Or should he cooperate to the extent that he ultimately "helps" the special agent find discrepancies, explaining then that these discrepancies came about not through fraudulent intent but rather through honest mistake? Or, if counsel feels that the government has a potentially strong case, should cooperation be offered with a view to ultimately seeking a light punishment?

On the other hand, if the taxpayer is not guilty of criminal wrongdoing, why not cooperate with the special agent, so that he will complete his investigation promptly and be on his way? But if you advise the latter, exposing your client to an examination more detailed than the usual I.R.S. audit, don't you thereby expose him to greater risk of I.R.S. discovery of more substantial nonfraud issues? And even if he is not guilty, is the taxpayer in an occupation where he might have difficulty getting a fair trial, or could circumstantial evidence and using quotations and facts out of context create an impression of guilt? Or, if you feel that the underlying case would not be strong enough to enable the government to secure a fraud conviction, doesn't your cooperation still leave the door open for the imposition of the 50 percent civil fraud penalty?

## CONSTITUTIONAL PROBLEMS

Aside from the practical decisions to be made along the lines just mentioned, the fraud area presents some unique challenges to the practitioner, involving concepts not ordinarily found in other aspects of tax practice. One such field is constitutional law.

Television drama has taught us that a law officer confronting his suspect must advise him that he has the right to obtain counsel, and that anything he says may be used against him. These rights arise under the Fifth and Sixth Amendments to the U. S. Constitution. In the landmark decision of *Miranda* v. *Arizona,* 384 U. S. 436, the Supreme Court held that statements made by a suspect in police custody (a nontax case) were not admissible against the suspect in the subsequent criminal trial, where the suspect-defendant was not given a full and effective warning of his rights under the Constitution at the outset of the interrogation process.

The facts of the *Miranda* case arose in police custody in an interrogation setting. Finding that such an "environment is created for no purpose other than to subjugate the individual to the will of his examiner," the Supreme Court held that the defendant may make statements not based upon voluntary judgment but rather by reason of the compelling atmosphere of the interrogation. On the other hand, it was noted, police (governmental authority, by way of analogy to our discussion) are not required to stop one from making voluntary confessions and other statements, and such truly voluntary disclosures are admissible.

*Miranda* and *Miranda*-type decisions normally do not apply to tax fraud cases.

The policies of special agents vary, not only between, but also within, Internal Revenue districts. Most special agents nowadays advise the taxpayers that they are criminal investigators. Some of them stop there; others follow through with complete–or nearly complete–*Miranda* warnings. But they don't have to.

Closely related to the right to remain silent, which arises from the privilege against self-incrimination under the Fifth Amendment, is the right to withhold one's books and records from the government in a criminal investigation. The taxpayer may properly resist even a summons issued by the government, under this privilege as well as under the Fourth Amendment, which prohibits unreasonable searches and seizures. However, not all records that may be harmful to the taxpayer are subject to this privilege. For example, copies of the transaction accounts of the taxpayer that are maintained by banks and brokers are not records of the taxpayer but rather records of the bank or broker. So the taxpayer will not ordinarily be successful in an attempt to intervene against his bank if it has been summoned by the I.R.S. to produce account records. Likewise, a corporation wholly owned by the taxpayer cannot successfully resist an I.R.S. summons on the grounds of self-incrimination of the taxpayer, as the corporation is a separate legal entity, while the self-incrimination privilege is personal to the individual.

In *Coopers & Lybrand,* 39 AFTR 2d 77-809, the I.R.S. was unsuccessful in compelling the accountants to produce a tax pool analysis file used in verifying their client's financial statements because it was not relevant to the preparation of the client's tax return. This case did not involve self-incrimination because the accountants had no responsibility for the client's tax matters. The Tenth Circuit distinguished this case from the Supreme Court's decision in *Couch* which approved a summons directing a taxpayer to produce records given to an accountant for the preparation of a tax return where taxpayer was denied the self-incrimination privilege.

## PRIVILEGED COMMUNICATION

Privileged communication between the attorney and his client is an ancient doctrine, deeply rooted in the English common law. In the law of evidence, a "communication" made to one's own attorney, in professional confidence and for the purpose of obtaining advice, is not permitted to be divulged by the attorney without the client's consent. Waiver of the privilege rests with the client, not with the attorney. It is this doctrine that prohibits the "other side" from calling your counsel as their witness to testify as to your statements to him about the case.

Since the role and importance of the accountant in business and tax matters is a function of modern times, there was no such doctrine for him in common law. It exists only in the several states that have enacted statutes conferring such a privilege, and in such states it exists only to the extent of such statutes, which are ordinarily narrowly construed.

The Federal Rules of Criminal Procedure provide that privileged communication exists only to the extent of common-law privilege. Hence, the accountant can normally be compelled to testify in federal courts as to what his client has communicated to him.

For the accountant who is about to refer his client to competent counsel for handling of the client's potential fraud case, it is a temptation to have a "heart-to-heart" with the client concerning the true state of facts relating to the fraud situation. The well-meaning accountant who discusses his client's case with him before counsel is engaged, or even without counsel's consent after he is engaged, may find himself the prosecution's "star witness."

The same admonition applies to the preparation of work papers for the client. As work papers usually belong to the accountant and not the client, the work papers may be subject to disclosure before the court. Thus, work papers and other analyses pertaining to a fraud case should be prepared by the accountant only under the advice and direction of counsel.

This same problem exists with regard to work papers prepared previous to and not in connection with the fraud case. These workpapers may be sought by the government in connection with the fraud case. The practitioner should consult the client's counsel as well as his own counsel as to what to do with these files, for voluntarily or unilaterally surrendering work papers to the government could prejudice the client and could subject the accountant to a civil damage suit by the client.

## THE BURDEN OF PROOF

In civil income tax litigation, the I.R.S. adopts its position on the issues and ultimately sets forth its conclusions in a final report to the taxpayer. The Commissioner's determination is presumptively correct, and the burden of proving him wrong lies with the taxpayer. See discussion of civil fraud penalty on page 444.

The contrary is true in the criminal fraud case. The government is the plaintiff and has the burden of proving the taxpayer guilty of fraud beyond a reasonable doubt. And as in all criminal cases, the defendant-taxpayer is presumed innocent until proved guilty. It is not sufficient for the government to prove that a liability is owing by the taxpayer. The essential element to be proved by the government is the willful attempt to evade tax. Obviously, the taxpayer who resolves a doubtful technical issue in his own favor in filing his income tax return is not criminally willful, compared to the taxpayer who intentionally siphons off gross income that is clearly gross income, with the intent of evading tax. The statute proscribes *evasion* of tax but does not, nor has it ever, prohibited *avoidance* of tax.

## DEFENDING THE FRAUD CASE

In order to understand the defense of the fraud case, you must have an understanding of the government's basic tools in prosecuting it.

### *The Prosecution*

From the government's point of view, the easiest case to prosecute is one involving specific items. That is to say, when the government has a case involving skimming of gross income over a period of several years, can find a clandestine bank account used by the taxpayer as the repository for the funds, can identify the specific deposits, and can even bring into court the customers who paid over such sums to testify that the payments were for sales made or services rendered by the taxpayer, the prosecutor need worry only about proving that the receipts did not find their way to the income tax return. Such a case is easy for a jury to understand. The taxpayer's willfulness can easily be inferred "beyond a reasonable doubt" from the facts and circumstances of the case.

Any prosecutor will tell you that these cases are few and far between. The posture of the usual case is that the taxpayer has an inordinate amount of unexplained bank deposits, or personal and living expenditures inconsistent with the income reported. The preparation and proof of these cases are laborious and detailed. The trial of them is lengthy. The prosecution runs the risk that proof of its case will be so complicated that comprehension by the jury will be limited.

The government's case is essentially built around the net-worth method of income determination or variations of it, such as the bank-deposit method or the statement of source and application of funds.

### *The Net-Worth Method*

The net-worth method of proving taxable income is based upon the theory that any increases or decreases in the taxpayer's net worth during a taxable period, adjusted for nontaxable income and nondeductible expenditures, must be the result of taxable income. In accounting, the income statement is the link between successive balance sheets. In the fraud case, the same is true, except that the "income statement" must be further adjusted in terms of taxable income before the net-worth increase or decrease can be compared with reported taxable income.

Successive balance sheets are prepared, using cost or the taxpayer's tax basis other than cost. They are prepared in accordance with the taxpayer's method of tax accounting. That is, if the taxpayer reports on the cash basis, beginning and ending balance sheets disregard accounts receivable; if the taxpayer reports on the installment method, the balance sheets are similarly prepared, and so on. The opening date of the first balance sheet coincides with the beginning of the taxpayer's taxable year, and the successive and final balance sheets close with the end of the taxable year.

The increase or decrease in net worth for the period is ascertained, and to such increase or decrease is added the taxpayer's personal living expenditures.

At this point, the figure obtained is roughly equal to gross income in the economic sense. The theory of the method is that every dollar acquired by the taxpayer can only be saved, spent to acquire an asset or reduce a liability, or spent for living expenses.

The "net worth" is then refined in terms of taxable income by adding nondeductible items, such as:

1. Federal income tax payments
2. Nondeductible portion of capital losses
3. Losses on sale of personal assets, if included as assets in the balance sheet

—and by subtracting items received that are nontaxable, such as:

1. Nontaxable portions of capital gains
2. Tax-exempt interest

3. Nontaxable pensions
4. Nontaxable proceeds from life insurance policies
5. Inheritances and gifts
6. Dividend exclusions, sick pay, etc.

Any difference between the computed taxable income and the reported taxable income is the unreported (or overreported) taxable income. Any understatement could be due to unreported gross income, overstated tax deductions, or a combination of both.

An example of the net-worth computation employed by the government in an actual case is set forth in Illustration 1 (pages 438-439, taken from *William G. Stratton* v. *Commissioner,* 54 TC No. 23). Although this case involved the civil fraud penalty, the net-worth computation is precisely the same type used in a criminal tax fraud proceeding. Illustration 2 (pages 440-442) shows the Tax Court's own computation of income under the same method after having taken testimony. Note that the total unreported income determined by the government for the nine-year period was $197,000, whereas the net unreported income for the same period was determined by the court to be $82,000. (In *Stratton,* incidentally, the taxpayer, an ex-governor of Illinois, had earlier been acquitted by a U.S. district court on a criminal charge of tax fraud.)

### *Variations of the Net-Worth Method*

The statement of source and application of funds traces increases and decreases in assets and liabilities as sources and applications of funds in the same manner as the statement does in accounting. It is essentially the same as the net-worth method, with the presentation changed to show that funds applied that cannot be accounted for in the sources of funds reported must have resulted from funds whose source was not reported.

The bank-deposit method is used primarily in cases where the net-worth method is impractical and/or in cases where it appears that a substantial portion of business or personal expenses were paid in cash.

The taxpayer's total bank deposits are first ascertained. Excluded from them are nontaxable income deposited, transfers among accounts, and so on. To the resultant net or "taxable-income deposits" amount is added the taxpayer's cash expenditures that were made from sources other than through his banking accounts. Any difference between the total so determined and the income reported is assumed to arise from income received and expended but never deposited nor reported. Sometimes the bank-deposit method is used as a "backup" to the net-worth method to support that the understatement developed by the net-worth method is attributable to unreported gross income rather than to overstated expenses.

Illustration 1

Exhibit A – Page 1 of 2

Computations of Unreported Income Determined by the Net Worth Plus Nondeductible Expenditures Method

| *Assets* | 12/31/52 | 12/31/53 | 12/31/54 | 12/31/55 | 12/31/56 | 12/31/57 | 12/31/58 | 12/31/59 | 12/31/60 |
|---|---|---|---|---|---|---|---|---|---|
| Warrants and checks on hand | $ 100.00 | $ 431.57 | $ 25.00 | $ 430.00 | $ 450.00 | $ 42.00 | $ 903.75 | $ 16.80 | $ 377.16 |
| Regular checking account First National Bank | 1,725.04 | 647.03 | 2,707.01 | 1,434.07 | 2,598.40 | 2,553.29 | 666.48 | 154.18 | 5,970.41 |
| L.T. checking account, First National Bank | -0- | -0- | -0- | -0- | -0- | 83.82 | 163.44 | 168.12 | 650.21 |
| Special checking account First National Bank | -0- | 79.27 | 606.95 | 1,430.66 | 1,114.90 | 169.06 | 849.77 | 492.66 | 1,146.01 |
| Savings account, First National Bank | 4,633.49 | 250.00 | 254.60 | 259.71 | 366.08 | 677.10 | 1,050.57 | 1,081.79 | 1,114.47 |
| Accounts receivable for oil run payments | -0- | 128.90 | 48.75 | 124.02 | 130.49 | 152.31 | 147.79 | 189.03 | 97.81 |
| Loan receivable from Donald J. Breckenridge | -0- | 470.00 | 145.00 | 1,560.00 | 1,065.00 | 735.00 | 470.00 | 730.00 | 680.00 |
| Investment in Bobbill Farm | -0- | 10,000.00 | 26,222.51 | 35,516.03 | 46,636.40 | 49,158.53 | 52,473.05 | 49,891.37 | 48,549.09 |
| Cost of Stock | -0- | 10,263.97 | 11,039.10 | 15,023.85 | 18,248.85 | 31,520.96 | 20,400.64 | 22,891.67 | 18,687.95 |
| Cost of lodge located in Sangamon County, Ill. | -0- | -0- | -0- | -0- | -0- | 18,316.43 | 60,917.82 | 62,741.68 | 63.093.94 |
| Cost of residence, Morris, Illinois | 8,300.00 | 8,300.00 | 8,300.00 | 8,300.00 | 8,300.00 | 8,300.00 | 8,300.00 | 8,300.00 | 8,300.00 |
| Cost of improvements to residence, Morris, Ill. | -0- | 3,134.44 | 15,632.67 | 15,632.67 | 19,455.50 | 19,455.50 | 19,455.50 | 19,455.50 | 19,455.50 |
| Investment in Pinney, Todd & Stratton (Exhibit B) | -0- | 1,648.69 | 1,519.77 | 1,390.85 | 1,508.24 | 1,354.65 | 1,320.97 | 1,173.75 | 1,026.53 |
| Cost of United States Savings Bonds | 18.75 | 56.25 | 468.75 | 468.75 | 468.75 | 468.75 | 468.75 | 468.75 | 468.75 |
| Cost of Morris Country Club Bond | -0- | -0- | -0- | -0- | 200.00 | 200.00 | 200.00 | 200.00 | 200.00 |
| Cost of State of Israel Bond | -0- | -0- | -0- | -0- | -0- | -0- | 100.00 | 100.00 | 100.00 |
| Cost of 1956 Lincoln | -0- | -0- | -0- | -0- | 4,677.75 | 4,677.75 | 4,677.75 | 4,677.75 | 4,677.76 |
| Cost of 1960 Chevrolet Station Wagon | -0- | -0- | -0- | -0- | -0- | -0- | -0- | -0- | 2,570.00 |
| Cost of Furniture and Furnishings | -0- | -0- | 700.00 | 700.00 | 1,108.00 | 1,108.00 | 8,788.03 | 11,358.10 | 12,503.87 |
| Cost of Framed Portraits | -0- | -0- | -0- | 3,500.00 | 7,432.56 | 7,432.56 | 7,432.56 | 7,432.56 | 7,432.56 |
| Cost of Houseboats & Boat Motors | -0- | -0- | -0- | -0- | 4,750.00 | 4,750.00 | 4,750.00 | 7,028.90 | 7,028.90 |
| Check in Transit to Reynolds & Co. | -0- | -0- | -0- | -0- | -0- | 1,492.50 | -0- | -0- | -0- |
| Accounts Receivable from Reynolds & Co. | -0- | -0- | -0- | -0- | -0- | -0- | -0- | -0- | 2,206.57 |
| Total Assets | $14,777.28 | $35,410.12 | $67,670.11 | $85,770.61 | $118,510.92 | $152,648.21 | $193,536.87 | $198,552.61 | $106,337.48 |
| *Liabilities* | | | | | | | | | |
| Account Payable - Reynolds & Co. | -0- | -0- | -0- | -0- | -0- | $ 1,501.53 | -0- | -0- | -0- |
| Accounts Payable - F.M. Pinney | -0- | $ 1,700.83 | $ 49.58 | $ 37.25 | $ 213.94 | 64.52 | $ 207.49 | $ 69.59 | 1,967.93 |
| Mortgage Payable - Marion Stratton Munyon | $ 4,000.00 | -0- | -0- | -0- | -0- | -0- | -0- | -0- | -0- |
| Mortgage Payable - Springfield Marine Bank | -0- | -0- | -0- | -0- | -0- | -0- | 8,468.66 | 3,140.08 | -0- |
| Total Liabilities | $ 4,000.00 | $ 1,700.83 | $ 49.58 | $ 37.25 | $ 213.94 | $ 1,566.05 | $ 8,676.15 | $ 3,209.67 | $ 1,967.93 |
| Net Worth at End of Each Year | $10,777.28 | $33,709.29 | $67,620.53 | $85,733.36 | $118,296.98 | $151,082.16 | $184,860.72 | $195,342.94 | $204,369.55 |
| Net Worth at End of Preceding Year | – | 10,777.28 | 33,709.29 | 67,620.53 | 85,733.36 | 118,296.98 | 151,082.16 | 184,860.72 | 195,342.94 |
| Net Worth Increase (Forward) | – | $22,932.01 | $33,911.24 | $18,112.83 | $ 32,563.62 | $ 32,785.18 | $ 33,778.56 | $ 10,482.22 | $ 9,026.61 |

Exhibit A – Page 2 of 2

Computations of Unreported Income Determined by the Net Worth Plus Nondeductible Expenditures Method – Continued

| | 12/31/53 | 12/31/54 | 12/31/55 | 12/31/56 | 12/31/57 | 12/31/58 | 12/13/59 | 12/31/60 |
|---|---|---|---|---|---|---|---|---|
| Net Worth Increase (Brought Forward) | $22,932.01 | $33,911.24 | $18,112.83 | $32,563.62 | $32,785.18 | $33,778.56 | $10,482.22 | $ 9,026.61 |
| Add: | | | | | | | | |
| Nondeductible expenditures paid by checks drawn on the Regular Account First National Bank (Exhibit C) | 14,927.51 | 11,951.23 | 15,791.48 | 12,980.49 | 9,364.89 | 9,790.35 | 13,259.24 | 13,669.28 |
| Nondeductible expenditures not paid by checks drawn on the Regular Account First National Bank (Exhibit D) | 2,764.13 | 6,107.43 | 1,890.49 | 11,147.67 | 14,204.33 | 12,822.47 | 8,398.36 | 7,569.92 |
| Federal income tax withheld by the State of Illinois | 3,960.30 | 3.894.48 | 3,894.58 | 3,894.48 | 3,894.48 | 3,894.48 | 3,894.48 | 3,894.48 |
| Nondeductible loss on sale of houseboat | | | | | | | 2,250.00 | |
| Nondeductible loss on sale of stock | | | | | | | | 1,044.43 |
| Retirement withheld by State of Illinois | 456.25 | 525.00 | 525.00 | 525.00 | 1,035.40 | 1,749.96 | 1,749.96 | 1,749.97 |
| Subtotal | $45,040.20 | $56,389.38 | $40,214.28 | $61,111.26 | $61,284.28 | $62,035.82 | $40,034.26 | $36,934.69 |
| Subtract: | | | | | | | | |
| Nontaxable gift of houseboat | | | | (4,750.00) | | | | |
| Nontaxable portion of long-term capital gain | | | | | (905.65) | (833.45) | | |
| Dividend exclusion claimed on income tax return | -0- | (50.00) | (50.00) | (50.00) | (50.00) | (75.00) | (100.00) | (100.00) |
| Distributive share of percentage depletion - Pinney, Todd and Stratton | -0- | (279.86) | (478.11) | (486.32) | (556.90) | (546.36) | (545.50) | (394.99) |
| Nontaxable insurance dividends from Veterans Administration | (66.00) | (64.80) | (64.80) | (62.40) | (73.20) | (70.80) | (70.80) | (69.60) |
| Deduction for state sales tax | (54.00) | (112.00) | (117.50) | (361.25) | (190.00) | (431.80) | (291.08) | (332.38) |
| Deduction for exemptions claimed on return | -0- | (3,000.00) | (3,000.00) | (3,000.00) | (3,000.00) | (3,000.00) | (2,400.00) | (1,800.00) |
| Remainder | $44,920.20 | $52,882.72 | $36,503.87 | $52,401.29 | $56,508.53 | $57,078.41 | $36,626.88 | $34,257.72 |
| Add (subtract) adjustments to reflect salary from the State of Illinois in the amounts reported on returns | -0- | (2,083.33) | 2,083.33 | -0- | (2,083.33) | 2,083.33 | (2,083.33) | -0- |
| Corrected net income (1953) or taxable income (1954 through 1960) | $44,920.20 | $50,799.39 | $38,587.20 | $52,401.29 | $54,425.20 | $59,161.74 | $34,543.55 | $34,257.72 |
| Net income (1953) or taxable income (1954 through 1960) reported on returns | 22,854.54 | 21,979.56 | 20,864.92 | 20,048.16 | 22,497.79 | 22,223.96 | 21,309.17 | 20,068.83 |
| Unreported Income | $22,065.66 | $28,819.83 | $17,722.28 | $32,353.13 | $31,927.41 | $36,937.78 | $13,234.38 | $14,188.89 |

Illustration 2

Exhibit A - Page 1 of 4

Computations of Unreported Income Determined by the Net-Worth Plus Nondeductible Expenditures Method

| *Assets* | 12/31/52 | 12/31/53 | 12/31/54 | 12/31/55 | 12/31/56 | 12/31/57 | 12/31/58 | 12/31/59 | 12/31/60 |
|---|---|---|---|---|---|---|---|---|---|
| Warrants and checks on hand | $ 100.00 | $ 431.57 | $ 25.00 | $ 430.00 | $ 450.00 | $ 42.00 | $ 903.75 | $ 16.80 | $ 377.16 |
| Regular checking acct. First National Bank | 1,725.04 | $ 647.03 | 2,707.01 | 1,434.07 | 2,598.40 | 2,553.29 | 666.48 | 154.18 | 5,970.41 |
| L.T. checking acct. First National Bank | -0- | -0- | -0- | -0- | -0- | 83.82 | 163.44 | 168.12 | 650.21 |
| Special checking acct. First National Bank | -0- | 79.27 | 606.95 | 1,430.66 | 1,114.90 | 169.06 | 849.77 | 492.66 | 1,146.01 |
| Savings acct. First National Bank | 4,633.49 | 250.00 | 254.60 | 259.71 | 366.08 | 677.10 | 1,050.57 | 1,081.79 | 1,114.47 |
| Other cash on hand 12/31/52 | 15,000.00 | -0- | -0- | -0- | -0- | -0- | -0- | -0- | -0- |
| Accts. Receivable for oil run payments | -0- | 128.90 | 48.75 | 124.02 | 130.49 | 152.31 | 147.79 | 189.03 | 97.81 |
| Loan Receivable from D.J. Breckenridge | -0- | 470.00 | 145.00 | 1,560.00 | 1,065.00 | 735.00 | 470.00 | 730.00 | 680.00 |
| Investment in Bobbill Farm | -0- | 10,000.00 | 26,222.51 | 35,516.03 | 46,636.40 | 49,158.53 | 52.473.05 | 49,891.37 | 48,549.09 |
| Cost of Stock | -0- | 10,263.97 | 11,039.10 | 15,023.85 | 18,248.85 | 31,520.96 | 20,400.64 | 22,891.67 | 18,687.95 |
| Cost of Lodge | -0- | -0- | -0- | -0- | -0- | 18,316.43 | 60,917.82 | 62,741.68 | 63,093.94 |
| Cost of Residence | 8,300.00 | 8,300.00 | 8,300.00 | 8,300.00 | 8,300.00 | 8,300.00 | 8,300.00 | 8,300.00 | 8,300.00 |
| Cost of improvements to residence | -0- | 3,134.44 | 15,632.67 | 15,632.67 | 19,455.50 | 19,455.50 | 19,455.50 | 19,455.50 | 19,455.50 |
| Investment in Pinney, Todd and Stratton Exhibit B | -0- | 1,648.69 | 1,519.77 | 1,390.85 | 1,508.24 | 1,354.65 | 1,320.97 | 1,173.75 | 1,026.53 |
| Cost of U.S. Savings Bonds | 18.75 | 56.25 | 468.75 | 468.75 | 468.75 | 468.75 | 468.75 | 468.75 | 468.75 |
| Cost of Morris Country Club Bond | -0- | -0- | -0- | -0- | 200.00 | 200.00 | 200.00 | 200.00 | 200.00 |
| Cost of State of Israel Bond | -0- | -0- | -0- | -0- | -0- | -0- | 100.00 | 100.00 | 100.00 |
| Depreciated cost of Chevrolet | -0- | -0- | -0- | -0- | -0- | -0- | -0- | -0- | 2,000.00 |
| Cost of furniture & furnishings | -0- | -0- | 700.00 | 700.00 | 1,108.00 | 1,108.00 | 8,788.03 | 11,358.10 | 12,503.87 |
| Cost of portrait of Shirley | -0- | -0- | -0- | 3,500.00 | 3,500.00 | 3,500.00 | 3,500.00 | 3,500.00 | 3,500.00 |
| Cost of frame for portrait | -0- | -0- | -0- | -0- | 207.73 | 207.73 | 207.73 | 207.73 | 207.73 |
| Cost of Houseboats and boat motors | -0- | -0- | -0- | -0- | 4,750.00 | 4,750.00 | 4,750.00 | 7,028.90 | 7,028.90 |
| Check in transit to Reynolds & Co. | -0- | -0- | -0- | -0- | -0- | 1,492.50 | -0- | -0- | -0- |
| Acct. Receivable from Reynolds & Co. | -0- | -0- | -0- | -0- | -0- | -0- | -0- | -0- | 2,206.57 |
| Total assets | $29,777.28 | $35,410.12 | $67,670.11 | $85,770.61 | $110.108.34 | $144.245.63 | $185,134.29 | $190,150.03 | $197.364.90 |

Exhibit A - Page 2 of 4

Computations of Unreported Income Determined by the Net-Worth Plus Nondeductible Expenditures Method

| *Liabilities* | 12/31/52 | 12/31/53 | 12/31/54 | 12/31/55 | 12/31/56 | 12/31/57 | 12/31/58 | 12/31/59 | 12/31/60 |
|---|---|---|---|---|---|---|---|---|---|
| Account Payable – Reynolds & Co. | -0- | -0- | -0- | -0- | -0- | $ 1,501.53 | -0- | -0- | -0- |
| Accounts Payable – F.M. Pinney | -0- | $ 1,700.83 | $ 49.58 | $ 37.25 | $ 213.94 | 64.52 | $ 207.49 | $ 69.59 | $ 1,967.93 |
| Mortgage Payable – Marion Stratton Munyon | $ 4,000.00 | -0- | -0- | -0- | -0- | -0- | -0- | -0- | -0- |
| Mortgage Payable – Springfield Marine Bank | -0- | -0- | -0- | -0- | -0- | -0- | 8,468.66 | 3,140.08 | -0- |
| Total Liabilities | $ 4,000.00 | $ 1,700.83 | $ 49.58 | $ 37.25 | $ 213.94 | $ 1,566.05 | $ 8,676.15 | $ 3,209.67 | $ 1,967.93 |
| Net worth at end of each year | $25,777.28 | $33,709.29 | $67,620.53 | $85,733.36 | $109,894.40 | $142,679.58 | $176,458.14 | $186,940.36 | $195,396.97 |
| Net worth at end of preceding year | -0- | 25,777.28 | 33,709.29 | 67,620.53 | 85,733.36 | 109.894.40 | 142,679.58 | 176,458.14 | 186,940.36 |
| Net worth increase (forward) | -0- | $ 7,932.01 | $33,911.24 | $18,112.83 | $ 24,161.04 | $ 32,785.18 | $ 33,778.56 | $ 10,482.22 | $ 8,456.61 |

Illustration 2
(Continued)

Exhibit A - Page 3 of 4
Computation of Unreported Income Determined by the Net Worth Plus Nondeductible Expenditures Method

| | 12/31/53 | 12/31/54 | 12/31/55 | 12/31/56 | 12/31/57 | 12/31/58 | 12/31/59 | 12/31/60 |
|---|---|---|---|---|---|---|---|---|
| Net-worth increase (brought forward) | $ 7,932.01 | $33,911.24 | $18,112.83 | $24,161.04 | $32,785.18 | $33,778,56 | $10,482.22 | $ 8,456.61 |
| Add: | | | | | | | | |
| Nondeductible expenditures paid by checks drawn on the regular acct. First National Bank | 13,169.68 | 10,725.17 | 13,182.41 | 10,688.50 | 8,492.69 | 8,754.27 | 10,465.15 | 10,180.62 |
| Nondeductible expenditures not paid by checks | 1,524.67 | 4,483.63 | 1,463.76 | 8,415.66 | 8,634.21 | 10,258.19 | 6,950.10 | 6,712.39 |
| Federal income tax withheld | 3,960.30 | 3,894.48 | 3,894.48 | 3,894.48 | 3,894.48 | 3,894.48 | 3,894.48 | 3,894.48 |
| Nondeductible loss on sale of houseboat | -0- | -0- | -0- | -0- | -0- | -0- | 2,250.00 | -0- |
| Nondeductible loss on sale of stock | -0- | -0- | -0- | -0- | -0- | -0- | -0- | 1,044.43 |
| Retirement Withheld from salary | 456.25 | 525.00 | 525.00 | 525.00 | 1,035.40 | 1,749.96 | 1,749.96 | 1,749.96 |
| Subtotal | $27,042.91 | $53,539.52 | $37,178.48 | $47,684.68 | $54,841.96 | $58,435.46 | $35,791.91 | $32,038.49 |
| Subtract: | | | | | | | | |
| Nontxable gift of houseboat | -0- | -0- | -0- | (4,750.00) | -0- | -0- | -0- | -0- |
| Other nontaxable gifts | (7,000.00) | (2,500.00) | (2,000.00) | (16,000.00) | (2,500.00) | (2,100.00) | (2,500.00) | (9,000.00) |
| Nontaxable portion of long-term capital gain | -0- | -0- | -0- | -0- | (905.65) | (833.45) | -0- | -0- |
| Dividend exclusions | -0- | (50.00) | (50.00) | (50.00) | (50.00) | (75.00) | (100.00) | (100.00) |
| Distributive share of percentage depletion | -0- | (279.86) | (478.11) | (486.32) | (556.90) | (546.36) | (545.50) | (394.99) |
| Nontaxable insurance dividends from Veterans Administration | (66.00) | (64.80) | (64.80) | (62.40) | (73.20) | (70.80) | (70.80) | (69.60) |
| Deduction for state sales tax | (54.00) | (112.00) | (117.50) | (361.25) | (190.00) | (431.80) | (291.08) | (332.38) |
| Itemized or standard deduction (less sales tax) | (1,000.00) | (1,241.79) | (1,591.07) | (2,486.83) | (1,628.48) | (2,779.46) | (2,077.87) | (2,147.52) |
| Exemptions claimed on return | -0- | (3,000.00) | (3,000.00) | (3,000.00) | (3,000.00) | (3,000.00) | (2,400.00) | (1,800.00) |
| Remainder | $18,922.91 | $46,291.07 | $29,877.00 | $20,487.88 | $45,937.73 | $48,598.59 | $27,806.66 | $18,194.00 |

Exhibit A - Page 4 of 4

Computation of Unreported Income Determined by the Net-Worth Plus Nondeductible Expenditures Method

| | 12/31/53 | 12/31/54 | 12/31/55 | 12/31/56 | 12/31/57 | 12/31/58 | 12/31/59 | 12/31/60 |
|---|---|---|---|---|---|---|---|---|
| Remainder (Brought Forward) | $18,922.91 | $46,291.07 | $29,877.00 | $20,487.88 | $45,937.73 | $48,598.59 | $27,806.66 | $18,194.00 |
| Add (subtract) adjustments to reflect salary from the State of Illinois in the amounts reported on returns | -0- | (2,083.33) | 2,083.33 | -0- | (2,083.33) | 2,083.33 | (2,083.33) | -0- |
| Corrected net income (1953) or taxable income (1954 through 1960) | $18,922.91 | $44,207.74 | $31,960.33 | $20,487.88 | $43,854.40 | $50,681.92 | $25,723.33 | $18,194.00 |
| Net income (1953) or taxable income (1954 through 1960) reported on returns | 22,854.54 | 21,979.56 | 20,864.92 | 20,048.16 | 22,497.79 | 22,223.96 | 21,309.17 | 20,068.83 |
| Unreported or (overreported) income | $ (3,931.63) | $22,228.18 | $11,095.41 | $ 439.72 | $21,356.61 | $28.457.96 | $ 4,414.16 | $ (1,874.83) |

### *The Defense*

The net-worth and related methods used by the government are ordinarily based to a large extent on approximations and assumptions. For example, in a case where the taxpayer makes personal expenditures in cash, the government will of necessity have to estimate many expenditures made, such as for groceries and other personal items not purchased via charge account. On the other hand, many items can be ascertained with great certainty, such as brokerage accounts and charge accounts in retail stores.

The basic imperfections of the reconstruction methods usually dictate that the government's case be based on a span of several years of net-worth computations. Thus, attempts by the taxpayer to shift items among intervening years will not help him in reducing the total understatement of income alleged.

In many court cases, the jury, usually unsophisticated in matters such as this, must hear step-by-step testimony concerning the net-worth and related computations. Objections to procedural and evidentiary matters by the defense during the government's case have distracted the jury at times when the light of understanding almost flickered.

But when all else has failed, the defense must be put on. The first attack is that the taxpayer really did not have the intent to defraud. The next attack is the accuracy of the opening balance sheet.

For example, the taxpayer had greater amounts of cash on hand at the beginning of the period than the government has computed. This cash, scraped together by the taxpayer over years of hard toil, provided the wherewithal for those living expenditures during the period.

The defense will also attack inconsistencies between the opening net worth and the closing net worth. The carrying value of the taxpayer's business autos may not have been correctly computed by the government under the basis rules. Did the government value securities held at the closing net-worth date in a fashion fully consistent with the opening valuation? What about stock dividends? These were nontaxable when received and should be valued at zero basis in the closing balance sheets.

Were all liabilities ascertained? Didn't the government go to greater lengths to find assets in the preparation of its case than to locate liabilities? After all, here are *four* charge accounts the government missed, although the assets acquired on credit were included.

And in the elimination from the net-worth increase, why didn't the government give the taxpayer the benefit of the large cash gifts that the taxpayer's father (now deceased) often bestowed upon the taxpayer?

The government's smallest errors and inconsistencies are magnified and remagnified until the jury is (one hopes) convinced that the computations can't be right enough to be the basis for punishment of the defendant. After all, the taxpayer is willing to pay the tax, isn't he?

## CONVICTION AND PUNISHMENT

Don't let the foregoing lull you into the belief that no one can ever be convicted of tax fraud. In fact, the government's record of convictions in cases tried is outstanding. For every taxpayer acquitted of tax fraud, 20 plead guilty or are convicted.

On the other hand, less than 20 percent of the potential fraud cases investigated are ever recommended for prosecution. Most are rejected by the special agents before or during preliminary investigation, owing to lack of convincing evidence of fraudulent intent or to immateriality of amounts involved. Others are dropped by the U.S. Attorney's office for similar reasons, or because of clear violations of taxpayers' constitutional rights, or because of anticipation of evidentiary and other practical problems of proof.

It is common knowledge that the government does not like to lose fraud cases, so it only tries the "best" ones. The reason is public relations. If the government freely tried tax fraud cases and lost substantial numbers of them, the tax fraud charge would not be so fearsome in the minds of the public. And confidence of the public in the I.R.S. would drop.

### *Civil Fraud Penalty*

In addition to the civil income tax asserted by the I.R.S., the so-called civil fraud penalty can be asserted. This penalty is 50 percent of the underpayment of income tax, if *any* part of the underpayment was due to fraud; and it can be properly assessed by the I.R.S. even when the taxpayer has been fined by reason of a criminal conviction. It can be properly assessed in lieu of criminal proceedings. Surprisingly to many, it can be properly assessed even in cases where the taxpayer has been tried and acquitted in the criminal-fraud proceeding!

The reason for this situation is that the government may have lost the criminal tax-fraud case simply because the evidence it presented did not amount to clear and convincing proof of guilt, *beyond a reasonable doubt.* In civil fraud, however, the evidence need only prove fraud by what is known as clear and convincing proof, which is a lesser burden of proof.

An example of the application of these principles is to be found in the case of *Helvering* v. *Mitchell,* 303 U. S. 391. The defendant, Mitchell, had been tried and acquitted of criminal fraud. Thereafter, the I.R.S. assessed an income tax, together with the 50 percent civil fraud penalty. Whether the civil fraud penalty was properly assessed was litigated and was ultimately decided by the Supreme Court. Mr. Justice Brandeis, speaking for the Court in 1938, said:

> The acquittal was "merely . . . an adjudication that the proof was not sufficient to overcome all reasonable doubt of the guilt of the accused.". . . It did not determine that Mitchell had not wilfully attempted

> to evade the tax. That acquittal on a criminal charge is not a bar to a civil action by the Government, remedial in its nature, arising out of the same facts on which the criminal proceedings was based has been long settled. . . .

The civil fraud penalty in the *Mitchell* case amounted to more than 364,000 1930's depression dollars.

In the reverse situation—that is, where the taxpayer has been convicted in the criminal proceeding—the taxpayer is estopped from later denying civil fraud because the government has already met the higher degree of proof required in the criminal trial.

### *Punishment*

The greatest value, in the social sense, of a jail sentence for tax fraud is the deterrent effect upon others who may be contemplating an exercise in tax evasion. At least this seems to be the general consensus of the federal judiciary

By and large, tax fraud is a "white-collar crime." Those accused are usually pillars of the community, respected businessmen or professional men. Their indictments, trials, convictions, and sentencing are indeed newsworthy.

Actually, it is easiest for these persons to perpetrate the tax fraud because their sources of income tend to be those not required to be reported to the I.R.S. Persons engaged as employees, particularly at the lower income levels, have little opportunity to engage in these practices (which is not to say that they would do so even if they had the opportunity).

In the garden variety of criminal case—say, for a crime of violence—there are considerations in sentencing that ordinarily do not apply in tax fraud cases. One reason advanced for sentencing a violator to prison is the removal of a dangerous person from society. This is the exception rather than the rule in a tax fraud case, where the violator is more often than not a respected member of society.

Another reason advanced in favor of imprisonment is that the incarceration gives society an opportunity to rehabilitate the offender. Again, this reason generally finds no niche in tax fraud cases, where the recidivism rate, even in suspended-sentence cases, is less than infinitesimal.

That sentencing to jail of the convicted tax fraud violator is considered by the federal judiciary to be a deterrent to others and therefore desirable seems borne out by the results of a survey of 92 chief judges of the United States district courts. This survey was conducted by the Honorable Walter E. Craig, United States District Judge for the District of Arizona. As reported by Judge Craig,[1] 70 of the 92 chief judges circularized responded, and of those respond-

[1] Presented to the Institute on Defending Tax Fraud Prosecutions of the Practicing Law Institute, Las Vegas, Nevada, December 12-13, 1969.

ing, 75 percent favored jail sentence as a deterrent to the public. Only 37 percent indicated that jail sentencing had a deterrent effect on the *defendant.*

As one federal judge put it, in sentencing a prominent citizen to 3 years in jail (one-half suspended) on a tax charge:

> The filing of fraudulent income tax returns is a serious matter. Income tax laws place the burden upon the individual to fairly state all of his income and expenses. On the basis of such returns he is obligated to pay his taxes. In the field of income taxes the Government must necessarily rely upon the honesty and good faith of the taxpayers. For more than 20 years, the defendant has enjoyed a good income. The theory of income taxes is that those with the greater incomes are in a better position to help defray the expenses of Government. Ordinarily, the greater the income, the greater the benefits the taxpayer receives from government services. By failing to pay his share of taxes as required by law, the defendant required others to bear a portion of the burden that should have been his.
>
> Many people of excellent standing in the community have urged me to be lenient to the defendant. In connection with another sentence, I recently stated that those members of society who are the best educated, who have the most material comforts, and who supply much of the community's leadership should be held to a higher rather than a lower standard of conduct.
>
> I cannot consider the defendant's activities in a vacuum. I must consider them in relation to those of millions of wage earners whose full income taxes are paid by means of payroll deductions and the millions of other taxpayers, both individual and corporate, who make full and frank disclosures of their incomes.

## CASE EXCERPTS

*U.S.* v. *William J. Troupe,* (CA8-1971) 27 AFTR 2d 71-660
*Lenske* v. *U.S.,* (CA9-1967) 21 AFTR 2d 436 (383 F. 2d 20)
*Lenske* v. *U.S.,* (CA9-1966) 18 AFTR 2d 5815
*U.S.* v. *Middlemiss,* 39 AFTR 2d 77-6389

### *U.S.* v. *William J. Troupe*
### (CA8-1971) 27 AFTR 2d 71-660

The summons was directed to William J. Troupe, an accountant, to produce accounting records and information relating to a corporate taxpayer, the B & C Meat Company, Inc. (hereinafter B & C Meat). The district court, over the government's objection, allowed the intervention of Carl Civella, who is a shareholder and an employee of B & C Meat. Civella challenged the issuance of the summons on the ground that it was issued to harass him, was vague and excessively broad, and that it had as its purpose criminal investigation of the intervenor himself. The intervenor also complained of limitations placed on his pretrial discovery by the district court. The district court held a full hearing. The court required the government to answer all interrogatories by oral testimony and allowed examination of government witnesses the intervenor wished to depose. The court concluded that the summons was issued for a legitimate purpose and entered its order of enforcement.

The primary argument presented on appeal is that the district court erred in its interpretation of *Reisman* v. *Caplin,* 375 U.S. 440 [13 AFTR 2d 457] (1964)[2] in requiring a showing that the sole purpose of investigation be criminal in nature before a challenge to the summons can be made. Intervenor contends that the present investigation is being carried on by special agent of the Intelligence Division, Department of Internal Revenue, acting as a criminal investigator rather than by the Audit Division, which traditionally investigates civil liability. The record demonstrates that an investigation was commenced because Civella was on a list of alleged underworld members and had reported income on his returns as "miscellaneous income." The government argues that it is necessary to investigate the B & C Meat records to determine whether any of this income came from the corporation and was properly reported on the corporate returns and whether Civella reported it accurately on his returns.

After oral argument in this court, the Supreme Court handed down the decision of *Donaldson* v. *United States,* [27 AFTR 2d 71-369] 39 U.S.L.W. 4139 (U.S., January 25, 1971). We find it controlling and dispositive of the substantive issues raised here. The Supreme Court held that there is no "meaningful line of distinction, for civil as compared with criminal purposes, at the point of a special agent's appearance." *Id.* at 4145. The Court further found authorization for "the use of the summons in investigating what may prove to be criminal conduct." *Ibid.* The *Donaldson* case makes it clear that the summons can be successfully challenged only when a criminal prosecution has been instituted and is pending at the time of the issuance of the summons or when criminal prosecution has been recommended. Thus, it is only when the sole purpose of the summons is for a criminal investigation that a challenge to the summons can be made.

Since it is undisputed that there is no related criminal prosecution pending and none had been recommended, the procedural complaints concerning the

[2]The Supreme Court in *Reisman* said: "[T]he witness may challenge the summons on any appropriate ground. This would include, as the circuits have held, the defenses that the material is sought for the improper purpose of obtaining evidence for use in a criminal prosecution, *Boren* v. *Tucker,* 239 F. 2d 757, 772-773 [50 AFTR 1217], as well as that it is protected by the attorney-client privilege, (citation omitted). 375 U. S. at 449.

trial court's alleged restriction on discovery must fall with the above disposition of the case.[3]

Judgment affirmed.

*Lenske* v. *U. S.*
(CA9-1967) 21 AFTR 2d 436 (383 F. 2d 20)

. . . The appellant Lenske will be referred to hereinafter as the defendant. In a trial without a jury in the district court he was convicted on three counts of evasion of federal income tax and on one count of wilfully subscribing to a false income tax return. No. 19539 is his appeal from his conviction. No. 20448 is his appeal from the order of the district court denying his motion for a new trial in the case in which he was convicted, and from the order denying his motion to disqualify the trial judge from sitting, on a remand directed by this court.

. . . In May 1959, a special agent was assigned to the defendant's case. He and the revenue agent who was already working on the collection aspects of the case devoted their full time for the following two and one-half years to the investigation of the defendant's case.

. . . The money that came in to Lenske went into his bank account. His payments were made by check. He furnished his cancelled checks to the special agent. The special agent and his assistant were, with the defendant's permission, installed in the small library of the defendant's law office for many weeks or months. The special agent called upon the defendant for particular files as they were needed, and the defendant directed his employees to find and turn over the desired files. There was no instance, apparently, in which any paper or record relating to the defendant's innumerable transactions was not delivered to the special agent. The special agent testified, rather petulantly, that on a few occasions there was some delay in getting the defendant to direct his employees to promptly find and deliver requested papers. The defendant did have a law practice and many business afairs to attend to.

[3]Assuming standing to complain, there is no merit to the intervenor's objection to the summons as being overly vague. See *United States* v. *Giordano,* 419 F. 2d 564 [25 AFTR 2d 70-346] (8 Cir. 1970) cert. denied 397 U. S. 1037. Nor is there merit to the complaint that the district court refused to place restrictions on the use of the evidence to be produced. See *United States* v. *Korel,* 397 U. S. 1 [21 AFTR 2d 1252] (1970); *United States* v. *Erdner,* 422 F. 2d 835 [25 AFTR 2d 70-691] (3 Cir. 1970). And as Mr. Justice Douglas makes clear in his concurring opinion in the *Donaldson* case, the intervenor has no basis to raise constitutional objections to the summons issued to the corporate taxpayer:
[I] t is difficult to see how the summoning of a third party, and the records of a third party, can violate the rights of the taxpayer, even if a criminal prosecution is contemplated or in progress. There is no right to be free from incrimination by the records or testimony of others." 39 U.S.L.W. at 4145.

The concurring opinion realistically appraises the investigation under circumstances existing in *Donaldson,* and as evidently exist here, as criminal in nature. Emphasis is there made that the individual taxpayer is entitled to be present at any examination, to confront and cross-examine witnesses and to offer rebuttal evidence. *Ibid.*

The special agent and his assistant spent many hours in the defendant's library hand-copying writings from the defendant's files and records. In these days of photostating machines that was a very wasteful process. But instead of frankly asking the defendant if they might, upon giving him a receipt for the writings, take them out and have them photographed, they concealed the writings in their brief cases when they left for lunch or at the end of the day, had them photographed, and sneaked them back into the defendant's files when they returned after lunch or the next morning.

We think the evidence shows that the special agent's conduct was not only irregular but was furtive and surreptitious, and far beneath the standard of what one expects from a public official.

The indictment stated that the defendant had attempted to evade and defeat his income taxes for the years 1955, 1957 and 1958 in designated large amounts, and that for the year 1956 he made a false return. The indictment gave no information as to which of his 90 properties, his numerous transactions, his thousands of documents, would be involved in the trial of the case. He knew that the Government had copies of all of his records and documents, because he had given them to the Government's agents. He knew that they had been studying them for two and one-half years. But even if he, like them, had had at his disposal all the resources of the United States, its Federal Bureau of Investigation and other investigating agencies, he could not have sought out and interviewed all the potential witnesses to all of his activities, to determine from which direction the attack would come, and then prepare his evidence to meet the attack. It would tax the imagination to conjure up a more frightening and frustrating situation than that in which his government has placed this citizen. The trial judge said to government counsel:

> The Government is the strongest litigant in the world. You have got the F.B.I. and all the government agencies available to you. You represent the strongest client in the world.

Nevertheless, in the first trial, the government counsel staunchly opposed the defendant's motion for a bill of particulars which would have given the defendant some little warning of what he was to be tried for. The court denied the defendant's motion.

Later in the trial, when the defendant sought to obtain copies of papers in the government files which might have been useful to the defense, government counsel said that he had regularly furnished exhibits to the defendant "the night before" they were used, that he resisted giving out things from the government files that the defendant should have no access to, that the defendant had even asked for statements of witnesses who had not testified. It thus seemed outrageous to counsel for "the strongest client in the world" that the client's citizen adversary should have even a moment's notice of what a witness would say to his detriment, or should be armed as government counsel was armed, with the prior statements of the witness, with which to confront him if he departed from them.

In the special agent's two and one-half years of investigation, he had interviewed some 500, perhaps as many as 1,500, persons. If any of those persons made statements which would have been helpful to Lenske, the Government's attitude was that Lenske had no right to know that, unless he found it out by his own effort and at his own expense.

The defendant presented an expert tax witness, Marx, whom the court regarded as an honest and highly competent tax expert. He, as an employee of the Internal Revenue Service, had had charge of supervising and training fourteen agents. After leaving the Internal Revenue Service he had set up an office and acted as a tax expert and witness for taxpayers and for the Government. In his 17 years in and out of the Government he had worked on more than 500 net-worth cases. Although Marx had had for only a short time the materials which the special agent had worked over for two and one-half years, one significant mistake became apparent to him within the first half hour of his study of the special agent's charts and exhibits. His testimony pointed out error after error in the special agent's treatment of transactions large and small. Many of his corrections were adopted by the Government when it revised its charts. But of particular significance is Marx's testimony with regard to the special agent's failure to follow leads which would have led to the right answers. Several instances were given by Marx. Many of his answers, obtained by following leads, were, as we have seen, accepted by the Government without further controversy. Marx spoke particularly about the special agent's failure to use the microfilms, which banks make and retain and which identify the bank on which a deposited check is drawn, to determine whether the deposit represented taxable income, or the repayment of a debt, or a deposit for investment, or the payment of an insurance loss, or whatever else it might represent. Marx testified that in seventeen years of tax practice he had not once been unable to so trace a deposit to its source. The special agent appears not to have made use of this important, practicable and reliable follow-up method.

It may be asked what harm is done, after all, by disregarding the admonitions of *Holland, supra,* putting everything into a chart showing increased net worth and having the special agent testify that it was prepared under his supervision and is right. There is still opportunity for cross-examination and for witnesses for the defense.

What is wrong, in addition to its being contrary to the law laid down by the Supreme Court, is that such a process is outrageously unfair. The Government uses its resources, here for two and one-half years, to build up its case and its charts. It then gets its indictment. The taxpayer still has no notice of wherein he is charged with criminal conduct. At the trial, or shortly before, he begins to learn the enormous amount of detail of the Government's case. If he is financially able, and is lucky, he may acquire a tax expert who, in helping him to cross-examine the Government's special agent, and in giving direct testimony for the defense, will largely demolish the Government's case. But, as in the instant case, it may leave a remnant, a vestigium somewhat above the level of *de minimis,* so he may still, as in this case, be headed for the penitentiary.

What has happened to him is that the Government has not assumed the burden of proving, beyond a reasonable doubt, that he is guilty. It has assumed only the burden, with its unlimited resources and time, of preparing a mass of documentary evidence and charts incomprehensible to a layman, all prepared by the Government itself, and saying to the taxpayer, "Your task is to prove that *all* of what is contained in the charts is false, not merely that it is 96 percent false, but that it is all false. You do not have the time nor the resources that the Government had, but that is your misfortune."

The appellant's conviction is reversed and the cause is remanded for further proceedings not inconsistent with this opinion.

Additional separate opinion of MADDEN, Judge:

On June 13, 1961, the special agent made his report to his superior, the District Director of Internal Revenue. The report consisted of 37 closely typewritten pages, followed by an appendix of 84 pages which listed 468 exhibits, and the names and addresses of 315 witnesses who would be available to testify for the prosecution if criminal proceedings were initiated. The report recommended criminal prosecution. Near the beginning of the report, under the heading, "History of Taxpayer," after stating, among other things, that Lenske had been born in Russia, reared in Minneapolis, had been a resident of Portland, Oregon, since 1925, had lived in the same house since 1936, and had no known criminal record, the report continued:

> Representatives of the Federal Bureau of Investigation, Portland, and the Intelligence Division of the Portland Police Department stated that they have reason to believe that Mr. Lenske is a Communist. In fact, they each maintain an extensive file on Mr. Lenske.

The report then stated that attached to the report were Exhibit 3A, a newspaper clipping stating that Lenske and another lawyer had called a meeting for the purpose of forming a local chapter of the Lawyers' Guild, and Exhibit 3B, which indicated "Mr. Lenske's thinking on the subject of Cuba, Laos, China, etc." I take judicial notice that the Lawyers' Guild is a national organization including many left-wing lawyers. I take judicial notice that there is in this country and in the world a great variety of "thoughts on Cuba, Laos, China, etc."

An examination of the exhibits shows that Exhibit 3A is a short news story stating that another lawyer and Lenske had called a meeting at a hotel for the purpose of organizing a local chapter of the Lawyers' Guild, and that a feature of the meeting would be the showing of a controversial film, "Operation

Abolition." Exhibit 3B is a rather long letter to the editor, from Lenske, in which Lenske expresses the thought that in "Cuba, Laos, China, etc." this country's actions had been in violation of our own laws and treaties, and in violation of international law.

I regard what I have recited above as a scandal of the first magnitude in the administration of the tax laws of the United States. It discloses nothing less than a witch-hunt, a crusade by the key agent of the United States in this prosecution, to rid our society of unorthodox thinkers and actors by using federal income tax laws and federal courts to put them in the penitentiary. No court should become an accessory to such a project.

When the special agent's report came in to his superiors, with his naive disclosure at the very beginning of his report that he placed high among the reasons why Lenske should be criminally prosecuted for income tax evasion Lenske's being a left-wing lawyer and having unorthodox political and social ideas, his superiors should have immediately removed him from the case and discarded every judgment which was contained in his recommendation. The special agent had given his superiors express notice that he was confused with regard to his duties and with regard to the basic ideals of his government. Discarding two and one-half years of dedicated endeavor of the special agent would have been a small price to pay to get the Government and its awesome taxing authority back on the path of fairness and decency.

The judgments which the special agent formed and embodied in his recommendations that Lenske be criminally prosecuted can only be described as grotesque. His two and one-half years of investigation had convinced him that Lenske had evaded taxes in the amount of $11,465.74 for the year 1955. The trial resulted in a finding that Lenske's taxes for 1955 would have been $414.78. The special agent determined Lenske's taxes to be 27 times as much as the court found them to be. On an examination testing his accuracy, the special agent would have scored less than 4 out of a possible 100. For the year 1957 the special agent's report said that Lenske had evaded $19,412.88 in taxes. The judgment of the court was that his taxes were $1,006.18. The special agent's report thus charged Lenske with nineteen times as much tax as the court found that he owed. The special agent's score was less than 6 out of a possible 100. For the year 1958, the report said Lenske should have paid $7,746.85. The court found that his taxes were $4,682.99, but that he had paid $2,000 in estimated tax. That left him owing $2,682.99. The special agent testified that he had, in his investigation, conducted perhaps 1,500 interviews. He might well have found time to look at the Government's record of Lenske's 1958 payments of $2,000 of estimated tax. The special agent's report thus attributed three times as much tax to Lenske as he owed for 1958. This was the special agent's best score, some 33 out of a possible 100. For 1956, the special agent's report said that Lenske should have paid a tax of $5,225.77. The court found that Lenske had no taxable income for 1956, but had a loss of $9,231.59. The special agent's examination score for 1956 would be, then, some almost incalculable number below zero.

The special agent was, so far as the record shows, technically competent and experienced. Such gross miscalculations as we have recited make it evident that some element foreign to the functions and duties of a government tax officer was corroding his judgment. Whether that corrosive element was that he had views differing from Lenske's about the Lawyers' Guild, or about "Cuba, Laos, China, etc." or about other political and social problems, or was something else that we cannot even imagine, the consequence is that no confidence whatever should be placed in the special agent's conclusions in this case. Yet he was not only the Government's investigator but the Government's principal witness in the trial. Under his supervision, the complicated charts and computations were prepared. He presented and explained them to the court. He testified that he interviewed more than 500 witnesses, perhaps as many as 1,500, and read "thousands, thousands" of documents.

CHAMBERS, Circuit Judge dissenting on petition for rehearing:

The district judge made 93 pages of findings of fact. I find them well supported by the record. To prove them well supported by the record I would have to attach about a thousand pounds of record and exhibits. Short of that, this case must stand on the different views of the evidence of the majority and myself.

The shortages of income not reported by the defendant were mainly in connection with real estate he was hiding out, not on simple oversights of reporting.

The district court resolved everything in Lenske's favor it could. He had the benefit of virtually all doubt. Still, that court found fraud beyond a reasonable doubt. And, so do I. As I have said before, and repeat, this case is so bad it ought to be affirmed *per curiam.*

The tragedy of the case is not that Lenske goes free. Internal Revenue can only catch and convict a few of those who cheat the public fisc. The tragedy is that someone might follow the case hereafter. I hope it can be treated as one of those "totality of circumstances" cases. A district court will not have another case exactly like this. Thus, it can find a different totality of circumstances.

As one begins to read the majority opinion and sees early therein the excoriation of the special agent for "sneaking" the files of Lenske out to have them photostated, one knows how the case will come out. Of course, Lenske had given permission to the agents to look. Before the majority opinion was written, I had always thought that permission to see is permission to copy. Further illustrating the hostility which the government has been up against here is the comment that "the special agent testified rather petulantly. . . ." I find the testimony not petulant.

As above, most of the majority opinion can be answered line for line, but such a course would only benefit the book publisher.

*Lenske* v. *U. S.*
(CA9-1966) 18 AFTR 2d 5815

CHAMBERS dissenting:

A proper appraisal of the case is this: Defendant is a lawyer. Part of the time he had a lawyer, but it is obvious he would not let the lawyer handle the case. Guilty as I believe the defendant is, a good lawyer, permitted to manage the case rather than the client running it, might have won the case. The defendant made his own bed and set it on fire. We pull him out of it.

*U.S.* v. *Middlemiss*
39 AFTR 2d 77-6389

The defense is that the defendant did not know that embezzled funds should be included as taxable income and, therefore, believed the tax returns filed to be true and correct as to every material matter when she filed them.

> In this statute, the word "willfully" generally connotes a voluntary, intentional violation of a known legal duty. [The Court]. . . has formulated the requirement of willfulness as "bad faith or evil intent," [*United States* v.] *Murdock,* 290 U.S. [389] at 398 [1933], or "evil motive and want of justification in view of all the financial circumstances of the taxpayer," *Spies* [v. *United States*], 317 U.S. [492] at 498 [1943], or knowledge that the taxpayer "should have reported more income than he did." *Sansone* [v. *United States*], 380 U.S. [343] at 353 [1965]. *United States* v. *Bishop,* 412 U.S. 346, 360 (1973).

* * *

The statute requires knowledge of a violation of the tax law, and the burden is on the Government to show that the defendant knew that the embezzled funds should be reported as taxable income. It is not the defendant's mere omission to report unearned income that the Government must prove, but that she made a knowing attempt to defraud the Government.

The defendant testified that she was a high school graduate with a knowledge of bookkeeping from high school. She had no accounting or tax training. She did not prepare any tax returns of her own. Her sister, who had formerly worked for the I.R.S., prepared her returns in the years that Shiro did not. It was her opinion that the total embezzlement came to $20,000, but she does not contest the amount computed by the I.R.S. In 1975, she went to see Attorney Beaumont, and, according to her testimony, he told her not to report any embezzled funds for the year 1975 since he did not know whether they were taxable or not. The defendant also testified that she had never read the instructions for filing Internal Revenue Form 1040 which contain a specific paragraph stating that embezzled funds are income.

The Supreme Court has twice made scholarly journeys into the nether world of whether embezzled funds are income. See *James* v. *United States,* 366 U.S. 213 (1961), and *Commissioner* v. *Wilcox,* 327 U.S. 404 (1946). It came up with two different conclusions, neither one of them unanimous. In the light of the failure of the Supreme Court to decipher, with unerring accuracy, the vagaries of this aspect of the Internal Revenue Code, it is not unlikely that the defendant, who probably never considered the issue at all, was quite unaware that the Government had commanded, in effect, that she confess to the embezzlement notwithstanding her right against self-incrimination.

Normally, in a prosecution under this statute, there is little problem with intent because the accused has deliberately understated income which was received legally.

While the defendant is clearly guilty of embezzlement, that is not the crime with which she is charged before this court.

I find and rule that the Government has not proven beyond a reasonable doubt that the defendant violated section 7206(1) of the Internal Revenue Code and deliberately failed to report income that she knew was supposed to be reported on her income tax returns.

The defendant stands acquitted.

## QUESTIONS AND PROBLEMS

1. Distinguish between a criminal fraud case and a civil fraud case in terms of:
   (a) The government's burden of proof
   (b) The nature of the penalties possible
   (c) The tribunal(s) involved
2. Explain the logic behind the statement that "a guilty finding on criminal fraud requires a finding of fraud in later civil tax litigation, but a not-guilty verdict does not prevent the government from trying to prove fraud in the civil case."
3. Explain why it would be improper to value a taxpayer's assets at their fair market values at all relevant dates in building up the data for a fraud prosecution using a net-worth approach.
4. ". . . the prosecution may pick and choose from the taxpayer's statement, relying on the favorable portion and throwing aside that which does not bolster its position," said the Court in one fraud case. An experienced tax lawyer says, "Most taxpayers convicted of criminal fraud actually convict themselves, either through what they say or the data which they voluntarily

turn over to the special agents." Relate these two statements to the problem of an innocent taxpayer being investigated for fraud who must decide whether to cooperate with the I.R.S.

5. Discuss the sentencing policy appropriate for convicted tax-law violators if the objective of a criminal tax fraud prosecution is:
   (a) To deter other taxpayers from cheating on their tax returns
   (b) To rehabilitate criminals and restore them to a productive place in society
   (c) To inflict punishment appropriate to the crime
   (d) To use the tax laws to remove undesirables from our midst (as per the *Lenske* case excerpt)
6. Evaluate the propriety of each of the objectives in Problem 5.
7. Distinguish between the efficacy of a state privileged-communication statute covering C.P.A.'s and the privileged communication accorded attorneys as it relates to a tax fraud case. What conclusions do you draw from this difference as to the proper role of the accountant in a matter that could eventually be a criminal fraud case?
8. Discuss the issue involved in the *Troupe* case (see excerpt) as it relates to the ability of the I.R.S. to subpoena the records of the taxpayer's accountant.
9. Contrast what happened to Mr. Lenske (case excerpt) with your personal concept(s) of civil rights and set forth what appear to you to be the assumptions underlying the three *Lenske* opinions (majority, Judge Madden concurring, and Judge Chambers dissenting).
10. On his 1977 return Mr. X initially reported the following:

| | | |
|---|---|---|
| Sales | | $57,271.16 |
| Less: Business expenses | | 40,221.16 |
| Net profit and adjusted gross income | | 17,050.00 |
| Less: Personal itemized deductions | $2,500.00 | |
| Personal exemption | 750.00 | 3,250.00 |
| Taxable income | | $13,800.00 |

You are a revenue agent engaged in auditing his tax return. Sales reported on the return can be traced to daily summaries maintained by the taxpayer, but you discover cash receipts were not deposited intact. Business expenses deducted are fully supported by receipts, but a perusal of the 1977 receipts indicates that they were for items sometimes paid in cash. Likewise, perusal of 1977 checking-account disbursements makes it clear that various personal expenses must have been paid with cash. The following information has been developed by you, and you are to determine the extent, if any, of the apparent understatement of gross receipts, using the bank-deposit method.

| | |
|---|---|
| Deposits per bank statements | $54,802.90 |
| Cash recorded as 1977 receipt, not deposited until 1978 | 1,000.00 |
| Cash recorded as 1976 receipt, deposited in 1977 | 2,000.00 |
| Money borrowed by taxpayer during 1977 and deposited | 2,000.00 |
| Balance per bank statement Dec. 31, 1976 | 18,317.00 |
| Balance per bank statement Dec. 31, 1977 | 27,479.50 |
| 1976 checks that cleared bank in 1977 | 500.00 |
| 1977 checks that did not clear bank until 1978 | 1,500.00 |
| Miscellaneous information: | |
| Refund of 1974 income taxes (deposited in bank) | 1,000.00 |
| 1977 payments on 1977 estimated income tax (paid by check) | 3,000.00 |
| Purchase of personal automobile (paid by check) | 4,000.00 |
| Other personal and living items (paid by check) | 10,000.00 |
| Estimated total personal and living expenses for 1977, including estimated tax, paid by cash and/or by check | 21,000.00 |
| Withdrawal from personal savings account, not deposited in checking account | 2,000.00 |

# 22

# Tax Research and Planning

## THE BASIC TAX SERVICE

How much of a tax library an accountant needs depends essentially on the nature of his practice and the availability of tax material elsewhere than in his own office. The bare minimum in an office, in almost any event, would be one of the standard tax services (for example, Prentice-Hall, CCH, or R.I.A.). These are kept current through an ingenious system of weekly replacement and addition pages. If these are kept up to date and used properly, they can provide answers to most of the routine tax problems encountered.

What is in the standard tax service?

First, there is the text of the Internal Revenue Code, in a separate volume. The Regulations, on the other hand, are scattered through the volumes of the service itself. Topically organized, the service contains in one place an integration of editorial comment, Internal Revenue Code, Regulations, rulings, and court decisions–although the rulings and court decisions are in some cases mere listings of items relevant to a particular topic, and at best are only brief summaries.

The key to effective use of the tax service is a methodical approach to a research problem:

1. Consult the topical index
2. Read the paragraphs to which you are referred
3. Look up the number of the text paragraphs you were reading in the Cross Reference Table (or Cumulative Index). This, in turn, will refer you to the paragraph numbers of new developments not reflected in the text you were reading.

Sometimes a little imagination may be required to find the heading under which your problem may be indexed. This relates partly to your ability to think in tax terms—a trait that is developed with experience. With experience behind you, there is an increasing tendency to view every factual situation from the standpoint of its tax aspects. And your terminology automatically falls into tax terminology. Thus, when a professional colleague purchases a farm and announces he is going to breed cattle, you might immediately have two thoughts—the *hobby loss* provisions of the law and the more basic question of whether the farm would constitute a *trade or business* being carried on for profit. He idly mentions that, of course, if the city keeps on expanding in his direction, the land might be suitable for ultimate residential use. You immediately think of the tax problems of *real estate subdivided for sale.*

In addition to the topical index and the cross-reference table to current developments, the tax service has other indexes. Knowing how to use them can save the accountant time and his clients money.

1. There is a list of court decisions by name, indicating the paragraph number of the service in which the decision is mentioned or discussed, as well as the volume and page of the decision itself. If you know the name of a decision in point, this index can save you a great deal of hunting around.

2. There are finding lists for code sections, regulations, and rulings. Agents frequently cite rulings, for instance, to support proposed disallowances. They seldom explain why the ruling applies. From this index, you can find where the ruling is mentioned, and perhaps discussed, in the text. In the same place, you are likely to find other rulings and cases mentioned. Some of them may even be contrary to the one cited by your agent.

3. Finally, there is an index to tax articles. This is arranged by the same paragraph numbers as the text of the service. Frequently, a well-researched and well-written article on a topic may greatly help to clarify your thinking on a problem.

## BEYOND THE BASIC SERVICE

Comprehensive though it is, the basic service can go only so far in a subject with such varied factual patterns as federal taxes. Beyond the basic service an accountant needs the cumulative bulletins, the cases, a record of changes in the Internal Revenue Code, and a citator.

### *Cumulative Bulletins*

The Internal Revenue Bulletin contains official rulings and procedures of the I.R.S. published Treasury Decisions, Executive Orders, Tax Conventions, legislation, agreements or disagreements with court decisions, and other items of general interest. Rulings and procedures reported in the bulletin do not have the force and effect of Treasury Department Regulations, but they may be used as precedents.

The cumulative bulletins from 1937-1 to date are still available from the Government Printing Office. Earlier volumes have been reprinted by private publishers. Some of the old GCM's, SM's, etc., keep on popping up as the most pertinent matter on a topic even yet. Thus, an investigation of the tax-exempt status of a trade association furnishing services to its members for fees would probably require you to dig back into SM (for Solicitor's Memorandum) 3413, CB 12-1, page 50, which involved a chamber of commerce that operated a traffic bureau. What would happen to the tax exemption of a country club that sold off land? Your research should probably include GCM9470, CB X-2, page 162, which involved denial of tax exemption to a country club in such a case.

### *Cases*

The cases you need fall into five possible categories:

1. All court cases (excluding those of the Tax Court and its predecessor, the Board of Tax Appeals) are, for instance, contained in *American Federal Tax Reports* and *American Federal Tax Reports, Second Series,* published by Prentice-Hall, Inc., and in *U. S. Tax Cases,* published by CCH. Current-year volumes come to you with your service.
2. Board of Tax Appeals cases, dating always prior to 1943, are available from the Government Printing Office.
3. BTA Memo decisions are available from Prentice-Hall.
4. Tax Court decisions are available on a current basis from Prentice-Hall and CCH as well as from the government itself on a subscription basis. Bound volumes are available from the Government Printing Office.
5. Tax Court Memorandum decisions are available from Prentice-Hall and CCH.

We will discuss the relative weight to be given different cases more fully later. You probably need the Tax Court material fully as much as you need the decisions of the other courts, even though it involves an additional service and additional costs. The Tax Court is the only tribunal you can go to without first paying the tax. An agent getting a signed 870, whatever your ultimate refund-claim intention may be, has disposed of the case; so he is apt to put greater weight on the type of precedent that directly affects most of his work. Furthermore, it is only as to Tax Court cases that you will find the formal seal of approval of the Commissioner of Internal Revenue—the acquiescence (acq. or A). It is hard for an agent to argue with a BTA or TC decision that has been acquiesced in, especially if your situation is on all fours with the decided case.

### *Code Changes*

The record of changes in the Internal Revenue Code is handled by the specialized Prentice-Hall service, appropriately titled *Cumulative Changes in the Internal Revenue Code and the Regulations.*

### *Citator*

The *Prentice-Hall Citator* is a separate service, consisting of bound volumes plus a loose-leaf volume maintained on a current basis. Cases reported by Prentice-Hall are broken down by the issues involved. The citator listing for a case is likewise broken down by the issues involved. Thus, the case of *Bingham's Trust* v. *Commissioner,* 33 AFTR 842, which was decided by the Supreme Court in 1945, involved 15 separate issues. In researching that case, you may be interested only in issue number 10. The *Prentice-Hall Citator* will separately list all those cases involving issue number 10 in which *Bingham* v. *Comm.* has been cited. For each case, it will indicate, with letter keys, what the nature of the citation was (whether the case cited was followed, distinguished, reversed, etc.). The listing for each case will be to the page in that opinion in which *Bingham* v. *Comm.* was mentioned. Obviously, the *Prentice-Hall Citator* makes it possible to do a thorough research job, even given a limited amount of time.

The *CCH Citator* is part of its regular service and merely cites cases without any breakdown by issues or indication of the nature of the citation.

In any event, no self-respecting tax man should rely on a case or a ruling that he hasn't checked through the citator for current developments. And from the citator, with one case as a starting point, dozens or even hundreds of cases pertinent to a specific issue can often be developed, including perhaps the one that disposes of the problem at hand.

### *Other Tax Publications*

Tax magazines, proceedings of tax meetings, and similar publications allow you to benefit from the research and experience of others. The AICPA's *Tax Adviser* and *The Journal of Taxation* are probably the two leading periodicals of this sort.

## EDUCATION FOR RESEARCH

People trained in law have an initial edge in tax research, because a substantial portion of legal education is essentially training in how to conduct research. Although formal research is emphasized in some accounting programs, it is not generally viewed as being an indispensable, intrinsic element of undergraduate training in accounting.

Yet a major function of professional education must really be to train a practitioner to educate himself. Certainly, this is true of the tax practitioner to an even greater extent than of most professionals. The most a professional tax education can normally do is to equip you with ways of approaching a problem, techniques for working out its solution, and skills to present the results of work persuasively and clearly to clients and other concerned parties. It will not give answers. If it tries to, it will only fail.

## SOME GENERAL THOUGHTS ON RESEARCH

Successful research can flow only from proper formulation of hypotheses. A hypothesis is an unproved assumption, and research, in the last analysis, consists of testing the validity of your hypotheses. But where do hypotheses come from? In tax research, they come mainly through a process of deductive reasoning, coupled with the use of analogies.

Thus, we read cases in doing tax research. We read the text of laws, regulations, committee reports. We are not merely searching for dicta that will dispose of our problem. We are trying to deduce the general principles that apply to a *type* of problem. If our deductions are to be valid, our research must cover all the relevant data. If our work is to be done economically, our research must be focussed only on the relevant.

Or we look at one factual situation and say, "This situation is similar to that situation, therefore the result should be similar." We reason by analogy. But analogies are dangerous. For instance, many practitioners have found a convenient way of thinking about a Subchapter S corporation through analogizing it to a partnership. This is useful, as long as we remember that we are dealing with an analogy, not with an identical situation.

The Internal Revenue Code spells out some of the differences in the Subchapter S situation. For instance, capital losses are not passed through to the owners of the Subchapter S corporation as they are in a partnership. But some of the differences require analogizing the Subchapter S corporation to the corporation instead of to the partnership. If a partnership were to collect tax-free interest income, this would pass through tax free to the partners. A corporation cannot pass through such characteristics generally, and the Subchapter S corporation is still a corporation, even though it is allowed by the I.R.C. to pass through ordinary income and losses and capital gains.

If a partnership were to collect the proceeds of life insurance carried on one of the partners, the proceeds could normally be distributed to the partners without any tax problems. But if the Subchapter S corporation collects the proceeds of a life insurance policy on one of its stockholders (say, its sole stockholder), it will find that its untaxed retained earnings have been increased and that distribution of these proceeds may be taxable as a dividend.

## THREE APPROACHES TO RESEARCH

For most of the rest of this section, we are going to develop an actual situation to illustrate the difference between doing research for purposes of planning (that is, at a time when what is done can still be altered), doing research for purposes of preparing a return (when what is done is done, although how we are to present what is done is still open to question), and doing research for purposes of contesting a proposed deficiency (when the fat is, so to speak, in the fire).

Our client is employed by a computer manufacturer. Unmarried, he travels constantly, although there is a regular pattern to his travels. He is away from his headquarters office for three to four months, and then in the office for a month to six weeks. Thus, out of a year, he will spend three to four months in his headquarters city and eight to nine months in various other locations. He is an employee for payroll tax and other purposes, but he views himself as an independent consultant, and his compensation depends indirectly upon his success in helping to close sales of his employer's products.

### *Research for Planning*

Assume that at the start of his employment the client comes to us and wants to know about the tax problems the employment may raise and how to minimize them. He has the feeling that he should be able to deduct all of his travel and living expenses, since he is constantly away from home. This immediately brings to our mind the vague memory of a case involving an itinerant musician who was held not to have a "home" for tax purposes, and who therefore was never away from "home" although he was always traveling. We tell the client that we will have to do some digging on this, but that probably the best he will be able to do is deduct his expenses while away from his headquarters city. He argues that the headquarters city is no different from anywhere else. Although he has some office space at the company, he maintains no permanent residence, but simply lives in an apartment hotel—and not always the same one—when he is in town. We tell him we will dig into it and see what we can recommend.

As we start doing a little reading on our problem, we discover that "a house is not a home" is certainly applicable to federal income taxes. We run across cases like that of *I. Jay Green,* 35 TC 764, in which the taxpayer claimed that his home was where his house was, but the government successfully contended that his home was Dayton, where his work was and where he actually spent 300 nights of the year. We encounter some old Tax Court Memo decisions dealing with salesmen (*Simeon J. Smith,* P-H Memo TC ¶ 43,438, and *Howard Murphy,* P-H Memo TC ¶ 43,120) who had no permanent places of abode, but who were nevertheless held to be away from home while away from, respectively, the headquarters city (where the salesman was an independent contractor) and the employer's business headquarters (where the salesman was an employee).

However, we also encounter a thread of thought running through some of the decisions (for example, *James* v. *U. S.,* D.C. (Nev.) 1959, 4 AFTR 2d 5214) that the entire rationale of allowing the deduction of travel and living expenses while away from home flows from an equity concept—that where a taxpayer has to maintain a home, and yet must travel away from this home in order to earn a living, it is only fair that he be allowed to deduct his travel expenses.

The tax service is of some help to us, especially in picking out the original material to read. This includes cases, regulations, revenue rulings, and some articles. The cases and the revenue rulings, through use of the citator, lead us in turn to more cases, and these to still more.

When we finish our work we draft for our client a memorandum in which we discuss several of the cases similar to his and point out the reasons underlying the taxpayer's success or failure. We conclude:

> As you can see, there is ample authority to support the idea that you would be entitled to deduct your expenses while away from Phoenix on business. On the other hand, the very frequency with which this question has been raised over the years, in factual circumstances somewhat similar to yours, indicates to us a need for caution. The perfect situation for deductibility of travel expenses while away from home on business is one where the headquarters city and the house of the taxpayer are in the same city. Where there is no house, there seems to be a tendency to suspect that there is no home. Thus, if we are to minimize the chance of controversy with the Treasury Department (and remember that such controversy is expensive even if we are ultimately successful), we would recommend that you maintain some sort of a "home" in the ordinary sense of that word.
>
> You might rent an apartment on an annual basis, with the right to sublease during the periods you are out of town. Depending on the months you have the apartment available for rental, you may well find that your out-of-pocket cost is no greater than a new location each time you are in town.

As you can see, in planning a transaction, the tax practitioner should tend toward the conservative approach. In most problems, and especially those involving taxes of not more than a few thousand dollars, the probable outcome if a case were taken to court usually becomes a minor factor because it is unlikely that it will ever go that far. So in planning the transaction, we must try to develop a plan that will stand up at the revenue-agent level. While the agent thinks in technical terms to a certain extent, in most cases where the technical side is ambiguous he is influenced quite heavily by commonsense standards of fairness.

Thus, our tax plan should always be real. Paper transactions, no matter how technically sound they may appear, should always be looked upon with suspicion. Our plan should make sense on a business or personal level, and not just on a tax level. Within the sometimes strained framework of tax logic, it should seem both fair and sensible. This is why we have recommended that our client establish a home of some sort, so that he can be away from "home" for tax purposes, even though such a home might technically make no difference at all.

### *Research for Preparing a Return*

Now let us assume that instead of his seeing us beforehand, our first contact with the client's problem of the deductibility of travel expenses comes when he shows up for a return-preparation interview. We learn that he has no "home" in the common meaning of that term, but we feel that he has a "home" in the tax meaning of that term. We prepare the return accordingly.

The client is meticulous about record keeping; he has a diary in which he enters his location and expenditures, and he keeps receipts for major items, such as hotel bills and transportation, for which receipts are reasonably obtainable. We summarize this in detail on a schedule (Form 2106). Although it is not required, filling in the schedule with some completeness seems to lessen the probability of the returns being audited. We also attach a statement on the question of "home," pointing out that the taxpayer is employed by the X Company, of Phoenix, Arizona; that his permanent headquarters is Phoenix; and that when he is away from Phoenix, he is away from home within the meaning of that word as defined by the Internal Revenue Service. We quote ¶ 11,366 of the Prentice-Hall Tax Service to the effect that ". . . the Revenue Service has consistently defined it [home] to mean the principal place of business, employment, or post of duty, regardless of where the family residence is maintained."

Now we have done what we can, without doing so much that our very attention to the matter raises suspicion, as far as the return is concerned. There remains the client. We point out to him that claiming the travel expenses while away from Phoenix is justified. However, we also point out to him that there is a possibility of disallowance of these deductions on the ground that he has no "home" from which he can be away. At this point, we might get involved in a planning discussion as to this year and future years. We make sure that the client fully understands what we are trying to tell him about the return itself, and that he is willing to assume the risk of possible controversy. We will probably work out for him a tax analysis schedule so that he can see, in dollar terms, exactly what we are talking about. We would also set up a tax savings "account" in his folder, and enter therein as a saving the tax reduction resulting from the travel expenses.

If the client seems the type of person who forgets easily, we would give him a written memorandum covering this "risky" deduction. The memorandum is stamped "CONFIDENTIAL" in red letters, and we hope that the client has enough sense to realize that he should never voluntarily make it available to the I.R.S.

A paid income tax return preparer is subject to a penalty for each return prepared in which an understatement of tax is due to the preparer's negligence or intentional disregard of rules and regulations. To avoid the penalty, a preparer may be required to make certain disclosures on the return if he disagrees with the rules or regulations of a statute and case law does not conflict with such interpretation.

### *Research for Contesting a Deficiency*

In spite of all our efforts, the client's return has been audited. Sure enough, the agent proposes to disallow the travel expenses on the ground that our client is an itinerant, with no home to be away from. Instead of pitying him for his homelessness, the revenue agent proposes to add financial suffering to the taxpayer's psychic discomfort. We draft a memo for the agent, since we hope that he can still be persuaded. As far as we know, he has a certain measure of discretion in this case. Certainly, Treasury Department policy is clear as to itinerants not getting travel expense deductions. But we feel that our facts remove the taxpayer from the category of "itinerant," and we hope to persuade the agent to feel the same. This is our memo:

> For tax purposes, the word "home" in the expression "away from home" in Section 162 (a) (2) has come to be a word of art. It has lost its common meaning of "abode" or "dwelling," and has come to mean "place of business, employment, or post or station at which he is employed" (*Josette J. F. Verrier Friedman,* 37 TC 557). The Commissioner has been quite successful in asserting this position, and the Tax Court has been consistent in its agreement that for purposes of travel-expense deductions, "home" is the principal place of employment (*Morton S. Cohen,* ¶ 57,110 P-H Memo TC).
>
> As is so often the case, though, the applicability of the general rule is complicated by specific facts. Thus, we have the problem of the construction worker who moves from place to place with his entire family, as he is able to find work with first one employer and then another. Rev. Rul. 60-189 recognizes that this man has no "home" to be away from, since he has no place of business, employment, or post or station other than where he happens to be at any given time.
>
> The itinerant musician is similar to the itinerant construction worker. He cannot be away from something he does not have and there-

fore cannot obtain travel-expense deductions (*Wilson John Fisher* v. *Commissioner,* CA7-1956, 49 AFTR 203).

But our facts are radically different from such situations. Mr.——— has a principal place of employment—Phoenix. Thus, his situation is not covered by any of these or similar rulings or cases.

To the contrary, our facts are quite similar to those involved in two revenue rulings and a Treasury interpretation. Says Rev. Rul. 54-497, "Where an employee conducts his trade or business each year at recurring seasonal places of employment, his business or 'tax home' does not shift during alternate seasons from one business location to the other but remains stationary at his principal post of duty during the taxable year. . . . [And] such an employee can deduct the cost of his meals and lodging only while his duties at his minor place of employment require him to remain away from his principal post of duty."

This point is driven home in answer number 5, Treasury Department Publication No. 300 (1956): "From these facts it is apparent that you have two recurring seasonal places of employment and that Cincinnati is your principal place of employment. You may deduct all of your traveling expenses while away from Cincinnati in pursuit of your minor employment including what you pay for your meals and lodging."

And the same point is reiterated in Rev. Rul. 54-497: "Where a taxpayer's business or employment is located in two or more separate areas, his 'home' for tax purposes is the area in which is located his principal place of business or employment."

In our discussions, we have agreed that if Mr.———were being independently employed in these various locations, his expenses while away from Phoenix would probably be deductible. But from the cases and rulings it would seem that his permanent employee status should enhance, rather than detract from, his right to a deduction.

Referring again to Rev. Rul. 54-497, it is pointed out that "if a member of a train crew receives a temporary, as distinguished from an indefinite, assignment to a run (whether or not 'overnight') which begins and ends at a terminal situated at a distance from his regular post of duty, he can deduct not only his expenses for meals and lodging while making runs from and to that terminal but all such expenses for the entire time during which his duties prevent him from returning to his regular post of duty. Likewise, any other railroad employee whose assignment away from his home terminal is strictly temporary (that is, its termination can be foreseen within a fixed or reasonably short period of time) is considered to be in travel status for the entire period during which his duties require him to remain away from his regular post of duty."

Is not this similar, with due allowance for the differences in the nature of his employment, to the situation of Mr.———? He, too, is absent from his regular place of employment on temporary assignments.

It appears to me that Mr.———is much more similar to a railroad employee or to a professional baseball player (the subject of Rev. Rul. 54-147) than he is to an itinerant construction worker or musician. Like the railroad worker or the baseball player, but unlike the construction worker or the musician, he has one employer, and his travel is at the direction of, and on business for, that one employer. Like the railroad worker or the baseball player, he has a fixed headquarters to which he returns, and which is his tax "home" within the meaning of that word as consistently interpreted by the Treasury Department and the Tax Court.

Notice that we call attention to the major points that the agent might make or has already made. It is from analyzing our weak spots that we can determine our strength, for these adverse rulings and cases are the ones about which we need to know the facts in order to show that our facts differ.

Also, we do not emphasize court decisions nearly as heavily as we do anything indicative of Treasury Department policy. The agent is not at all worried about what the Court of Appeals for the Sixth Circuit would say—and is especially unworried if we are not in the Sixth Circuit. He is worried about what will happen on review. If he has correctly applied Treasury Department policy, then review will be happy with his work. Our job is to convince him that Treasury Department policy is on our side. Until we reach the appellate division—and usually we don't go that far—we find that emphasizing the litigating chances of our position is mainly wasted effort.

## HOW TO EVALUATE CASES

The Internal Revenue Code is the basic source of the rules of tax accounting. To the uninitiated, it comes as a shock to learn that in its torrents of words there are more questions raised than answers provided. The Regulations are the Treasury Department's attempt to provide these answers. Some Regulations do an admirable job, some produce other results. For most tax-practice purposes, the Regulations and the Code constitute basic authority. A revenue agent will follow the Regulations until the Treasury Department changes them, if they appear to be clear on a particular point.

Revenue Rulings likewise constitute basic authority within the Treasury Department. If a Ruling is "on all fours" with your situation, it is unlikely that you will find Treasury Department personnel willing to ignore it.

At the court-case level, though, matters get muddied a bit. Cases get to court in the first place only as the result of conflict between the taxpayer and the Treasury Department. So if you see a constant stream of cases on the same basic issue (such as capital gain versus ordinary income on the sale of realty), you should realize that there is apparently a prevailing policy that encourages such litigation.

Congressional committee reports and court decisions are particularly important when you get involved in litigation. In dealing with the Treasury Department, though, the cases that furnish the most assistance are the Tax Court cases that have been formally acquiesced in. The congressional committee reports are of practically no use unless an area is involved that is not yet covered by Regulations. Tax Court cases that have been non-acquiesced in are of negative use at the audit level and may indicate a Treasury Department desire for more litigation on a particular subject.

Where the Commissioner has not spoken on a Tax Court decision, it is usually worth citing to the agent. District court decisions, until you get to the appellate-division level, usually carry no weight at all—and only when you are dealing with a refund claim do they carry much weight even there. However, district court decisions can be useful if they are the only ones on a particular point, and no Regulation or Ruling covers that precise point.

Decisions of the Court of Claims are so few, and the function of the Court of Claims is so little understood among Treasury Department personnel, that in general citing it may be somewhat a waste of time. However, in some areas, such as capital gains on realty, the Court of Claims may have such carefully developed opinions that their decisions carry weight simply from the persuasive power of the reasoning.

The decisions of the U. S. circuit courts of appeal carry substantial weight among Treasury Department personnel. At the appellate-division level, especially, the decisions of the court of appeals for the taxpayer's circuit are often key factors in evaluating the ultimate possibility of a favorable settlement. Finally, of course, the decisions of the U. S. Supreme Court are the law of the land.

Unfortunately for the practitioner, decisions do not come in the fashion most useful for planning purposes. Tax Court and Court of Claims decisions usually give a fairly comprehensive factual background and an opinion that is detailed. District-court decisions, on the other hand, vary considerably. If a jury verdict is involved, you may simply have available to you the charge to the jury and a statement of the verdict. This is usually of little value.

Since your objective in analyzing cases will be, in part, to find similarities between your facts and the favorable decisions, and differences between your facts and the unfavorable decisions, careful analysis of the facts becomes all-important. You also have to determine whether the applicable law was the same, and whether subsequent cases might have been critical of the particular decision.

In reading a trial court decision, it is important to distinguish between those decisions where the applicable law was relatively clear but the taxpayer was unable to carry his burden of proving sufficient facts to bring his situation within it, and those cases where the facts were relatively clear and the argument was over the law. Thus, in *Sterno, Inc.,* TC Memo 1959-241, the Tax Court held that commissions that were paid to a related sales corporation were not deductible to the extent that they exceeded the amount of salaries, commissions, and expenses paid out by the sales corporation. This case was decided on the basis that the taxpayer had not carried his burden of proving that the determination of the I.R.S. was wrong. But for a later year, in TC Memo 1965-023, the same taxpayer was able to satisfy its burden of proof and the sales commission payments were allowed as a deduction.

A refund claim was then filed by the taxpayer who had received the payments in the year when the Tax Court disallowed a portion of them for deduction purposes; the claim was filed on the basis that the amounts it had received were not compensation for services rendered but were dividends from its subsidiary. The difference is substantial, inasmuch as the corporation receiving a dividend gets an 85 percent dividends-received deduction, and thus the parent corporation would have been entitled to a substantial refund. However, the U.S. Court of Claims denied the refund claim, stating that the Tax Court's decision had merely been that the paying corporation had not proved the payments were reasonable—the Tax Court had not determined that the payments were dividends. (*Sterno Sales Corporation* v. *U. S.* [1965] 15 AFTR 2d 979.)

It is also important to read decisions of courts of appeal with some care as to what they are actually deciding. A court of appeals will normally not find that a lower court's findings of fact should be reversed unless there is a very clear error being made by the lower court. Thus you will find appeals courts affirming lower-court decisions on the basis that they are not satisfied that the factual determinations of the lower court were clearly erroneous. On the other hand, an appeals court takes no such attitude about the way the lower court has applied the law. If the appeals court disagrees with the lower court as to the application of the law, it will reverse without the necessity of finding the lower-court decision clearly erroneous. It is quite possible for two very similar cases to be differently decided by trial courts based upon their peculiar facts, and for both decisions to be affirmed by the appeals court involved. Appeals court decisions are most valuable when they deal with questions of law and are probably least valuable in most tax-planning and controversy situations, where they are dealing only with the question of whether the trial court made erroneous findings of fact.

## HOW TO GET AND USE PRIVATE RULINGS

All the research in the world cannot answer certain types of tax questions. The big question that research finds difficult to answer is "What is the present Treasury Department attitude on this point?"

The purpose of a private ruling from the I.R.S. is to buy insurance. Although rulings may be modified or revoked, there will usually be no retroactive change as to the particular taxpayer who obtained a ruling if the ruling request correctly stated the facts, the transaction was carried out in the manner indicated in the ruling request, and the law itself has not been changed.

There are, of course, some areas in which the Treasury Department simply will not rule. Mainly, these deal with factual determinations, but they also deal with situations in which there is conflict in court decisions or with areas where the Treasury Department simply does not want to encourage taking advantage of tax "gimmicks."

The practitioner contemplating requesting a ruling must ask himself these questions:

1. Is it likely that the Treasury Department will rule on this situation?
2. Is the transaction one that can be changed, if change is necessary to obtain a favorable ruling?
3. Is the transaction one that can be abandoned, if a favorable ruling simply is not obtainable?

The ruling procedure puts the practitioner without a Washington office or correspondent at a disadvantage. Frequently, an informal discussion with people in the I.R.S. national offices can give the tax person a good idea of whether a request for ruling will prove productive of a favorable ruling, and he may also get some idea of modifications necessary in the tax plan to enhance the likelihood of the ruling being favorable. I.R.S. does publish its rulings, so a search of these published private rulings can prove helpful. Since some 40,000 rulings are issued each year, a great deal of precedent already exists in many areas, and often rather clear policies are in force, although they may not be generally known except to the I.R.S. people handling ruling requests.

Likewise, the taxpayer has a right, if he so requests, to have a conference on the ruling. Such conferences can be extremely useful in arriving at modifications to the basic plan that will make a favorable ruling possible.

The request for ruling must contain the name, address, and account number of the taxpayer requesting the ruling, as well as all other parties to the transaction. It must include the specific nature and details of the transactions that are to be the subject of the ruling. Rulings are not issued to practitioners, but only to taxpayers. Usually, a power of attorney is obtained from the taxpayer, and the power directs that all correspondence be mailed to the practitioner.

If there are documents involved, copies of them should be submitted with the ruling request. In addition, the ruling request should present an argument for the particular tax result desired by the taxpayer, citing pertinent authorities. If no particular result is desired, the request must still state what the taxpayer thinks the tax result should be.

The request must also state whether the taxpayer or his representative knows whether the identical issue in any case is pending in any field office of the I.R.S. Where the identical issue is pending at the field-office level, the likelihood of obtaining a ruling is nil.

It is probably a good idea to put into the ruling request a statement that the right is reserved to withdraw the request for ruling if an adverse ruling is going to be forthcoming. While the National Office may still furnish its views on the ruling request to the office where the taxpayer's return will be filed, it may neglect to do so—and, in any event, there is no adverse ruling outstanding. Perhaps nothing is gained by withdrawal, but then neither is anything lost.

To maintain some confidentiality on rulings received, a taxpayer must attach to the ruling request either a statement referring to the proposed deletions including name, address and taxpayer identifying number, and setting forth the statutory basis for each proposed deletion, or a statement that no information other than names, address and taxpayer identifying numbers need be deleted. This statement must be a separate document.

## RESEARCH METHODOLOGY

Approach your tax research methodically. Head up a sheet of paper with your initials and the date in the upper right-hand corner. Show the name of the client, and indicate the nature of the problem. List specifically each step you perform, what paragraph numbers you looked up, what cases you read. Excerpts should be on separate sheets of paper, attached to the basic sheet.

There are several reasons why you should make a record of your research. First, it tends to make you do a more thorough job. Second, if you are training someone to do research, it makes the training much easier. Third, in explaining to a client the reason why the bill he's getting is so high, you can run over the complexity of the work you did much more convincingly with a record of that work in front of you. Fourth, if the question is ever raised of why you handled a certain item in a certain way or made a certain recommendation, you have the answer right in your file. The tax services change each week, each year, and the recommendation you made two years ago may look pretty silly based on the present state of things unless you can show what the state of things was when you were doing your analysis.

## HOW TO ANALYZE TAX-PLANNING PROBLEMS

Some tax-planning problems have a single solution; others could be solved in any of several ways, with varying tax and business results. In some problems, the facts initially available may be insufficient. In a real-world situation, you might be able to ascertain the missing facts, once you realized their importance. In a school situation you should set forth what facts you feel are necessary, and then make such reasonable assumptions regarding those facts for purposes of your solution as are not inconsistent with the rest of the problem.

The first step, therefore, is to see what the problem is. There may be a business objective to be achieved with a minimum of tax expense. There may be a situation where a tax benefit is available through taking some sort of action.

Once the problem is at least tentatively defined, you should gather as much data as you can about the problem. This mainly involves seeing what facts you are given that are relevant, what facts (if any) you have to obtain or assume, and what applicable tax provisions deal with this type of situation.

Only a limited number of tax factors can be involved in any given situation. If income tax minimization is to be achieved, we have to (1) avoid the recognition of income, (2) increase the deductible expense, (3) reduce the applicable tax rates (directly or by obtaining a credit or special deduction), or (4) affect the timing of items of income or expense.

Avoiding the recognition of income can be illustrated by setting up a transaction so that it is an exchange of property subject to a mortgage for property, rather than an exchange of property for property plus cash. Deductible expenses can be increased by leasing land rather than owning it. Applicable tax rates can be reduced by operating a business in a corporate form rather than as a sole proprietorship. Electing to report a sale on the installment basis is one of innumerable examples of minimizing taxes by affecting the timing of reporting items.

One or more of these four factors will be involved in any income tax plan. In addition, of course, a tax plan must be fully documented, so that the taxpayer can prove that he did what he purported to do. The plan should make business sense, should be adaptable to possible future changes in the taxpayer's situation, and should not expose the taxpayer to risks that are beyond his ability to bear. Two individuals, each owning 50 percent of the stock of a corporation and desiring to split the one corporation into two separate corporations so that each could go his own way, would need to be quite careful. They have a sound business purpose, but there is a risk that the attempt to split the business in two might result in having the value of at least one of the resulting corporations taxed to the shareholder as a dividend. Such an outcome would result in almost confiscatory taxes—with the proceeds of liquidating the corporation perhaps not even being enough to pay the taxes.

You are now ready to set up alternative ways in which the problem could be handled or the situation disposed of. Here is where your imagination comes into play. Some of the alternatives you dream up may be ridiculous. These can be eliminated as you start critically evaluating the alternatives.

Based on the facts you have and what you can determine about the tax rules, ask, for each alternative, "What would happen if this were done?" You will probably have to go back to your reference books a number of times to clarify points that are vague in your thinking.

Let us illustrate how this works, and how to use elementary reference material with a specific simple example.

*Example:*

You are the financial vice-president of the Alamo Corporation. The corporate business is manufacturing toys and games. The seasonal pattern of the business is such that inventory builds up from January until about September, putting a drain on cash that is met by short-term bank borrowing. Starting with September, inventories fall, while receivables rise as merchandise is shipped to jobbers, wholesalers, chains, and large department stores. By December, receivables start falling and in January are back to their normal level. From January until June, there is usually a cash surplus. In previous years, these surpluses have been invested in tax-anticipation warrants of the local city which paid 4 percent interest and were paid off on June 15.

The 4 percent interest rate seems quite low to you. You know that you could invest in at least four more attractive vehicles offering equal safety but a higher rate of return. You could purchase discount United States bonds paying about 5 percent. You could buy obligations of finance companies that would pay 6 percent. Preferred stock, paying a 6 percent per annum dividend, is available. Also available is stock of a corporation that pays tax-free dividends, inasmuch as it has no current or accumulated earnings and profits for tax purposes. The dividends on this will run about 7 percent per annum. The market prices of the stocks remain stable except just prior to the ex-dividend date, when they move up by the amount of the dividend and then drop back.

The corporation has available an estimated $2 million that it can invest from January 1 through June 30 of the coming year. The applicable tax rate is 48 percent.

Your problem is to maximize your after-tax return on the investment of this surplus cash—an investment of $2 million for half a year. This will produce $40,000 if invested in tax-anticipation warrants, $50,000 if in United States bonds, and $60,000 if in the finance-company notes. Assuming that quarterly dividend dates are March 31 and June 30, it will produce $60,000 in preferred-stock dividends and $70,000 in dividends that are not a taxable distribution. It is possible, in the case of the stock investments, to sell the stock just before it goes ex-dividend, or else to wait until after it goes ex-dividend, receive the dividend, and sell the stock for the amount paid for it. So you have seven possible alternatives:

1. Four percent tax-anticipation warrants
2. Five percent United States bonds
3. Six percent finance-company notes
4. Six percent preferred stock, receiving both dividends
5. Six percent preferred stock, receiving one dividend, with the second dividend reflected as an increase in the selling price
6. Seven percent common stock of the loss corporation, receiving both dividends
7. Seven percent common stock of the loss corporation, receiving the first dividend, but letting the second dividend be reflected in the selling price

Your next step is to check the tax status of these alternatives. You might use the *Prentice-Hall Federal Tax Handbook* for this research. If it failed to provide answers, you might then use the *Federal Tax Service* into which it is cross-referenced.

1. You look up "Warrants, tax-anticipation" in your index and find nothing. Then you try "Tax-anticipation warrants." Nothing. You recall that earlier in this book the obligations of cities and states, or their subdivisions, were called "municipal bonds." You try "Municipalities" and find that under "obligations, interest," you are referred to *Handbook* paragraphs 1314 and 1623. These tell you, as you already suspected, that interest on the obligations of any political subdivision of a state is wholly exempt from tax. Paragraph 1623 of the *Handbook* further tells you that gain on disposition is taxable and loss is deductible, but this is irrelevant to your problem.

2. The logical place to find out about United States bonds would appear to be under the heading "Bonds, U.S." The index tells you to see "Federal obligations." Under that general heading, you find a subheading, "Discount, issued at," which refers you to *Handbook* paragraph 1314. This tells you that the discount element in savings bonds is taxed as interest. It also refers you to paragraphs 2715 (b) and (c).

The discount is interest income, you discover, and the discount is not income until the obligation matures. This last point is of no importance in your present problem, but you can note that here would seem to be an opportunity for shifting income into whichever of two periods one wanted it to fall in. This would be accomplished by buying a discounted non-interest-bearing short-term United States obligation with a maturity just a few days into the next fiscal year, if you wanted the income on the next year's tax return rather than this year's.

3. Finance-company notes have no special treatment as far as you can determine. Therefore, the entire $60,000 would be subject to the 48 percent tax, and the tax would be $28,800.

4. Try as you may, you find no special tax provisions dealing with dividends received on preferred stock of a domestic manufacturing company. You thus conclude that the dividends will give rise to the special dividends-received deduction of 85 percent that is applicable, as you discover at *Handbook* paragraph 3108 (a). You are forced, in order to reach this conclusion, to make the assumption that the corporation involved is a domestic corporation but not a public utility. Of your $60,000 of dividends, only $9,000 (15 percent) will be subject to income tax. At a 48 percent rate, the tax will be $4,320.

5. If you receive one dividend but let the amount of the second dividend be reflected in the selling price of the stock, then your dividends-received deduction will be on only $30,000 of dividends, leaving $4,500 (15 percent) taxable as ordinary income. The remaining $30,000 will be a short-term capital gain taxable at 48 percent, as per *Handbook* paragraph 3204. The total tax will be $2,160 plus $14,400, or $16,560. This alternative might as well be eliminated as being inferior to number 4, you conclude.

6. The dividend paid by the corporation that has neither current nor accumulated taxable income (for example, as the result of substantial intangible drilling and development costs, which are expensed for tax purposes but capitalized for book purposes) suggests that you look in the index under

"Dividends, profits available for," which leads you to *Handbook* paragraph 1701. There you learn that a dividend other than from earnings for tax purposes (which is a slightly different concept from retained earnings for accounting purposes) is not taxable. Instead, the amounts received reduce the tax basis of the stock on which the dividend is received. Thus, if you receive $70,000 in dividends, your basis in the stock will be reduced from $2,000,000 to $1,930,000. When you then sell the stock for $2,000,000, you will have a $70,000 gain. Assuming that you hold the stock less than one year, that short-term gain will be taxed at 48 percent—or a tax of $33,600.

7. If you receive only the first dividend, you will reduce your tax basis by $35,000—to $1,965,000. The selling price of the stock, increased by the amount of the second dividend, will be $2,035,000. Your gain will be $70,000, your tax will be 48 percent, or $33,600. Alternatives 6 and 7, in other words, are substantially equal to each other. Neither looks too good.

Now that you have gathered the relevant facts concerning each alternative and have tried to determine the tax rules applicable, you can array the results of adopting each of the alternatives that you are still considering—numbers 1, 2, 3, and 4.

| | *Income* | *Tax* | *After taxes* |
|---|---|---|---|
| 1. Four percent tax warrants | $40,000 | -0- | $40,000 |
| 2. Five percent United States bonds | 50,000 | $24,000 | 26,000 |
| 3. Six percent finance notes | 60,000 | 28,800 | 31,200 |
| 4. Six percent preferred | 60,000 | 4,320 | 55,680 |

It would thus appear that alternative 4 would best accomplish your objective of maximizing the after-tax return on your temporary investment. Intangible factors that probably need consideration include the possibility of undesirable damage to your community relations by failing to buy the tax-anticipation warrants of the city as you have done in prior years. You should also recognize that, even if the preferred stock has had a stable price history, there is more downside risk to it than to fixed-dollar obligations with definite maturity dates. Within the framework of your problem, however, you cannot easily quantify these. You can only mention them.

## CASE EXCERPT

*Ragland Investment Co.* v. *U. S.*
(CA6-1970) 26 AFTR 2d 70-5898

Trial court's finding of fact that dividend rather than interest income resulted from redemption of preferred stock that had been issued to taxpayer in exchange for his business is not clearly erroneous, and is not reviewable as a matter of law.

. . . The buying corporation issued preferred stock to the seller. This preferred stock thereafter was redeemed. The taxpayers contend that the payments received by them were dividend income. The Commissioner asserts that these payments were interest. The Tax Court found that the cumulative preferred stocks in the buying corporation issued to the sellers represented an equity investment and that payments made with respect to it were dividends.

The Commissioner asserts that the ultimate question of whether the preferred stock issued to the taxpayers by the buying corporation is equity or debt for tax purposes is a question of law and not a question of fact, and that the clearly erroneous standard of review does not apply. The Commissioner undertakes to distinguish *Commissioner* v. *Duberstein*, 363 U. S. 278, and asks this Court to reverse decisions in which we have followed *Duberstein* in applying the clearly erroneous standard of review in cases presenting comparable factual situations. See, e. g., *Austin Village, Inc.*, v. *U. S.*, DER No. 195 of 1970 (6th Cir. 1970); *Berthold* v. *Commissioner,* 404 F. 2d 119 (6th Cir.); *Fellinger* v. *U. S.*, 363 F. 2d 826 (6th Cir.); *R. C. Owen Co.* v. *Commissioner,* 351 F. 2d 410, DER No. 197 of 1965 (6th Cir.), cert. denied, 383 U. S. 967; and *Foresun* v. *Commissioner,* 348 F. 2d 1006, DER No. 143 of 1965.

Although *Duberstein* dealt with tax concepts of "gifts" versus "compensation" and the present case involves tax concepts of "dividend income" versus "interest," this Court is convinced that the reasoning of the majority opinion in *Duberstein* affords no meaningful distinction on factual grounds so far as the standard of review is concerned.

In *Berthold, Foresun* and other cases where the clearly erroneous standard favored the collection of the tax by the Government, the Commissioner argued that the determination involved an issue of fact requiring application of the clearly erroneous standard.

In the present case, where the decision of the Tax Court is adverse to the Government, we are invited (as we were in *Austin Village*) to hold that the conclusions of the finder of facts are erroneous as a matter of law.

The Commissioner should not "blow hot or cold, depending on which standard of review would require payment of the tax" (concurring opinion of Judge Edwards in *Austin Village, Inc.* v. *U. S., supra*). It seems that if the Commissioner now is convinced that the findings of the trial tribunal in this type of case should be reviewed as a matter of law, the logical step is to seek reversal of *Duberstein,* which this Court has no power to do. We decline to reverse the decisions of this Court following *Duberstein.*

We hold that the findings of the Tax Court in this case are findings of fact. On this appeal this Court will not disturb these findings unless they are clearly erroneous.

The Commissioner further urges that even if the clearly erroneous standard of review is applicable, the findings of the Tax Court are clearly erroneous. We hold that the findings of the Tax Court are not clearly erroneous, but to the contrary are supported by substantial evidence as set forth in the majority opinion of the Tax Court.

## QUESTIONS AND PROBLEMS

In each of these situations, you are given certain facts. From them, you are to determine what tax problems may be anticipated in achieving the business results that are apparently desired. Your answer should set forth the facts given, plus the facts assumed; the nature of the problem posed; some of the alternative approaches that might be taken; a discussion of the tax law that would be applicable; a projection and/or evaluation of each alternative; and a final recommendation.

1. Miller wants to sell the stock in his wholly owned corporation. Corporate retained earnings are $80,000. One of the corporate assets is a claim to an income tax refund. The claim is on the books for $40,000, but the prospective purchaser of the stock is unwilling to ascribe a $40,000 value to it in arriving at a price for the stock. When he and Miller are unable to agree on a valuation, Miller suggests that the contract for sale of the stock state that any amount received on this refund claim should be paid directly to Miller. Miller is in a 50 percent tax bracket, has a tax basis in the stock of $30,000, and has held the stock ten years. Selling price, excluding the refund claim as a corporate asset, would be $100,000, payable in cash.
2. Larry Woods owns 40 percent of the stock of the Baraboo Corporation. Another 40 percent is owned by Herman Finger, and the remaining 20 percent is split among four of the long-time corporation employees. Baraboo Corporation has no excess of cash on hand, but it does have an untapped line of credit at the bank sufficient to allow it to raise approximately $100,000. Finger comes to Woods and offers to sell him his entire stock interest for $60,000. He knows that Woods does not have that much cash, but he suggests that the corporation can borrow the cash from the bank and Woods can then borrow it from the corporation. With Finger no longer drawing a salary, the increase in corporate earnings should be enough to allow the bank loan to be paid off in a few years. In turn, Woods can increase his own salary, because he will control 80 percent of the stock, and pay off the money he has borrowed from the corporation.
3. The Athens Piston Company has almost $600,000 in accumulated earnings. From 1957 through 1977, it has paid less than $2,000 a year in dividends. The shareholders would like to get their cash out but quail at the thought of paying ordinary income tax on dividends. If they could only sell the stock to someone! They would be happy to sell for only $650,000–far less than

the appraised value of the assets. But they want cash. Interested persons lack the cash, whereas those with cash are not interested.

Mr. Kramer, an insurance broker who also specializes in arranging financing, makes this offer to the stockholders. He will form the Douglas Corporation, in which he will invest $1,000. Douglas will then contract to buy all the stock of Athens Piston. What will it use for cash? On the day the sale is closed, Athens will borrow enough cash from banks, secured by receivables, inventory, land, buildings, and machinery, for Douglas to pay for the stock it is buying.

To Kramer's great surprise, the Athens Piston shareholders agree to this plan. Kramer is now concerned with carrying this through in a way that will give him and/or Douglas Corporation optimum tax results. He feels that some wrong move could result in his losing the entire package to the tax collector.

4. Earl Bryan started the *Middletown Post* as a weekly newspaper 30 years ago, with $2,000 borrowed from his friends and relatives. Today, the *Post* is the only daily in Middle County and an institution with its roots and its influence spread throughout its territory. But it is hard to be an institution as you grow older. Mr. Bryan, now 64, feels that his community deserves a more aggressive management and that he needs a change of scenery. His wife dead, his children grown, he wants to chuck civic cares and operational headaches and start writing the book that he has never quite got around to.

   Horace Hocks, president of a chain of small-town newspapers, has offered Mr. Bryan $150,000 for the stock of Post Publishers, Inc., plus $5,000 per year for ten years for writing a weekly column and acting as a consultant. It is understood that the consulting activities will not take up more than six weeks a year. The $150,000 is divided into two parts under the proposed contract–$75,000 as payment for the stock, and $75,000 as "compensation for an agreement not to compete for ten years." Bryan is quite sure there is room for bargaining over the offer. He knows that Hocks prefers buying the corporation's assets rather than its stock.

   Mr. Bryan's salary from the *Post* has been $17,500 a year. His investments produce about $5,000 a year dividend income, and he takes the standard deduction. His stock in the *Post* has a tax basis to him of $20,000. A condensed balance sheet of the *Post* at September 30, 1977, shows:

| | | | |
|---|---|---|---|
| Current assets | $15,000 | Current liabilities | $10,000 |
| Plant and equipment (net) | 75,000* | Stockholders' equity | 80,000 |
| Total assets | $90,000 | Total liabilities | $90,000 |

*Accumulated depreciation includes $10,000 taken since January 1, 1962 on equipment. No acquisitions subject to the investment credit have been made.

5. John Taylor and his two brothers support their mother. They each give her $1,500 a year. She receives another $1,200 from Social Security. Her medical expenses are high: they average around $2,000 a year. John and his brothers would like to get the maximum tax advantage from the payments they make. All are in a 26 percent bracket and itemize deductions on their returns.
6. James Montgomery, a staff assistant with a C.P.A. firm, has been selected to appear on a television quiz show. The plan of the show is such that, each week he is on the show, he may win $5,000, and if he manages to stay on for eight weeks, he will win $100,000. The TV producer has informed Montgomery that he can enter into an agreement, before appearing on the show, to take any amounts he may win in equal monthly payments, spread out over not less than 25 nor more than 100 months.
7. Ralph Keck, a loyal alumnus of both Mid-American University and the Alpha Beta Gamma fraternity, wishes to make money available to the fraternity to finance a new chapter house, *if* he can get a tax deduction for his contribution. He has contemplated making a gift directly to the fraternity chapter, as well as making a contribution to Mid-American specifically earmarked as a low-interest loan fund for an Alpha Beta Gamma fraternity house.
8. Jones bought some Acme Corporation stock in Jan. 1978 for $5,000 (1,000 shares at $5 per share). By December 1978, the stock had dropped to $2.50 per share. Jones still has faith in Acme, but he would like to take advantage of that loss on his 1978 tax return. He also wants to maintain his position in Acme stock.
9. Skyline is a nonprofit corporation, organized to conduct a country club. It owns land in excess of its country club needs. So far, it has made no improvements of any type. To finance the golf course and the club house, it proposes to sell building lots to its members. Some of its founding members, in recognition of their assignment to the corporation of options they held on the land, will be given lots without charge.
10. Dr. White, a dentist, wants to purchase the professional practice of elderly Dr. Brown. They have agreed on a price of $16,000, with an immediate cash payment of $2,000 plus payment by Dr. White to Dr. Brown of 25 percent of all fees received until the full $16,000 has been paid. Dr. Brown agrees to render whatever services are necessary in order to facilitate the transfer of the practice to Dr. White. Dr. White's only concern is how to set up the transaction so that the payments he makes to Dr. Brown will be deductible for tax purposes. He figures that he will be in a 45 percent tax bracket. Dr. Brown is unconcerned about tax treatment and appears willing to go along with any arrangement that will not inconvenience him.
11. Henderson Corporation owns unimproved real estate that it is purchasing on contracts. It needs $70,000 in order to keep its contract payments on

the real estate from going into default during the next three years. During the three years, it plans to subdivide the land–and before the three-year period is up, to raise more than enough cash to pay off both the purchase contracts and any interim financing.

Mr. Dough is willing to lend Henderson the $70,000, but only if he can get capital gains treatment on the amount that he will receive as "interest." He is unwilling to take the risk involved for only ordinary income when he will have a capital loss if he sustains a loss on the deal.

12. Alpha Corporation (a retailer) is owned by Mr. Barnes. In advertising, in signs, and so forth, the name "Alpha Corporation" does not appear; instead, "Barnes Market" is used. The name "Barnes Market" is registered under state law, both as a trade name and as a trademark. Mr. Barnes owns the trade name and the trademark, but has hitherto made them available free of charge to the corporation. He now plans on selling the business as a going concern. The corporate assets will be sold at a slight loss from book value. The trade name, which has a $50 tax basis to Mr. Barnes but which has been given value by 20 years of advertising and promotion paid for by the Alpha Corporation, will be sold by Mr. Barnes for $30,000.

13. Mr. Chutter has an agreement with his employer that if Chutter dies while still an employee of the company, his family will receive $40,000. To cover its potential liability to Chutter, the corporation has taken out a $40,000 life insurance policy on Chutter. They have given Chutter a letter, "As long as you are in our employment, the proceeds of this policy will be turned over to your family."

    Chutter tells his wife, "It's the same as though I was carrying $40,000 of life insurance with you as the beneficiary."

14. Beta Corporation is an Electing Small Business Corporation. It was formed in November 1969, and at that time it acquired an operating ranch. In May 1978 it is contemplating the sale of its land, which has increased 50 percent in value because of the development of a country club and subdivision adjacent to its acreage. The corporation has operated at a loss during its existence and at the present time is not operating at all, in the sense of having any cattle. The three stockholders are in relatively high tax brackets, but none is a real estate dealer for tax purposes; they would prefer to have the corporation continue in existence as an Electing Small Business corporation. The proposed sales contract on the land calls for a minimal down payment, payments on the basis of a release clause, and guaranteed minimum annual payments that would pay the contract out in ten years even if the land were never subdivided. It also calls for interest on the unpaid balance at 8 percent, which would produce interest income in 1978 of $8,000 versus capital gains of $5,000. Both Beta and the proposed buyer are cash-basis taxpayers and unrelated.

15. John Fredericks owns a house located on a ten-acre tract in the Catalina

Foothills area. Cost of the property was approximately $50,000, although present market value is $100,000. Mr. Fredericks is a widower, with an annual net taxable income of $40,000 and an estate with a value (net of all deductions and exemptions) of $1,000,000.

Upon his death, he would like his home to go to the Mountain View Presbyterian Church, to be used as a retreat and for such other purposes as the church might desire. Fredericks is now 60 years old. The value of a life interest in a male aged 60 is 40 percent of the total value.

Mr. Fredericks has thought of two ways in which he can give the property to the church. He might donate it now, retaining the right to full use of the property as his personal residence for the remainder of his life. Or he might leave the property to the church in his will.

16. The Bliss Design Company manufactures store displays. Their business is highly seasonal, being greatly influenced by the demands of their largest customer, a national shoe chain. From December through April is their peak production period.

    Charles Bliss, the president and largest stockholder, was quite dismayed to learn that the land on which the corporation's manufacturing plant stands is to be taken to construct a new highway interchange. He has been unable to find out exactly when the land will be taken over. However, he feels that the company's safest course of action is to immediately start construction of a new plant and to transfer its equipment to it in an orderly fashion so as to interrupt production as little as possible. He particularly dreads the possibility of having to make the move during the peak season and creating customer-relations problems by inability to meet tight delivery schedules.

    The tax basis of the land and buildings amounts to $450,000. Mr. Bliss has been able to locate a buyer willing to pay $700,000 for the property, in the hope that more than this could be obtained from the government. An appraisal valued the property at $750,000, but Mr. Bliss feels that this was somewhat optimistic. A new plant would cost $725,000.

# 23

# Tax Reform

Tax reform is not only a current issue but an ancient problem. Thus, we read in I Kings 12 of Rehoboam, the son of Solomon, of whom the people demanded a lighter tax burden. Rehoboam responded, "My father made your yoke heavy, but I will add to your yoke." The result? The Kingdom was split by a tax revolt into Israel and Judah, with Rehoboam losing Israel and retaining only Judah.

In the beginning of this book, the *Prologue* fictionalized some of the concepts and problems of taxation in order to give you an easily grasped frame of reference. Now we return to some of the same concepts, but without the story-telling gloss.

What is the purpose of the U.S. tax system?

It is possible to conceive of that purpose as being solely the collection of revenue. A tax law based on such a purpose would provide a minimum of special benefits and incentives—that would be difficult to get into the law and difficult to keep in the law. A revenue-only tax law would seldom change in essence, although it might change frequently in its rates. It would be relatively simple and its impact would be relatively predictable, because past experience with the very same law would help predict the effect of altering those few variables which would be changed from time to time.

Such a tax law would attempt to be neutral, in that it would have as one of its goals a minimum of either incentive or penalty. Transactions that would seem advantageous relative to other transactions absent a tax law would still seem as advantageous after reflecting the impact of the tax law. Property values would be affected only minimally by tax law changes, since all types of property would be affected about the same.

That is not, of course, the present tax law in the United States. Special incentives, relief provisions for various categories of taxpayers, and attempts to provide equity and social insurance cost an estimated $100 billion annually through what are called "tax expenditures." Constant tinkering with the law contributes to an adversary climate in tax administration which partly causes uncertainty as to what particular tax provisions actually mean.

Thus, one school of critics of the present U.S. tax system would eliminate most or all nonbusiness itemized deductions of individuals, do away with special incentive provisions, and then lower the rate of tax on what would then be a much larger base of income.

Another school focuses on the lack of operational progressivity revealed by tax statistics as compared to the apparent progressivity of the tax rate tables. Especially if the burden of all taxes is analyzed, there is relatively little progressivity[1] in the combined federal, state, and local tax structures in the U.S. This is offensive to many people on ideological grounds, and these people would also advocate doing away with itemized deductions, special credits, and other incentives—but with primary focus on those of major benefit to upper-income taxpayers.

And then there are the defenders of the *status quo*. They would point out that the U.S. tax system has evolved over a period of 65 years to its present status, and that it provides a tool for fiscal and economic fine-tuning that has become increasingly important as government has played a larger and larger role in the U.S. economy. One does not simply abandon such a tax system on theoretical and ideological grounds.

Thus, the answers to questions of tax reform are not answers that can be provided by specialists in public finance, or economists, or C.P.A.s, or lawyers, or by any group of technicians. They are answers that come from the values and perceived self-interest of the various groups and individuals concerned about tax reform—or, to be even more precise, from the perception by those involved in enacting tax laws as to the values and the self-interest of their particular constituencies.

Throughout this book, different tax reform issues have been discussed in the context of the provisions involved. Over and over, the evolutionary nature of U.S. tax provisions has been stressed. While it is relatively easy to get general agreement on broad characteristics of a "good" tax system, applying such agreed-upon criteria to specific tax change proposals does not produce an easy concensus. The sort of standards or principles which serve as a starting point would likely include:

*1. Equity:*

Every practicable effort should be made to treat all persons who are in the same economic situation, for example, those with the same annual income, in the same way (sometimes referred to as "horizontal equity"). Also, appropriate

[1]Pechman, Joseph A., and Okner, Benjamin A., *Who Bears the Tax Burden,* The Brookings Institution, 1974.

and fair distinctions should be made in the treatment of those who are in different economic circumstances (sometimes referred to as "vertical equity" or "progressivity"). The most common illustrative example of progressivity is a graduated tax whose rates increase as the level of income increases, thus relating the tax to the taxpayer's presumptive ability to pay.

*2. Moral Integrity:*

In structure, administration, and enforcement, the tax system should foster honest and conscientious self-assessment. Integrity of the system–an understanding that it operates as intended, fairly toward all–will tend to produce integrity in the taxpaying public. Under this criterion, emphasis is placed on the taxpayer's being treated fairly and with dignity in the administration of the tax rules. The privacy of tax returns is of importance to the taxpayer and should be protected. The relationship between the government tax-collecting agency and the taxpayer should not *ipso facto* be an adversary one. The rules by which administrative proceedings are conducted should not assume wrongful intent or behavior by the taxpayer.

*3. Simplicity:*

The tax system should be made as simple as practicable so that taxpayers, tax administrators, and legislators all can understand the rules and confidently apply them themselves or comply with them. Simple provisions and rules are more likely to be uniformly applied, and the results of such uniform application not affected by individual judgment, interpretation, or circumstances.

*4. Efficiency:*

A good tax system should contribute to or at least not hinder, the economy's obtaining from its limited resources the highest possible output not only of goods and services but also of those intangibles making up the "quality of life."

*5. Political Acceptability:*

Political acceptability, as used here, refers more to acceptance by the electorate than it does to feasibility of passage by the legislature. A tax system would not be acceptable, but would be rejected, evaded, or ignored, if the public perceived it to be unfair, overly complex, or inefficient in operation. Included in political acceptability is not only the concept and general effect of the tax, but is implementation and administration, as well.

*6. Flexibility:*

The tax laws should have built-in provisions for their periodic legislative review. This is especially desirable if the tax system is to be used to accomplish economic and social objectives as well as to raise revenues.

Laws enacted to solve the problems of a given time period tend to become obsolete. Tax laws are no exception. The criterion of flexibility is intended to make the revenue-raising mechanism, and the law itself, responsive to and reflective of changing economic and social priorities.

These criteria conflict with each other. For example, equity often is achievable only with a loss of simplicity, while too heavy-handed an emphasis on moral integrity may lead to a zealousness that threatens political acceptability. There must inevitably be some trading-off.

The nature of the U.S. political process is such that an extensive scrapping of the present system and substitution of a philosophically coherent approach (e.g., elimination of all incentive provisions, itemized deductions for individuals, and lowering of tax rates) is not politically likely. Each provision in the tax law has its own constituency. Its proposed repeal generates heated opposition, regardless of what else is being done to any other provisions. Politicians don't like heated opposition, so legislation tends to focus on specific tax provisions, and on their modification rather than their abolition.

For example, when the use of accelerated depreciation on business real estate was criticized as creating excessive tax benefits, a first response was to provide for a partial recapture, as ordinary income, of some part of the gain on disposition of the realty that would otherwise be capital gain. Originally, holding the property for at least ten years eliminated entirely any ordinary income recapture. Later, property was categorized (low-income housing, other residential, and commercial) and different holding periods were required in order to avoid any ordinary income upon sale. Most recently, the ability to eliminate ordinary income by a long-enough holding period was abolished for all but low-income housing. Determining the tax effects of a sale of realty that has been held for some time is now quite complicated, since each of the changes treats differently the depreciation taken before and after a cut-off date. In addition, since the ordinary income portion of the gain is based upon the excess of accelerated over straight-line depreciation, the passage of time impacts the calculation inasmuch as there comes a point in the depreciation of the realty where the "accelerated" method is producing less than the straight-line would have, and thus the potential ordinary income is being reduced year by year.

However, Congress was not content with this rather complicated approach to this particular tax question. Along the line, it also decreed that the annual excess of accelerated over straight-line depreciation on realty would constitute a tax preference item. This now means that it may be subject to up to an additional 15 percent tax, depending upon the particular tax situation of the taxpayer, and it may affect the maximum tax on earned income and thus add as much as an additional 20 percent tax.

The history of other tax provisions could be similarly sketched. The result is a mosaic of rules, exceptions to the rules, special provisions, exceptions to the special provisions, etc. Powers and interests are not so much balanced as placated, while the costs and effects of changes are not only misunderstood by the citizenry but are often incomprehensible to the legislators and technicians who formulate the statutory provisions and to the lawyers and C.P.A.s who attempt to counsel taxpayers on their impact.

There are many consequences to such a state of affairs. Such confusion is wastefully expensive, requiring the efforts of thousands of people; it has a devastating impact on people's perception of their ability to cope with the demands of their society; it contributes to governmental corruption in tax legislation and administration. As to balancing powers and interests, the confusion and complexity of the magnitude of the present federal income tax law puts increasing power into the hands of legislators and of special interest groups without any balancing force capable of dealing adequately with how that power is exercised.

Complexity warps the perception of the taxpayer. Add to complexity, tax rules that seem to be in a constant state of change, and the average taxpayer simply abandons trying to understand how the tax law affects him. He recognizes that his efforts to control his income tax liability may be at least as important to his after-tax economic well-being as are the efforts he makes to earn his income. So he may conclude that the capriciousness, complexity, and constant change of the tax law justify taking any action or making any claim which would be unlikely to result in criminal charges. He may rationalize that "everyone's doing it," and so join the insistent clamor for tax benefits and privileges for whatever groups he identifies with. Can he be fairly criticized for all this? He is behaving as the system assumes he will behave and encourages him to behave.

Abstractly, this is "bad." It is the essence of the just society that it encourage good rather than evil, selflessness rather than selfishness, cooperation rather than destructive aggrandizement. Thus, complexity and constant change must be viewed as not being in the public good, all other things being equal. But, of course, all other things are seldom equal.

Thus, in spite of the negative aspects of the present system, there are positive arguments for the retention of its essential features.

### *1. A Tax Incentive Is Not an Expenditure*

A tax incentive is not the same thing as a governmental expenditure. The tax incentive allows people to retain what they already have, but there is a subtle difference between keeping what you have and instituting a program of governmental subsidy for yourself. There is probably less damage done if taxpayers get to keep too much of their own money than if a governmental program funnels funds to the wrong recipients, or squanders money in bureaucratic foolishness, or is "taken" by chiselers.

Some would also argue that equating tax incentives and governmental expenditures requires the presumption that the federal government has an ownership claim to income superior to that of the taxpayer who is actually receiving or earning that income. While the ability to levy an income tax probably encompasses the legal power to tax 100 percent (or even more) of income, there is probably substantial agreement that, even if such a power exists, its exercise would be unconscionable, and that an individual's right to his or her income is a property right that should be jealously and zealously safeguarded. An analogy is sometimes drawn between the government and an armed robber. The robber may have the *power* to take your money, but that does not mean he has the *right* to do so.

There is also the measurement problem. In the context of equating tax expenditures with incentives, the impossibility of accurately measuring the cost of tax incentives tends to make much of the discussion difficult. However, even if tax expenditures could be measured with high accuracy, the measurement would suffer from the *ceteris peribus* (all other things being equal) problem. For example, the tax expenditure for charitable contributions is estimated on the assumption that all other tax system elements would be the same without the tax provision as with it. But that is patently, although unmeasurably, absurd. If the incentive does encourage contributions, then eliminating the deduction will reduce the contributions. Charitable organizations will have less to spend, fewer employees, etc., and their employees and suppliers will thus have less taxable income and pay less tax.

Finally, there are real legal differences between what can be done with appropriations as compared to tax incentives. For example, the charitable contribution deduction can provide a tax incentive for contributions to religious organizations, while a direct money appropriation from the federal government would violate the constitutional separation of church and state.

### 2. *Tax Incentive Advantages*

Tax incentives are simpler, speedier, more direct, and more efficiently administered than are other incentive programs. Although it could stand improvement, the Internal Revenue Service administers an apparatus that has great flexibility, at low administrative cost per dollar involved, whereas other incentive programs generally lead to expansion of governmental agencies and are frequently accompanied by long time delays in field implementation as well as substantial over-all inefficiency in accomplishing their objectives.

### *3. Tax Incentives Conform to Human Nature*

There is the belief that taxpayers will try to lessen or avoid taxes no matter what the tax system, and therefore natural human game-playing tendency should be channelled into socially desirable activity. If people will do things to cut their taxes anyway, let them do socially desirable things (like putting their money into residential housing). Related to this is the belief that in many areas of economic behavior, a tax incentive may have more impact than a cash subsidy (i.e., a dollar saved may be worth more than a dollar earned, if the dollar saved is a tax dollar).

### *4. Tax Incentives Have a Built-in System of Checks and Balances*

Many believe that the intimate involvement of most citizens with the federal income tax process leads to a relatively high level of knowledge of tax incentives as compared to the public knowledge of other types of incentive programs. This, in turn, results in a built-in contribution to the system of checks and balances comparable in its effect to the safeguards built into the appropriation process.

Given such an environment, what are some of the key tax reform issues in these latter years of the 1970's?

## DOUBLE TAXATION OF CORPORATIONS

Who bears the burden of an income tax imposed on business? The economics and the politics of taxation are affected by one's perception of the answer to this question. Since business entities are merely conduits, the answer has to be that the burden of the corporate income tax falls on the corporate shareholder, the worker, and the consumer. The proportion that each pays varies, of course, among industries as well as among different periods of time.

Coupled with an apparent upcoming shortage of investment capital, the reality of double taxation leads many to conclude that elimination of the double taxation would help solve the capital shortage. Elimination would probably involve one or a combination of both:

1. allowing corporations a deduction for dividends paid, or
2. taxing corporate income to shareholders as earned rather than as distributed, with the shareholder getting a credit for the income tax paid as a deposit on behalf by his corporation.

The probable direct effect of either approach would seem, in part, to be the shift of the tax impact to the shareholders. Alternative 1 presumably would force corporations to pay most of their current earnings in dividends, subjecting these dividends to tax in the hands of taxpaying shareholders and sending the corporations back to the equity markets to get the cash they now obtain through retaining earnings.

In the second approach, corporate cash flow would not change, but investors in marginal tax brackets higher than the corporate would find their after-tax return decreased.

Pension funds, churches, and other tax-exempt investors likely would benefit from the first alternative as their cash flow from dividends was increased, and also would benefit from the second alternative if their dividend credit could produce a cash refund. But the net impact, because of the tax-exempts, would be to reduce total income tax receipts. That reduction would have to be balanced by tax increases somewhere. Only when the question is answered as to where those tax dollars will come from can the ultimate impact of eliminating double taxation be evaluated.

## U.S. TAXATION OF FOREIGN INCOME

U.S. taxpayers are allowed to take a credit against their U.S. tax for foreign income taxes paid. Presumably, the U.S. taxpayer is indifferent as to whether he pays a dollar of tax to the United States or to a foreign country, so long as the foreign tax rate does not exceed the amount for which he can obtain a credit. The rationale for the foreign tax credit is equity to the taxpayer and neutrality of the tax system in making international investment decisions.

From the standpoint of the U.S. national interest, some contend, there is a great difference between a dollar in taxes paid to a foreign country and the same dollar paid to the United States. In fact, since the use of foreign corporations allows U.S. persons to defer tax on foreign earnings, there is a positive incentive for U.S. persons to invest abroad in countries where the income tax rate is substantially less than the U.S. income tax rate.

Which viewpoint a particular individual may adopt will likely depend on whether he believes that the U.S. tax loss is more than made up by the advantage to U.S. national interests of having U.S. business actively engaged around the world.

## CREDITS INSTEAD OF DEDUCTIONS

If tax rates rise as income rises, then the value of a tax deduction will be greater, in terms of after-tax dollars, to someone with higher income. A credit, by contrast, is worth the same dollars to all taxpayers with a tax liability against which the credit will apply. If the credit is refundable (i.e., if the credit exceeds the tax liability, the government writes the taxpayer a check). Then truly all taxpayers, even those who have no tax to pay, are being treated alike.

One deduction often proposed for change to credit status is the personal exemption. By definition, every person is entitled to the personal exemption deduction for himself, at least, so that it is the most universal tax deduction in the system. A major argument for changing it to a credit is that the personal exemption is the community's way of sharing or subsidizing the cost of a human being's supporting himself and others who are dependent upon him. Therefore, why should the community subsidize one human being more heavily than another merely because of a higher income level? In fact, from the standpoint of community concern for the individual, why not subsidize on a basis where the subsidy declines as the income rises?

It is possible, though, to view the personal exemption differently. Instead of focusing on how taxpayers at different income levels are treated, think of the personal exemption in terms of the taxation of taxpayers having the same adjusted gross income. If, as discussed in Chapter 6, some concept of "disposable income" seems to influence the tax deductions allowed individuals, then personal exemptions can be viewed as a way of adjusting a given level of income for some minimal amount of annual expense that needs to be incurred for each person who must be supported out of that income. Only after such an adjustment has been made can disposable income properly subject to income tax be determined. Would it be fair to impose the same income tax on a single person with $20,000 of income as a family of eight with $20,000?

## CAPITAL RECOVERY ALLOWANCES

As demonstrated in the Appendix, expensing capital investments at the time made would produce an after-tax rate of return on those investments equal to the before-tax, all other things being equal. Making the investment non-deductible forever, by contrast, would reduce the after-tax return on investment to the same percentage of the before-tax as the complement of the tax rate.

Some types of investments (e.g., research and development expenditures) can be charged to expense when incurred. Others (e.g., purchased goodwill) are never deductible. Most are recovered over some period of time and in some pattern (e.g., useful life, or not less than 80 percent of ADR guideline life, for machinery and equipment, using depreciation that can be heavier in the early years than in the later).

The issue is whether incentives are needed for business to make investments. One argument points out that business will not, in fact, make investments unless they perceive potential profits. Hence it is concluded that tax incentives are not as useful in stimulating investment when consumer demand is weak as they are in changing the perceived profitability of different competing investments when consumer demand is strong.

A contrary argument points to the infinite complexity of the world economy. Projects compete with projects, but the dollars also compete with the costs of financing and the returns on passive as well as active investment in all corners of the globe. Hence, anything that will improve the perceived profitability of investments which, for instance, create jobs in the U.S., should be good for the U.S. economy in the long run.

There is also the question of business "climate." It is argued that regardless of actual effect, policies (e.g., an increase in the investment credit, which increases the perceived profitability of a project by lowering the after-tax investment) which show business that government is cooperative and supportive increase the likelihood of investments being made by reducing uncertainty and risk as to unfavorable future tax legislation.

## NEGATIVE INCOME TAX

Properly speaking, the negative income tax proposal is a social welfare proposal and not a tax matter at all. But the tax law is concerned with all sorts of matters, as has been frequently pointed out, so it is not *just* a tax law anyway.

At the extreme if fully implemented, the negative income tax would result in every person (or at least every family group) either writing checks to the I.R.S. or getting checks from I.R.S. Those who have positive taxable income would write checks, while those with negative taxable income would receive them. Instead of making payments on estimated taxes, those with negative taxable income would receive estimated tax refund checks.

The argument is that the tax collecting and administration structure is much more efficient than the multitude of welfare agencies and programs now in operation. Thus the costs of welfare per dollar distributed could be dramatically slashed. Beyond that, the negative income tax proposal represents an acceptance of the proposition that solely by virtue of being a U.S. resident a person has a right to some minimum level of income regardless of the reasons why he or she has no more income.

The opposition to this approach to welfare includes people of several different viewpoints. One viewpoint is that without controls over the use of funds, persons being subsidized will be victimized (by their own weaknesses and through being exploited by others) so that there will still be a need for special programs to look out for, e.g., dependent children, and thus many of the anticipated savings will not materialize.

Some are concerned that the magnitude of the negative income tax program will swamp the I.R.S., leading to a decline in the efficiency and effectiveness of its over-all program. When forced to deal with "welfare chiselers," will I.R.S. inherit all the problems of administration of present programs, so that rather than create efficiency in welfare the change will produce chaos in tax collections?

## CAPITAL GAIN PROVISIONS

Some argue that capital gains should be taxed no differently than any other form of income. Others argue that they should not be taxed at all. With the minimum tax and the maximum tax, some high-income taxpayers with high levels of personal service income find that capital gains are being taxed at a shade under 50 percent while their personal service income is being taxed at 50 percent, and hence for them the tax distinction is disappearing. Other taxpayers, with only small amounts of capital gain, find that capital gains cost them only half as much tax as if they received ordinary income.

To some, the significance of the special tax treatment accorded capital gains lies in the importance of wide participation in the securities markets of the United States. Rather than seeing the states use lotteries and casino gambling to raise revenues, they would prefer to see tax-exemption or tax shelter accorded security profits to provide a continuing stimulant to small investor participation in the U.S. system of financing business. Business expansion, it is argued, would lead to higher levels of tax collection, more than offsetting the modest revenue losses from not taxing security gains.

## ADAPTING TO INFLATION

A tax law with dollar amounts specified as limits or floors for many items, with a progressive rate structure, and with a variety of objectives inevitably is subjected to stresses and strains during inflation. Is a $750 personal exemption adequate? How come people who have not had an increase in real income pay sharply higher income taxes? Should not depreciation allowances be adjusted for changes in the value of the dollar so that we are not taxing capital and destroying the ability of business to replace its plant and equipment?

The attempt to maintain relative equities during inflation can only serve to complicate an already complicated law. Yet failure to do some things will be perceived by the voters as callous indifference to their problems. The real answer would be to keep inflation under reasonable control, and thus eliminate the problem. Failing that, there is some support for the idea that key elements in the individual tax structure, and capital recovery in the business area, might be linked to price indexes so as to automatically mirror inflation.

## RELIANCE ON OTHER TAXES

The idea of putting a "lid" on the tax rates applicable to individuals seems to be gaining support. The maximum tax on personal service income was, in reality, a big step toward accomplishing this idea. In the past, it was believed that tax reductions and incentives did not cost tax revenue in the long run because of their stimulating effect on the economy. Increased income meant that the lower tax rates produced more dollars.

Now there is less faith in the growth potential of the U.S. economy. Where do the dollars come from to support expanding governmental expenditures if not from the income tax? Where do the dollars come from to support a reduction in income taxes?

A prime candidate is the excise or sales tax. Many feel that the European experience with the Value Added Tax (VAT) has been favorable, and that such a tax is the logical next step for the U.S. as well. See Chapter 18 for a discussion of the VAT. Property taxes create administrative problems, but excise taxes fit into an existing framework and are relatively easy to implement. Main arguments against excise taxes (including VAT) reflect their lack of progressivity, in the sense that ability-to-pay is not a direct factor. Selective excise taxes can partially overcome that complaint (e.g., retail sales taxes that exempt basic necessities).

## CONCLUSION

Tax reform is obviously not a simple, black and white, good or bad, problem. Perhaps that is why it is discussed so much, and done so little; and perhaps that is why what tax reform legislation there is tends to be painfully complex. Thus, there may be more con to tax reform than the so-called pros are willing to admit.

### EXCERPT

### TAX EXPENDITURE ESTIMATES, 1977-82

A number of tax provisions are not treated as tax expenditures. The general tax rate structure is not part of tax expenditure analysis: the structure of graduated tax rates and taxable income brackets in the individual income tax and separate tax structures for single persons, married persons filing separately, heads-of-households and income splitting for married persons. Other such items are the personal exemption—one per taxpayer and each dependent—and the minimum standard deduction. On the other hand, included as tax expenditures are the additional personal exemptions for the aged and blind, itemized personal deductions, and the excess of the percentage standard deduction over the minimum standard deduction.

In the business tax area, the combined corporate normal and surtax tax rate is not classified as a tax expenditure. The surtax exemption is treated as a departure designed to foster small corporations, and therefore it is treated as a tax expenditure.

There is no provision for negative tax expenditures, and no provisions are classified as disincentives. Thus, the corporate surtax rate is treated as the basic provision and not a departure from the normal tax. The limitation on the deduction of a net long-term capital loss is a limit to the incentive made available through the special treatment for capital gains.

Imputations of income in kind received from the services of durable assets are not treated as income in the tax code and are not here classified as tax expenditures. They might be considered as income under other concepts of income for tax purposes. Measurement of the imputed income-in-kind would be a formidable task. The imputed income from an owner-occupied home is the most prominent of these items, and among the others are the income that could be imputed to household furniture and appliances, books and art collections and automobiles. Food stamps are a form of income in kind that also is omitted from this listing.

Foreign tax credits are not classified here as tax expenditures since they are generally considered as the way of taking into account the interrelationship of domestic and foreign tax systems. In addition, this analysis does not attempt to go behind the current legal acceptance and attribution of payments by U.S. corporations to foreign governments as taxes (e.g., it does not attempt to treat any as royalties as in the case of oil income), when the payments are designated in that way by those governments. Treating credits for some of these payments as tax expenditures might be appropriate, but they would be difficult to measure.

*Measurement of Tax Expenditures*

Estimates of tax expenditures are difficult to determine and are subject to important limitations.

Each tax expenditure is measured in isolation. The amount of the deduction is added back in the calculation of taxable income, which raises its level. The difference in tax liabilities between the existing structure of tax rates and this new higher level of tax liabilities is taken as the amount of the tax expenditure. For this computation and in keeping with the general practice of revenue estimating, it is assumed that nothing else changes: neither the behavior of the taxpayer, nor the economic variables that might signal an adjustment in business behavior, nor tax, fiscal or monetary policies. The estimates also do not take into account any effects that the removal of one or more of the items might have on investment patterns, consumption, or other aspects of economic activity. In other words, the estimates shown do not take into account the induced effects of changing the provisions. Repeal of a provision, therefore, would not necessarily raise the revenue associated with removal of that provision.

There are other aspects of this kind of analysis.

First, if two or more items were to be eliminated, the result of the combination of changes being made at the same time might produce a lesser or greater revenue effect than the sum of the amounts shown for each item separately. This is why totals are not shown for table 1, except in a footnote.

Second, in some cases if a tax expenditure item were to be eliminated, it is possible that Congress would, at least to some extent, desire to deal with the underlying problem by a direct expenditure or loan program. The effect of any such program is not taken into account in the estimates shown. A direct expenditure could become a tax expenditure if it takes the form of a payment to an individual or business that is not included in income subject to taxation. In addition, if some of these provisions were removed from the tax laws, this removal might be accompanied by revisions in tax rates, personal exemptions or the minimum standard deduction, as has happened in the past. Other fiscal and monetary policies might be adopted to offset a tax change. None of these possibilities has been taken into account in the estimates.

TABLE 1.—TAX EXPENDITURE ESTIMATES BY FUNCTION AND SUBFUNCTION[1]

[Fiscal years; in millions of dollars]

| Function and subfunction | Corporations 1977 | 1978 | 1979 | 1980 | 1981 | 1982 | Individuals 1977 | 1978 | 1979 | 1980 | 1981 | 1982 |
|---|---|---|---|---|---|---|---|---|---|---|---|---|
| National defense: | | | | | | | | | | | | |
| Military personnel: | | | | | | | | | | | | |
| Exclusion of benefits and allowances to Armed Forces personnel | | | | | | | 1,095 | 1,260 | 1,360 | 1,470 | 1,585 | 1,715 |
| Exclusion of military disability pensions | | | | | | | 105 | 115 | 120 | 130 | 135 | 145 |
| International affairs: | | | | | | | | | | | | |
| International financial programs: | | | | | | | | | | | | |
| Exclusion of income earned abroad by U.S. citizens | | | | | | | 120 | 135 | 150 | 160 | 170 | 185 |
| Deferral of income of domestic international sales corporations (DISC) | 1,030 | 1,190 | 1,360 | 1,455 | 1,475 | 1,545 | | | | | | |
| Deferral of income of controlled foreign corporations | 410 | 410 | 410 | 410 | 410 | 410 | | | | | | |
| Special rate for Western Hemisphere trade corporations | 35 | 25 | 15 | 5 | | | | | | | | |
| Natural resources, environment, and energy: | | | | | | | | | | | | |
| Conservation and land management: Capital gains treatment of certain timber income | 300 | 325 | 340 | 355 | 375 | 395 | 95 | 100 | 105 | 110 | 115 | 125 |
| Pollution control and abatement: | | | | | | | | | | | | |
| Exclusion of interest on State and local government pollution control bonds | 170 | 220 | 265 | 300 | 330 | 355 | 75 | 100 | 125 | 145 | 160 | 175 |
| Exclusion of payments in aid of construction of water and sewage utilities | 15 | 10 | 10 | 10 | 10 | 10 | | | | | | |
| 5-year amortization on pollution control facilities | −80 | −130 | −45 | 40 | 130 | 180 | | | | | | |
| Energy: | | | | | | | | | | | | |
| Expensing of exploration and development costs | 610 | 600 | 610 | 635 | 675 | 735 | 105 | 150 | 155 | 185 | 200 | 230 |
| Excess of percentage over cost depletion | 1,035 | 1,060 | 1,135 | 1,220 | 1,295 | 1,360 | 275 | 300 | 330 | 360 | 400 | 410 |
| Other natural resources: Capital gains treatment of royalties on coal and iron ore | 20 | 20 | 25 | 25 | 30 | 30 | 45 | 50 | 60 | 70 | 80 | 90 |
| Agriculture: | | | | | | | | | | | | |
| Farm income stabilization: | | | | | | | | | | | | |
| Capital gains treatment of certain ordinary income | 10 | 15 | 15 | 15 | 15 | 15 | 330 | 350 | 365 | 385 | 405 | 425 |
| Expensing of certain capital outlays | 80 | 70 | 75 | 80 | 80 | 85 | 370 | 440 | 460 | 475 | 490 | 510 |
| Deductibility of noncash patronage dividends and certain other items of farm cooperatives | 455 | 490 | 535 | 570 | 610 | 655 | −165 | -170 | −180 | −190 | −200 | −210 |
| See footnotes at end of table. | | | | | | | | | | | | |
| Commerce and transportation: | | | | | | | | | | | | |
| Mortgage credit and thrift insurance: | | | | | | | | | | | | |
| Exemption of credit union income | 165 | 185 | 200 | 225 | 250 | 275 | | | | | | |
| Excess bad debt reserves of financial institutions | 560 | 645 | 860 | 875 | 945 | 925 | | | | | | |
| Deductibility of mortgage interest on owner-occupied homes | | | | | | | 5,435 | 6,030 | 6,695 | 7,430 | 8,250 | 9,160 |
| Deductibility of property tax on owner-occupied homes | | | | | | | 4,560 | 4,995 | 5,545 | 6,155 | 6,830 | 7,580 |
| Deductibility of interest on consumer credit | | | | | | | 2,310 | 2,565 | 2,845 | 3,160 | 3,505 | 3,895 |
| Credit for purchase of new homes | | | | | | | 100 | | | | | |
| Deferral of capital gains on home sales | | | | | | | 890 | 935 | 980 | 1,030 | 1,080 | 1,135 |
| Other advancement and regulation of commerce: | | | | | | | | | | | | |
| Dividend exclusion | | | | | | | 410 | 425 | 450 | 470 | 495 | 520 |
| Corporate surtax exemption | 4,650 | 4,250 | 3,655 | 3,915 | 4,205 | 4,485 | | | | | | |
| Capital gains (other than farming, timber, iron ore and coal) | 555 | 550 | 550 | 585 | 615 | 650 | 7,030 | 7,360 | 7,710 | 8,265 | 8,855 | 9,495 |
| Capital gains at death | | | | | | | 7,280 | 8,120 | 8,975 | 9,910 | 10,945 | 12,090 |
| Depreciation on rental housing in excess of straight line | 100 | 100 | 105 | 105 | 105 | 105 | 405 | 425 | 450 | 470 | 490 | 515 |
| Depreciation on buildings (other than rental housing) in excess of straight line | 210 | 200 | 190 | 185 | 180 | 175 | 185 | 175 | 170 | 165 | 160 | 155 |
| Expensing of research and development expenditures | 1,395 | 1,450 | 1,520 | 1,610 | 1,695 | 1,715 | 30 | 30 | 30 | 30 | 35 | 35 |
| Exclusion of interest on State and local industrial development bonds | 195 | 235 | 270 | 315 | 355 | 400 | 90 | 110 | 130 | 150 | 170 | 190 |
| Excess first-year depreciation | 45 | 45 | 50 | 50 | 55 | 55 | 135 | 145 | 155 | 160 | 170 | 180 |
| Expensing of construction period interest and taxes | 475 | 500 | 525 | 555 | 585 | 615 | 150 | 140 | 90 | 140 | 160 | 205 |
| Investment credit | 8,640 | 9,670 | 10,375 | 10,910 | 9,380 | 7,380 | 1,970 | 2,205 | 2,430 | 2,595 | 2,595 | 1,725 |
| Asset depreciation range | 1,630 | 1,825 | 2,000 | 2,095 | 2,115 | 2,115 | 175 | 195 | 220 | 230 | 235 | 235 |

| | | | | | | | | | | | | |
|---|---|---|---|---|---|---|---|---|---|---|---|---|
| Ground transportation: | | | | | | | | | | | | |
| 5-year amortization on railroad rolling stock | —35 | —40 | —40 | —40 | —40 | —40 | | | | | | |
| Deductibility of nonbusiness State gasoline taxes | | | | | | | 795 | 880 | 980 | 1,085 | 1,205 | 1,340 |
| Water transportation: Deferral of tax on shipping companies | 90 | 70 | 60 | 50 | 40 | 35 | | | | | | |
| Community and regional development: | | | | | | | | | | | | |
| Community development: | | | | | | | | | | | | |
| 5-year amortization for housing rehabilitation | 10 | 5 | 5 | (2) | (2) | —5 | 20 | 10 | 5 | (2) | (2) | —5 |
| Tax incentives for preservation of historic structures | (2) | (2) | 5 | 5 | 5 | 5 | (2) | (2) | 5 | 5 | 10 | 10 |
| Education, training, employment, and social services: | | | | | | | | | | | | |
| Higher education: | | | | | | | | | | | | |
| Exclusion of scholarship and fellowship income | | | | | | | 250 | 285 | 375 | 400 | 420 | 445 |
| Parental personal exemption for students age 19 or over | | | | | | | 750 | 770 | 790 | 815 | 840 | 865 |
| Deductibility of charitable contributions (education) | 215 | 240 | 265 | 300 | 335 | 365 | 540 | 565 | 595 | 625 | 655 | 690 |
| Training and employment: | | | | | | | | | | | | |
| Credit for child- and dependent-care expenses | | | | | | | 840 | 870 | 960 | 1,050 | 1,155 | 1,270 |
| Deduction for eliminating barriers for the handicapped | 5 | 10 | 10 | 5 | (2) | (2) | | | | | | |
| 5-year amortization on child-care facilities | (2) | (2) | (2) | (2) | (2) | (2) | | | | | | |
| Credit for employment of AFDC recipients and public assistance recipients under work incentive programs | 15 | 15 | 20 | 20 | 20 | 20 | | | | | | |
| Other labor services: | | | | | | | | | | | | |
| Exclusion of employee meals and lodging (other than military) | | | | | | | 330 | 350 | 370 | 395 | 420 | 445 |
| Maximum tax on personal service income | | | | | | | 730 | 855 | 1,025 | 1,235 | 1,480 | 1,775 |
| Exclusion of contributions to prepaid legal services plans | | | | | | | 5 | 10 | 15 | 20 | 35 | 50 |
| Investment credit for ESOP's | 245 | 255 | 305 | 330 | 190 | | | | | | | |
| Social services: Deductibility of charitable contributions to other than education and health | 270 | 295 | 330 | 370 | 415 | 450 | 3,985 | 4,510 | 5,100 | 5,755 | 6,490 | 7,310 |
| Health: | | | | | | | | | | | | |
| Health-care services: | | | | | | | | | | | | |
| Exclusion of employer contributions for medical insurance premiums and medical care | | | | | | | 5,195 | 5,840 | 6,560 | 7,375 | 8,290 | 9,320 |
| Deductibility of medical expenses | | | | | | | 2,585 | 2,870 | 3,185 | 3,535 | 3,920 | 4,355 |
| Health research and education: Deductibility of charitable contributions (health) | 135 | 150 | 165 | 185 | 205 | 225 | 915 | 965 | 1,010 | 1,060 | 1,115 | 1,170 |
| Income security: | | | | | | | | | | | | |
| General retirement and disability insurance: | | | | | | | | | | | | |
| Exclusion of social security benefits: | | | | | | | | | | | | |
| Disability insurance benefits | | | | | | | 380 | 430 | 485 | 540 | 600 | 665 |
| OASI benefits for retired workers | | | | | | | 3,125 | 3,460 | 3,795 | 4,155 | 4,500 | 4,870 |
| Benefits for dependents and survivors | | | | | | | 730 | 795 | 875 | 955 | 1,035 | 1,120 |
| Exclusion of railroad retirement system benefits | | | | | | | 200 | 205 | 215 | 220 | 230 | 235 |
| Exclusion of workmen's compensation benefits | | | | | | | 705 | 810 | 935 | 1,070 | 1,235 | 1,420 |
| Exclusion of special benefits for disabled coal miners | | | | | | | 50 | 50 | 50 | 55 | 55 | 55 |
| Net exclusion of pension contributions and earnings: | | | | | | | | | | | | |
| Employer plans | | | | | | | 8,715 | 9,940 | 11,335 | 12,925 | 14,740 | 16,815 |
| Plans for self-employed and others | | | | | | | 1,305 | 1,535 | 1,760 | 2,025 | 2,325 | 2,670 |
| Exclusion of other employee benefits: | | | | | | | | | | | | |
| Premiums on group term life insurance | | | | | | | 800 | 835 | 870 | 900 | 940 | 975 |
| Premiums on accident and accidental death insurance | | | | | | | 70 | 75 | 80 | 85 | 85 | 95 |
| Exclusion of capital gains on home sales for persons age 65 and over | | | | | | | 40 | 70 | 70 | 70 | 70 | 75 |
| Additional exemption for elderly | | | | | | | 1,220 | 1,280 | 1,345 | 1,410 | 1,480 | 1,555 |
| Tax credit for the elderly | | | | | | | 495 | 440 | 435 | 430 | 425 | 420 |
| Exclusion of interest on life insurance savings | | | | | | | 1,815 | 1,995 | 2,185 | 2,400 | 2,630 | 2,885 |
| Exclusion of sick pay | | | | | | | 50 | 55 | 60 | 60 | 65 | 70 |
| Unemployment insurance: | | | | | | | | | | | | |
| Exclsuion of unemployment insurance benefits | | | | | | | 2,745 | 2,445 | 2,240 | 2,125 | 2,070 | 2,035 |
| Exclusion of income of trusts to finance supplementary unemployment benefits | | | | | | | 10 | 10 | 10 | 10 | 10 | 10 |
| Public assistance: | | | | | | | | | | | | |
| Exclusion of public assistance benefits | | | | | | | 100 | 105 | 110 | 115 | 125 | 130 |
| Excess of percentage standard deduction over minimum standard deduction | | | | | | | 1,285 | 1,410 | 1,555 | 1,710 | 1,880 | 2,070 |
| Additional exemption for the blind | | | | | | | 20 | 20 | 20 | 20 | 20 | 20 |
| Earned income credit: | | | | | | | | | | | | |
| Nonrefundable portion | | | | | | | 395 | 380 | | | | |
| Refundable portion | | | | | | | 1,015 | 970 | | | | |
| Deductibility of casualty losses | | | | | | | 345 | 380 | 425 | 470 | 520 | 580 |

TABLE 1.—TAX EXPENDITURE ESTIMATES BY FUNCTION AND SUBFUNCTION[1]—Conitnued

[Fiscal years; in millions of dollars]

| Function and subfunction | Corporations | | | | | | Individuals | | | | | |
|---|---|---|---|---|---|---|---|---|---|---|---|---|
| | 1977 | 1978 | 1979 | 1980 | 1981 | 1982 | 1977 | 1978 | 1979 | 1980 | 1981 | 1982 |
| Veterans benefits and services: | | | | | | | | | | | | |
| Income security for veterans: | | | | | | | | | | | | |
| Exclusion of veterans disability compensation | | | | | | | 655 | 690 | 690 | 685 | 685 | 685 |
| Exclusion of veterans pensions | | | | | | | 30 | 35 | 35 | 35 | 35 | 35 |
| Veterans education, training, and rehabilitation: Exclusion of GI bill benefits | | | | | | | 255 | 240 | 220 | 190 | 160 | 135 |
| General government—Other general government: Credits and deductions for political contributions | | | | | | | 40 | 35 | 40 | 40 | 45 | 45 |
| Revenue sharing and general purpose fiscal assistance: | | | | | | | | | | | | |
| Other general purpose fiscal assistance: | | | | | | | | | | | | |
| Exclusion of interest on general purpose State and local debt | 3, 105 | 3, 470 | 3, 865 | 4, 305 | 4, 780 | 5, 310 | 1, 680 | 1, 880 | 2, 095 | 2, 335 | 2, 595 | 2, 880 |
| Tax credit for corporations doing business in U.S. possessions[3] | 285 | 310 | 330 | 350 | 370 | 390 | | | | | | |
| Deductibility of nonbusiness State and local taxes (other than on owner-occupied homes and gasoline) | | | | | | | 8, 095 | 8, 990 | 9, 975 | 11, 075 | 12, 290 | 13, 645 |
| Interest—Interest on the public debt: Deferral of interest on savings bonds | | | | | | | 565 | 625 | 685 | 755 | 820 | 890 |

[1] All estimates are based on the Internal Revenue Code as of Jan. 1, 1977.
[2] Less than $2,500,000.
[3] Includes the effect of sec. 931 exclusion for individuals doing business in certain U.S. possessions.

Note: Limitations on the use of totals are explained in the text:

SUM OF THE TAX EXPENDITURE ITEMS BY TYPE OF TAXPAYER AND FISCAL YEAR*

[In millions of dollars]

| Fiscal year | Corporations and individuals | Corporations | Individuals |
|---|---|---|---|
| 1977 | 114, 470 | 27, 050 | 87, 465 |
| 1978 | 124, 395 | 28, 740 | 95, 710 |
| 1979 | 133, 865 | 30, 370 | 103, 545 |
| 1980 | 146, 285 | 32, 425 | 113, 935 |
| 1981 | 157, 460 | 32, 240 | 125, 280 |
| 1982 | 168, 465 | 31, 425 | 137, 100 |

*These totals represent the mathematical sum of the estimated fiscal year effect of each of the 85 tax expenditure items included in this table.

Source: Staffs of the Treasury Department and the Joint Committee on Taxation.

Third, when tax expenditure items have been added to the tax law in the past, they did not become fully effective until the lapse of several years. As a result, the eventual annual cost of some items is not fully reflected until some time in the future. Conversely, if various items now in the law were to be eliminated, it is unlikely, in many cases, that the full revenue effects shown would be realized until an extended period of years had passed.

Fourth, differences in personal income levels and corporate profits can also account for differences in the cost of tax expenditure items from year to year. Thus, some tax expenditure items themselves may be larger or smaller from year to year, wholly independent of tax considerations.

Fifth, in the case of many of the items, especially those for which information is not available on tax returns, it is necessary to obtain information from whatever sources are available and, when sources are limited, to make assumptions on which to base the estimates.

# Appendix: Quantitative Aspects of Decision Making

What makes a successful manager? If we were to do something as risky as to name one characteristic in answer to this question, that one would probably be this: *He makes decisions that stand up.* They may not always be the right decisions; we do not say that the successful manager never makes mistakes. No, he is not infallible. But his decisions do stand up in the sense that they are consistent. His decisions contribute to his goals.

Some people have acquired an ability along this line that they apply without any conscious recognition that they are using any particular technique in decision making. Most of us need to work at our decision making, or we shall find problems mastering us instead of our mastering them.

There is no mystery about the steps in decision making. Although they may be classified in various ways, the following will do for our purposes.

1. Identification of the problem
2. The search for alternative approaches
3. Gathering of information relative to the alternatives
4. Quantification of the alternatives
5. Elimination of unsatisfactory alternatives
6. Qualitative review of alternatives
7. Decision
8. Follow-through

Our concern with decision making in this appendix is focused on item 4, the quantification of the alternatives. How do tax considerations affect the quantitative aspects of alternatives in a problem situation?

## IDENTIFICATION OF THE PROBLEM

Every business has problems. At first glance, they are easy to identify. We're short of cash. Obviously, we need more cash. But is cash the problem, or is it just the symptom? If it is just the symptom, then getting more cash merely means postponing the day when we shall have to face the real problem. Perhaps the real problem is that we have an inefficient operation. How can we find out? If our selling prices are about the same as those of everyone else in our line of business, perhaps we need to look a bit more closely at our business mix.

Assume, for example, that we are in the pest-control business. Maybe our volume is heavy on original termite treatments and cleanouts, but we don't hang onto the customers afterward for termite renewals and monthly pest-control services. Original termite treatments consist of treating a house that has never been treated against termites. Cleanouts involve chemically killing all insect and rodent life in an infested house. Termite renewals are periodic treatments, somewhat like tetanus booster shots. Thus, instead of a good, steady backbone of repeat month-in-and-month-out business, we have hard-to-get, one-shot jobs. This gives us peaks of heavy work and valleys of slack work, making it hard for us to hold our men. And having relatively inexperienced men, in turn, makes it harder to hold the repeat business.

Or maybe we need to look at our expenses, compared with those of our competitors. Perhaps our buying isn't as sharp as it could be. Maybe we aren't too careful how much material we use. How do our men stack up against each other on expenses? How do the cost figures on separate but similar jobs stack up against each other? In cost control, the rule is *divide and conquer.* If we divide our costs into meaningful groupings (by man, by territory, by function, and so forth), we will have taken the first step in conquering those costs, because we can start to see the shape of our problems.

## THE SEARCH FOR ALTERNATIVE APPROACHES

This might be thought of as the brainstorming aspect of problem solving. The key thing here is *not to evaluate, not to criticize.* We jot down the ideas as they come to us. The farther out the idea is, the better. The more approaches that are tossed into the hopper, the better. If one must do this alone, it is best to cut off the phone, lean back, and let fly. Jot down or record the ideas as they come, and then go back to digging for new ideas. If one can have several people work on this with him, all the better. One man's idea acts as a stimulant to the next person.

## INFORMATION AND QUANTIFICATION

Once the alternative approaches are all set out, we have to start working on them. Our question is: What would happen if we were to do such-and-such? Later in this appendix we shall illustrate, in simple, two-alternative situations, how this might be done.

## QUALITATIVE REVIEW OF ALTERNATIVES

Alternatives whose figures seem satisfactory will still contain aspects that cannot be reduced to numbers. Here we return to the idea of goals. Our decisions and our goals have a step-type relationship:

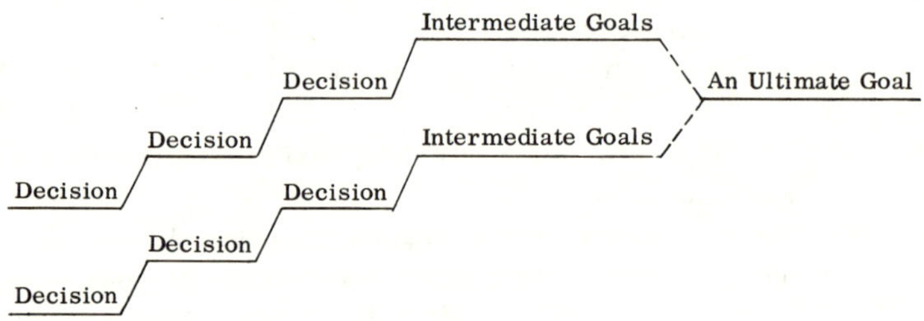


The ultimate goals tend to be big . . . and vague. Some people argue that *profit* is the ultimate goal of every business. Although this is doubtful, let us assume that profit is the goal. What is profit? What time period are we using to measure profit? Is it simply this year's profit? If we intend that this business go on for an indefinite time into the future, then we must plan for at least enough profit to keep it going indefinitely. Although we plan to have enough profit in good years to ride out the bad years, we must also avoid doing such a job earning this year's profit that we hurt our prospects for next year and for the years after that.

Assuming, then, that our ultimate (long-run) goal is profit, then our intermediate goals might be certain things that we feel would contribute to the ultimate goal:

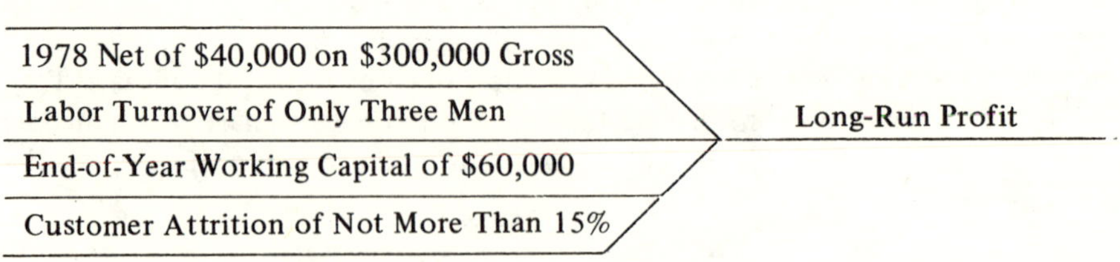

Any specific alternative decision we propose making, then, can be measured against these intermediate goals. Will this alternative help more to achieve one or more of these goals than another available alternative would help?

## FOLLOW-THROUGH

Follow-through in business, as in tennis, is what makes a decision work. If the information on the alternative that is finally adopted has been carefully gathered and logically evaluated, most of the steps necessary to implement the decision are clear. These steps should be spelled out and responsibility for their execution assigned. As the decision is carried out, there should be a feeding back of information on what actually happens to be checked against the assumptions we made when we arrived at the decision. For instance, we take a pretreating contract. A pretreating contract involves treating the foundations of new homes against termites. Where a substantial real estate project is involved, these contracts are let on a highly competitive basis. We estimated labor cost as so much per house, material cost as so much, and so on. As the work goes along, we should be comparing the costs of the job as it develops with our cost estimates. If things aren't coming along as we expected, then *now,* while something can still be done, is the time to act. Perhaps the contractor isn't adhering to the schedule he gave us, and this throws our labor scheduling out of line. Let's argue with him now and get the matter straightened out *before* we have a heavy loss, not after.

If we know what assumptions entered into our decision, if we know what other alternatives were open to us, our operations can become flexible. Although unexpected things will still happen to us, we shall not be caught entirely unaware by them. We shall have the decision-making equivalent of a good sprinkler system, instead of trying to put out fires with cups of water.

## ILLUSTRATIVE SITUATIONS

The two illustrative situations that follow are based on the Pest Control Company profit and loss schedule shown in Table A-1. These two situations deal, respectively, with (1) a proposal to expand volume by cutting prices, and (2) a choice between leasing and buying a new truck.

In the interests of simplicity, we have eliminated in these first illustrations many factors, including tax considerations, that would certainly have to be considered in any real-world situation. Our objective with these examples is simply to show the general type of approach that might be adapted to the quantification of alternatives. Then we shall discuss the ways in which tax considerations might be reflected.

### *Expanding Volume by Cutting Prices*

A review of Table A-1, indicates that we have, for a time period involving a year or so, three types of expenses:

TABLE A-1

Hypothetical Company
Pest Control Profit and Loss Schedule

| | | |
|---|---|---|
| Income | $220,000 | 100% |
| Direct Expenses: | | |
| Direct material and supplies | 35,200 | 16% |
| Direct labor | 74,800 | 34% |
| Truck expenses | 22,000 | 10% |
| Total | 132,000 | 60% |
| Gross Profit | 88,000 | 40% |
| Indirect Expenses: | | |
| Truck depreciation | $8,400 | 4% |
| Equipment depreciation | 2,100 | 1% |
| Auto depreciation–5 year (straight-line) | 1,200 | |
| Office supplies and expense | 800 | |
| Office salaries | 7,200 | 3% |
| Insurance–disability | 240 | |
| Insurance–truck, equipment, and liability | 4,000 | 2% |
| Rent | 3,600 | 2% |
| Taxes (including own F.I.C.A.) | 8,800 | 4% |
| Advertising | 10,000 | 5% |
| Telephone | 720 | |
| Utilities | 480 | |
| Travel | 2,000 | 1% |
| Professional services | 1,200 | 1% |
| Interest–trucks | 1,080 | |
| Interest–equipment | 440 | |
| Interest–auto | 240 | |
| Other | 800 | |
| Total | $ 53,300 | 24% |
| Profit | $ 34,700 | 16% |

1. Direct expenses–running 60 cents per dollar of revenue
2. Indirect out-of-pocket expenses, most of which are not materially affected by fluctuations in revenue–running about $42,000 ($41,600)
3. Depreciation–running almost $12,000 ($11,700)

We now have seven men, each with his own territory. Each man's compensation is a percentage of the revenue of his territory. Several of the men feel that lower prices could boost the revenue they generate (and, of course, their own compensation). Management believes that in perhaps one out of eight calls we lose the job strictly on a price basis. If prices were cut on new business, this, they feel, would force a cut on present business as well. Cutting 10 percent would be necessary to make us fully competitive with the lowest-priced competition. Of course, the result of our price cut could be a retaliatory price cut by our competition, but this risk is believed to be minimal.

| | *Present* | *After Cut* |
|---|---|---|
| Revenue ($220,000 – $22,000 [10%] + $24,750 [12½%]) | $220,000 | $222,750 |
| Direct costs | 132,000 | 140,084* |
| Gross profit | 88,000 | 82,666 |
| Indirect costs | 53,300 | 53,300 |
| Net profit | $ 34,700 | $ 29,366 |

*Labor, 34 percent of revenue ($75,734). Other direct expense ($64,350) based on 26 percent of revenue adjusted for price cut ($247,500).

Based upon our assumptions, it does not appear that a price cut is a rational move. Let us change our assumptions and see how our analysis changes.

One of our territories is a separate community. Present revenue from this territory is $15,000, and the direct expenses in this territory are the same proportion of revenue as for the entire company. Management feels that a price change in this territory will not require price changes in the other territories, and that a 10 percent price reduction would lead to a 40 percent expansion in physical volume.

| | *Present* | *After Cut* |
|---|---|---|
| Territory revenue | $15,000 | $18,900 |
| Direct costs | 9,000 | 11,912* |
| Contribution to company indirect costs | $ 6,000 | $ 6,988 |

*Direct labor, 34 percent of revenue ($6,426); other expenses ($5,486), 26 percent of revenue adjusted for price cut.

Based upon these assumptions, the price cut on this selective basis might appear attractive as a short-run pricing policy.

### *Buy or Lease*

We have decided to get a new truck. Cost would be $6,000. We estimate that we could use it for four years, at the end of which time its resale value would be $1,200. We can lease the same truck for $2,000 per year.

| | *Buy* | *Lease* | *Difference* |
|---|---|---|---|
| Investment | $6,000.00 | –0– | $6,000.00 |
| Operating expenses, per year | X | X | –0– |
| Rent, per year | –0– | $2,000.00 | $2,000.00 |
| Resale value | $1,200.00 | –0– | $1,200.00 |

Let us postulate that we could find an equally risky investment paying 12 percent. We might ask ourselves how leasing the truck rates as an alternative to investing, at 12 percent a year. The investment is $6,000; the return consists of the four years of rent saved, plus the $1,200 resale value at the end of four years.

| | |
|---|---|
| Invested @ 12% | $6,000.00 |
| First-year earnings | 720.00 |
| Available | 6,720.00 |
| First-year rent | 2,000.00 |
| Reinvested | 4,720.00 |
| Second-year earnings | 560.00 |
| Available | 5,280.00 |
| Second-year rent | 2,000.00 |
| Reinvested | 3,280.00 |
| Third-year earnings | 400.00 |
| Available | 3,680.00 |
| Third-year rent | 2,000.00 |
| Reinvested | 1,680.00 |
| Fourth-year interest | 200.00 |
| Available | 1,880.00 |
| Fourth-year rent | 2,000.00 |
| Shortage | 120.00 |
| Resale value of truck, if not leased | 1,200.00 |
| Advantage of ownership over leasing | $1,320.00 |

What does this tell us? It tells us that if our two alternatives were to (1) buy the truck, or (2) lease the truck and invest the amount we would otherwise have used to buy the truck in a 12 percent investment, then buying the truck would be the better alternative. How much better? Better by $1,320! This is a useful answer. But it is a useful answer only as long as we are comparing just these two things. What if we are going to have to compare several things involving unlike investments? Won't we need to express our return on buying the truck over leasing it in a form that relates the amount of return to both the amount of investment required to achieve it and the length of time for which that investment is required?

This type of result can be obtained by calculating the return on investment of the buying alternative, using the "Difference" column figures.

Although this calculation may be done in a variety of ways, the essential idea underlying all of them is the determination of a discount rate that equates the present investment with the present value of the cash inflows to be realized on that investment. We can tell from our calculation above, which used a 12 percent rate, that the actual rate that would result in ownership and leasing being equal would have to be greater than 12 percent. Through trial and error, using different rates of return greater than 12 percent, we can determine that the rate we need to use is more than 15 percent and less than 20 percent—a bit closer to 20 than to 15. When we "try" 18 percent, we find this result:

| | |
|---|---|
| Investment | $6,000.00 |
| Present value, at 18% of $2,000 per year for 4 years (see Table A-2 on page 513) | 5,380.00 |
| Present value of $1,200 4 years from now ($1,200 x .516) – from Table A-2 | 620.00 |
| Total | $6,000.00 |

In terms of our previous example, our 18 percent return means this:

| | *Year 1* | *Year 2* | *Year 3* | *Year 4* |
|---|---|---|---|---|
| Investment | $6,000 | $5,080 | $3,994 | $2,714 |
| Interest at 18% | 1,080 | 914 | 720 | 486 |
| Available | 7,080 | 5,994 | 4,714 | 3,200 |
| Rent | 2,000 | 2,000 | 2,000 | 2,000 |
| To reinvest | $5,080 | $3,994 | $2,714 | $1,200 |
| Resale of truck | | | | 1,200 |
| Difference between leasing and investing at 18% | | | | –0– |

This general technique can be described as the "discounted cash flow" approach to quantifying investment alternatives. It is based on the idea that a business has a limited supply of funds to invest, and profit will be maximized if they are invested in those alternatives promising the greatest return. The example we have been working through illustrates a variant of this general approach—the "internal rate of return" method. This method suffers from one serious defect: its use implies an assumption that the cash inflows in each alternative will be invested at the rate of return applicable to that alternative. But this assumption makes little sense; cash inflows will be invested in whatever opportunities are available, regardless of the particular source of cash.

More rational to many people, easier to apply, and producing more meaningful distinctions among alternatives is the "profitability index" method of applying the "discounted cash flow" approach. Its basic idea is to equate the time element involved in diverse investments. If I have to invest $5,000 today in order to get $500 at the end of one year, $1,000 after the second year, $2,000 at the end of the third year, $3,000 at the end of the fourth year, and $4,000 at the end of the fifth year, I have a total return of $10,500. Although this total amount is the same as I would get if my $5,000 investment paid me $10,000 at the end of year 1 and $500 at the end of year 5, I would normally much prefer the latter, all other things being equal. How do I quantify such a situation, so that my preference can be objectively expressed?

One way is to assume a rate of return that I could earn investing such cash flows as become available. If I can earn 10 percent on any such amounts, then the present value to me of $1 in 5 years is the amount I would have to invest now that, earning compound interest at 10 percent, would amount to $1 in 5 years. Table A-2, page 503, shows that amount to be $0.621. We can easily check this:

| *Year* | *Beginning Balance* | *Interest* | *Ending Balance* |
|---|---|---|---|
| 1 | 0.621 | 0.062 | 0.683 |
| 2 | 0.683 | 0.068 | 0.751 |
| 3 | 0.751 | 0.075 | 0.826 |
| 4 | 0.826 | 0.083 | 0.909 |
| 5 | 0.909 | 0.091 | 1.000 |

The present value of $1 in 5 years is $0.621 if money is worth 10 percent per year to us.

The use of the present-value concept gives us a useful tool for reducing dollars at various points in time to a common denominator that makes them comparable to one another.

In the profitability-index approach, the company selects a rate of return as its estimated or desired rate of return. It may use its estimated cost of capital, or it may use a target return on investment. The cash inflows and outflows of each alternative are reduced to their present values based on this percentage and the use of present-value tables. The cash inflows are then divided by the outflows. If the result is exactly 1, then the rate of return is the target rate of return and is the same result that would be obtained under the "internal rate of return" method. If the result is less than 1, the return is unsatisfactory and it is irrelevant what the percentage might actually be. If the result is greater than 1, the degree to which it is greater than 1 measures the relative profitability of the alternative.

Let us return to our "buy of lease" illustration. Assume now that we are dealing with a company that has a target rate of return of 10 percent.

| | *Unadjusted* *$* | *Discounted* *@ 10%* |
|---|---|---|
| Outflow (year 0) | $6,000 | $6,000 |
| Inflows: | | |
| $2,000 per year for 4 years | $8,000 | $6,340 |
| $1,200 after 4 years | $1,200 | 820 |
| Total | | $7,160 |
| Profitability index | | $ 1.19 |

Buying would appear to be indicated, as contrasted with leasing, in this example.

We are not emphasizing this approach because of an academic preoccupation with an intriguing technique. A majority of large businesses in this country use some variation of the discounted cash-flow approach to equipment-investment decisions. Without some grasp of this way of thinking, it is practically impossible to see how some types of tax rules affect business decisions.

## REFLECTING THE TAX FACTOR

Now let us return to our two examples and complicate life a bit for our little pest-control business. We now have to deal with a tax rate of 60 percent applied to the net income of the business.

### *Expanding Volume*

The direct impact of introducing tax considerations into the question of expanding volume through cutting prices will be to scale our net profit figures down to 40 percent of what they were. Assuming, as we are for this illustration, that there is no difference between the accounting concept of income involved here and the tax concept of income, the income tax will keep everything in its relative position vis-à-vis everything else. A price cut will still appear undesirable if the cut must be on present business as well as on new business. The price cut might still be attractive if we can make it in just one territory.

It is also likely that, to the extent that the tax rate reduces the dollars of profit potential, it may reduce the incentive to take any action disturbing the status quo if the present situation is reasonably satisfactory. The decision to make no change will depend in part upon the ability of the business to utilize losses and upon any discrimination the tax system may make in the rates applicable to gains and to losses.

### *Buy or Lease*

Our problems become more involved in the buy-or-lease alternative. The key variable here is the timing of the deductibility of the $6,000 invested in the truck if we buy it. First, let us see what would happen to our profitability index if we take a tax deduction of $1,200 per year for our investment in the truck. We shall save $2,000 per year for 4 years by buying the truck rather than leasing it. But we shall have a deduction of $1,200 per year; thus, only $800 of the saving will be subject to our 60 percent tax. Hence, the tax will be $480 and our after-tax savings will be $1,520 per year. Our investment will still be $6,000, and after 4 years we shall still have a $1,200 inflow, which will not be taxable because it will be offset by the unrecovered investment of $1,200 ($6,000 less four times $1,200).

| | *Unadjusted* $ | *Discounted* @ *10%* |
|---|---|---|
| Outflow (year 0) | $6,000 | $6,000 |
| Inflows: | | |
| $1,520 per year for 4 years | 6,080 | $4,820 |
| $1,200 after 4 years | 1,200 | 820 |
| Total | | $5,640 |
| Profitability index | | .94 |

As we can see, our profitability index now indicates that this is an unacceptable alternative, compared with our previous 1.19.

What if our entire $6,000 investment were deductible in the year it was made? How would this affect our profitability index? Note that this would mean that the actual cash outflow for the investment would result in an immediate tax reduction of 60 percent of the outflow itself. Thus, the investment would be reduced by 60 percent, from $6,000 to only $2,400. The $2,000 per year of annual savings and the $1,200 of resale proceeds would all be subject to tax at 60 percent, and thus would be scaled down to $800 and $480, respectively.

| | *Unadjusted* $ | *Discounted* @ *10%* |
|---|---|---|
| Outflow | $2,400 | $2,400 |
| Inflows: | | |
| $800 per year for 4 years | 3,200 | $2,536 |
| $480 after 4 years | 480 | 328 |
| Total | | $2,864 |
| Profitability index | | 1.19 |

Our profitability index would, not too surprisingly, remain the same after taxes as it was before taxes.

Thus, even ignoring special credits, special deductions, and differences in concept between accounting income and tax income, the factor of the timing of items can make a substantial difference in their relative investment attractiveness.

## CONCLUSION

So how do income tax considerations affect the relative attractiveness of alternative decisions? We can perceive these different possibilities:

1. The rate applicable to gains and losses is the same, and the items are reflected in the tax computation in the periods in which cash flows in or out. In such a situation, the income tax is neutral. The most attractive alternative before tax will be the most attractive after tax, and the rate of return or the profitability index will be the same after tax as before.
2. A different rate applies to either the gains or the losses of some alternatives but not of others, or the tax effect of some alternatives is reflected in periods other than those in which cash flows in or out. In these situations, the after-tax appearance of alternatives will differ from their before-tax appearance, and the income tax will tend to steer people toward certain courses of action and away from others.

The latter is precisely the situation with *our* federal income tax. We have a great variety of provisions that affect the timing of the incidence of the income tax or the benefit of a deduction. We have a number of provisions that apply, directly or indirectly, tax rates to some types of income that are different from the rates applied to other types of income. Some transactions may be entirely free of any tax incidence. Other transactions may be subjected to almost confiscatory taxes.

Thus, to understand the relationship between the federal tax structure and the decisions that people would make *if* they made decisions rationally, we had to explore the details of these various provisions. That is what most of the rest of this book was about.

By adopting this approach, we do not mean to imply that we think that anyone makes every decision in a completely rational manner. Even for a perfectly adjusted person, a complete rationality would probably be an almost intolerable strain. And, in fact, all of us are a little neurotic and quite a few of us are extremely irrational about many things.

Furthermore, complete conformance to our model of rationality in business decisions would assume that the decision maker had complete knowledge of all the relevant factors affecting his decision. Many areas of taxes, however, are so imprecise that no one can be sure what the applicable tax rule will be in a specific situation at a specific time.

What we *do* mean by assuming that people will make decisions in a rational manner, even when we know that often they will not, is that we *believe* that there is a tendency for tax provisions to affect decisions in a discernible manner. Or, tax provisions *tend* to push the decisions in the direction that a rational approach would seem to indicate rather than in any other direction. Experience indicates that business people and investors *are* influenced by tax considerations, consciously and subconsciously. We therefore conclude, although we cannot prove, that such influence is along the lines we are indicating.

There is, of course, a possibility that the very complexity of the tax law discourages many persons from any attempt to reflect tax considerations. Although there may be some merit to this thought in individual situations, the prosperous existence of scores of thousands of tax consultants would seem to indicate that many people are at least attempting to reflect tax considerations in their thinking.

What complexity does is to increase attempts at simplification. The profitability index (PI) that we discussed earlier is the result of an attempt to derive one number that will summarize a complex situation. "Earnings per share" (EPS) is another attempt to summarize a complex reality. Projections of after-tax results showing the PI or the EPS boil down all the uncertainties and complexities of the tax and business realities into one number. Bayesian statistical approaches (subjective probability) to tax planning and controversy problems do the same thing. The technicians resolve the uncertainties, and the PI, EPS, or "value" of the alternative comes out as a solid, specific dollar figure. Thus, the nonexpert can cope with the complexity.

At the level of national tax policy, there *is* an implicit assumption that people do tend to behave in a rational manner. This assumption is the reason why there are so many special tax treatments of various items. Some of these, like the accelerated depreciation put into the law in 1954 or the investment credit inserted in 1962 and reinstated in 1971, are designed to encourage certain types of action, such as business investments in plant and equipment. Other provisions are designed to discourage certain types of action; still others, to relieve inequities. All, however, appear to have some effect on some decisions, some of the time.

And even if there are people whose decisions are made in bland disregard of the federal tax structure, this merely means that there will be that much more competitive advantage lodged with the persons who make their decisions rationally, taking tax considerations as well as other considerations into account.

TABLE A-2

Table of Present Value of $1

| *N* | *N years from now* | | | *Per year for N years* | | |
|---|---|---|---|---|---|---|
| *(Year)* | *10%* | *12%* | *18%* | *10%* | *12%* | *18%* |
| 1 | .909 | .893 | .847 | .909 | .893 | .847 |
| 2 | .826 | .797 | .718 | 1.736 | 1.690 | 1.566 |
| 3 | .751 | .712 | .609 | 2.487 | 2.402 | 2.174 |
| 4 | .683 | .636 | .516 | 3.170 | 3.037 | 2.690 |
| 5 | .621 | .567 | .437 | 3.791 | 3.605 | 3.127 |
| 6 | .564 | .507 | .370 | 4.355 | 4.111 | 3.498 |
| 7 | .513 | .452 | .314 | 4.868 | 4.564 | 3.812 |
| 8 | .467 | .404 | .266 | 5.335 | 4.968 | 4.078 |
| 9 | .424 | .361 | .225 | 5.759 | 5.328 | 4.303 |
| 10 | .386 | .322 | .191 | 6.145 | 5.650 | 4.494 |

# Index


Accelerated depreciation, 169, 170, 205, 207-9, 212, 215, 249, 250
Accident insurance, 305
Accounting:
  accrual basis, 40, 185, 242, 367
  cash basis, 194, 242, 283-84
  completed-contract basis, 187, 188
  cost depletion basis, 237, 238
  income concept of, 35-41
  for investment credit, 226-27
  LIFO, 320
  in partnerships, 107
  percentage-depletion basis, 237-42, 250-51
  percentage-of-completion basis, 187-88
  professional practice of 23-24
  for research and development costs, 72
Accounting firms, 22
Accounting Principles Board, 226, 227
*Accounting Trends and Techniques,* 321
Accrual basis of accounting, 40, 185, 242, 367
Adams, Samuel Hopkins, 55
*Adolph Posner,* Tax Court Memo, 139-40
*Alderson v. Commissioner,* 287-88
*All-Steel Equipment Inc. v. Commissioner, 328-30*
*American Federal Tax Reports, 460*
*American Federal Tax Reports, Second Series,* 460
American Institute of Certified Public Accountants, 13, 38, 321
Analogy, reasoning by, 462-63
Annuities, 300
  commercial, 305-6
  for employees of tax-exempt organizations, 303
  tax treatment of, 301, 305-6
Appeals procedure, 14-15, 423-25
Appellate Division conferences, 14, 15, 421-23
Armed Services Procurement Regulations, 213
Asset Depreciation Range (ADR), 209-11, 250
"At risk" rules, 279-80, 283, 284
Attorneys, 12-14, 22-24
Audits, 415-27
  appeals procedure, 14-15, 423-25
  appellate-division conference, 14, 15, 421-23
  case excerpts, 425-27
  district conference, 420-21
  field, 415-20
  research for contesting a deficiency, 466-68
  selection of returns for, 16-17
  statute of limitations and, 22
  unqualified preparers of returns and, 15-16
Automatic Data Processing (ADP), 16-17

Bad-debt expense, 250
Balance sheets:
  corporate return, 60-62, 67

Balance Sheets (*cont.*)
in criminal net-worth case, 33
Small Business Corporation return, 79, 82, 83
*Barron's,* 38-39
Benefit plans, *see* Employee benefit plans
Board of Tax Appeals, 12, 460
*See also* Tax Court
Bonds:
municipal, 274-75
United States, 272-73
"Boot," 346-47
Brandeis, Louis D., 444-45
British Companies Acts, 36
Burden of proof:
on government, 435
on taxpayer, 20-21, 32, 41
Business decisions, income concepts and, 38-39
Business income of individuals, 118-20
Bypass trusts, 393-94

Call options, 276-77
Capital assets:
characterization of, 164-65
preferential treatment of, 164, 175
Capital budgeting, depreciation and, 211-13
Capital gains, 163-77, 262
case excerpts, 175-77
coal and iron ore royalties as, 172
in corporate liquidations, 347
of corporations, 164, 166-69
decisions and, 173-75
depreciable property and, 169-70, 209-10
of fiduciaries, 167
foreign tax credit and, 369-70
historical review of, 173
of individuals, 163-66, 252-54
interest income from bonds as, 272-73
on livestock, 164, 172, 284-85
minimum tax effect on, 250-54, 257-58
offsetting capital losses against, 165, 168-69
of partnerships, 167
on patents, 172, 173
sale of property used in trade or business as, 164, 171, 262
security profits as, 164, 270
in simple trusts, 147
of Small Business Corporations, 79, 167-68
special provisions, 170-73
Capital gains (*cont.*)
stockholder earnings as, 275, 341-42, 347
tax reform and, 492-93
on timber crops, 171-72
Capital losses, 165, 168-69
decisions and, 173-75
historical review of, 173
from sale of property used in trade or business, 171
of Small Business Corporations, 167, 169
Capital recovery allowance, 491-92
*Carl E. Mathena v. U.S.,* 176-77
Cases, tax research and, 460, 468-70
Cash basis of accounting, 194, 242, 283-84
Casualty and theft losses, 190
Cattle investments, 283-85
Certified Public Accountants, 12-14, 23-25
Charitable contributions, 63, 399
estate tax and, 394
on individual returns, 118, 119, 128-29
*Chartier Real Estate Co., Inc.,* 175-76
Civil fraud penalty, 21, 430, 444-45
Clifford trust, 399-400
Coal royalties, capital gains treatment of, 172
Code of Federal Regulations, 19
Collapsible corporations, 347-49
Commercial annuities, 305-6
Commissioner of Internal Revenue, 460
*Commissioner v. Newman,* 25, 26
*Commissioner v. Pepsi-Cola Niagara Bottling Corp.,* 308-9
Community income, 126
Community property:
estate taxes and, 390
separate returns and, 126
Completed-contract basis of accounting, 187, 188
Complex trusts:
defined, 148-49, 154
exemptions for, 147
income tax savings with, 149-51
return, 150
Conference Committee, 18
Congress, 17-18, 39-41, 84, 121, 302, 302, 206, 468
*See also* House of Representatives; Senate; Tax law
*Congressional Record,* 18, 56
Consolidated return, 339-41
Consumption as income, 34-35
Contract for deed, 185-86, 277
Contractors, accounting procedures for, 187-88

Copyrights, taxation on earned income from, 164, 172-73
Corporate stocks, 270
Corporation income tax, 55-72
 balance sheet, 60-62, 67
 capital gains provisions, 164, 166-69
 complicated return, 63-66
 consolidated return, 339-41
 exceptions to simple situation, 62-63
 fiscal policy and, 69
 historic role of, 68-69
 internal investment and, 69-70
 minimum tax on tax preferences and, 251, 281
 of 1909, 55-56
 of 1913, 56-57
 1977 receipts, 133
 operating losses and, 189-92
 pricing policy and, 70-72
 rationale of, 57-58
 simple return, 58-66
 unreasonable accumulation of earnings and, 66-68, 84-85
 *See also* Corporations
Corporations:
 collapsible, 347-49
 distributions, 341-43, 347
 dividend policy of, 69-70
 double taxation of, 62-63, 69-70, 87, 489-90
 dummy, 100
 foreign operations of, 371-73
 foreign tax credit of, 374-77
 formation of, 336-37, 346
 as investment vehicle, 280-82
 liquidations, 344-48
 multiple, 192-93
 one-shot election, 167-68
 partnerships distinguished from, 100
 professional, 108
 real estate syndicates taxed as, 265
 regulated investment companies, 273-74
 reorganization of, 337-41, 346-52
 Small Business, *see* Small Business Corporations
 small business investment, 270-71
Cost depletion, 237, 238
Cost depreciation, *see* Depreciation
Cost recovery, 185-86
Court of Claims, 14, 15, 20, 24, 423, 424, 469-70
Craig, Walter E., 445-46
Credits:
 deductions versus, 490-91
Credits (*cont.*)
 dependent care, 128-30
 for the elderly 306-7
 foreign tax, *see* Foreign tax credit
 investment, *see* Investment credit
 new jobs, 230
 past-service, 297-98
Criminal fraud, *see* Tax fraud
Cumulative bulletins, 459-60
*Cumulative Changes in the Internal Revenue Code and the Regulations,* 461

*D. G. Haley, et al. v. Commissioner,* 110-12
Decedent, tax problems of, 151-52
Decision making, quantitative aspects of, 500-13
Declining-balance depreciation, 206-9, 215
Deductions:
 burden of proof for, 41
 in community property states, 126
 credits versus, 221, 490-91
 depreciation, *see* Depreciation
 employee benefits contributions, 297, 298
 employee life, health, and accident insurance policies, 304-5
 of fiduciaries, 154
 itemized, *see* Itemized deductions
 marital, *see* Marital deduction
 operating losses, 189-92
 pricing policy and, 71
 standard, 124, 127-28
 trusteed benefit plan contributions, 296
Dental expenses, 122
Dependent care credit, 128-30
Depletion:
 cost, 237, 238
 discovery-value, 239
 minimum tax and, 250-51
 oil and gas, 239-40
 percentage, 237-42, 250-51
Depreciation, 202-18
 accelerated, 169, 170, 205, 207-9, 212, 215, 249, 250
 accounting problems and, 215-16
 Asset Depreciation Range (ADR), 209-11, 250
 based on cost, implications of, 204-7
 capital budgeting and, 211-13
 case excerpts, 216-18
 declining-balance, 206-9, 215
 depletion versus, 237-39
 patterns of, 207-9

Depreciation (*cont.*)
of personal property, 169-70, 209-10, 250, 251
of real estate, 164, 170, 203, 209, 210, 262-64
recapture, 170, 209-10, 214
sale and leaseback transaction, 214-15
selling prices and, 213-14
straight-line, 170, 207-8, 250
sum-of-the-years'-digits, 208-9, 215
in tax accounting, 202-4
useful life, 210-11
Development costs, 240-41 250
Discount mortgage, 277-78
Discovery-value depletion, 239
Disposable income, 129
Distribution schedule, 79, 81
District conference, 420-21
District courts, 14, 15, 21, 24, 423, 424
Dividend income:
from foreign corporations, 368
on individual returns, 118, 119, 122
of partnership, 103, 106
of Small Business Corporations, 86
Dividends:
common stocks, 343
unreasonable accumulation of earnings and, 66-68, 84-85
Dividends paid deduction, 274
Dividends received deduction, 62-63, 65
Dollar-value method of inventory valuation, 317-19, 321
Domestic International Sales Corporation (DISC), 375-77
Double taxation of corporations, 62-63, 69-70, 87, 489-90
foreign taxes and, 367, 373
value added tax as, 375

*Earl A. Phillips v. Frank,* 285-86
Earned income, foreign exclusion of, 360-66
Education for research, 461-62
Edwards, James Wyatt, 223
*Edwin D. Davis,* 91-94
Elderly, credit for, 306-7
Electing Small Business Corporations:
defined, 271
foreign tax matters and, 363
net operating losses, 191
*See also* Small Business Corporations
*Eli Lilly & Co. v. U.S.,* 379-82
Employee benefit plans:
annuities, *see* Annuities
case excerpts, 308-9
employee stock ownership, 299-300
life, health, and accident insurance, 304-5
small businesses and, 307-8
tax treatment of distributions, 300-301
trusteed, 296-98
*See also* Retirement Income
Employee expenses, 122
Employee stock ownership plans (ESOPs), 299-300
*Estate of Charles T. Franklin,* 288-91
*Estate of Edward A. Tully, Sr. v. U.S.,* 406-8
Estate tax, 146
bypass trusts and, 393-94
charitable beneficiaries and, 394
corporate mergers and, 349
extension of time for payment of, 397-98
integrated with gift tax 388
*inter vivos* gifts and, 391-92
marital deduction, 390-91
1977 receipts, 133
of nonresident aliens, 370-71
rates, 137-38, 389-90
redemption of stock to pay, 398
state law and, 398
transfer tax credit and, 388, 396-97
Estate tax attorney 22, 23
*Estelle Morris Trusts,* 156-57
Estimated tax:
declaration of, 131
underpayment of, 21
Excise tax, 494
on corporate income, 55-56
1977 receipts, 133
Exemptions:
for dependents, 127
for married taxpayers, 124
on municipal bonds, 274
personal, 490-91
for trusts, 147
Expenditure approach to defining income, 35
Exploration costs, 240-41, 250

Fair market value, defined, 34
Federal Rules of Criminal Procedure, 434
*Federal Tax Service,* 474
*Federated Department Stores, Inc. v. Commissioner,* 41, 45-47

Federal Reserve System, 272
*Fetzer Refrigerator Co.,* 197-98
Fiduciaries, 151
  capital gains of, 167
  defined, 147, 152
  executor of decedent as, 151-52
  *See also* Fiduciary income tax
Fiduciary income tax, 146-48
  case excerpts, 155-58
  complex trusts, *see* Complex trusts
  deductions for, 154
  income tax savings, 149-51
  operation of the trust, 147-49
  returns, 146-50, 153-55
  simple trusts, 147-48
  tax problems of decedent, 151-52
Field audit, 415-20
Fifth Amendment, 433
Filing requirements, 128
Financial Accounting Standards Board (FASB), 38
Flat-rate tax, 35
Foreign tax credit, 251, 490
  corporations, 374-77
  individuals, 366-70
Foreign taxes, 360-84
  case excerpts, 378-84
  foreign tax credit, *see* Foreign tax credit
  international tax planning, 377-78
  nonresident alien and U.S. taxes, 370-71
  tax treaties, 377
  U.S. citizens abroad, 360-66
  U.S. corporation operations abroad, 371-73
Form 870 (Waiver of Restrictions on Assessment), 418
Form 870AD (Appellate Division Settlement), 422
Form 872 (Consent Fixing Period of Limitation Upon Assessment of Income and Profits Tax), 419-20
Form 1040 (U.S. Individual Income Tax Return), 119, 121, 123-25
Form 1040A (Short Form), 130-31
Form 1041 (U.S. Fiduciary Income Tax Return), 148, 150, 155
Form 1065 (U.S. Partnership Return of Income), 104, 105
Form 1120 (U.S. Corporation Income Tax Return), 59, 61, 65, 67
Form 1120S (U.S. Small Business Corporation), 80-83
Form 3468 (Computation of Investment Credit), 225
Form L-191 (30-day letter), 421
Fraud, *see* Tax fraud
*Fred A. Berzon,* 404-6

Gifts:
  reduction of estate taxes with, 391-93
  reduction of income tax with, 399-400
Gift tax:
  integrated with estate tax, 388
  marital deduction, 391-93
  1977 receipts, 133
  rates, 389-90
  state law and, 398
  transfer tax credit and, 388, 394-96
*Gregory v. Helvering,* 89, 355-56
Group insurance plan, 307
*Grunebaum v. Commissioner,* 378-79

H.R. 10 Bill, 302
Halvorson, Gay, 222, 223
Head of household, 126-27, 134-35
Health insurance, 305
*Helvering v. Clifford,* 402-3
Historical cost approach, 37-38
Holding companies, 280-82, 372
House of Representatives, 17, 18, 56, 302
    Ways and Means Committee, 17, 18, 254
  *See also* Congress
Hughes, Charles Evans, 55
*Hutzler Brothers Company v. Commissioner,* 325-27
Hypotheses, formulation of, 462

Income, 32-50
  accounting concepts of, 35-41
  business decisions and, 38-39
  case excerpts, 41-50
  consumption as, 34-35
  fiduciary accounting of, 147, 149-51, 154
  of foreign base-company, 372
  of individuals, 122-26, 131
  net-worth approach to, 32-34, 436-37, 443
  of partnerships, 103-7
  personal service, *see* Maximum tax on personal service income
  of proprietorship, 118-20

Income (*cont.*)
in respect of a decedent, 152
tax versus accounting concepts of, 39-41
timing of, *see* Timing of income
*See also* Net Income
Income averaging, 188-89, 255
Income tax:
negative, 492
*See also* Corporation income tax; Fiduciary income tax; Foreign taxes; Individual income tax; Partnerships; Small Business Corporations
Income tax law, *see* Tax law
Individual income tax, 118-40
business income, 118-20
business losses, 190-91
capital gains provisions, 163-66, 252-54
case excerpts, 138-40
declaration of estimated tax, 131
deductions, 127-28
filing requirements, 128
foreign tax credit and, 366-70
joint versus separate returns, 124-27
maximum, *see* Maximum tax on personal service income
1977 receipts, 133
returns, 122-27, 130-31
self-employed, social security tax on, 106-7, 120-21
tax-law concepts for, 128-30
tax rates, 132-38
Inflation, adaptation to, 493
Installment sales, reporting of, 183-85
Insurance policies, 307, 400-402
Interest:
as itemized deduction, 21, 122
on state and local investments, 63, 64, 274-75
on tax deficiencies, 21
on United States bonds, 272-73
tax-free, 66
Internal investment, 69-70
Internal Revenue, Bureau of, 312, 316, 317, 320
Internal Revenue Bulletin, 459-60
Internal Revenue Code, 11, 17, 39, 208-9, 239-40, 353, 360, 371-73, 377, 458, 461, 468
Internal Revenue Service, 13, 19, 128, 278, 302, 303, 349, 372-73, 419, 488
Appellate Division, 14, 15, 421-23
Audit Division, *see* Audits
Internal Revenue Service (*cont.*)
employment in, 22-23
Intelligence Division, 431-32
litigation policy adopted by, 19-20
private rulings of, 19, 470-72
Regional Counsel's Office, 24
statute of limitations and, 22
International tax planning, 377-78
*Inter vivos* gifts, 391-92
*Inter vivos* trusts, 147, 153
Inventories:
in cattle tax shelters, 283-84
*See also* LIFO (last-in, first-out) method of inventory valuation
Investment credit, 212, 251
accounting for, 226-27
computation of, 225
conditions for, 227-29
deduction versus, 221
effectiveness of, 222-24
for employee stock ownership plan contributions, 299
investment decisions and, 229-30
maximum allowed, 227
tax law and, 224, 230-31
Investment trusts, 273-74
Involuntary conversions, gains on, 175
Iron ore royalties, capital gains treatment of, 172
Itemized deductions:
criteria for taking, 127
deferred payments on, 127
divided between foreign and U.S. income, 368-69
excess, minimum tax on, 249
types of, 122

*James L. Stinnett, Jr., et al,* 88-89
*James v. U.S.*, 41, 42-44
*Joe E. Borg,* 90-91
*John W. Meyers, Jr.,* 243-44
Joint Committee on Internal Revenue Taxation, 17
Joint returns, 124-26, 134
Joint ventures, 101-2
*Joseph B. Ferguson v. Commissioner,* 425-26
*Journal of Taxation, The,* 461
*Jungle, The* (Sinclair), 55
Justice, Department of, 20, 24, 39

Kennedy Administration, 224
Kennedy, John F., 175
Keogh plan, 302
*Klein Chocolate Company v. Commissioner,* 327-28
*Kramertown Co., Inc. v. Commissioner,* 231-33
*Kurio v. U.S.,* 25-27

*Lazarus v. U.S.,* 287
Legislation, *see* Tax law
*Lenske v. U.S.,* 448-54
Life insurance policies, 304-5, 400-402
LIFO (last-in, first-out) method of inventory valuation, 314-32
  case excerpts, 324-32
  case study, 314-19
  effects of adopting, 320-24
  tax LIFO versus accounting LIFO, 320
Livestock:
  capital gains treatment of, 164, 172, 284-85
  investment credit on, 227
Long-term capital gains:
  of corporations, 166-67, 168-69, 270
  minimum tax on, 250-54
  of noncorporate taxpayers, 165-66, 168
Loophole-closing legislation, 87, 210
  personal capital gains, 169
  trust tax provisions, 151
  *See also* Maximum tax on personal service income; Minimum tax on tax preferences
Losses:
  capital, *see* Capital losses
  casualty and theft, 190
  as itemized deductions, 122
  operating, 189-92, 266, 344-46, 348
  by Small Business Corporations, 85, 190, 191
Lower-of-cost-or-market method of inventory valuation, 320, 322

*McGowan v. Commissioner,* 25, 27-29
Macy's (R. H. Macy & Company), 314-19
*Madonna J. and James E. Colwell v. Commissioner,* 41, 44-45
*Marineland of the Pacific, Inc.,* 233-34
Marital deduction:
  estate tax, 390-91
  gift tax, 391-93
Married taxpayers, 131
  dependent care credit and, 128, 129-30
  filing requirements, 128
  joint versus separate returns, 124-26
  tax rates for, 133-34, 136-37
*Massey Motors, Inc. v. U.S.,* 216-18
Maximum tax on personal service income, 254-58, 493
  computation of, 255-57
  impact of, 257-58
  provisions, 255-58
Meat Inspection Act, 55
Medical expenses, 122, 126, 128, 129
Medicare, 120, 121
*Merchants National Bank of Topeka v. Commissioner, The,* 218
Mergers, 338-39
  accounting for, 349-52
  operating losses and, 345-46
  statutory, 347
  tax law and, 348-49
Mineral resources:
  case excerpts, 243-47
  depletion, 239-40
  exploration and development costs, 240-41
Minimum tax on tax preferences:
  computation of, 253-54
  corporations and, 251, 281
  gifts within family and, 396
  impact of, 257-58
  recapture and, 251-54
  tax preference items, 249-51
*Miranda* warnings, 433
Money, time-adjusted value of, 71-72
Mortgages:
  discount, 277-78
  installment transaction, 184
  sales versus, 267
Multiple entities, 192-93
Municipal bonds, 274-75
Mutual funds, 273-74

National Industrial Conference Board, 316
Natural resources:
  investment in, 279
  *See also* Mineral resources; Oil and gas

Negative income tax, 492
Net income:
  concept of, 38
  of partnerships, 103, 106, 108
  of Small Business Corporations, 84, 86, 103, 107
Net operating loss, 189-92
Net-worth method of income determination, 32-34, 436-37, 443
  variations of, 437-43
New jobs credit, 230
*Nilssen Estate v. U.S.,* 157-58
90-day letter, 422-23
Nonresident alien, U.S. taxes and, 370-71

Oil and gas:
  depletion, 239-40
  exploration and development costs, 240-41
  investors in, 241-42
One-shot election, 167-68
Operating losses, 189-92, 266, 344-46, 348
Option contracts, 276-77
Ordinary income, defined, 103
Ordinary Loss Small Business Corporations, 271
  *See also* Small Business Corporations

Partnerships, 99-112
  aggregate concept of, 102
  capital gains of, 167
  case excerpts, 108-12
  conduit nature of returns, 102-5
  corporations distinguished from, 100
  defined, 101-2
  entity concept of, 107
  foreign taxes of, 364
  net operating loss, 191
  partners' salaries and interest payments, 106
  reconciliation schedule, 105-6
  relative importance of, 107-8
  return, 102-6
  self-employment income, 106-7
  Small Business Corporation return compared to, 102-3
Past-service credit, 297-98
Patents, capital gains treatment of, 172, 173
Penalty provisions in tax law, 21, 66-67, 85, 131
Pension plans:
  for employees, 297-98
  for the self-employed and professionals, 302-3
  Small Business Corporations and, 85
  tax treatment of, 301
Percentage depletion, 237-42, 250-51
Percentage-of-completion basis of accounting, 187-88
Personal exemption, 490-91
Personal property:
  depreciation of, 169-70, 209-10, 250, 251
  installment method of reporting, 184
  investment credit on, 224, 227-30
  restricted, 186-87
  useful life of, 210-11
Personal residence, gain on sale of, 175
Personal service income, maximum tax on, *See* Maximum tax on personal service income
Pooling-of-interest concept, 350-52
Pools, 101
*PPG Industries, Inc.,* 382-84
*Prentice-Hall Citator,* 461
*Prentice-Hall Federal Tax Handbook,* 474-76
Prentice-Hall Tax Service, 458, 465
Prices:
  corporation income tax and, 70-72
  depreciation and, 213-14
Private rulings, 19, 470-72
Privileged communication, 434-35
Professional corporations, 108
Professionals, pension plans for, 302-3
Profit-sharing plans, 85, 298, 301
Progressive tax, 35
Property, *See* Personal property; Real estate
Proprietorship profit, 118-20
Public underwriting, 343
Pure Food and Drug Act of 1906, 55
Put options, 276-77

*Ragland Investment Co. v. U.S.,* 476-78
Railroad Retirement System, 306, 307
Real estate:
  depreciation of, 164, 170, 203, 209, 210, 262-64
  dividing up the fee, 269
  installment method of reporting, 183-84
  mortgaging versus selling, 267

Real estate (*cont.*)
rental property, 107, 203, 209, 262-64
sales as capital gains, 164, 171, 262
syndicates, 264-65
tax law and, 261-70, 285-91
trading versus selling, 267-68
transfer to corporations, 342, 346
Real estate investment trusts (REIT), 265-66
Reconciliation schedule:
partnership return, 105-6
Small Business Corporation return, 81-84
Refunds, 16, 20-22
Regulated investment companies, 273-74
Rental property, 107, 203, 209, 262-64
Research, *see* Tax research
Research and development costs, accounting for, 72
Residence abroad, U.S. citizen, 360-66
Restricted property, 186-87
Retirement income:
annuities, *see* Annuities
pension plans, *see* Pension plans
tax treatment of, 300-301
Return on investment, 70-72
Returns:
corporation, 58-68, 339-41
fiduciary, 146-50, 153-55
individual, 122-27, 130-31
late, 21
partnership, 102-6
research for preparing, 465-66
selection for audits, 16-17
Small Business Corporation, 79-84, 102-3
*See also* Tax specialists
Revenue Act of 1913, 56-57
Revenue agents, 14, 15, 17, 20, 22, 23, 431
*See also* Audits
Rinfret, Pierre A., 222*n*
Root, Elihu, 17
Royalties, capital gains treatment of, 172

Salaries of partners, 106
Sales and leaseback, 214-15
Sales tax, 494
Salvage value, 207-8
*Schlude v. Commissioner,* 41, 47-50
Securities:
business combinations and, 337-43, 346-52
employee ownership plans, 299-300
purchase and sales as capital gain, 164, 270
puts and calls, 276-77
Securities (*cont.*)
short sales, 275
stock-bonus plans, 298
stock redemption, 341-42, 347, 398
stock transfers, 186-87
tax law and, 270-78
wash sales, 276
*See also* Bonds
Securities and Exchange Commission, 56, 226
Seidler, Lee J., 205*n*
Self-employed:
declaration of estimated tax, 131-32
income of, 86, 106-7
pension plans for, 302-3
Social Security tax for, 106-7, 120-21
Selling prices, depreciation and, 213-14
Senate, 18, 56, 302
Finance Committee, 18, 226-27
Separate returns, 126, 136-37
Shareholders:
capital accumulation of, 69-70
of Small Business Corporations, 78
taxes on investments of, 347
tax law effects on, 270
undistributed taxable income of, 81-84
*See also* Securities
Short sales, 275
Short-term capital loss, 168
Short-term trusts, 399-400
Simple trusts, 147-48, 154
Sinclair, Upton, 55
Small Business Corporations, 78-94
capital gains of, 79, 167-68
capital losses of, 167, 169
case excerpts, 88-94
reduced incentive toward partnership and, 108
retained earnings, 81-84
return, 79-84, 102-3
shareholders of, 78
tax advantages of, 84-87
tax disadvantages of, 87-88
*See also* Electing Small Business Corporations; Ordinary Loss Small Business Corporations; Small Business Investment Corporations
Small businesses, employee benefit plans and, 307-8
Small Business Investment Act of 1958, 271
Small Business Investment Corporations, 270-71

Social Security benefits, 86, 120, 306, 307
Social Security numbers, 16
Social Security tax:
  in partnerships, 106-7
  on self-employed, 120-21
Special agents, 22, 23, 32-33, 431-32
"Split-dollar" insurance, 304-5
Standard deduction, 124, 127-28
Standard tax service, 458
*Stanley C. Orrisch,* 108-10
Statute of limitations, 22
Statutory mergers, 347
Stock, *see* Securities
Straight-line depreciation, 170, 207-8, 250
Subchapter S corporations, *see* Small Business Corporations
Subsidiaries:
  acquisition of, 337-39
  foreign, 371-73
Sum-of-the-years'-digits depreciation, 208-9, 215
Supreme Court, 15, 20, 36, 55, 433-34, 469
Syndicates, 101, 264-65

Taft, William Howard, 55-56
Taxable income, 39-41, 103, 368
*Tax Adviser,* 461
Tax allocation, 215-16
Tax audits, *see* Audits
Tax concepts of income, 39-41
Tax Court, 12, 14, 15, 20, 24, 130, 317, 422-25, 460, 468-70
Tax-exempt organizations, 303-4
Tax expenditure estimates, 1977-82, 494-99
Tax fraud, 21, 33, 430-55
  burden of proof, 435
  case excerpts, 446-55
  civil fraud penalty, 21, 430, 444-45
  constitutional law and, 432-34
  conviction for, 444
  defense of, 443
  investigation of, 431-32
  privileged communication and, 434-35
  prosecution of, 435-42
  punishment for, 445-46
Tax incentive, 487-89
Tax law:
  "at risk" rule, 279-80
  capital gains provisions, 164-68
Tax law: (*cont.*)
  cattle investments and, 283-85
  complexity of, 486-87
  Congress and, 17-18
  depletion and, 238-40
  discouragement factors in, 174-75
  essential features of, 487-90
  foreign operations of corporations and, 371-73
  holding companies and, 280-82
  individual income tax and, 128-30
  investment credit and, 224, 230-31
  mergers and, 348-49
  natural resources and, 279
  penalty provisions in, 21, 66-67, 85, 131
  real estate and, 261-70, 285-91
  securities and, 270-78
  statute of limitations, 22
  timing of income and, 182
  U.S. citizens abroad and, 361-62
  *See also* Loophole-closing legislation
Tax-option corporations, *see* Small Business Corporations
Tax planning:
  analysis of problems, 472-76
  international, 377-78
  research for, 463-65
Tax practice as profession, 22-25
Tax preferences, minimum tax on, *see* Minimum tax on tax preferences
Tax publications, 461
Tax rates:
  capital gains provisions and, 163
  for estate tax, 137-38, 389-90
  for fiduciaries, 154
  for individuals, 132-38
  timing of income and, 182
Tax Reduction Act of 1975, 240
Tax Reduction and Simplification Act of 1977, 230
Tax reform, 483-99
  complexity of present law, 486-87
  essential features of present law, 487-90
  key issues of, 489-94
  standards for, 484-86
  tax expenditure estimates, 177-82, 494-99
Tax Reform Act of 1969, 170, 209, 249, 254
Tax Reform Act of 1976, 130, 170, 249, 262, 275, 279, 284, 361-62, 368, 464
Tax research, 458-72
  analogies, 462-63

Tax research (*cont.*)
basic tax service, 458-59
case excerpt, 476-78
cases, 460, 468-70
code changes, 461
for contesting a deficiency, 466-68
cumulative bulletins, 459-60
education for, 461-62
hypothesis formulation, 462
methodology, 472
*Prentice-Hall Citator,* 461
for preparing returns, 465-66
private rulings, 470-72
for tax planning, 463-65
tax publications, 461
Tax returns, *see* Returns
Tax services, 458-59
Tax shelter investments, 261, 280-82
Tax specialists:
attorneys, 12-14, 24
certified public accountants, 12-14, 23-25
in corporate employment, 24
unqualified persons as, 13-16
Tax treaties, 377
Testamentary trust, 147, 153
30-day letter, 421
*Thor Power Tool Co.,* 330-32
Throwback rules in trust taxation, 149-50
Timber crop, capital gains treatment of, 171-72
Time-adjusted value of money, 71-72
Timing of income, 182-98
case excerpts, 194-98
cash basis accounting, 194
contractors, 187-88
cost recovery, 185-86
income averaging, 188-89
installment sales, 183-85
multiple entities, 192-93
operating losses, 189-92
restricted property, 186-87
tax rates and, 182
*Towne v. Eisner,* 36, 41-42
Trades, realty, 267-68
Transactional approach to taxes, 41
Transfer tax, 388-90
*See also* Estate tax; Gift tax
Treasury Department, 13, 15, 17-20, 108, 210, 239, 302, 320, 415, 417-18, 419, 466, 468, 470-72
Treasury Regulations, 18-19
Trueblood report, 38
Trusts:
bypass, 393-94
employee benefit plans, 296-98
*inter vivos,* 147, 153
operation of, 147-49
real estate investment, 265-66
short-term, 399-400
tax rates for, 137-38
testamentary, 147, 153

Unimproved land, 262
United States bonds, 272-73
*U.S. et al. v. Coopers & Lybrandt,* 426-27
United States Steel Corporation, 55, 202, 204-5
*U.S. Tax Cases,* 460
*U.S. v. McCormick,* 25
*U.S. v. Marvin Shurbet, et ux.,* 244-47
*U.S. v. Middlemiss,* 454-55
*U.S. v. William J. Troupe,* 446-48
Unlimited throwback rule, 149-50
Useful life:
depreciation and, 210-11
investment credit and, 224, 227, 228

Value added tax (VAT), 374-75, 494
Vintage accounts, 210

*W. Roland* and *Stella H. Cooper v. U.S.,* 138-39
*Wall Street Journal, The,* 38-39
*Warren Jones Co. v. Commissioner,* 195-96
Wash sales, 276
Weil doctrine, 176
*Wilford E. Thatcher v. Commissioner,* 352, 354
*Woodward v. U.S.,* 196-97